# NEW JERSEY CODE OF CRIMINAL JUSTICE

## A Practical Manual

ON LINE

Kenneth Del Vecchio, Esq.

**PEARSON**

Prentice
Hall

Upper Saddle River, New Jersey 07458

**Library of Congress Cataloging-in-Publication Data**

Del Vecchio, Kenneth.
New Jersey Code of Criminal Justice: a practical manual / Kenneth Del Vecchio.
    p. cm.
    Includes index.
    ISBN 0-13-112224-X
    1. Criminal law—New Jersey. 2. Criminal procedure—New Jersey. I. New Jersey. New
Jersey Code of Criminal Justice. II. Title.

KFN2361.A3339D45 2005
345.749—dc22

2003064684

**Editor-in-Chief:** Stephen Helba
**Executive Editor:** Frank Mortimer, Jr.
**Assistant Editor:** Korrine Dorsey
**Marketing Manager:** Tim Peyton
**Editorial Assistant:** Barbara Rosenberg
**Managing Editor:** Mary Carnis
**Production Liaison:** Brian Hyland
**Production Editor:** Janet Bolton
**Director of Manufacturing
   and Production:** Bruce Johnson

**Manufacturing Manager:** Ilene Sanford
**Manufacturing Buyer:** Cathleen Petersen
**Cover Design:** Amy Rosen
**Composition:** Integra
**Printing and Binding:** Von Hoffman, Owensille
**Proofreader:** Maine Proofreading Services
**Copy Editor:** Maine Proofreading Services

Pearson Education LTD.
Pearson Education Australia PTY, Limited
Pearson Education Singapore, Pte. Ltd.
Pearson Education North Asia Ltd.
Pearson Education Canada, Ltd.
Pearson Educacion de Mexico, S.A. de C.V.
Pearson Education—Japan
Pearson Education Malaysia, Pte. Ltd.
Pearson Education, Upper Saddle River, New Jersey

10  9  8  7  6  5  4  3  2  1
ISBN 0-13-112224-X

*This book is dedicated to two distinguished
New Jersey barristers,
Walter R. Dewey and Miles R. Feinstein.*

# CONTENTS

# PREFACE

*New Jersey Code of Criminal Justice: A Practical Manual* serves as a comprehensive and detailed work to assist those who are attempting to understand and apply New Jersey's criminal statutes. This codebook is written to decipher and explain the statutes for police officers charging under them, to educate police academy trainees and other students studying law, to interpret the statutes' meanings for lawyers and judges, and to generally make the criminal codebook a more interesting and educational tool.

This book contains, in complete verbatim text, every statute found in Title 2C, New Jersey's code of criminal justice. Preceding each statutory chapter or group of chapters is a fictional fact pattern. The characters and incidents portrayed and the names herein are fictitious, and any similarity to the name, character, or history of any persons or entity is entirely coincidental and unintentional. Following each statute that defines a crime, disorderly persons offense and petty disorderly persons offense, is a practical application section. These sections draw on the fact patterns to explain the statutes. Readers can utilize the fact patterns and practical applications to understand the language of the statutes and, thereafter, determine how to appropriately charge pursuant to them.

Although *New Jersey Code of Criminal Justice: A Practical Manual* primarily tackles the substantive statutes defining crimes, disorderly persons offenses, and petty disorderly persons offenses, it also explains many of the other related statutes, such as defenses and general provisions. Statutory language defining the offenses, the elements pertaining to them, and the differences among the offenses are addressed in detail. In total, every statute that defines a crime, disorderly persons offense, and petty disorderly persons offense has a practical application section that explains it. Several other statutes are afforded practical application sections as well. Sentencing and administrative statutes are not the focus of this book; therefore, practical application sections are not provided for these statutes.

This codebook is practical and necessary for police officers, who are presented daily with real-life criminal circumstances and need to know how to correctly charge pursuant to each peculiar and unique situation. It is equally important for trainees at the academies who must learn the criminal laws of New Jersey and be able to apply them once they graduate and "hit the streets." Similarly, it is a valuable tool for other students studying law, and even for lawyers and judges, who are looking for mechanisms to better understand the often confusing and convoluted statutory language.

# ACKNOWLEDGMENTS

My wife, Francine, dedicated countless hours of typing, grammatical proofreading, and research-related work to this book. As I completed each chapter, she read and examined it with me. Her honest excitement for my writing holds an intangible quality that I can't quite describe in this acknowledgment. Francine's unyielding efforts were modestly provided in face of the challenges and rigors she herself endured as an Ivy League doctoral student (Teachers College, Columbia University) and as a full-time public school teacher. I thank her, with all my heart, for her loyalty and stamina.

Van Tracy, a Fordham Law School student, served as my research assistant for this book. He not only delivered quality, valuable research but also demonstrated an impressive understanding of New Jersey's criminal statutes. Van was a contributing writer for the practical application sections in Chapter 21 and the computer-related theft section in Chapter 20. He should be proud of his work.

Several New Jersey law enforcement officers and attorneys contributed their time and expertise to review *New Jersey Code of Criminal Justice: A Practical Manual*. I am grateful for their thoughts. Their ranks include Mahwah Chief of Police James Batelli; Dan Frier, Esq.; Hawthorne Chief of Police Martin Boyd; Miles R. Feinstein, Esq.; Bergen County Police Academy Director Frank Del Vecchio; Jon Kearney, Esq.; Mahwah Patrolman Russell Read; Michael Borao, Esq.; Newark Police Department Sargeant Michael Goitiandia; and Doctor. Janice Joseph, Richard Stockton College of New Jersey.

I thank Prentice Hall and Pearson Education for giving me the opportunity to be their author of this important book. I owe special thanks to Frank Mortimer, Jr., and Korrine Dorsey for their guidance and professional ingenuity as I authored the work. I also want to thank Kim Davies and Mark Dantzker for believing in me and getting me started with *New Jersey Code of Criminal Justice: A Practical Manual*. Similarly, I want to thank those who contributed important services during the final stages: Janet Bolton, Deborah Leighton, and Eugene O'Connor. And lastly, I thank Sarah Hayday for introducing me to Prentice Hall and Pearson Education.

# ABOUT THE AUTHOR

Kenneth Del Vecchio is a criminal lawyer who has tried nearly 400 cases, serving as both a prosecutor and defense attorney. He is also a critically acclaimed filmmaker whose movies have won awards and received national and international distribution. In addition, Del Vecchio is a published novelist.

As a lawyer, Del Vecchio is credited with being one of the youngest attorneys in New Jersey history to try and win a felony jury trial. Since then, Del Vecchio has handled literally thousands of criminal cases as both a prosecutor and criminal defense attorney.

Kenneth Del Vecchio currently serves as the Prosecutor for the Borough of Hawthorne; he previously was the Prosecutor of the City of Clifton. On the defense side, he represents clients in criminal matters all across the State of New Jersey, with the exception of Passaic County where he prosecutes. He is a member of the New Jersey and Pennsylvania bars, being admitted to both states in 1994.

Often headlined as a Renaissance Man, Kenneth Del Vecchio has been the subject of hundreds of national magazine and newspaper articles. He has been called The Triple Threat: Prosecutor, Film Producer, Author by print and television media.

His independent films, primarily focusing on criminal law, include *The Drum Beats Twice*, *Tinsel Town*, *Pride & Loyalty* and *Rules for Men*.

In addition to his filmmaking career, Kenneth Del Vecchio is a published novelist, having authored the criminal suspense novels *Revelation in the Wilderness* and *Pride & Loyalty*. He resides in the Borough of Hawthorne with his wife Francine.

# 1

# PRELIMINARY

## FACT PATTERN (PERTAINS TO CHAPTERS 1 TO 7)

Over an 18-month period, 30 separate armed robberies involving a masked assailant occurred on the New Jersey state highways. Similarities in each case ended with the unifying factor of the perpetrator's mask—a white handkerchief. Race and ethnicity varied, ages were different, as well as hair color. Some perpetrators were men, others women. English language was used, as well as Spanish, Hebrew, Arabic, and Italian. The weapon in each case was different; sometimes a gun was used, other times a knife or baseball bat. The robberies spanned the Garden State Parkway, New Jersey Turnpike, and several of their intersecting state roadways. Getaway cars ranged from domestic models to Japanese and German imports. And the accompanying crimes in each case were distinct from one another, almost to the point of being bizarre.

Initially, law enforcement officials entertained a theory that a string of copycat masked robberies had occurred. However, that idea was quickly disbanded when five of the suspected felons were arrested—all of whom ultimately admitted under interrogation that they were part of a singular, intricate, organized crime outfit headed by one mastermind operative. Learning the identity of this criminal chieftain was the subject of a series of meetings convened by New Jersey State Police Colonel Frank Winters. Winters formed a council of several high-ranking law enforcement officers, hailing from municipalities from Cape May to Mahwah. Together, these men and women determined to locate the group's leader and ascertain the purpose and goals of these criminal activities.

The first order of business was for each officer to recount the crimes that occurred in his or her jurisdiction. The Borough of Carlstadt was the site of the first robbery, a venture that netted masked gunman Michael Westmont almost $100,000. Carlstadt Police Chief Andrew Beaumont explained the unusual circumstances as the other panel members listened intently.

On Route 17 North, less than one mile from the Meadowlands Sports Complex, two intoxicated football players argued furiously inside the Seventeen Diner. They knocked a plate of spaghetti and marinara sauce on the floor and tossed their respective drinks at each other. Their cursing was so loud it could be heard outside the restaurant's entrance doors. In an effort to satisfy the diner's other customers and end the argument, management called the Carlstadt police. Their arrival and presence, however, was not sufficient to quell the argument, as it actually swelled into a fistfight when one of the players slapped the other in the face. As the fight ensued, with the patrol officers attempting to break it up, the situation took a strange turn of events—a dark-haired Caucasian male, draping a white handkerchief across his face, entered the establishment. He brandished a sawed-off shotgun and fired a few shots into the air. In English, the man ordered everyone to lie face down on the floor. Everyone complied, including the police officers, as they had no other recourse because their backs were to the gunman. The assailant then proceeded to the now-docile football players and reached into the front pocket of one of the men's leather jacket. He removed the man's car keys and exited the Seventeen Diner as quickly as he had entered. The assailant then sped off in the athlete's brand-new Mercedes. It was later learned that a suitcase containing $95,000 in U.S. currency was hidden in the vehicle's trunk.

The two football players were arrested at the scene for violating state statutes related to their tumultuous behavior in the diner. The patrol officers, suspicious of the evening's events, probed the two men about the nature of their fight and the source of the large amount of cash in the one gentleman's automobile. The quick arrival of the athletes' defense attorneys thwarted the police questioning, however, but not their follow-up investigation. Were either of the players involved in the robbery? If so, for what reason?

The Carlstadt police chief summed up what had happened. Rodney Crawson, the player whose car was stolen, had owed Bill McNichol, the other player, $200,000 in gambling debts. Crawson had placed bets with McNichol and lost. McNichol was attempting to collect the funds the evening of the argument. Although he was aware that Crawson had a portion of the cash debt in his Mercedes, McNichol feared he would not turn the money over. This fear resulted in McNichol's contacting an underworld friend, who arranged for the robbery of Crawson's car and cash. McNichol allowed the masked assailant to retain the proceeds related to the stolen automobile, but the cash was to be split between them.

In order to obtain a more lenient plea deal, McNichol cooperated with authorities and advised that Michael Westmont was the man wearing the white handkerchief. McNichol admitted, however, that Westmont was not the person responsible for planning the robbery. Westmont, of course, was still arrested. Both men refused to identify the name of the man who put them together.

Following standard protocol, the Carlstadt police fingerprinted McNichol and Westmont and ran an NCIC report to ascertain their respective criminal histories. While the cumulative results of the NCIC searches resulted in no criminal convictions, Chief Beaumont reported that Michael Westmont's fingerprints matched those of an individual sought for a 35-year-old New Jersey murder of a nursing student.

After probing further, Beaumont and his detectives learned that Westmont was a former medical doctor who was a fugitive from justice for allegedly performing first-trimester abortions in the 1960s—a time when the medical procedure was illegal in the state of New Jersey. He also found that the doctor had been convicted of sexual assault in 1959 under the alias "Roger Ponot." Westmont/Ponot had never registered as a sex offender in the municipality where he resided. Chief Beaumont advised that Westmont would be charged appropriately for these various crimes.

In the southwest part of the state, West Deptford police officers recently arrested Jacques Vandermeit, charging him with armed robbery, aggravated assault, and other related offenses. West Deptford's chief of police, M. P. Ironstone, explained the circumstances that led to Vandermeit's arrest—an arrest he personally performed.

While traveling to headquarters on an early Thursday morning, Ironstone bypassed his daily stop at his favorite highway coffee shop. His attention had been diverted by the strange appearances of two men in a jewelry store parking lot across the highway. One man was wearing a white handkerchief over his face and the other was shirtless and barefoot, only sporting blue jeans. Ironstone immediately notified his on-duty patrol officers and headed to the closest U-turn, which was about two miles south of his current location. As he looked in his rearview mirror, Ironstone saw the men enter the jewelry establishment. Minutes later, he arrived alone at the store, witnessing a violent chain of events.

As he approached, Ironstone saw the masked man rip the jewelry clerk over a glass countertop and begin beating him on the upper body and face with a baseball bat. The half-naked man looked on, chanting and screaming for him to "knock the dude out." He then stuffed a handful of diamonds into the masked man's coat pocket. At this, Ironstone burst through the door, gun drawn, and ordered the assailants to hit the floor with arms and legs outstretched. The masked man seemingly complied with the chief's directive, dropping the baseball bat and falling to the ground. As he did so, however, his shirtless companion tripped over him and fell directly into Ironstone. The felon and police officer simultaneously crashed to the ground, allowing the face-covered man to escape through a back exit. Ironstone immediately ascertained that the jewelry clerk, although apparently injured, was not in a life-threatening condition. He handcuffed the one robbery suspect and then chased after the other.

A 20-minute foot pursuit followed where Ironstone tracked the assailant across the highway, through wooded areas, into residential backyards, and finally into a super-market. Once inside the grocery store, Ironstone tackled the fleeing felon before any more danger could occur. Backup officers arrived moments later, and the suspect, who was later identified as Jacques Vandermeit, was transported to the West Deptford police headquarters. There, $500,000 in diamonds, rubies, and emeralds was confiscated from his person.

Vandermeit's accomplice, however, never made it to the police station. Ironstone advised that the jewelry clerk had shot and killed the man before police made it to the gem store. Apparently, although the shirtless man was handcuffed, he was able to reach into his pants where he was attempting to remove a solid black instrument. The clerk, frightened and believing it was a gun, grabbed a pistol he kept stashed behind the counter. The gun accidentally went off as the clerk pointed it at the handcuffed man in an attempt to prevent him from reaching it. The solid black instrument turned out to be a hairbrush. The dead man's family subsequently argued that the clerk should be charged with manslaughter. The West Deptford Police Department and the Gloucester County Prosecutor's Office denied their request. Ironstone also noted that an autopsy of the shirtless man showed that he had high levels of both PCP and alcohol in his bloodstream.

In Jersey City, Hudson County Prosecutor Francine Colongero had recently success-fully indicted Jillian Peterson for armed robbery and attempted murder. She described to her group of colleagues the circumstances that led to this indictment.

The Jersey City police received a late afternoon report that a red Camaro was traveling in excess of 100 miles per hour on Route 1&9, a busy commuter highway. Several independent witnesses verified that the vehicle's lone occupant was a woman whose face was masked with a white handkerchief. Two patrol cars were dispatched to the stretch of roadway where the vehicle was traveling. One of the units located the

Camaro but did not find it violating any motor vehicle statutes. To the contrary, the vehicle was parked at a local car dealership. The suspect driver was not visible from the patrol officer's highway purview.

Aware of the reports that the Camaro driver was masked, the officer was naturally cautious and drove past the dealership and parked in the lot of an adjoining business. Moments later, he heard screaming and two loud thuds. Following the sounds of this violent eruption, the officer raced to the dealership's showroom. There, he found the masked woman alone. Two machetes were lodged in a wall leading down a staircase; the woman stood motionless, holding a black leather suitcase. The officer ordered her to freeze, pointing his pistol at her. She responded by saying, "Queen Elizabeth told me to steal this cash. I am flying to the moon with her tomorrow to start a cheese factory." Upon the completion of her statements, she reached inside her overcoat and produced a hand grenade. As she was about to pull the explosive device's pin, the police officer lunged at her, knocking the grenade from her hand and allowing it to fall harmlessly to the floor. The woman, who was later identified as Jillian Peterson, was arrested on the spot.

A subsequent investigation revealed that Peterson was a martial arts enthusiast, whose particular expertise was sword and knife fighting, skills she employed in her failed robbery attempt of the car dealership. Wielding two machetes, she ordered the business's general manager to turn over the company's $500,000 cash reserve, which she advised she knew was hidden in a safe in the back office. The manager complied and immediately led her to the money. When they returned to the showroom, Peterson waved the machetes and told the manager, "Thanks for the cash. I'm going to kill you with these machetes anyway." The manager, who was so close to Peterson that the knives could touch him, quickly dropped to the floor, rolling through an open doorway and down a staircase. As he was doing this, Peterson whipped the knives at him, narrowly missing the man's head. Though the man fled, she stayed in place, staring at the knives stuck in the wall. She later told the police that she was so distraught having missed the general manager that she was initially unable to move. Peterson provided no further statements, and the Hudson County Prosecutor's Office prepared to succeed in their various felony charges against her.

## 2C:1-1.    Short title; rules of construction

a.  This Title shall be known and may be cited as the "New Jersey Code of Criminal Justice."

b.  Except as provided in subsections c. and d. of this section, the code does not apply to offenses committed prior to its effective date and prosecutions and dispositions for such offenses shall be governed by the prior law, which is continued in effect for that purpose, as if this code were not in force. For the purposes of this section, an offense was committed after the effective date of the code if any of the elements of the offenses occurred subsequent thereto.

c.  In any case pending on or initiated after the effective date of the code involving an offense committed prior to such date:

   (1)  The procedural provisions of the code shall govern, insofar as they are justly applicable and their application does not introduce confusion or delay;

   (2)  The court, with the consent of the defendant, may impose sentence under the provisions of the code applicable to the offense and the offender.

   (3)  The court shall, if the offense committed is no longer an offense under the provisions of the code, dismiss such prosecution.

d. (1) The provisions of the code governing the treatment and the release or discharge of prisoners, probationers and parolees shall apply to persons under sentence for offenses committed prior to the effective date of the code, except that the minimum or maximum period of their detention or supervision shall in no case be increased.

(2) Any person who is under sentence of imprisonment on the effective date of the code for an offense committed prior to the effective date which has been eliminated by the code or who has been sentenced to a maximum term of imprisonment for an offense committed prior to the effective date which exceeds the maximum established by the code for such an offense and who, on said effective date, has not had his sentence suspended or been paroled or discharged, may move to have his sentence reviewed by the sentencing court and the court may impose a new sentence, for good cause shown as though the person had been convicted under the code, except that no period of detention or supervision shall be increased as a result of such resentencing.

e. The provisions of the code not inconsistent with those of prior laws shall be construed as a continuation of such laws.

f. The classification and arrangement of the several sections of the code have been made for the purpose of convenience, reference and orderly arrangement, and therefore no implication or presumption of a legislative construction is to be drawn therefrom.

g. In the construction of the code, or any part thereof, no outline or analysis of the contents of said title or of any subtitle, chapter, article or section, no cross-reference or cross-reference note and no headnote or source note to any section shall be deemed to be a part of the code.

h. If said title or any subtitle, chapter, article or section of the code, or any provision thereof, shall be declared to be unconstitutional, invalid or inoperative in whole or in part, by a court of competent jurisdiction, such title, subtitle, chapter, article, section or provision shall, to the extent that it is not unconstitutional, invalid or inoperative, be enforced and effectuated, and no such determination shall be deemed to invalidate or make ineffectual the remaining provisions of the title, or of any subtitle, chapter, article or section of the code.

## PRACTICAL APPLICATION OF STATUTE

The Carlstadt Police Department would be in error if they charged Michael Westmont for performing first-trimester abortions in the 1960s even though he violated the law at that time. Given that this code of criminal justice became generally effective in 1979 and that there is no provision currently outlawing first-trimester abortions in the code, nor any continued law prohibiting said abortions that existed prior to the enactment of the code, under 2C:1-1 Westmont cannot be prosecuted in New Jersey for his 1960s abortions.

2C:1-1c.(3) specifically addresses the above issue. With regard to any case pending after the effective date of the code that involves "an offense committed prior to such date," "the court shall, if the offense committed is no longer an offense under the provisions of the code, dismiss such prosecution."

2C:1-2.        **Purposes; principles of construction**

a. The general purposes of the provisions governing the definition of offenses are:

(1) To forbid, prevent, and condemn conduct that unjustifiably and inexcusably inflicts or threatens serious harm to individual or public interests;

      (2)  To insure the public safety by preventing the commission of offenses through the deterrent influence of the sentences authorized, the rehabilitation of those convicted, and their confinement when required in the interests of public protection;

      (3)  To subject to public control persons whose conduct indicates that they are disposed to commit offenses;

      (4)  To give fair warning of the nature of the conduct proscribed and of the sentences authorized upon conviction;

      (5)  To differentiate on reasonable grounds between serious and minor offenses; and

      (6)  To define adequately the act and mental state which constitute each offense, and limit the condemnation of conduct as criminal when it is without fault.

b.  The general purposes of the provisions governing the sentencing of offenders are:

      (1)  To prevent and condemn the commission of offenses;

      (2)  To promote the correction and rehabilitation of offenders;

      (3)  To insure the public safety by preventing the commission of offenses through the deterrent influence of sentences imposed and the confinement of offenders when required in the interest of public protection;

      (4)  To safeguard offenders against excessive, disproportionate or arbitrary punishment;

      (5)  To give fair warning of the nature of the sentences that may be imposed on conviction of an offense;

      (6)  To differentiate among offenders with a view to a just individualization in their treatment;

      (7)  To advance the use of generally accepted scientific methods and knowledge in sentencing offenders; and

      (8)  To promote restitution to victims.

c.  The provisions of the code shall be construed according to the fair import of their terms but when the language is susceptible of differing constructions it shall be interpreted to further the general purposes stated in this section and the special purposes of the particular provision involved. The discretionary powers conferred by the code shall be exercised in accordance with the criteria stated in the code and, insofar as such criteria are not decisive, to further the general purposes stated in this section.

d.  Nothing contained in this code shall limit the right of a defendant and, subject only to the Federal and State constitutions, the right of the State to appeal or seek leave to appeal pursuant to law and Rules of Court.

## 2C:1-3.      Territorial applicability

a.  Except as otherwise provided in this section, a person may be convicted under the law of this State of an offense committed by his own conduct or the conduct of another for which he is legally accountable if:

      (1)  Either the conduct which is an element of the offense or the result which is such an element occurs within this State;

      (2)  Conduct occurring outside the State is sufficient under the law of this State to constitute an attempt to commit a crime within the State;

      (3)  Conduct occurring outside the State is sufficient under the law of this State to constitute a conspiracy to commit an offense within the State and an overt act in furtherance of such conspiracy occurs within the State;

(4) Conduct occurring within the State establishes complicity in the commission of, or an attempt, or conspiracy to commit, an offense in another jurisdiction which also is an offense under the law of this State;

(5) The offense consists of the omission to perform a legal duty imposed by the law of this State with respect to domicile, residence or a relationship to a person, thing or transaction in the State; or

(6) The offense is based on a statute of this State which expressly prohibits conduct outside the State, when the conduct bears a reasonable relation to a legitimate interest of this State and the actor knows or should know that his conduct is likely to affect that interest.

b.  Subsection a.(1) does not apply when either causing a specified result or a purpose to cause or danger of causing such a result is an element of an offense and the result occurs or is designed or likely to occur only in another jurisdiction where the conduct charged would not constitute an offense, unless a legislative purpose plainly appears to declare the conduct criminal regardless of the place of the result.

c.  Except as provided in subsection g., subsection a.(1) does not apply when causing a particular result is an element of an offense and the result is caused by conduct occurring outside the State which would not constitute an offense if the result had occurred there, unless the actor purposely or knowingly caused the result within the State.

d.  When the offense is homicide, either the death of the victim or the bodily impact causing death constitutes a "result," within the meaning of subsection a.(1) and if the body of a homicide victim is found within the State, it may be inferred that such result occurred within the State.

e.  This State includes the land and water, including the waters set forth in N.J.S. 40A:13-2 and the air space above such land and water with respect to which the State has legislative jurisdiction. It also includes any territory made subject to the criminal jurisdiction of this State by compacts between it and another state or between it and the Federal Government.

f.  Notwithstanding that territorial jurisdiction may be found under this section, the court may dismiss, hold in abeyance for up to 6 months, or, with the permission of the defendant, place on the inactive list a criminal prosecution under the law of this State where it appears that such action is in the interests of justice because the defendant is being prosecuted for an offense based on the same conduct in another jurisdiction and this State's interest will be adequately served by a prosecution in the other jurisdiction.

g.  When the result which is an element of an offense consists of inflicting a harm upon a resident of this State or depriving a resident of this State of a benefit, the result occurs within this State, even if the conduct occurs wholly outside this State and any property that was affected by the offense was located outside this State.

## PRACTICAL APPLICATION OF STATUTE

The Carlstadt Police Department obviously has jurisdiction to charge Bill McNichol and Michael Westmont with armed robbery for their combined efforts in illegally heisting $100,000 in cash from Crawson. The actual robbery took place in New Jersey; therefore, these defendants would appropriately be charged for this offense in the Garden State. What if, however, the actual robbery did not occur within the territorial boundaries of New Jersey? Could McNichol and Westmont have been charged for robbery under that scenario? The answer may be yes, due to the planning involved in their illegal undertakings.

The crime of conspiracy is key to determining whether the defendants could be prosecuted in New Jersey even if the actual offense did not occur in this state. For instance, if the facts were modified to the extent that the diner and parking lot where the armed robbery occurred were in Connecticut or New York, but the defendants had conspired (planned) to commit the crime in New Jersey, then New Jersey could be the jurisdiction where charges could be levied—but only if an overt act in furtherance of the conspiracy to commit robbery also occurred in New Jersey. A sufficient overt act in this case could be McNichol paying off Westmont in New Jersey or Westmont purchasing the robbery gun within the confines of this state. In sum, McNichol and Westmont could be charged with the armed robbery in New Jersey where they conspired and planned the crime in the state and furthered the conspiracy by payment or another overt act in the Garden State even if the actual offense had actually been carried out in a different state.

**2C:1-4.**          **Classes of offenses**

    a.  An offense defined by this code or by any other statute of this State, for which a sentence of imprisonment in excess of 6 months is authorized, constitutes a crime within the meaning of the Constitution of this State. Crimes are designated in this code as being of the first, second, third or fourth degree.

    b.  An offense is a disorderly persons offense if it is so designated in this code or in a statute other than this code. An offense is a petty disorderly persons offense if it is so designated in this code or in a statute other than this code. Disorderly persons offenses and petty disorderly persons offenses are petty offenses and are not crimes within the meaning of the Constitution of this State. There shall be no right to indictment by a grand jury nor any right to trial by jury on such offenses. Conviction of such offenses shall not give rise to any disability or legal disadvantage based on conviction of a crime.

    c.  An offense defined by any statute of this State other than this code shall be classified as provided in this section or in section 2C:43-1 and, except as provided in section 2C:1-5b and chapter 43, the sentence that may be imposed upon conviction thereof shall hereafter be governed by this code. Insofar as any provision outside the code declares an offense to be a misdemeanor when such offense specifically provides a maximum penalty of 6 months' imprisonment or less, whether or not in combination with a fine, such provision shall constitute a disorderly persons offense.

    d.  Subject to the provisions of section 2C:43-1, reference in any statute, rule, or regulation outside the code to the term "high misdemeanor" shall mean crimes of the first, second, or third degree and reference to the term "misdemeanor" shall mean all crimes.

## PRACTICAL APPLICATION OF STATUTE

Throughout the codebook, offenses are classified as either crimes, disorderly persons offenses, or petty disorderly persons offenses. The primary differentiating factor among these classifications is the penalty that each category can yield along with the different rights attached to the same.

For example, an individual charged with a crime, such as murder, armed robbery, or theft, is entitled to an indictment by a grand jury and a jury trial. A person charged with simple assault, a disorderly persons offense, however, has no such rights. This defendant will simply be served a complaint and then face a singular judge as his trier of fact.

The penalty for a disorderly persons offense cannot exceed six months of imprisonment; 30 days is the maximum prison term for a conviction of a petty disorderly persons offense. The rationale behind this light sentencing structure is simple: the offenses are considered less serious in nature. Examples of disorderly persons offenses and petty disorderly persons offenses are harassment, shoplifting, disorderly conduct, and simple assault. The football players' various antics in the diner would be disorderly persons offenses, while the subsequent armed robbery would be a crime.

Offenses become crimes when the potential prison sentence attached to the offense exceeds six months; sentences for the most serious crimes in New Jersey may reach 25 years in prison, life in prison, or even the death penalty (see 2C:43-6 for sentences of imprisonment for crimes). Crimes are gradated according to their degree. First degree crimes, such as murder, kidnapping, and aggravated sexual assault, are the most serious offenses and carry the greatest possible prison terms. Fourth degree crimes (e.g., reckless endangerment, certain theft offenses, certain forgery offenses) are the least serious, and although a prison term up to 18 months may be imposed, individuals convicted of these offenses often will escape prison sentences.

**2C:1-5.**        **Abolition of common law crimes; all offenses defined by statute; application of general provisions of the code; limitation of local government laws**

    a. Common law crimes are abolished and no conduct constitutes an offense unless the offense is defined by this code or another statute of this State.

    b. The provisions of subtitle 1 of the code are applicable to offenses defined by other statutes. The provisions of subtitle 3 are applicable to offenses defined by other statutes but the maximum penalties applicable to such offenses, if specifically provided in the statute defining such offenses, shall be as provided therein, rather than as provided in this code, except that if the non-code offense is a misdemeanor with a maximum penalty of more than 18 months imprisonment, the provisions of section 2C:43-1b. shall apply.

    c. This section does not affect the power to punish for contempt, either summarily or after indictment, or to employ any sanction authorized by law for the enforcement of an order or a civil judgment or decree.

    d. Notwithstanding any other provision of law, the local governmental units of this State may neither enact nor enforce any ordinance or other local law or regulation conflicting with, or preempted by, any provision of this code or with any policy of this State expressed by this code, whether that policy be expressed by inclusion of a provision in the code or by exclusion of that subject from the code.

**2C:1-6.**        **Time limitations**

    a. A prosecution for any offense set forth in N.J.S.2C:11-3, N.J.S.2C:11-4, N.J.S.2C:14-2 or sections 1 through 5 of P.L.2002, c. 26 (C.2C:38-1 et seq.) may be commenced at any time.

    b. Except as otherwise provided in this section, prosecutions for other offenses are subject to the following periods of limitations:

        (1) A prosecution for a crime must be commenced within five years after it is committed;

        (2) A prosecution for a disorderly persons offense or petty disorderly persons offense must be commenced within one year after it is committed;

        (3) A prosecution for any offense set forth in N.J.S.2C:27-2, N.J.S.2C:27-4, N.J.S.2C:27-6, N.J.S.2C:27-7, N.J.S.2C:29-4, N.J.S.2C:30-2, N.J.S.2C:30-3, or any attempt or conspiracy

to commit such an offense, must be commenced within seven years after the commission of the offense;

(4) A prosecution for an offense set forth in N.J.S.2C:14-3 or N.J.S.2C:24-4, when the victim at the time of the offense is below the age of 18 years, must be commenced within five years of the victim's attaining the age of 18 or within two years of the discovery of the offense by the victim, whichever is later;

(5) A prosecution for any offense set forth in paragraph (2) of subsection a. of N.J.S.2C:17-2, section 9 of P.L.1970, c. 39 (C.13:1E-9), section 20 of P.L.1989, c. 34 (C.13:1E-48.20), section 19 of P.L.1954, c. 212 (C.26:2C-19), section 10 of P.L.1984, c. 173 (C.34:5A-41), or section 10 of P.L.1977, c. 74 (C.58:10A-10) must be commenced within ten years after the date of discovery of the offense by a local law enforcement agency, a county prosecutor, or the Department of Environmental Protection either directly by any of those entities or indirectly by notice given to any of those entities.

c. An offense is committed either when every element occurs or, if a legislative purpose to prohibit a continuing course of conduct plainly appears, at the time when the course of conduct or the defendant's complicity therein is terminated. Time starts to run on the day after the offense is committed, except that when the prosecution is supported by physical evidence that identifies the actor by means of DNA testing or fingerprint analysis, time does not start to run until the State is in possession of both the physical evidence and the DNA or fingerprint evidence necessary to establish the identification of the actor by means of comparison to the physical evidence.

d. A prosecution is commenced for a crime when an indictment is found and for a nonindictable offense when a warrant or other process is issued, provided that such warrant or process is executed without unreasonable delay. Nothing contained in this section, however, shall be deemed to prohibit the downgrading of an offense at any time if the prosecution of the greater offense was commenced within the statute of limitations applicable to the greater offense.

e. The period of limitation does not run during any time when a prosecution against the accused for the same conduct is pending in this State.

f. The limitations in this section shall not apply to any person fleeing from justice.

g. Except as otherwise provided in this code, no civil action shall be brought pursuant to this code more than five years after such action accrues.

## PRACTICAL APPLICATION OF STATUTE

2C:1-6a. provides that there is no time limitation to prosecute individuals who have committed murder (2C:11-3), aggravated manslaughter or manslaughter (2C:11-4), or sexual assault (2C:14-2). In other words, a person can be charged with murder, manslaughter, or sexual assault even if the criminal offense occurred ten years ago, 25 years ago, or 100 years ago. Accordingly, with receipt of Michael Westmont's matching fingerprints, law enforcement authorities may appropriately charge him with the nursing student murder that was 35 years old. They are not barred by any statute of limitations provision.

If Westmont, however, had merely punched the nursing student in the face, thereby committing a simple assault, or stabbed the nursing student in the arm, committing an aggravated assault, authorities would be barred from prosecuting him at this time. Under 2C:1-6b.(1), prosecutions for crimes must be commenced within five years of their commission. Since aggravated assault is defined as a crime under the code, authorities would not be able to charge Westmont for an aggravated assault that is 35 years old.

Similarly, Westmont could not be charged currently for a 35-year-old simple assault. The time limitation to commence prosecution of simple assault, a disorderly persons offense, is even shorter than for a crime. 2C:1-6b.(2) provides that a prosecution for a disorderly persons offense or petty disorderly persons offense must be commenced within one year after it is committed. While Westmont cannot get away with murder, he could certainly get away with committing other violent crimes such as aggravated assault and simple assault if enough time passes.

Please note that there are a few crimes where the statute of limitations is extended to seven years (see subsection b.(3)) and a couple where prosecution "must be commenced within ten years after the date of discovery of the offense" (see subsection b.(5)). Also, per subsection b.(4), there are a few crimes where prosecution "must be commenced within five years of the victim's attaining the age of 18 or within two years of the discovery of the offense by the victim, whichever is later."

It is also important to note that the statutory limitations on prosecutions as stated in 2C:1-6 only act as bars to the *initiation* or *commencement* of prosecutions. In other words, if in 1975 an indictment had been handed down against Michael Westmont for an aggravated assault or a warrant had been issued charging him with simple assault, Westmont would not be able to escape facing either of these charges if he had fled and become a fugitive of justice. Currently, the state would still be able to prosecute him for those already-charged offenses.

---

**2C:1-7.**     **Blank**

**2C:1-8.**     **Method of prosecution when conduct constitutes more than one offense**

a. **Prosecution for multiple offenses; limitation on convictions**. When the same conduct of a defendant may establish the commission of more than one offense, the defendant may be prosecuted for each such offense. He may not, however, be convicted of more than one offense if:

   (1) One offense is included in the other, as defined in subsection d. of this section;

   (2) One offense consists only of a conspiracy or other form of preparation to commit the other;

   (3) Inconsistent findings of fact are required to establish the commission of the offenses; or

   (4) The offenses differ only in that one is defined to prohibit a designated kind of conduct generally and the other to prohibit a specific instance of such conduct. The provisions of this paragraph (4) of subsection a. of this section or any other provision of law notwithstanding, no State tax offense defined in Title 54 of the Revised Statutes or Title 54A of the New Jersey Statutes, as amended and supplemented, shall be construed to preclude a prosecution for any offense defined in this code.

   A determination barring multiple convictions shall be made by the court after verdict or finding of guilt.

b. **Limitation on separate trials for multiple offenses**. Except as provided in subsection c. of this section, a defendant shall not be subject to separate trials for multiple criminal offenses based on the same conduct or arising from the same episode, if such offenses are known to the appropriate prosecuting officer at the time of the commencement of the first trial and are within the jurisdiction and venue of a single court.

c. **Authority of court to order separate trials**. When a defendant is charged with two or more criminal offenses based on the same conduct or arising from the same episode, the court may order any such charges to be tried separately in accordance with the Rules of Court.

d. **Conviction of included offense permitted**. A defendant may be convicted of an offense included in an offense charged whether or not the included offense is an indictable offense. An offense is so included when:

   (1) It is established by proof of the same or less than all the facts required to establish the commission of the offense charged; or

   (2) It consists of an attempt or conspiracy to commit the offense charged or to commit an offense otherwise included therein; or

   (3) It differs from the offense charged only in the respect that a less serious injury or risk of injury to the same person, property or public interest or a lesser kind of culpability suffices to establish its commission.

e. **Submission of included offense to jury**. The court shall not charge the jury with respect to an included offense unless there is a rational basis for a verdict convicting the defendant of the included offense.

**2C:1-9.**          **When prosecution barred by former prosecution for the same offense**

A prosecution of a defendant for a violation of the same provision of the statutes based upon the same facts as a former prosecution is barred by such former prosecution under the following circumstances:

a. The former prosecution resulted in an acquittal by a finding of not guilty by the trier of fact or in a determination that there was insufficient evidence to warrant a conviction. A finding of guilty of a lesser included offense is an acquittal of the greater inclusive offense, although the conviction is subsequently set aside.

b. The former prosecution was terminated, after the complaint had been filed or the indictment found, by a final order or judgment for the defendant, which has not been set aside, reversed, or vacated and which necessarily required a determination inconsistent with a fact or a legal proposition that must be established for conviction of the offense. This subsection shall not apply to an order or judgment quashing an indictment prior to trial.

c. The former prosecution resulted in a conviction. There is a conviction if the prosecution resulted in a judgment of conviction which has not been reversed or vacated, a verdict of guilty which has not been set aside and which is capable of supporting a judgment, or a plea of guilty accepted by the court. In the latter two cases failure to enter judgment must be for a reason other than a motion of the defendant.

d. The former prosecution was improperly terminated. Except as provided in this subsection, there is an improper termination of a prosecution if the termination is for reasons not amounting to an acquittal, and it takes place after the jury was impaneled and sworn or, in a trial before a court without a jury, after the first witness was sworn but before findings were rendered by the trier of facts. Termination under any of the following circumstances is not improper:

   (1) The defendant consents to the termination or waives, by motion to dismiss or otherwise, his right to object to the termination.

   (2) The trial court finds that the termination is necessary because of the failure of the jury to agree upon a verdict after a reasonable time for deliberation has been allowed.

   (3) The trial court finds that the termination is required by a sufficient legal reason and a manifest or absolute or overriding necessity.

**2C:1-10.**     **When prosecution barred by former prosecution for different offense**

A prosecution of a defendant for a violation of a different provision of the statutes or based on different facts than a former prosecution is barred by such former prosecution under the following circumstances:

    a. The former prosecution resulted in an acquittal or in a conviction as defined in section 2C:1-9 and the subsequent prosecution is for:

        (1) Any offense of which the defendant could have been convicted on the first prosecution; or

        (2) Any offense for which the defendant should have been tried on the first prosecution under section 2C:1-8 unless the court ordered a separate trial of the charge of such offense; or

        (3) The same conduct, unless (a) the offense of which the defendant was formerly convicted or acquitted and the offense for which he is subsequently prosecuted each requires proof of a fact not required by the other and the law defining each of such offenses is intended to prevent a substantially different harm or evil, or (b) the second offense was not consummated when the former trial began.

    b. The former prosecution was terminated, after the complaint was filed or the indictment found, by an acquittal or by a final order or judgment for the defendant which has not been set aside, reversed or vacated and which acquittal, final order or judgment necessarily required a determination inconsistent with a fact which must be established for conviction of the second offense.

    c. The former prosecution was improperly terminated, as improper termination is defined in section 2C:1-9, and the subsequent prosecution is for an offense of which the defendant could have been convicted had the former prosecution not been improperly terminated.

    d. Nothing in this section shall bar the disposition of a nonindictable complaint after disposition of an indictable offense except as required by the Federal and State constitutions.

**2C:1-11.**     **Former prosecution in another jurisdiction: when a bar**

When conduct constitutes an offense within the concurrent jurisdiction of this State and of the United States, a prosecution in the District Court of the United States is a bar to a subsequent prosecution in this State under the following circumstances:

    a. The first prosecution resulted in an acquittal or in a conviction, or in an improper termination as defined in section 2C:1-9 and the subsequent prosecution is based on the same conduct, unless (1) the offense of which the defendant was formerly convicted or acquitted and the offense for which he is subsequently prosecuted each requires proof of a fact not required by the other and the law defining each of such offenses is intended to prevent a substantially different harm or evil or (2) the offense for which the defendant is subsequently prosecuted is intended to prevent a substantially more serious harm or evil than the offense of which he was formerly convicted or acquitted or (3) the second offense was not consummated when the former trial began; or

    b. The former prosecution was terminated, after the information was filed or the indictment found, by an acquittal or by a final order or judgment for the defendant which has not been set aside, reversed or vacated and which acquittal, final order or judgment necessarily required a determination inconsistent with a fact which must be established for conviction of the offense of which the defendant is subsequently prosecuted.

**2C:1-12.**  **Former prosecution before court lacking jurisdiction or when fraudulently procured by the defendant**

A prosecution is not a bar within the meaning of sections 2C:1-9, 10 and 11 under any of the following circumstances:

a. The former prosecution was before a court which lacked jurisdiction over the defendant or the offense tried in that court; or

b. The former prosecution was procured by the defendant without the knowledge of the appropriate prosecuting officer; or

c. The former prosecution resulted in a judgment of conviction which was held invalid in a subsequent proceeding on a petition for post-conviction relief or similar process, except that any bar as to reprosecution for a greater inclusive offense created by section 2C:1-9a. shall apply.

**2C:1-13.**  **Proof beyond a reasonable doubt; affirmative defenses; burden of proving fact when not an element of an offense**

a. No person may be convicted of an offense unless each element of such offense is proved beyond a reasonable doubt. In the absence of such proof, the innocence of the defendant is assumed.

b. Subsection a. of this section does not:

   (1) Require the disproof of an affirmative defense unless and until there is evidence supporting such defense; or

   (2) Apply to any defense which the code or another statute requires the defendant to prove by a preponderance of evidence or such other standard as specified in this code.

c. A defense is affirmative, within the meaning of subsection b.(1) of this section, when:

   (1) It arises under a section of the code which so provides; or

   (2) It relates to an offense defined by a statute other than the code and such statute so provides; or

d. When the application of the code depends upon the finding of a fact which is not an element of an offense, unless the code otherwise provides:

   (1) The burden of proving the fact is on the prosecution or defendant, depending on whose interest or contention will be furthered if the finding should be made; and

   (2) The fact must be proved to the satisfaction of the court or jury, as the case may be.

e. When the code or other statute defining an offense establishes a presumption with respect to any fact which is an element of an offense, it has the meaning accorded it by the law of evidence.

f. In any civil action commenced pursuant to any provision of this code the burden of proof shall be by a preponderance of the evidence.

**2C:1-14.**  **General definitions**

In this code, unless a different meaning plainly is required:

a. "Statute" includes the Constitution and a local law or ordinance of a political subdivision of the State;

b. "Act" or "action" means a bodily movement whether voluntary or involuntary;

c. "Omission" means a failure to act;

d. "Conduct" means an action or omission and its accompanying state of mind, or, where relevant, a series of acts and omissions;

e. "Actor" includes, where relevant, a person guilty of an omission;

f. "Acted" includes, where relevant, "omitted to act";

g. "Person," "he," and "actor" include any natural person and, where relevant, a corporation or an unincorporated association;

h. "Element of an offense" means (1) such conduct or (2) such attendant circumstances or (3) such a result of conduct as

    (a) Is included in the description of the forbidden conduct in the definition of the offense;

    (b) Establishes the required kind of culpability;

    (c) Negatives an excuse or justification for such conduct;

    (d) Negatives a defense under the statute of limitations; or

    (e) Establishes jurisdiction or venue;

i. "Material element of an offense" means an element that does not relate exclusively to the statute of limitations, jurisdiction, venue or to any other matter similarly unconnected with (1) the harm or evil, incident to conduct, sought to be prevented by the law defining the offense, or (2) the existence of a justification or excuse for such conduct;

j. "Reasonably believes" or "reasonable belief" designates a belief the holding of which does not make the actor reckless or criminally negligent;

k. "Offense" means a crime, a disorderly persons offense or a petty disorderly persons offense unless a particular section in this code is intended to apply to less than all three;

l. (Deleted by amendment, P.L.1991, c. 91).

m. "Amount involved," "benefit," and other terms of value. Where it is necessary in this act to determine value, for purposes of fixing the degree of an offense, that value shall be the fair market value at the time and place of the operative act.

n. "Motor vehicle" shall have the meaning provided in R.S.39:1-1.

o. "Unlawful taking of a motor vehicle" means conduct prohibited under N.J.S.2C:20-10 when the means of conveyance taken, operated or controlled is a motor vehicle.

p. "Research facility" means any building, laboratory, institution, organization, school, or person engaged in research, testing, educational or experimental activities, or any commercial or academic enterprise that uses warm-blooded or cold-blooded animals for food or fiber production, agriculture, research, testing, experimentation or education. A research facility includes, but is not limited to, any enclosure, separately secured yard, pad, pond, vehicle, building structure or premises or separately secured portion thereof.

q. "Communication" means any form of communication made by any means, including, but not limited to, any verbal or written communication, communications conveyed by any electronic communication device, which includes but is not limited to, a wire, radio, electromagnetic, photoelectric or photo-optical system, telephone, including a cordless, cellular or digital telephone, computer, video recorder, fax machine, pager, or any other means of transmitting voice or data and communications made by sign or gesture.

# 2

# GENERAL PRINCIPLES OF LIABILITY

**2C:2-1.**  **Requirement of voluntary act; omission as basis of liability; possession as an act**

a. A person is not guilty of an offense unless his liability is based on conduct which includes a voluntary act or the omission to perform an act of which he is physically capable. A bodily movement that is not a product of the effort or determination of the actor, either conscious or habitual, is not a voluntary act within the meaning of this section.

b. Liability for the commission of an offense may not be based on an omission unaccompanied by action unless:

(1) The omission is expressly made sufficient by the law defining the offense; or

(2) A duty to perform the omitted act is otherwise imposed by law, including but not limited to, laws such as the "Uniform Fire Safety Act," P.L.1983, c. 383 (C.52:27D-192 et seq.), the "State Uniform Construction Code Act," P.L.1975, c. 217 (C.52:27D-119 et seq.), or any other law intended to protect the public safety or any rule or regulation promulgated thereunder.

c. Possession is an act, within the meaning of this section, if the possessor knowingly procured or received the thing possessed or was aware of his control thereof for a sufficient period to have been able to terminate his possession.

## PRACTICAL APPLICATION OF STATUTE

The one football player slapping the other is a voluntary act and therefore makes him culpable for simple assault. However, if the facts were modified, wherein the ballplayer's striking conduct was the result of an epileptic seizure, his bodily movement would not be considered legally voluntary and, accordingly, it would be inappropriate to charge him with simple assault.

**2C:2-2.**  **General requirements of culpability**

a. **Minimum requirements of culpability.** Except as provided in subsection c.(3) of this section, a person is not guilty of an offense unless he acted purposely, knowingly, recklessly or negligently, as the law may require, with respect to each material element of the offense.

b. **Kinds of culpability defined.**

   (1) *Purposely.* A person acts purposely with respect to the nature of his conduct or a result thereof if it is his conscious object to engage in conduct of that nature or to cause such a result. A person acts purposely with respect to attendant circumstances if he is aware of the existence of such circumstances or he believes or hopes that they exist. "With purpose," "designed," "with design" or equivalent terms have the same meaning.

   (2) *Knowingly.* A person acts knowingly with respect to the nature of his conduct or the attendant circumstances if he is aware that his conduct is of that nature, or that such circumstances exist, or he is aware of a high probability of their existence. A person acts knowingly with respect to a result of his conduct if he is aware that it is practically certain that his conduct will cause such a result. "Knowing," "with knowledge" or equivalent terms have the same meaning.

   (3) *Recklessly.* A person acts recklessly with respect to a material element of an offense when he consciously disregards a substantial and unjustifiable risk that the material element exists or will result from his conduct. The risk must be of such a nature and degree that, considering the nature and purpose of the actor's conduct and the circumstances known to him, its disregard involves a gross deviation from the standard of conduct that a reasonable person would observe in the actor's situation. "Recklessness," "with recklessness" or equivalent terms have the same meaning.

   (4) *Negligently.* A person acts negligently with respect to a material element of an offense when he should be aware of a substantial and unjustifiable risk that the material element exists or will result from his conduct. The risk must be of such a nature and degree that the actor's failure to perceive it, considering the nature and purpose of his conduct and the circumstances known to him, involves a gross deviation from the standard of care that a reasonable person would observe in the actor's situation. "Negligently" or "negligence" when used in this code, shall refer to the standard set forth in this section and not to the standards applied in civil cases.

c. **Construction of statutes with respect to culpability requirements.**

   (1) Prescribed culpability requirement applies to all material elements. When the law defining an offense prescribes the kind of culpability that is sufficient for the commission of an offense, without distinguishing among the material elements thereof, such provision shall apply to all the material elements of the offense, unless a contrary purpose plainly appears.

   (2) Substitutes for kinds of culpability. When the law provides that a particular kind of culpability suffices to establish an element of an offense such element is also established if a person acts with higher kind of culpability.

   (3) Construction of statutes not stating culpability requirement. Although no culpable mental state is expressly designated in a statute defining an offense, a culpable mental state may nevertheless be required for the commission of such offense, or with respect to some or all of the material elements thereof, if the proscribed conduct necessarily involves such culpable mental state. A statute defining a crime, unless clearly indicating a legislative intent to impose strict liability, should be construed as defining a crime with the culpability defined in paragraph b.(2) of this section. This provision applies to offenses defined both within and outside of this code.

d. **Culpability as to illegality of conduct.** Neither knowledge nor recklessness nor negligence as to whether conduct constitutes an offense or as to the existence, meaning or application of the law determining the elements of an offense is an element of such offense, unless the definition of the offense or the code so provides.

e. **Culpability as determinant of grade of offense.** When the grade or degree of an offense depends on whether the offense is committed purposely, knowingly, recklessly or criminally negligently, its grade or degree shall be the lowest for which the determinative kind of culpability is established with respect to any material element of the offense.

**2C:2-3.**   **Causal relationship between conduct and result; divergence between result designed, contemplated or risked and actual result**

a. Conduct is the cause of a result when:

(1) It is an antecedent but for which the result in question would not have occurred; and

(2) The relationship between the conduct and result satisfies any additional causal requirements imposed by the code or by the law defining the offense.

b. When the offense requires that the defendant purposely or knowingly cause a particular result, the actual result must be within the design or contemplation, as the case may be, of the actor, or, if not, the actual result must involve the same kind of injury or harm as that designed or contemplated and not be too remote, accidental in its occurrence, or dependent on another's volitional act to have a just bearing on the actor's liability or on the gravity of his offense.

c. When the offense requires that the defendant recklessly or criminally negligently cause a particular result, the actual result must be within the risk of which the actor is aware or, in the case of criminal negligence, of which he should be aware, or, if not, the actual result must involve the same kind of injury or harm as the probable result and must not be too remote, accidental in its occurrence, or dependent on another's volitional act to have a just bearing on the actor's liability or on the gravity of his offense.

d. A defendant shall not be relieved of responsibility for causing a result if the only difference between what actually occurred and what was designed, contemplated or risked is that a different person or property was injured or affected or that a less serious or less extensive injury or harm occurred.

e. When causing a particular result is a material element of an offense for which absolute liability is imposed by law, the element is not established unless the actual result is a probable consequence of the actor's conduct.

**2C:2-4.**   **Ignorance or mistake**

a. Ignorance or mistake as to a matter of fact or law is a defense if the defendant reasonably arrived at the conclusion underlying the mistake and:

(1) It negatives the culpable mental state required to establish the offense; or

(2) The law provides that the state of mind established by such ignorance or mistake constitutes a defense.

b. Although ignorance or mistake would otherwise afford a defense to the offense charged, the defense is not available if the defendant would be guilty of another offense had the situation been as he supposed. In such case, however, the ignorance or mistake of the defendant shall reduce the grade and degree of the offense of which he may be convicted to those of the offense of which he would be guilty had the situation been as he supposed.

c. A belief that conduct does not legally constitute an offense is a defense to a prosecution for that offense based upon such conduct when:

(1) The statute defining the offense is not known to the actor and has not been published or otherwise reasonably made available prior to the conduct alleged; or

(2) The actor acts in reasonable reliance upon an official statement of the law, afterward determined to be invalid or erroneous, contained in (a) a statute, (b) judicial decision, opinion, judgment, or rule, (c) an administrative order or grant of permission, or (d) an official interpretation of the public officer or body charged by law with responsibility for the interpretation, administration or enforcement of the law defining the offense; or

(3) The actor otherwise diligently pursues all means available to ascertain the meaning and application of the offense to his conduct and honestly and in good faith concludes his conduct is not an offense in circumstances in which a law-abiding and prudent person would also so conclude.

The defendant must prove a defense arising under subsection c. of this section by clear and convincing evidence.

## PRACTICAL APPLICATION OF STATUTE

The Gloucester County Prosecutor's Office and West Deptford Police Department were correct in their decision in declining to prosecute the jewelry clerk for manslaughter after he had shot and killed the shirtless man handcuffed in his store. Sound rationale to decline prosecution is that the clerk would be successful in a defense of mistake.

2C:2-4 provides that a mistake as to a matter of fact is a defense if an individual "reasonably arrived at the conclusion underlying the mistake" and such mistake negates an offense's required mental state.

Manslaughter and aggravated manslaughter require an individual to manifest a mental state of "recklessness" in order to be convicted for either of these offenses. In other words, a person must act recklessly in causing another's death.

A review of the circumstances that led to the shirtless man's death shows that the jewelry clerk did not act recklessly in grabbing a gun to protect himself. The clerk had just been robbed by an armed assailant who repeatedly struck him with a baseball bat. The shirtless man clearly was involved in the robbery, egging the masked man on and calling for him to "knock the dude out." Even though the half-clothed man was handcuffed, he reached for an item that reasonably could appear to be a gun. Unfortunately, the item turned out to be a hairbrush, and the clerk's gun accidentally fired.

The jewelry clerk's *mistake of fact*—that the robbery suspect was actually reaching for a brush and not a gun—was reasonable under the totality of the circumstances. It gave rise to him appropriately grabbing a gun to protect himself as he feared for his life. This reasonable conclusion negates manslaughter's required culpable mental state of recklessness. Under New Jersey law, recklessness and mistake of fact have a mirror relationship. Where a person makes a reasonable mistake, he cannot act recklessly. Accordingly, while defenses are generally raised at trial to ward off a state-sought conviction, it would be fundamentally unfair to charge the jewelry clerk in this case—given the reasonableness of his mistake.

As a special note, generally courts will find that a *mistake of law* or *ignorance of the law* is no defense. Special exceptions will occur, however, in circumstances where a defendant has relied on an erroneous statute or judicial opinion of an official interpretation of the law by a sanctioned body. For example, if the New Jersey state attorney general or a county prosecutor specifically advised a pharmacist that it was legal to prescribe cocaine to individuals suffering from depression, then the state would be hard-pressed to charge that pharmacist with illegal drug distribution (under Title 2C:35 of the codebook) if he did indeed fulfill a prescription for cocaine for a depressed patient.

In most cases, however, individuals are responsible for knowing the criminal laws that govern in the state. Arguments that lack of knowledge or insufficient notice of the law is present almost always will be rejected. Rarely, if ever, should law enforcement officers not charge an individual with an offense because a defendant, or his attorney, claims ignorance of the law. If such a defense exists, it is a matter for the courts to determine.

**2C:2-5.**          **Defenses generally**

Conduct which would otherwise be an offense is excused or alleviated by reason of any defense now provided by law for which neither the code nor other statutory law defining the offense provides exceptions or defenses dealing with the specific situation involved and a legislative purpose to exclude the defense claimed does not otherwise plainly appear.

**2C:2-6.**          **Liability for conduct of another; complicity**

a. A person is guilty of an offense if it is committed by his own conduct or by the conduct of another person for which he is legally accountable, or both.

b. A person is legally accountable for the conduct of another person when:

    (1) Acting with the kind of culpability that is sufficient for the commission of the offense, he causes an innocent or irresponsible person to engage in such conduct;

    (2) He is made accountable for the conduct of such other person by the code or by the law defining the offense;

    (3) He is an accomplice of such other person in the commission of an offense; or

    (4) He is engaged in a conspiracy with such other person.

c. A person is an accomplice of another person in the commission of an offense if:

    (1) With the purpose of promoting or facilitating the commission of the offense; he

        (a) Solicits such other person to commit it;

        (b) Aids or agrees or attempts to aid such other person in planning or committing it; or

        (c) Having a legal duty to prevent the commission of the offense, fails to make proper effort so to do; or

    (2) His conduct is expressly declared by law to establish his complicity.

d. A person who is legally incapable of committing a particular offense himself may be guilty thereof if it is committed by another person for whose conduct he is legally accountable, unless such liability is inconsistent with the purpose of the provision establishing his incapacity.

e. Unless otherwise provided by the code or by the law defining the offense, a person is not an accomplice in an offense committed by another person if:

    (1) He is a victim of that offense;

    (2) The offense is so defined that his conduct is inevitably incident to its commission; or

    (3) He terminates his complicity under circumstances manifesting a complete and voluntary renunciation as defined in section 2C:5-1d. prior to the commission of the offense. Termination by renunciation is an affirmative defense which the defendant must prove by a preponderance of the evidence.

f. An accomplice may be convicted on proof of the commission of the offense and of his complicity therein, though the person claimed to have committed the offense has not been prosecuted or convicted or has been convicted of a different offense or degree of offense or has an immunity to prosecution or conviction or has been acquitted.

## PRACTICAL APPLICATION OF STATUTE

### Accountable as an Accomplice—Soliciting an Offense

Bill McNichol should be charged with the armed robbery of his football player teammate, Rodney Crawson. While McNichol did not actually tote the gun or physically steal the cash from Crawson's automobile, under 2C:2-6c.(1)(a), McNichol is an accomplice to the robbery because he solicited Westmont to commit the offense.

2C:2-6b.(3) provides that a "person is legally accountable for the conduct of another person" when he is an "accomplice of such other person in the commission of an offense." McNichol is an accomplice to the armed robbery, due to his solicitation of Michael Westmont's criminal activities as aforementioned. Accordingly, McNichol's status as an accomplice makes him legally accountable for the armed robbery to the same extent as Westmont.

### Accountable as an Accomplice—Aiding an Offense

In the same vein, had the shirtless man lived, he would have been appropriately charged for armed robbery even though Jacques Vandermeit brandished the weapon and took the gems. What makes the shirtless man an accomplice to the offense is not that he solicited Vandermeit to commit the crime, but that he *aided* Vandermeit in the commission of it.

2C:2-6c.(1)(b) states that a person is an accomplice of another person in the commission of an offense if . . . "he aids or agrees or attempts to aid such other person in planning or committing it." The shirtless man drove to the crime location with Vandermeit. He accompanied him into the jewelry store and urged Vandermeit to knock the victim out during the baseball-bat beating. And he stuffed a handful of diamonds in his masked partner's pocket. The sum total of these actions demonstrates that the shirtless man aided Vandermeit in committing the armed robbery of the jewelry store. Accordingly, he would be an accomplice to the offense and legally accountable for Vandermeit's armed robbery conduct. But would the shirtless man be held legally accountable for the separate offense of aggravated assault? For Vandermeit's beating of the jewelry clerk? The answer is probably yes.

Even though the shirtless man did not physically partake in hitting the clerk with the baseball bat, he actively urged Vandermeit to strike him. The shirtless man called for him to "knock the dude out." Although case law is a bit gray in this area, New Jersey courts have routinely found this kind of conduct to amount to complicity, making an individual an accomplice to the offense. As such, the shirtless man would have been appropriately charged with aggravated assault had he not been killed by the jewelry clerk.

### Accountable Due to Conspiracy

In both the football player heist and the jewelry store robbery, the criminal mastermind sought by state and local police would be legally accountable for the armed robberies—as a conspirator.

2C:2-6b.(4) sets forth that a person is legally accountable for the conduct of another person if "he is engaged in a conspiracy with such other person." The elements necessary to charge someone with conspiracy will be discussed later in this book. However, simply, the mastermind's planning and arrangement with Michael Westmont (in the football player case) and Jacques Vandermeit (in the jewelry store case) to commit their respective armed robberies, make him a co-conspirator in those offenses. Being culpable in this manner, the mastermind is legally accountable for both armed robberies to the same extent as Westmont and Vandermeit. He would be appropriately charged with both crimes.

**2C:2-7.**        **Liability of corporations and persons acting, or under a duty to act, in their behalf**

    a. A corporation may be convicted of the commission of an offense if:

        (1) The conduct constituting the offense is engaged in by an agent of the corporation while acting within the scope of his employment and in behalf of the corporation unless the offense is one defined by a statute which indicates a legislative purpose not to impose criminal liability on corporations. If the law governing the offense designates the agents for whose conduct the corporation is accountable or the circumstances under which it is accountable, such provisions shall apply;

        (2) The offense consists of an omission to discharge a specific duty of affirmative performance imposed on corporations by law; or

        (3) The conduct constituting the offense is engaged in, authorized, solicited, requested, commanded, or recklessly tolerated by the board of directors or by a high managerial agent acting within the scope of his employment and in behalf of the corporation.

    b. As used in this section:

        (1) "Corporation" does not include an entity organized as or by a governmental agency for the execution of a governmental program;

        (2) "Agent" means any director, officer, servant, employee or other person authorized to act in behalf of the corporation;

        (3) "High managerial agent" means an officer of a corporation or any other agent of a corporation having duties of such responsibility that his conduct may fairly be assumed to represent the policy of the corporation.

    c. In any prosecution of a corporation for the commission of an offense included within the terms of subsection a. (1) of this section, other than an offense for which absolute liability has been imposed, it shall be a defense if the defendant proves by a preponderance of evidence that the high managerial agent having supervisory responsibility over the subject matter of the offense employed due diligence to prevent its commission. This paragraph shall not apply if it is plainly inconsistent with the legislative purpose in defining the particular offense.

    d. Nothing in this section imposing liability upon a corporation shall be construed as limiting the liability for an offense of an individual by reason of his being an agent of the corporation.

**2C:2-8.**        **Intoxication**

    a. Except as provided in subsection d. of this section, intoxication of the actor is not a defense unless it negatives an element of the offense.

    b. When recklessness establishes an element of the offense, if the actor, due to self-induced intoxication, is unaware of a risk of which he would have been aware had he been sober, such unawareness is immaterial.

c. Intoxication does not, in itself, constitute mental disease within the meaning of chapter 4.

d. Intoxication which (1) is not self-induced or (2) is pathological is an affirmative defense if by reason of such intoxication the actor at the time of his conduct did not know the nature and quality of the act he was doing, or if he did know it, that he did not know what he was doing was wrong. Intoxication under this subsection must be proved by clear and convincing evidence.

e. **Definitions.** In this section unless a different meaning plainly is required:

(1) "Intoxication" means a disturbance of mental or physical capacities resulting from the introduction of substances into the body;

(2) "Self-induced intoxication" means intoxication caused by substances which the actor knowingly introduces into his body, the tendency of which to cause intoxication he knows or ought to know, unless he introduces them pursuant to medical advice or under such circumstances as would afford a defense to a charge of crime;

(3) "Pathological intoxication" means intoxication grossly excessive in degree, given the amount of the intoxicant, to which the actor does not know he is susceptible.

## PRACTICAL APPLICATION OF STATUTE

When charging an individual with offenses, law enforcement officers may want to take intoxication into consideration. However, this is a defense and, as such, really is a matter for the trier of fact to determine at the time of trial. In any case, had the shirtless man survived the aftermath of the jewelry store robbery, intoxication may have been a valid defense for the offenses he was involved with that day. Autopsy results showed he had high levels of PCP and alcohol in his blood.

In order to prevail in this defense, the shirtless man would need to show that either his intoxication was not self-induced or that it was pathological, meaning that it was "grossly excessive in degree." Furthermore, subsection d. of the statute provides that he would need to demonstrate that this intoxication resulted in an inability to know the nature and quality of his actions, or if he did know it, that he did not know what he was doing was wrong.

Was the shirtless man's intoxication not self-induced, meaning that the masked man, Jacques Vandermeit, injected PCP into his system and forced him to consume alcohol? Evidence at trial could show that. If his intoxication was self-induced, was it grossly excessive in degree? An expert at trial could testify to this. Self-induced or not, grossly excessive or not, did the intoxication cause the shirtless man to not know the nature and quality of his acts or to not know what he was doing was wrong? Again, an expert at trial may be able to convince a jury of this. Get the picture?

Although the West Deptford Police Department and Gloucester County Prosecutor's Office certainly would want to take into consideration the shirtless man's intoxication, for evidentiary purposes, they shouldn't avoid charging him, or anyone for that matter, because of their findings of intoxication. Intoxication, as a defense, should be left to the court system for determination.

As a special note, intoxication can be a defense to murder, reducing the offense to the lesser homicide statute of manslaughter. Courts have concluded that intoxication can negate the necessary mental states of murder, "purposeful" or "knowledge." However, intoxication can not be a defense to manslaughter, as it cannot negate one of manslaughter's crucial elements—an actor's "reckless" mental state. So while a defendant may be able to use the intoxication defense to lower his charge from murder to manslaughter, he cannot escape a homicide conviction altogether because he was drunk or high.

**2C:2-9.**        **Duress**

    a.  Subject to subsection b. of this section, it is an affirmative defense that the actor engaged in the conduct charged to constitute an offense because he was coerced to do so by the use of, or a threat to use, unlawful force against his person or the person of another, which a person of reasonable firmness in his situation would have been unable to resist.

    b.  The defense provided by this section is unavailable if the actor recklessly placed himself in a situation in which it was probable that he would be subjected to duress. The defense is also unavailable if he was criminally negligent in placing himself in such a situation, whenever criminal negligence suffices to establish culpability for the offense charged. In a prosecution for murder, the defense is only available to reduce the degree of the crime to manslaughter.

    c.  It is not a defense that a woman acted on the command of her husband, unless she acted under such coercion as would establish a defense under this section. The presumption that a woman, acting in the presence of her husband, is coerced is abolished.

## PRACTICAL APPLICATION OF STATUTE

Whether duress is a defense in a given case is a matter for the courts to determine. A modification of the facts involving the shirtless man, however, can exemplify where this defense may be applicable.

If Jacques Vandermeit, the masked criminal, had stripped the shirtless man of his clothing and forced him at gunpoint to be part of the jewelry store heist, then the shirtless man probably would be successful in a defense of duress. 2C:2-9a. provides that duress is an affirmative defense where an individual is coerced by the use of, or threat to use, unlawful force to commit a crime—"which a person of reasonable firmness in his situation would have been unable to resist." Here, again, the code sets forth a reasonableness requirement. Certainly, a person of reasonable firmness would have accompanied Vandermeit into the jewelry store robbery if forced to do so by gunpoint. Therefore, under these circumstances, duress would be an affirmative defense for the shirtless man. Would duress be an affirmative defense, however, if the shirtless man was aware that the masked man was about to commit the robbery and actively sought to drive with him to the jewelry store? And once there the masked man forced him at gunpoint to join him in the robbery? It's unlikely that the defense would be available here.

2C:2-9b. provides that the defense of duress is "unavailable if the actor recklessly placed himself in a situation in which it was probable that he would be subjected to duress." Under the aforementioned fact pattern, the shirtless man's own decision to travel with the masked man to a robbery location likely would be found to be reckless. Accordingly, he would lose any defense of duress.

**2C:2-10.**        **Consent**

    a.  **In general.** The consent of the victim to conduct charged to constitute an offense or to the result thereof is a defense if such consent negatives an element of the offense or precludes the infliction of the harm or evil sought to be prevented by the law defining the offense

b. **Consent to bodily harm.** When conduct is charged to constitute an offense because it causes or threatens bodily harm, consent to such conduct or to the infliction of such harm is a defense if:

(1) The bodily harm consented to or threatened by the conduct consented to is not serious; or

(2) The conduct and the harm are reasonably foreseeable hazards of joint participation in a concerted activity of a kind not forbidden by law; or

(3) The consent establishes a justification for the conduct under chapter 3 of the code.

c. **Ineffective consent.** Unless otherwise provided by the code or by the law defining the offense, assent does not constitute consent if:

(1) It is given by a person who is legally incompetent to authorize the conduct charged to constitute the offense; or

(2) It is given by a person who by reason of youth, mental disease or defect or intoxication is manifestly unable or known by the actor to be unable to make a reasonable judgment as to the nature of harmfulness of the conduct charged to constitute an offense; or

(3) It is induced by force, duress or deception of a kind sought to be prevented by the law defining the offense.

## PRACTICAL APPLICATION OF STATUTE

The West Deptford Police Department would be correct in charging Jacques Vandermeit with aggravated assault even if they learned that the jewelry clerk consented to Vandermeit's baseball-bat beating. While 2C:2-10b.(1) provides a defense for the infliction of bodily injury which is consented to, it only permits it under circumstances where "the bodily harm consented to . . . is not serious." Given that the jewelry clerk was struck multiple times with the baseball bat, the bodily harm likely would be quite serious. Accordingly, in this situation, consent would not be a defense.

A person, however, probably could prevail through a consent defense if another had consented to a slap in the face or a punch to the arm. Interestingly, the statute provides language in subsection b.(2) for a consent defense in circumstances of "joint participation in a concerted activity of a kind not forbidden by law." This is why people are not prosecuted for participating in a boxing or wrestling match—the opponent's consent to his beating is a valid defense in those situtations.

**2C:2-11.**          **De minimis infractions**

The assignment judge may dismiss a prosecution if, having regard to the nature of the conduct charged to constitute an offense and the nature of the attendant circumstances, it finds that the defendant's conduct:

a. Was within a customary license or tolerance, neither expressly negated by the person whose interest was infringed nor inconsistent with the purpose of the law defining the offense;

b. Did not actually cause or threaten the harm or evil sought to be prevented by the law defining the offense or did so only to an extent too trivial to warrant the condemnation of conviction; or

c. Presents such other extenuations that it cannot reasonably be regarded as envisaged by the Legislature in forbidding the offense. The assignment judge shall not dismiss a prosecution under this section without giving the prosecutor notice and an opportunity to be heard. The prosecutor shall have a right to appeal any such dismissal.

**2C:2-12.**          **Entrapment**

    a.  A public law enforcement official or a person engaged in cooperation with such an official or one acting as an agent of a public law enforcement official perpetrates an entrapment if for the purpose of obtaining evidence of the commission of an offense, he induces or encourages and, as a direct result, causes another person to engage in conduct constituting such offense by either:

        (1)  Making knowingly false representations designed to induce the belief that such conduct is not prohibited; or

        (2)  Employing methods of persuasion or inducement which create a substantial risk that such an offense will be committed by persons other than those who are ready to commit it.

    b.  Except as provided in subsection c. of this section, a person prosecuted for an offense shall be acquitted if he proves by a preponderance of evidence that his conduct occurred in response to an entrapment. The issue of entrapment shall be tried by the trier of fact.

    c.  The defense afforded by this section is unavailable when causing or threatening bodily injury is an element of the offense charged and the prosecution is based on conduct causing or threatening such injury to a person other than the person perpetrating the entrapment.

## PRACTICAL APPLICATION OF THE STATUTE

Entrapment is a defense that is rarely successful in its imposition. However, it is a legally viable mechanism for an accused individual to avoid conviction, and therefore it is important to understand the narrow scenarios that allow it to be invoked.

As subsection c. of the statute provides, the defense is unavailable when an element of the charged offense involves "causing or threatening bodily injury." With this being the case, none of the accused armed robbers—Westmont, Vandermeit, or Peterson—could avail himself/herself of the defense since bodily injury was caused or threatened in all of their incidents. But what if the facts were modified in one of their cases? For instance, what if Michael Westmont merely snuck into Rodney Crawson's car and stole his cash? And he was solicited to commit this nonviolent theft not by professional football star Bill McNichol, but by an undercover police officer—could Westmont claim entrapment? Perhaps.

For an entrapment defense to prevail, the statute necessitates that the underlying crime must be "induced" or "encouraged" by a "public law enforcement official." This inducement must directly cause an individual to commit the crime. Even more so, for the entrapment defense to work, the defendant must prove that the law enforcement officer made "knowingly false representations" that the conduct constituting the offense is not prohibited or employed methods of inducement that created a "substantial risk" that a person not ready to commit the offense would thereafter commit it.

Based on the aforesaid, Michael Westmont could not succeed in an entrapment defense merely because an undercover officer solicited his thievery conduct. But he could be victorious via the defense if he proved that the undercover cop purposely lied to him, advising that taking Crawson's cash was not illegal because the money had been abandoned and belonged to no one. Westmont could also be victorious if he were able to prove that he would have never normally been predisposed to commit the theft, but the undercover officer's methods of persuasion were so severe that they changed his perspective, thereby causing him to steal Crawson's cash. As one can see, the burden of proof here is on the defendant, and it is a very difficult burden to meet. This is why the defense is rarely invoked, and also why triers of fact rarely accept it. Still, law enforcement officers should be wary of engaging in certain crime-inducement activities. Otherwise, their charges may not stick.

# 3

# General Principles of Justification

**2C:3-1.**  **Justification an affirmative defense; civil remedies unaffected**

a. In any prosecution based on conduct which is justifiable under this chapter, justification is an affirmative defense.

b. The fact that conduct is justifiable under this chapter does not abolish or impair any remedy for such conduct which is available in any civil action.

**2C:3-2.**  **Necessity and other justifications in general**

a. **Necessity.** Conduct which would otherwise be an offense is justifiable by reason of necessity to the extent permitted by law and as to which neither the code nor other statutory law defining the offense provides exceptions or defenses dealing with the specific situation involved and a legislative purpose to exclude the justification claimed does not otherwise plainly appear.

b. **Other justifications in general.** Conduct which would otherwise be an offense is justifiable by reason of any defense of justification provided by law for which neither the code nor other statutory law defining the offense provides exceptions or defenses dealing with the specific situation involved and a legislative purpose to exclude the justification claimed does not otherwise plainly appear.

**2C:3-3.**  **Execution of public duty**

a. Except as provided in subsection b. of this section, conduct is justifiable when it is required or authorized by:

    (1) The law defining the duties or functions of a public officer or the assistance to be rendered to such officer in the performance of his duties;

    (2) The law governing the execution of legal process;

    (3) The judgment or order of a competent court or tribunal;

    (4) The law governing the armed services or the lawful conduct of war; or

    (5) Any other provision of law imposing a public duty.

b. The other sections of this chapter apply to:

    (1) The use of force upon or toward the person of another for any of the purposes dealt with in such sections; and

(2) The use of deadly force for any purpose, unless the use of such force is otherwise expressly authorized by law.

c.  The justification afforded by subsection a. of this section applies:

    (1) When the actor reasonably believes his conduct to be required or authorized by the judgment or direction of a competent court or tribunal or in the lawful execution of legal process, notwithstanding lack of jurisdiction of the court or defect in the legal process; and

    (2) When the actor reasonably believes his conduct to be required or authorized to assist a public officer in the performance of his duties, notwithstanding that the officer exceeded his legal authority.

## 2C:3-4.  Use of force in self-protection

a.  Use of force justifiable for protection of the person. Subject to the provisions of this section and of section 2C:3-9, the use of force upon or toward another person is justifiable when the actor reasonably believes that such force is immediately necessary for the purpose of protecting himself against the use of unlawful force by such other person on the present occasion.

b.  Limitations on justifying necessity for use of force.

    (1) The use of force is not justifiable under this section:

        (a) To resist an arrest which the actor knows is being made by a peace officer in the performance of his duties, although the arrest is unlawful, unless the peace officer employs unlawful force to effect such arrest; or

        (b) To resist force used by the occupier or possessor of property or by another person on his behalf, where the actor knows that the person using the force is doing so under a claim of right to protect the property, except that this limitation shall not apply if:

            (i) The actor is a public officer acting in the performance of his duties or a person lawfully assisting him therein or a person making or assisting in a lawful arrest;

            (ii) The actor has been unlawfully dispossessed of the property and is making a reentry or recaption justified by section 2C:3-6; or

            (iii) The actor reasonably believes that such force is necessary to protect himself against death or serious bodily harm.

    (2) The use of deadly force is not justifiable under this section unless the actor reasonably believes that such force is necessary to protect himself against death or serious bodily harm; nor is it justifiable if:

        (a) The actor, with the purpose of causing death or serious bodily harm, provoked the use of force against himself in the same encounter; or

        (b) The actor knows that he can avoid the necessity of using such force with complete safety by retreating or by surrendering possession of a thing to a person asserting a claim of right thereto or by complying with a demand that he abstain from any action which he has no duty to take, except that:

            (i) The actor is not obliged to retreat from his dwelling, unless he was the initial aggressor; and

            (ii) A public officer justified in using force in the performance of his duties or a person justified in using force in his assistance or a person justified in using force in making an arrest or preventing an escape is not obliged to desist from efforts to perform such duty, effect such arrest or prevent such escape because of resistance or threatened resistance by or on behalf of the person against whom such action is directed.

(3) Except as required by paragraphs (1) and (2) of this subsection, a person employing protective force may estimate the necessity of using force when the force is used, without retreating, surrendering possession, doing any other act which he has no legal duty to do or abstaining from any lawful action.

c. (1) Notwithstanding the provisions of N.J.S.2C:3-5, N.J.S.2C:3-9, or this section, the use of force or deadly force upon or toward an intruder who is unlawfully in a dwelling is justifiable when the actor reasonably believes that the force is immediately necessary for the purpose of protecting himself or other persons in the dwelling against the use of unlawful force by the intruder on the present occasion.

(2) A reasonable belief exists when the actor, to protect himself or a third person, was in his own dwelling at the time of the offense or was privileged to be thereon and the encounter between the actor and intruder was sudden and unexpected, compelling the actor to act instantly and:

    (a) The actor reasonably believed that the intruder would inflict personal injury upon the actor or others in the dwelling; or

    (b) The actor demanded that the intruder disarm, surrender or withdraw, and the intruder refused to do so.

(3) An actor employing protective force may estimate the necessity of using force when the force is used, without retreating, surrendering possession, withdrawing or doing any other act which he has no legal duty to do or abstaining from any lawful action.

## Practical Application of Statute

The car dealership manager would have been justified to use force—even deadly force—to protect himself from machete-wielding Jillian Peterson. The Hudson County Prosecutor's Office would be in error if they indicted the manager for homicide had he shot Peterson after she threatened to kill him with the machetes.

The code, in 2C:3-4a., provides that an individual is justified to use force against another when the "actor reasonably believes that such force is immediately necessary" to protect himself against the use of unlawful force by another. To use deadly force, the person must reasonably believe it is necessary to protect himself against death or serious bodily harm. The courts have clarified this part of the statute by determining that the defense of deadly force can only be used when a threat of death is imminent. Also, one cannot justify one's use of such force unless he can show that the only way to preserve his life was by killing his assailant.

Certainly, the dealership manager would have manifested a reasonable belief that force was immediately necessary to protect his own life. First, Peterson had just completed the theft of thousands of dollars, giving her a potent motive to not be identified. Next, she was waving two deadly weapons at the man. And she actually told him that she was going to kill him. Under these circumstances, death would appear imminent to any reasonable person, providing justification to utilize deadly force as the only means to save his life. Had the dealership manager shot and killed Peterson, instead of fleeing, it is almost definite that no law enforcement agency would charge him for murder or any homicide statute. Deadly force, in that situation, would have been justified.

### Deadly Force Not Justified If Person Can Retreat

It is important to note, however, that under 2C:3-4b.(2)(b), the use of deadly force is not justifiable if an individual knows that he can retreat with complete safety. For example, if the dealership manager was not only next to a doorway but 100 feet from Peterson, he probably would not be able to avail himself of a self-defense argument. Why? Because under those circumstances, he most likely could have avoided shooting Peterson and retreated with complete safety. However, because the actual facts have Peterson right next to the manager—where the machetes were so close they could actually touch him—Peterson had no obligation to retreat. The fact that he actually did was just fortuitous for Peterson.

### No Requirement to Retreat from Dwelling

The requirement to retreat instead of using deadly force changes when the person threatened with violence is in his own dwelling or "privileged to be in someone else's dwelling." Per 2C:3-4b.(2)(b)(i), an "actor is not obliged to retreat from his dwelling, unless he was the initial aggressor." Under subsection c. of the statute, an actor may use force or deadly force against an intruder in his dwelling if he "reasonably believes that the force is immediately necessary for the purpose of protecting himself or other persons in the dwelling against the use of unlawful force." In other words, even if the dwelling occupant can retreat safely, he can use force or deadly force to ward off an intruder if he reasonably believes the intruder would inflict personal injury on an occupant in the home.

What is a reasonable belief and when a person should retreat, however, are to be measured by an objective standard and not what a particular actor finds reasonable. These are questions to be resolved by a jury.

---

**2C:3-5.**        **Use of force for the protection of other persons**

  a. Subject to the provisions of this section and of section 2C:3-9, the use of force upon or toward the person of another is justifiable to protect a third person when:

  (1) The actor would be justified under section 2C:3-4 in using such force to protect himself against the injury he believes to be threatened to the person whom he seeks to protect; and

  (2) Under the circumstances as the actor reasonably believes them to be, the person whom he seeks to protect would be justified in using such protective force; and

  (3) The actor reasonably believes that his intervention is necessary for the protection of such other person.

  b. Notwithstanding subsection a. of this section:

  (1) When the actor would be obliged under section 2C:3-4 b. (2)(b) to retreat or take other action he is not obliged to do so before using force for the protection of another person, unless he knows that he can thereby secure the complete safety of such other person, and

  (2) When the person whom the actor seeks to protect would be obliged under section 2C:3-4b (2)(b) to retreat or take similar action if he knew that he could obtain complete

safety by so doing, the actor is obliged to try to cause him to do so before using force in his protection if the actor knows that he can obtain complete safety in that way; and

(3) Neither the actor nor the person whom he seeks to protect is obliged to retreat when in the other's dwelling to any greater extent than in his own.

## PRACTICAL APPLICATION OF STATUTE

An individual may use force to protect others for the same reasons he can use force to protect himself as defined in 2C:3-4. A caveat to this, however, is that individual must also reasonably believe that force "is necessary for the protection of such other person" (see 2C:3-5a,(3)) and that the other person must be justified himself "in using such protective force" (see 2C:3-5a.(2)). A modification of the facts of the car dealership robbery can exemplify this.

The dealership manager is still right next to Jillian Peterson and her machetes. Salesperson Sarah Sunshine, though, is 100 feet away from them. Although she can safely retreat, she fires a pistol at Peterson, killing her immediately. Here, Sarah Sunshine is justified in her use of deadly force against Peterson. Objectively speaking, Sunshine's force was necessary to protect the manager's life. In the same vein, the manager would have been justified himself to use the same protective force. With these two prongs met, Sunshine's shooting of Peterson is justifiable deadly force. And, as this statute provides in subsection b., Sunshine was not obligated to retreat herself. This is because she could not reasonably know that she could secure the manager's complete safety without using force.

**2C:3-6.**          **Use of force in defense of premises or personal property**

a. **Use of force in defense of premises.** Subject to the provisions of this section and of section 2C:3-9, the use of force upon or toward the person of another is justifiable when the actor is in possession or control of premises or is licensed or privileged to be thereon and he reasonably believes such force necessary to prevent or terminate what he reasonably believes to be the commission or attempted commission of a criminal trespass by such other person in or upon such premises.

b. **Limitations on justifiable use of force in defense of premises.**

(1) Request to desist. The use of force is justifiable under this section only if the actor first requests the person against whom such force is used to desist from his interference with the property, unless the actor reasonably believes that

(a) Such request would be useless;

(b) It would be dangerous to himself or another person to make the request; or

(c) Substantial harm will be done to the physical condition of the property which is sought to be protected before the request can effectively be made.

(2) Exclusion of trespasser. The use of force is not justifiable under this section if the actor knows that the exclusion of the trespasser will expose him to substantial danger of serious bodily harm.

(3) Use of deadly force. The use of deadly force is not justifiable under subsection a. of this section unless the actor reasonably believes that:

(a) The person against whom the force is used is attempting to dispossess him of his dwelling otherwise than under a claim of right to its possession; or

    (b)  The person against whom the force is used is attempting to commit or consummate arson, burglary, robbery or other criminal theft or property destruction; except that

    (c)  Deadly force does not become justifiable under subparagraphs (a) and (b) of this subsection unless the actor reasonably believes that:

        (i)  The person against whom it is employed has employed or threatened deadly force against or in the presence of the actor; or

        (ii)  The use of force other than deadly force to terminate or prevent the commission or the consummation of the crime would expose the actor or another in his presence to substantial danger of bodily harm. An actor within a dwelling shall be presumed to have a reasonable belief in the existence of the danger. The State must rebut this presumption by proof beyond a reasonable doubt.

c.  **Use of force in defense of personal property.** Subject to the provisions of subsection d. of this section and of section 2C:3-9, the use of force upon or toward the person of another is justifiable when the actor reasonably believes it necessary to prevent what he reasonably believes to be an attempt by such other person to commit theft, criminal mischief or other criminal interference with personal property in his possession or in the possession of another for whose protection he acts.

d.  **Limitations on justifiable use of force in defense of personal property.**

    (1)  Request to desist and exclusion of trespasser. The limitations of subsection b. (1) and (2) of this section apply to subsection c. of this section.

    (2)  Use of deadly force. The use of deadly force in defense of personal property is not justified unless justified under another provision of this chapter.

## PRACTICAL APPLICATION OF STATUTE

When an individual has the legal right to use force in defense of property is quite subjective to the peculiar circumstances of his case. The statute governing these matters, 2C:3-6a., permits an actor to employ force when "he reasonably believes such force necessary to prevent or terminate what he reasonably believes to be the commission" of a criminal trespass on premises which he controls or possesses. However, subsection b. of the statute requires that the person must first request that the trespasser "desist from his interference with the property." Exceptions to the desist requirement are enumerated later in the subsection. For instance, per 2C:3-6b.(1)(b), a property owner does not have to request that the trespasser desist if he reasonably believes that "it would be dangerous to himself or another person to make the request." Masked assailant Jillian Peterson's case, modified, sheds light on how this statute functions.

    Let's say that Peterson arrives at the car dealership unarmed, surreptitiously entering through the back door. Inside, she is discovered by the manager. The manager notes that she is without weaponry, but nonetheless wants her to vacate the premises as it is after hours. Here, the manager would not be justified if he employed force without first requesting that Peterson desist and immediately vacate the store. If, however, Peterson did not leave after a request for her to do so, then the manager would be permitted to use force under the statute.

    The manager would not be required to make the desist request if Peterson visibly carried a knife. Under that scenario, it would be dangerous for the manager to stop and make such a request. There, he would be justified in simply reacting with force to stop her from trespassing upon the premises which he controlled. Similarly, if the manager stumbled upon Peterson smashing an automobile with a hammer, he would be justified in using force against her without first asking her to stop her criminal activities. 2C:3-6b.(1)(c) eliminates the desist request where an individual reasonably believes that substantial harm will be done to the physical property sought to be protected before a desist request can effectively be made.

The manager surely would have a reasonable belief that substantial physical harm would occur to the car if he didn't immediately act with force to stop her hammering of it. Accordingly, he would not be required to ask her to desist before using force there. But could the manager use deadly force to protect his property in this situation? No way.

### Deadly Force in Defense of Property

While 2C:3-6b.(3) provides that deadly force may be used to defend property, in practicality, deadly force may *not* be employed in these cases. More specifically, in the defense of property alone, deadly force is not justifiable. The statute only permits lethal action where deadly force has been "employed or threatened" against the actor or in his presence (2C:3-6b.(3)(c)(i)) or where the use of force other than deadly force will expose the actor or another to "substantial danger of bodily harm" (2C:3-6b.(3)(c)(ii)). In other words, deadly force may only be used to protect oneself or another—not the property.

---

**2C:3-7.**          **Use of force in law enforcement**

a. **Use of force justifiable to effect an arrest.** Subject to the provisions of this section and of section 2C:3-9, the use of force upon or toward the person of another is justifiable when the actor is making or assisting in making an arrest and the actor reasonably believes that such force is immediately necessary to effect a lawful arrest.

b. **Limitations on the use of force.**

(1) The use of force is not justifiable under this section unless:

   (a) The actor makes known the purpose of the arrest or reasonably believes that it is otherwise known by or cannot reasonably be made known to the person to be arrested; and

   (b) When the arrest is made under a warrant, the warrant is valid or reasonably believed by the actor to be valid.

(2) The use of deadly force is not justifiable under this section unless:

   (a) The actor effecting the arrest is authorized to act as a peace officer or has been summoned by and is assisting a person whom he reasonably believes to be authorized to act as a peace officer; and

   (b) The actor reasonably believes that the force employed creates no substantial risk of injury to innocent persons; and

   (c) The actor reasonably believes that the crime for which the arrest is made was homicide, kidnapping, an offense under 2C:14-2 or 2C:14-3, arson, robbery, burglary of a dwelling, or an attempt to commit one of these crimes; and

   (d) The actor reasonably believes:

      (i) There is an imminent threat of deadly force to himself or a third party; or

      (ii)  The use of deadly force is necessary to thwart the commission of a crime as set forth in subparagraph (c) of this paragraph; or

      (iii)  The use of deadly force is necessary to prevent an escape.

c.  **Use of force to prevent escape from custody.** The use of force to prevent the escape of an arrested person from custody is justifiable when the force could, under subsections a. and b. of this section, have been employed to effect the arrest under which the person is in custody. A correction officer or other person authorized to act as a peace officer is, however, justified in using any force including deadly force, which he reasonably believes to be immediately necessary to prevent the escape of a person committed to a jail, prison, or other institution for the detention of persons charged with or convicted of an offense so long as the actor believes that the force employed creates no substantial risk of injury to innocent persons.

d.  **Use of force by private person assisting an unlawful arrest.**

    (1)  A private person who is summoned by a peace officer to assist in effecting an unlawful arrest is justified in using any force which he would be justified in using if the arrest were lawful, provided that he does not believe the arrest is unlawful.

    (2)  A private person who assists another private person in effecting an unlawful arrest, or who, not being summoned, assists a peace officer in effecting an unlawful arrest, is justified in using any force which he would be justified in using if the arrest were lawful, provided that (a) he reasonably believes the arrest is lawful, and (b) the arrest would be lawful if the facts were as he believes them to be and such belief is reasonable.

e.  **Use of force to prevent suicide or the commission of a crime.** The use of force upon or toward the person of another is justifiable when the actor reasonably believes that such force is immediately necessary to prevent such other person from committing suicide, inflicting serious bodily harm upon himself, committing or consummating the commission of a crime involving or threatening bodily harm, damage to or loss of property or a breach of the peace, except that:

    (1)  Any limitations imposed by the other provisions of this chapter on the justifiable use of force in self-protection, for the protection of others, the protection of property, the effectuation of an arrest or the prevention of an escape from custody shall apply notwithstanding the criminality of the conduct against which such force is used; and

    (2)  The use of deadly force is not in any event justifiable under this subsection unless the actor reasonably believes that it is likely that the person whom he seeks to prevent from committing a crime will endanger human life or inflict serious bodily harm upon another unless the commission or the consummation of the crime is prevented and that the use of such force presents no substantial risk of injury to innocent persons.

## PRACTICAL APPLICATION OF STATUTE

Chief Ironstone was justified in using force against Jacques Vandermeit when arresting him for his armed robbery and aggravated assault of the jewelry store. Under subsection a. of 2C:3-7, a law enforcement officer may use force in making an arrest when he "reasonably believes that such force is immediately necessary to effect a lawful arrest."

When Chief Ironstone finally caught up to Vandermeit after chasing him for several minutes, force was objectively necessary to effectuate the arrest. Ironstone held a reasonable belief that tackling Vandermeit was the only means available to finally arrest him, and therefore his use of force was justifiable. But would he have been justified to employ deadly force against Vandermeit? The answer is probably yes.

## Use of Deadly Force in Law Enforcement

Law enforcement officers, and others assisting law enforcement officers, should be careful in using deadly force. However, there are many circumstances where such force is necessary and justifiable. Under the provisions of 2C:3-7, Chief Ironstone would have been justified to use deadly force against Jacques Vandermeit for a number of reasons.

The statute specifically enumerates the necessary factors that need to exist in order for deadly force to be justifiable in law enforcement. First, the actor must be a law enforcement officer or an individual authorized to assist an officer (2C:3-7b.(2)(a)). Second, the actor must reasonably believe that the force employed creates no substantial risk of injury to innocent persons (2C:3-7b.(2)(b)). Next, the crime involved must be homicide, kidnapping, sexual assault, criminal sexual assault, arson, robbery, or burglary of a dwelling—an attempt of any of these crimes will suffice (2C:3-7b.(2)(c)). The actor must also have a reasonable belief that one of the following situations exists: There is an imminent threat of deadly force to himself or a third party, the use of deadly force is necessary to thwart any of the aforementioned crimes, or deadly force is necessary to prevent an escape (2C:3-7b.(2)(d)(i),(ii), and (iii)).

After reviewing the above-listed elements, it appears that Chief Ironstone would have been within the boundaries of the law if he had employed deadly force against Jacques Vandermeit. Ironstone is a law enforcement officer. He witnessed a robbery in progress and thereafter chased a fleeing felon who was escaping an arrest. Vandermeit also was violently beating the jewelry clerk with a baseball bat, which reasonably could have been construed as an attempted murder. It is quite likely that at multiple times during the incident—inside the jewelry store and during the ensuing chase—that Ironstone held a reasonable belief that employing deadly force created no substantial risk of injury to innocent persons. Chief Ironstone could have shot Vandermeit without putting the jewelry clerk or any passersby at risk. A shooting by the chief likely would ultimately be considered justified, as he held a reasonable belief for all three prongs of subsection b.(2)(d) of the statute: there was an imminent threat of deadly force against the jewelry clerk, his use of deadly force was necessary to thwart Vandermeit's armed robbery and attempted murder, and it may have been necessary to prevent his escape.

While it appears accurate that Chief Ironstone could have legally utilized deadly force to thwart Jacques Vandermeit's criminal activities and preserve the safety of innocent victim(s), such use of force is truly reserved for only the most grave and serious situations. In other words, though the statute seems to permit the use of deadly force to thwart a burglary of a dwelling, a law enforcement officer may want to strongly consider other options before shooting, or otherwise killing, the suspect burglar. Without an imminent threat of deadly force to the officer himself, or third party, or the presence of a violent crime such as sexual assault or kidnapping, courts may find that deadly force was not justifiable—and then a law enforcement officer finds himself charged with a felony.

---

**2C:3-8.**          **Use of force by persons with special responsibility for care, discipline or safety of others**

The use of force upon or toward the person of another is justifiable as permitted by law or as would be a defense in a civil action based thereon where the actor has been vested or entrusted with special responsibility for the care, supervision, discipline or safety of another or of others and the force is used for the purpose of and, subject to section 2C:3-9b., to the extent necessary to further that responsibility, unless:

  a. The code or the law defining the offense deals with the specific situation involved; or

  b. A legislative purpose to exclude the justification claimed otherwise plainly appears; or

  c. Deadly force is used, in which case such force must be otherwise justifiable under the provisions of this chapter.

**2C:3-9.     Mistake of law as to unlawfulness of force or legality of arrest; reckless or negligent use of excessive but otherwise justifiable force; reckless or negligent injury or risk of injury to innocent persons**

  a. The justification afforded by sections 2C:3-4 to 2C:3-7 is unavailable when:

  (1) The actor's belief in the unlawfulness of the force or conduct against which he employs protective force or his belief in the lawfulness of an arrest which he endeavors to effect by force is erroneous; and

  (2) His error is due to ignorance or mistake as to the provisions of the code, any other provisions of the criminal law or the law governing the legality of an arrest or search.

  b. (Deleted by amendment; P.L.1981, c. 290.)

  c. When the actor is justified under sections 2C:3-3 to 2C:3-8 in using force upon or toward the person of another but he recklessly or negligently injures or creates a risk of injury to innocent persons, the justification afforded by those sections is unavailable in a prosecution for such recklessness or negligence towards innocent persons.

**2C:3-10.     Justification in property crimes**

Conduct involving the appropriation, seizure or destruction of, damage to, intrusion on, or interference with, property is justifiable under circumstances which would establish a defense of privilege in a civil action based thereon, unless:

  a. The code or the law defining the offense deals with the specific situation involved; or

  b. A legislative purpose to exclude the justification claimed otherwise plainly appears.

**2C:3-11.     Definitions**

In this chapter, unless a different meaning plainly is required:

  a. "Unlawful force" means force, including confinement, which is employed without the consent of the person against whom it is directed and the employment of which constitutes an offense or actionable tort or would constitute such offense or tort except for a defense (such as the absence of intent, negligence, or mental capacity; duress, youth, or diplomatic status) not amounting to a privilege to use the force. Assent constitutes consent, within the meaning of this section, whether or not it otherwise is legally effective, except assent to the infliction of death or serious bodily harm.

  b. "Deadly force" means force which the actor uses with the purpose of causing or which he knows to create a substantial risk of causing death or serious bodily harm. Purposely firing a firearm in the direction of another person or at a vehicle, building or structure in which another person is believed to be constitutes deadly force. A threat to cause death or serious bodily harm, by the production of a weapon or otherwise, so long as the actor's purpose is limited to creating an apprehension that he will use deadly force if necessary, does not constitute deadly force.

  c. "Dwelling" means any building or structure, though movable or temporary, or a portion thereof, which is for the time being the actor's home or place of lodging except that, as used in 2C:3-7, the building or structure need not be the actor's own home or place of lodging.

d. "Serious bodily harm" means bodily harm which creates a substantial risk of death or which causes serious, permanent disfigurement or protracted loss or impairment of the function of any bodily member or organ or which results from aggravated sexual assault or sexual assault.

e. "Bodily harm" means physical pain, or temporary disfigurement, or impairment of physical condition.

# 4

# RESPONSIBILITY

**2C:4-1.**          **Insanity defense**

A person is not criminally responsible for conduct if at the time of such conduct he was laboring under such a defect of reason, from disease of the mind as not to know the nature and quality of the act he was doing, or if he did know it, that he did not know what he was doing was wrong. Insanity is an affirmative defense which must be proved by a preponderance of the evidence.

## PRACTICAL APPLICATION OF STATUTE

Jillian Peterson perhaps could succeed in an insanity defense. This woman attempted to rob a car dealership while wearing a white handkerchief and manipulating two sharp machetes. Upon her failed attempt to strike her intended victim with the heavy knives, she stood motionless, incapable of movement as she was distraught with herself. Even more so, she advised law enforcement officers that "Queen Elizabeth told me to steal this cash. I am flying to the moon with her tomorrow to start a cheese factory." While she sounds nuts, was she legally insane at the time of her crimes?

    2C:4-1 provides that a person is not criminally responsible for his conduct due to insanity if he did not "know the nature and quality of the act he was doing" or "if he did know it, that he did not know what he was doing was wrong." This is clearly a question for a jury to decide. However, did Peterson understand what she was doing—the nature and quality of her act? Probably. She told the car dealership manager that she was going to kill him and then immediately threw machetes at him, attempting to complete that task. She also actively sought out to heist cash from the business, even having knowledge where the money was stored. This seems to add up to a person knowing the nature and quality of her ill acts to rob and murder. But did she know that her criminal activities were wrong? Maybe not. She did mention that Queen Elizabeth told her to steal the cash and that she was flying to the moon with her to start a cheese factory. This may be enough for her to prove by a preponderance of the evidence that she was legally insane. Ultimately though, psychiatric expert witnesses would duel this matter out in the courtroom. Thereafter, a jury would decide the fate of Peterson's insanity defense.

**2C:4-2.** **Evidence of mental disease or defect admissible when relevant to element of the offense**

Evidence that the defendant suffered from a mental disease or defect is admissible whenever it is relevant to prove that the defendant did not have a state of mind which is an element of the offense. In the absence of such evidence, it may be presumed that the defendant had no mental disease or defect which would negate a state of mind which is an element of the offense.

**2C:4-3.** **Requirement of notice**

a. If a defendant intends to claim insanity pursuant to section 2C:4-1 or the absence of a requisite state of mind pursuant to section 2C:4-2, he shall serve notice of such intention upon the prosecuting attorney in accordance with the Rules of Court.

b. When a defendant is acquitted on the ground of insanity, the verdict and judgment shall so state.

**2C:4-4.** **Mental incompetence excluding fitness to proceed**

a. No person who lacks capacity to understand the proceedings against him or to assist in his own defense shall be tried, convicted or sentenced for the commission of an offense so long as such incapacity endures.

b. A person shall be considered mentally competent to stand trial on criminal charges if the proofs shall establish:

(1) That the defendant has the mental capacity to appreciate his presence in relation to time, place and things; and

(2) That his elementary mental processes are such that he comprehends:

(a) That he is in a court of justice charged with a criminal offense;

(b) That there is a judge on the bench;

(c) That there is a prosecutor present who will try to convict him of a criminal charge;

(d) That he has a lawyer who will undertake to defend him against that charge;

(e) That he will be expected to tell to the best of his mental ability the facts surrounding him at the time and place where the alleged violation was committed if he chooses to testify and understands the right not to testify;

(f) That there is or may be a jury present to pass upon evidence adduced as to guilt or innocence of such charge or, that if he should choose to enter into plea negotiations or to plead guilty, that he comprehend the consequences of a guilty plea and that he be able to knowingly, intelligently, and voluntarily waive those rights which are waived upon such entry of a guilty plea; and

(g) That he has the ability to participate in an adequate presentation of his defense.

**2C:4-5.** **Psychiatric or psychological examination of defendant with respect to fitness to proceed**

a. Whenever there is reason to doubt the defendant's fitness to proceed, the court may on motion by the prosecutor, the defendant or on its own motion, appoint at least one qualified psychiatrist or licensed psychologist to examine and report upon the mental condition of the defendant. The psychiatrist or licensed psychologist so appointed shall be either:

(1) From a list agreed to by the court, the prosecutor and the defendant; or

(2) Agreed to by the court, prosecutor and defendant.

Alternatively, the court may order examination of a defendant for fitness to proceed by the Department of Human Services. The department shall provide or arrange for examination of the defendant at a jail, prison or psychiatric hospital. However, to ensure that a defendant is not unnecessarily hospitalized for the purpose of the examination, a defendant shall not be admitted to a State psychiatric hospital for an examination regarding his fitness to proceed unless a qualified psychiatrist or licensed psychologist designated by the commissioner determines that hospitalization is clinically necessary to perform the examination. Whenever the qualified psychiatrist or licensed psychologist determines that hospitalization is clinically necessary to perform the examination, the court shall order the defendant to be committed to the custody of the Commissioner of Human Services for placement in a State psychiatric hospital designated for that purpose for a period not exceeding 30 days.

A qualified psychiatrist or licensed psychologist retained by the defendant or by the prosecutor shall, if requested, be permitted to examine a defendant who has been admitted to a State psychiatric hospital.

b. The report of the examination shall include at least the following: (1) a description of the nature of the examination; (2) a diagnosis of the mental condition of the defendant; (3) an opinion as to the defendant's capacity to understand the proceedings against him and to assist in his own defense. The person or persons conducting the examination may ask questions respecting the crime charged when such questions are necessary to enable formation of an opinion as to a relevant issue, however, the evidentiary character of any inculpatory statement shall be limited expressly to the question of competency and shall not be admissible on the issue of guilt.

c. If the examination cannot be conducted by reason of the unwillingness of the defendant to participate therein, the report shall so state and shall include, if possible, an opinion as to whether such unwillingness of the defendant was the result of mental incompetence. Upon the filing of such a report, the court may permit examination without cooperation, may appoint a different psychiatrist or licensed psychologist, or may commit the defendant for observation for a period not exceeding 30 days except on good cause shown, or exclude or limit testimony by the defense psychiatrist or licensed psychologist.

d. The report of the examination shall be sent by the psychiatrist or licensed psychologist to the court, the prosecutor and counsel for the defendant.

**2C:4-6.**     **Determination of fitness to proceed; effect of finding of unfitness; proceedings if fitness is regained; post-commitment hearing**

a. When the issue of the defendant's fitness to proceed is raised, the issue shall be determined by the court. If neither the prosecutor nor counsel for the defendant contests the finding of the report filed pursuant to section 2C:4-5, the court may make the determination on the basis of such report. If the finding is contested or if there is no report, the court shall hold a hearing on the issue. If the report is received in evidence upon such hearing, either party shall have the right to summon and examine the psychiatrists or licensed psychologists who joined in the report and to offer evidence upon the issue.

b. If the court determines that the defendant lacks fitness to proceed, the proceeding against him shall be suspended, except as provided in subsection c. of this section. At this time, the court may commit him to the custody of the Commissioner of Human Services to be placed in an appropriate institution if it is found that the defendant is so dangerous to himself or others as to require institutionalization, or it shall proceed to determine whether placement in an out-patient setting or release is appropriate; provided, however, that no commitment to any institution shall be in excess of such period of time during which it can be determined whether it is substantially probable that the defendant could regain his competence within the foreseeable future.

    If the court determines that the defendant is fit to proceed, but suffers from mental illness, as defined in section 2 of P.L.1987, c. 116 (C.30:4-27.2), that does not require institutionalization, the court shall order the defendant to be provided appropriate treatment in the jail or prison in which the defendant is incarcerated. Where the defendant is incarcerated in a county correctional facility, the county shall provide or arrange for this treatment. The Department of Corrections shall reimburse the county for the reasonable costs of treatment, as determined by the Commissioner of Corrections, provided that the county has submitted to the commissioner such documentation and verification as the commissioner shall require.

c. If the defendant has not regained his fitness to proceed within three months, the court shall hold a hearing on the issue of whether the charges against him shall be dismissed with prejudice or held in abeyance.

    The hearing shall be held only upon notice to the prosecutor and with an opportunity for the prosecutor to be heard. When the charges are not dismissed, each defendant's case shall be specifically reviewed by the court at six-month intervals until an order is made by the court that the defendant stand trial or that the charges be dismissed.

    There shall be a presumption that charges against a defendant who is not competent to proceed shall be held in abeyance. The presumption can be overcome only if the court determines, using the factors set forth in this subsection, that continuing the criminal prosecution under the particular circumstances of the case would constitute a constitutionally significant injury to the defendant attributable to undue delay in being brought to trial.

    In determining whether the charges shall be held in abeyance or dismissed, the court shall weigh the following factors: the defendant's prospects for regaining competency; the period of time during which the defendant has remained incompetent; the nature and extent of the defendant's institutionalization; the nature and gravity of the crimes charged; the effects of delay on the prosecution; the effects of delay on the defendant, including any likelihood of prejudice to the defendant in the trial arising out of the delay; and the public interest in prosecuting the charges.

d. When the court, on its own motion or upon application of the commissioner, his designee or either party, determines after a hearing, if a hearing is requested, that the defendant has regained fitness to proceed, the proceedings shall be resumed.

e. (Deleted by amendment, P.L.1996, c. 133.)

f. The fact that the defendant is unfit to proceed does not preclude determination of any legal objection to the prosecution which is susceptible of fair determination prior to trial and without the personal participation of the defendant.

## 2C:4-7.      Disposition

If a defendant is acquitted by reason of insanity the court shall dispose of the case as provided for in section 2C:4-8 of this chapter.

## 2C:4-8.      Commitment of a person by reason of insanity

a. After acquittal by reason of insanity, the court shall order that the defendant undergo a psychiatric examination by a psychiatrist of the prosecutor's choice. If the examination cannot take place because of the unwillingness of the defendant to participate, the court shall proceed as in section 2C:4-5c. The defendant, pursuant to this section, may also be examined by a psychiatrist of his own choice.

b. The court shall dispose of the defendant in the following manner:

   (1) If the court finds that the defendant may be released without danger to the community or himself without supervision, the court shall so release the defendant; or

   (2) If the court finds that the defendant may be released without danger to the community or to himself under supervision or under conditions, the court shall so order; or

   (3) If the court finds that the defendant cannot be released with or without supervision or conditions without posing a danger to the community or to himself, it shall commit the defendant to a mental health facility approved for this purpose by the Commissioner of Human Services to be treated as a person civilly committed. In all proceedings conducted pursuant to this section and pursuant to section N.J.S.2C:4-6 concerning a defendant who lacks the fitness to proceed, including any periodic review proceeding, the prosecuting attorney shall have the right to appear and be heard. The defendant's continued commitment, under the law governing civil commitment, shall be established by a preponderance of the evidence, during the maximum period of imprisonment that could have been imposed, as an ordinary term of imprisonment, for any charge on which the defendant has been acquitted by reason of insanity. Expiration of that maximum period of imprisonment shall be calculated by crediting the defendant with any time spent in confinement for the charge or charges on which the defendant has been acquitted by reason of insanity.

c. No person committed under this section shall be confined within any penal or correctional institution or any part thereof.

## 2C:4-9.     Release of persons committed by reason of insanity

a. If a person has been committed pursuant to section 2C:4-8 or section 2C:4-6 and if the commissioner, or his designee, or the superintendent of the institution to which the person has been committed, is of the view that a person committed to his custody, pursuant to section 2C:4-8 or section 2C:4-6, may be discharged or released on condition without danger to himself or to others, or that he may be transferred to a less restrictive setting for treatment, the commissioner or superintendent shall make application for the discharge or release of such person in a report to the court by which such person was committed and shall transmit a copy of such application and report to the prosecutor, the court, and defense counsel. The court may, in its discretion, appoint at least two qualified psychiatrists, neither of whom may be on the staff of the hospital to which the defendant had been committed, to examine such person and to report within 30 days, or such longer period as the court determines to be necessary for the purpose, their opinion as to his mental condition.

b. The court shall hold a hearing to determine whether the committed person may be safely discharged, released on condition without danger to himself or others, or treated as in civil commitment. The hearing shall be held upon notice to the prosecutor and with the prosecutor's opportunity to be heard. Any such hearing shall be deemed a civil proceeding. According to the determination of the court upon the hearing, the court shall proceed as in section 2C:4-8b. (1), (2) or (3).

c. A committed person may make application for his discharge or release to the court by which he was committed, and the procedure to be followed upon such application shall be the same as that prescribed above in the case of an application by the commissioner.

d. Each defendant's case shall be specifically reviewed as provided by the law governing civil commitment.

**2C:4-10.**  **Statements for purposes of examination or treatment inadmissible except on issue of mental condition**

A statement made by a person subjected to psychiatric or psychological examination or treatment pursuant to section 2C:4-5, 2C:4-6 or 2C:4-9 for the purposes of such examination or treatment shall not be admissible in evidence against him in any criminal proceeding on any issue other than that of his mental condition but it shall be admissible upon that issue, whether or not it would otherwise be deemed a privileged communication. When such a statement constitutes an admission of guilt of the crime charged or of an element thereof, it shall only be admissible where it appears at trial that conversations with the examining psychiatrist or licensed psychologist were necessary to enable him to form an opinion as to a matter in issue.

**2C:4-11.**  **Immaturity excluding criminal conviction; transfer of proceedings to family court**

    a.  A person shall not be tried for or convicted of an offense if:

        (1)  At the time of the conduct charged to constitute the offense he was less than 14 years of age, in which case the family court shall have exclusive jurisdiction unless pursuant to section 8 of the "New Jersey Code of Juvenile Justice" the juvenile has demanded indictment and trial by jury; or

        (2)  At the time of the conduct charged to constitute the offense he was 14, 15, 16 or 17 years of age, unless

            (a)  The family court has no jurisdiction over him;

            (b)  The family court has, pursuant to section 7 of "New Jersey Code of Juvenile Justice," entered an order waiving jurisdiction and referring the case to the county prosecutor for the institution of criminal proceedings against him;

            (c)  The juvenile has, pursuant to section 8 of the "New Jersey Code of Juvenile Justice," demanded indictment and trial by jury.

    b.  No court shall have jurisdiction to try and convict a person of an offense if criminal proceedings against him are barred by subsection a. of this section. When it appears that a person charged with the commission of an offense may be of such an age that proceedings may be barred under subsection a. of this section, the court shall hold a hearing thereon, and the burden shall be on such person to establish to the satisfaction of the court that the proceeding is barred upon such grounds. If the court determines that the proceeding is barred, custody of the person charged shall be surrendered to the family court and the case, including all papers and processes relating thereto shall be transferred.

# 5

# INCHOATE CRIMES

**2C:5-1.**    **Criminal attempt**

    a.  **Definition of attempt.** A person is guilty of an attempt to commit a crime if, acting with the kind of culpability otherwise required for commission of the crime, he:

        (1)  Purposely engages in conduct which would constitute the crime if the attendant circumstances were as a reasonable person would believe them to be;

        (2)  When causing a particular result is an element of the crime, does or omits to do anything with the purpose of causing such result without further conduct on his part; or

        (3)  Purposely does or omits to do anything which, under the circumstances as a reasonable person would believe them to be, is an act or omission constituting a substantial step in a course of conduct planned to culminate in his commission of the crime.

    b.  **Conduct which may be held substantial step under subsection a. (3).** Conduct shall not be held to constitute a substantial step under subsection a. (3) of this section unless it is strongly corroborative of the actor's criminal purpose.

    c.  **Conduct designed to aid another in commission of a crime.** A person who engages in conduct designed to aid another to commit a crime which would establish his complicity under section 2C:2-6 if the crime were committed by such other person, is guilty of an attempt to commit the crime, although the crime is not committed or attempted by such other person.

    d.  **Renunciation of criminal purpose.** When the actor's conduct would otherwise constitute an attempt under subsection a. (2) or (3) of this section, it is an affirmative defense which he must prove by a preponderance of the evidence that he abandoned his effort to commit the crime or otherwise prevented its commission, under circumstances manifesting a complete and voluntary renunciation of his criminal purpose. The establishment of such defense does not, however, affect the liability of an accomplice who did not join in such abandonment or prevention.

        Within the meaning of this chapter, renunciation of criminal purpose is not voluntary if it is motivated, in whole or in part, by circumstances, not present or apparent at the inception of the actor's course of conduct, which increase the probability of detection or apprehension or which make more difficult the accomplishment of the criminal purpose. Renunciation is not complete if it is motivated by a decision to postpone the criminal conduct until a more advantageous time or to transfer the criminal effort to another but similar objective or victim. Renunciation is also not complete if mere abandonment is insufficient to accomplish avoidance of the offense in which case the defendant must have taken further and affirmative steps that prevented the commission thereof.

## PRACTICAL APPLICATION OF STATUTE

### Criminal Attempt

The Hudson County Prosecutor's Office would be correct in charging Jillian Peterson with attempted murder. 2C:5-1 sets forth the elements necessary for a person to be charged, and ultimately convicted, for attempting to commit an offense. This statute, under subsection a.(3), specifically provides that a "substantial step" must be taken by an individual in his planned course of criminal conduct in order for him to be guilty of a criminal attempt. Subsection b. further clarifies the "substantial step" requirement by adding that it must be "strongly corroborative of the actor's criminal purpose."

Jillian Peterson did not kill the car dealership manager. However, she intended to cause his death. She not only advised the manager that she was going to kill him, but she also threw two large machetes at him, narrowly missing him. Peterson also had a motive to kill the man—to escape being caught for armed robbery of the dealership.

Peterson identified her criminal intent and purpose by telling the manager that she was going to kill him. She took a substantial step in reaching this goal by whipping the machetes at him—this action is certainly "strongly corroborative" of her criminal purpose to kill him. Accordingly, Peterson should be charged for her attempt to murder the car dealership manager. But what if Peterson had an accomplice with her? A cohort waiting in a getaway car? Should this accomplice also be charged with attempted murder? The answer is probably yes.

### Conduct Designed to Aid Another in Commission of a Crime

2C:5-1c. is the component of the criminal attempt statute that addresses the culpability of accomplices. Basically, the subsection determines that if a person solicits or aids another in the planning or commission of a crime, he "is guilty of an attempt to commit the crime, although the crime is not committed or attempted by such other person." With this being the case, a companion of Peterson's likely would be charged with attempted murder.

For example, if Peterson and another individual, George, arrived at the car dealership together, planning to rob it and to kill the manager, George would be guilty of attempted murder just the same as Peterson. Why? Because George is an accomplice—someone who aided Peterson in planning and carrying out the crime.

It is interesting to note here that George probably would be convicted of attempted murder even if he did not actively plan with Peterson to kill the manager. This is due to the provisions of 2C:11-3a.(3), which outlines the elements for a felony murder conviction. As will be discussed in more detail later in this book, a person is guilty of murder if he is engaged in one of several different felonies (including robbery) where a death occurs during the commission of or flight from one of these crimes. If the person at least knows that another participant is armed with a deadly weapon, he can be convicted of murder if death occurs during one of the enumerated felonies. Accordingly, had Peterson succeeded in killing the manager, George could be charged with murder. Following this, per the language of 2C:5-1c., he could be charged with attempted murder if he at least knew that Peterson was armed with the machetes.

## Renunciation Affirmative Defense

George could escape an attempted murder charge if he abandoned his efforts to commit the criminal activities with Peterson or outright prevented the crimes. 2C:5-1d. sets forth the necessary elements to allow a defendant to succeed in this defense, a decision which ultimately should be determined by a jury. However, law enforcement agencies could consider renunciation evidence when deciding to charge a person with criminal attempt.

For instance, if ample evidence was presented that showed that George refused to drive with Peterson to the car dealership but thereafter arrived and physically stopped her from throwing the machetes at the manager, he should not be charged or indicted for attempted murder. Similarly, if evidence showed that although he initially intended to be a participant of the robbery, he completely and voluntarily removed himself from the crime, then he likely should not be charged. Specifically, if George contacted Peterson and told her in no uncertain terms that he was not going to participate in the robbery, then he likely would succeed in a renunciation defense and avoid an attempted murder conviction. Once again, while this may be best left for a jury to determine, the police or prosecutor's office certainly may take such renunciation evidence into consideration when deciding what charges to institute or further by seeking an indictment.

---

**2C:5-2.**          ## Conspiracy

    a. **Definition of conspiracy.** A person is guilty of conspiracy with another person or persons to commit a crime if with the purpose of promoting or facilitating its commission he:

        (1) Agrees with such other person or persons that they or one or more of them will engage in conduct which constitutes such crime or an attempt or solicitation to commit such crime; or

        (2) Agrees to aid such other person or persons in the planning or commission of such crime or of an attempt or solicitation to commit such crime.

    b. **Scope of conspiratorial relationship.** If a person guilty of conspiracy, as defined by subsection a. of this section, knows that a person with whom he conspires to commit a crime has conspired with another person or persons to commit the same crime, he is guilty of conspiring with such other person or persons, whether or not he knows their identity, to commit such crime.

    c. **Conspiracy with multiple objectives.** If a person conspires to commit a number of crimes, he is guilty of only one conspiracy so long as such multiple crimes are the object of the same agreement or continuous conspiratorial relationship. It shall not be a defense to a charge under this section that one or more of the objectives of the conspiracy was not criminal; provided that one or more of its objectives or the means of promoting or facilitating an objective of the conspiracy is criminal.

    d. **Overt act.** No person may be convicted of conspiracy to commit a crime other than a crime of the first or second degree or distribution or possession with intent to distribute a controlled dangerous substance or controlled substance analog as defined in chapter 35 of this title, unless an overt act in pursuance of such conspiracy is proved to have been done by him or by a person with whom he conspired.

    e. **Renunciation of purpose.** It is an affirmative defense which the actor must prove by a preponderance of the evidence that he, after conspiring to commit a crime, informed the authority of the existence of the conspiracy and his participation therein, and thwarted or caused to be thwarted the commission of any offense in furtherance of the conspiracy, under circumstances manifesting a complete and voluntary renunciation of criminal purpose as defined in N.J.S.2C:5-1d.; provided, however, that an attempt as defined in N.J.S.2C:5-1 shall not be considered an offense for purposes of renunciation under this subsection.

f. **Duration of conspiracy.** For the purpose of N.J.S.2C:1-6d.:

(1) Conspiracy is a continuing course of conduct which terminates when the crime or crimes which are its object are committed or the agreement that they be committed is abandoned by the defendant and by those with whom he conspired; and

(2) Such abandonment is presumed with respect to a crime other than one of the first or second degree if neither the defendant nor anyone with whom he conspired does any overt act in pursuance of the conspiracy during the applicable period of limitation; and

(3) If an individual abandons the agreement, the conspiracy is terminated as to him only if and when he advises those with whom he conspired of his abandonment or he informs the law enforcement authorities of the existence of the conspiracy and of his participation therein.

g. **Leader of organized crime.** A person is a leader of organized crime if he purposefully conspires with others as an organizer, supervisor, manager or financier to commit a continuing series of crimes which constitute a pattern of racketeering activity under the provisions of N.J.S. 2C:41-1, provided, however, that notwithstanding 2C:1-8a. (2), a conviction of leader of organized crime shall not merge with the conviction of any other crime which constitutes racketeering activity under 2C:41-1. As used in this section, "financier" means a person who provides money, credit or a thing of value with the purpose or knowledge that it will be used to finance or support the operations of a conspiracy to commit a series of crimes which constitute a pattern of racketeering activity, including but not limited to the purchase of materials to be used in the commission of crimes, buying or renting housing or vehicles, purchasing transportation for members of the conspiracy or otherwise facilitating the commission of crimes which constitute a pattern of racketeering activity.

## PRACTICAL APPLICATION OF STATUTE

### Conspiracy

The criminal mastermind sought by State Police Colonel Frank Winters and all of the individuals involved in the string of masked robberies (i.e., Jacques Vandermeit, Michael Westmont, Bill McNichol, Jillian Peterson) should be charged under the conspiracy statute. 2C:5-2 provides that a person is guilty of conspiracy when he agrees with other person(s) to commit a crime or aids other person(s) in committing a crime. A person also may be convicted of conspiracy for soliciting or attempting a crime.

Per subsection b. of the statute, an individual can be found guilty of conspiracy with other person(s) even if he does not know their identity—provided that he conspired with a separate individual(s) who had conspired with those unknown person(s) to commit the same crime. Confusing? Maybe not.

Remember the case of the two football players arguing in the diner? Bill McNichol hired Michael Westmont to rob his football player friend, Rodney Crawson. Westmont, sporting a white handkerchief over his face and armed with a sawed-off shotgun, heisted Crawson's car keys and then stole his automobile which held almost $100,000 cash in the trunk. Before the actual robbery, McNichol had never met Westmont. They were introduced by the mysterious underworld mastermind sought by New Jersey's top law enforcement bosses.

In this case, each of the men—Westmont, McNichol, and the mastermind—could be charged with robbery. They also all could be charged with conspiring with one another. McNichol solicited the mastermind to aid him in his theft of Crawson. The mastermind solicited Westmont to carry out the actual robbery. Even though McNichol did not know the identity of Westmont until after the robbery, he is still guilty of conspiring with this masked gunman. Even more so, under the statute, McNichol would be guilty of conspiring with Westmont even if he had never learned the identity of Westmont at all. Simply, because McNichol conspired with the mastermind to commit the robbery, who in turn conspired with Westmont to commit the same crime, all three are guilty of conspiring with each other.

Following the above rationale, it is also true that Jacques Vandermeit (jewelry store robbery) and Jillian Peterson (car dealership robbery) could be charged with conspiring with Westmont, McNichol, and the mastermind. Why? Because they were all engaged in a continuing course of criminal conduct under one organized crime outfit. Remember Colonel Frank Winters's goal: to locate the group's leader and ascertain the purpose and goals of their criminal activities. While law enforcement did not know their exact goal, they did know that all these individuals were working together to raise money for a particular purpose. Accordingly, under the statute, they all could be charged with conspiring with each other—even though they did not know each other and even though they committed separate, distinct robberies.

### One Charge of Conspiracy When Continuous Conspiratorial Relationship Exists

It is likely that the mastermind and his gang would only each be charged with one count of conspiracy. Subsection c. of the conspiracy statute provides that "If a person conspires to commit a number of crimes, he is guilty of only one conspiracy so long as such multiple crimes are the object of the same agreement or continuous conspiratorial relationship." Since the bandits' individual robberies were the object of a singular, continuous conspiratorial relationship—a string of crimes arranged by the mastermind to net money for their organized crime outfit—each conspirator should be charged with only one count of conspiracy.

### Overt Act

The conspiracy statute sets forth an "overt act" requirement in order for a defendant to be found guilty of conspiracy. However, there is a caveat to this requirement: An overt act in furtherance of the conspiracy is not a necessary element for conspiracies involving crimes of the first or second degree, or for conspiracies to commit drug distribution offenses. First, what is an "overt act" and when does it apply?

An overt act is some kind of behavior, by either the accused, or a co-conspirator, that furthers the crime which they have agreed to commit. And it may not even be an action that is directly related to the actual commission of the crime.

A modification of the car dealership facts demonstrates this point. Let's say that prior to the dealership robbery, Jillian Peterson had discussed her plan with a man named Bart Sampson. Sampson, sympathetic to her cause, agrees with her that he is interested in assisting her in the robbery. For weeks, though, he does nothing about the pending crime. But two days before the robbery, he purchases two machetes and provides Peterson with them. Sampson's discussion with Peterson about aiding her in the robbery, on its own, does not constitute an overt act in furtherance of the conspiracy. However, his providing the machetes to her clearly is an overt act that furthered the crime. But what if Sampson had purchased the machetes for Peterson but was unable to get them to her before she carried out the robbery? Or what if Peterson was arrested before she was able to actually commit the crime? Could Sampson still be found guilty of conspiracy?

Sampson's purchase alone should satisfy the overt act requirement, because it was an action that openly and clearly was taken to further their conspiracy. Interestingly, though, in this case, Sampson could be charged with conspiracy even if he had not committed an overt act at all. As aforementioned, conspiracies involving crimes of the first or second degree do not require an overt act for a person to be found guilty of conspiracy. Accordingly, with armed robbery being a crime of the first degree, Sampson's simple agreement with Peterson to assist her in the crime would suffice for him to be guilty of conspiracy. His only way to avoid conviction: if he had completely and voluntarily renounced his involvement in the crime as per subsection e. of the statute.

### Leader of Organized Crime

As per 2C:5-2g., the individual who masterminded the masked robberies should be charged as a "leader of organized crime." The mastermind purposely organized and conspired with Westmont, Vandermeit, and Peterson to carry out their respective robberies. Law enforcement similarly suspects him of supervising and leading numerous other illegal activities. This series of organized, continuing criminal events could constitute a pattern of racketeering activity under 2C:41-1 (a section that will be dealt with later in this book). Accordingly, the mastermind, if he eventually is identified, would appropriately be charged with "leader of organized crime," which is a separate and distinct criminal offense.

---

**2C:5-3.**  **Incapacity, irresponsibility or immunity of party to conspiracy**

    a. **In general.** Except as provided in subsection b. of this section, it is immaterial to the liability of a person who conspires with another to commit a crime that:

        (1) He or the person with whom he conspires does not occupy a particular position or have a particular characteristic which is an element of such crime, if he believes that one of them does; or

        (2) The person with whom he conspires is irresponsible or has an immunity to prosecution or conviction for the commission of the crime.

    b. **Exceptions to subsection a.: Victims, behavior inevitably incident to the commission of the crime.** It is a defense to a charge of conspiracy to commit a crime that if the object of the conspiracy were achieved, the person charged would not be guilty of a crime under the law defining the crime or as an accomplice under section 2C:2-6e. (1) or (2).

**2C:5-4.**  **Grading of criminal attempt and conspiracy; mitigation in cases of lesser danger**

    a. Grading. Except as provided in subsections c. and d., an attempt or conspiracy to commit a crime of the first degree is a crime of the second degree; except that an attempt or conspiracy to commit murder or terrorism is a crime of the first degree, provided, however, that if the person attempted or conspired to murder five or more persons, the person shall be sentenced by the court to a term of 30 years, during which the person shall not be eligible for parole, or to a specific term of years which shall be between 30 years and life imprisonment, of which the person shall serve not less than 30 years before eligibility for parole. Otherwise an attempt is a crime of the same degree as the most serious crime which is attempted, and conspiracy is a crime of the same degree as the most serious crime which is the object of the conspiracy; provided that, leader of organized crime is a crime of the second degree. An attempt or conspiracy to commit an offense defined by a statute outside the code shall be graded as a crime of the same degree as the offense is graded pursuant to N.J.S.2C:1-4 and N.J.S.2C:43-1.

b. Mitigation. The court may impose sentence for a crime of a lower grade or degree if neither the particular conduct charged nor the defendant presents a public danger warranting the grading provided for such crime under subsection a. because:

(1) The criminal attempt or conspiracy charged is so inherently unlikely to result or culminate in the commission of a crime; or

(2) The conspiracy, as to the particular defendant charged, is so peripherally related to the main unlawful enterprise.

c. Notwithstanding the provisions of subsection a. of this section, conspiracy to commit a crime set forth in subsection a., b., or d. of N.J.S.2C:17-1 where the structure which was the target of the crime was a church, synagogue, temple or other place of public worship is a crime of the first degree.

d. Notwithstanding the provisions of subsection a. of this section, conspiracy to commit a crime as set forth in P.L.1994, c. 121 (C.2C:21-23 et seq.) is a crime of the same degree as the most serious crime that was conspired to be committed.

## PRACTICAL APPLICATION OF STATUTE

### Attempt/Conspiracy to Commit First Degree Crime Is a Second Degree Crime—Murder and Terrorism Are the Exceptions

Jillian Peterson conspired to heist cash from a car dealership. In the process, she attempted to kill the dealership manager by whipping machetes at him. Michael Westmont wielded a shotgun at diner patrons and police officers. He fled the scene after stealing nearly $100,000 from a professional football player's automobile. This theft was also the product of a conspiracy. So how should Westmont and Peterson be charged? Were their conspiracies crimes of the first degree or second degree, or even lower?

Jillian Peterson should be charged with first degree robbery and first degree attempted murder but second degree conspiracy for her robbery of the car dealership. Michael Westmont should be charged with first degree robbery and second degree conspiracy for his offenses at the diner. Why are their conspiracy charges lower degree crimes than their robberies? Why is Peterson's attempted murder charge a first degree offense?

2C:5-4 provides for grading of criminal attempt and conspiracy offenses. In part, this section states, "an attempt or conspiracy to commit a crime of the first degree is a crime of the second degree." Under that language, Peterson's attempt to kill the dealership manager would only be a second degree crime even though murder is a first degree crime. However, the statute provides two singular exceptions to that rule: "an attempt or conspiracy to commit murder or terrorism is a crime of the first degree." Accordingly,

Peterson's attempted murder of the dealership manager is a first degree offense. Similarly, if she conspired to commit murder, then her conspiracy charge would be one of the first degree.

Now let's look at the robbery conspiracies. As stated above, the statute generally provides that a conspiracy to commit a crime of the first degree is a crime of the second degree. Therefore, Peterson's and Westmont's conspiracies to commit first degree crimes—robbery in each of their cases—are appropriately graded as second degree conspiracy offenses.

### All Other Degree Crimes—Attempt/Conspiracy Same Degree as Underlying Crime

One should note, however, that for all other degree offenses, "an attempt is a crime of the same degree as the most serious crime which is attempted" and a "conspiracy is a crime of the same degree as the most serious crime which is the object of the conspiracy." For example, if an individual conspires with others to commit a third degree burglary, then he should be charged with third degree conspiracy to commit burglary. Similarly, if he attempts to commit a third degree burglary but is caught, he should be charged with third degree attempted burglary.

**2C:5-5.**     **Burglar's tools**

    a. Any person who manufactures or possesses any engine, machine, tool or implement adapted, designed or commonly used for committing or facilitating any offense in chapter 20 of this Title or offenses involving forcible entry into premises.

        (1) Knowing the same to be so adapted or designed or commonly used; and

        (2) With either a purpose so to use or employ it, or with a purpose to provide it to some person who he knows has such a purpose to use or employ it, is guilty of an offense.

    b. Any person who publishes plans or instructions dealing with the manufacture or use of any burglar tools as defined above, with the intent that such publication be used for committing or facilitating any offense in chapter 20 of this Title or offenses involving forcible entry into premises is guilty of an offense.

    The offense under a. or b. of this section is a crime of the fourth degree if the defendant manufactured such instrument or implements or published such plans or instructions; otherwise it is a disorderly persons offense.

### PRACTICAL APPLICATION OF STATUTE

2C:5-5 makes the possession or manufacture of burglar tools an illegal offense. Specifically, if a person manufactures burglar tools, implements them during a burglary/theft, or publishes plans or instructions detailing how to manufacture burglar tools, he is guilty of a fourth degree crime. It should be noted, however, that the manufacture of such tools or publication of plans alone technically is not an offense. The individual must know that the tools are commonly used for burglary/theft purposes and must have an intent to use these tools, or provide them to others, for use in a burglary/theft offense. Similarly, an individual publishing plans or instructions on the manufacturing of burglar tools must intend for said plans to be used to aid others in a burglary/theft in order to be convicted under this statute.

A person who merely possesses burglar tools but hasn't manufactured or implemented them is guilty of a disorderly persons offense. Again, possession alone is not sufficient for a conviction. It must also be proved that the person knew the tools were commonly used for illegal activity and that he intended to use them at some point. This isn't an easy task.

A modification of the facts involving Jacques Vandermeit and the jewelry store robbery will exemplify the above. Instead of Chief M. P. Ironstone arriving at the store during the robbery, he pulls over Vandermeit's car for speeding. Vandermeit is alone and not wearing a handkerchief. Lying in the passenger seat, however, is an oddly sharpened screwdriver, a device commonly used in the illegal entry of dwellings and other structures. Based on this observation alone, should Ironstone arrest and charge Vandermeit? Maybe, maybe not.

A crucial element of this offense is proof of intent to use the tool in the commission of a burglary/theft. If Ironstone elicited or found corroborating evidence that demonstrated Vandermeit's intent to use the screwdriver in a theft-type activity, then it is likely that Vandermeit would be convicted of a burglar tools offense. Without such corroboration, however, a guilty verdict is unlikely, and an arrest may be futile.

**2C:5-6.**     **Motor vehicle master keys**

    a. Any person who knowingly possesses a motor vehicle master key or device designed to operate a lock or locks on motor vehicles or to start a motor vehicle without an ignition key is guilty of a crime of the fourth degree.

    b. Any person who offers or advertises for sale, sells or gives to any person other than those excepted in subsection c. a motor vehicle master key or device designed to operate a lock or locks on a motor vehicle or to start a motor vehicle without an ignition key is guilty of a crime of the fourth degree.

    c. Subsection a. shall not apply to a law enforcement officer, constable, locksmith or dealer, distributor or manufacturer of motor vehicles or motor vehicle locks, a garage keeper, or a person engaged in the business of lending on the security of motor vehicles, or in the business of acquiring by purchase evidence of debt secured by interests in motor vehicles, and his employees and agents.

**2C:5-7.**     **Key to lock in or on real property owned or leased by state**

Any person who knowingly uses, distributes, manufactures, duplicates or possesses a key designed to be used in a lock in or on real property owned or leased by the State without conforming to the rules and regulations established according to section 2 of this act is guilty of a disorderly persons offense.

# 6

# BAIL

**2C:6-1.**    **Persons accused of minor offenses**

No person charged with a crime of the fourth degree, a disorderly persons offense or a petty disorderly persons offense shall be required to deposit bail in an amount exceeding $2,500.00, unless the court finds that the person presents a serious threat to the physical safety of potential evidence or of persons involved in circumstances surrounding the alleged offense or unless the court finds bail of that amount will not reasonably assure the appearance of the defendant as required. The court may for good cause shown impose a higher bail; the court shall specifically place on the record its reasons for imposing bail in an amount exceeding $2,500.00.

# 7

# REGISTRATION
# AND NOTIFICATION
# OF RELEASE
# OF CERTAIN OFFENDERS

**2C:7-1.**      **Legislative findings and declaration**

The Legislature finds and declares:

a. The danger of recidivism posed by sex offenders and offenders who commit other predatory acts against children, and the dangers posed by persons who prey on others as a result of mental illness, require a system of registration that will permit law enforcement officials to identify and alert the public when necessary for the public safety.

b. A system of registration of sex offenders and offenders who commit other predatory acts against children will provide law enforcement with additional information critical to preventing and promptly resolving incidents involving sexual abuse and missing persons.

**2C:7-2.**      **Registration of sex offenders; definition; requirements**

a. (1) A person who has been convicted, adjudicated delinquent or found not guilty by reason of insanity for commission of a sex offense as defined in subsection b. of this section shall register as provided in subsections c. and d. of this section.

(2) A person who in another jurisdiction is required to register as a sex offender and (a) is enrolled on a full-time or part-time basis in any public or private educational institution in this State, including any secondary school, trade or professional institution, institution of higher education or other post-secondary school, or (b) is employed or carries on a vocation in this State, on either a full-time or a part-time basis, with or without compensation, for more than 14 consecutive days or for an aggregate period exceeding 30 days in a calendar year, shall register in this State as provided in subsections c. and d. of this section. A person who fails to register as required under this act shall be guilty of a crime of the fourth degree.

b. For the purposes of this act a sex offense shall include the following:

(1) Aggravated sexual assault, sexual assault, aggravated criminal sexual contact, kidnapping pursuant to paragraph (2) of subsection c. of N.J.S.2C:13-1 or an attempt to commit any of these crimes if the court found that the offender's conduct was characterized by a pattern of repetitive, compulsive behavior, regardless of the date of the commission of the offense or the date of conviction;

(2) A conviction, adjudication of delinquency, or acquittal by reason of insanity for aggravated sexual assault; sexual assault; aggravated criminal sexual contact; kidnapping pursuant to paragraph (2) of subsection c. of N.J.S.2C:13-1; endangering the welfare of a child by engaging in sexual conduct which would impair or debauch the morals of the child pursuant to subsection a. of N.J.S.2C:24-4; endangering the welfare of a child pursuant to paragraph (4) of subsection b. of N.J.S.2C:24-4; luring or enticing pursuant to section 1 of P.L.1993, c.291 (C.2C:13-6); criminal sexual contact pursuant to N.J.S.2C:14-3b. if the victim is a minor; kidnapping pursuant to N.J.S.2C:13-1, criminal restraint pursuant to N.J.S.2C:13-2, or false imprisonment pursuant to N.J.S.2C:13-3 if the victim is a minor and the offender is not the parent of the victim; knowingly promoting prostitution of a child pursuant to paragraph (3) or paragraph (4) of subsection b. of N.J.S.2C:34-1; or an attempt to commit any of these enumerated offenses if the conviction, adjudication of delinquency or acquittal by reason of insanity is entered on or after the effective date of this act or the offender is serving a sentence of incarceration, probation, parole or other form of community supervision as a result of the offense or is confined following acquittal by reason of insanity or as a result of civil commitment on the effective date of this act;

(3) A conviction, adjudication of delinquency or acquittal by reason of insanity for an offense similar to any offense enumerated in paragraph (2) or a sentence on the basis of criteria similar to the criteria set forth in paragraph (1) of this subsection entered or imposed under the laws of the United States, this State or another state.

c. A person required to register under the provisions of this act shall do so on forms to be provided by the designated registering agency as follows:

(1) A person who is required to register and who is under supervision in the community on probation, parole, furlough, work release, or a similar program, shall register at the time the person is placed under supervision or no later than 120 days after the effective date of this act, whichever is later, in accordance with procedures established by the Department of Corrections, the Department of Human Services, the Juvenile Justice Commission established pursuant to section 2 of P.L.1995, c.284 (C.52:17B-170) or the Administrative Office of the Courts, whichever is responsible for supervision;

(2) A person confined in a correctional or juvenile facility or involuntarily committed who is required to register shall register prior to release in accordance with procedures established by the Department of Corrections, the Department of Human Services or the Juvenile Justice Commission;

(3) A person moving to or returning to this State from another jurisdiction shall register with the chief law enforcement officer of the municipality in which the person will reside or, if the municipality does not have a local police force, the Superintendent of State Police within 120 days of the effective date of this act or 10 days of first residing in or returning to a municipality in this State, whichever is later;

(4) A person required to register on the basis of a conviction prior to the effective date who is not confined or under supervision on the effective date of this act shall register within 120 days of the effective date of this act with the chief law enforcement officer of the municipality in which the person will reside or, if the municipality does not have a local police force, the Superintendent of State Police;

(5) A person who in another jurisdiction is required to register as a sex offender and who is enrolled on a full-time or part-time basis in any public or private educational institution in this State, including any secondary school, trade or professional institution,

institution of higher education or other post-secondary school shall, within ten days of commencing attendance at such educational institution, register with the chief law enforcement officer of the municipality in which the educational institution is located or, if the municipality does not have a local police force, the Superintendent of State Police;

(6) A person who in another jurisdiction is required to register as a sex offender and who is employed or carries on a vocation in this State, on either a full-time or a part-time basis, with or without compensation, for more than 14 consecutive days or for an aggregate period exceeding 30 days in a calendar year, shall, within ten days after commencing such employment or vocation, register with the chief law enforcement officer of the municipality in which the employer is located or where the vocation is carried on, as the case may be, or, if the municipality does not have a local police force, the Superintendent of State Police;

(7) In addition to any other registration requirements set forth in this section, a person required to register under this act who is enrolled at, employed by or carries on a vocation at an institution of higher education or other post-secondary school in this State shall, within ten days after commencing such attendance, employment or vocation, register with the law enforcement unit of the educational institution, if the institution has such a unit.

d. Upon a change of address, a person shall notify the law enforcement agency with which the person is registered and shall re-register with the appropriate law enforcement agency no less than 10 days before he intends to first reside at his new address. Upon a change of employment or school enrollment status, a person shall notify the appropriate law enforcement agency no later than five days after any such change. A person who fails to notify the appropriate law enforcement agency of a change of address or status in accordance with this subsection is guilty of a crime of the fourth degree.

e. A person required to register under paragraph (1) of subsection b. of this section or under paragraph (3) of subsection b. due to a sentence imposed on the basis of criteria similar to the criteria set forth in paragraph (1) of subsection b. shall verify his address with the appropriate law enforcement agency every 90 days in a manner prescribed by the Attorney General. A person required to register under paragraph (2) of subsection b. of this section or under paragraph (3) of subsection b. on the basis of a conviction for an offense similar to an offense enumerated in paragraph (2) of subsection b. shall verify his address annually in a manner prescribed by the Attorney General. One year after the effective date of this act, the Attorney General shall review, evaluate and, if warranted, modify pursuant to the "Administrative Procedure Act," P.L.1968, c.410 (C.52:14B-1 et seq.) the verificaion requirement.

f. Except as provided in subsection g. of this section, a person required to register under this act may make application to the Superior Court of this State to terminate the obligation upon proof that the person has not committed an offense within 15 years following conviction or release from a correctional facility for any term of imprisonment imposed, whichever is later, and is not likely to pose a threat to the safety of others.

g. A person required to register under this section who has been convicted of, adjudicated delinquent, or acquitted by reason of insanity for more than one sex offense as defined in subsection b. of this section or who has been convicted of, adjudicated delinquent, or acquitted by reason of insanity for aggravated sexual assault pursuant to subsection a. of N.J.S.2C:14-2 or sexual assault pursuant to paragraph (1) of subsection c. of N.J.S.2C:14-2 is not eligible under subsection f. of this section to make application to the Superior Court of this State to terminate the registration obligation.

## PRACTICAL APPLICATION OF STATUTE

Michael Westmont, the masked gunman who stormed the Seventeen Diner and ultimately stole nearly $100,000 from a professional football player, should be charged with a fourth degree "Megan's Law" crime for failing to register as a sex offender, in addition to the multiple other serious felonies he committed. Westmont's charge under 2C:7-2 arises out of his 1959 conviction of sexual assault and his failure to ever register as a sex offender in the municipality where he resided.

Subsection b. of 2C:7-2 defines what offenses are sex offenses for purposes of this act. Among the crimes included are aggravated criminal sexual contact, kidnapping offenses, multiple offenses related to minors, and, of course, sexual assault and aggravated sexual assault. Subsections c. and d. provide for the appropriate locations and timetables within which sex offenders must register their status as a sex offender. Particularly, subsection c.(4) provides that a person who was convicted of a sex offense prior to the effective date of the act and who was not confined or under supervision on the effective date of the act "shall register within 120 days of the effective date of this act with the chief law enforcement officer of the municipality in which the person will reside."

Michael Westmont was convicted of sexual assault in 1959. His term of incarceration had expired years before 2C:7-2's 1994 effective date. Westmont, however, failed to register his status as a convicted sex offender within 120 days of the act's 1994 effective date. In fact, he never registered with the chief law enforcement officer of the New Jersey municipality where he resided. Accordingly, it would be correct for the police to charge him with a fourth degree crime for violating 2C:7-2's registration requirements.

It is important to note that subsections c. and d. provide for varied registration requirements, depending on the sex offender's confinement status and his residential living arrangements. For example, per c.(1), a sex offender under a supervisory program, such as probation or parole, is required to register "at the time the person is placed under supervision." Under subsection d., a sex offender who changes his address "must re-register with the appropriate law enforcement agency no less than 10 days before he intends to first reside at his new address." It is also important to note that under 2C:7-22, an individual cannot avoid sex offender registration if his sex offense conviction occurred as a minor. (Convictions as a minor are correctly referred to as "adjudicated delinquent.") Similarly, if he was "acquitted by reason of insanity" for commission of a sex offense, he still must register per the requirements of the statute.

<br>

**2C:7-3.**     **Notice of obligation to register as sex offender**

Notice of the obligation to register shall be provided as follows:

(1) A court imposing a sentence, disposition or order of commitment following acquittal by reason of insanity shall notify the defendant of the obligation to register pursuant to section 2 of this act.

(2) The Department of Corrections, the Administrative Office of the Courts, the Juvenile Justice Commission established pursuant to section 2 of P.L.1995, c. 284 (C.52:17B-170) and the Department of Human Services shall (a) establish procedures for notifying persons

under their supervision of the obligation to register pursuant to this act and (b) establish procedures for registration by persons with the appropriate law enforcement agency who are under supervision in the community on probation, parole, furlough, work release or similar program outside the facility, and registration with the appropriate law enforcement agency of persons who are released from the facility in which they are confined without supervision.

(3) The Division of Motor Vehicles in the Department of Law and Public Safety shall provide notice of the obligation to register pursuant to this section in connection with each application for a license to operate a motor vehicle and each application for an identification card issued pursuant to section 2 of P.L.1980, c. 47 (C.39:3-29.3).

(4) The Attorney General shall cause notice of the obligation to register to be published in a manner reasonably calculated to reach the general public within 30 days of the effective date of this act.

## 2C:7-4.    Registration forms; contents; transmission of form

a. Within 60 days of the effective date of this act, the Superintendent of State Police, with the approval of the Attorney General, shall prepare the form of registration statement as required in subsection b. of this section and shall provide such forms to each organized full-time municipal police department, the Department of Corrections, the Administrative Office of the Courts and the Department of Human Services. In addition, the Superintendent of State Police shall make such forms available to the Juvenile Justice Commission established pursuant to section 2 of P.L.1995, c. 284 (C.52:17B-170).

b. The form of registration required by this act shall include:

(1) A statement in writing signed by the person required to register acknowledging that the person has been advised of the duty to register and reregister imposed by this act and including the person's name, social security number, age, race, sex, date of birth, height, weight, hair and eye color, address of legal residence, address of any current temporary residence, date and place of employment; and any anticipated or current school enrollement, including but not limited to enrollment at or employment by any institution of higher education

(2) Date and place of each conviction, adjudication or acquittal by reason of insanity, indictment number, fingerprints, and a brief description of the crime or crimes for which registration is required; and

(3) Any other information that the Attorney General deems necessary to assess risk of future commission of a crime, including criminal and corrections records, nonprivileged personnel, treatment, and abuse registry records, and evidentiary genetic markers when available.

c. Within three days of receipt of a registration pursuant to subsection c. of section 2 of this act, the registering agency shall forward the statement and any other required information to the prosecutor who shall, as soon as practicable, transmit the form of registration to the Superintendent of State Police, and, if the registrant will reside in a different county, to the prosecutor of the county in which the person will reside. The prosecutor of the county in which the person will reside shall transmit the form of registration to the law enforcement agency responsible for the municipality in which the person will reside and other appropriate law enforcement agencies. The superintendent shall promptly transmit the conviction data and fingerprints to the Federal Bureau of Investigation.

d. The Superintendent of State Police shall maintain a central registry of registrations provided pursuant to this act.

**2C:7-5.**         **Records; access; immunity**

    a. Records maintained pursuant to this act shall be open to any law enforcement agency in this State, the United States or any other state. Law enforcement agencies in this State shall be authorized to release relevant and necessary information regarding sex offenders to the public when the release of the information is necessary for public protection in accordance with the provisions of P.L.1994, c. 128 (C.2C:7-6 et seq.).

    b. An elected public official, public employee, or public agency is immune from civil liability for damages for any discretionary decision to release relevant and necessary information, unless it is shown that the official, employee, or agency acted with gross negligence or in bad faith. The immunity provided under this section applies to the release of relevant information to other employees or officials or to the general public.

    c. Nothing in this act shall be deemed to impose any liability upon or to give rise to a cause of action against any public official, public employee, or public agency for failing to release information as authorized in subsection d. of this section.

    d. Nothing in this section shall be construed to prevent law enforcement officers from notifying members of the public exposed to danger of any persons that pose a danger under circumstances that are not enumerated in this act.

**2C:7-6.**         **Notification of community of intent of sex offender released from correctional facility or adjudicated delinquent to reside in municipality**

Within 45 days after receiving notification pursuant to section 1 of P.L.1994, c. 135 (C.30: 4-123.53a.) that an inmate convicted of or adjudicated delinquent for a sex offense as defined in section 2 of P.L.1994, c. 133 (C.2C:7-2.) is to be released from incarceration and after receipt of registration as required therein, the chief law enforcement officer of the municipality where the inmate intends to reside shall provide notification in accordance with the provisions of section 3 of this act of that inmate's release to the community. If the municipality does not have a police force, the Superintendent of State Police shall provide notification.

**2C:7-7.**         **Chief law enforcement officer to provide notification to community**

After receipt of notification and registration pursuant to P.L.1994, c. 133 (C.2C:7-1 et al.) that a person required to register pursuant to that act intends to change his address, the chief law enforcement officer of the municipality to which the person is relocating shall provide notification of that relocation to the community pursuant to section 3 of this act. If the municipality does not have a police force, the Superintendent of State Police shall provide notification.

**2C:7-8.**         **Notification guidelines; identification of factors relevant to risk of re-offense**

    a. After consultation with members of the advisory council established pursuant to section 6 of this act and within 60 days of the effective date, the Attorney General shall promulgate guidelines and procedures for the notification required pursuant to the provisions of this act. The guidelines shall identify factors relevant to risk of re-offense and shall provide for three levels of notification depending upon the degree of the risk of re-offense.

    b. Factors relevant to risk of re-offense shall include, but not be limited to, the following:

        (1) Conditions of release that minimize risk of re-offense, including but not limited to whether the offender is under supervision of probation or parole; receiving counseling, therapy or treatment; or residing in a home situation that provides guidance and supervision;

        (2) Physical conditions that minimize risk of re-offense, including but not limited to advanced age or debilitating illness;

(3) Criminal history factors indicative of high risk of re-offense, including:

   (a) Whether the offender's conduct was found to be characterized by repetitive and compulsive behavior;

   (b) Whether the offender served the maximum term;

   (c) Whether the offender committed the sex offense against a child;

(4) Other criminal history factors to be considered in determining risk, including:

   (a) The relationship between the offender and the victim;

   (b) Whether the offense involved the use of a weapon, violence, or infliction of serious bodily injury;

   (c) The number, date and nature of prior offenses;

(5) Whether psychological or psychiatric profiles indicate a risk of recidivism;

(6) The offender's response to treatment;

(7) Recent behavior, including behavior while confined or while under supervision in the community as well as behavior in the community following service of sentence;

(8) Recent threats against persons or expressions of intent to commit additional crimes.

c. The regulations shall provide for three levels of notification depending upon the risk of re-offense by the offender as follows:

(1) If risk of re-offense is low, law enforcement agencies likely to encounter the person registered shall be notified;

(2) If risk of re-offense is moderate, organizations in the community including schools, religious and youth organizations shall be notified in accordance with the Attorney General's guidelines, in addition to the notice required by paragraph (1) of this subsection;

(3) If risk of re-offense is high, the public shall be notified through means in accordance with the Attorney General's guidelines designed to reach members of the public likely to encounter the person registered, in addition to the notice required by paragraphs (1) and (2) of this subsection.

d. In order to promote uniform application of the notification guidelines required by this section, the Attorney General shall develop procedures for evaluation of the risk of re-offense and implementation of community notification. These procedures shall require, but not be limited to, the following:

(1) The county prosecutor of the county where the person was convicted and the county prosecutor of the county where the registered person will reside, together with any law enforcement officials that either deems appropriate, shall assess the risk of re-offense by the registered person;

(2) The county prosecutor of the county in which the registered person will reside, after consultation with local law enforcement officials, shall determine the means of providing notification.

e. The Attorney General's guidelines shall provide for the manner in which records of notification provided pursuant to this act shall be maintained and disclosed.

**2C:7-9.**     **Immunity from civil and criminal liability for providing or failing to provide relevant public information**

Notwithstanding any other provision of law to the contrary, any person who provides or fails to provide information relevant to the procedures set forth in this act shall not be liable in any civil or criminal action. Nothing herein shall be deemed to grant any such immunity to any person for his willful or wanton act of commission or omission.

**2C:7-10.**          **Notification concerning other dangerous circumstances unaffected**

Nothing in this act shall be construed to prevent law enforcement officers from providing community notification concerning any person who poses a danger under circumstances that are not provided for in this act.

**2C:7-11.**          **Notification advisory council established; qualification of members**

A notification advisory council is established to consult with and provide recommendations to the Attorney General concerning the guidelines to be promulgated pursuant to section 3 of this act. The council shall consist of 12 persons who, by experience or training, have a personal interest or professional expertise in law enforcement, crime prevention, victim advocacy, criminology, psychology, parole, public education or community relations. The members of the council shall be appointed in the following manner: four shall be appointed by the Governor, of whom no more than two shall be of the same political party; four shall be appointed by the President of the Senate, of whom no more than two shall be of the same political party; and four shall be appointed by the Speaker of the General Assembly, of whom no more than two shall be of the same political party. Any vacancies occurring in the membership shall be filled in the same manner as the original appointments.

One year after the effective date of this act, the Attorney General and the council shall conduct a comprehensive review of the guidelines to determine whether any changes or revisions should be promulgated. Upon completion of that review and the submission of any recommendations thereon, the council shall expire.

**2C:7-12.**          **Legislative findings**

The Legislature finds and declares that the public safety will be enhanced by making information about certain sex offenders contained in the sex offender central registry established pursuant to section 4 of P.L.1994, c. 133 (C.2C:7-4) available to the public through the Internet. Knowledge of whether a person is a convicted sex offender at risk of re-offense could be a significant factor in protecting oneself and one's family members, or those in care of a group or community organization, from recidivist acts by the offender. The technology afforded by the Internet would make this information readily accessible to parents and private entities, enabling them to undertake appropriate remedial precautions to prevent or avoid placing potential victims at risk. Public access to registry information is intended solely for the protection of the public, and is not intended to impose additional criminal punishment upon any convicted sex offender. The Legislature further finds and declares that, in some instances, countervailing interests support a legislative determination to exclude from the Internet registry the registration information of certain sex offenders. For example, the interest in facilitating rehabilitation of juveniles who have been adjudicated delinquent for the commission of one sex offense, but who do not present a relatively high risk of re-offense, justifies the decision to limit public access to information about such juveniles through the Internet. Other instances where the Legislature has determined that making sex offender registry information available to the general public through the Internet would not necessarily serve the public safety purposes of the law include moderate risk offenders whose sole sex offense involved incest or consensual sex. However, in such cases, the legislature deems it appropriate and consistent with the public safety purposes of the law to provide a process that permits inclusion of information about these individuals in the Internet registry where public access would be warranted, based on the relative risk posed by the particular offender.

**2C:7-13.**        **Information in central registry to be made available on the Internet**

a. Pursuant to the provisions of this section, the Superintendent of State Police shall develop and maintain a system for making certain information in the central registry established pursuant to subsection d. of section 4 of P.L.1994, c. 133 (C.2C:7-4) publicly available by means of electronic Internet technology.

b. The public may, without limitation, obtain access to the Internet registry to view an individual registration record, any part of, or the entire Internet registry concerning all offenders whose risk of re-offense is high or for whom the court has ordered notification in accordance with paragraph (3) of subsection c. of section 3 of P.L.1994, c. 128 (C.2C:7-8), regardless of the age of the offender.

c. Except as provided in subsection d. of this section, the public may, without limitation, obtain access to the Internet registry to view an individual registration record, any part of, or the entire Internet registry concerning offenders whose risk of re-offense is moderate and for whom the court has ordered notification in accordance with paragraph (2) of subsection c. of section 3 of P.L.1994, c. 128 (C.2C:7-8).

d. The individual registration record of an offender whose risk of re-offense has been determined to be moderate and for whom the court has ordered notification in accordance with paragraph (2) of subsection c. of section 3 of P.L.1994, c. 128 (C.2C:7-8) shall not be made available to the public on the Internet registry if the sole sex offense committed by the offender which renders him subject to the requirements of P.L.1994, c. 133 (C.2C:7-1 et seq.) is one of the following:

   (1) An adjudication of delinquency for any sex offense as defined in subsection b. of section 2 of P.L.1994, c. 133 (C.2C:7-2);

   (2) A conviction or acquittal by reason of insanity for a violation of N.J.S.2C:14-2 or N.J.S.2C:14-3 under circumstances in which the offender was related to the victim by blood or affinity to the third degree or was a foster parent, a guardian, or stood in loco parentis within the household; or

   (3) A conviction or acquittal by reason of insanity for a violation of N.J.S.2C:14-2 or N.J.S.2C:14-3 in any case in which the victim assented to the commission of the offense but by reason of age was not capable of giving lawful consent.

e. Notwithstanding the provisions of paragraph d. of this subsection, the individual registration record of an offender to whom an exception enumerated in paragraph (1), (2) or (3) of subsection d. of this section applies shall be made available to the public on the Internet registry if the State establishes by clear and convincing evidence that, given the particular facts and circumstances of the offense and the characteristics and propensities of the offender, the risk to the general public posed by the offender is substantially similar to that posed by offenders whose risk of re-offense is moderate and who do not qualify under the enumerated exceptions.

f. The individual registration records of offenders whose risk of re-offense is low or of offenders whose risk of re-offense is moderate but for whom the court has not ordered notification in accordance with paragraph (2) of subsection c. of section 3 of P.L.1994, c. 128 (C.2C:7-8) shall not be available to the public on the Internet registry.

g. The information concerning a registered offender to be made publicly available on the Internet shall include: the offender's name and any aliases the offender has used or under which the offender may be or may have been known; any sex offense as defined in subsection b. of section 2 of P.L.1994, c.133 (C.2C:7-2) for which the offender was convicted, adjudicated delinquent or acquitted by reason of insanity, as the case may be; the date and location of disposition; a brief description of any such offense, including the victim's gender and indication of whether the victim was less than 18 years old or less than 13 years old; a general description of the offender's modus operandi, if any; the determination of whether the risk of re-offense by the offender is moderate or high; the offender's age, race, sex, date of birth, height, weight, hair, eye color and any distinguishing scars or tattoos; a photograph of the offender and the date on which the photograph was entered into the registry; the make, model, color, year and license plate number of any vehicle operated by the offender; and the street address, zip code, municipality and county in which the offender resides.

**2C:7-14.**          **Duties of the Attorney General**

The Attorney General shall:

a. Ensure that the Internet registry contains warnings that any person who uses the information contained therein to threaten, intimidate or harass another, or who otherwise misuses that information may be criminally prosecuted;

b. Ensure that the Internet registry contains an explanation of its limitations, including statements advising that a positive identification of an offender whose registration record has been made available may be confirmed only by fingerprints; that some information contained in the registry may be outdated or inaccurate; and that the Internet registry is not a comprehensive listing of every person who has ever committed a sex offense in New Jersey;

c. Strive to ensure the information contained in the Internet registry is accurate, and that the data therein is revised and updated as appropriate in a timely and efficient manner; and

d. Provide in the Internet registry information designed to inform and educate the public about sex offenders and the operation of Megan's Law, as well as pertinent and appropriate information concerning crime prevention and personal safety, with appropriate links to relevant web sites operated by the State of New Jersey.

**2C:7-15.**          **Failure to investigate or disclose any information from the registry**

No action shall be brought against any person for failure to investigate or disclose any information from the registry that is compiled or made available to the citizens of this State pursuant to P.L.2001, c. 167 (C.2C:7-12 et seq.).

**2C:7-16.**          **Use of disclosed information**

a. Any information disclosed pursuant to this act may be used in any manner by any person or by any public, governmental or private entity, organization or official, or any agent thereof, for any lawful purpose consistent with the enhancement of public safety.

b. Any person who uses information disclosed pursuant to this act to commit a crime shall be guilty of a crime of the third degree. Any person who uses information disclosed pursuant to this act to commit a disorderly persons or petty disorderly persons offense shall be guilty of a disorderly persons offense and shall be fined not less than $500 or more than $1,000, in addition to any other penalty or fine imposed.

c. Except as authorized under any other provision of law, use of any of the information disclosed pursuant to this act for the purpose of applying for, obtaining, or denying any of the following, is prohibited:

(1) Health insurance;

(2) Insurance;

(3) Loans;

(4) Credit;

(5) Education, scholarships, or fellowships;

    (6)  Benefits, privileges, or services provided by any business establishment, unless for a purpose consistent with the enhancement of public safety; or

    (7)  Housing or accommodations.

  d.  Whenever there is reasonable cause to believe that any person or group of persons is engaged in a pattern or practice of misuse of the information disclosed pursuant to this act, the Attorney General, or any county or municipal prosecutor having jurisdiction, or any person aggrieved by the misuse of that information is authorized to bring a civil action in the appropriate court requesting preventive relief, including an application for a permanent or temporary injunction, restraining order, or other order against the person or group of persons responsible for the pattern or practice of misuse. The foregoing remedies shall be independent of and in addition to any other remedies or procedures that may be available under other provisions of law.

  e.  Evidence that a person obtained information about an offender from the Internet registry within one year prior to committing a criminal offense against that offender shall give rise to an inference that the person used information in violation of subsection b. of this section.

## 2C:7-17.     Provisions are severable

The provisions of this act shall be deemed to be severable, and if any phrase, clause, sentence, word or provision of this act is declared to be unconstitutional, invalid or inoperative in whole or in part, or the applicability thereof to any person is held invalid, by a court of competent jurisdiction, the remainder of this act shall not thereby be deemed to be unconstitutional, invalid or inoperative and, to the extent it is not declared unconstitutional, invalid or inoperative, shall be effectuated and enforced.

## 2C:7-18.     Internet Registry Advisory Council

An Internet Registry Advisory Council is established to consult with and provide recommendations to the Attorney General concerning the making of sex offender registration records available to the public on the Internet. The council shall consist of nine persons who, by experience or training, have a personal interest or professional expertise in law enforcement, crime prevention, victim advocacy, criminology, psychology, parole, public education or community relations. The members of the council shall be appointed in the following manner: three shall be appointed by the Governor, of whom no more than two shall be of the same political party; three shall be appointed by the President of the Senate, of whom no more than two shall be of the same political party; and three shall be appointed by the Speaker of the General Assembly, of whom no more than two shall be of the same political party. Any vacancies occurring in the membership shall be filled in the same manner as the original appointments. The council shall hold at least two meetings per year to review the implementation and operations of the Internet registry.

## 2C:7-19.     Short title

This act and the system of registration and community notification provided pursuant to P.L.1994, c. 133 and P.L.1994, c. 128 (C.2C:7-1 through 11) shall be known and may be cited as "Megan's Law."

**Chapters 8 to 10—Reserved**

# 11

# CRIMINAL HOMICIDE

## FACT PATTERN

The New Jersey Attorney General called a special meeting at his Trenton office to discuss four seemingly unrelated homicides. Invited were the detectives leading the investigations in the separate cases: a New Jersey state trooper, a Clifton lieutenant, a Cherry Hill detective, and a Bergen County Prosecutor's Office investigator. Each officer provided a short summary of his/her investigation to the state's top law enforcement official.

While on patrol during a late evening winter shift, Trooper Gene Knollwood responded to a radio report that a toll collector on the New Jersey Turnpike had just been robbed at gunpoint by a male traveling in a black SUV with a dented rear bumper. The crime occurred at Exit 16W and the assailant fled toward Route 3 West.

Minutes after the crime, Knollwood located a SUV matching the description and activated his overhead lights and sirens, ordering the automobile to stop. Instead, the suspect accelerated and a pursuit followed. The chase ended abruptly, however, when the driver made a sudden erratic turn, crossing from the left lane to the right, attempting to exit onto the off-ramp leading to Route 17. At this location, the vehicle struck a stranded motorist, killing him upon impact. The suspect, Jeff Weiss, was arrested on the scene.

Weeks earlier, in Hackensack, the county seat of Bergen County, a fight broke out between two strangers in an upscale bar/restaurant directly after the bartender had announced "last call." When Hackensack patrol officers arrived at the location, they found a late twenties male, later identified as George Carmichael, dead in a pool of blood. Witnesses advised that he was physically beaten by an unknown man in his late twenties after the two argued over who was next in line for a drink. According to the witnesses, the assailant had thrown the first punch and fled when he saw Carmichael fall to the floor. No weapons were used during the altercation. During the following week, an investigation led by Sheila Talamico of the Bergen County Prosecutor's Office resulted in the arrest of Larry Kelleher. Kelleher, under interrogation, admitted that he had struck Carmichael at the bar, but was unaware that his blows had resulted in the man's demise.

Across the state, near Philadelphia, the Cherry Hill Police Department investigated the disappearance of a middle-aged lawyer for nearly three weeks. The search ended when his body was located in a wooded area under a pile of rocks and tree branches. The makeshift grave confirmed Detective Sergeant Nicholas Sane's fears that the man had been murdered. But by what means?

The lawyer's physical body, except for decomposition, was not harmed. An autopsy, however, revealed that the man had ingested an alarming amount of arsenic over time, wherein he died several weeks after his final ingestion. A subsequent investigation, involving a joint task force of DEA, Camden County Prosecutor's Office investigators, and Cherry Hill police personnel, led to the attorney's sister, Brigitte Madison, who was the beneficiary of his lucrative life insurance policy and all of his assets. Although she denied any wrongdoing, the investigators found traces of rodent poison in her garbage can. The poison's key ingredient was arsenic. Also, a forensic analysis of hair strands found on the decedent's body matched Madison's hair. Similarly, her fingerprints were found on her brother's watch, which was on his wrist when he was uncovered at his nature deathbed. Finally, passages in Madison's diary mentioned jealousy of her brother's wealth and her desire to see him dead. She even had described a fantasy plot to murder the barrister, which was to be carried out by poisoning him.

On the same day the Cherry Hill police arrested Brigitte Madison, the Clifton Police Department found Cindy Lemon, an early thirties woman, shot to death in her newly built town house. Immediately, the police suspected her live-in boyfriend to be the perpetrator, given reports of a tumultuous relationship. Lieutenant Mario Axel headed a manhunt for her missing boyfriend. However, his search was unwarranted, as the man arrived by his own volition at the Clifton Police Department, hysterical after learning that his girlfriend was dead. He had been in Europe on business; airline personnel and other witnesses verified his out-of-the-country alibi, and accordingly the investigation turned to Lemon's former roommate, Maggie Harkins.

Harkins had filed a lawsuit against Lemon, alleging that she had fraudulently duped her out of $30,000, which was later used as a down payment for the town house. Harkins's case subsequently was dismissed by a superior court judge; the dismissal occurred just hours before Lemon was found riddled with bullets in her home. Axel learned, through a neighbor's account, that Harkins was seen arriving at the town house that afternoon but couldn't advise when she departed. With this information, Axel asked Harkins to voluntarily come to police headquarters to discuss the matter with him. She complied, and there admitted to shooting Lemon in a "blind rage."

After Axel completed explaining the Harkins case, the four officers sat silent with Attorney General Christian Taylor, confused as to any possible connection among their cases. There were no similarities in victims. The fact patterns were totally unrelated: the causes of death in each case were unique; the homicide locales were in different parts of the state; and there appeared to be a definitive, distinct rationale for all killings.

The relationship, Taylor ultimately advised, was that all four perpetrators—Jeff Weiss, Larry Kelleher, Brigitte Madison, and Maggie Harkins—were part of a violent, underground anti-social group, RS, which was purportedly planning a massive bombing of an unknown public building. Indeed, these homicides were unrelated to their activities in RS. However, the attorney general's office and the FBI were obviously greatly concerned about the pending massacre and wanted to capitalize on these fortuitous arrests, perhaps enticing one, if not all, of the defendants to "flip" on the bombing's masterminds.

Taylor explained that deals could be offered, amending each of their charges to lesser included offenses, if they cooperated and provided integral details. Accordingly, it was important for him to learn as much as possible about these individuals. Who is the type to cooperate, who has a motive to cooperate, and who may need to cooperate.

The investigating officers could provide this insight. The first necessary factor to analyze was under what homicide statute each defendant was charged. With that information, Attorney General Taylor could determine what lower charges, if any, could ultimately be offered upon cooperation. New Jersey's homicide statutes were then reviewed.

---

**2C:11-1.**     **Definitions**

In chapters 11 through 15, unless a different meaning plainly is required:

    a. "Bodily injury" means physical pain, illness or any impairment of physical condition;

    b. "Serious bodily injury" means bodily injury which creates a substantial risk of death or which causes serious, permanent disfigurement, or protracted loss or impairment of the function of any bodily member or organ;

    c. "Deadly weapon" means any firearm or other weapon, device, instrument, material or substance, whether animate or inanimate, which in the manner it is used or is intended to be used, is known to be capable of producing death or serious bodily injury or which in the manner it is fashioned would lead the victim reasonably to believe it to be capable of producing death or serious bodily injury;

    d. "Significant bodily injury" means bodily injury which creates a temporary loss of the function of any bodily member or organ or temporary loss of any one of the five senses.

**2C:11-2.**     **Criminal homicide**

    a. A person is guilty of criminal homicide if he purposely, knowingly, recklessly or, under the circumstances set forth in section 2C:11-5, causes the death of another human being.

    b. Criminal homicide is murder, manslaughter or death by auto.

**2C:11-2.1.**     **Elapse of time between assault and death, prosecution for criminal homicide**

The length of time which has elapsed between the initial assault and the death of the victim shall not be a bar to prosecution of the actor for criminal homicide.

## Practical Application of Statute

---

Many times a victim does not die immediately after a homicidal assault occurs. This statute prevents a defendant from escaping a criminal homicide charge where a significant time lapse occurs between the assault and death.

New Jersey case law has held that if a person perishes within a year and a day after the assault, a defendant can be convicted of homicide, whether he was charged with murder, aggravated assault, or another homicide statute. Accordingly, in Brigitte Madison's case, she will be unable to avoid a homicide conviction because her brother died weeks after his lethal intake of arsenic.

---

**2C:11-3.**     **Murder**

    a. Except as provided in N.J.S.2C:11-4, criminal homicide constitutes murder when:

       (1) The actor purposely causes death or serious bodily injury resulting in death; or

       (2) The actor knowingly causes death or serious bodily injury resulting in death; or

(3) It is committed when the actor, acting either alone or with one or more other persons, is engaged in the commission of, or an attempt to commit, or flight after committing or attempting to commit robbery, sexual assault, arson, burglary, kidnapping, carjacking, criminal escape or terrorism pursuant to section 2 of P.L. 2002, c.26 (C.2C.38-2), and in the course of such crime or of immediate flight therefrom, any person causes the death of a person other than one of the participants; except that in any prosecution under this subsection, in which the defendant was not the only participant in the underlying crime, it is an affirmative defense that the defendant:

    (a) Did not commit the homicidal act or in any way solicit, request, command, importune, cause or aid the commission thereof; and

    (b) Was not armed with a deadly weapon, or any instrument, article or substance readily capable of causing death or serious physical injury and of a sort not ordinarily carried in public places by law-abiding persons; and

    (c) Had no reasonable ground to believe that any other participant was armed with such a weapon, instrument, article or substance; and

    (d) Had no reasonable ground to believe that any other participant intended to engage in conduct likely to result in death or serious physical injury.

b. (1) Murder is a crime of the first degree but a person convicted of murder shall be sentenced, except as provided in subsection c. of this section, by the court to a term of 30 years, during which the person shall not be eligible for parole, or be sentenced to a specific term of years which shall be between 30 years and life imprisonment of which the person shall serve 30 years before being eligible for parole.

(2) If the victim was a law enforcement officer and was murdered while performing his official duties or was murdered because of his status as a law enforcement officer, the person convicted of that murder shall be sentenced, except as otherwise provided in subsection c. of this section, by the court to a term of life imprisonment, during which the person shall not be eligible for parole.

(3) A person convicted of murder and who is not sentenced to death under this section shall be sentenced to a term of life imprisonment without eligibility for parole if the murder was committed under all of the following circumstances:

    (a) The victim is less than 14 years old; and

    (b) The act is committed in the course of the commission, whether alone or with one or more persons, of a violation of N.J.S.2C:14-2 or N.J.S.2C:14-3.

(4) If the defendant was subject to sentencing pursuant to subsection c. and the jury or court found the existence of one or more aggravating factors, but that such factors did not outweigh the mitigating factors found to exist by the jury or court or the jury was unable to reach a unanimous verdict as to the weight of the factors, the defendant shall be sentenced by the court to a term of life imprisonment during which the defendant shall not be eligible for parole. With respect to a sentence imposed pursuant to this subsection, the defendant shall not be entitled to a deduction of commutation and work credits from that sentence.

c. Any person convicted under subsection a.(1) or (2) who committed the homicidal act by his own conduct; or who as an accomplice procured the commission of the offense by payment or promise of payment of anything of pecuniary value; or who, as a leader of a narcotics trafficking network as defined in N.J.S.2C:35-3 and in furtherance of a conspiracy enumerated in N.J.S.2C:35-3, commanded or by threat or promise solicited the commission of the offense, or, if the murder occurred during the commission of the crime of terrorism, any person who committed the crime of terrorism, shall be sentenced as provided hereinafter:

(1) The court shall conduct a separate sentencing proceeding to determine whether the defendant should be sentenced to death or pursuant to the provisions of subsection b. of this section.

Where the defendant has been tried by a jury, the proceeding shall be conducted by the judge who presided at the trial and before the jury which determined the defendant's guilt, except that, for good cause, the court may discharge that jury and conduct the proceeding before a jury empaneled for the purpose of the proceeding. Where the defendant has entered a plea of guilty or has been tried without a jury, the proceeding shall be conducted by the judge who accepted the defendant's plea or who determined the defendant's guilt and before a jury empaneled for the purpose of the proceeding. On motion of the defendant and with consent of the prosecuting attorney the court may conduct a proceeding without a jury. Nothing in this subsection shall be construed to prevent the participation of an alternate juror in the sentencing proceeding if one of the jurors who rendered the guilty verdict becomes ill or is otherwise unable to proceed before or during the sentencing proceeding.

(2) (a) At the proceeding, the State shall have the burden of establishing beyond a reasonable doubt the existence of any aggravating factors set forth in paragraph (4) of this subsection. The defendant shall have the burden of producing evidence of the existence of any mitigating factors set forth in paragraph (5) of this subsection but shall not have a burden with regard to the establishment of a mitigating factor.

(b) The admissibility of evidence offered by the State to establish any of the aggravating factors shall be governed by the rules governing the admission of evidence at criminal trials. The defendant may offer, without regard to the rules governing the admission of evidence at criminal trials, reliable evidence relevant to any of the mitigating factors. If the defendant produces evidence in mitigation which would not be admissible under the rules governing the admission of evidence at criminal trials, the State may rebut that evidence without regard to the rules governing the admission of evidence at criminal trials.

(c) Evidence admitted at the trial, which is relevant to the aggravating and mitigating factors set forth in paragraphs (4) and (5) of this subsection, shall be considered without the necessity of reintroducing that evidence at the sentencing proceeding; provided that the fact finder at the sentencing proceeding was present as either the fact finder or the judge at the trial.

(d) The State and the defendant shall be permitted to rebut any evidence presented by the other party at the sentencing proceeding and to present argument as to the adequacy of the evidence to establish the existence of any aggravating or mitigating factor.

(e) Prior to the commencement of the sentencing proceeding, or at such time as he has knowledge of the existence of an aggravating factor, the prosecuting attorney shall give notice to the defendant of the aggravating factors which he intends to prove in the proceeding.

(f) Evidence offered by the State with regard to the establishment of a prior homicide conviction pursuant to paragraph (4) (a) of this subsection may include the identity and age of the victim, the manner of death and the relationship, if any, of the victim to the defendant.

(3) The jury, or if there is no jury, the court shall return a special verdict setting forth in writing the existence or nonexistence of each of the aggravating and mitigating factors set forth in paragraphs (4) and (5) of this subsection. If any aggravating factor is found to exist, the verdict shall also state whether it outweighs beyond a reasonable doubt any one or more mitigating factors.

    (a) If the jury or the court finds that any aggravating factors exist and that all of the aggravating factors outweigh beyond a reasonable doubt all of the mitigating factors, the court shall sentence the defendant to death.

    (b) If the jury or the court finds that no aggravating factors exist, or that all of the aggravating factors which exist do not outweigh all of the mitigating factors, the court shall sentence the defendant pursuant to subsection b.

    (c) If the jury is unable to reach a unanimous verdict, the court shall sentence the defendant pursuant to subsection b.

(4) The aggravating factors which may be found by the jury or the court are:

    (a) The defendant has been convicted, at any time, of another murder. For purposes of this section, a conviction shall be deemed final when sentence is imposed and may be used as an aggravating factor regardless of whether it is on appeal;

    (b) In the commission of the murder, the defendant purposely or knowingly created a grave risk of death to another person in addition to the victim;

    (c) The murder was outrageously or wantonly vile, horrible or inhuman in that it involved torture, depravity of mind, or an aggravated assault to the victim;

    (d) The defendant committed the murder as consideration for the receipt, or in expectation of the receipt of any thing of pecuniary value;

    (e) The defendant procured the commission of the murder by payment or promise of payment of anything of pecuniary value;

    (f) The murder was committed for the purpose of escaping detection, apprehension, trial, punishment or confinement for another offense committed by the defendant or another;

    (g) The murder was committed while the defendant was engaged in the commission of, or an attempt to commit, or flight after committing or attempting to commit murder, robbery, sexual assault, arson, burglary, kidnapping, carjacking or the crime of contempt in violation of N.J.S.2C:29-9b;

    (h) The defendant murdered a public servant, as defined in N.J.S.2C:27-1, while the victim was engaged in the performance of his official duties, or because of the victim's status as a public servant;

    (i) The defendant: (i) as a leader of a narcotics trafficking network as defined in N.J.S.2C:35-3 and in furtherance of a conspiracy enumerated in N.J.S.2C:35-3, committed, commanded or by threat or promise solicited the commission of the murder or (ii) committed the murder at the direction of a leader of a narcotics trafficking network as defined in N.J.S.2C:35-3 in furtherance of a conspiracy enumerated in N.J.S.2C:35-3;

    (j) The homicidal act that the defendant committed or procured was in violation of paragraph (1) of subsection a. of N.J.S.2C:17-2;

    (k) The victim was less than 14 years old; or

    (l) The murder was committed during the commission of, or an attempt to commit, or flight after committing or attempting to commit, terrorism pursuant to section 2 of P.L. 2002, c.26 (C.2C:38-2).

    (5) The mitigating factors which may be found by the jury or the court are:

        (a) The defendant was under the influence of extreme mental or emotional disturbance insufficient to constitute a defense to prosecution;

        (b) The victim solicited, participated in or consented to the conduct which resulted in his death;

        (c) The age of the defendant at the time of the murder;

        (d) The defendant's capacity to appreciate the wrongfulness of his conduct or to conform his conduct to the requirements of the law was significantly impaired as the result of mental disease or defect or intoxication, but not to a degree sufficient to constitute a defense to prosecution;

        (e) The defendant was under unusual and substantial duress insufficient to constitute a defense to prosecution;

        (f) The defendant has no significant history of prior criminal activity;

        (g) The defendant rendered substantial assistance to the State in the prosecution of another person for the crime of murder; or

        (h) Any other factor which is relevant to the defendant's character or record or to the circumstances of the offense.

    (6) When a defendant at a sentencing proceeding presents evidence of the defendant's character or record pursuant to subparagraph (h) of paragraph (5) of this subsection, the State may present evidence of the murder victim's character and background and of the impact of the murder on the victim's survivors. If the jury finds that the State has proven at least one aggravating factor beyond a reasonable doubt and the jury finds the existence of a mitigating factor pursuant to subparagraph (h) of paragraph (5) of this subsection, the jury may consider the victim and survivor evidence presented by the State pursuant to this paragraph in determining the appropriate weight to give mitigating evidence presented pursuant to subparagraph (h) of paragraph (5) of this subsection. As used in this paragraph "victim and survivor evidence" may include the display of a photograph of the victim taken before the homicide.

d.  The sentencing proceeding set forth in subsection c. of this section shall not be waived by the prosecuting attorney.

e.  Every judgment of conviction which results in a sentence of death under this section shall be appealed, pursuant to the Rules of Court, to the Supreme Court. Upon the request of the defendant, the Supreme Court shall also determine whether the sentence is disproportionate to the penalty imposed in similar cases, considering both the crime and the defendant. Proportionality review under this section shall be limited to a comparison of similar cases in which a sentence of death has been imposed under subsection c. of this section. In any instance in which the defendant fails, or refuses to appeal, the appeal shall be taken by the Office of the Public Defender or other counsel appointed by the Supreme Court for that purpose.

f.  Prior to the jury's sentencing deliberations, the trial court shall inform the jury of the sentences which may be imposed pursuant to subsection b. of this section or the defendant if the defendant is not sentenced to death. The jury shall also be informed that a failure to reach a unanimous verdict shall result in sentencing by the court pursuant to subsection b.

g.  A juvenile who has been tried as an adult and convicted of murder shall not be sentenced pursuant to the provisions of subsection c. but shall be sentenced pursuant to the provisions of subsection b. of this section.

h.  In a sentencing proceeding conducted pursuant to this section, no evidence shall be admissible concerning the method or manner of execution which would be imposed on a defendant sentenced to death.

i. For purposes of this section the term "homicidal act" shall mean conduct that causes death or serious bodily injury resulting in death.

j. In a sentencing proceeding conducted pursuant to this section, the display of a photograph of the victim taken before the homicide shall be permitted.

## PRACTICAL APPLICATION OF STATUTE

### The Intent to Kill

Brigitte Madison could appropriately be charged with murder under subsections a.(1) or a.(2) of the statute. This is a crime of the first degree, wherein she would face life in prison or even death if convicted. But why should she face this type of punishment? What is it about her actions that makes her susceptible to a murder conviction? As in most New Jersey criminal statutes, the key element of the offense is the actor's criminal intent or *mens rea*. Here she must manifest either a criminal intent of "purpose" or "knowledge"—the intent to kill. If the prosecution can prove that Madison poisoned her brother "purposely," intending to cause his death, or "purposely" intending to cause his serious bodily injury which resulted in his death, then she will be convicted of murder. Similarly, if the prosecution can prove the lesser intent of "knowledge"—that she poisoned her brother "knowing" her actions would cause his death or that his serious bodily injury would result in his death—then she will be convicted of murder.

Assuming the prosecution can prove that Madison did indeed poison her brother, through the evidence of her hair strands, fingerprints, diary entries, etc., it is an almost guarantee that she will be convicted of murder, and not under a lesser homicide statute. Why? Because common sense dictates that she had to, at minimum, "know" that her act of poisoning her brother with arsenic would result in his death. More likely, however, she acted "purposely" to cause his death—remember, she was the beneficiary of his huge life insurance policy and the recipient of all his assets. Accordingly, murder is the correct statute to charge Brigitte Madison under. This gives the attorney general a lot of room to downgrade to a lesser homicide statute, such as aggravated manslaughter, though it is most likely the best deal she would be offered is a plea to murder with a stipulation that the state would not seek the death penalty.

### Felony Murder

Jeff Weiss was indicted for murder, even though the prosecution would be unable to prove that he "purposely" or "knowingly" intended to kill the stranded motorist. How? Under subsection a.(3) of the statute, which is commonly known as the "felony murder statute."

In order to secure this first degree conviction, the state must prove that two criminal actions occurred: the killing of another individual and an *underlying* felony. Simply, for the charge to be valid a defendant must cause a person's death while committing a felony or during his flight after committing a felony. Only certain felonies apply, however: robbery, sexual assault, arson, burglary, kidnapping, criminal escape, and terrorism.

Since Weiss first stole money from the toll collector at gunpoint, one of the requisite underlying felony offenses, robbery, exists. Immediately thereafter, during his flight from the robbery, he caused the stranded motorist's death by striking the man with his vehicle. With these two elements met, Weiss is ripe to be charged with murder.

It is interesting to note that if Weiss had an accomplice who was killed during the automobile accident, he would not be charged with that person's murder. The statute provides an exception for deaths of other participants of the felony crimes. What's even more interesting is that the statute provides an "affirmative defense" to a charge of felony murder under subsections a.(3)(a) through a.(3)(d).

This defense only applies where the defendant is "not the only participant" involved in the felony act. Further, the elements are extremely difficult to meet for the defendant, given that four prongs must be present:

1. The defendant did not actually commit the homicidal act or solicit it in any way;
2. The defendant was not armed with a deadly weapon;
3. The defendant had no reason to believe that another participant in the felony was armed with a deadly weapon; and
4. The defendant had no reason to believe that another participant intended to act in a way that would likely cause death.

Changing the facts in Jeff Weiss's case will provide an example where a defendant should not be charged with murder even though a death occurred during a felony such as robbery. Weiss and a second man, Sanford Lennox, plan to rob the tollbooth. They approach the money collector on foot and pass him a note demanding the monetary funds. The toll collector refuses to turn over the money. This angers Weiss and he reaches into the booth, grabbing two rolls of quarters, smashing them repeatedly across the man's head and screaming, "Die. Die. I want you dead." Lennox stands motionless, horrified at what has occurred. The toll collector crumbles to the ground, dead, as the two men flee.

Here, Weiss clearly should be charged with murder, but not Sanford Lennox. Lennox not only did not commit the homicidal act, but he stood silently to the side, not soliciting it in any way. He was not armed with a deadly weapon. Further, he did not have any reason to believe Weiss was armed with a deadly weapon or that Weiss intended to engage in an act likely to cause death—they planned to use a note to illegally obtain the toll money. With all these elements present, Lennox has an affirmative defense under the murder statute.

Court challenges to the "felony murder" component of the statute occur frequently. However, the subsection has been upheld as legal. An individual, therefore, can be convicted of a first degree charge of murder in cases where he does not manifest the specific intent to kill. Simply, if a person is killed during the commission of one of the enumerated felonies or flight therefrom, an individual in many cases will be charged and convicted of murder even though he may not have intended to kill anyone.

---

**2C:11-3a.**          **Adoption of court rules concerning photos of homicide victim**

The Supreme Court may adopt court rules pertaining to the display of a photograph of a homicide victim in court as permitted in N.J.S.2C:11-3 concerning murder and in section 3 of P.L. 1985, c. 249 (C.52:4B-36) concerning other homicide prosecutions. These court rules may include, but shall not be limited to, the following matters to ensure uniformity in all homicide prosecutions:

a.  the size of the photograph;

b.  the duration of the display;

c.  the location of the photograph in the courtroom

**2C:11-4.**        **Manslaughter**

    a. Criminal homicide constitutes aggravated manslaughter when:

       (1) The actor recklessly causes death under circumstances manifesting extreme indifference to human life; or

       (2) The actor causes the death of another person while fleeing or attempting to elude a law enforcement officer in violation of subsection b. of N.J.S.2C:29-2. Notwithstanding the provision of any other law to the contrary, the actor shall be strictly liable for a violation of this paragraph upon proof of a violation of subsection b. of N.J.S.2C:29-2 which resulted in the death of another person. As used in this paragraph, "actor" shall not include a passenger in a motor vehicle.

    b. Criminal homicide constitutes manslaughter when:

       (1) It is committed recklessly; or

       (2) A homicide which would otherwise be murder under section 2C:11-3 is committed in the heat of passion resulting from a reasonable provocation.

    c. Aggravated manslaughter under paragraph (1) of subsection a. of this section is a crime of the first degree and upon conviction thereof a person may, notwithstanding the provisions of paragraph (1) of subsection a. of N.J.S.2C:43-6, be sentenced to an ordinary term of imprisonment between 10 and 30 years. Aggravated manslaughter under paragraph (2) of subsection a. of this section is a crime of the first degree. Manslaughter is a crime of the second degree.

## PRACTICAL APPLICATION OF STATUTE

### Aggravated Manslaughter

Under 2C:11-4a., a defendant is guilty of aggravated manslaughter, a first degree crime, when he "recklessly" causes death "under circumstances manifesting extreme indifference to human life." What exactly does this mean?

    First, the statute does not require the "intent to kill" as does murder under 2C:11-3. The defendant does not need to act "purposely" or "knowing" that his actions will result in death. The requisite *mens rea*, or mental state, here falls just short of that high level of intent.

    For example, Maggie Harkins could be charged with aggravated manslaughter if the facts showed that she intended to fire her gun "only in the vicinity" of Cindy Lemon and not directly at her. In that scenario, she did not intend to kill Lemon, perhaps only seeking to frighten her. However, pointing a firearm, a deadly weapon, and firing it near someone certainly is "reckless" behavior which manifests "extreme indifference to human life." While Harkins may not have acted with purpose or knowledge that her actions would cause Lemon's death, could anything be more callous or uncaring toward another's life, especially when the result was that the bullets not only struck Lemon but did indeed kill her?

    If the facts showed, however, that she purposely fired the gun at Lemon, then she would be ripe for a murder conviction. Ironically, though, under the circumstances of her case, the most appropriate charge may be an offense lower than both murder and aggravated manslaughter—manslaughter.

### Manslaughter

Whereas aggravated manslaughter is a crime of the first degree, manslaughter is a second degree crime wherein the prison term upon conviction can be significantly less. The reason is again predicated upon the actor's intent or mental state.

The difference between aggravated manslaughter and manslaughter primarily rests in the omission of the language "under circumstances manifesting extreme indifference to human life." Manslaughter simply requires that the defendant causes a death while acting "recklessly." Manslaughter is the correct statute for the Bergen County Prosecutor's Office to seek an indictment against Larry Kelleher. An indictment of aggravated manslaughter in his case would be overreaching.

Kelleher did not cause George Carmichael's death under circumstances manifesting extreme indifference to human life. He didn't repeatedly strike him on the head with a baseball bat or fire a gun in his direction. Kelleher, rather, acted just "recklessly": a drunkard in a bar fight, lacking any intent to kill, but seeking to cause some bodily injury to his adversary. Unfortunately, his reckless fighting behavior resulted in Carmichael's death and therefore he is facing the criminal homicide charge of manslaughter. The Attorney General, with broad sentencing range, could fairly offer Kelleher a minimal prison term if he cooperated with information about the pending RS bombing. Conversely, if Kelleher didn't cooperate, he could seek the maximum term. However, as noted above, it would be inappropriate for the state to threaten a greater charge, such as aggravated manslaughter or murder, as the facts of the case don't meet the elements of those offenses.

### Manslaughter—Heat of Passion

Maggie Harkins's matter, however, provides more charging options. As discussed earlier, she could be indicted for aggravated manslaughter if the facts proved she only intended to fire near Cindy Lemon. Conversely, if the facts showed she fired directly at her victim, then Harkins could be indicted for murder because she acted "purposely" or "knowing" that her actions would result in death. But under these latter facts, even with the intent to kill present, Harkins could avoid a murder charge and face only manslaughter—under 2C:11-4b.(2), the "heat of passion" provision. The following facts could substantiate a manslaughter charge.

Maggie Harkins and Cindy Lemon were former roommates. Their relationship apparently had gone awry, to the extent that Harkins filed a lawsuit against Lemon, alleging that Lemon had fraudulently duped her out of $30,000. Harkins's lawsuit quickly gets dismissed, and she confronts Lemon at her town house, the property Lemon bought with the money she heisted from her old friend. Harkins brings a gun with her but doesn't intend to use it. However, an argument immediately ensues between the two, wherein Harkins not only learns that her accusations of theft were true but also that Lemon had engaged in a sexual relationship with her boyfriend. In a "blind rage" she shoots Lemon.

The statute provides that in order for this act to be manslaughter and not murder, the homicide must occur in the "heat of passion resulting from a reasonable provocation." Would Harkins's "blind rage" shooting equate to an act perpetrated in the heat of passion? Probably. From the mouth of Lemon, Harkins learned that she did indeed steal from her. And even more so that she had sexual relations with Harkins's boyfriend. This, all in the town house that was partially bought with the stolen funds. Given their previous friendship and the nature of the information abruptly learned by Harkins, her actions would likely be viewed as occurring in the heat of passion—and with reasonable provocation. Accordingly, Attorney General Taylor could downgrade Harkins's charge from murder to manslaughter in order to obtain the information and testimony he wants about RS and its bombing masterminds. This would be quite advantageous to Harkins, who could avoid a potential death sentence or life in prison and instead face a more moderate term of incarceration.

### Manslaughter—Death Caused While Eluding Police

2C:11-4a.(2) is distinguished from the felony murder statute under 2C:11-3a.(3) in that it involves flight from a law enforcement officer in all matters other than robbery, sexual assault, arson, burglary, kidnapping, carjacking, criminal escape, and terrorism. In other words, if a defendant causes another person's death while eluding the police after a simple assault or running a red light, he is guilty of manslaughter. Simply, if the state can prove the defendant committed the underlying offense of eluding (2C:29-2b.) and that another person's death is caused during the defendant's eluding of police, then that defendant is strictly liable for manslaughter.

---

**2C:11-5.**     **Death by auto or vessel**

   a. Criminal homicide constitutes vehicular homicide when it is caused by driving a vehicle or vessel recklessly.

   Proof that the defendant fell asleep while driving or was driving after having been without sleep for a period in excess of 24 consecutive hours may give rise to an inference that the defendant was driving recklessly. Proof that the defendant was driving while intoxicated in violation of R.S.39:4-50 or was operating a vessel under the influence of alcohol or drugs in violation of section 3 of P.L.1952, c.157 (C.12:7-46) shall give rise to an inference that the defendant was driving recklessly. Nothing in this section shall be construed to in any way limit the conduct or conditions that may be found to constitute driving a vehicle or vessel recklessly.

   b. Except as provided in paragraph (3) of this subsection, vehicular homicide is a crime of the second degree.

   (1) If the defendant was operating the auto or vessel while under the influence of any intoxicating liquor, narcotic, hallucinogenic or habit-producing drug, or with a blood alcohol concentration at or above the prohibited level as prescribed in R.S.39:4-50, or if the defendant was operating the auto or vessel while his driver's license or reciprocity privilege was suspended or revoked for any violation of R.S.39:4-50, section 2 of P.L.1981, c. 512 (C.39:4-50.4a.), by the Director of the Division of Motor Vehicles pursuant to P.L.1982, c. 85 (C.39:5-30a et seq.), or by the court for a violation of R.S.39:4-96, the defendant shall be sentenced to a term of imprisonment by the court. The term of imprisonment shall include the imposition of a minimum term. The minimum term shall be fixed at, or between, one-third and one-half of the sentence imposed by the court or three years, whichever is greater, during which the defendant shall be ineligible for parole.

   (2) The court shall not impose a mandatory sentence pursuant to paragraph (1) of this subsection unless the grounds therefore have been established at a hearing. At the hearing, which may occur at the time of sentencing, the prosecutor shall establish by a preponderance of the evidence that the defendant was operating the auto or vessel while under the influence of any intoxicating liquor, narcotic, hallucinogenic or habit-producing drug, or with a blood alcohol concentration at or above the level prescribed in R.S.39:4-50 or that the defendant was operating the auto or vessel while his driver's license or reciprocity privilege was suspended or revoked for any violation of

R.S.39:4-50, section 2 of P.L. 1981, c. 512 (C:39:4-50.4a.), by the Director of the Division of Motor Vehicles pursuant to P.L. 1982, c .85 (C:39:5-30a. et seq.), or by the court for a violation of R.S.39:4-96. In making its findings, the court shall take judicial notice of any evidence, testimony or information adduced at the trial, plea hearing, or other court proceedings and shall also consider the presentence report and any other relevant information.

(3) Vehicular homicide is a crime of the first degree if the defendant was operating the auto or vessel while in violation of R.S.39:4-50 or section 2 of P.L. 1982, c. 512 (C.39:4-50,4a.) while:

    (a) on any school property used for school purposes which is owned by or leased to any elementary or secondary school or school board, or within 1,000 feet of such school property;

    (b) driving through a school crossing as defined in R.S.39:1-1 if the municipality, by ordinance or resolution, has designated the school crossing as such; or

    (c) driving through a school crossing as defined in R.S.39:1-1 knowing that juveniles are present if the municipality has not designated the school crossing as such by ordinance or resolution.

    A map or true copy of a map depicting the location and boundaries of the area on or within 1,000 feet of any property used for school purposes which is owned by or leased to any elementary or secondary school or school board produced pursuant to section 1 of P.L. 1997, c. 101 (C.2C:35-7) may be used in a prosecution under subparagraph (a) of this paragraph.

    It shall be no defense to a prosecution for a violation of subparagraphs (a) or (b) of this paragraph that the defendant was unaware that the prohibited conduct took place while on or within 1,000 feet of any school property or while driving through a school crossing. Nor shall it be a defense to a prosecution under subparagraphs (a) or (b) of this paragraph that no juveniles were present on the school property or crossing zone at the time of the offense or that the school was not in session.

(4) If the defendant was operating the auto or vessel in violation of R.S.39:4-50 or section 2 of P.L. 1981, c. 512 (C.39:4-50.4a.), the defendant's license to operate a motor vehicle shall be suspended for a period of between five years and life, which period shall commence upon completion of any prison sentence imposed upon that person.

c. For good cause shown, the court may, in accepting a plea of guilty under this section, order that such plea not be evidential in any civil proceeding.

d. Nothing herein shall be deemed to preclude, if the evidence so warrants, an indictment and conviction for aggravated manslaughter under the provisions of subsection a. of N.J.S.2C:11-4.

    As used in this section, "auto or vessel" means all means of conveyance propelled otherwise than by muscular power.

e. Any person who violates paragraph (3) of subsection b. of this section shall forfeit the auto or vessel used in the commission of the offense, unless the defendant can establish at a hearing , which may occur at the time of sentencing, by a preponderance of the evidence that such forfeiture would constitute a serious hardship to the family of the defendant that outweighs the need to deter such conduct by the defendant and others. In making its findings, the court shall take judicial notice of any evidence, testimony or information adduced at the trial, plea hearing, or other court proceedings and shall also consider the presentence report and any other relevant information. Forfeiture pursuant to this subsection shall be in addition to, and not in lieu of, civil forfeiture pursuant to chapter 64 of this title.

## PRACTICAL APPLICATION OF STATUTE

Notwithstanding the robbery element of Jeff Weiss's case, he committed vehicular homicide, a second degree offense. Weiss raced from the left lane to the right on Route 3 in an attempt to exit onto Route 17. He did this even though a stranded motorist stood near the off-ramp. His "reckless" driving resulted in death and therefore, under 2C:11-5a., he is guilty of vehicular homicide.

Under subsection b. of the statute, the punishment becomes more severe if the defendant commits vehicular homicide while also violating one of two New Jersey motor vehicle violations: driving while intoxicated, commonly known as DWI (39:4-50), or driving while on the revoked list (39:3-40). It is interesting to note that the penalties are only enhanced for driving on the revoked list if the defendant is on the revoked list because of a DWI conviction or because of a conviction of reckless driving under (39:4-96). Accordingly, Jeff Weiss would be charged under subsection b., rather than subsection a., if his vehicular homicide occurred in conjunction with a DWI or a violation of driving on the revoked list as discussed above.

The punishment becomes even harsher, with the offense growing to a crime of the first degree under paragraph (3) of subsection b. Weiss would be charged here if he commits a vehicular homicide while intoxicated (DWI) and if it occurs on school property, within 1,000 feet of school property, or while he is driving through a school crossing. Law enforcement officers are to ignore whether the defendant was aware that he was in a school zone or school crossing when charging under this statute.

Additionally, the statute provides that the state is not precluded from also charging a defendant with aggravated manslaughter if the evidence so warrants. Accordingly, Attorney General Taylor has a wide range of possible plea offers to make to Jeff Weiss—murder, aggravated manslaughter, and different degrees of vehicular homicide—depending on his sobriety, motor vehicle standing, and the location of the incident.

## 2C:11-5.1  Knowingly leaving scene of motor vehicle accident resulting in death, third degree crime; sentencing

A motor vehicle operator who knows he is involved in an accident and knowingly leaves the scene of that accident under circumstances that violate the provisions of R.S.39:4-129 shall be guilty of a crime of the third degree if the accident results in the death of another person. The presumption of nonimprisonment set forth in N.J.S.2C:44-1 shall not apply to persons convicted under the provisions of this section.

If the evidence so warrants, nothing in this section shall be deemed to preclude an indictment and conviction for aggravated manslaughter under the provisions of N.J.S.2C:11-4 or for vehicular homicide under the provisions of N.J.S.2C:11-5.

Notwithstanding the provisions of N.J.S.2C:1-8 or any other provisions of law, a conviction arising under this section shall not merge with a conviction for aggravated manslaughter under the provisions of N.J.S.2C:11-4 or for vehicular homicide under the provisions of N.J.S.2C:11-5 and a separate sentence shall be imposed upon each such conviction.

Notwithstanding the provisions of N.J.S.2C:44-5 or any other provisions of law, when the court imposes multiple sentences of imprisonment for more than one offense, those sentences shall run consecutively.

For the purposes of this section, neither knowledge of the death nor the knowledge of the violation are elements of the offense and it shall not be a defense that the operator of the motor vehicle was unaware of the death or of the provisions of R.S.39:4-129.

## PRACTICAL APPLICATION OF STATUTE

This third degree crime is primarily predicated upon a New Jersey motor vehicle statute, leaving the scene of an accident (39:4-129). Quite clearly, if Jeff Weiss left the scene of the accident after he struck and killed the stranded motorist, he would be convicted under this criminal homicide statute.

This offense, like the motor vehicle offense, requires the mental state of knowledge. The defendant must "know" that he was involved in a motor vehicle accident and "know" that he left the motor vehicle accident after it occurred. It is not an element of the offense, however, that the defendant knew that he killed someone. The State just needs to prove that the defendant knew he was in an accident and that he knowingly left the accident.

In Jeff Weiss's case, obviously he knew he was in a motor vehicle accident; such a fatal impact could not be missed. In fact, the motor vehicle statute imputes knowledge of the accident to any individual involved in a motor vehicle accident where death occurs. 39:4-129e. provides, "The driver of any motor vehicle involved in an accident resulting in injury or death to any person or damage in the amount of $250 or more to any vehicle or property shall be presumed to have knowledge that he was involved in such accident, and such presumption shall be rebuttable in nature."

Given Weiss's "knowledge," he is guilty of violating 2C:11-5.1.

**2C:11-6.**      **Aiding suicide**

A person who purposely aids another to commit suicide is guilty of a crime of the second degree if his conduct causes such suicide or an attempted suicide, and otherwise of a crime of the fourth degree.

## PRACTICAL APPLICATION OF STATUTE

With the facts slightly changed, Brigitte Madison could be charged with aiding suicide rather than murder. If instead of purposely poisoning her brother with arsenic in an attempt to gain his monetary wealth, she "purposely" aided him to commit suicide, then she would be guilty of this lesser homicide statute. This would be a crime of the second degree, as her conduct caused the suicide.

2C:11-6 is a rarely invoked statute, given the minimal occurrences where individuals assist others in suicides. However, it is a viable statute and will be upheld where the facts are proven and meet the elements of the offense.

# 12

# ASSAULT; RECKLESS ENDANGERING; THREATS

## FACT PATTERN

In Newark, police Sergeant Samuel Paterson recently arrested two brothers in connection with the beating of a 50-year-old grocer. While on routine patrol, Paterson waited at a red light in a long line of traffic. As the automobiles ahead of him slowly started to move, he heard a low rumble of commotion through his cruiser's closed window. Turning to his left, he witnessed two men, later identified as Lance and Stanley Jones, violently beating another individual with golf clubs in front of a grocery store. They repeatedly struck the man in the body and face with the clubs.

Paterson, in full uniform, immediately exited his vehicle in an effort to stop the trauma. As he approached, however, Lance Jones reached into his coat pocket and produced a pistol. He aimed the weapon at Paterson; as he did so, a red laser beam raced from the gun's barrel toward the police officer. At the same time, Stanley Jones ran at Paterson and struck him in the head with a closed fist. Then Stanley turned around and pointed his own gun at a group of bystanders. He nodded to his brother and said, "Let's go, bro."

The two brothers, still pointing their guns, walked backwards to a nearby Ford Mustang, entered the vehicle, and fled. Stanley was the driver. Sergeant Paterson immediately radioed for assistance and pursued them in his cruiser, keeping safe distance from the felons, with his sirens blaring and lights flashing. Stanley weaved in and out of traffic, driving in excess of 80 miles per hour down the busy Newark streets. After only a few minutes, however, the Jones brothers crashed their speeding vehicle into a parked car while attempting to avoid a maroon minivan that had crossed the double yellow line. Inside the parked vehicle was an elderly woman. The jolt of the crash caused her to lunge forward, wherein she smashed her forehead into her car's windshield. The minivan similarly struck a parked vehicle; the impact of this crash caused the unoperated car to jump the curb and hit a pedestrian.

The Jones brothers, uninjured, exited their vehicle and fled on foot. Fortunately, however, they were apprehended only two blocks from the motor vehicle accident. Backup officers caught up with them as they were attempting to mount a fence. They were handcuffed and transported to the closest precinct for processing. Also arrested at the site of the accident was Pedro Munoz, the driver of the minivan that crossed the double yellow lines. Field sobriety tests and a strong odor of alcohol led Sergeant Paterson to believe that Munoz was driving while intoxicated.

All victims of the Jones brothers' rampage, including Sergeant Paterson, were rushed to the hospital for medical treatment. A tally of their injuries resulted in the following: the man beaten outside the grocery store turned out to be the store's owner. The strikes from the golf clubs were so severe that he was rendered unconscious and required over 40 stitches to his head. He also suffered several broken ribs. The elderly woman injured by the Jones's vehicle cracked her skull so hard that she fell into a coma where she remained for two weeks. Fortunately, she recovered afterward; her injuries, though, required a metal plate to be placed in her head as well as numerous staples. The pedestrian struck via Pedro Munoz's accident suffered only scrapes and bruises. Sergeant Paterson likewise only suffered a bruise to his face.

Once at police headquarters, Sergeant Paterson ran the criminal histories of both Jones brothers. He found that there was an open warrant against Stanley Jones involving a woman who Jones had once dated. The woman alleged that Jones had slipped a drug in a beverage that she was consuming. The drink tranquilized her, causing her to become disoriented. Thereafter, in the same evening, she stated that Jones sexually assaulted her.

She also claimed that Jones appeared in front of her house on five subsequent occasions and followed her when she drove to and from work. On each occasion, he verbally advised her not to report the sexual assault and twice threatened to kill her, her mother, and her sister. Appropriate charges were filed against Stanley Jones, which were now the subject of this warrant. Sergeant Peterson also found that Jones had over twenty prior convictions, including convictions for arson, aggravated assault, and burglary. At the time of the arrest, he was on parole for an arson conviction.

Lance Jones had ten prior convictions including burglary and theft offenses. He also was once convicted of taking a pistol from a uniformed police officer's person. The officer was attempting to arrest Jones, but was thwarted in his efforts when Jones wrangled the gun from him and discharged the weapon in the process.

---

**2C:12-1.**     **Assault**

    a.  Simple assault. A person is guilty of assault if he:

        (1)  Attempts to cause or purposely, knowingly or recklessly causes bodily injury to another; or

        (2)  Negligently causes bodily injury to another with a deadly weapon; or

        (3)  Attempts by physical menace to put another in fear of imminent serious bodily injury. Simple assault is a disorderly persons offense unless committed in a fight or scuffle entered into by mutual consent, in which case it is a petty disorderly persons offense.

    b.  Aggravated assault. A person is guilty of aggravated assault if he:

        (1)  Attempts to cause serious bodily injury to another, or causes such injury purposely or knowingly or under circumstances manifesting extreme indifference to the value of human life recklessly causes such injury; or

        (2)  Attempts to cause or purposely or knowingly causes bodily injury to another with a deadly weapon; or

        (3)  Recklessly causes bodily injury to another with a deadly weapon; or

(4) Knowingly under circumstances manifesting extreme indifference to the value of human life points a firearm, as defined in section 2C:39-1f., at or in the direction of another, whether or not the actor believes it to be loaded; or

(5) Commits a simple assault as defined in subsection a. (1), (2) or (3) of this section upon:

    (a) Any law enforcement officer acting in the performance of his duties while in uniform or exhibiting evidence of his authority or because of his status as a law enforcement officer; or

    (b) Any paid or volunteer fireman acting in the performance of his duties while in uniform or otherwise clearly identifiable as being engaged in the performance of the duties of a fireman; or

    (c) Any person engaged in emergency first-aid or medical services acting in the performance of his duties while in uniform or otherwise clearly identifiable as being engaged in the performance of emergency first-aid or medical services; or

    (d) Any school board member, school administrator, teacher, school bus driver or other employee of a school board while clearly identifiable as being engaged in the performance of his duties or because of his status as a member or employee of a school board or any school bus driver employed by an operator under contract to a school board while clearly identifiable as being engaged in the performance of his duties or because of his status as a school bus driver; or

    (e) Any employee of the Division of Youth and Family Services while clearly identifiable as being engaged in the performance of his duties or because of his status as an employee of the division; or

    (f) Any justice of the Supreme Court, judge of the Superior Court, judge of the Tax Court or municipal judge while clearly identifiable as being engaged in the performance of judicial duties or because of his status as a member of the judiciary; or

    (g) Any operator of a motorbus or the operator's supervisor or any employee of a rail passenger service while clearly identifiable as being engaged in the performance of his duties or because of his status as an operator of a motorbus or as the operator's supervisor or as an employee of a rail passenger service; or

(6) Causes bodily injury to another person while fleeing or attempting to elude a law enforcement officer in violation of subsection b. of N.J.S.2C:29-2 or while operating a motor vehicle in violation of subsection c. of N.J.S.2C:20-10. Notwithstanding any other provision of law to the contrary, a person shall be strictly liable for a violation of this subsection upon proof of a violation of subsection b. of N.J.S.2C:29-2 or while operating a motor vehicle in violation of subsection c. of N.J.S.2C:20-10 which resulted in bodily injury to another person; or

(7) Attempts to cause significant bodily injury to another or causes significant bodily injury purposely or knowingly or, under circumstances manifesting extreme indifference to the value of human life recklessly causes such significant bodily injury; or

(8) Causes bodily injury by knowingly or purposely starting a fire or causing an explosion in violation of N.J.S.2C:17-1 which results in bodily injury to any emergency services personnel involved in fire suppression activities, rendering emergency medical services resulting from the fire or explosion or rescue operations, or rendering any necessary assistance at the scene of the fire or explosion, including any bodily injury sustained while responding to the scene of a reported fire or explosion. For purposes of this subsection, "emergency services personnel" shall include, but not be limited to, any paid or volunteer fireman, any person engaged in emergency first-aid or medical services and any law enforcement officer. Notwithstanding any other pro-

vision of law to the contrary, a person shall be strictly liable for a violation of this paragraph upon proof of a violation of N.J.S.2C:17-1 which resulted in bodily injury to any emergency services personnel; or

(9) Knowingly, under circumstances manifesting extreme indifference to the value of human life, points or displays a firearm, as defined in subsection f. of N.J.S.2C:39-1, at or in the direction of a law enforcement officer; or

(10) Knowingly points, displays or uses an imitation firearm, as defined in subsection f. of N.J.S.2C:39-1, at or in the direction of a law enforcement officer with the purpose to intimidate, threaten or attempt to put the officer in fear of bodily injury or for any unlawful purpose; or

(11) Uses or activates a laser sighting system or device, or a system or device which, in the manner used, would cause a reasonable person to believe that it is a laser sighting system or device, against a law enforcement officer acting in the performance of his duties while in uniform or exhibiting evidence of his authority. As used in this paragraph, "laser sighting system or device" means any system or device that is integrated with or affixed to a firearm and emits a laser light beam that is used to assist in the sight alignment or aiming of the firearm.

Aggravated assault under subsections b. (1) and b. (6) is a crime of the second degree; under subsections b. (2), b. (7), b. (9) and b. (10) is a crime of the third degree; under subsections b. (3) and b. (4) is a crime of the fourth degree; and under subsection b. (5) is a crime of the third degree if the victim suffers bodily injury, otherwise it is a crime of the fourth degree. Aggravated assault under subsection b.(8) is a crime of the third degree if the victim suffers bodily injury; if the victim suffers significant bodily injury or serious bodily injury it is a crime of the second degree. Aggravated assault under subsection b.(11) is a crime of the third degree.

c. (1) A person is guilty of assault by auto or vessel when the person drives a vehicle or vessel recklessly and causes either serious bodily injury or bodily injury to another. Assault by auto or vessel is a crime of the fourth degree if serious bodily injury results and is a disorderly persons offense if bodily injury results.

(2) Assault by auto or vessel is a crime of the third degree if the person drives the vehicle while in violation of R.S.39:4-50 or section 2 of P.L.1981, c. 512 (C.39:4-50.4a.) and serious bodily injury results and is a crime of the fourth degree if the person drives the vehicle while in violation of R.S.39:4-50 or section 2 of P.L.1981, c. 512 (C.39:4-50.4a.) and bodily injury results.

(3) Assault by auto or vessel is a crime of the second degree if serious bodily injury results from the defendant operating the auto or vessel while in violation of R.S.39:4-50 or section 2 of P.L.1981, c. 512 (C.39:4-50.4a.) while

(a) on any school property used for school purposes which is owned by or leased to any elementary or secondary school or school board, or within 1,000 feet of such school property;

(b) driving through a school crossing as defined in R.S.39:1-1 if the municipality, by ordinance or resolution, has designated the school crossing as such; or

(c) driving through a school crossing as defined in R.S.39:1-1 knowing that juveniles are present if the municipality has not designated the school crossing as such by ordinance or resolution.

Assault by auto or vessel is a crime of the third degree if bodily injury results from the defendant operating the auto or vessel in violation of this paragraph.

A map or true copy of a map depicting the location and boundaries of the area on or within 1,000 feet of any property used for school purposes which is owned by or leased to any elementary or secondary school or school board produced pursuant to section 1 of P.L.1987, c. 101 (C.2C:35-7) may be used in a prosecution under subparagraph (a) of paragraph (3) of this section.

It shall be no defense to a prosecution for a violation of subparagraph (a) or (b) of paragraph (3) of this subsection that the defendant was unaware that the prohibited conduct took place while on or within 1,000 feet of any school property or while driving through a school crossing. Nor shall it be a defense to a prosecution under subparagraph (a) or (b) of paragraph (3) of this subsection that no juveniles were present on the school property or crossing zone at the time of the offense or that the school was not in session.

As used in this section, "vessel" means a means of conveyance for travel on water and propelled otherwise than by muscular power.

d. A person who is employed by a facility as defined in section 2 of P.L.1977, c. 239 (C.52:27G-2) who commits a simple assault as defined in paragraph (1) or (2) of subsection a. of this section upon an institutionalized elderly person as defined in section 2 of P.L.1977, c. 239 (C.52:27G-2) is guilty of a crime of the fourth degree.

e. (Deleted by amendment, P.L.2001, c. 443.)

f. A person who commits a simple assault as defined in paragraph (1), (2) or (3) of subsection a. of this section in the presence of a child under 16 years of age at a school or community sponsored youth sports event is guilty of a crime of the fourth degree. The defendant shall be strictly liable upon proof that the offense occurred, in fact, in the presence of a child under 16 years of age. It shall not be a defense that the defendant did not know that the child was present or reasonably believed that the child was 16 years of age or older. The provisions of this subsection shall not be construed to create any liability on the part of a participant in a youth sports event or to abrogate any immunity or defense available to a participant in a youth sports event. As used in this act, "school or community sponsored youth sports event" means a competition, practice or instructional event involving one or more interscholastic sports teams or youth sports teams organized pursuant to a nonprofit or similar charter or which are member teams in a youth league organized by or affiliated with a county or municipal recreation department and shall not include collegiate, semi-professional or professional sporting events.

## PRACTICAL APPLICATION OF STATUTE

### Simple Assault

If the Jones brothers had merely punched or slapped the grocer in the face, they would be guilty of simple assault. Similarly, if they had merely waved their golf clubs at the grocer's head, instead of striking him, they would be guilty of simple assault. Per the actual facts, however, they are guilty of an aggravated assault of the grocer. As will be discussed later, the defining factors that elevate their offense to aggravated assault are that they used a deadly weapon to actually beat the man and the fact that they caused *serious* bodily injury.

Under 2C:12-1a.(1), a person is guilty of simple assault if he "attempts to cause or purposely, knowingly or recklessly causes bodily injury to another." The Jones brothers would be guilty of simple assault under this provision if they had punched or slapped the grocer in the face. Why? Because their actions would have only resulted in *bodily injury* to the man, not *serious* bodily injury.

Per subsection a.(3), a person is guilty of simple assault if he "attempts by physical menace to put another in fear of imminent serious bodily injury." The Jones brothers would be convicted of simple assault under this subsection if they had just waved the golf clubs at the grocer but never actually struck him. Please note that this subsection has a *serious* bodily injury component, as opposed to just bodily injury. Here, their physical menace of waving deadly weapons at him would have put the man in imminent fear of *serious* bodily injury. A person having golf clubs swung in front of his face would reasonably not just fear bodily injury but would fear *serious* bodily injury. Accordingly, such actions would render the Jones brothers guilty of simple assault— even though no actual injury occurred.

### Aggravated Assault—Generally

The aggravated assault statute is a complicated and diverse statute providing for numerous situations where an individual may be convicted of aggravated assault. The statute, in its various subsections, often differentiates among "bodily injury," significant bodily injury," and "serious bodily injury," as well as the various mental states (i.e., "purposely," "knowingly," and "recklessly") that must be present for a conviction. It is also important to note that aggravated assaults range from fourth degree crimes to second degree crimes and many times are differentiated by the victim's occupation status. Each subsection has its own unique requirements. All of this, and more, will be examined in the following practical application sections.

### Second Degree Aggravated Assault—Causing Serious Bodily Injury

The Jones brothers could be convicted of multiple counts of aggravated assault for their violent tirade in Newark. Their first count of aggravated assault arises out of their golf clubbing the grocer.

2C:12-1b.(1) provides that an individual is guilty of aggravated assault if he "attempts to cause serious bodily injury to another, or causes such injury purposely or knowingly." An actor may also be convicted under this subsection of the statute if he acted "recklessly" in causing serious bodily injury. The reckless mental state requirement, though, necessitates that the defendant must act "under circumstances manifesting extreme indifference to the value of human life." Whatever the mental state—purposely, knowingly, or recklessly—the actor must cause (or attempt to cause) *serious* bodily injury, not just bodily injury, in order to be convicted under this subsection of the statute.

Lance and Stanley Jones repeatedly swung golf clubs at the grocer's body and head. The strikes were so severe that their victim was rendered unconscious, suffered broken ribs, and required over 40 stitches to his head. This is "*serious* bodily injury." Not only is it clear, by their actions, that they attempted to cause serious bodily injury to the grocer, it is equally evident that they purposely intended to cause these serious injuries. Any person knows that repeatedly striking another in the body and head with golf clubs will result in serious bodily injury. Accordingly, the Jones brothers should be charged with aggravated assault, under 2C:12-1b.(1), for their beating of the grocer. This is a crime of the second degree.

Now, what does acting "under circumstances manifesting extreme indifference to the value of human life" mean? Where would this "reckless" mental state fit in? Perhaps if the Jones brothers only struck the grocer in the body, but not the head, then it may be difficult to prove that they purposely or knowingly caused serious bodily injury. However, in repeatedly hitting the man in the body with golf clubs, they could have killed him by rupturing an internal organ. Accordingly, this behavior would surely be deemed as acting with "extreme indifference" to the value of human life. Any serious bodily injury resulting therefrom would certainly have been, at minimum, recklessly caused. Under these circumstances, the Joneses would still appropriately be charged under 2C:12-1b.(1).

It is interesting to note that under 2C:12-1b.(7), an individual is guilty of a crime of the *third* degree if he "purposely or knowingly or, under circumstances manifesting extreme indifference to the value of human life recklessly causes" *significant* bodily injury to another. This subsection provides for an offense that falls between simple assault and second degree aggravated assault under 2C:12-1b.(1). The differential factor is *significant* bodily injury, which is something less than *serious* bodily injury, but something more than just bodily injury. Law enforcement officers determining under which statute to charge simply must use their judgment.

### Bodily Injury Caused by a Deadly Weapon—Third or Fourth Degree Crime Depending Upon Mental State

An individual who causes bodily injury, but not serious bodily injury, with a deadly weapon is guilty of a third degree crime if he causes this bodily injury "purposely" or "knowingly." He is guilty of a lesser fourth degree crime if such bodily injury is "recklessly" caused via the use of a deadly weapon. A modification of the grocer's golf club beating can exemplify how these statutes should be implemented.

Instead of repeatedly beating the grocer with the golf clubs, Stanley Jones strikes him once in the arm, breaking the man's wrist. Here, a deadly weapon—the golf club—was utilized to "purposely" cause bodily injury. Therefore, under 2C:12-1b.(2), Stanley Jones would appropriately be charged with aggravated assault. Here this is a crime of the third degree.

In a similar vein, if Stanley Jones simply intended to scare the grocer by swinging the clubs wildly in the air but accidentally struck him in the wrist, he should still be charged with aggravated assault. But why? If he didn't intend to hit the man, why should he be charged with aggravated assault? Because all three elements of 2C:12-1b.(3) have been met in this scenario. The golf club, a deadly metal weapon, was utilized by Jones in a manner that was clearly reckless. Wildly swinging the instrument in the air posed a dangerous situation to any individuals in its close proximity. Indeed, the net result was bodily injury to the grocer—the club struck him in the wrist. For his reckless assault with a deadly weapon, Stanley Jones would be charged with a fourth degree crime under 2C:12-1b.(3).

### Simple Assault of Law Enforcement Officers and Other Public Officials Automatically Becomes a Third Degree Aggravated Assault

Stanley Jones's punch to Sergeant Paterson's face is not a disorderly persons offense. It is not a simple assault, as it would be if Paterson was just some person who Jones happened to hit in a street fight. But how is this so?

Subsection (5) of the aggravated assault statute enumerates multiple scenarios where a simple assault automatically is elevated to the status of a third degree aggravated assault. One of the scenarios is where a defendant commits a simple assault upon "any law enforcement officer acting in the performance of his duties." Since Jones punched Paterson in the face while he was performing his duties as a Newark police officer, Jones simply could be convicted of third degree aggravated assault. The reality, though, is that many times these charges will be downgraded to simple assault and resolved in the municipal court. Often where an officer only suffers bodily injury such as bumps and bruises, the case will be remanded and handled as a simple assault just like other similar matters involving minor injuries.

Other situations under subsection (5), where a simple assault automatically becomes an aggravated assault, include simple assaults of firemen, first-aid workers, school board members, teachers, Division of Youth and Family Services employees, judges, and even bus drivers and rail service operators. Of special note, though, is that the position alone does not necessitate the elevated charge to aggravated assault: The victim must either be assaulted while performing in his position (i.e., a police officer on the job, a teacher instructing a class) or because of his position (i.e., a police officer is assaulted because of his status as a police officer). In other words, a person who punches an off-duty police officer or teacher during a bar fight will only be charged with simple assault—as long as the basis for the simple assault was other than the officer's or teacher's status.

### Pointing Firearm at Law Enforcement Officer, Third Degree Crime; Pointing Firearm at Other Persons, Fourth Degree Crime

Lance Jones is guilty of third degree aggravated assault for pointing his pistol at Sergeant Paterson—per the provisions of 2C:12-1b.(9). Interestingly, though, the Jones brothers are guilty of a fourth degree aggravated assault for pointing their guns at the crowd of bystanders under 2C:12-1b.(4). Again, the code makes an assault offense more serious in degree if the intended victim is a law enforcement officer rather than a layperson.

### Pointing Imitation Firearm at Law Enforcement Officer—Third Degree Crime

It is also interesting to note that even if the gun pointed at Sergeant Paterson was an imitation, Lance Jones could be convicted of a third degree aggravated assault. 2C:12-1b.(10) provides that an individual who knowingly points an imitation firearm at a law enforcement officer "with the purpose to intimidate, threaten or attempt to put the officer in fear of bodily injury or for any unlawful purpose" is guilty of a third degree aggravated assault.

Obviously, Lance Jones pointed his pistol at Sergeant Paterson in an effort to intimidate and threaten him. His goal, of course, was an unlawful purpose—to put the officer in fear of bodily injury and to be able to flee from arrest. Accordingly, even if the gun turned out to be fake, Lance Jones should be charged with a third degree crime under 2C:12-1b.(10).

### Firearm Laser System Activated Upon Law Enforcement Officer—Third Degree Aggravated Assault

Lance Jones should be charged with an additional count of third degree aggravated assault for the red laser beam that ran from his gun at Sergeant Paterson. 2C:12-1b.(11) defines a separate and distinct count of aggravated assault to cover situations where a person activates a laser sighting system that is affixed to a firearm at a law enforcement officer. Once again, this subsection only pertains to individuals performing within their duties as law enforcement officers.

Lance Jones emitted a red laser beam at Sergeant Paterson, who was working as a police officer at the time. The red beam flowed from a device affixed to his pistol. Accordingly, he is ripe to be charged with a third degree aggravated assault under subsection b.(11) of the aggravated assault statute.

### Bodily Injury Caused While Fleeing/Eluding Law Enforcement Officer—Second Degree Aggravated Assault

Stanley Jones, if not both brothers, should be charged with second degree aggravated assault under 2C:12-1b.(6) for the injuries they caused to the elderly woman when they struck her vehicle. This charge should be levied even though the automobile crash was not purposeful and actually was probably just accidental.

Statute 2C:12-1b.(6) provides that a defendant who "causes bodily injury to another person while fleeing or attempting to elude a law enforcement officer in violation of subsection b. of N.J.S.2C:29-2" is guilty of second degree aggravated assault. N.J.S.2C:29-2b. is the eluding statute, setting forth that an individual is guilty of the same where he knowingly eludes a law enforcement officer in a motor vehicle after having received a signal to stop the vehicle.

Sergeant Paterson attempted to arrest the Jones brothers while they were beating the grocer. Instead of submitting to the officer's demands, the brothers fled. Even more so, they entered a motor vehicle and refused to stop in the face of the officer's signals of a blaring siren and flashing lights. Their automobile only halted because it crashed into the parked car where the elderly woman was sitting. The impact of this crash caused the woman serious bodily injury, including a lapse into a coma.

The elderly woman's injuries were caused while the Jones brothers were fleeing and attempting to elude Sergeant Paterson. They knowingly eluded the officer, aware that he was signaling them to stop their motor vehicle. With these elements met, Stanley Jones should be charged with second degree aggravated assault under 2C:12-1b.(6). His brother Lance probably should similarly be charged under this subsection, due to his accomplice status and because the injuries occurred during flight from Sergeant Paterson that included his flight as well as Stanley's.

It is important to note here that under this subsection, it is irrelevant that the elderly woman's injuries were so serious. Simple "bodily injury" is sufficient for an individual to face charges of this second degree crime. Therefore, if the woman had only suffered a broken finger or even a black and blue eye, the Jones brothers could still face a count of second degree aggravated assault. Also interesting to note is that this subsection does not require an intent to injure—the actor does not have to purposely, knowingly, or even recklessly, cause injury. The actor simply is "strictly liable" under this subsection; he is guilty of the second degree aggravated assault just as long as bodily injury is caused while he is fleeing or attempting to elude a law enforcement officer.

### Assault by Auto

Pedro Munoz should be charged with fourth degree assault by auto for striking the pedestrian with his car. 2C:12-1c.(2) provides that assault by auto is a crime of the fourth degree if the "person drives the vehicle while in violation of R.S.39:4-50" and *bodily injury* occurs. It is a crime of the third degree if *serious* bodily injury occurs while the person drives the vehicle in violation of 39:4-50.

As is clear from above, the degree of this offense becomes more serious as the injuries increase: bodily injury earns a fourth degree offense; serious bodily injury, a third degree offense. The other defining element of subsection c.(2) is the person driving in violation of 39:4-50 (i.e., driving while intoxicated). Subsection c.(1) does not have the DWI requirement. C.(1) simply sets forth that if an individual is caused bodily injury due to another's reckless driving, it is a disorderly persons offense; if *serious* bodily injury is caused due to reckless driving, it is a fourth degree crime.

Pedro Munoz should be charged under subsection c.(2), and not c.(1), because he was operating his motor vehicle while intoxicated. His charge should only be a fourth degree offense because, fortunately, the pedestrian struck only suffered bodily injury—scrapes and bruises.

It is important to note that in certain circumstances assault by auto automatically becomes a second degree offense. Under subsection c.(3), if an intoxicated motor vehicle operator drives on property connected to schools or school crossings and *serious* bodily injury is caused by him, then he is guilty of second degree assault by auto. He is guilty of third degree assault by auto if only bodily injury results pursuant to the circumstances described in this paragraph.

### Simple Assault Upgraded to Aggravated Assault at Youth Sports Events

2C:12-1f. is a brand-new addition to the aggravated assault statute, enacted in August 2002. Basically, this provision upgrades a simple assault to a fourth degree aggravated assault where a person commits a simple assault in the presence of a child under 16 at a youth sports event.

For example, Stanley Jones is sitting in the stands of a high school football game, watching his nephew return punts and play free safety. He gets upset when the referee penalizes his nephew's team for an apparent personal foul committed by his nephew. Jones, enraged, runs onto the field and punches the referee in the stomach. Ordinarily, this action would constitute a simple assault. Now, however, the assault would be elevated from its usual disorderly persons offense status to a fourth degree crime. Why? Because at this high school football game, both in the stands and on the field, would be children under 16. Committing the simple assault in their presence automatically makes this a fourth degree aggravated assault under this newly added section.

But what about if an 18-year-old senior linebacker punches a 17-year-old junior halfback during the game or after it ended? This simple assault would be in the presence of the same children under 16. Should the high school linebacker be charged with aggravated assault? Is that what the legislators intended when they enacted the provision? Technically, it appears that the appropriate charge would be a fourth degree aggravated assault, but in practice this kind of case would probably be downgraded back to a simple assault and remanded to the municipal court for handling.

| 2C:12-1.1. | **Knowingly leaving scene of motor vehicle accident resulting in serious bodily injury, fourth degree crime; sentencing** |
|---|---|

A motor vehicle operator who knows he is involved in an accident and knowingly leaves the scene of that accident under circumstances that violate the provisions of R.S.39:4-129 shall be guilty of a crime of the fourth degree if the accident results in serious bodily injury to another person. The presumption of nonimprisonment set forth in N.J.S.2C:44-1 shall not apply to persons convicted under the provisions of this section.

If the evidence so warrants, nothing in this section shall be deemed to preclude an indictment and conviction for aggravated assault or assault by auto under the provisions of N.J.S.2C:12-1.

Notwithstanding the provisions of N.J.S.2C:1-8 or any other provisions of law, a conviction arising under this section shall not merge with a conviction for aggravated assault or assault by auto under the provisions of N.J.S.2C:12-1 and a separate sentence shall be imposed upon each conviction.

Notwithstanding the provisions of N.J.S.2C:44-5 or any other provisions of law, whenever in the case of such multiple convictions the court imposes multiple sentences of imprisonment for more than one offense, those sentences shall run consecutively.

For the purposes of this section, neither knowledge of the serious bodily injury nor knowledge of the violation are elements of the offense and it shall not be a defense that the driver of the motor vehicle was unaware of the serious bodily injury or provisions of R.S.39:4-129.

## PRACTICAL APPLICATION OF STATUTE

This statute is a criminal counterpart to 39:4-129, the motor vehicle statute for leaving the scene of an accident. The Jones brothers should be charged under this criminal statute, which is a fourth degree crime. Simply, the brothers *knew* they were involved in an accident—they crashed into a parked car. Immediately thereafter, they *knowingly* fled the scene. An elderly victim inside the parked car suffered *serious* bodily injury (she fell into a coma and required dozens of stitches), which are the types of injuries necessary for conviction under the statute. Accordingly, with all of the aforesaid elements met, the Joneses would be found guilty for violating this statute.

It is interesting to note that even if the brothers had no knowledge of the woman's serious injuries, they would still be convicted under this statute. Their cause of her injuries, coupled with their knowledge of the accident and their knowing flight from the scene, is sufficient for a guilty verdict.

**2C:12-1.2.** **Endangering an injured victim**

a. A person is guilty of endangering an injured victim if he causes bodily injury to any person or solicits, aids, encourages, or attempts or agrees to aid another, who causes bodily injury to any person, and leaves the scene of the injury knowing or reasonably believing that the injured person is physically helpless, mentally incapacitated or otherwise unable to care for himself.

b. As used in this section, the following definitions shall apply:

(1) "Physically helpless" means the condition in which a person is unconscious, unable to flee, or physically unable to summon assistance;

(2) "Mentally incapacitated" means that condition in which a person is rendered temporarily or permanently incapable of understanding or controlling one's conduct, or of appraising or controlling one's condition, which incapacity shall include but is not limited to an inability to comprehend one's own peril;

(3) "Bodily injury" shall have the meaning set forth in N.J.S.2C:11-1.

c. It is an affirmative defense to prosecution for a violation of this section that the defendant summoned medical treatment for the victim or knew that medical treatment had been summoned by another person, and protected the victim from further injury or harm until emergency assistance personnel arrived. This affirmative defense shall be proved by the defendant by a preponderance of the evidence.

d. A person who violates the provisions of this section shall be guilty of a crime of the third degree. Notwithstanding the provisions of N.J.S.2C:1-8 or any other provision of law, a conviction arising under this subsection shall not merge with a conviction of the crime that rendered the person physically helpless or mentally incapacitated, nor shall such other conviction merge with a conviction under this section. Notwithstanding the provisions of N.J.S.2C:44-5 or any other provision of law, the sentence imposed pursuant to this section shall be ordered to be served consecutively to that imposed for any conviction of the crime that rendered the person physically helpless or mentally incapacitated.

e. Nothing herein shall be deemed to preclude, if the evidence so warrants, an indictment and conviction for murder, manslaughter, assault or any other offense.

## PRACTICAL APPLICATION OF STATUTE

The Jones brothers are guilty of endangering an injured victim after they left the grocer to flee police capture. This is a third degree crime.

A crime has been committed under 2C:12-1.2 where three elements are met. First, the defendant must cause bodily injury to a person or aid, solicit, or encourage another in causing bodily injury to a person. Next, the defendant must leave the scene of the injury. Finally, he must leave the injury scene "knowing" or "reasonably believing" that the injured person is physically helpless, mentally incapacitated, or otherwise unable to care for himself.

The Jones brothers caused bodily injury—in fact, serious bodily injury—to the grocer by beating him in the face and body with golf clubs. The grocer was rendered unconscious by their beating and required 40 stitches to his head. Nonetheless, the brothers left the scene of the injury when Sergeant Paterson arrived. Given the extent of the grocer's injuries, the brothers obviously had to "know" (or at least "reasonably believe") that the grocer was physically helpless and unable to care for himself—the man was unconscious and in a pool of blood. Accordingly, the Joneses are guilty of the third degree crime of endangering an injured victim.

---

**2C:12-2.**    **Reckless endangerment**

a. A person who purposely or knowingly does any act, including putting up a false light, which results in the loss or destruction of a vessel commits a crime of the third degree.

b. A person commits a crime of the fourth degree if he:

(1) Manufactures or sells a golf ball containing acid or corrosive fluid substance; or

(2) Purposely or knowingly offers, gives or entices any person to take or accept any treat, candy, gift, food, drink or other substance that is intended to be consumed which is poisonous, intoxicating, anesthetizing, tranquilizing, disorienting, deleterious or harmful to the health or welfare of such person, without the knowledge of the other person as to the identity and effect of the substance, except that it is a crime of the third degree if the actor violates the provisions of this paragraph with the purpose to commit or facilitate the commission of another criminal offense.

Notwithstanding the term of imprisonment provided under N.J.S. 2C:43-6, and the provisions of subsection e. of N.J.S.2C:44-1, if a person is convicted of a crime of the fourth degree under paragraph (2) of this subsection, the sentence imposed shall include a fixed minimum sentence of not less than six months during which the defendant shall not be eligible for parole. If a person is convicted of a crime of the third degree under paragraph (2) of this subsection, the sentence imposed shall include a fixed minimum sentence of not less than eighteen months during which the defendant shall not be eligible for parole. The court may not suspend or make any other noncustodial disposition of that person. Notwithstanding the provisions of N.J.S.2C:1-8 or any other provision of law, a conviction arising under this subsection shall not merge with a conviction for any offense that the defendant intended to commit or facilitate, when the defendant violated the provisions of this section, nor shall any such other conviction merge with a conviction under this section. Notwithstanding the provisions of N.J.S.2C:44-5 or any other provision of law, the sentence for a crime of the third degree imposed pursuant to this paragraph shall be ordered to be served consecutively to that imposed for a conviction of the offense that the defendant intended to commit or facilitate when the defendant violated the provisions of this subsection.

## PRACTICAL APPLICATION OF STATUTE

Based on the allegations made by Stanley Jones's ex-girlfriend, he should be charged with reckless endangerment under 2C:12-2b.(2). According to this woman, Jones laced her beverage with an intoxicating drug that caused her to become tranquilized and disoriented. Thereafter, he sexually assaulted her.

2C:12-2b.(2) states that when an individual "purposely" or "knowingly" gives another person food or drink which is "poisonous, intoxicating, anesthetizing, tranquilizing, disorienting, deleterious or harmful" to the health of such person, then he is guilty of fourth degree reckless endangerment. He is guilty of third degree reckless endangerment if he performs the aforesaid actions "with the purpose to commit or facilitate the commission of another criminal offense."

If the prosecution can prove that Jones "purposely" or "knowingly" slipped an "intoxicating . . . tranquilizing, disorienting" substance into his ex-girlfriend's drink, then he will be convicted of fourth degree reckless endangerment. If the prosecution can further prove that Jones dropped in the substance in an effort to sexually assault the woman, then his crime will be elevated to third degree reckless endangerment.

**2C:12-3.**          **Terroristic threats**

a. A person is guilty of a crime of the third degree if he threatens to commit any crime of violence with the purpose to terrorize another or to cause evacuation of a building, place of assembly, or facility of public transportation, or otherwise to cause serious public inconvenience, or in reckless disregard of the risk of causing such terror or inconvenience. A violation of this subsection is a crime of the second degree if it occurs during a declared period of national, State or county emergency. The actor shall be strictly liable upon proof that the crime occurred, in fact, during a declared period of national, State or county emergency. It shall not be a defense that the actor did not know that there was a declared period of emergency at the time the crime occurred.

b. A person is guilty of a crime of the third degree if he threatens to kill another with the purpose to put him in imminent fear of death under circumstances reasonably causing the victim to believe the immediacy of the threat and the likelihood that it will be carried out.

## PRACTICAL APPLICATION OF STATUTE

Stanley Jones is ripe for a conviction of terroristic threats per the language of 2C:12-3b. This subsection provides that a person is guilty of a third degree offense "if he threatens to kill another with the purpose to put him in imminent fear of death." The statute also sets forth a "reasonableness" requirement—that the victim reasonably believes the immediacy of the threat and that it will likely be carried out.

Jones's ex-girlfriend had already been drugged by him and sexually assaulted. Subsequent to this, he continually appeared at her home and followed her. He even verbally threatened to kill her. Given these circumstances, it would be reasonable for this woman to believe that his threat to kill was serious and that he could immediately carry it out. Accordingly, Jones should be charged with the third degree crime of terroristic threats.

It is interesting to note that under subsection a. of this statute, an individual can be convicted of terroristic threats if he threatens to commit "any crime of violence with purpose to terrorize another or to cause evacuation of a building" or places of assembly. Therefore, one who threatens to blow up a building, even if he is fabricating, is guilty of this third degree crime.

**2C:12-4**　　　**Repealed**
**to 2C:12-9.**

**2C:12-10.**　　　**Definitions; stalking designated a crime; degrees**

a. As used in this act:

(1) "Course of conduct" means repeatedly maintaining a visual or physical proximity to a person or repeatedly conveying, or causing to be conveyed, verbal or written threats or threats conveyed by any other means of communication or threats implied by conduct or a combination thereof directed at or toward a person.

(2) "Repeatedly" means on two or more occasions.

(3) "Immediate family" means a spouse, parent, child, sibling or any other person who regularly resides in the household or who within the prior six months regularly resided in the household.

b. A person is guilty of stalking, a crime of the fourth degree, if he purposefully or knowingly engages in a course of conduct directed at a specific person that would cause a reasonable person to fear bodily injury to himself or a member of his immediate family or to fear the death of himself or a member of his immediate family.

c. A person is guilty of a crime of the third degree if he commits the crime of stalking in violation of an existing court order prohibiting the behavior.

d. A person who commits a second or subsequent offense of stalking against the same victim is guilty of a crime of the third degree.

e. A person is guilty of a crime of the third degree if he commits the crime of stalking while serving a term of imprisonment or while on parole or probation as the result of a conviction for any indictable offense under the laws of this State, any other state or the United States.

f.  This act shall not apply to conduct which occurs during organized group picketing.

## PRACTICAL APPLICATION OF STATUTE

Three phrases of language are important to a conviction under the stalking statute: "course of conduct," "repeatedly," and "immediate family." A person is guilty of stalking if he engages in a "course of conduct" that consists of him "repeatedly" maintaining visual or physical proximity to another which in turn causes that other individual to *reasonably* fear bodily injury to himself or a member of his "immediate family." Similarly, an accused is guilty of stalking if the "course of conduct" consists of "repeatedly" conveying threats. "Repeatedly" is defined as two or more occasions.

As the statute indicates, however, repeated proximity to another or repeated threats are not, alone, sufficient for a conviction. These courses of conduct must be so severe that they would cause a *reasonable* person to fear bodily injury to himself or a member of his immediate family. An immediate family member is defined as a spouse, parent, child, sibling, or any other person who has regularly resided in the household within the prior six months.

Stanley Jones is guilty of stalking his ex-girlfriend. First, he engaged in a "course of conduct" that violates the statute. He "repeatedly" maintained physical and visual proximity to her by appearing in front of her house five times. Even more so, he twice threatened to kill her, her mother, and her sister. And remember, Jones had previously drugged and sexually assaulted the woman. This course of conduct certainly would make any *reasonable* person fear bodily injury to herself and her "immediate family" members—her mother and sister. With these facts existing, Stanley Jones would normally be convicted of a fourth degree stalking charge; Jones's charge, however, should be elevated to a third degree offense under subsection e. of this statute.

Per subsection e., a person is guilty of third degree stalking if he commits the crime "while serving a term of imprisonment or while on parole or probation as the result of a conviction for any indictable offense." Since Stanley Jones was on parole from an arson conviction (an indictable offense) at the time he stalked his ex-girlfriend, his charge should be elevated to a third degree offense pursuant to the requirements of subsection e. of this statute.

It is important to note here that stalking also becomes a third degree offense under subsections c. and d. as well. If a person stalks in violation of an existing court order (e.g., a restraining order), he is guilty of a third degree crime. Likewise, if he commits a second or subsequent stalking offense, he is guilty of a third degree crime.

**2C:12-10.1.**     **Conviction for stalking, permanent restraining order**

a.  A judgment of conviction for stalking shall operate as an application for a permanent restraining order limiting the contact of the defendant and the victim who was stalked.

b.  A hearing shall be held on the application for a permanent restraining order at the time of the verdict or plea of guilty unless the victim requests otherwise. This hearing shall be in Superior Court. A permanent restraining order may grant the following specific relief:

    (1) An order restraining the defendant from entering the residence, property, school, or place of employment of the victim and requiring the defendant to stay away from any specified place that is named in the order and is frequented regularly by the victim.

    (2) An order restraining the defendant from making contact with the victim, including an order forbidding the defendant from personally or through an agent initiating any communication likely to cause annoyance or alarm including, but not limited to, personal, written, or telephone contact with the victim, the victim's employers, employees, or fellow workers, or others with whom communication would be likely to cause annoyance or alarm to the victim.

c. The permanent restraining order entered by the court subsequent to a conviction for stalking as provided in this act may be dissolved upon the application of the stalking victim to the court which granted the order.

d. Notice of permanent restraining orders issued pursuant to this act shall be sent by the clerk of the court or other person designated by the court to the appropriate chiefs of police, members of the State Police and any other appropriate law enforcement agency or court.

e. Any permanent restraining order issued pursuant to this act shall be in effect throughout the State, and shall be enforced by all law enforcement officers.

f. A violation by the defendant of an order issued pursuant to this act shall constitute an offense under subsection a. of N.J.S.2C:29-9 and each order shall so state. Violations of these orders may be enforced in a civil or criminal action initiated by the stalking victim or by the court, on its own motion, pursuant to applicable court rules. Nothing in this act shall preclude the filing of a criminal complaint for stalking based on the same act which is the basis for the violation of the permanent restraining order.

## 2C:12-10.2.  Temporary restraining order for alleged stalking; conditions

a. In any case involving an allegation of stalking where the victim is a child under the age of 18 years or is developmentally disabled as defined in section 3 of P.L.1977, c.200 (C.5:5-44.4) or where the victim is 18 years of age or older and is mentally defective as defined in N.J.S. 2C:14-1, the court may issue a temporary restraining order against the defendant which limits the contact of the defendant and the victim.

b. The provisions of subsection a. of this section are in addition to, and not in lieu of, the provisions of section 3 of P.L.1996, c. 39 (C.2C:12-10.1) which provide that a judgment of conviction for stalking shall operate as an application for a permanent restraining order limiting the contact of the defendant and the victim.

c. The parent or guardian of the child or the person described in subsection a. of this section may file a complaint with the Superior Court in conformity with the rules of court seeking a temporary restraining order against a person alleged to have committed stalking against the child or the person described in subsection a. of this section. The parent or guardian may seek emergency, ex parte relief. A decision shall be made by the judge regarding the emergency relief forthwith. If it appears that the child or the person described in subsection a. of this section is in danger of being stalked by the defendant, the judge shall issue a temporary restraining order pursuant to subsection e. of this section.

d. A conviction of stalking shall not be a prerequisite for the grant of a temporary restraining order under this act.

e. A temporary restraining order issued under this act shall limit the contact of the defendant and the child or the person described in subsection a. of this section who was stalked and in addition may grant all other relief specified in section 3 of P.L.1996, c. 39 (C.2C:12-10.1).

f. A hearing shall be held in the Superior Court within 10 days of the issuance of any temporary restraining order which was issued on an emergency, ex parte basis. A copy of the complaint shall be served on the defendant in conformity with the rules of court. At the hearing the standard for continuing the temporary restraining order shall be by a preponderance of the evidence.

g. If the court rules that the temporary restraining order shall be continued, the order shall remain in effect until either:

(1) the defendant is convicted of stalking, in which case the court shall hold a hearing on the issue of whether a permanent restraining order shall be entered pursuant to section 3 of P.L.1996, c. 39 (C.2C:12-10.1); or

(2) the victim's parent or guardian or, in the case of a victim who has reached the age of 18, the victim, requests that the restraining order be dismissed and the court finds just cause to do so.

**2C:12-11.**        **Disarming a law enforcement, corrections officer; crime; degrees**

a. A person who knowingly takes or attempts to exercise unlawful control over a firearm or other weapon in the possession of a law enforcement or corrections officer when that officer is acting in the performance of his duties, and either is in uniform or exhibits evidence of his authority, is guilty of a crime of the second degree.

b. A person violating the provisions of subsection a. of this section shall be guilty of a crime of the first degree if:

(1) The person fires or discharges the firearm;

(2) The person uses or threatens to use the firearm or weapon against the officer or any other person; or

(3) The officer or another person suffers serious bodily injury.

## PRACTICAL APPLICATION OF STATUTE

Lance Jones's actions in disarming a uniformed police officer, and thereafter firing his gun, constitute a crime of the first degree pursuant to the language of 2C:12-11b.(1). Under the basic requirements of this statute, however, disarming a law enforcement officer (or corrections officer) makes a person guilty of a second degree crime. The charge becomes a first degree offense under subsection b. (as in Jones's case) if the person discharges the firearm or threatens to use it against someone or if another suffers serious bodily injury as a result of the person's disarming activities.

As a special note, a conviction under this statute does not necessitate the taking of a firearm; other weapons, such as a knife or even a nightstick, may suffice. Also, the officer need not be in uniform when disarmed; the officer simply must be acting in the performance of his duties and exhibiting evidence of his authority.

**2C:12-12.**        **Definitions relative to certain acts of inmates, parolees**

As used in this act:

"Bodily fluid" means saliva, blood, urine, feces, seminal fluid or any other bodily fluid.

"Department of Corrections employee" means any corrections officer, parole officer or other employee of the New Jersey Department of Corrections and any person under contract to provide services to the department.

**2C:12-13.**     **Throwing bodily fluid at certain law enforcement officers deemed aggravated assault; grading, sentence**

A person who throws a bodily fluid at a Department of Corrections employee, county corrections officer, juvenile corrections officer, juvenile detention staff member, any sheriff, undersheriff or sheriff's officer or any municipal, county or State law enforcement officer while in the performance of his duties or otherwise purposely subjects such employee to contact with a bodily fluid commits an aggravated assault. If the victim suffers bodily injury, this shall be a crime of the third degree. Otherwise, this shall be a crime of the fourth degree. A term of imprisonment imposed for this offense shall run consecutively to any term of imprisonment currently being served and to any other term imposed for another offense committed at the time of the assault. Nothing herein shall be deemed to preclude, if the evidence so warrants, an indictment and conviction for a violation or attempted violation of chapter 11 of Title 2C of the New Jersey Statutes or subsection b. of N.J.S.2C:12-1 or any other provision of the criminal laws.

## PRACTICAL APPLICATION OF STATUTE

Simply, one who throws bodily fluid at a law enforcement officer while he is performing his duties is guilty of aggravated assault. It is a third degree crime if the officer suffers bodily injury; otherwise, it is a fourth degree crime. One item of note: The bodily fluid does not necessarily need to be "thrown" for conviction. It is sufficient if the actor just "subjects such employee to contact with a bodily fluid."

# 13

# KIDNAPPING AND RELATED OFFENSES: COERCION

## FACT PATTERN (PERTAINS TO CHAPTERS 13 AND 14)

In Middlesex County, the New Brunswick Police Department, working in conjunction with the county prosecutor's office, recently arrested Mercury Anderson for a variety of serious criminal offenses. Anderson's arrest resulted from an 18-month investigation predicated on an anonymous tip delivered to New Brunswick Lieutenant Sanford Stokes. The high-ranking police official had been advised that Anderson was taking women and children by force, committing various sexual offenses upon them, and then turning his victims back into the community. Although none of the victims was able to identify Anderson because of an array of disguises and professional makeup he wore, an exhaustive investigation finally netted overwhelming physical evidence and taped conversations where Anderson made several incriminating admissions. The cases included the following victims and facts:

**Candice Wesley**: Ms. Wesley, 29, was Anderson's first victim. Anderson snatched Wesley from her automobile and forcibly brought her to an apartment located in East Brunswick. There, Anderson contacted Wesley's family and advised that she would be returned to them for a fee of $50,000. Six hours later, Anderson apparently got nervous and released Wesley, unharmed, at a local diner. He never received the payment he demanded.

**Jerri Sloane**: Just the same as Candice Wesley, Ms. Sloane, 15, was abducted from an automobile and brought to the East Brunswick apartment. However, once there Anderson engaged in nonconsensual sexual intercourse with her and beat her violently, breaking her nose with the butt of a handgun. Thereafter, he took Sloane to a park and left her there.

**Eric Mesos**: Anderson invaded Mesos's car, advising him that if he left the vehicle, Mesos's mother would be killed. Mesos remained in the car with Anderson for 15 minutes. During this time period, Anderson twice exposed his genitals to Mesos. Then Anderson left the vehicle. Mesos was 20 at the time of the incident.

**Frank Pileggi**: Anderson lured Pileggi, 10, into a pickup truck by offering Pileggi a set of baseball cards. Once inside the truck, Anderson rubbed his hands over Pileggi's buttocks and groin area. Pileggi was then told to leave the vehicle.

**Samantha Cora**: Anderson met Cora, 12, at a carnival. He bought her cotton candy and ice cream and then asked if she would join him at his apartment. Cora agreed, and at the apartment she consensually engaged in sexual intercourse with him.

After Anderson was arrested, the police also learned that three years earlier he had taken his own 10-year-old daughter from the child's mother. She had sole legal and physical custody of the minor but was never advised of her child's whereabouts. Authorities had been unable to solve the child's disappearance due to their inability to locate Anderson. Now, Mercury Anderson, 52, was criminally charged for this abduction, as well as for repeatedly sexually assaulting his daughter immediately upon her taking. He was also charged with multiple other offenses for his string of violent unlawful activities.

Once Lieutenant Stokes processed Anderson, bail was set at $1 million. Although Anderson was unable to post the bail and be released, he contacted Stokes, via phone, at his private home. During their phone conversation, he threatened to kill Stokes if he testified at trial or furthered his case in any way. Anderson also threatened to reveal to the public a private secret of Stokes's—that the lieutenant had schizophrenia and was treated multiple times at a local hospital for the disease. Anderson, as well, threatened to publicly accuse Stokes of beating him while in custody. Lieutenant Stokes neither suffered from schizophrenia nor had he beaten Anderson while in custody.

---

## 2C:13-1.          Kidnapping

a. **Holding for ransom, reward or as a hostage.** A person is guilty of kidnapping if he unlawfully removes another from the place where he is found or if he unlawfully confines another with the purpose of holding that person for ransom or reward or as a shield or hostage.

b. **Holding for other purposes.** A person is guilty of kidnapping if he unlawfully removes another from his place of residence or business, or a substantial distance from the vicinity where he is found, or if he unlawfully confines another for a substantial period, with any of the following purposes:

   (1) To facilitate commission of any crime or flight thereafter;

   (2) To inflict bodily injury on or to terrorize the victim or another;

   (3) To interfere with the performance of any governmental or political function; or

   (4) To permanently deprive a parent, guardian or other lawful custodian of custody of the victim.

c. **Grading of kidnapping.**

   (1) Except as provided in paragraph (2) of this subsection, kidnapping is a crime of the first degree and upon conviction thereof, a person may, notwithstanding the provisions of paragraph (1) of subsection a. of N.J.S.2C:43-6, be sentenced to an ordinary term of imprisonment between 15 and 30 years. If the actor releases the victim unharmed and in a safe place prior to apprehension, it is a crime of the second degree.

   (2) Kidnapping is a crime of the first degree and upon conviction thereof, an actor shall be sentenced to a term of imprisonment by the court, if the victim of the kidnapping is less than 16 years of age and if during the kidnapping:

      (a) A crime under N.J.S.2C:14-2 or subsection a. of N.J.S.2C:14-3 is committed against the victim;

   (b) A crime under subsection b. of N.J.S.2C:24-4 is committed against the victim; or

   (c) The actor sells or delivers the victim to another person for pecuniary gain other than in circumstances which lead to the return of the victim to a parent, guardian or other person responsible for the general supervision of the victim.

   Notwithstanding the provisions of paragraph (1) of subsection a. of N.J.S.2C:43-6, the term of imprisonment imposed under this paragraph shall be either a term of 25 years during which the actor shall not be eligible for parole, or a specific term between 25 years and life imprisonment, of which the actor shall serve 25 years before being eligible for parole; provided, however, that the crime of kidnapping under this paragraph and underlying aggravating crimes listed in subparagraph (a), (b) or (c) of this paragraph shall merge for purposes of sentencing. If the actor is convicted of the criminal homicide of a victim of a kidnapping under the provisions of chapter 11, any sentence imposed under provisions of this paragraph shall be served consecutively to any sentence imposed pursuant to the provisions of chapter 11.

d. **"Unlawful" removal or confinement.** A removal or confinement is unlawful within the meaning of this section and of sections 2C:13-2 and 2C:13-3, if it is accomplished by force, threat or deception, or, in the case of a person who is under the age of 14 or is incompetent, if it is accomplished without the consent of a parent, guardian or other person responsible for general supervision of his welfare.

e. It is an affirmative defense to a prosecution under paragraph (4) of subsection b. of this section, which must be proved by clear and convincing evidence, that:

   (1) The actor reasonably believed that the action was necessary to preserve the victim from imminent danger to his welfare. However, no defense shall be available pursuant to this subsection if the actor does not, as soon as reasonably practicable but in no event more than 24 hours after taking a victim under his protection, give notice of the victim's location to the police department of the municipality where the victim resided, the office of the county prosecutor in the county where the victim resided, or the Division of Youth and Family Services in the Department of Human Services;

   (2) The actor reasonably believed that the taking or detaining of the victim was consented to by a parent, or by an authorized State agency; or

   (3) The victim, being at the time of the taking or concealment not less than 14 years old, was taken away at his own volition by his parent and without purpose to commit a criminal offense with or against the victim.

f. It is an affirmative defense to a prosecution under paragraph (4) of subsection b. of this section that a parent having the right of custody reasonably believed he was fleeing from imminent physical danger from the other parent, provided that the parent having custody, as soon as reasonably practicable:

   (1) Gives notice of the victim's location to the police department of the municipality where the victim resided, the office of the county prosecutor in the county where the victim resided, or the Division of Youth and Family Services in the Department of Human Services; or

   (2) Commences an action affecting custody in an appropriate court.

g. As used in subsections e. and f. of this section, "parent" means a parent, guardian or other lawful custodian of a victim.

## PRACTICAL APPLICATION OF STATUTE

### Kidnapping—First and Second Degree Offenses

2C:13-1 contains an array of circumstances that permit a charge of kidnapping. The offense generally is a crime of the first degree but may be lowered to a second degree offense if the defendant "releases the victim unharmed and in a safe place prior to apprehension." Per this exception, which can be found in subsection c. of the statute, Mercury Anderson should be charged with second degree kidnapping for his crime involving Candice Wesley.

Ms. Wesley, an adult, was taken from her automobile against her will. She was brought to an apartment, and a ransom of $50,000 was demanded. For some reason, Anderson released her at a diner six hours later unharmed. Under subsection a. of the statute, a person is guilty of kidnapping if he "unlawfully removes another from the place where he is found," confines this person unlawfully, and demands a ransom. Since Anderson unlawfully removed Wesley from her car, confined her in his apartment, and then demanded a $50,000 ransom, he is guilty of kidnapping. The crime is a second degree offense because he released her unharmed and at the safe location of a diner.

It is important to note that Anderson could be convicted of kidnapping even if his crime was predicated on purposes other than obtaining a ransom. Subsection a. also provides that if Anderson removed and held his victim to be utilized as a "shield" (e.g., from gunfire by law enforcement) or as a "hostage," he could be convicted of kidnapping.

Under subsection b., he is guilty of kidnapping if he confines someone for a "substantial" period of time (or takes someone to another location and confines him) for a number of reasons, including facilitating a crime, inflicting bodily injury on the victim, interfering with a government function, or attempting to permanently deprive a parent of lawful custody. Accordingly, if Anderson had taken Wesley to his apartment to beat her, rather than demand a ransom, he would still be convicted of kidnapping. Similarly, if his purpose in removing her from her car and confining her was to stop the State Assembly from legislating for a day, he is guilty of kidnapping. Finally, if Anderson had not actually taken Wesley to his apartment but instead simply confined her in a car while he beat her, he is guilty of kidnapping as long as the confinement was for a "substantial" period of time. But what is a "substantial" period of time? Courts have ruled as little as 30 minutes.

### Permanently Depriving Lawful Custodian of Custody

Mercury Anderson also should be charged with kidnapping under subsection b. for the abduction of his own daughter. The child's mother had sole physical and legal custody of this juvenile. Anderson took the child from her and kept the minor in his custody for three years, never advising the mother of her child's whereabouts. This obviously was an effort to permanently deprive the mother of her lawful custody. Since Anderson did not release the child prior to his apprehension, he is guilty of first degree kidnapping of his daughter.

Under subsection e., it is an affirmative defense to the above form of kidnapping if the actor "reasonably believed that the action was necessary to preserve the victim from imminent danger." This defense is not available, though, if the actor does not notify the police or other appropriate authorities of the victim's location within 24 hours of the taking. It is also an affirmative defense if the actor reasonably believed that the child's parent or an authorized state agency consented to the taking or if the child is 14 years (or older) and consents to his own taking.

The above-listed defenses are not available to Mercury Anderson, however. He had no reason to believe his daughter was in imminent danger, and he never notified anyone of her location. Moreover, neither the child's mother nor any state agency consented to her taking. Also, the child was under 14 at the time of the taking, and there is no evidence that she joined Anderson of her own volition.

It should further be noted that even if Anderson's daughter was 14 or older and consented to going with him, he still would not have an affirmative defense to kidnapping. Subsection e.(3) sets forth that this type of affirmative defense is only available if the taking is "without purpose to commit a criminal offense with or against the victim." Given that Anderson repeatedly sexually assaulted his daughter, he certainly acted with a purpose to commit a criminal offense upon the taking of his child. Therefore, even if his daughter was 14 or older and consented to his taking of her, Anderson would still be guilty of kidnapping. His failure to notify the child's mother (or any appropriate state agency) of her whereabouts for three years in and of itself may also be a crime sufficient to vitiate such a defense, even in fact of a child being 14 or older and consenting to the taking.

### Special First Degree Kidnapping Provisions When Victim Is Under 16

Kidnapping is always a crime of the first degree, per subsection c.(2) of this statute, when the victim is under 16 years of age *and* one of the following crimes occurs during the kidnapping: aggravated sexual assault or sexual assault (2C:14-2), aggravated criminal sexual contact (2C:14-3a.), child pornography offenses (2C:24-4b.), or selling the child for monetary gain. A defendant who commits any of the aforesaid crimes during a kidnapping will receive an enhanced prison term—above and beyond the ordinary term of imprisonment for first degree offenses.

Mercury Anderson's kidnapping of Jerri Sloane is violative of subsection c.(2). Sloane was 15 at the time of her abduction. During the kidnapping, Anderson forced her to engage in nonconsensual sexual intercourse. Accordingly, he should be charged with this first degree kidnapping and be sentenced to the enhanced incarceration.

---

**2C:13-2.**    **Criminal restraint**

A person commits a crime of the third degree if he knowingly:

  a. Restrains another unlawfully in circumstances exposing the other to risk of serious bodily injury; or

  b. Holds another in a condition of involuntary servitude.

The creation by the actor of circumstances resulting in a belief by another that he must remain in a particular location shall for purposes of this section be deemed to be a holding in a condition of involuntary servitude.

In any prosecution under subsection b., it is an affirmative defense that the person held was a child less than 18 years old and the actor was a relative or legal guardian of such child and his sole purpose was to assume control of such child.

## PRACTICAL APPLICATION OF STATUTE

Mercury Anderson's actions beset against Eric Mesos constitute a criminal restraint, a third degree crime. An individual is guilty of criminal restraint if he restrains another unlawfully, thereby exposing that person to serious bodily injury (subsection a.) or if he holds another in "involuntary servitude" (subsection b.). Creating a set of circumstances that makes someone believe that he must remain in a particular location is an "involuntary servitude" under this statute.

Anderson invaded Mesos's automobile, advising him that if he left the vehicle, his mother would be killed. These threats levied by Anderson made Mesos believe that he couldn't leave the automobile. Mesos remained in the car for 15 minutes until Anderson vacated. Accordingly, Anderson held Mesos in an involuntary servitude and therefore violated subsection b. of this statute.

If the facts were tweaked to the extent that Anderson duct-taped Mesos's mouth and stuffed him in the trunk of the car for 15 minutes—in an effort to restrain him—Anderson would still be convicted of criminal restraint. As subsection a. of the statute provides, a person is guilty of this offense if he restrains "another unlawfully in circumstances exposing the other to risk of serious bodily injury." Thus, Anderson's suffocating actions, which could cause serious bodily injury to Mesos, would make him guilty of criminal restraint. It should be noted, though, that if Anderson kept Mesos in this confined condition for much longer, he could be charged with kidnapping instead of criminal restraint.

**2C:13-3.**       **False imprisonment**

A person commits a disorderly persons offense if he knowingly restrains another unlawfully so as to interfere substantially with his liberty. In any prosecution under this section, it is an affirmative defense that the person restrained was a child less than 18 years old and that the actor was a relative or legal guardian of such child and that his sole purpose was to assume control of such child.

## PRACTICAL APPLICATION OF STATUTE

False imprisonment is a disorderly persons offense, as it is basically a lesser form of criminal restraint. The statute requires that an actor knowingly restrain someone unlawfully so as to interfere substantially with his liberty. A modification of Mercury Anderson's restraint of Eric Mesos can exemplify this offense.

If Anderson entered Mesos's car and locked the doors, refusing to allow Mesos to exit, he would be ripe for a false imprisonment conviction. Here, Anderson's restraint would be substantially interfering with Mesos's liberty to move about freely. As long as the restraint did not subject Mesos to the risk of serious bodily injury, Anderson's actions would constitute a false imprisonment offense rather than criminal restraint.

**2C:13-4.          Interference with custody**

   a. Custody of children. A person, including a parent, guardian or other lawful custodian, is guilty of interference with custody if he:

     (1) Takes or detains a minor child with the purpose of concealing the minor child and thereby depriving the child's other parent of custody or parenting time with the minor child; or

     (2) After being served with process or having actual knowledge of an action affecting marriage or custody but prior to the issuance of a temporary or final order determining custody and parenting time rights to a minor child, takes, detains, entices or conceals the child within or outside the State for the purpose of depriving the child's other parent of custody or parenting time, or to evade the jurisdiction of the courts of this State;

     (3) After being served with process or having actual knowledge of an action affecting the protective services needs of a child pursuant to Title 9 of the Revised Statutes in an action affecting custody, but prior to the issuance of a temporary or final order determining custody rights of a minor child, takes, detains, entices or conceals the child within or outside the State for the purpose of evading the jurisdiction of the courts of this State; or

     (4) After the issuance of a temporary or final order specifying custody, joint custody rights or parenting time, takes, detains, entices or conceals a minor child from the other parent in violation of the custody or parenting time order.

     Interference with custody is a crime of the second degree if the child is taken, detained, enticed or concealed: (i) outside the United States or (ii) for more than 24 hours Otherwise, interference with custody is a crime of the third degree but the presumption of non-imprisonment set forth in subsection e. of N.J.S.2C:44-1 for a first offense of a crime of the third degree shall not apply.

   b. Custody of committed persons. A person is guilty of a crime of the fourth degree if he knowingly takes or entices any committed person away from lawful custody when he is not privileged to do so. "Committed person" means, in addition to anyone committed under judicial warrant, any orphan, neglected or delinquent child, mentally defective or insane person, or other dependent or incompetent person entrusted to another's custody by or through a recognized social agency or otherwise by authority of law.

   c. It is an affirmative defense to a prosecution under subsection a. of this section, which must be proved by clear and convincing evidence, that:

     (1) The actor reasonably believed that the action was necessary to preserve the child from imminent danger to his welfare. However, no defense shall be available pursuant to this subsection if the actor does not, as soon as reasonably practicable but in no event more than 24 hours after taking a child under his protection, give notice of the child's location to the police department of the municipality where the child resided, the office of the county prosecutor in the county where the child resided, or the Division of Youth and Family Services in the Department of Human Services;

     (2) The actor reasonably believed that the taking or detaining of the minor child was consented to by the other parent, or by an authorized State agency; or

     (3) The child, being at the time of the taking or concealment not less than 14 years old, was taken away at his own volition and without purpose to commit a criminal offense with or against the child.

   d. It is an affirmative defense to a prosecution under subsection a. of this section that a parent having the right of custody reasonably believed he was fleeing from imminent physical danger from the other parent, provided that the parent having custody, as soon as reasonably practicable:

  (1)  Gives notice of the child's location to the police department of the municipality where the child resided, the office of the county prosecutor in the county where the child resided, or the Division of Youth and Family Services in the Department of Human Services; or

  (2)  Commences an action affecting custody in an appropriate court.

e.  The offenses enumerated in this section are continuous in nature and continue for so long as the child is concealed or detained.

f.  (1)  In addition to any other disposition provided by law, a person convicted under subsection a. of this section shall make restitution of all reasonable expenses and costs, including reasonable counsel fees, incurred by the other parent in securing the child's return.

  (2)  In imposing sentence under subsection a. of this section the court shall consider, in addition to the factors enumerated in chapter 44 of Title 2C of the New Jersey Statutes:

     (a)  Whether the person returned the child voluntarily; and

     (b)  The length of time the child was concealed or detained.

g.  As used in this section, "parent" means a parent, guardian or other lawful custodian of a minor child.

## PRACTICAL APPLICATION OF STATUTE

Interference with custody is a charge often filed during child custody battles occurring in the family courts. Many times, law enforcement personnel appropriately find that parents' complaints involving the taking or concealing of their children do not meet the elements of kidnapping, but rather are offenses under 2C:13-4. Other times, actions appearing to amount to interference with custody may not be crimes at all and this should be noted. A review of family court proceedings and related orders is integral when charging under this statute.

Mercury Anderson is guilty of kidnapping his own daughter because he took the girl from her mother, *permanently* depriving the woman of her lawful custody. Anderson kept the child concealed from the mother for three years, never revealing her location. However, if the facts were changed slightly, he would be guilty of interference with custody, a third degree offense, instead of kidnapping.

The interference with custody charge would be proper if Anderson's taking of the child did not result in a permanent loss of custody or parenting by the mother. This charge would be valid just if the taking and concealing of the daughter resulted in any significant depriving of the woman's custody or parenting time.

Interference with custody is generally a third degree crime. It becomes a crime of the second degree if the child is taken outside the United States or taken for more than 24 hours. If a child is taken for more than 24 hours, though, and a law enforcement officer considers it serious enough to warrant a second degree interference with custody charge, then perhaps the true crime is kidnapping. In other words, does it sound right that a parent who takes his child for 25 (or 48 or 72) hours should be charged with a second degree offense? For such a serious charge, circumstances of a more illicit nature probably should be occurring, and therefore kidnapping may be the correct charge.

**2C:13-5.**          **Criminal coercion**

a. Offense defined. A person is guilty of criminal coercion if, with purpose unlawfully to restrict another's freedom of action to engage or refrain from engaging in conduct, he threatens to:

(1) Inflict bodily injury on anyone or commit any other offense;

(2) Accuse anyone of an offense;

(3) Expose any secret which would tend to subject any person to hatred, contempt or ridicule, or to impair his credit or business repute;

(4) Take or withhold action as an official, or cause an official to take or withhold action;

(5) Bring about or continue a strike, boycott or other collective action, except that such a threat shall not be deemed coercive when the restriction compelled is demanded in the course of negotiation for the benefit of the group in whose interest the actor acts;

(6) Testify or provide information or withhold testimony or information with respect to another's legal claim or defense; or

(7) Perform any other act which would not in itself substantially benefit the actor but which is calculated to substantially harm another person with respect to his health, safety, business, calling, career, financial condition, reputation or personal relationships.

It is an affirmative defense to prosecution based on paragraphs (2), (3), (4), (6) and (7) that the actor believed the accusation or secret to be true or the proposed official action justified and that his purpose was limited to compelling the other to behave in a way reasonably related to the circumstances which were the subject of the accusation, exposure or proposed official action, as by desisting from further misbehavior, making good a wrong done, or refraining from taking any action or responsibility for which the actor believes the other disqualified.

b. Grading. Criminal coercion is a crime of the fourth degree unless the threat is to commit a crime more serious than one of the fourth degree or the actor's purpose is criminal, in which cases the offense is a crime of the third degree.

## PRACTICAL APPLICATION OF STATUTE

The New Brunswick Police Department should charge Mercury Anderson with criminal coercion for his threats to falsely accuse Lieutenant Stokes of beating him while in custody and to expose the Lieutenant to possible ridicule by revealing to the public that Stokes has schizophrenia. Anderson's threats are crimes of criminal coercion, as they were levied in an effort to prevent Stokes from testifying at his trial. Ordinarily, criminal coercion is a crime of the fourth degree; Anderson's aforesaid actions amount to this grading level.

Mercury Anderson should also be charged with a third degree criminal coercion for his threat to kill Stokes if the officer testified against him or furthered his case in any way. Under subsection b. of the statute, criminal coercion is elevated from a fourth degree offense to a third degree offense where "the threat is to commit a crime more serious than one of the fourth degree." Since Anderson threatened to kill Stokes (murdering someone is a first degree crime), he threatened to commit a crime more serious than a fourth degree offense. Accordingly, Anderson is here guilty of a third degree criminal coercion.

Generally, a threat to kill will simply fall under the terroristic threats statute. Indeed, Anderson's threat to kill Lieutenant Stokes is a terroristic threat. However, it is also an act of criminal coercion. Subsection a. of this statute defines criminal coercion as an unlawful, purposeful action intended "to restrict another's freedom of action to engage or refrain from engaging in conduct." Because Anderson's intent in threatening to kill Stokes was to prevent him from testifying—"to restrict his freedom of action"—he is guilty of criminal coercion. This same rationale holds true as to why Anderson should face criminal coercion charges for his threats to publicly expose Stokes's schizophrenia and his in-custody beating—the threats were made for the unlawful purpose of preventing him from testifying. Anderson should also be charged with witness tampering, which is a separate and distinct crime that will be discussed later in this book.

---

**2C:13-6.**     **Luring, enticing child by various means, attempts; crime of third degree; subsequent offense, mandatory imprisonment**

A person commits a crime of the third degree if he attempts, via electronic or any other means, to lure or entice a child or one who he reasonably believes to be a child into a motor vehicle, structure or isolated area, or to meet or appear at any other place, with a purpose to commit a criminal offense with or against the child.

"Child" as used in this act means a person less than 18 years old.

"Electronic means" as used in this section includes, but is not limited to, the Internet, which shall have the meaning set forth in N.J.S. 2C:24-4.

"Structure" as used in this act means any building, room, ship, vessel or airplane and also means any place adapted for overnight accommodation of persons, or for carrying on business therein, whether or not a person is actually present.

Nothing herein shall be deemed to preclude, if the evidence so warrants, an indictment and conviction for attempted kidnapping under the provisions of N.J.S.2C:13-1.

A person convicted of a second or subsequent offense under this section shall be sentenced to a term of imprisonment. Notwithstanding the provisions of paragraph (3) of subsection a. of N.J.S.2C:43-6, the term of imprisonment shall include, unless the person is sentenced pursuant to the provisions of N.J.S.2C:43-7, a mandatory minimum term of one-third to one-half of the sentence imposed, or two years, whichever is greater, during which time the defendant shall not be eligible for parole. If the person is sentenced pursuant to N.J.S.2C:43-7, the court shall impose a minimum term of one-third to one-half of the sentence imposed, or three years, whichever is greater. The court may not suspend or make any other non-custodial disposition of any person sentenced as a second or subsequent offender pursuant to this section. For the purposes of this section an offense is considered a second or subsequent offense if the actor has at any time been convicted pursuant to this section, or under any similar statute of the United States, this State or any other state for an offense that is substantially equivalent to this section.

## PRACTICAL APPLICATION OF STATUTE

Mercury Anderson is guilty of violating 2C:13-6 for luring Frank Pileggi into his automobile. Per the statute, a person commits this third degree offense if he attempts to lure or entice a child into a motor vehicle or other isolated area with a purpose to commit a criminal offense with or against the child.

Frank Pileggi, 10, was lured into a motor vehicle via Mercury Anderson's offering a set of baseball cards. Once inside the automobile, Anderson committed the offense of aggravated criminal sexual contact by rubbing Pileggi's buttocks and groin area. Accordingly, in addition to being charged with sexual assault, Anderson should be charged under 2C:13-6 for luring this 10-year-old child into his automobile and sexually violating him therein.

# 14

# SEXUAL OFFENSES

**2C:14-1.** **Definitions**

The following definitions apply to this chapter:

a. "Actor" means a person accused of an offense proscribed under this act;

b. "Victim" means a person alleging to have been subjected to offenses proscribed by this act;

c. "Sexual penetration" means vaginal intercourse, cunnilingus, fellatio or anal intercourse between persons or insertion of the hand, finger or object into the anus or vagina either by the actor or upon the actor's instruction. The depth of insertion shall not be relevant as to the question of commission of the crime.

d. "Sexual contact" means an intentional touching by the victim or actor, either directly or through clothing, of the victim's or actor's intimate parts for the purpose of degrading or humiliating the victim or sexually arousing or sexually gratifying the actor. Sexual contact of the actor with himself must be in view of the victim whom the actor knows to be present.

e. "Intimate parts" means the following body parts: sexual organs, genital area, anal area, inner thigh, groin, buttock or breast of a person;

f. "Severe personal injury" means severe bodily injury, disfigurement, disease, incapacitating mental anguish or chronic pain;

g. "Physically helpless" means that condition in which a person is unconscious or is physically unable to flee or is physically unable to communicate unwillingness to act;

h. "Mentally defective" means that condition in which a person suffers from a mental disease or defect which renders that person temporarily or permanently incapable of understanding the nature of his conduct, including, but not limited to, being incapable of providing consent.

i. "Mentally incapacitated" means that condition in which a person is rendered temporarily incapable of understanding or controlling his conduct due to the influence of a narcotic, anesthetic, intoxicant, or other substance administered to that person without his prior knowledge or consent, or due to any other act committed upon that person which rendered that person incapable of appraising or controlling his conduct.

j. "Coercion" as used in this chapter shall refer to those acts which are defined as criminal coercion in section 2C:13-5(1), (2), (3), (4), (6) and (7).

**2C:14-2.** **Sexual assault**

a. An actor is guilty of aggravated sexual assault if he commits an act of sexual penetration with another person under any one of the following circumstances:

(1) The victim is less than 13 years old;

(2) The victim is at least 13 but less than 16 years old; and

(a) The actor is related to the victim by blood or affinity to the third degree, or

(b) The actor has supervisory or disciplinary power over the victim by virtue of the actor's legal, professional, or occupational status, or

(c) The actor is a foster parent, a guardian, or stands in loco parentis within the household;

(3) The act is committed during the commission, or attempted commission, whether alone or with one or more other persons, of robbery, kidnapping, homicide, aggravated assault on another, burglary, arson or criminal escape;

(4) The actor is armed with a weapon or any object fashioned in such a manner as to lead the victim to reasonably believe it to be a weapon and threatens by word or gesture to use the weapon or object;

(5) The actor is aided or abetted by one or more other persons and the actor uses physical force or coercion;

(6) The actor uses physical force or coercion and severe personal injury is sustained by the victim;

(7) The victim is one whom the actor knew or should have known was physically helpless, mentally defective or mentally incapacitated.

Aggravated sexual assault is a crime of the first degree.

b. An actor is guilty of sexual assault if he commits an act of sexual contact with a victim who is less than 13 years old and the actor is at least four years older than the victim.

c. An actor is guilty of sexual assault if he commits an act of sexual penetration with another person under any one of the following circumstances:

(1) The actor uses physical force or coercion, but the victim does not sustain severe personal injury;

(2) The victim is on probation or parole, or is detained in a hospital, prison or other institution and the actor has supervisory or disciplinary power over the victim by virtue of the actor's legal, professional or occupational status;

(3) The victim is at least 16 but less than 18 years old and:

(a) The actor is related to the victim by blood or affinity to the third degree; or

(b) The actor has supervisory or disciplinary power of any nature or in any capacity over the victim; or

(c) The actor is a foster parent, a guardian, or stands in loco parentis within the household;

(4) The victim is at least 13 but less than 16 years old and the actor is at least four years older than the victim.

Sexual assault is a crime of the second degree.

## PRACTICAL APPLICATION OF STATUTE

### Aggravated Sexual Assault—Generally

Aggravated sexual assault is a crime of the first degree. A variety of actions constitute the commission of this offense. Under some circumstances, an actor is guilty only where sexual penetration was not consented to; in other circumstances, however, consent is not a required element of the offense. In all cases, an act of sexual penetration must occur for a conviction under this statute. Sexual penetration, as defined under

2C:14-1, means vaginal intercourse, cunnilingus, fellatio, anal intercourse between persons or the insertion of the hand, finger, or object into the anus or vagina of another. The actor need not conduct the insertion himself; his instruction of an insertion will suffice to constitute an act of sexual penetration.

Regardless of age, an individual is guilty of aggravated sexual assault if he commits an act of sexual penetration during the commission of violent crimes such as robbery, kidnapping, or murder (see 2C:14-2a.(3)). He is similarly guilty of aggravated sexual assault where he utilizes a weapon to force another into an act of sexual penetration (see 2C:14-2a.(4)). This first degree crime is also committed where the actor uses physical force *and* "severe personal injury" is sustained by the victim (see 2C:14-2a.(6)). Likewise, an actor who uses physical force *and* is "aided or abetted by one or more other persons" is guilty of aggravated sexual assault (see 2C:14-2a.(5)).

Mercury Anderson is guilty of aggravated sexual assault for his nonconsensual sexual penetration of Jerri Sloane. First, he violated 2C:14-2a.(3), as he had sexual intercourse with Sloane during her kidnapping. He is guilty of the offense, per the tenets of 2C:14-2a.(4), because he armed himself with a handgun while he sexually penetrated her. Neither of these two subsections requires that personal injury result from the sexual act. Anderson, however, is also guilty of aggravated sexual assault under 2C:14-2a.(6). Why? Because he used physical force against Sloane *and* personal injury resulted. Anderson beat her violently, breaking her nose with the butt of a handgun.

If Anderson had been aided by an accomplice and used physical force to have sexual intercourse with Sloane, he would have violated 2C:14-2a.(5). This subsection though, as in a.(3) and a.(4), again does not require personal injury to be caused for an aggravated sexual assault conviction.

### Aggravated Sexual Assault—Victim Under 13

Mercury Anderson is guilty of aggravated sexual assault for having sexual intercourse with Samantha Cora, even though she consented to the act. Under 2C:14-2a., an actor is guilty of aggravated sexual assault if he commits an act of "sexual penetration" with a victim less than 13 years old. This is a crime of strict liability, here meaning that it is irrelevant if the offender knew the victim was under 13 or if the victim consented to the sexual penetration.

Samantha Cora, 12 years old, consented to having sexual intercourse, an act of sexual penetration, with Mercury Anderson. However, her consent is not a defense to 2C:14-2a.(1). Simply, having sexual intercourse with an individual under 13 makes an actor guilty of aggravated sexual assault. Accordingly, Mercury Anderson should be charged with this first degree crime for having sexual intercourse with Samantha Cora.

### Aggravated Sexual Assault—Victim at Least 13, but Under 16

If Samantha Cora was 15 rather than 12, Mercury Anderson could still be charged with aggravated sexual assault for his sexual intercourse with the girl. However, in addition to the minor's age being 13, 14, or 15, one of three factors must be present for a conviction. If the actor was related by blood to a victim whose age is 13, 14 or 15, he is guilty. If Anderson had supervisory or disciplinary powers over a victim whose age is 13, 14, or 15, he is guilty. If he was a foster parent, or otherwise had guardian control of a victim with an age of 13, 14, or 15, he is guilty.

In sum, if any of the factors mentioned in the above paragraph existed, in addition to Samantha Cora being 15 years old, Mercury Anderson would be guilty of aggravated sexual assault for having sexual intercourse with this girl even though she consented to the act. If none of the aforesaid additional factors were present, however, an act of sexual penetration with a person 13, 14, or 15 years old is the lesser crime of sexual assault. This crime will be discussed later in this practical application section.

### Aggravated Sexual Assault—Mentally Defective or Incapacitated Victim

Under 2C:14-2a.(7), a defendant is guilty of aggravated sexual assault if the "victim is one whom the actor knew or should have known was physically helpless, mentally defective or mentally incapacitated." This is a crime of strict liability where consent is not a defense. Many of the terms of this subsection make the conviction of a defendant dependent upon expert testimony. Although "mentally defective" and "mentally incapacitated" are defined in 2C:14-1, expert psychological testimony is a must to determine whether or not an individual "knew" or "should have known" the victim's condition. Accordingly, even before charging an individual under this subsection, law enforcement officers should have a viable reason to believe that the victim was "mentally incapacitated," "mentally defective," or "physically helpless."

### Sexual Assault—Generally

Like aggravated sexual assault, there are multiple scenarios that amount to the commission of sexual assault. The offenses range from situations involving nonconsensual sexual penetration where an actor uses force to situations of consensual sexual penetration where a victim is 13, 14, or 15. Each type of offense, though, has special circumstances in order for the act to be considered a sexual assault.

As set forth in the previous sections, Mercury Anderson is guilty of aggravated sexual assault for the forced sexual intercourse he had with Jerri Sloane. However, if the facts were modified, he would face the lesser charge of sexual assault instead. For example, Anderson would be guilty of sexual assault, under 2C:14-2c.(1), if he used physical force to have nonconsensual sexual intercourse with Jerri Sloane, an adult, in her own home or another location. For him to be guilty of sexual assault under these circumstances, rather than aggravated sexual assault, Sloane could not have suffered "severe personal injury" due to the forceful attack. Also, for the charge to be the lesser offense of sexual assault, there could be no kidnapping involved. Remember, an act of sexual penetration that occurs during the commission of crimes such as kidnapping, murder, and robbery automatically becomes an aggravated sexual assault.

### Sexual Assault—Sexual Contact with Victim Under 13

Mercury Anderson should be charged with sexual assault, and not the lower crime of criminal sexual contact for his touching of 10-year-old Frank Pileggi's buttocks and groin area. Sexual contact, as defined in 2C:14-1, means "intentional touching" by the victim or actor, either directly or through clothing, of the victim's or actor's intimate parts. Intimate parts include genitals, anal area, buttocks, groin, breast, and inner thigh. Also, for the contact to be illegal, it must be perpetrated for the purpose of "degrading or humiliating the victim" or "sexually arousing or gratifying the actor."

2C:14-2b. elevates a "sexual contact," as described above, from a charge of criminal sexual contact to sexual assault where the victim is less than 13 years old. Mercury Anderson lured a 10-year-old boy, Frank Pileggi, into his automobile. There, Anderson touched the boy's groin and buttocks through his clothing. Anderson had no appropriate purpose to conduct these sexual contacts; obviously the touching was conducted to sexually arouse and gratify Anderson. Accordingly, Anderson would be charged with the second degree crime of sexual assault for this illegal contact with Frank Pileggi. Given Pileggi's youthful age, this charge is appropriate even if the boy consented to the contact.

### Sexual Assault—Actor Has Supervisory Power Over Victim in Institution or on Parole

Under 2C:14-2c.(2), a corrections officer or medical doctor is guilty of sexual assault if he engages in an act of sexual penetration with an inmate or detained hospital patient. This subsection provides that an individual having supervisory/disciplinary power over a person on probation or parole is guilty of sexual assault if he engages in an act of sexual penetration with that supervised person. Similarly, an individual having supervisory/disciplinary power over a detained prison inmate or hospital patient is guilty of sexual assault if he engages in an act of sexual penetration with that confined person.

The subsection does not require force or coercion as an element of the offense. Accordingly, it seems that if a parole officer has sexual intercourse—even if it is consensual—with a parolee, he is guilty of the second degree crime of sexual assault. Similarly, a prison guard who engages in fellatio (an act of sexual penetration) with an inmate is guilty of sexual assault. And a medical doctor who engages in cunnilingus (an act of sexual penetration) with a detained hospital patient is guilty of sexual assault.

**2C:14-2.1.**      **Victim of sexual assault may consult with prosecutor on plea negotiations**

Whenever there is a prosecution for a violation of N.J.S.A.2C:14-2, the victim of the sexual assault shall be provided an opportunity to consult with the prosecuting authority prior to the conclusion of any plea negotiations.

Nothing contained herein shall be construed to alter or limit the authority or discretion of the prosecutor to enter into any plea agreement which the prosecutor deems appropriate.

**2C:14-3.**      **Aggravated criminal sexual contact; criminal sexual contact**

     a. An actor is guilty of aggravated criminal sexual contact if he commits an act of sexual contact with the victim under any of the circumstances set forth in 2C:14-2a. (2) through (7).

     Aggravated criminal sexual contact is a crime of the third degree.

     b. An actor is guilty of criminal sexual contact if he commits an act of sexual contact with the victim under any of the circumstances set forth in section 2C:14-2c. (1) through (4).

     Criminal sexual contact is a crime of the fourth degree.

## PRACTICAL APPLICATION OF STATUTE

### Aggravated Criminal Sexual Contact and Criminal Sexual Contact

Per the definitions set forth under 2C:14-1, sexual contact is an intentional touching by the victim or actor, either directly or through clothing, of the victim's or actor's intimate parts. Intimate parts include genitals, anal area, buttocks, groin, breast, and inner thigh. Also, for the contact to be illegal, it must be perpetrated for the purpose of "degrading or humiliating the victim" or "sexually arousing or sexually gratifying the actor."

2C:14-3 has two subsections. Subsection a. sets forth the provisions for the third degree crime of aggravated sexual contact, and subsection b. covers the fourth degree crime of sexual contact. Basically, aggravated sexual contact is a lower form of aggravated sexual assault, and sexual contact is the lesser version of sexual assault. Aggravated criminal sexual contact follows the same circumstances set forth in the aggravated sexual assault statute 2C:14-2a.(2) through (7). Criminal sexual contact follows the same circumstances set forth in the sexual assault statute 2C:14-2c.(1) through (4). The difference lies in that a sexual contact must occur rather than a sexual penetration.

Examples of aggravated criminal sexual contact include a football coach touching a 15-year-old boy's groin in an effort to gratify himself; a man rubbing a woman's breasts over her shirt during a kidnapping; a woman wielding a knife while she touches another woman's genitals; a man accompanied by two other men who uses physical force to rub a woman's genitals over her pants; a man using physical force to rub another man's buttocks and causing severe personal injury to that victim; and a man who fondles the breasts of a woman who he knows is mentally incapacitated.

Examples of criminal sexual contact include a man using physical force to rub another man's buttocks but severe personal injury is not suffered by the victim; a prison guard rubbing the breasts of an inmate; a high school teacher touching a 17-year-old student's genitals over her pants; and a 25-year-old man rubbing the groin of a 15-year-old girl.

It is important to note that, just like the provisions of the aggravated sexual assault and the sexual assault statutes, in many cases an actor is guilty of aggravated criminal sexual contact and criminal sexual contact even where a victim consents. Many of the above examples fall within this framework (e.g., the high school teacher cannot claim a defense of consent where he touches his 17-year-old student's genitals over her pants; the 25-year-old man is still guilty of criminal sexual contact even if the 15-year-old girl consented to him rubbing her groin).

**2C:14-4.**     **Lewdness**

   a. A person commits a disorderly persons offense if he does any flagrantly lewd and offensive act which he knows or reasonably expects is likely to be observed by other nonconsenting persons who would be affronted or alarmed.

   b. A person commits a crime of the fourth degree if:

       (1) He exposes his intimate parts for the purpose of arousing or gratifying the sexual desire of the actor or of any other person under circumstances where the actor knows or reasonably expects he is likely to be observed by a child who is less than 13 years of age where the actor is at least four years older than the child.

(2) He exposes his intimate parts for the purpose of arousing or gratifying the sexual desire of the actor or of any other person under circumstances where the actor knows or reasonably expects he is likely to be observed by a person who because of mental disease or defect is unable to understand the sexual nature of the actor's conduct.

c. As used in this section:

"lewd acts" shall include the exposing of the genitals for the purpose of arousing or gratifying the sexual desire of the actor or of any other person.

## PRACTICAL APPLICATION OF STATUTE

### Lewdness as a Disorderly Persons Offense

Mercury Anderson is guilty of the disorderly persons offense of lewdness for exposing his genitals to 20-year-old Eric Mesos. Lewdness is a disorderly persons offense where a person performs any flagrantly lewd and offensive act which he knows or reasonably expects to be observed by other nonconsenting persons who would be alarmed by the act. Lewd acts include exposing the genitals for the purpose of arousing or gratifying the sexual desires of the actor or another.

Anderson twice exposed his genitals to Eric Mesos while the two were seated in an automobile. Mesos did not consent to these acts, as he was only in the automobile under the threat that his mother would be killed if he left. Clearly, Anderson only exposed his genitals for his own sexual gratification, and he had to reasonably expect these lewd acts would alarm Mesos. Accordingly, Mercury Anderson is guilty of the disorderly persons offense of lewdness.

### Lewdness as a Fourth Degree Crime

Lewdness becomes a fourth degree crime under two circumstances: where an actor exposes his genitals to a child under 13 (and the actor is at least four years older than the child) and where an actor exposes his genitals to a person who is mentally defective (a person who has a mental disease or defect which makes him unable to understand the sexual nature of the actor's conduct). In both cases, the actor must expose his genitals for the purpose of arousing or gratifying his own sexual desires or the sexual desires of another. Mercury Anderson's flashing of his genitals to Eric Mesos would therefore be elevated to a fourth degree lewdness if Mesos had been either under 13 or if he was proven to be mentally defective.

**2C:14-5.**     **Provisions generally applicable to Chapter 14**

a. The prosecutor shall not be required to offer proof that the victim resisted, or resisted to the utmost, or reasonably resisted the sexual assault in any offense proscribed by this chapter.

b. No actor shall be presumed to be incapable of committing a crime under this chapter because of age or impotency or marriage to the victim.

c. It shall be no defense to a prosecution for a crime under this chapter that the actor believed the victim to be above the age stated for the offense, even if such a mistaken belief was reasonable.

**2C:14-6.**     **Sentencing**

If a person is convicted of a second or subsequent offense under sections 2C:14-2 or 2C:14-3a., the sentence imposed under those sections for the second or subsequent offense shall, unless the person is sentenced pursuant to the provisions of 2C:43-7, include a fixed minimum sentence of not less than 5 years during which the defendant shall not be eligible for parole. The court may not suspend or make any other non-custodial disposition of any person sentenced as a second or subsequent offender pursuant to this section. For the purpose of this section an offense is considered a second or subsequent offense, if the actor has at any time been convicted under sections 2C:14-2 or 2C:14-3a. or under any similar statute of the United States, this state, or any other state for an offense that is substantially equivalent to sections 2C:14-2 or 2C:14-3a.

**2C:14-7.**     **Victim's previous sexual conduct; manner of dress**

a. In prosecutions for aggravated sexual assault, sexual assault, aggravated criminal sexual contact, criminal sexual contact, endangering the welfare of a child in violation of N.J.S.2C:24-4 or the fourth degree crime of lewdness in violation of subsection b. of N.J.S.2C:14-4, evidence of the victim's previous sexual conduct shall not be admitted nor reference made to it in the presence of the jury except as provided in this section. When the defendant seeks to admit such evidence for any purpose, the defendant must apply for an order of the court before the trial or preliminary hearing, except that the court may allow the motion to be made during trial if the court determines that the evidence is newly discovered and could not have been obtained earlier through the exercise of due diligence. After the application is made, the court shall conduct a hearing in camera to determine the admissibility of the evidence. If the court finds that evidence offered by the defendant regarding the sexual conduct of the victim is relevant and highly material and meets the requirements of subsections c. and d. of this section and that the probative value of the evidence offered substantially outweighs its collateral nature or the probability that its admission will create undue prejudice, confusion of the issues, or unwarranted invasion of the privacy of the victim, the court shall enter an order setting forth with specificity what evidence may be introduced and the nature of the questions which shall be permitted, and the reasons why the court finds that such evidence satisfies the standards contained in this section. The defendant may then offer evidence under the order of the court.

b. In the absence of clear and convincing proof to the contrary, evidence of the victim's sexual conduct occurring more than one year before the date of the offense charged is presumed to be inadmissible under this section.

c. Evidence of previous sexual conduct with persons other than the defendant which is offered by any lay or expert witness shall not be considered relevant unless it is material to proving the source of semen, pregnancy or disease.

d. Evidence of the victim's previous sexual conduct with the defendant shall be considered relevant if it is probative of whether a reasonable person, knowing what the defendant knew at the time of the alleged offense, would have believed that the alleged victim freely and affirmatively permitted the sexual behavior complained of.

e. Evidence of the manner in which the victim was dressed at the time an offense was committed shall not be admitted unless such evidence is determined by the court to be relevant and admissible in the interest of justice, after an offer of proof by the proponent of such evidence outside the hearing of the jury or at such hearing as the court may require, and a statement by the court of its findings of fact essential to its determination. A statement by the court of its findings shall also be included in the record.

f. For the purposes of this section, "sexual conduct" shall mean any conduct or behavior relating to sexual activities of the victim, including but not limited to previous or subsequent experience of sexual penetration or sexual contact, use of contraceptives, sexual activities reflected in gynecological records, living arrangement and life style.

2C:14-8.        **Juveniles in need of supervision (J.I.N.S.) law not affected**

Nothing in this chapter shall be deemed to limit the jurisdiction of the court under P.L.1973, c. 306 (C. 2A:4-42 et seq.).

# 15

# ROBBERY

## FACT PATTERN (PERTAINS TO CHAPTERS 15 TO 17)

Investigative reporter Chang Lee contacted Paterson Police Captain Sterling Marley after he uncovered the hideout of Mickey Vice, a deranged parolee who had recently committed a tirade of violent thefts and property damage. Marley headed Paterson's elite robbery squad and had been seeking Vice's capture for several weeks, following a chain of criminal events that were not similar to any other in his 25-year career. Accordingly, Captain Marley immediately met with the reporter to learn Vice's location. At their meeting Marley recounted Vice's crimes—off the record.

Mickey Vice orchestrated and carried out five separate criminal actions over a five-week period. His first victim, Horace Wille, a 50-year-old American Indian, was punched in the face several times as Vice stole $500 from the man's wallet. While beating Wille, Vice told him that "This is payback for all the money your Indian casinos steal from us. Indians stink."

Exactly one week later, Vice entered Nelson Simone's BMW, pointed a pistol at him, and ordered, "Listen, you homosexual, go into your glovebox and hand me the $100 bill that I know is in there." After Simone turned over the money, Vice violently beat him with the gun, knocking the man unconscious. Then Vice pushed Simone out of his car and fled. Nelson Simone was hospitalized but survived the incident.

For the third week's crime, Vice appeared at his prior residence on Fifth Street in Paterson. Still living at the home was his estranged wife, Carrie. According to Carrie, Vice initially was calm, even congenial, toward her. Things, however, became "odd," as she described it, when Vice suggested that "they burn down the house to collect insurance money and to avoid Paterson's requirement that they pay to have fire escapes erected and junk removed from the backyard." When Carrie refused, Vice forced her to have sexual intercourse with him, then hit her over the head with a baseball bat, causing her to become unconscious. Immediately thereafter, he poured gasoline in the home's living room and lit a match to it. Vice's house, as well as the two row houses connected to it, burned to the ground. Carrie and the other dwellings' occupants were all rescued by Paterson firefighters.

In the fourth week, Vice's criminal activities began with a simple car theft. His first order of business began with the removal of the automobile's vehicle identification number. After he completed this task, Vice attempted to start the car. However, his skills had apparently deteriorated and he was unable to ignite the engine. Angry, Vice exited the vehicle, repeatedly kicked its doors and smashed all of its windows. The total losses resulting from this damage were $1,550. His attention then turned to a multi-unit building located across the street. He found the structure particularly interesting because it was owned by Carrie's father. Two hours later, Vice returned to the building with dynamite and exploded the same at the base of the building. Although, miraculously, no one was killed, 17 people suffered serious bodily injuries, such as broken bones and loss of eyesight, and over 30 homes were destroyed.

Vice, excited by his recent widespread damage, concocted a particularly vile plan for his fifth week's crimes. Posing as a government nuclear radiation inspector, he gained entrance into a newly constructed nuclear power plant in the industrial section of Paterson. Once inside, Vice spray-painted in a woman's bathroom "I am the king. I hate all people who are not just like me." He then released a container of poisonous gas in the facility's hallway, causing most of the workers to flee to open air. As the employees exited, Vice raced to the plant's off-limits area—where the machinery generating the nuclear power was located. There, he fired shots at the men and women remaining at their job sites and threw a stick of dynamite into the machinery, hoping to release radiation. Fortunately, the dynamite failed to cause any significant damage, and no one was injured by his gunfire. Vice escaped, however, utilizing the melee to avoid capture.

As Captain Marley concluded his last words about Vice's violent five-week tirade, Chang Lee passed him a napkin with an address. Marley cordially thanked the reporter, then raced to his police cruiser. Within 30 minutes, Vice's hideout, an apartment situated atop a hamburger restaurant, was surrounded by over 50 law enforcement personnel. He surrendered, but not without incident. After two hours of gunfire directed at the police officers, he ran out of ammunition. Suddenly, he appeared on the street with his hands raised above his head. Captain Marley personally subdued Vice and took him into custody.

## 2C:15-1.    Robbery

a. **Robbery defined.** A person is guilty of robbery if, in the course of committing a theft, he:

(1) Inflicts bodily injury or uses force upon another; or

(2) Threatens another with or purposely puts him in fear of immediate bodily injury; or

(3) Commits or threatens immediately to commit any crime of the first or second degree.

An act shall be deemed to be included in the phrase "in the course of committing a theft" if it occurs in an attempt to commit theft or in immediate flight after the attempt or commission.

b. **Grading.** Robbery is a crime of the second degree, except that it is a crime of the first degree if in the course of committing the theft the actor attempts to kill anyone, or purposely inflicts or attempts to inflict serious bodily injury, or is armed with, or uses or threatens the immediate use of a deadly weapon.

### PRACTICAL APPLICATION OF STATUTE

Robbery can be either a first or second degree offense. The determining factor to make it a crime of the first degree is whether a deadly weapon is utilized during the commission of theft or if a defendant attempts to kill someone or purposely inflicts or attempts to inflict *serious* bodily injury during a theft. Robbery is a lesser second degree offense where the offender threatens or inflicts bodily injury during a theft, or in circumstances where force (without a deadly weapon) is used during the commission of a theft. The statute also provides that an offender is guilty of second degree robbery if, during the commission of a theft, he threatens to commit any first or second degree crime such as kidnapping, arson, or sexual assault.

Mickey Vice is guilty of the second degree robbery of Horace Wille. Vice lifted $500 from the man. During this theft, he caused bodily injury to Wille by punching him in the face several times. Serious bodily injury did not result from the beating, nor was Wille's life threatened by Vice. A deadly weapon was not utilized in the crime. Accordingly, this strong armed robbery is a second degree offense.

Vice's robbery of Nelson Simone, however, is a crime of the first degree. Nelson Simone watched, horrified, as Mickey Vice pointed a gun at him and stole $100. The crime didn't end there, though, as Vice pistol-whipped his victim about the head, causing Simone to be rendered unconscious. This is a first degree robbery for two reasons: a deadly weapon was used during the theft, and serious bodily injury resulted from Vice's purposeful beating.

It is important to note that Vice would be guilty of first degree robbery if he simply threatened to use a deadly weapon during the theft or if he attempted to cause serious bodily injury during the offense. "Threatened" and "attempted' are the key words here. Accordingly, had Vice never brandished a weapon but instead threatened, "I will shoot you with a gun," he still would be guilty of first degree robbery. Similarly, had Vice's violent gun-whipping merely resulted in a couple of stitches, he still could be charged with the higher graded crime. Why? Because repeatedly beating someone in the head with a pistol is a purposeful attempt to cause serious bodily injury.

## 2C:15-2. Carjacking

a. **Carjacking defined.** A person is guilty of carjacking if in the course of committing an unlawful taking of a motor vehicle, as defined in R.S.39:1-1, or in an attempt to commit an unlawful taking of a motor vehicle he

   (1) inflicts bodily injury or uses force upon an occupant or person in possession or control of a motor vehicle;

   (2) threatens an occupant or person in control with, or purposely or knowingly puts an occupant or person in control of the motor vehicle in fear of, immediate bodily injury;

   (3) commits or threatens immediately to commit any crime of the first or second degree; or

   (4) operates or causes said vehicle to be operated with the person who was in possession or control or was an occupant of the motor vehicle at the time of the taking remaining in the vehicle.

   An act shall be deemed to be "in the course of committing an unlawful taking of a motor vehicle" if it occurs during an attempt to commit the unlawful taking of a motor vehicle or during an immediate flight after the attempt or commission.

b. **Grading.** Carjacking is a crime of the first degree and upon conviction thereof a person may, notwithstanding the provisions of paragraph (1) of subsection a. of N.J.S.2C:43-6, be sentenced to an ordinary term of imprisonment between 10 and 30 years. A person convicted of carjacking shall be sentenced to a term of imprisonment and that term of imprisonment shall include the imposition of a minimum term of at least five years during which the defendant shall be ineligible for parole.

## PRACTICAL APPLICATION OF STATUTE

Mickey Vice is guilty of carjacking, a first degree crime, for his unlawful taking of Nelson Simone's BMW. But why isn't Vice guilty of just theft or robbery?

2C:15-2 elevates a theft or robbery of an automobile to carjacking if the unlawful taking of the vehicle involves one of several violent actions or threats beset upon an occupant or person in control of the vehicle. For instance, under subsection a.(1), if the thief inflicts bodily injury or uses force, the crime is carjacking. Under a.(2), if he threatens the victim with immediate bodily injury, it is a carjacking. Per a.(3), if the actor commits or threatens any first or second degree crime (e.g., aggravated assault, sexual assault, arson), he is guilty of carjacking. Finally, pursuant to a.(4), the actor is guilty of carjacking if he forces the victim to remain in the vehicle, either as driver or passenger, at the time of the unlawful taking.

Per the provisions of subsection a.(1), Mickey Vice should be convicted of carjacking. He entered Nelson Simone's BMW and stole $100 from him. Immediately thereafter, he inflicted bodily injury upon the man by beating him in the head with a pistol. Vice then pushed his victim from the BMW and fled in the vehicle. Vice's unlawful taking of Nelson Simone's automobile, coupled with his infliction of bodily injury, make him guilty of carjacking.

# 16

# BIAS CRIMES

**2C:16-1.**  **Bias intimidation**

a.  **Bias Intimidation.** A person is guilty of the crime of bias intimidation if he commits, attempts to commit, conspires with another to commit, or threatens the immediate commission of an offense specified in chapters 11 through 18 of Title 2C of the New Jersey Statutes; N.J.S.2C:33-4; N.J.S.2C:39-3; N.J.S.2C:39-4 or N.J.S.2C:39-5,

   (1)  with a purpose to intimidate an individual or group of individuals because of race, color, religion, gender, handicap, sexual orientation, or ethnicity; or

   (2)  knowing that the conduct constituting the offense would cause an individual or group of individuals to be intimidated because of race, color, religion, gender, handicap, sexual orientation, or ethnicity; or

   (3)  under circumstances that caused any victim of the underlying offense to be intimidated and the victim, considering the manner in which the offense was committed, reasonably believed either that (a) the offense was committed with a purpose to intimidate the victim or any person or entity in whose welfare the victim is interested because of race, color, religion, gender, handicap, sexual orientation, or ethnicity, or (b) the victim or the victim's property was selected to be the target of the offense because of the victim's race, color, religion, gender, handicap, sexual orientation, or ethnicity.

b.  **Permissive inference concerning selection of targeted person or property.** Proof that the target of the underlying offense was selected by the defendant, or by another acting in concert with the defendant, because of race, color, religion, gender, handicap, sexual orientation, or ethnicity shall give rise to a permissive inference by the trier of fact that the defendant acted with a purpose to intimidate an individual or group of individuals because of race, color, religion, gender, handicap, sexual orientation, or ethnicity.

c.  **Grading.** Bias intimidation is a crime of the fourth degree if the underlying offense referred to in subsection a. is a disorderly persons offense or petty disorderly persons offense. Otherwise, bias intimidation is a crime one degree higher than the most serious underlying crime referred to in subsection a., except that where the underlying crime is a crime of the first degree, bias intimidation is a first-degree crime and the defendant upon conviction thereof may, notwithstanding the provisions of paragraph (1) of subsection a. of N.J.S.2C:43-6, be sentenced to an ordinary term of imprisonment between 15 years and 30 years, with a presumptive term of 20 years.

d.  **Gender exemption in sexual offense prosecutions.** It shall not be a violation of subsection a. if the underlying criminal offense is a violation of chapter 14 of Title 2C of the New Jersey Statutes and the circumstance specified in paragraph (1), (2) or (3) of subsection a. of this section is based solely upon the gender of the victim.

e. **Merger.** Notwithstanding the provisions of N.J.S.2C:1-8 or any other provision of law, a conviction for bias intimidation shall not merge with a conviction of any of the underlying offenses referred to in subsection a. of this section, nor shall any conviction for such underlying offense merge with a conviction for bias intimidation. The court shall impose separate sentences upon a conviction for bias intimidation and a conviction of any underlying offense.

## PRACTICAL APPLICATION OF STATUTE

Mickey Vice should be charged with first degree bias intimidation for his offenses perpetrated against Horace Wille. It is Vice's personal motivation behind his criminal actions that permits a charge under 2C:16-1. It is the seriousness of his offenses against Wille that makes the bias intimidation charge one of the first degree.

The bias intimidation statute basically creates a separate and distinct crime for committing certain offenses based on a victim's race, color, religion, gender, handicap, sexual orientation, or ethnicity. Subsection a. of the statute enumerates the only underlying offenses that can give rise to a bias intimidation charge. These offenses are all those found in Chapters 11 to 18 of the code (e.g., murder, manslaughter, assault, kidnapping, criminal restraint, sexual assault, robbery, arson, criminal mischief, burglary).

If during the commission of one of the above enumerated offenses, an offender acts with a purpose to intimidate the victim based on his background (e.g., race, religion), the offender is guilty of bias intimidation. Likewise, if during the commission of one of the enumerated offenses, the offender knows his conduct would cause the victim to be intimidated because of his background, he is guilty of bias intimidation. What does all this mean? It means that a defendant's personal motivations for committing a crime, in some instances, can give rise to a separate and distinct charge of bias intimidation. In other instances, however, a defendant's personal motivations will not result in an additional charge. For example, if a victim is stabbed because he is a Mormon or a homosexual, then the offender will be charged with aggravated assault and bias intimidation. However, if the victim was stabbed because the offender lost a chess game to him, then the offender will be charged with only one crime, aggravated assault. So what about Mickey Vice? What should he be charged with for his actions beset against Horace Wille?

Mickey Vice committed a second degree robbery of Horace Wille, an American Indian. Vice stole cash from Wille and punched him in the face several times. And he told his victim that "This is payback for all the money your Indian casinos steal from us. Indians stink." Clearly, Vice committed the crime of robbery with a purpose to intimidate Wille because of his background as an American Indian. At minimum, Vice knew his conduct would cause his victim to be intimidated because of his race; Vice told him the robbery was payback for the Indian casinos. Accordingly, Mickey Vice is guilty of first degree bias intimidation as well as the second degree robbery offense. But why is this a first degree crime when the underlying offense is a second degree crime?

Subsection c. of the statute provides the grading of bias intimidation offenses. Bias intimidation is a fourth degree crime if the underlying offense is a disorderly persons offense. In all other situations, "bias intimidation is a crime one degree higher than the most serious underlying crime" committed against the victim. Since the most serious crime Vice committed upon Wille was a second degree robbery, his separate and distinct bias intimidation charge would appropriately be a first degree offense—one degree higher than the underlying second degree robbery.

## Gender Exemption

Mickey Vice should not be charged with the separate crime of bias intimidation based on the aggravated sexual assault of his estranged wife, Carrie. Subsection d. of the statute provides a gender exemption, which prohibits prosecution for bias intimidation where the underlying offense is of sexual nature and the defendant's actions are "based solely upon the gender of the victim." Given that no factor listed in 2C:16-1, other than perhaps gender, was a motivation behind Vice's rape of Carrie, he should not be charged with bias intimidation. However, he should, of course, face a charge of aggravated sexual assault.

# 17

# Arson, Criminal Mischief, and Other Property Destruction

**2C:17-1.** **Arson and related offenses**

a. **Aggravated arson.** A person is guilty of aggravated arson, a crime of the second degree, if he starts a fire or causes an explosion, whether on his own property or another's:

(1) Thereby purposely or knowingly placing another person in danger of death or bodily injury; or

(2) With the purpose of destroying a building or structure of another; or

(3) With the purpose of collecting insurance for the destruction or damage to such property under circumstances which recklessly place any other person in danger of death or bodily injury; or

(4) With the purpose of destroying or damaging a structure in order to exempt the structure, completely or partially, from the provisions of any State, county or local zoning, planning or building law, regulation, ordinance or enactment under circumstances which recklessly place any other person in danger of death or bodily injury; or

(5) With the purpose of destroying or damaging any forest.

b. **Arson.** A person is guilty of arson, a crime of the third degree, if he purposely starts a fire or causes an explosion, whether on his own property or another's:

(1) Thereby recklessly placing another person in danger of death or bodily injury; or

(2) Thereby recklessly placing a building or structure of another in danger of damage or destruction; or

(3) With the purpose of collecting insurance for the destruction or damage to such property; or

(4) With the purpose of destroying or damaging a structure in order to exempt the structure, completely or partially, from the provisions of any State, county or local zoning, planning or building law, regulation, ordinance or enactment; or

(5) Thereby recklessly placing a forest in danger of damage or destruction.

c. **Failure to control or report dangerous fire.** A person who knows that a fire is endangering life or a substantial amount of property of another and either fails to take reasonable measures to put out or control the fire, when he can do so without substantial risk to himself, or to give prompt fire alarm, commits a crime of the fourth degree if:

   (1) He knows that he is under an official, contractual, or other legal duty to prevent or combat the fire; or

   (2) The fire was started, albeit lawfully, by him or with his assent, or on property in his custody or control.

d. Any person who, directly or indirectly, pays or accepts or offers to pay or accept any form of consideration including, but not limited to, money or any other pecuniary benefit, regardless of whether any consideration is actually exchanged for the purpose of starting a fire or causing an explosion in violation of this section commits a crime of the first degree.

e. Notwithstanding the provisions of any section of this Title to the contrary, if a person is convicted of aggravated arson pursuant to the provisions of subsection a. of this section and the structure which was the target of the offense was a health care facility or a physician's office, the sentence imposed shall include a term of imprisonment. The court may not suspend or make any other noncustodial disposition of a person sentenced pursuant to the provisions of this subsection.

f. **Definitions.** "Structure" is defined in section 2C:18-1. Property is that of another, for the purpose of this section, if any one other than the actor has a possessory, or legal or equitable proprietary interest therein. Property is that of another for the purpose of this section, if anyone other than the actor has a legal or equitable interest in the property including, but not limited to, a mortgage, pledge, lien or security interest therein. If a building or structure is divided into separately occupied units, any unit not occupied by the actor is an occupied structure of another.

As used in this section, "forest" means and includes any forest, brush land, grass land, salt marsh, wooded area and any combination thereof, including but not limited to, an open space area, public lands, wetlands, park lands, natural habitats, a State conservation area, a wildlife refuge area or any other designated undeveloped open space whether or not it is subject to specific protection under law.

As used in this section, "health care facility" means health care facility as defined in section 2 of P.L.1971, c.136 (C.26:2H-2).

g. Notwithstanding the provisions of any section of this Title to the contrary, if a person is convicted pursuant to the provisions of subsection a., b. or d. of this section and the structure which was the target of the offense was a church, synagogue, temple or other place of public worship, that person commits a crime of the first degree and the sentence imposed shall include a term of imprisonment. The term of imprisonment shall include a minimum term of 15 years, during which the defendant shall be ineligible for parole. The court may not suspend or make any other noncustodial disposition of a person sentenced pursuant to the provisions of this subsection.

## PRACTICAL APPLICATION OF STATUTE

### Aggravated Arson and Arson Generally

The primary difference between aggravated arson and arson rests in the mental state of the defendant. For example, if an actor starts a fire "purposely" or "knowingly," thus placing another person in danger of death or bodily injury, he is guilty of aggravated arson, a second degree crime. However, if he starts the fire "recklessly," placing another person in danger of death or bodily injury, he is guilty of the lesser third degree crime, arson.

This "purposeful"/"knowing" differentiation from "recklessness" becomes convoluted, however, when the actor's reason for committing the fire either involves collecting insurance or avoiding zoning/building laws. For example, if an actor sets a fire in order to collect insurance on the property *and* thereby "recklessly" places another in danger of death or bodily injury, he is guilty of aggravated arson. If he starts the fire to collect insurance and no one is placed in such danger, however, then he is only guilty of arson.

Please note that aggravated arson and arson are considered to be committed in circumstances where an actor starts a fire or causes an explosion. Also, one can commit either of these offenses whether on his own property or another's property.

### Aggravated Arson—Purposely/Knowingly Placing Another in Danger

Under 2C:17-1a.(1), Mickey Vice is guilty of aggravated arson for the fire he started at his own house. Vice started this fire after he had sexually assaulted his estranged wife, Carrie. He knocked her unconscious and then poured gasoline in the home's living room, striking a match to the scene. Leaving the woman in the house as it burned to the ground, he necessarily "purposely," or at least "knowingly," placed her in danger of death or bodily injury. Accordingly, Mickey Vice is guilty of aggravated arson under subsection a.(1) of the statute.

### Aggravated Arson—Purposely Destroying a Building of Another

Subsection a.(2) provides that a person is guilty of aggravated arson if he starts a fire or causes an explosion "with the purpose of destroying a building or structure of another." Mickey Vice is guilty of aggravated arson under this subsection for the explosion he carried out at his father-in-law's multi-unit building.

Vice purposely placed and detonated dynamite at the base of the building. Over 30 homes were destroyed and numerous people suffered serious bodily injuries. Certainly, Vice's purpose in exploding the dynamite was to destroy his father-in-law's building. Therefore, he should be charged and convicted of aggravated arson for this brutal act.

### Aggravated Arson—Starting a Fire to Collect Insurance or to Avoid Zoning/Building Laws

Mickey Vice is guilty of aggravated arson under both subsections a.(3) and a.(4) for the fire he started at his own house. 2C:17-1a.(3) provides that an actor has committed aggravated arson when he starts a fire to collect insurance. 2C:17-1a.(4) makes the fire-starter guilty of aggravated arson when his purpose was to destroy the structure to have it exempt from a zoning or building law. Under both a.(3) and a.(4), the actor's fire must "recklessly" place another person in danger of death or bodily injury for the crime to be aggravated arson and not just arson.

When Vice started the fire at his house, his wife was unconscious. Not only did he leave her for dead in the burning structure, the fire spread to two adjoining row houses where people lived. In starting this fire, Vice recklessly placed his neighbors in danger of death or bodily injury, for he had to know that the fire could easily spread to the homes connected to his house—certainly any reasonable person would know this. Vice's actions rise above recklessness as he "purposely" or "knowingly" placed his wife in danger of death by starting the fire. With all this being the case, the reckless element of a.(3) and a.(4) is met. But why did Vice start the fire?

Mickey Vice told his wife that they should "burn down the house to collect insurance money and to avoid Paterson's requirement that they pay to have fire escapes erected and junk removed from the backyard." Accordingly, he is guilty of a.(3), because part of his purpose in starting the fire was to collect insurance for the destruction of the property. Likewise, he is guilty of a.(4), because he also started the fire to avoid building ordinances of erecting a fire escape and removing junk from the yard.

Vice would be guilty of third degree arson rather than second degree aggravated arson if he had started the fire for the same reasons as above (to collect insurance or to avoid zoning/building laws) and no persons were recklessly placed in danger. Under b.(3) of the statute, an actor is guilty of arson if he starts a fire to collect insurance. Under b.(4), he is guilty of arson if he starts a fire to avoid a building or zoning law.

### Arson—Recklessly Placing Another in Danger

Subsection b.(1) provides that an actor is guilty of arson if he starts a fire that "recklessly" places another in danger of death or bodily injury. Changing the facts in Mickey Vice's burning of his home can exemplify this type of arson.

Let's say Vice never argued with his wife on the day of the fire, that he never even saw her. However, ignorant of her whereabouts, he starts the fire at his house. Under these circumstances—not knowing if she was in the house—he would be recklessly placing his wife in danger of death or bodily injury. Similarly, Vice's actions would recklessly place his neighbors in danger, given the design of their homes as row houses which are connected to each other. It is quite possible that the fire would spread, which would put them in danger of death or bodily injury. Accordingly, under these circumstances, Vice would be guilty of arson under 2C:17-1b.(1).

### Arson—Recklessly Placing the Building of Another in Danger of Destruction

Vice should be charged with arson under subsection b.(2) for recklessly placing his neighbors' homes in danger of destruction. As stated above, their row houses were connected to Vice's. Given this type of structure, Vice had to reasonably know that the fire he started at his own home would likely spread to his neighbors' homes. Accordingly, he is guilty of arson under this subsection.

### Fire Placing a Forest in Danger

An actor who starts a fire to "purposely" destroy a forest is guilty of aggravated arson under subsection a.(5). If he starts a fire that "recklessly" places a forest in danger of destruction, he is guilty of arson under b.(5).

### Paying to Start a Fire

If Mickey Vice had paid another person (or been the one who was paid) to start the fire at his home, he would be guilty of a first degree offense. Under subsection d. of the statute, aggravated arson and arson are elevated to a first degree crime where money or pecuniary value is exchanged to start a fire. Both the person who pays the money and the one who accepts it are guilty per this provision. It is important to note that the money does not actually need to be exchanged for conviction hereunder; an agreement for the same simply must be in place.

### Failure to Control or Report a Dangerous Fire

Subsection c. of the statute is interesting as it is somewhat akin to a "Good Samaritan" law. As examples, the following people would be guilty of a fourth degree offense per the elements of this subsection: a fireman who does nothing while he watches a house filled with people burn to the ground even though he could have taken measures to control the fire without putting himself at substantial risk; and a police officer who does not notify the fire department of a raging building fire which likely will destroy the property. Another example: John Smith starts a controlled burn of a leaf pile in the far corner of his yard, and after an unexpected gust of wind, several burning leaves fly off the pile and onto his old tool shed, igniting the roof and quickly engulfing the entire shed. Despite having a cell phone and easy access to a garden hose, which could have easily been used to quench the smoldering leaves on the roof, he runs inside his home and watches the flames spread to the neighboring property. A final example: at a corporate Christmas party, Jim Exec lights a fire in the fireplace of his deluxe office into which he and his guests proceed to throw napkins and other combustibles. One of these napkins falls outside the hearth, starting a small fire on the Persian rug. Despite knowing that he has a fire extinguisher in his office, Jim and his guests run out to the street and watch the building burn to the ground—and don't even bother to report it.

| | |
|---|---|
| **2C:17-2.** | **Causing or risking widespread injury or damage** |

    a.   (1)  A person who, purposely or knowingly, unlawfully causes an explosion, flood, avalanche, collapse of a building, release or abandonment of poison gas, radioactive material or any other harmful or destructive substance commits a crime of the second degree. A person who, purposely or knowingly, unlawfully causes widespread injury or damage in any manner commits a crime of the second degree.

         (2)  A person who, purposely or knowingly, unlawfully causes a hazardous discharge required to be reported pursuant to the "Spill Compensation and Control Act," P.L.1976, c. 141 (C.58:10-23.11 et seq.) or any rules and regulations adopted pursuant thereto, or who, purposely or knowingly, unlawfully causes a release or abandonment of hazardous waste as defined in section 1 of P.L.1976, c.99 (C.13:1E-38) or a toxic pollutant as defined in section 3 of P.L.1977, c. 74 (C.58:10A-3) commits a crime of the second degree. Any person who recklessly violates the provisions of this paragraph is guilty of a crime of the third degree.

    b.  A person who recklessly causes widespread injury or damage is guilty of a crime of the third degree.

    c.  A person who recklessly creates a risk of widespread injury or damage commits a crime of the fourth degree, even if no such injury or damage occurs. A violation of this subsection is a crime of the third degree if the risk of widespread injury or damage results from the reckless handling or storage of hazardous materials. A violation of this subsection is a crime of the second degree if the handling or storage of hazardous materials violated any law, rule or regulation intended to protect the public health and safety.

d. A person who knowingly or recklessly fails to take reasonable measures to prevent or mitigate widespread injury or damage commits a crime of the fourth degree, if:

    (1) He knows that he is under an official, contractual or other legal duty to take such measures; or

    (2) He did or assented to the act causing or threatening the injury or damage.

e. For purposes of this section, widespread injury or damage means serious bodily injury to five or more people or damage to five or more habitations or to a building which would normally have contained 25 or more persons at the time of the offense.

## PRACTICAL APPLICATION OF STATUTE

Mickey Vice should be charged with causing widespread injury and damage under 2C:17-2a. for the dynamite blasting of his father-in-law's building. This statute provides that a person who "purposely" or "knowingly"—and unlawfully—causes disasters, such as an explosion, collapse of a building, avalanche, or flood, is guilty of a second degree offense. Per subsection e., widespread injury or damage has occurred if an actor caused serious bodily injury to five or more people or damage to five or more habitations.

Vice purposely placed dynamite at the base of his father-in-law's building. After setting it there, he detonated the explosives. Although no one was killed, 17 people suffered serious bodily injuries (broken bones, loss of eyesight) and over 30 homes were destroyed. Given this massive destruction carried out by Vice, he should be charged with a second degree crime under 2C:17-2.

It should be noted that the statute sets forth lower degree crimes where a less culpable mental state is involved and where damage does not actually occur. For example, under subsection b., if the defendant "recklessly" causes widespread injury or damage, he is guilty of a third degree offense. Under subsection c., if he "recklessly" creates a *risk* of widespread injury or damage, he is guilty of a fourth degree crime even if no such injury or damage occurs.

**2C:17-3.**    **Criminal mischief**

a. **Offense defined.** A person is guilty of criminal mischief if he:

    (1) Purposely or knowingly damages tangible property of another or damages tangible property of another recklessly or negligently in the employment of fire, explosives or other dangerous means listed in subsection a. of N.J.S.2C:17-2; or

    (2) Purposely, knowingly or recklessly tampers with tangible property of another so as to endanger person or property.

b. **Grading.**

    (1) Criminal mischief is a crime of the third degree if the actor purposely or knowingly causes pecuniary loss of $2,000.00 or more, or a substantial interruption or impairment of public communication, transportation, supply of water, gas or power, or other public service.

    (2) Criminal mischief is a crime of the fourth degree if the actor causes pecuniary loss in excess of $500.00. It is a disorderly persons offense if the actor causes pecuniary loss of $500.00 or less.

    (3) Criminal mischief is a crime of the third degree if the actor damages, defaces, eradicates, alters, receives, releases or causes the loss of any research property used by

the research facility, or otherwise causes physical disruption to the functioning of the research facility. The term "physical disruption" does not include any lawful activity that results from public, governmental, or research facility employee reaction to the disclosure of information about the research facility.

    (4) Criminal mischief is a crime of the fourth degree if the actor damages, removes or impairs the operation of any device, including, but not limited to, a sign, signal, light or other equipment, which serves to regulate or ensure the safety of air traffic at any airport, landing field, landing strip, heliport, helistop or any other aviation facility; however, if the damage, removal or impediment of the device recklessly causes bodily injury or damage to property, the actor is guilty of a crime of the third degree, or if it recklessly causes a death, the actor is guilty of a crime of the second degree.

    (5) Criminal mischief is a crime of the fourth degree if the actor interferes or tampers with any airport, landing field, landing strip, heliport, helistop or any other aviation facility; however if the interference or tampering with the airport, landing field, landing strip, heliport, helistop or other aviation facility recklessly causes bodily injury or damage to property, the actor is guilty of a crime of the third degree, or if it recklessly causes a death, the actor is guilty of a crime of the second degree.

    (6) Criminal mischief is a crime of the third degree if the actor tampers with a grave, crypt, mausoleum or other site where human remains are stored or interred, with the purpose to desecrate, destroy or steal such human remains or any part thereof.

c.  A person convicted of an offense of criminal mischief that involves an act of graffiti may, in addition to any other penalty imposed by the court, be required to pay to the owner of the damaged property monetary restitution in the amount of the pecuniary damage caused by the act of graffiti and to perform community service, which shall include removing the graffiti from the property, if appropriate. If community service is ordered, it shall be for either not less than 20 days or not less than the number of days necessary to remove the graffiti from the property.

d.  As used in this section:

    (1) "Act of graffiti" means the drawing, painting or making of any mark or inscription on public or private real or personal property without the permission of the owner.

    (2) "Spray paint" means any paint or pigmented substance that is in an aerosol or similar spray container.

## PRACTICAL APPLICATION OF STATUTE

### Criminal Mischief

Criminal mischief can be a third degree offense, fourth degree offense, or a disorderly persons offense. The seriousness of the charge primarily depends upon the monetary loss a defendant causes to property that he damages. Losses of $2,000 or more mean the defendant is guilty of a third degree crime. Losses in excess of $500 but less than $2,000 make the defendant susceptible to a fourth degree crime. If the defendant causes damage that results in a pecuniary loss of $500 or less, he is guilty of only a disorderly persons offense.

    Mickey Vice is guilty of two counts of criminal mischief. First, after Vice failed to hot-wire an automobile, he repeatedly kicked its doors and smashed in all its windows. For this damage, he should be charged with fourth degree criminal mischief as the total losses were $1,550—in excess of $500 but less than $2,000. Vice should also be convicted of a disorderly persons offense of criminal mischief for the spray-painting he did in the women's bathroom at the nuclear power plant. The costs to remedy the graffiti would likely be under $500, and therefore the charge would appropriately be a disorderly persons offense.

### Third or Fourth Degree Criminal Mischief Automatic for Specific Types of Damage

It is interesting to note that specific types of damages will automatically render a third or fourth degree charge regardless of the monetary loss. These specific damages are itemized in subsections b.(1) through b.(6). For instance, under subsection b.(1), a person is guilty of third degree criminal mischief if he purposely or knowingly causes a substantial interruption of public services such as gas, water, or transportation. Under b.(6), a third degree offense is committed in circumstances where damage is purposely caused to places where human remains are kept (e.g., grave, crypt, mausoleum).

---

**2C:17-3.1.**     **Traffic sign, signal damage, removal, violation**

A person who purposely, knowingly, recklessly or negligently defaces, injures or removes an official traffic sign or signal described in Title 39 of the Revised Statutes is guilty of a disorderly persons offense.

If a juvenile who is adjudicated delinquent for an act which, if committed by an adult, would constitute a violation of this section is assessed a fine and the court determines that the juvenile is unable to pay the fine, the juvenile's parents or legal guardian shall be responsible for the imposed fine.

### PRACTICAL APPLICATION OF STATUTE

---

An example of an offense under 2C:17-3.1 would be Mickey Vice "purposely" ripping down a stop sign. Another example is if, "for kicks," he climbed up a traffic light and while swinging on the light, he "recklessly" causes it to snap and crash to the ground. Both of these acts are disorderly persons offenses per 2C:17-3.1.

---

**2C:17-4,**     **Repealed**
**2C:17-5.**

**2C:17-6.**     **Motor vehicles; removal or alteration of identification number or mark; possession; penalty**

    a. A person who removes, defaces, alters, changes, destroys, covers or obliterates any trademark, distinguishing or identification number, serial number or mark on or from any motor vehicle for an unlawful purpose, is guilty of a crime of the third degree.

    b. A person who for an unlawful purpose knowingly possesses any motor vehicle, or any of the parts thereof, from or on which any trademark, distinguishing or identification number, or serial number or mark has been removed, covered, altered, changed, defaced, destroyed or obliterated, is guilty of an offense, unless, within 10 days after the motor vehicle or any part thereof shall have come into his possession, he files with the Director of the Division of Motor Vehicles in the Department of Law and Public Safety a verified statement showing: the source of his title, the proper trademark, identification or distinguishing number, or serial number or mark, if known, and if known, the manner of and reason for the mutilation, change, alteration, concealment or defacement, the length of time the motor vehicle or part has been held and the price paid therefor.

    If the value of the motor vehicle or parts possessed exceeds $500.00 the offense is a crime of the third degree; if the value is at least $200.00 but does not exceed $500.00 it is a crime of the fourth degree; if the value is less than $200.00 it is a disorderly persons offense.

c.  As used in this section, "motor vehicle" includes motor bicycles, motorcycles, automobiles, trucks, tractors or other vehicles designed to be self-propelled by mechanical power, and otherwise than by muscular power, except motor vehicles running upon or guided by rails or tracks.

## PRACTICAL APPLICATION OF STATUTE

For removing the vehicle identification number of an automobile he attempted to steal, Mickey Vice is guilty of a third degree offense. Simply, 2C:17-6a. provides that any person who removes or defaces any trademark or serial number from a motor vehicle, for an unlawful purpose, is guilty of a third degree crime. Vice removed the vehicle identification number for the unlawful purpose of hiding the automobile's identity after he stole it. Accordingly, he is guilty of this third degree crime.

**2C:17-7.**        **Tampering, damage involving nuclear electric generating plant; crime of first degree**

The provisions of N.J.S.2C:17-2 to the contrary notwithstanding, any person who purposely or knowingly damages or tampers with any machinery, device, or equipment at a nuclear electric generating plant with the purpose to cause or threaten to cause an unauthorized release of radiation commits a crime of the first degree, and may be sentenced to an extended term of imprisonment as set forth in paragraph (2) of subsection a. of N.J.S.2C:43-7, notwithstanding the provisions of N.J.S. 2C:44-3; provided, however, that if the defendant is not sentenced to an extended term of imprisonment, the defendant shall be sentenced to an ordinary term of imprisonment between 15 and 30 years.

## PRACTICAL APPLICATION OF STATUTE

Mickey Vice has violated the provisions of 2C:17-7 for his attempt to release radiation during his melee at the nuclear power plant. The charge is valid even though no radiation was actually released.

    2C:17-7 provides that any person who purposely or knowingly damages machinery at a nuclear generating plant, with the intent to release radiation, is guilty of a first degree crime. Mickey Vice shot at power plant employees and threw a stick of dynamite into nuclear generating machinery, hoping to release radiation. Accordingly, even though he failed in his attempt, Vice is guilty of a 2C:17-7 first degree offense.

**2C:17-8.**     **Nuclear electric generating plant; damaging or tampering with equipment which results in death; crime of first degree**

Any person who purposely or knowingly damages or tampers with any machinery, device, or equipment at a nuclear electric generating plant which results in the death of another due to exposure to radiation commits a crime of the first degree, and may be sentenced to an extended term of imprisonment as set forth in paragraph (2) of subsection a. of N.J.S. 2C:43-7, notwithstanding the provisions of N.J.S. 2C:44-3.

## PRACTICAL APPLICATION OF STATUTE

If Mickey Vice had succeeded in his quest to release radiation and death had resulted from his damage, then he would be guilty of a first degree crime per 2C:17-8.

**2C:17-9.**     **Nuclear electric generating plant; damaging or tampering with equipment which results in injury; crime of second degree**

Any person who purposely or knowingly damages or tampers with any machinery, device, or equipment at a nuclear electric generating plant which results in the injury of another due to exposure to radiation commits a crime of the second degree, and may be sentenced to an extended term of imprisonment as set forth in paragraph (3) of subsection a. of N.J.S. 2C:43-7, notwithstanding the provisions of N.J.S. 2C:44-3.

## PRACTICAL APPLICATION OF STATUTE

If Mickey Vice had succeeded in his attempt to release radiation and at least one other person was injured by his damages, then he would be guilty of a second degree crime per 2C:17-9.

# 18

# BURGLARY AND OTHER CRIMINAL INTRUSION

## FACT PATTERN (PERTAINS TO CHAPTERS 18 TO 20)

As a personal birthday present, Ignacio Marini determined to obtain a wish list of items: fifty thousand dollars in cash. A Mercedes. A gold pinky ring. A diamond earring. A moose. Two kilograms of cocaine. One pound of marijuana. A gerbil. The mechanical repair of his lawn mower. And a box of Devil Dogs. Marini determined that two days' worth of activities would net him all his desired presents.

### Day One

To carry out his goals, Marini procured a stocking from his sister's bedroom and exited his Hackensack co-op home. His first stop—a supermarket approximately six blocks from his residence. The man was hungry.

Once inside, Marini surreptitiously traveled down several of the store's aisles. He stopped when he reached the baked goods. There he quickly grabbed a box of 16 Devil Dogs and stuffed the pastry items into his coat pocket. He then exited the store with swift calculation.

Outside, Marini spotted a brand-new, white, convertible Mercedes Benz. He gave a cursory glance at his surroundings, forced a Devil Dog in his mouth, swallowed it with two bites, and then hot-wired the vehicle, which was valued at $85,000.

From the supermarket's parking lot, Marini traveled one municipality to the town of Paramus. Checking notes to himself, he arrived at a home on Century Road. At this location, he affixed a tie to his shirt, procured a briefcase, approached the door, and rang the bell. Moments later, 73-year-old Fanny Moses answered. Marini advised her that he was the township's tax collector and that he was there to collect $52,500, the amount she was overdue in her property taxes. Ms. Moses was not in any arrears in her taxes, and Marini knew this. Similarly, Marini was not the township's tax collector nor the member of any government agency. He was aware, however, that Ms. Moses suffered from Alzheimer's disease. Ms. Moses handed over a check without objection. Ignacio's next stop was two doors away at the home of Sandy Jerusalem.

At Mr. Jerusalem's residence, Marini removed his tie and placed a top hat on his head. He then banged furiously on the door until Jerusalem responded. Once the greeting was complete, Marini simply told Jerusalem, "Kindly turn over your gold pinky ring to me or I will advise the media that you regularly frequent a nudist camp in South Jersey." Jerusalem immediately removed his pinky ring, valued at $3,500, and handed it to his blackmailer.

Marini then reentered his new Mercedes and traveled north to Mahwah, where he stopped on a quiet residential street just after night fell. Placing a stocking over his head, Marini walked briskly to the street's last house. There he utilized a screwdriver to pry open a screen. Once through the open window, he went directly to the home's only juvenile room. It was empty except for a caged gerbil who was enjoying a relaxing moment on a pile of wood chips. Marini heisted the tiny animal and exited.

### Day Two

Bright and early the next morning, Marini rose from a pleasant night's sleep and immediately traveled to a Rochelle Park mechanical repair shop. Posing as a local councilman, Marini asked to have his lawn mower repaired by day's end and to have an invoice sent to his home. The shop owner agreed. Marini, of course, never paid the invoice which amounted to $165.

A shipping center in the town of Maywood was Marini's next stop. At this store, Marini maintained a box to receive mail. Waiting for him was a single letter addressed to "Ignacio B. Marini." Marini, aware that this letter was sent to him by mistake (his uncle was "Ignacio B. Marini" and he himself was "Ignacio S. Marini"), opened the letter anyway. Inside was an insurance check for $25,000. Marini expeditiously deposited the check into his personal bank account and then drove to a friend's house.

Although Marini was over 40, his closest friend was Charles Bigby, a 17-year-old high school dropout. Bigby was elated with Marini's new stolen car; his older pal, noting this, asked Bigby to come along for "some more fun."

Simply driving down the block from Bigby's house, the two arrived at a horse farm. Even though the property was marked with "No Trespassing" signs, the friends bypassed the same and jumped on two horses. They galloped off, riding the saddled animals on the city streets of Hackensack for nearly an hour. When they were finished, they tied the horses to a tree and proceeded to a late-model BMW.

Marini coaxed Bigby to hot-wire the automobile and to thereafter meet him at Mickey's Auto Body Shop in East Rutherford. Bigby agreed, and 30 minutes later they were each paid $10,000 by Mickey Morabito, an unassuming man in his sixties who ran an intricate auto theft ring. Under his control were over 50 men who routinely stole automobiles for payment. Morabito, in turn, would either resell the automobiles for a huge profit or chop them up for parts and then sell them.

Before Marini and Bigby left Morabito's headquarters, they ducked into the conference room. There, Marini enlisted Bigby to assist him in carrying two heavy boxes, one box containing nearly a pound of marijuana and the other two kilograms of cocaine. They avoided detection by Morabito and his employees, jumped into a pickup truck owned by a regular shop customer, and fled. Laughing raucously as they counted their money and drugs, Marini ran stop lights and drove at excessive speeds. They sideswiped two parked automobiles and then finally arrived back at the horse farm, about 15 minutes after leaving Morabito's.

Once again posing as a Rochelle Park councilman, Marini presented the owner of the horse farm with a handshake and the promise to make four payments of $1,000. The future payments were supposed to be in exchange for a prize moose which the horse farm held on its premises. Per their agreement, Marini was required to make the four payments of $1,000 on the first of the month for four consecutive months. The moose was then loaded onto the pickup truck. Of course, no payments were ever delivered.

Tired by the day's events and late for supper, Bigby asked to be taken home. Marini complied, driving his young friend to his doorstep. Before Marini could depart, however, Bigby presented him with his birthday gift: a brand-new, 32-inch color television set valued at $1,000. Bigby told his mentor, "It's a little hot, but I chiseled off the serial numbers. Enjoy." Marini thanked his best friend and then departed.

Driving with both the moose and television set, Marini decided to make his final stop at BB's Home of Appliances. Upon entering the establishment, he was immediately greeted by Franz Bellenwood. The two sipped espresso as Marini explained that he had a $750 television set with the serial numbers removed. Bellenwood directed Marini to follow normal business procedure and bring the set around back.

Moments later, the two men met at the rear of the building. Marini then followed Bellenwood to the basement where he placed the television set next to hundreds of other appliances and electronic equipment with similarly defaced serial numbers. In exchange for the TV, Bellenwood supplied Marini with a half-carat diamond earring.

Satisfied that all his birthday gifts had been received, Marini asked Bellenwood to join him for a celebratory dinner. Bellenwood consented and prepared to lock up his basement of goods. All of a sudden, however, a battalion of Hackensack police officers and investigators from the Bergen County Prosecutor's Office entered the room armed with arrest warrants. Marini shared a glass of tap water and a bologna sandwich with Bellenwood as the birthday celebration was carried out in the Bergen County Jail.

## 2C:18-1.    Definition

In this chapter, unless a different meaning plainly is required, "structure" means any building, room, ship, vessel, car, vehicle or airplane, and also means any place adapted for overnight accommodation of persons, or for carrying on business therein, whether or not a person is actually present.

## 2C:18-2.    Burglary

a. **Burglary defined.** A person is guilty of burglary if, with purpose to commit an offense therein he

   (1) Enters a research facility, structure, or a separately secured or occupied portion thereof unless the structure was at the time open to the public or the actor is licensed or privileged to enter; or

   (2) Surreptitiously remains in a research facility, structure, or a separately secured or occupied portion thereof knowing that he is not licensed or privileged to do so.

b. **Grading.** Burglary is a crime of the second degree if in the course of committing the offense, the actor:

   (1) Purposely, knowingly or recklessly inflicts, attempts to inflict or threatens to inflict bodily injury on anyone; or

   (2) Is armed with or displays what appear to be explosives or a deadly weapon.

Otherwise burglary is a crime of the third degree. An act shall be deemed "in the course of committing" an offense if it occurs in an attempt to commit an offense or in immediate flight after the attempt or commission.

## PRACTICAL APPLICATION OF STATUTE

Burglary is an offense primarily predicated upon two basic elements: entering a structure with a purpose to commit an offense once inside it. The offense inside, however, need not actually be committed; an attempt is sufficient for conviction under this statute. Ignacio Marini is guilty of burglary for his break-in and gerbil theft at the Mahwah home.

Marini planned to obtain a gerbil as one of his birthday presents. In order to accomplish this goal, he used a screwdriver to pry open a screen and illegally enter the home in Mahwah. His purpose in entering this home was to commit the offense of theft, the theft of the gerbil. Accordingly, Marini is guilty of burglary, which is a third degree offense in this case.

Marini's aforementioned burglary is a third degree crime because he neither injured another during the offense nor was armed with a deadly weapon. In burglaries where a defendant inflicts (or threatens to inflict) bodily injury or is armed with a deadly weapon, the defendant is guilty of second degree burglary.

**2C:18-3.**    **Unlicensed entry of structures; defiant trespasser; peering into dwelling places; defenses**

a. **Unlicensed entry of structures.** A person commits an offense if, knowing that he is not licensed or privileged to do so, he enters or surreptitiously remains in any research facility structure, or separately secured or occupied portion thereof. An offense under this subsection is a crime of the fourth degree if it is committed in a school or on school property. The offense is a crime of the fourth degree if it is committed in a dwelling. An offense under this section is a crime of the fourth degree if it is committed in a research facility. Otherwise it is a disorderly persons offense.

b. **Defiant trespasser.** A person commits a petty disorderly persons offense if, knowing that he is not licensed or privileged to do so, he enters or remains in any place as to which notice against trespass is given by:

   (1) Actual communication to the actor; or

   (2) Posting in a manner prescribed by law or reasonably likely to come to the attention of intruders; or

   (3) Fencing or other enclosure manifestly designed to exclude intruders.

c. **Peering into windows or other openings of dwelling places.** A person commits a crime of the fourth degree if, knowing that he is not licensed or privileged to do so, he peers into a window or other opening of a dwelling or other structure adapted for overnight accommodation for the purpose of invading the privacy of another person and under circumstances in which a reasonable person in the dwelling or other structure would not expect to be observed.

d. **Defenses.** It is an affirmative defense to prosecution under this section that:

   (1) A structure involved in an offense under subsection a. was abandoned;

   (2) The structure was at the time open to members of the public and the actor complied with all lawful conditions imposed on access to or remaining in the structure; or

(3) The actor reasonably believed that the owner of the structure, or other person empowered to license access thereto, would have licensed him to enter or remain, or, in the case of subsection c. of this section, to peer.

## PRACTICAL APPLICATION OF STATUTE

### Unlicensed Entry of Structures

If Marini had no intent to steal the gerbil or commit any other crime in the Mahwah home he entered, then he would be guilty of fourth degree trespassing rather than burglary. 2C:18-3a. sets forth the elements that make it illegal to enter a structure without license or privilege to do so. Key to this offense is the mental state of "knowledge": the actor must know that he has no right to enter the structure. Criminal trespass is a fourth degree crime if the structure entered is a dwelling, school, or research facility. Otherwise, it is a disorderly persons offense.

Marini entered the house in Mahwah. He did so by prying open a window and climbing through the vacated space. He obviously knew he was not licensed to enter this dwelling. Accordingly, had he just remained in the house and watched television (and never stole the gerbil or committed any other crime), then he would only be guilty of fourth degree trespassing.

### Defiant Trespass

Per the provisions of 2C:18-3b., Marini and his friend Charles Bigby are guilty of the petty disorderly persons offense of defiant trespass. This is due to their entry onto the horse farm in face of the posted "No Trespassing" signs.

Defiant trespass covers the many different types of property not enumerated in subsection a. of the statute. A person commits this offense if he enters any property where "notice against trespass is given." Notice can be afforded through actual communication or a posting that is clear. Individuals intending to enter property should also regard fencing (or other similar closures) as notice not to trespass.

The horse farm was clearly marked with "No Trespassing" signs. Marini and Bigby saw the signs, ignored them, and entered the property. Accordingly, they are guilty of defiant trespass, one of the lowest graded offenses under the code as it is a petty disorderly persons offense. Their horse thefts, of course, make them guilty of separate, more serious offenses.

### Peering into Windows

Simply, one who peers into the windows (or other openings) of a dwelling without permission of the occupants is guilty of a fourth degree crime. Two elements, however, must be present for a conviction: the peering is "for the purpose of invading privacy" and a "reasonable person in the dwelling would not expect to be observed."

An example of this crime is the typical Peeping Tom. Linda is undressing in her bedroom. Tom climbs a ladder and peeks through the curtains. Tom is guilty of a fourth degree offense under 2C:18-3c.

## Defenses

It is important to note that the criminal trespass statute provides specific affirmative defenses to the offenses defined therein. If a structure such as a dwelling or research facility was abandoned at the time of entry, the abandonment is an affirmative defense. Likewise, if the structure was open to members of the public at the time of entry and the actor was not required to leave by any law, then he has an affirmative defense to trespass. Finally, if the actor reasonably believed that he was licensed to enter the property, then he cannot be convicted of an offense under this statute.

**2C:18-4.**    **Lands defined**

As used in this act, "lands" means agricultural or horticultural lands devoted to the production for sale of plants and animals useful to man, encompassing plowed or tilled fields, standing crops or their residues, cranberry bogs and appurtenant dams, dikes, canals, ditches and pump houses, including impoundments, man-made reservoirs and the adjacent shorelines thereto, orchards, nurseries, and lands with a maintained fence for the purpose of restraining domestic livestock. "Lands" shall also include lands in agricultural use, as defined in section 3 of P.L. 1983, c. 32 (C. 4:1C-13), where public notice prohibiting trespass is given by actual communication to the actor, conspicuous posting, or fencing or other enclosure manifestly designed to exclude intruders.

**2C:18-5.**    **Knowingly or recklessly operating motor vehicle or riding horseback on lands of another without written permission, or damaging or injuring tangible property**

It is an offense under this act to:
  a. Knowingly or recklessly operate a motorized vehicle or to ride horseback upon the lands of another without obtaining and in possession of the written permission of the owner, occupant, or lessee thereof.
  b. Knowingly or recklessly damage or injure any tangible property, including, but not limited to, any fence, building, feedstocks, crops, live trees, or any domestic animals, located on the lands of another.

## PRACTICAL APPLICATION OF STATUTE

### Operating Motor Vehicle/Riding Horseback on Another's Property

2C:18-5 is an interesting statute, as it is rarely invoked and because it only states that an "offense" is committed upon its violation. The law is broken where an individual "knowingly" or "recklessly" operates a motor vehicle or rides horseback on another's property without proper permission. The offense should be deemed a petty disorderly persons offense, but no such classification is actually provided in the statute. It is important to note, though, that per 2C:43-1, "an offense declared to be a crime, without specification of degree, is of the fourth degree." Given that there is no language in 2C:18-5 declaring the offense a crime, the presumption should be in favor of the defendant that the offense is of the lowest grade—a petty disorderly persons offense.

## Damaging Tangible Property

Under subsection b. of this statute, an individual can be convicted of a third degree crime, fourth degree crime, or disorderly persons offense for causing damage to tangible property such as buildings, homes, crops, domestic animals, and live trees. The difference among the gradation of offenses is defined in the subsequent statute, 2C:18-6, and depends upon the monetary amount of damage caused by the defendant. If there is a pecuniary loss of $2,000 or more, a third degree crime has been committed. A fourth degree crime has occurred if damages are between $500 and $2,000. And the defendant is guilty of a disorderly persons offense if he causes monetary loss of $500 or less.

This statute is remarkably similar to criminal mischief as set forth in 2C:17-3. A minor difference appears to be in the language "knowingly or *recklessly*" damaging the tangible property of another. Criminal mischief has a subsection that allows for a conviction with a "reckless" mental state, but it requires that the actor damage the tangible property "so as to endanger person or property." The statute here has no such requirement: Simply damaging tangible property through reckless behavior renders a person guilty.

---

**2C:18-6.**      ### Offenses; penalties; restitution

    a. An offense pursuant to section 2 of this act is a crime of the third degree if the actor causes pecuniary loss of $2,000.00 or more; a crime of the fourth degree if the actor causes pecuniary loss in excess of $500.00 but less than $2,000.00; and a disorderly persons offense if he causes pecuniary loss of $500.00 or less.

    b. The provisions of N.J.S. 2C:43-3 to the contrary notwithstanding, in addition to any other sentence which the court may impose, a person convicted of an offense under this act shall be sentenced to make restitution, and to pay a fine of not less than $500.00 if the offense is a crime of the third degree; to pay a fine of not less than $200.00 if the offense is a crime of the fourth degree; and to pay a fine of not less than $100.00 when the conviction is of a disorderly persons offense.

### Chapter 19—Reenacted as Chapter 15 of Title 2C by P.L. 1979, c.178

# 20

# THEFT AND RELATED OFFENSES

## I. GENERAL PROVISIONS

**2C:20-1.**    **Definitions**

In chapters 20 and 21, unless a different meaning plainly is required:

a. "Deprive" means: (1) to withhold or cause to be withheld property of another permanently or for so extended a period as to appropriate a substantial portion of its economic value, or with purpose to restore only upon payment of reward or other compensation; or (2) to dispose or cause disposal of the property so as to make it unlikely that the owner will recover it.

b. "Fiduciary" means an executor, general administrator of an intestate, administrator with the will annexed, substituted administrator, guardian, substituted guardian, trustee under any trust, express, implied, resulting or constructive, substituted trustee, executor, conservator, curator, receiver, trustee in bankruptcy, assignee for the benefit of creditors, partner, agent or officer of a corporation, public or private, temporary administrator, administrator, administrator pendente lite, administrator ad prosequendum, administrator ad litem or other person acting in a similar capacity.

c. "Financial institution" means a bank, insurance company, credit union, savings and loan association, investment trust or other organization held out to the public as a place of deposit of funds or medium of savings or collective investment.

d. "Government" means the United States, any state, county, municipality, or other political unit, or any department, agency or subdivision of any of the foregoing, or any corporation or other association carrying out the functions of government.

e. "Movable property" means property the location of which can be changed, including things growing on, affixed to, or found in land, and documents, although the rights represented thereby have no physical location. "Immovable property" is all other property.

f. "Obtain" means: (1) in relation to property, to bring about a transfer or purported transfer of a legal interest in the property, whether to the obtainer or another; or (2) in relation to labor or service, to secure performance thereof.

g. "Property" means anything of value, including real estate, tangible and intangible personal property, trade secrets, contract rights, choses in action and other interests in or claims to wealth, admission or transportation tickets, captured or domestic animals, food and drink, electric, gas, steam or other power, financial instruments, information, data, and computer software, in either human readable or computer readable form, copies or originals.

h. "Property of another" includes property in which any person other than the actor has an interest which the actor is not privileged to infringe, regardless of the fact that the actor also has an interest in the property and regardless of the fact that the other person might be precluded from civil recovery because the property was used in an unlawful transaction or was subject to forfeiture as contraband. Property in possession of the actor shall not be deemed property of another who has only a security interest therein, even if legal title is in the creditor pursuant to a conditional sales contract or other security agreement.

i. "Trade secret" means the whole or any portion or phase of any scientific or technical information, design, process, procedure, formula or improvement which is secret and of value. A trade secret shall be presumed to be secret when the owner thereof takes measures to prevent it from becoming available to persons other than those selected by the owner to have access thereto for limited purposes.

j. "Dealer in property" means a person who buys and sells property as a business.

k. "Traffic" means:

(1) To sell, transfer, distribute, dispense or otherwise dispose of property to another person; or

(2) To buy, receive, possess, or obtain control of or use property, with intent to sell, transfer, distribute, dispense or otherwise dispose of such property to another person.

l. "Broken succession of title" means lack of regular documents of purchase and transfer by any seller except the manufacturer of the subject property, or possession of documents of purchase and transfer by any buyer without corresponding documents of sale and transfer in possession of seller, or possession of documents of sale and transfer by seller without corresponding documents of purchase and transfer in possession of any buyer.

m. "Person" includes any individual or entity or enterprise, as defined herein, holding or capable of holding a legal or beneficial interest in property.

n. "Anything of value" means any direct or indirect gain or advantage to any person.

o. "Interest in property which has been stolen" means title or right of possession to such property.

p. "Stolen property" means property that has been the subject of any unlawful taking.

q. "Enterprise" includes any individual, sole proprietorship, partnership, corporation, business trust, association, or other legal entity, and any union or group of individuals associated in fact, although not a legal entity, and it includes illicit as well as licit enterprises and governmental as well as other entities.

r. "Attorney General" includes the Attorney General of New Jersey, his assistants and deputies. The term shall also include a county prosecutor or his designated assistant prosecutor, if a county prosecutor is expressly authorized in writing by the Attorney General to carry out the powers conferred on the Attorney General by this chapter.

s. "Access device" means property consisting of any telephone calling card number, credit card number, account number, mobile identification number, electronic serial number, personal identification number, or any other data intended to control or limit access to telecommunications or other computer networks in either human readable or computer readable form, either copy or original, that can be used to obtain telephone service.

t. "Defaced access device" means any access device, in either human readable or computer readable form, either copy or original, which has been removed, erased, defaced, altered, destroyed, covered or otherwise changed in any manner from its original configuration.

u. "Domestic companion animal" means any animal commonly referred to as a pet or one that has been bought, bred, raised or otherwise acquired, in accordance with local ordinances and State and federal law for the primary purpose of providing companionship to the owner, rather than for business or agricultural purposes.

    v. "Personal identifying information" means any name, number or other information that may be used, alone or in conjunction with any other information, to identify a specific individual and includes, but is not limited to, the name, address, telephone number, date of birth, social security number, official State issued identification number, employer or taxpayer number, place of employment, employee identification number, demand deposit account number, savings account number, credit card number, mother's maiden name, unique biometric data, such as fingerprint, voice print, retina or iris image or other unique physical representation, or unique electronic identification number, address or routing code of the individual.

**2C:20-1.1.**    **Offense involving access device; presumption of unlawful purpose**

In any prosecution for an offense enumerated in chapter 20 of Title 2C of the New Jersey Statutes involving a defaced access device, any removal, erasure, defacement, alteration, destruction, covering or other change in such access device from its original configuration performed by any person other than an authorized manufacturer of, or service provider to access devices shall be presumed to be for an unlawful purpose.

**2C:20-2.**    **Consolidation of theft offenses; grading; provisions applicable to theft generally**

    a. Consolidation of Theft and Computer Criminal Activity Offenses. Conduct denominated theft or computer criminal activity in this chapter constitutes a single offense, but each episode or transaction may be the subject of a separate prosecution and conviction. A charge of theft or computer criminal activity may be supported by evidence that it was committed in any manner that would be theft or computer criminal activity under this chapter, notwithstanding the specification of a different manner in the indictment or accusation, subject only to the power of the court to ensure fair trial by granting a bill of particulars, discovery, a continuance, or other appropriate relief where the conduct of the defense would be prejudiced by lack of fair notice or by surprise.

    b. Grading of theft offenses.

        (1) Theft constitutes a crime of the second degree if:

            (a) The amount involved is $75,000.00 or more;

            (b) The property is taken by extortion;

            (c) The property stolen is a controlled dangerous substance or controlled substance analog as defined in N.J.S.2C:35-2 and the quantity is in excess of one kilogram;

            (d) The property stolen is a person's benefits under federal or State law, or from any other source, which the Department of Human Services or an agency acting on its behalf has budgeted for the person's health care and the amount involved is $75,000 or more; or

            (e) The property stolen is human remains or any part thereof.

        (2) Theft constitutes a crime of the third degree if:

            (a) The amount involved exceeds $500.00 but is less than $75,000.00;

            (b) The property stolen is a firearm, motor vehicle, vessel, boat, horse, domestic companion animal or airplane;

            (c) The property stolen is a controlled dangerous substance or controlled substance analog as defined in N.J.S.2C:35-2 and the amount involved is less than $75,000.00 or is undetermined and the quantity is one kilogram or less;

            (d) It is from the person of the victim;

    (e)  It is in breach of an obligation by a person in his capacity as a fiduciary;

    (f)  It is by threat not amounting to extortion;

    (g)  It is of a public record, writing or instrument kept, filed or deposited according to law with or in the keeping of any public office or public servant;

    (h)  The property stolen is a person's benefits under federal or State law, or from any other source, which the Department of Human Services or an agency acting on its behalf has budgeted for the person's health care and the amount involved is less than $75,000;

    (i)  The property stolen is any real or personal property related to, necessary for, or derived from research, regardless of value, including, but not limited to, any sample, specimens and components thereof, research subject, including any warm-blooded or cold-blooded animals being used for research or intended for use in research, supplies, records, data or test results, prototypes or equipment, as well as any proprietary information or other type of information related to research;

    (j)  The property stolen is a New Jersey Prescription Blank as referred to in R.S.45:14-14; or

    (k)  The property stolen consists of an access device or a defaced access device.

  (3)  Theft constitutes a crime of the fourth degree if the amount involved is at least $200.00 but does not exceed $500.00. If the amount involved was less than $200.00 the offense constitutes a disorderly persons offense.

  (4)  The amount involved in a theft shall be determined by the trier of fact. The amount shall include, but shall not be limited to, the amount of any State tax avoided, evaded or otherwise unpaid, improperly retained or disposed of. Amounts involved in thefts committed pursuant to one scheme or course of conduct, whether from the same person or several persons, may be aggregated in determining the grade of the offense.

c.  Claim of right. It is an affirmative defense to prosecution for theft that the actor:

  (1)  Was unaware that the property or service was that of another;

  (2)  Acted under an honest claim of right to the property or service involved or that he had a right to acquire or dispose of it as he did;

  (3)  Took property exposed for sale, intending to purchase and pay for it promptly, or reasonably believing that the owner, if present, would have consented.

d.  Theft from spouse. It is no defense that theft or computer criminal activity was from or committed against the actor's spouse, except that misappropriation of household and personal effects, or other property normally accessible to both spouses, is theft or computer criminal activity only if it occurs after the parties have ceased living together.

## PRACTICAL APPLICATION OF STATUTE

### Grading of Theft Offenses

Theft can be a second, third, or fourth degree crime, as well as a disorderly persons offense. The grading differences are primarily determined by the pecuniary loss suffered, but also may be the consequence of other substantive matters.

An individual who commits a theft involving a pecuniary loss of $75,000 or more is guilty of second degree theft. Similarly, if the property is taken by extortion or if a person steals over one kilogram of a controlled dangerous substance (CDS), he is guilty of a second degree crime. The theft of human remains is also a crime of the second degree.

Third degree thefts include the theft of firearms, motor vehicles, boats, airplanes, dogs, cats, and other domestic companion animals. Thefts from the person (purse snatching), CDSs under a kilogram in weight, and blank prescriptions are also third degree crimes. If the amount involved in any theft exceeds $500, but is less than $75,000, a crime of the third degree has been committed.

A fourth degree theft has occurred when the amount involved is between $200 and $500. It is a disorderly persons offense when an actor has stolen matter with a value less than $200. Particular types of theft offenses will be discussed in detail in the practical application sections following each category in this chapter (e.g., theft by deception, theft of services).

**2C:20-2.1.**          **Additional penalties for theft or unlawful taking of motor vehicle**

a. In addition to any other disposition authorized by law, a person convicted under the provisions of this chapter of theft or unlawful taking of a motor vehicle shall be subject

  (1) For the first offense, to a penalty of $500.00 and to the suspension or postponement of the person's license to operate a motor vehicle over the highways of this State for a period of one year.

  (2) For a second offense, to a penalty of $750.00 and to the suspension or postponement of the person's license to operate a motor vehicle over the highways of this State for a period of two years.

  (3) For a third or subsequent offense, to a penalty of $1,000.00, and to the suspension or postponement of the person's license to operate a motor vehicle over the highways of this State for 10 years.

b. The suspension or postponement of the person's license to operate a motor vehicle pursuant to subsection a. of this section shall commence on the day the sentence is imposed. In the case of any person who at the time of the imposition of sentence is less than 17 years of age, the period of the suspension of driving privileges authorized herein, including a suspension of the privilege of operating a motorized bicycle, shall commence on the day the sentence is imposed and shall run for a period as fixed by the court of one year for a first offense, two years for a second offense or 10 years for a third offense calculated from the day after the day the person reaches the age of 17 years. If the driving privilege of any person is under revocation, suspension, or postponement for a violation of any provision of this Title or Title 39 of the Revised Statutes at the time of any conviction or adjudication of delinquency for a violation of any offense defined in this chapter or chapter 36 of this Title, the revocation, suspension, or postponement period imposed herein shall commence as of the date of termination of the existing revocation, suspension, or postponement.

Upon conviction the court shall collect forthwith the New Jersey driver's licenses of the person and forward such license or licenses to the Director of the Division of Motor Vehicles along with a report indicating the first and last day of the suspension or postponement period imposed by the court pursuant to this section. If the court is for any reason unable to collect the license or licenses of the person, the court shall cause a report of the conviction or adjudication of delinquency to be filed with the director. That report shall include the complete name, address, date of birth, eye color, and sex of the person and shall indicate the first and last day of the suspension or postponement period imposed by the court pursuant to this section. The court shall inform the person orally and in writing that if the person is convicted of personally operating a motor vehicle during the period of license suspension or postponement imposed pursuant to this section the person shall, upon conviction, be subject to the penalties set forth in R.S.39:3-40. A person shall be required to acknowledge receipt of the written notice in writing. Failure to receive a written notice or failure to acknowledge in writing the receipt of a written notice shall not be a defense to a subsequent charge of a violation of R.S.39:3-40. If the person is the holder of a driver's license from another jurisdiction, the court shall not collect the license but shall notify the director who shall notify the appropriate officials in the licensing jurisdiction. The court shall, however, in accordance with the provisions of this section, revoke the person's non-resident driving privileges in this State.

c. All penalties provided for in this section shall be collected as provided for the collection of fines and restitutions in section 3 of P.L.1979, c. 396 (C.2C:46-4), and shall be distributed in accordance with the provisions of N.J.S.2C:64-6 as if the collected monies were the proceeds of property forfeited pursuant to the provisions of chapter 64. However, the distributed monies are to be used for law enforcement activities related to auto theft.

## 2C:20-2.2.    Additional fine for auto theft

Notwithstanding the provisions of N.J.S.2C:43-3, if the fair market value of the automobile and its contents at the time it was stolen exceeds $7,500.00 and the automobile is not recovered, the court may sentence the defendant to pay a fine for that higher amount.

## 2C:20-3.    Theft by unlawful taking or disposition

a. **Movable property.** A person is guilty of theft if he unlawfully takes, or exercises unlawful control over, movable property of another with purpose to deprive him thereof.

b. **Immovable property.** A person is guilty of theft if he unlawfully transfers any interest in immovable property of another with purpose to benefit himself or another not entitled thereto.

### PRACTICAL APPLICATION OF STATUTE

#### Movable Property

Ignacio Marini's theft of the convertible Mercedes is a theft of movable property by unlawful taking. This theft would normally be a third degree crime, as thefts of motor vehicles automatically are graded as third degree offenses. However, it is a second degree offense here because the value of the automobile exceeds $75,000. (The Mercedes was worth $85,000 at the time it was unlawfully taken.)

Other movable property stolen by Marini included two kilograms of cocaine, a pound of marijuana, and the gerbil. The theft of the cocaine is a second degree offense because it is a CDS that exceeds one kilogram in weight. The marijuana heist is a crime of the third degree because its weight is less than one kilogram. The gerbil theft is also a third degree theft, as a gerbil is a domestic companion animal.

Under all of the above circumstances, Marini is guilty of theft by unlawful taking under 2C:20-3a. This is because he unlawfully heisted the movable property with the purpose to deprive the owner of it.

#### Immovable Property

Thefts of immovable property include the transfer of health benefits and titles in real estate property. The seriousness of the offense depends upon the amount of pecuniary loss involved in the theft.

**2C:20-4.**    **Theft by deception**

A person is guilty of theft if he purposely obtains property of another by deception. A person deceives if he purposely:

a. Creates or reinforces a false impression, including false impressions as to law, value, intention or other state of mind, and including, but not limited to, a false impression that the person is soliciting or collecting funds for a charitable purpose; but deception as to a person's intention to perform a promise shall not be inferred from the fact alone that he did not subsequently perform the promise;

b. Prevents another from acquiring information which would affect his judgment of a transaction; or

c. Fails to correct a false impression which the deceiver previously created or reinforced, or which the deceiver knows to be influencing another to whom he stands in a fiduciary or confidential relationship.

The term "deceive" does not, however, include falsity as to matters having no pecuniary significance, or puffing or exaggeration by statements unlikely to deceive ordinary persons in the group addressed.

## PRACTICAL APPLICATION OF STATUTE

For his theft of a $52,500 check from Alzheimer's sufferer Fanny Moses, Marini should be charged with theft by deception. This is a crime of the third degree because the pecuniary loss involved exceeds $500 but is less than $75,000.

Theft by deception in its simplest sense involves deceiving another in order to obtain items of value. Under subsection a., an actor deceives if he "creates or reinforces a false impression." Under subsection b., he deceives if he "prevents another from acquiring information which would affect his judgment of a transaction." Finally, per subsection c., a deception has occurred if the con man "fails to correct a false impression" that he previously created or if he knows that the false impression is "influencing another to whom he stands in a fiduciary or confidential duty."

Marini's guilt lies in deceptive behavior best defined in subsection a. Posing as the Paramus tax collector, Marini advised 73-year-old Fanny Moses that she was $52,500 in arrears in her property taxes. Marini created a false impression as to his identity, for he was actually not the town's tax collector. And he created a false impression as to Ms. Moses's property taxes—she was not in any arrears. Marini's ultimate receipt of Moses's $52,500 check, therefore, constitutes a theft by deception.

The fact that Ms. Moses suffered from Alzheimer's disease only makes his crime that much more egregious. And it negates any defense that his statements would be unlikely to deceive an ordinary person in her situation.

**2C:20-5.**    **Theft by extortion**

A person is guilty of theft by extortion if he purposely and unlawfully obtains property of another by extortion. A person extorts if he purposely threatens to:

a. Inflict bodily injury on or physically confine or restrain anyone or commit any other criminal offense;

b. Accuse anyone of an offense or cause charges of an offense to be instituted against any person;

c. Expose or publicize any secret or any asserted fact, whether true or false, tending to subject any person to hatred, contempt or ridicule, or to impair his credit or business repute;

d. Take or withhold action as an official, or cause an official to take or withhold action;

e. Bring about or continue a strike, boycott or other collective action, if the property is not demanded or received for the benefit of the group in whose interest the actor purports to act;

f. Testify or provide information or withhold testimony or information with respect to another's legal claim or defense; or

g. Inflict any other harm which would not substantially benefit the actor but which is calculated to materially harm another person.

It is an affirmative defense to prosecution based on paragraphs b, c, d or f that the property obtained was honestly claimed as restitution or indemnification for harm done in the circumstances or as lawful compensation for property or services.

## PRACTICAL APPLICATION OF STATUTE

Sandy Jerusalem is the victim of a theft by extortion arising out of Ignacio Marini's taking of his gold pinky ring. This theft is automatically a second degree crime, regardless of the pecuniary value of the ring, because it was stolen through extortion measures.

In order to be guilty of theft by extortion, the defendant's actions must be "purposeful." A defendant extorts if he purposely threatens to inflict bodily injury, accuses another of a criminal offense, or exposes a secret that would subject another to hatred, contempt, or ridicule.

Marini appeared at Sandy Jerusalem's home with the intent to steal his gold pinky ring, one of the items Marini determined to obtain as a birthday present for himself. Marini told Jerusalem, "Kindly turn over your gold pinky ring to me or I will advise the media that you regularly frequent a nudist camp in South Jersey." Jerusalem then, in turn, handed over the ring. Marini's purposeful threat certainly would expose a secret that would subject Jerusalem to public contempt and ridicule. Accordingly, this is a theft by extortion, and even though the value of the ring was only $3,500, it is a second degree offense.

## 2C:20-6. Theft of property lost, mislaid, or delivered by mistake

A person who comes into control of property of another that he knows to have been lost, mislaid, or delivered under a mistake as to the nature or amount of the property or the identity of the recipient is guilty of theft if, knowing the identity of the owner and with purpose to deprive said owner thereof, he converts the property to his own use.

## PRACTICAL APPLICATION OF STATUTE

The correct charge for Marini's depositing of his uncle's insurance check is under 2C:20-6, as he took control of a check that was delivered to him by mistake. This is a third degree crime because the amount of the check was $25,000—in excess of $500 but less than $75,000.

This statute makes the taking of property illegal where the actor knows that the property was lost, mislaid, or delivered by mistake *and* where he knows the identity of the owner. Also, the actor must convert the property to his own use with the "purpose" to deprive the owner of it.

A $25,000 insurance check was delivered to Marini by mistake. The true recipient of the check was supposed to be Marini's uncle and he knew this. With the purpose to deprive his uncle of the proceeds of the check, Marini deposited the funds into his personal bank account. Accordingly, he is guilty of theft under 2C:20-6.

**2C:20-7.**          **Receiving stolen property**

a. **Receiving.** A person is guilty of theft if he knowingly receives or brings into this State movable property of another knowing that it has been stolen, or believing that it is probably stolen. It is an affirmative defense that the property was received with purpose to restore it to the owner. "Receiving" means acquiring possession, control or title, or lending on the security of the property.

b. **Presumption of knowledge.** The requisite knowledge or belief is presumed in the case of a person who:

(1)  Is found in possession or control of two or more items of property stolen on two or more separate occasions; or

(2)  Has received stolen property in another transaction within the year preceding the transaction charged; or

(3)  Being a person in the business of buying or selling property of the sort received, acquires the property without having ascertained by reasonable inquiry that the person from whom he obtained it had a legal right to possess and dispose of it; or

(4)  Is found in possession of two or more defaced access devices.

## PRACTICAL APPLICATION OF STATUTE

### Generally

Ignacio Marini should be convicted of theft under 2C:20-7 for his receipt of a television set that he knew to be stolen. Since the television set's value was more than $500, but less than $75,000, this is a third degree crime.

A person is guilty of receiving stolen property if "he knowingly receives or brings into this State movable property of another knowing that it has been stolen, or believing that it is probably stolen." Marini's best friend, Charles Bigby, gave him a brand-new 32-inch color television set, valued at $1,000, as a birthday present. Bigby told Marini, "It's a little hot, but I chiseled off the serial numbers. Enjoy." Marini knowingly received the television set, which he knew was stolen. This being the case, he is guilty of receiving stolen property, a third degree theft offense given the TV's $1,000 value.

### Presumption of Knowledge

It is important to note that the receiving stolen property statute provides that there is a "presumption of knowledge" (that the property is stolen) under certain circumstances. Per subsection b. of the statute, a person is "presumed" to know—or believe that an item is probably stolen—in four scenarios.

An example where knowledge of stolen property is presumed is as follows: Mark the Manipulator is in the pawnbroker business. He regularly buys items of jewelry, television sets, stereo systems, and home appliances. Jerry, a man who Mark knows to be a drug addict, stops by his store with a diamond ring. Mark neither asks Jerry for proof of ownership of the ring (i.e., a receipt or warranty) nor asks where he obtained the ring. Mark simply buys the ring from Jerry. The ring turns out to be stolen.

2C:20-7b.(3) provides that knowledge or belief is presumed in the case of a person who, "being a person in the business of buying or selling property of the sort received, acquires the property without having ascertained by reasonable inquiry that the person from whom he obtained it had a legal right to possess or dispose of it." Mark was in the business of buying diamond rings. When Jerry attempted to sell the diamond ring to him, Mark did not make any reasonable inquiry into whether Jerry had a legal right to possess or dispose of the ring. Accordingly, per subsection b.(3), Mark may be "presumed" to have knowledge that the diamond ring was stolen.

---

**2C:20-7.1.**        **Fencing**

   a. **Possession of altered property.** Any dealer in property who knew or should have known that the identifying features such as serial numbers and permanently affixed labels of property in his possession have been removed or altered without the consent of the manufacturer is guilty of possession of altered property. It is a defense to a prosecution under this subsection that a person lawfully possesses the usual indicia of ownership in addition to mere possession.

   b. **Dealing in stolen property.** A person is guilty of dealing in stolen property if he traffics in, or initiates, organizes, plans, finances, directs, manages or supervises trafficking in stolen property.

   c. The value of the property involved in the violation of this section shall be determined by the trier of fact. The value of the property involved in the violation of this section may be aggregated in determining the grade of the offense where the acts or conduct constituting a violation were committed pursuant to one scheme or course of conduct, whether from the same person or several persons.

   d. It is an affirmative defense to a prosecution under this section that the actor:

      (1) Was unaware that the property or service was that of another;

      (2) Acted under an honest claim of right to the property or service involved or that he had a right to acquire or dispose of it as he did.

   e. In addition to the presumptions contained in N.J.S. 2C:20-7b. the following presumptions are available in the prosecution for a fencing offense:

      (1) Proof of the purchase or sale of property at a price substantially below its fair market value, unless satisfactorily explained, gives rise to an inference that the person buying or selling the property knew that it had been stolen;

      (2) Proof of the purchase or sale of property by a dealer in that property, out of the regular course of business, or without the usual indicia of ownership other than mere possession, or the property or the job lot of which it is a part was bought, received, possessed or controlled in broken succession of title, so that it cannot be traced, by appropriate documents, in unbroken succession to the manufacturer,

in all cases where the regular course of business reasonably indicates records of purchase, transfer or sale, unless satisfactorily explained, gives rise to an inference that the person buying or selling the property knew that it had been stolen; and

(3) Proof that a person buying or selling property of the sort received obtained such property without having ascertained by reasonable inquiry that the person from whom he obtained it had a legal right to possess or control it gives rise to an inference that such person knew that it had been stolen.

## PRACTICAL APPLICATION OF STATUTE

Franz Bellenwood, Ignacio Marini's intended fence for his stolen television set, is guilty of a third degree crime as the value of the TV was $1,000. Bellenwood's guilt is predicated upon his personal knowledge that the television was stolen; however, knowledge could be imputed to him, under 2C:20-7.1, for a variety of reasons.

The fencing statute differs from receiving stolen property in that it specifically prohibits criminal behavior involving "dealers," individuals who sell property for a living. Subsection a. of the statute makes it illegal for a dealer to possess property which he "knew or should have known" has identifying features (such as serial numbers) that have been altered. Subsection b., the more serious component of the statute, sets forth the elements that make a dealer guilty of "dealing" in stolen property. If he "traffics in, or initiates, organizes, plans, finances, directs, manages or supervises trafficking in stolen property," he has violated subsection b. of the fencing statute.

Bellenwood is guilty of fencing under subsection b. of the statute. Marini met Bellenwood at his place of business. He explained to Bellenwood that the TV had defaced serial numbers and that he wished to sell it to him. Bellenwood responded by bringing Marini to the business's basement where numerous stolen appliances with defaced serial numbers were stored. There the television set was exchanged for a half-carat diamond earring. Given that Bellenwood obviously engaged in a business of dealing in stolen property, he is guilty of a third degree crime under 2C:20-7.1b.

Law enforcement officers charging under 2C:20-7.1 should take note that subsection e. of the statute provides the prosecution with several "presumptions of knowledge" that the items in question were stolen. For example, e.(1) provides that if property is either purchased or sold at a price "substantially below its fair market value," there is a presumption that the dealer knew the property was stolen. This presumption of knowledge exists unless the dealer can "satisfactorily explain" the low purchase cost or sale price. While these presumptions should certainly be taken into consideration by law enforcement personnel investigating individuals and charging pursuant to the statute, the ultimate determination of "knowledge" is a legal question and will be determined by the trier of fact—a jury or judge.

**2C:20-8.**     **Theft of services**

    a. A person is guilty of theft if he purposely obtains services which he knows are available only for compensation, by deception or threat, or by false token, slug, or other means, including but not limited to mechanical or electronic devices or through fraudulent statements, to avoid payment for the service. "Services" include labor or professional service; transportation, telephone, telecommunications, electric, water, gas, cable television, or other public service; accommodation in hotels, restaurants or elsewhere; entertainment; admission to exhibitions; use of vehicles or other movable property. Where compensation for service is ordinarily paid immediately upon the rendering of such service, as in the case of hotels and restaurants, absconding without payment or offer to pay gives rise to a presumption that the service was obtained by deception as to intention to pay.

b. A person commits theft if, having control over the disposition of services of another, to which he is not entitled, he knowingly diverts such services to his own benefit or to the benefit of another not entitled thereto.

c. Any person who, without permission and for the purpose of obtaining electric current, gas or water with intent to defraud any vendor of electricity, gas or water or a person who is furnished by a vendor with electric current, gas or water:

(1) Connects or causes to be connected by wire or any other device with the wires, cables or conductors of any such vendor or any other person; or

(2) Connects or disconnects the meters, pipes or conduits of such vendor or any other person or in any other manner tampers or interferes with such meters, pipes or conduits, or connects with such meters, pipes or conduits by pipes, conduits or other instruments—is guilty of a disorderly persons offense.

The existence of any of the conditions with reference to meters, pipes, conduits or attachments, described in this subsection, is presumptive evidence that the person to whom gas, electricity or water is at the time being furnished by or through such meters, pipes, conduits or attachments has, with intent to defraud, created or caused to be created with reference to such meters, pipes, conduits or attachments, the condition so existing; provided, however, that the presumption shall not apply to any person so furnished with gas, electricity or water for less than 31 days or until there has been at least one meter reading.

A violation of this subsection shall be deemed to be a continuing offense as long as the conditions described in this subsection exist.

d. Any person who, without permission or authority, connects or causes to be connected by wires or other devices, any meter erected or set up for the purpose of registering or recording the amount of electric current supplied to any customer by any vendor of electricity within this State, or changes or shunts the wiring leading to or from any such meter, or by any device, appliance or means whatsoever tampers with any such meter so that the meter will not measure or record the full amount of electric current supplied to such customer, is guilty of a disorderly persons offense.

The existence of any of the conditions with reference to meters or attachments described in this subsection is presumptive evidence that the person to whom electricity is at the time being furnished by or through such meters or attachments has, with intent to defraud, created or caused to be created with reference to such meters or attachments, the condition so existing; provided, however, that the presumption shall not apply to any person so furnished with electricity for less than 31 days or until there has been at least one meter reading.

A violation of this subsection shall be deemed to be a continuing offense as long as the conditions described in this subsection exist.

e. Any person who, with intent to obtain cable television service without payment, in whole or in part, of the lawful charges therefor, or with intent to deprive another of the lawful receipt of such service, damages, cuts, tampers with, installs, taps or makes any connection with, or who displaces, removes, injures or destroys any wire, cable, conduit, apparatus or equipment of a cable television company operating a CATV system; or who, without authority of a cable television company, intentionally prevents, obstructs or delays, by any means or contrivance, the sending, transmission, conveyance, distribution or receipt of programming material carried by equipment of the cable television company operating a CATV system, is a disorderly person.

The existence of any of the conditions with reference to wires, cables, conduits, apparatus or equipment described in this subsection is presumptive evidence that the person to whom cable television service is at the time being furnished has, with intent to obtain cable television service without authorization or compensation or to otherwise defraud, created or caused to be created the condition so existing.

f. Any person who purposely or knowingly manufactures, constructs, sells, offers for sale, distributes or installs any equipment, device or instrument designed or intended to facilitate the interception, decoding or receipt of any cable television service with intent to obtain such service and avoid the lawful payment of the charges therefor to the provider, in whole or in part, is a disorderly person.

Any communications paraphernalia prohibited under this subsection shall be subject to forfeiture and may be seized by the State or any law enforcement officer in accordance with the provisions of N.J.S.2C:64-1 et seq.

g. Any person who purposely or knowingly maintains or possesses any equipment, device or instrument of the type described in subsection f. of this section or maintains or possesses any equipment, device or instrument actually used to facilitate the interception, decoding or receipt of any cable television service with intent to obtain such service and avoid the lawful payment, in whole or in part, of the charges therefor to the provider, is a disorderly person.

Any communications paraphernalia prohibited under this subsection shall be subject to forfeiture and may be seized by the State or any law enforcement officer in accordance with the provisions of N.J.S.2C:64-1 et seq.

h. Any person who, with the intent of depriving a telephone company of its lawful charges therefor, purposely or knowingly makes use of any telecommunications service by means of the unauthorized use of any electronic or mechanical device or connection, or by the unauthorized use of billing information, or by the use of a computer, computer equipment or computer software, or by the use of misidentifying or misleading information given to a representative of the telephone company is guilty of a crime of the third degree.

The existence of any of the conditions with reference to electronic or mechanical devices, computers, computer equipment or computer software described in this subsection is presumptive evidence that the person to whom telecommunications service is at the time being furnished has, with intent to obtain telecommunications service without authorization or compensation or to otherwise defraud, created or caused to be created the condition so existing.

i. Any person who purposely or knowingly manufactures, constructs, sells, offers for sale, distributes, installs, or otherwise provides any service, equipment, device, computer, computer equipment, computer software or instrument designed or intended to facilitate the receipt of any telecommunications service and avoid the lawful payment of the charges therefor to the provider, in whole or in part, is guilty of a crime of the third degree.

Any communications paraphernalia, computer, computer equipment or computer software prohibited under this subsection shall be subject to forfeiture and may be seized by the State or any law enforcement officer in accordance with the provisions of N.J.S. 2C:64-1 et seq.

j. Any person who purposely or knowingly maintains or possesses any equipment, device, computer, computer equipment, computer software or instrument of the type described in subsection i. of this section, or maintains or possesses any equipment, device, computer, computer equipment, computer software or instrument actually used to facilitate the receipt of any telecommunications service with intent to obtain such service and avoid the lawful payment, in whole or in part, of the charges therefor to the provider, is guilty of a crime of the third degree.

Any communications paraphernalia, computer, computer equipment or computer software prohibited under this subsection shall be subject to forfeiture and may be seized by the State or any law enforcement officer in accordance with the provisions of N.J.S. 2C:64-1 et seq.

k. In addition to any other disposition authorized by law, and notwithstanding the provisions of N.J.S. 2C:43-3, every person who violates this section shall be sentenced to make restitution to the vendor and to pay a minimum fine of $500.00 for each offense. In determining the amount of restitution, the court shall consider the costs expended by the vendor, including but not limited to the repair and replacement of damaged equipment, the cost of the services unlawfully obtained, investigation expenses, and attorney fees.

l. The presumptions of evidence applicable to offenses defined in subsections c., d., e. and h. of this section shall also apply in any prosecution for theft of services brought pursuant to the provisions of subsection a. or b. of this section.

## PRACTICAL APPLICATION OF STATUTE

The appropriate charge for Ignacio Marini's trickery with the lawn mower repair shop owner is theft of services. Given that the total owed but never recovered was $165, this theft constitutes a disorderly persons offense.

Although 2C:20-8 is a statute containing considerable language, it primarily provides that a person is guilty of theft of services if he fraudulently dupes another to provide labor or services with no intention to pay for said services. Basically, any services stolen through deception will result in a conviction under this statute. However, many items are specifically enumerated, including professional services (e.g., lawyers, doctors), transportation, telecommunications, restaurants, hotels, and entertainment. Subsections c., d., e., f., g., h., i., j. set forth special provisions for thefts involving gas, electric, cable television, and telecommunication services.

Marini didn't rip off any large private corporation or government agency in order to obtain repairs to his lawn mower. He did, however, defraud a small business owner. Posing as a Rochelle Park councilman, Marini asked to have his lawn mower repaired and to thereafter have an invoice sent to his home. Marini, of course, was neither a Rochelle Park councilman nor did he ever intend to pay the bill. Accordingly, because he deceived the business owner, causing him to provide services that were never paid for, Marini is guilty of theft of services.

**2C:20-9.**     **Theft by failure to make required disposition of property received**

A person who purposely obtains or retains property upon agreement or subject to a known legal obligation to make specified payment or other disposition, whether from such property or its proceeds or from his own property to be reserved in equivalent amount, is guilty of theft if he deals with the property obtained as his own and fails to make the required payment or disposition. The foregoing applies notwithstanding that it may be impossible to identify particular property as belonging to the victim at the time of the actor's failure to make the required payment or disposition. An officer or employee of the government or of a financial institution is presumed: (a) to know any legal obligation relevant to his criminal liability under this section, and (b) to have dealt with the property as his own if he fails to pay or account upon lawful demand, or if an audit reveals a shortage or falsification of accounts. The fact that any payment or other disposition was made with a subsequently dishonored negotiable instrument shall constitute prima facie evidence of the actor's failure to make the required payment or disposition, and the trier of fact may draw a permissive inference therefrom that the actor did not intend to make the required payment or other disposition.

## Practical Application of Statute

Theft by failure to make required disposition is predicated upon the mental state of "purpose." One who "purposely" obtains or retains property upon a known agreement to make payment (a disposition) is guilty of theft under this statute if he maintains the property as his own and fails to make said disposition. Marini is guilty of theft per the elements of 2C:20-9 for his taking of the prize moose from the farm owner.

Marini and the owner of the horse farm shook hands on a deal that required Marini to make four payments of $1,000 in exchange for the prize moose. The farm owner delivered on his promise and provided Marini the moose. Marini took the moose, never intending to make the required payments for the animal. Given that he "purposely" obtained this property, the prize moose, upon a known agreement to make a disposition (four payments of $1,000) and thereafter retained the moose without ever making the payments, he is guilty of theft under 2C:20-9. This is a third degree crime, as the amount of money involved exceeds $500 but is less than $75,000.

**2C:20-10.**     **Unlawful taking of means of conveyance**

a. A person commits a disorderly persons offense if, with purpose to withhold temporarily from the owner, he takes, operates, or exercises control over any means of conveyance, other than a motor vehicle, without consent of the owner or other person authorized to give consent. "Means of conveyance" includes but is not limited to motor vehicles, bicycles, motorized bicycles, boats, horses, vessels, surfboards, rafts, skimobiles, airplanes, trains, trams and trailers. It is an affirmative defense to prosecution under subsections a., b. and c. of this section that the actor reasonably believed that the owner or any other person authorized to give consent would have consented to the operation had he known of it.

b. A person commits a crime of the fourth degree if, with purpose to withhold temporarily from the owner, he takes, operates or exercises control over a motor vehicle without the consent of the owner or other person authorized to give consent.

c. A person commits a crime of the third degree if, with purpose to withhold temporarily from the owner, he takes, operates or exercises control over a motor vehicle without the consent of the owner or other person authorized to give consent and operates the motor vehicle in a manner that creates a risk of injury to any person or a risk of damage to property.

d. A person commits a crime of the fourth degree if he enters and rides in a motor vehicle knowing that the motor vehicle has been taken or is being operated without the consent of the owner or other person authorized to consent.

## PRACTICAL APPLICATION OF STATUTE

### Theft of Means of Conveyance

Ignacio Marini is guilty of the third degree crime of unlawful taking of a means of conveyance for his taking of the pickup truck from Mickey's Auto Body Shop. This is not considered a normal auto theft given the "temporary" taking of the motor vehicle. In Marini's case, the crime reaches the third degree level only because he drove the automobile in a manner that created a "risk of injury" to others.

Pursuant to subsection c. of 2C:20-10, a person who purposely "temporarily" withholds or operates another's motor vehicle without consent is guilty of a third degree crime if he operates the vehicle "in a manner that creates a risk of injury to any person or a risk of damage to property." After stealing cocaine and marijuana from Mickey Morabito, Marini and Bigby drove away in a pickup truck owned by one of Mickey's customers. They did not have the owner's consent to drive the vehicle. Laughing raucously as they counted their heisted money and drugs, Marini ran stop signs and drove at excessive speeds. During this rampage, he even sideswiped two parked cars. The siege of the truck, though, lasted merely 15 minutes.

Here, all elements of the offense have been met. The pickup truck was only heisted "temporarily" (15 minutes), but it was taken without the owner's consent. In addition, Marini's driving clearly put other people at risk of injury and he actually caused property damage. Accordingly, he is guilty of a third degree crime under 2C:20-10c.

It is interesting to note that under subsection b. of the statute, had Marini not driven in a "risky" manner, he would only be guilty of a fourth degree crime. Also per subsection a., if he had taken a means of conveyance other than a motor vehicle (e.g., a bike or horse), he would be guilty of only a disorderly persons offense.

### Knowingly Riding in Motor Vehicle That Is Being Operated Without Owner's Consent

Per subsection d. of 2C:20-10, an individual is guilty of a fourth degree crime if he "knowingly" rides in a motor vehicle that is being operated without the owner's consent. Given that Bigby "knew" that he and Marini were driving in the pickup truck without the owner's consent, he is guilty of this fourth degree offense.

**2C:20-11.** **Shoplifting**

a. Definitions. The following definitions apply to this section:

(1) "Shopping cart" means those push carts of the type or types which are commonly provided by grocery stores, drug stores or other retail mercantile establishments for the

use of the public in transporting commodities in stores and markets and, incidentally, from the stores to a place outside the store;

(2) "Store or other retail mercantile establishment" means a place where merchandise is displayed, held, stored or sold or offered to the public for sale;

(3) "Merchandise" means any goods, chattels, foodstuffs or wares of any type and description, regardless of the value thereof;

(4) "Merchant" means any owner or operator of any store or other retail mercantile establishment, or any agent, servant, employee, lessee, consignee, officer, director, franchisee or independent contractor of such owner or proprietor;

(5) "Person" means any individual or individuals, including an agent, servant or employee of a merchant where the facts of the situation so require;

(6) "Conceal" means to conceal merchandise so that, although there may be some notice of its presence, it is not visible through ordinary observation;

(7) "Full retail value" means the merchant's stated or advertised price of the merchandise;

(8) "Premises of a store or retail mercantile establishment" means and includes but is not limited to, the retail mercantile establishment; any common use areas in shopping centers and all parking areas set aside by a merchant or on behalf of a merchant for the parking of vehicles for the convenience of the patrons of such retail mercantile establishment;

(9) "Under-ring" means to cause the cash register or other sale recording device to reflect less than the full retail value of the merchandise;

(10) "Antishoplifting or inventory control device countermeasure" means any item or device which is designed, manufactured, modified, or altered to defeat any antishoplifting or inventory control device.

b. Shoplifting. Shoplifting shall consist of any one or more of the following acts:

(1) For any person purposely to take possession of, carry away, transfer or cause to be carried away or transferred, any merchandise displayed, held, stored or offered for sale by any store or other retail mercantile establishment with the intention of depriving the merchant of the possession, use or benefit of such merchandise or converting the same to the use of such person without paying to the merchant the full retail value thereof.

(2) For any person purposely to conceal upon his person or otherwise any merchandise offered for sale by any store or other retail mercantile establishment with the intention of depriving the merchant of the processes, use or benefit of such merchandise or converting the same to the use of such person without paying to the merchant the value thereof.

(3) For any person purposely to alter, transfer or remove any label, price tag or marking indicia of value or any other markings which aid in determining value affixed to any merchandise displayed, held, stored or offered for sale by any store or other retail mercantile establishment and to attempt to purchase such merchandise personally or in consort with another at less than the full retail value with the intention of depriving the merchant of all or some part of the value thereof.

(4) For any person purposely to transfer any merchandise displayed, held, stored or offered for sale by any store or other retail merchandise establishment from the container in or on which the same shall be displayed to any other container with intent to deprive the merchant of all or some part of the retail value thereof.

(5) For any person purposely to under-ring with the intention of depriving the merchant of the full retail value thereof.

(6) For any person purposely to remove a shopping cart from the premises of a store or other retail mercantile establishment without the consent of the merchant given at the time of such removal with the intention of permanently depriving the merchant of the possession, use or benefit of such cart.

c. Gradation.

(1) Shoplifting constitutes a crime of the second degree under subsection b. of this section if the full retail value of the merchandise is $75,000.00 or more.

(2) Shoplifting constitutes a crime of the third degree under subsection b. of this section if the full retail value of the merchandise exceeds $500.00 but is less than $75,000.00.

(3) Shoplifting constitutes a crime of the fourth degree under subsection b. of this section if the full retail value of the merchandise is at least $200.00 but does not exceed $500.00

(4) Shoplifting is a disorderly persons offense under subsection b. of this section if the full retail value of the merchandise is less than $200.00. Additionally, notwithstanding the term of imprisonment provided in N.J.S.2C:43-6 or 2C:43-8, any person convicted of a shoplifting offense shall be sentenced to perform community service as follows: for a first offense, at least ten days of community service; for a second offense, at least 15 days of community service; and for a third or subsequent offense, a maximum of 25 days of community service and any person convicted of a third or subsequent shoplifting offense shall serve a minimum term of imprisonment of not less than 90 days.

d. Presumptions. Any person purposely concealing unpurchased merchandise of any store or other retail mercantile establishment, either on the premises or outside the premises of such store or other retail mercantile establishment, shall be prima facie presumed to have so concealed such merchandise with the intention of depriving the merchant of the possession, use or benefit of such merchandise without paying the full retail value thereof, and the finding of such merchandise concealed upon the person or among the belongings of such person shall be prima facie evidence of purposeful concealment; and if such person conceals, or causes to be concealed, such merchandise upon the person or among the belongings of another, the finding of the same shall also be prima facie evidence of willful concealment on the part of the person so concealing such merchandise.

e. A law enforcement officer, or a special officer, or a merchant, who has probable cause for believing that a person has willfully concealed unpurchased merchandise and that he can recover the merchandise by taking the person into custody, may, for the purpose of attempting to effect recovery thereof, take the person into custody and detain him in a reasonable manner for not more than a reasonable time, and the taking into custody by a law enforcement officer or special officer or merchant shall not render such person criminally or civilly liable in any manner or to any extent whatsoever.

Any law enforcement officer may arrest without warrant any person he has probable cause for believing has committed the offense of shoplifting as defined in this section.

A merchant who causes the arrest of a person for shoplifting, as provided for in this section, shall not be criminally or civilly liable in any manner or to any extent whatsoever where the merchant has probable cause for believing that the person arrested committed the offense of shoplifting.

f. Any person who possesses or uses any antishoplifting or inventory control device countermeasure within any store or other retail mercantile establishment is guilty of a disorderly persons offense.

## PRACTICAL APPLICATION OF STATUTE

### Shoplifting

Shoplifting isn't just stealing candy, batteries, and T-shirts. The offense actually ranges from a disorderly persons offense all the way to a second degree crime. This range depends upon the amount of monetary loss involved in the theft. In the case of Ignacio Marini, however, he is only guilty of the lowest level shoplifting offense as he merely took a box of Devil Dogs from his local supermarket.

Subsection b. of the statute enumerates the different types of acts that constitute shoplifting. They include the following: taking/carrying away merchandise offered for sale (b.(1)); concealing merchandise (b.(2)); altering price tags (b.(3)); transferring merchandise from one container to another (b.(4)); under-ringing at the register (b.(5)); and removing a shopping cart from a store (b.(6)). All forms of shoplifting require that the thief act "purposely."

Marini could appropriately be charged with shoplifting under b.(1) or b.(2) for his theft of the Devil Dogs. After entering his local supermarket, Marini proceeded to the store's aisle that contained baked goods. There he grabbed a box of Devil Dogs and stuffed them in his coat pocket. He then exited the store without paying for the items.

Marini "purposely" took possession of the Devil Dogs and carried them away from the store. His intent was obviously to deprive the merchant of possession of these items without paying for the same. Accordingly, he could be charged with shoplifting under b.(1) of the statute. Likewise, Marini could be charged under b.(2) as he "purposely" concealed the merchandise upon his person. Since he did this in an effort to deprive the supermarket of the benefit of the items and did not pay for them, he could be convicted per this subsection. So which subsection should Marini be charged under? Really, either fits. However, b.(1) is probably the better choice as b.(2) is more geared toward situations where thieves get caught (i.e., he concealed the box in his clothes but never actually made it out of the store).

### Grading

Subsection c. of the statute sets forth the requirements for grading shoplifting offenses. Basically, they fall under the same parameters as other theft offenses. If the full retail value of the item(s) stolen is $75,000 or more, a second degree crime has been committed. Shoplifting constitutes a third degree crime if the value exceeds $500 but is less than $75,000. It is a fourth degree crime where the value of the merchandise is between $200 and $500. A disorderly persons offense is committed if the merchandise is worth less than $200. Marini's shoplifting offense is just this, as the Devil Dogs' full retail value was well under $200.

### Detaining Shoplifting Suspects

Pursuant to the provisions of subsection e., a law enforcement officer, special officer, or a merchant may detain a shoplifting suspect upon having probable cause to believe that the suspect has "willfully concealed unpurchased merchandise." Also, the detainer must believe that "he can recover the merchandise by taking the person into custody."

It is crucial to note that the above referenced custody must be performed in a "reasonable manner" and can occur for "not more than a reasonable time." If the tenets of this subsection are handled "reasonably" and with probable cause, then any officer or merchant effectuating such a detention cannot be held criminally or civilly liable for his conduct. But one should be careful, because what is considered a "reasonable manner" of detention and a "reasonable time" of detention are matters to be interpreted by the courts.

### Possessing/Using Antishoplifting Countermeasure—Disorderly Persons Offense

As provided in subsection f., one who possesses or uses any "antishoplifting or inventory control device countermeasure" within any store is guilty of a disorderly persons offense. What is such an item? Subsection a. of the statute, which provides definitions pertaining to special terms contained in it, doesn't do much to define this phrase. However, examples of "antishoplifting or inventory control device countermeasures" are devices that change bar codes and devices that de-magnetize magnetic antishoplifting strips. Given that their purpose is to defeat antishoplifting devices, their possession and/or use (within a store) is a disorderly persons offense.

---

**2C:20-11.1.        Guidelines for prosecution of shoplifting offenses**

The Attorney General shall develop, no later than the 120th day after the effective date of this act, guidelines to ensure that the prosecution of shoplifting offenses is conducted in a uniform manner throughout the State.

**2C:20-12.        Definitions for sections 2-4**

The following definitions apply to sections 2 through 4 of this act as they relate to the theft of library material:

  a. "Library material" means any material, regardless of physical form or characteristics, or any part thereof, belonging to, on loan to, or otherwise in the custody of a library facility;

  b. "Library facility" means any public library, any library of an educational, historical, or charitable institution, organization or society, or any museum.

**2C:20-13.        Concealment of material**

Any person who purposely conceals, on or off the premises of the library facility, upon his person or among his belongings, or upon the person or among the belongings of another, any library material shall be prima facie presumed to have concealed the material for the purpose of depriving the library facility of its use or benefit.

**2C:20-14.        Detention on probable cause**

  a. A law enforcement officer, a special officer, or an employee of a library facility who has probable cause for believing that a person has willfully concealed library material and that he can recover the material by taking the person into custody, may, for the purpose of attempting to recover the material, take the person into custody and detain him in a reasonable manner for a reasonable time. Taking the person into custody shall not render the law enforcement officer, the special officer, or the employee of a library facility civilly or criminally liable.

    b. Any law enforcement officer who has probable cause for believing that a person has committed the offense of theft of library material may arrest the person without warrant.

    c. An employee of a library facility who causes the arrest of a person for theft of library material, as provided for in this act, shall not be civilly or criminally liable where the employee has probable cause for believing that the person arrested committed the offense of theft of library material.

## 2C:20-15.    Sign required

All library facilities shall post at their primary entrances and exits a conspicuous sign to read as follows: IN ORDER TO PREVENT THE THEFT OF BOOKS AND LIBRARY MATERIAL, STATE LAW AUTHORIZES THE DETENTION FOR A REASONABLE PERIOD OF ANY PERSON USING THESE FACILITIES WHO IS SUSPECTED OF COMMITTING A THEFT OF LIBRARY MATERIAL.

## 2C:20-16.    Operation of facility for sale of stolen automobile parts, penalties

    a. A person who knowingly maintains or operates any premises, place or facility used for the remodeling, repainting, or separating of automobile parts for resale of any stolen automobile is guilty of a crime of the second degree.

    b. Notwithstanding any provision of law to the contrary, any person convicted of a violation of this section shall forthwith forfeit his right to operate a motor vehicle in this State for a period to be fixed by the court at not less than three nor more than five years. The court shall cause a report of the conviction to be filed with the Director of the Division of Motor Vehicles.

### PRACTICAL APPLICATION OF STATUTE

Mickey Morabito is guilty of maintaining a facility for selling stolen automobiles and their parts. This is a crime of the second degree.

    Simply, one who "knowingly" maintains or operates a facility used for reselling stolen automobiles or for chopping up stolen automobiles and reselling the parts is guilty of violating this statute. In East Rutherford, Morabito maintained such a facility. Posing as a legitimate auto body shop owner, Morabito routinely brought in stolen cars, which he either immediately resold for a huge profit or chopped up into parts and then resold the individual items. The Mercedes and BMW sold to him by Marini and Bigby were just examples of his huge enterprise. Accordingly, since Morabito actively engaged in this business, he is guilty of a second degree crime under 2C:20-16.

## 2C:20-17.    Use of juvenile in theft of automobiles, penalty

    a. A person who is at least 18 years of age who knowingly uses, solicits, directs, hires or employs a person who is in fact 17 years of age or younger to commit theft of an automobile is guilty of a crime of the second degree. Notwithstanding the provisions of N.J.S. 2C:1-8, a conviction under this section shall not merge with a conviction for theft of an automobile. Nothing contained in this act shall prohibit the court from imposing an extended term pursuant to N.J.S. 2C:43-7; nor shall this act be construed in any way to preclude or limit the prosecution or conviction of any person for conspiracy under N.J.S. 2C:5-2, or any prosecution or conviction for any other offense.

b. It shall be no defense to a prosecution under this section that the actor mistakenly believed that the person which the actor used, solicited, directed, hired or employed was older than 17 years of age, even if such mistaken belief was reasonable.

## PRACTICAL APPLICATION OF STATUTE

Ignacio Marini's use of his 17-year-old friend Charles Bigby to steal a BMW renders him guilty of a second degree crime per the elements of 2C:20-17. It is not a defense if Marini wasn't aware of Bigby's age or if Bigby willingly engaged in the theft.

2C:20-17, in a nutshell, provides that any person who is at least 18 who knowingly uses, solicits, or employs someone 17 or younger to steal an automobile is guilty of a second degree crime. Marini asked Bigby to hot-wire and drive away a late-model BMW. Bigby agreed and thereafter took the stolen car to Mickey's Auto Body Shop where they received a $10,000 payment for it. Given that Marini is well over 18 and that he solicited 17-year-old Bigby to steal the BMW, Marini is guilty of violating this statute.

**2C:20-18.**          **Leader of auto theft trafficking network, penalty**

A person is a leader of an auto theft trafficking network if he conspires with others as an organizer, supervisor, financier or manager, to engage for profit in a scheme or course of conduct to unlawfully take, dispose of, distribute, bring into or transport in this State automobiles as stolen property. Leader of auto theft trafficking network is a crime of the second degree. Notwithstanding the provisions of subsection a. of N.J.S. 2C:43-3, the court may impose a fine not to exceed $250,000.00 or five times the retail value of the automobiles seized at the time of the arrest, whichever is greater.

Notwithstanding the provisions of N.J.S. 2C:1-8, a conviction of leader of auto theft trafficking network shall not merge with the conviction for any offense which is the object of the conspiracy. Nothing contained in this act shall prohibit the court from imposing an extended term pursuant to N.J.S. 2C:43-7; nor shall this act be construed in any way to preclude or limit the prosecution or conviction of any person for conspiracy under N.J.S. 2C:5-2, or any prosecution or conviction for any other offense.

It shall not be necessary in any prosecution under this act for the State to prove that any intended profit was actually realized. The trier of fact may infer that a particular scheme or course of conduct was undertaken for profit from all of the attending circumstances, including but not limited to the number of persons involved in the scheme or course of conduct, the actor's net worth and his expenditures in relation to his legitimate sources of income, the number of automobiles involved, or the amount of cash or currency involved.

It shall not be a defense to a prosecution under this act that the automobile was brought into or transported in this State solely for ultimate distribution in another jurisdiction; nor shall it be a defense that any profit was intended to be made in another jurisdiction.

## PRACTICAL APPLICATION OF STATUTE

To be convicted of being a leader of an auto theft trafficking network, the defendant must "conspire" with others as an "organizer, supervisor, financier or manager" to make a profit from the theft of automobiles. Mickey Morabito could be convicted of this second degree crime.

Morabito maintained and operated a chop shop in East Rutherford, where he routinely bought stolen automobiles. He either immediately resold the vehicles for a huge profit or chopped them up and then sold the stolen parts. The fact that he maintained such a facility and made a profit from the stolen vehicles alone does not make him guilty of violating 2C:20-18, though. The evidence must show that Morabito "conspired" with others and that he somehow headed the theft ring.

Because his business necessarily involved paying thieves, such as Marini and Bigby, for stolen automobiles, it is clear that Morabito conspired with others. Similarly, it would probably be easy to show that he organized and/or supervised the network, as he was the individual responsible for paying for the vehicles and reselling them. The sum total of his actions, therefore, makes it likely that he would be convicted of being a leader of an auto theft trafficking network if he was indeed charged with this offense.

**2C:20-19.**     **Reserved**

**2C:20-20.**     **Civil actions**

    a. Any person damaged in his business or property by reason of a violation of section 7 of this amendatory and supplementary act may sue therefor in any appropriate court and shall recover threefold any damages he sustains and the cost of the suit, including a reasonable attorney's fee, costs of investigation and litigation.

    b. (1) All persons who have possessed or obtained control of stolen property are liable as principals and may be sued jointly or severally, whether or not possession or control was joint.

    (2) Any person held liable for possession or control of stolen property under chapter 20 of Title 2C of the New Jersey Statutes shall have standing to bring a civil action for contribution from any person who possessed or exercised control over the stolen property and who knew, had reason to know, or was reckless with regard to the risk that it was stolen.

    c. Any action for damages under chapter 20 of Title 2C of the New Jersey Statutes shall be maintained in the Superior Court sitting without a jury.

**2C:20-21.**     **Injunctive relief by state; other persons**

    a. In addition to any other action or proceeding authorized by law, the Attorney General or a person alleging injury or loss, may bring an action in the Superior Court to enjoin violations of chapter 20 of Title 2C of the New Jersey Statutes, or to enjoin any acts in furtherance thereof. The Superior Court, in any action brought pursuant to this section, shall, after making due provision for the rights of innocent persons such as prior lienholders or other valid lienholders whose rights are prior to those of the State, grant relief as may be appropriate in the circumstances, including but not limited to:

    (1) Ordering any defendant to divest himself of any interest in any enterprise, including real estate;

    (2) Imposing reasonable restrictions upon the future activities or investments of any defendant, including but not limited to, prohibiting any defendant from engaging in the same type of endeavor as the enterprise in which he was engaged in violation of chapter 20 of Title 2C of the New Jersey Statutes; or

    (3) Ordering the dissolution or reorganization of any enterprise; or

(4) Ordering the suspension or revocation of any license, permit, or prior approval granted to any enterprise by any department or agency of the State; or

(5) Ordering the forfeiture of the charter of a corporation organized under the laws of this State or the revocation of a certificate authorizing a foreign corporation to conduct business within this State, upon finding that the board of directors or a managerial agent acting on behalf of the corporation, in conducting the affairs of the corporation, has authorized or engaged in conduct in violation of chapter 20 of Title 2C of the New Jersey Statutes and that, for the prevention of future criminal activity, the public interest requires the charter of the corporation forfeited and the corporation dissolved or the certificate revoked.

b.  In any action the Attorney General or injured person shall move as soon as practicable for a hearing and determination. Pending final determination, the Superior Court may enter temporary orders, including restraints and prohibitions, or take other actions as are in the interest of justice.

## 2C:20-22.      Estoppel

A final judgment rendered in favor of the Attorney General or other person in any criminal action, or proceeding under chapter 20 of Title 2C of the New Jersey Statutes, shall estop the defendant in the action or proceeding in any subsequent civil action or proceeding under chapter 20 of Title 2C of the New Jersey Statutes as to all matters as to which the judgment in the action or proceeding would be an estoppel as between the parties to it.

# II. COMPUTER-RELATED CRIMES

## 2C:20-23.      Definitions

As used in this act:

a.  "Access" means to instruct, communicate with, store data in, retrieve data from, or otherwise make use of any resources of a computer, computer storage medium, computer system, or computer network.

b.  "Computer" means an electronic, magnetic, optical, electrochemical or other high speed data processing device or another similar device capable of executing a computer program, including arithmetic, logic, memory, data storage or input-output operations and includes all computer equipment connected to such a device, computer system or computer network, but shall not include an automated typewriter or typesetter or a portable, hand-held calculator.

c.  "Computer equipment" means any equipment or devices, including all input, output, processing, storage, software, or communications facilities, intended to interface with the computer.

d.  "Computer network" means the interconnection of communication lines, including microwave or other means of electronic communications, with a computer through remote terminals, or a complex consisting of two or more interconnected computers, and shall include te Internet.

e.  "Computer program" means a series of instructions or statements executable on a computer, which directs the computer system in a manner to produce a desired result.

f.  "Computer software" means a set of computer programs, data, procedures, and associated documentation concerned with the operation of a computer system.

g. "Computer system" means a set of interconnected computer equipment intended to operate as a cohesive system.

h. "Data" means information, facts, concepts, or instructions contained in a computer, computer storage medium, computer system, or computer network. It shall also include, but not be limited to, any alphanumeric, hexadecimal, octal or binary code.

i. "Data base" means a collection of data.

j. "Financial instrument" includes but is not limited to a check, draft, warrant, money order, note, certificate of deposit, letter of credit, bill of exchange, credit or debit card, transaction authorization mechanism, marketable security and any computer representation of these items.

k. "Services" includes but is not limited to the use of a computer system, computer network, computer programs, data prepared for computer use and data contained within a computer system or computer network.

l. "Personal identifying information" shall have the meaning set forth in subsection a. of N.J.S.2C:21-17, and shall also include passwords and other codes that permit access to any data, data base, computer, computer storage medium, computer program, computer software, computer equipment, computer system or computer network, where access is intended to be secure, restricted or limited.

m. "Internet" means the international computer network of both federal and non-federal interoperable packet switched data networks.

n. "Alter," "damage" or "destroy" shall include, but not be limited to, any change or impairment to the integrity or availability of any data or other information, data base, computer program, computer software, computer equipment, computer, computer storage medium, computer system, or computer network by any means including introduction of a computer contaminant.

o. "User of computer services" shall include, but not be limited to, any person, business, computer, computer network, computer system, computer equipment or any other device which makes use of any resources of a computer, computer network, computer system, computer storage medium, computer equipment, data or data base.

p. "Computer contaminant" means any set of computer instructions that are designed to alter, damage, destroy, record or transmit information within a computer, computer system or computer network without the authorization of the owner of the information. They include, but are not limited to, a group of computer instructions commonly called viruses or worms, that are self-replicating or self-propagating and are designed to contaminate other computer programs or computer data, consume computer resources, alter, damage, destroy, record or transmit data or in some other fashion usurp the normal operation of the computer, computer program, computer operations, computer services or computer network.

q. "Authorization" means permission, authority or consent given by a person who possesses lawful authority to grant such permission, authority or consent to another person to access, operate, use, obtain, take, copy, alter, damage or destroy a computer, computer network, computer system, computer equipment, computer software, computer program, computer storage medium, or data. An actor has authorization if a reasonable person would believe that the act was authorized.

**2C:20-24.**    **Value of property of services; additional measures**

For the purposes of this act, the value of any property or services, including the use of computer time, shall be their fair market value, if it is determined that a willing buyer and willing seller exist.

Value shall include the cost of repair or remediation of any damage caused by an unlawful act and the gross revenue from any lost business opportunity caused by the unlawful act. The value of any lost business opportunity may be determined by comparison to gross revenue generated before the unlawful act that resulted in the lost business opportunity. Value shall include, but not be limited to, the cost of generating or obtaining data and storing it within a computer or computer system.

**2C:20-25.**    **Computer criminal activity; degree of crime; sentencing**

A person is guilty of computer criminal activity if the person purposely or knowingly and without authorization, or in excess of authorization:

a. Accesses any data, data base, computer storage medium, computer program, computer software, computer equipment, computer, computer system or computer network;

b. Alters, damages or destroys any data, data base, computer, computer storage medium, computer program, computer software, computer system or computer network, or denies, disrupts or impairs computer services, including access to any part of the Internet, that are available to any other user of the computer services;

c. Accesses or attempts to access any data, data base, computer, computer storage medium, computer program, computer software, computer equipment, computer system or computer network for the purpose of executing a scheme to defraud, or to obtain services, property, personal identifying information, or money, from the owner of a computer or any third party;

d. (Deleted by amendment, P.L.2003, c.39).

e. Obtains, takes, copies or uses any data, data base, computer program, computer software, personal identifying information, or other information stored in a computer, computer network, computer system, computer equipment or computer storage medium; or

f. Accesses and recklessly alters, damages or destroys any data, data base, computer, computer storage medium, computer program, computer software, computer equipment, computer system or computer network.

g. A violation of subsection a. of this section is a crime of the third degree. A violation of subsection b. is a crime of the second degree. A violation of subsection c. is a crime of the third degree, except that it is a crime of the second degree if the value of the services, property, personal identifying information, or money obtained or sought to be obtained exceeds $5,000. A violation of subsection e. is a crime of the third degree, except that it is a crime of the second degree if the data, data base, computer program, computer software, or information:

(1) is or contains personal identifying information, medical diagnoses, treatments or other medical information concerning an identifiable person;

(2) is or contains governmental records or other information that is protected from disclosure by law, court order or rule of court; or

(3) has a value exceeding $5,000.

A violation of subsection f. is a crime of the fourth degree, except that it is a crime of the third degree if the value of the damage exceeds $5,000.

A violation of any subsection of this section is a crime of the first degree if the offense results in:

(1) a substantial interruption or impairment of public communication, transportation, supply of water, gas or power, or other public service. The term "substantial interruption or impairment" shall mean such interruption or impairment that:

(a) affects 10 or more structures or habitations;

(b) lasts for two or more hours; or

(c) creates a risk of death or significant bodily injury to any person;

(2) damages or loss in excess of $250,000; or

    (3)  significant bodily injury to any person.

        Every sentence of imprisonment for a crime of the first degree committed in violation of this section shall include a minimum term of one-third to one-half of the sentence imposed, during which term the defendant shall not be eligible for parole.

  h.  Every sentence imposed upon a conviction pursuant to this section shall, if the victim is a government agency, include a period of imprisonment. The period of imprisonment shall include a minimum term of one-third to one-half of the sentence imposed, during which term the defendant shall not be eligible for parole. The victim shall be deemed to be a government agency if a computer, computer network, computer storage medium, computer system, computer equipment, computer program, computer software, computer data or data base that is a subject of the crime is owned, operated or maintained by or on behalf of a governmental agency or unit of State or local government or a public authority. The defendant shall be strictly liable under this subsection and it shall not be a defense that the defendant did not know or intend that the victim was a government agency, or that the defendant intended that there be other victims of the crime.

        A violation of any subsection of this section shall be a distinct offense from a violation of any other subsection of this section, and a conviction for a violation of any subsection of this section shall not merge with a conviction for a violation of any other subsection of this section or section 10 of P.L.1984, c.184 (C.2C:20-31), or for conspiring or attempting to violate any subsection of this section or section 10 of P.L.1984, c.184 (C.2C:20-31), and a separate sentence shall be imposed for each such conviction.

        When a violation of any subsection of this section involves an offense committed against a person under 18 years of age, the violation shall constitute an aggravating circumstance to be considered by the court when determining the appropriate sentence to be imposed.

## PRACTICAL APPLICATION OF STATUTE

Allen, Bob, and Charles are three disgruntled employees of Arnoldi Asset Management, Inc. After recent cuts in pay and the looming threat of job loss due to a sagging economy, the three employees decide to sabotage the company before all mutually quit their jobs within the next month. Using Allen's building key, the three individuals enter Arnoldi's offices late one evening without authorization. The lone security guard is accustomed to employees coming in at random hours and doesn't give it a second thought. Bob, one of the tech administrators, leads the group to the computer area where the group splits up to execute their plan.

    Allen, a member of the marketing department, logs on to marketing's database of current and potential high-net-worth investors and saves the list to a zip disk so that he may later solicit these individuals to invest in a scam he intends to set up. Bob, the tech administrator, logs on to the network and plants a malicious virus which is designed to completely erase the hard drive of the network and cripple the company's e-mail capabilities. Finally, Charles, one of the traders, transfers the profiles of the department's Lexis/Nexis users from the local computer in the trading room to his personal laptop so that he may access the service at home for his own purposes without paying the normal fee.

    Despite each individual's computer prowess, they were all easily caught soon after things started going wrong. Each individual was charged with computer-related theft, but each under a different subsection of 2C:20-25.

    While all three's actions meet the criteria of "purposely or knowingly and without authorization," their specific actions lie within the four separate subsections. Allen should be charged under 2C:20-25a. for taking the investor database for his own use. Bob should be charged under subsection b. for damaging or destroying the actual computer system or computer network when he planted the malicious virus. Charles should be charged under subsection c. because he accessed a computer for the purpose of executing a scheme to wrongfully obtain services, the Lexis-Nexis application, from the company's computer.

**2C:20-26**
**to 2C:20-30.**    **Repealed**

**2C:20-31.**    **Wrongful access, disclosure of information; degree of crime; sentencing**

a. A person is guilty of a crime of the third degree if the person purposely or knowingly and without authorization, or in excess of authorization, accesses any data, data base, computer, computer storage medium, computer software, computer equipment, computer system and knowingly or recklessly discloses or causes to be disclosed any data, data base, computer software, computer programs or personal identifying information.

b. A person is guilty of a crime of the second degree if the person purposely or knowingly and without authorization, or in excess of authorization, accesses any data, data base, computer, computer storage medium, computer software, computer equipment, computer system or computer network and purposely or knowingly discloses or causes to be disclosed any data, data base, computer software, computer program or other information that is protected from disclosure by any law, court order or rule of court. Every sentence imposed upon a conviction pursuant to this subsection shall include a period of imprisonment. The period of imprisonment shall include a minimum term of one-third to one-half of the sentence imposed, during which term the defendant shall not be eligible for parole.

## PRACTICAL APPLICATION OF STATUTE

Michele, while temping at Big Dude's Auto, is exposed to a computer program that can simulate riding in the new Turbo-Pro model cars planned to go into production in the coming months. Without authorization, Michele decides to play around with the program a little, and in the process inadvertently accesses the design plans for a top-secret stealth car that is being researched for the military. In an effort to impress several friends, she saves the program to disk and over the next week shows the program to a few acquaintances. Daniel, whose computer Michele had accessed, notices the unauthorized use and realizes that the top-secret file has been accessed and saved. He reports the incident to his superiors who eventually trace the breach to Michele.

Here, Michele could be charged under 2C:20-31 for disclosure of data from wrongful access, a crime of the third degree. A conviction of this offense can occur despite the fact that damages could not be assessed.

**2C:20-32.**    **Repealed**

**2C:20-33.**    **Obtaining, copying, accessing program, software valued at $1,000 or less**

It is an affirmative defense to a prosecution pursuant to subsection e. of section 4 of P.L.1984, c.184 (C.2C:20-25), which shall be proved by clear and convincing evidence, that the actor obtained, copied or accessed a computer program or computer software that had a retail value of less than $1,000 and the actor did not disseminate or disclose the program or software to any other person.

## PRACTICAL APPLICATION OF STATUTE

Tom and his buddies are typical teenagers with too much time on their hands. Through instructions easily found online, they have figured out how to use their CD burner to make copies of their favorite games and DVDs on disk. Here, their conduct does not constitute theft per the language of 2C:20-33. Why? Because the teenagers are not mass-producing these copies for resale, and the retail value of their copied material is under $1,000.

**2C:20-34.    Situs of offense; determination**

For the purpose of prosecution under this act, and in addition to determining the situs of the offense pursuant to the provisions of N.J.S.2C:1-3, the situs of an offense of computer criminal activity shall also be the location of the computer, computer storage medium, computer program, computer software, computer equipment, computer system or computer network which is accessed, or where the computer, computer storage medium, computer program, computer software, computer equipment, computer system, computer network or other device used in the offense is situated, or where the actual damage occurs.

**2C:20-35.    Definitions**

As used in this act:

"ATP card" means a document issued by a State or federal agency, to a certified household, to show the food stamp allotment a household is authorized to receive on presentation.

"Benefit card" means a card used or intended for use to access Work First New Jersey, food stamp or other benefits as determined by the Commissioner of Human Services under the electronic benefit distribution system established pursuant to the "Public Assistance Electronic Benefit Distribution System Act," P.L.1985, c. 501 (C.44:10-5.1 et seq.) and continued pursuant to P.L.1997, c. 37 (C.44:10-71 et al.).

"Department" means the Department of Human Services.

"Food stamp coupon" means any coupon or stamp used or intended for use in the purchase of food pursuant to the federal food stamp program authorized by Title XIII of the "Food and Agriculture Act of 1977," Pub.L.95-113 (7 U.S.C.s.2011 et seq.), or the New Jersey Supplementary Food Stamp Program established pursuant to P.L.1998, c. 32 (C.44:10-79 et al.).

**2C:20-36.    Misuse of food stamp coupons, ATP card, benefit card, value equal or greater than $150**

If the face value of food stamp coupons or an ATP card or benefit card is equal to or greater than $150, an individual shall be guilty of a crime of the fourth degree if he purposely or knowingly and without authorization:

a. Receives or uses the proceeds of food stamp coupons or an ATP card or benefit card for which he has not applied or has not been approved by the department to use;

b. Engages in any transaction to convert food stamp coupons or an ATP card or benefit card to other property contrary to federal and State government rules and regulations governing the Work First New Jersey program, the federal food stamp program, the New Jersey Supplementary Food Stamp Program, or any other program included in the electronic benefit distribution system; or

c. Transfers food stamp coupons or an ATP card or benefit card to another person who is not lawfully entitled or approved by the department to use the coupons or ATP card or benefit card.

## PRACTICAL APPLICATION OF STATUTE

Daniel Deadbeat has been collecting food stamp coupons since he lost his job nearly a year ago. Instead of using the coupons for food, however, Daniel regularly "sells" his $250 stamp on the black market for slightly less than its face value in order to buy alcohol and cigarettes. Through a sting operation set up to catch this sort of behavior, Daniel ends up "selling" his stamps to an undercover officer.

Daniel should be charged under 2C:20-36b., with a crime of the fourth degree, for engaging "in any transaction to convert food stamp coupons or an ATP card or benefit card to other property contrary to federal and State government rules and regulations governing the Work First New Jersey program, the federal food stamp program, the New Jersey Supplementary Food Stamp Program, or any other program included in the electronic benefit distribution system," where the face value of the food stamp coupon is "equal to or greater than $150."

If Daniel had been selling his $250 coupons to an individual (rather than an undercover officer) and that individual used the coupons for his own unauthorized use, he would be guilty of a fourth degree crime under subsection a. of this same statute. Why? Because this individual received "the proceeds of food stamp coupons or an ATP card or benefit card for which he has not applied or has not been approved by the department to use," where the food stamp has a face value equal to or greater than $150.

---

**2C:20-37.**          **Misuse of food stamp coupons, ATP card, benefit card, value less than $150**

If the face value of food stamp coupons or an ATP card or benefit card is less than $150, an individual shall be guilty of a disorderly persons offense if he purposely or knowingly and without authorization:

   a. Receives or uses the proceeds of food stamp coupons or an ATP card or benefit card for which he has not applied or has not been approved, by the department, to use;

   b. Engages in any transaction to convert food stamp coupons or an ATP card or benefit card to other property contrary to federal and State government rules and regulations governing the Work First New Jersey program, the federal food stamp program, the New Jersey Supplementary Food Stamp Program, or any other program included in the electronic benefit distribution system; or

   c. Transfers food stamp coupons or an ATP card or benefit card to another person who is not lawfully entitled or approved, by the department, to use the coupons or ATP card or benefit card.

## PRACTICAL APPLICATION OF STATUTE

Daniel's offense (as described in 2C:20-36's Practical Application section) would be considered a disorderly persons offense if, under the same circumstances, the face value of the food stamp coupons was less than $150.

# 21

# FORGERY AND FRAUDULENT PRACTICES

## FACT PATTERN (PERTAINS TO CHAPTERS 21 AND 22)

At the urging of the mayor of Cranford and the Union County Prosecutor, Christian Star was appointed to be the new director of the Union County Police Academy. Star's appointment was quite a feat given that he was only 33 years old at the time of the announcement. Accomplishing great things at a young age, though, was nothing new to Christian Star. He had already moved from patrolman to sergeant to lieutenant to captain in the Cranford Police Department. And he had personally cracked the largest forgery and fraudulent business scam in the state of New Jersey. This is what led to his police academy director post—who better to train the county's recruits? The first class under his leadership listened closely as one of the academy's instructors explained the story of Director Star's monumental bust.

Maxwell Borscht, a former Ivy League valedictorian, resigned an executive position with a top corporate firm in Chicago, Illinois, after a power struggle with other bosses. Borscht told family, friends, and business colleagues that he intended to pursue a career in acting as he was "finished with corporate America." He said he was moving to New York City. Borscht, though, was lying.

Trading in his Chicago penthouse for a spacious Victorian home in Cranford, New Jersey, Borscht assumed the name "Kalman Greenwald" and began operating "Jackpot Entertainment Insurance," which he held out to be a specialized subsidiary company of one of the nation's largest insurance companies, The Pellman Group. The problem was, Jackpot Entertainment Insurance was as fake as his new name.

Borscht had acquired his alias, Kalman Greenwald, through an arranged meeting with Elizabeth businessman Michael "The Hunk" Pardemena. The Hunk made a career of manufacturing various phony forms of identification, as well as obtaining some genuine items. For example, he had recently purchased an Elizabeth police badge from his friend, Manny Rando. On the same day, The Hunk "restructured" Rando's father's will to make Rando the sole beneficiary of his dad's estate. The Hunk did this by dissolving the printed ink and replacing it with language favorable to Rando.

The Hunk also visited the home of Rando's father-in-law. There, he destroyed the man's will, which left all his assets to a charity. The purpose of this destruction was so that the man would die intestate, thereby requiring that his assets would go to his closest living immediate family member, which was Manny's wife.

Now, back to The Hunk's dealings with Borscht. The Hunk, on the spot, made a New Jersey driver's license for Borscht which falsely purported Borscht to be Kalman Greenwald. The Hunk sold the license to Borscht for $500. In the same transaction, The Hunk sold Borscht a fake motor vehicle insurance card.

Ironically, Christian Star's first interaction with Borscht was on the evening Borscht purchased his illicit identification cards from The Hunk. Star, in his supervisor cruiser, pulled Borscht over, who presented the newly purchased driver's license and insurance card. The cards, even to an expert eye, appeared authentic; Borscht went on his way with a warning for speeding.

The following days were dedicated to setting up and financing Borscht's fictitious business, Jackpot Entertainment Insurance. In an unusual move to obtain start-up capital, Borscht created a manuscript that he claimed to be an authentic writing of Ernest Hemingway. It was handwritten, yet the writing so closely resembled Hemingway's that knowledgeable collectors were fooled by it. The highest bidder took it home for $50,000. Borscht's next order of business was to alter actual records pertaining to Kalman Greenwald. Greenwald was indeed a real person.

Borscht changed an important diagnosis made by Greenwald's cardiologist. The document was altered to read that Greenwald had "chronic heart disease . . . which necessitated a heart transplant." The real diagnosis was a "heart murmur." Borscht took this diagnostic record to sympathetic, wealthy members of Union County's Chamber of Commerce and solicited over $25,000 in funds to pay costs that insurance would not cover in the "heart transplant." Borscht then went to a doctor friend, Elias Williamson, M.D., who acted as if he had performed the surgery. Williamson submitted claims to Greenwald's insurance company and then split the proceeds of the insurance payments with Borscht.

Borscht continued his fund-raising campaign by the use of credit cards. His first act was to simply pluck two credit cards from the Cape May home of Kalman Greenwald. Greenwald, a former business associate of Borscht, was moving to Portugal, and Borscht attended his "going away" party. Borscht then maxed out the cards via cash advances. He later used them, along with his phony driver's license, as part of the application process to obtain additional credit cards. In those applications, he falsely purported to be Kalman Greenwald, signing Greenwald's name to the paperwork and listing phony business references.

Utilizing Greenwald's identity, Borscht visited several businesses in northern New Jersey that were familiar with Greenwald's reputation but not his physical appearance. Borscht's false pretense allowed him to obtain several items of value on invoice, including office furniture, equipment, and handmade suits. Borscht, as Greenwald, agreed to pay the vendors within 30 days; payment of course was never remitted. During these visits, Borscht actually paid for an item, a large jar of "anti-aging" pills. The merchant claimed on the jar's label that the pills were made from a coral found only off the coast of Australia, when in fact he produced them in his basement, utilizing various ingredients from his own kitchen. When Borscht found out he was misled, he returned to the store and issued a check for $3,500 in exchange for various livestock that the merchant retained at a farm in Sussex County. The merchant wasn't pleased, though, when he learned the check was from a bank account that had been closed for nearly a year. Borscht laughed heartily, knowing the account no longer existed.

Fully funded and equipped, Borscht was now ready to begin work. At the headquarters of the insurance conglomerate, The Pellman Group, Borscht met with Sandi Ireland, one of the company's Board of Directors. Ireland had previously worked hand in hand with none other than Kalman Greenwald, Pellman's recently retired chief financial officer.

Borscht paid Ireland $50,000 to form a subsidiary company named Jackpot Entertainment Insurance, which actually wouldn't be started for 24 months, as it would take that period of time to clear the internal bureaucratic red tape and administrative matters. The name, though, would be in place and tied to The Pellman Group. Anyone checking into Jackpot could confirm this. Borscht convinced Ireland that she was at no risk because if things went afoul, Ireland could easily claim that Borscht simply stole the name. Ireland took the money and had the subsidiary company formed, even though she knew it could be to the detriment of Pellman and its shareholders. At the same board of directors meeting where she proposed the formation of Jackpot, Ireland agreed with other board members to issue each board member a $150,000 dividend, holding it out to be a "President's Day bonus," although they knew the corporation didn't allow for such a dividend distribution.

Borscht then began soliciting high-level film production companies, purporting to sell them liability and other entertainment insurance policies for their film productions. Posing as Kalman Greenwald, former CFO of The Pellman Group and now CEO of Jackpot, Borscht met with the top executives of numerous production companies. Because The Pellman Group had never sold such insurance, the executives were interested in meeting with Borscht/Greenwald. They immediately purchased the insurance because the rates were so much lower than those of competitors.

To avoid any detection of fraud, Borscht created policy documents that replicated in letterhead, typesetting, and stock language other documents delivered by The Pellman Group. He issued the policies under the name "Jackpot Entertainment Insurance— A Subsidiary of The Pellman Group," and he signed Kalman Greenwald's name to each policy. He did all this even though he had no consent whatsoever from Greenwald or The Pellman Group to issue such policies. As a special touch, Borscht applied The Pellman Group's signatory wax seal; he had created equipment that perfectly matched the seal.

Within six months of opening shop, Borscht had sold such a large number of fictitious insurance policies to New Jersey production companies that he had netted himself over $3 million. At this point, he was committed to wind up the business, as claims were beginning to come in. Heat was sure to be coming, as he had absolutely no plans to pay any of the claims. He had one problem, however. Cranford Police Officer Christian Star.

The young captain responded to a call from a local restaurateur that a "new guy in town" was dancing on one of his tables, screaming, "I'm 53 but only look 35 . . . Don't you all love me?" When Star arrived, Borscht was off the table but rolling on the floor instead, yelling, "I'm in the movie business . . . rich and handsome . . . rich and handsome." Star immediately recognized him as a man he had previously pulled over. Having an incredible memory, he tapped Borscht on the shoulder and said, "Mr. Greenwald, could you stand up?"

Borscht didn't stand but lifted his head and said, "I'm Borscht . . . Would you like an apple martini?" Captain Star noted the name change, but also noted Borscht's drunkenness. He lifted the man up from the floor, threw him over his shoulder, and carried him to his police vehicle. Then he gave him a courtesy ride home.

On instinct, Star ran a check on the "new guy in town." He quickly learned that a Kalman Greenwald had recently sold his home in Cape May. He also learned that

Greenwald was previously the CFO of The Pellman Group. Human resources advised that he had just retired and thought that he had moved out of the country. They mentioned, though, that Greenwald was a private man, and perhaps wanted to remain anonymous in the United States for a while. This seemed to conflict with the behavior Star just witnessed at the restaurant, but he had no real resason to suspect Greenwald of a crime so he thought he would just monitor the man. That was, until he got a call from Sandi Ireland.

The Pellman Group director freaked when she heard that law enforcement was inquiring about Kalman Greenwald. Did they know about Borscht's subsidiary company? Were they onto the bribe? Was it possible that Borscht killed Kalman Greenwald? Ireland didn't want to face culpability for any of this so she made an appointment with Captain Star and spilled everything.

An arrest of Borscht was not easy, however. By the time that Star had arrived with an arrest warrant, Borscht was gone. The home, though, did provide clues as to his whereabouts. Above a ceiling panel, Star found several thousands of dollars in cash which Borscht had forgotten in his rush to leave. Underneath a floor tile, Star discovered where the money was derived from—three pizza parlors in Hunterdon County.

Borscht had bought the establishments in his real name before scheming the Jackpot insurance scam. What Star ultimately learned was that Borscht was selling heroin when he first came to New Jersey. He utilized the pizza places to disguise the real manner that he earned funds. His goal was to act like the money was made legitimately via the restaurants, sending it through those businesses' records as if an enormous number of pizzas and calzones were sold.

Star then hooked up with investigators from the Hunterdon County Prosecutor's Office to have surveillance set up at the various pizza parlors. Borscht, however, never appeared. At this point, Star thought that perhaps Borscht simply fled the country with the millions he deceptively earned. But then he thought about something Sandi Ireland said in her babbling confession: a great uncle of Borscht's was buried in an unmarked grave in Cherry Hill. The significance was that there was a family myth that buried along with the uncle was $5 million in gold bullion.

Star, discouraged with the Hunterdon County stakeouts, drove across state to Cherry Hill, figuring he'd stop in Philadelphia to catch a Phillies game if nothing turned up at the cemeteries. But something did. As he approached his third graveyard, he found Borscht, shovel in hand, breaking open a pine box casket in an unmarked grave. Borscht pulled the human remains from the box, tossed them aside, and threw up his hands. He then kicked the unfortunate, unnamed man's skeleton and cried, "Where's the bullion, you bony fool?" At this point, Christian Star pointed his pistol at Borscht, dangling handcuffs from his free hand.

The young officer had captured his man. And the police academy promotion came just one month later.

---

**2C:21-1.**  **Forgery and related offenses**

   a. **Forgery.** A person is guilty of forgery if, with purpose to defraud or injure anyone, or with knowledge that he is facilitating a fraud or injury to be perpetrated by anyone, the actor:

     (1) Alters or changes any writing of another without his authorization;

     (2) Makes, completes, executes, authenticates, issues or transfers any writing so that it purports to be the act of another who did not authorize that act or of a fictitious

person, or to have been executed at a time or place or in a numbered sequence other than was in fact the case, or to be a copy of an original when no such original existed; or

(3) Utters any writing which he knows to be forged in a manner specified in paragraph (1) or (2).

"Writing" includes printing or any other method of recording information, money, coins, tokens, stamps, seals, credit cards, badges, trademarks, access devices, and other symbols of value, right, privilege, or identification, including retail sales receipts, universal product code (UPC) labels and checks. This section shall apply without limitation to forged, copied or imitated checks.

As used in this section, "information" includes, but is not limited to, personal identifying information as defined in subsection v. of N.J.S.2C:20-1.

b. **Grading of forgery.** Forgery is a crime of the third degree if the writing is or purports to be part of an issue of money, securities, postage or revenue stamps, or other instruments, certificates or licenses issued by the government, New Jersey Prescription Blanks as referred to in R.S.45:14-14, or part of an issue of stock, bonds or other instruments representing interest in or claims against any property or enterprise, personal identifying information or an access device. Forgery is a crime of the third degree if the writing is or purports to be a check. Forgery is a crime of the third degree if the writing is or purports to be 15 or more forged or altered retail sales receipts or universal product code labels.

Otherwise forgery is a crime of the fourth degree.

c. **Possession of forgery devices.** A person is guilty of possession of forgery devices, a crime of the third degree, when with purpose to use, or to aid or permit another to use the same for purposes of forging written instruments, including access devices and personal identifying information, he makes or possesses any device, apparatus, equipment, computer, computer equipment, computer software or article specially designed or adapted to such use.

## PRACTICAL APPLICATION OF STATUTE

Michael "The Hunk" Pardemena could appropriately be found guilty of forgery under subsection a.(1) of the above statute due to his "restructuring" of Rando's father's will. In The Hunk's case, this would be a crime of the third degree.

Subsection b. of this statute makes the offense of forgery a crime of the third degree under certain listed circumstances and a crime of the fourth degree in all remaining instances. Circumstances in which forgery is a crime of the third degree include matters such as where the forged documents are government-issued certificates or licenses (i.e., money, securities, or postage stamps), stocks or bonds, New Jersey Prescription Blanks, and "instruments representing interest in or claims against any property or enterprise."

Although the statute does not specifically mention wills, it could certainly be argued that a will could fall into the category of an "instrument representing an interest in property," therefore making The Hunk's actions a crime of the third degree.

At its core, the crime of forgery consists of two elements: (1) the intent to defraud; and (2) the false making or material altering of any writing that, if genuine, would have some legal effect upon the rights of others. Although intent can occasionally be a tricky element, the very act of forgery itself is probably sufficient to imply an intent to defraud. In The Hunk's case, both elements are met. First, he clearly intended to defraud the two beneficiaries of Rando's father—he dissolved the printed ink of the will and replaced it with language favorable to Rando. Second, the material altering of the will would certainly have a legal effect on others, as it would deprive the true beneficiaries of the will's grants and proceeds. Accordingly, The Hunk is guilty of third degree forgery per subsection a.(1) of the statute.

### Possession of Forgery Devices

Maxwell Borscht is guilty of possessing forgery devices as part of his phony insurance company, Jackpot Entertainment Insurance. This is a crime of the third degree.

Per subsection c. of 2C:21-1, a person who possesses any device, apparatus, or equipment with a purpose to use the same to aid in forging written instruments is guilty of a third degree crime. Borscht had created equipment that perfectly matched the signature wax seal of one of the nation's largest insurance companies, The Pellman Group. Borscht used this equipment in an effort to make his own phony insurance documents look authentic. Since he used this seal device with a purpose to aid in forging written instruments, Borscht is guilty of violating subsection c. of 2C:21-1.

**2C:21-2.**        **Criminal simulation**

A person commits a crime of the fourth degree if, with purpose to defraud anyone or with knowledge that he is facilitating a fraud to be perpetrated by anyone, he makes, alters or utters any object so that it appears to have value because of antiquity, rarity, source, or authorship which it does not possess.

### PRACTICAL APPLICATION OF STATUTE

When Maxwell Borscht created his sham Ernest Hemingway manuscript, he committed the fourth degree crime of criminal simulation. This statute simply requires that a person (with purpose to defraud) make or alter any object so that it appears to have value because of "antiquity, rarity, source, or authorship which it does not possess." By forging an Ernest Hemingway manuscript for the sole purpose of pawning it off as an original, and subsequently reaping the ill-received gains from an unknowing bidder, Borsht falls squarely within the statute. Accordingly, he is guilty of a fourth degree crime as defined in 2C:21-2.

**2C:21-2.1.**        **Offenses involving false government documents, degree of crime**

    a. A person who knowingly sells, offers or exposes for sale, or otherwise transfers, or possesses with the intent to sell, offer or expose for sale, or otherwise transfer, a document, printed form or other writing which falsely purports to be a driver's license or other document issued by a governmental agency and which could be used as a means of verifying a person's identity or age or any other personal identifying information is guilty of a crime of the second degree.

    b. A person who knowingly makes, or possesses devices or materials to make, a document or other writing which falsely purports to be a driver's license or other document issued by a governmental agency and which could be used as a means of verifying a person's identity or age or any other personal identifying information is guilty of a crime of the second degree.

    c. A person who knowingly exhibits, displays or utters a document or other writing which falsely purports to be a driver's license or other document issued by a governmental agency and which could be used as a means of verifying a person's identity or age or any other personal identifying information is guilty of a crime of the third degree. A violation of R.S.33:1-81 or section 6 of P.L.1968, c.313 (C.33:1-81.7) for using the personal identifying information of another to illegally purchase an alcoholic beverage or for using the personal identifying information of another to misrepresent his age for the purpose of obtaining tobacco or other consumer product denied to persons under 18 years of age shall not constitute an offense under this subsection if the actor received only that benefit or service and did not perpetrate or attempt to perpetrate any additional injury or fraud on another.

d. A person who knowingly possesses a document or other writing which falsely purports to be a driver's license or other document issued by a governmental agency and which could be used as a means of verifying a person's identity or age or any other personal identifying information is guilty of a crime of the fourth degree.

e. In addition to any other disposition authorized by this Title, the provisions of section 24 of P.L.1982, c.77 (C.2A:4A-43), or any other statute indicating the dispositions that may be ordered for an adjudication of delinquency, and, notwithstanding the provisions of subsection c. of N.J.S.2C:43-2, every person convicted of or adjudicated delinquent for a violation of any offense defined in this section shall forthwith forfeit his right to operate a motor vehicle over the highways of this State for a period to be fixed by the court at not less than six months or more than two years which shall commence on the day the sentence is imposed. In the case of any person who at the time of the imposition of the sentence is less than 17 years of age, the period of the suspension of driving privileges authorized herein, including a suspension of the privilege of operating a motorized bicycle, shall commence on the day the sentence is imposed and shall run for a period as fixed by the court of not less than six months or more than two years after the day the person reaches the age of 17 years. If the driving privilege of any person is under revocation, suspension, or postponement for a violation of any provision of this Title or Title 39 of the Revised Statutes at the time of any conviction or adjudication of delinquency for a violation of any offense defined in this chapter or chapter 36 of this Title, the revocation, suspension, or postponement period imposed herein shall commence as of the date of termination of the existing revocation, suspension or postponement.

The court before whom any person is convicted of or adjudicated delinquent for a violation of any offense defined in this section shall collect forthwith the New Jersey driver's license or licenses of that person and forward the license or licenses to the Director of the Division of Motor Vehicles along with a report indicating the first and last day of the suspension or postponement period imposed by the court pursuant to this section. If the court is for any reason unable to collect the license or licenses of the person, the court shall cause a report of the conviction or adjudication of delinquency to be filed with the director. The report shall include the complete name, address, date of birth, eye color and sex of the person and shall indicate the first and last day of the suspension or postponement period imposed by the court pursuant to this section. The court shall inform the person orally and in writing that if the person is convicted of personally operating a motor vehicle during the period of license suspension or postponement imposed pursuant to this section, the person shall, upon conviction, be subject to the penalties set forth in R.S.39:3-40. A person shall be required to acknowledge receipt of the written notice in writing. Failure to receive a written notice or failure to acknowledge in writing the receipt of a written notice shall not be a defense to a subsequent charge of a violation of R.S.39:3-40. If the person is the holder of a driver's license from another jurisdiction, the court shall not collect the license, but shall notify forthwith the director who shall notify the appropriate officials in that licensing jurisdiction. The court shall, however, in accordance with the provisions of this section, revoke the person's non-resident driving privileges in this State.

In addition to any other condition imposed, a court, in its discretion, may suspend, revoke or postpone the driving privileges of a person admitted to supervisory treatment under N.J.S.2C:36A-1 or N.J.S.2C:43-12 without a plea of guilty or finding of guilt.

## PRACTICAL APPLICATION OF STATUTE

Section 2C:21-2.1 generally makes it a crime to sell, make, exhibit, or possess any document which falsely purports to be a driver's license or other document issued by the government that could be used as a means of verifying a person's identity or age. Subsections a. and b. specify that it is a crime of the second degree to "sell" or "make" such IDs.

Subsection c. makes it a crime of the third degree to "display" or "exhibit" the IDs. Finally, per subsection d., it is a crime of the fourth degree for a person to knowingly "possess" a fake ID.

The Hunk and Maxwell Borscht are both guilty of crimes under this statute. The Hunk should be found guilty of the more severe second degree offenses found under subsections a. and b. of 2C:21-2.1. Why? Because he both made and sold Borscht a fake New Jersey driver's license which falsely purported Borscht to be Kalman Greenwald.

Borscht's possession of this ID makes him guilty of a fourth degree crime under subsection d. Later, when he presented it to Police Lieutenant Christian Star at a motor vehicle stop, Borscht's offense rose to a crime of the third degree as provided for in subsection c. of the statute.

**2C:21-2.1a.**  **[Reallocated as § 2C:21-2.3]**

**2C:21-2.2.**  **Ban on police badge transfers**

It shall be a disorderly persons offense to:
a. Sell a law enforcement agency badge, the prescribed form of which is presently in use or has been in use in New Jersey during any of the five years preceding the sale, to a person other than a member of a law enforcement agency who presents a letter authorizing the purchase, signed by the commanding officer of that law enforcement agency;
b. Purchase a law enforcement agency badge, described in subsection a. of this section, unless the purchaser is a member of a law enforcement agency who presents a letter authorizing the purchase, signed by the commanding officer of that law enforcement agency; or
c. Give or lend a law enforcement agency badge described in subsection a. of this section, unless the person to whom a badge was given or loaned is a member of a law enforcement agency who presents a letter authorizing the transfer, signed by the commanding officer of that law enforcement agency.

## PRACTICAL APPLICATION OF STATUTE

The Hunk continues his stroll down fraudulent lane by violating section 2C:21-2.2.b., which makes it a disorderly persons offense for non-law enforcement personnel to buy a law enforcement agency badge. This act is an offense when the badge is either presently in use or has been in use in New Jersey during any of the five years prior to the sale.

Manny Rando, the seller of the badge, is also in violation of the statute. This is so because subsection a. forbids the sale of any such badge to anyone but authorized law enforcement personnel who present a letter authorizing the purchase, signed by the commanding officer of that law enforcement agency. Rando is not a law enforcement officer, and even if he was, he did not have the appropriate authorization to sell an Elizabeth badge to The Hunk. Accordingly, he is guilty of a disorderly persons offense under 2C:21-2.2.

The only issue that might get these two off the hook is if it turned out that the Elizabeth police badge that Rando sold to The Hunk had not been in use for more than five years prior to the sale. If this was the case, it appears the statute provides that there would be no offense.

Christian Star and the other law enforcement officers should take note of subsection c. of this statute, which proscribes giving or loaning their badges to anyone except a fellow member of a law enforcement agency. Even in that case, the law enforcement officer must present a letter authorizing the transfer, signed by the commanding officer of that law enforcement agency. Anyone, officer or civilian, can be found guilty of a disorderly persons offense if they are in violation of this subsection.

**2C:21-2.3.**    **Producing, selling, offering, displaying, possessing, fraudulent motor vehicle insurance ID cards; penalties**

a. A person who knowingly produces, sells, offers or exposes for sale a document, printed form or other writing which simulates a motor vehicle insurance identification card is guilty of a crime of the third degree. In addition to any other penalty imposed, a person convicted under this section shall be ordered by the court to perform community service for a period of 30 days.

b. A person who exhibits or displays to a law enforcement officer or a person conducting a motor vehicle inspection pursuant to chapter 8 of Title 39 of the Revised Statutes a falsely made, forged, altered, counterfeited or simulated motor vehicle insurance identification card, knowing that the insurance identification card was falsely made, forged, altered, counterfeited or simulated, commits a crime of the fourth degree.

c. A person who possesses a falsely made, forged, altered, counterfeited or simulated motor vehicle insurance identification card, knowing that the insurance identification card was falsely made, forged, altered, counterfeited or simulated, commits a disorderly persons offense.

## PRACTICAL APPLICATION OF STATUTE

The Hunk and Maxwell Borscht violated 2C:21-2.3 during their illicit transactions in which The Hunk also produced and sold a fake motor vehicle insurance card to Borscht. Subsection a. makes it a third degree crime for a person to knowingly produce, sell, offer, or expose for sale a fake motor vehicle insurance identification card. The Hunk actually is guilty of two counts under this statute since he both produced and sold the bogus ID.

Subsections b. and c distinguish between the act of knowingly displaying a fake insurance ID card to a law enforcement officer (or motor vehicle inspector) and merely possessing such ID with the knowledge that it was falsely made. In the former subsection, the crime is of the fourth degree, whereas mere possession is considered a disorderly persons offense. Obviously, Borscht could be found guilty of both. He bought and subsequently displayed to Christian Star this fake insurance card knowing full well that it was bogus.

**2C:21-2.4.**  **Possession of certain fraudulent receipts, universal product code (UPC) labels and checks**

a. Except as provided in subsection b. of this section, any person who knowingly possesses a forged or altered retail sales receipt, universal product code (UPC) label or check for the purpose of defrauding a retail merchant shall be guilty of a disorderly persons offense.

b. Any person who knowingly possesses 15 or more forged or altered retail sales receipts, universal product code labels or checks for the purpose of defrauding a retail merchant shall be guilty of a crime of the fourth degree.

## PRACTICAL APPLICATION OF STATUTE

Let's say the facts in Maxwell Borscht's case were a bit different. Instead of creating the bogus Hemingway manuscript to obtain start-up capital, Borscht obtained hundreds of fake universal product code (UPC) labels and sales receipts for MacroHard computer software that just so happened to be offering a $300 rebate to anyone sending in their UPC code and sales receipt. His intent was to send in the items in order to reap the monetary benefits of the rebate.

If the above was the case, Borscht would be guilty of an offense under 2C:21-2.4 for possession of forged or altered receipts and UPC labels. The grifter would be guilty of the fourth degree version of this crime under subsection b. since he knowingly possessed 15 or more such items with the purpose of defrauding a retail merchant. If under the same circumstances, Borscht had possessed less than 15 of the forged items, he would be guilty of a disorderly persons offense as per subsection a. of the statute.

**2C:21-3.**  **Frauds relating to public records and recordable instruments**

a. **Fraudulent destruction, removal or concealment of recordable instruments.** A person commits a crime of the third degree if, with purpose to deceive or injure anyone, he destroys, removes or conceals any will, deed, mortgage, security instrument or other writing for which the law provides public recording.

b. **Offering a false instrument for filing.** A person is guilty of a disorderly persons offense when, knowing that a written instrument contains a false statement or false information, he offers or presents it to a public office or public servant with knowledge or belief that it will be filed with, registered or recorded in or otherwise become a part of the records of such public office or public servant.

## PRACTICAL APPLICATION OF STATUTE

The Hunk tops off his devious activities with a visit to the home of Rando's father-in-law, where he destroys the man's will with the purpose of leaving him intestate. This would require that the man's assets go to his closest living immediate family member,

Rando's wife. This action plainly violates subsection a. of 2C:21-3, which makes it a third degree crime if, with purpose to deceive or injure anyone, a person destroys, removes, or conceals any will, deed, mortgage, security investment, or other writing for which the law provides public recording.

Rando's father-in-law had determined that all his assets would be transferred to charitable organizations upon his death. In destroying the man's will, The Hunk certainly had a purpose to deceive and injure the charities, which would have otherwise received the man's wealth. Accordingly, The Hunk is guilty of a third degree crime as set forth in subsection a. of 2C:21-3. This subsection makes it a third degree crime if, with purpose to deceive or injure anyone, he destroys, removes, or conceals any will, deed, mortgage, security instrument, or other writing for which the law provides public recording. The Hunk certainly had a purpose to injure the charities, which would have otherwise received the proceeds of the will, by destroying the will.

Subsection b. of this statute does not apply in this case. However, it should be noted that any individual who offers a document he knows contains false information for filing with any public office is guilty of a disorderly persons offense. This subsection, though, applies only where the individual did not actually and intentionally make the false statement or record but only has the knowledge that the information contained in the document is false. An example would be where someone noticed a typo in a boundary line agreement yet proceeded to file the agreement with the state in hopes that he might receive the benefit of the error. Remember that the actual making of such false statements or documents is a third degree offense of forgery under 2C:21-1.

| 2C:21-4. | **Falsifying or tampering with records** |
|---|---|

a. Except as provided in subsection b. of this section, a person commits a crime of the fourth degree if he falsifies, destroys, removes, conceals any writing or record, or utters any writing or record knowing that it contains a false statement or information, with purpose to deceive or injure anyone or to conceal any wrongdoing.

b. **Issuing a false financial statement.** A person is guilty of issuing a false financial statement, a crime of the third degree, when, with purpose to deceive or injure anyone or to conceal any wrongdoing; he by oath or affirmation.

   (1) Knowingly makes or utters a written instrument which purports to describe the financial condition or ability to pay of some person and which is inaccurate in some substantial respect; or

   (2) Represents in writing that a written instrument purporting to describe a person's financial condition or ability to pay as of a prior date is accurate with respect to such person's current financial condition or ability to pay, whereas, he knows it is substantially inaccurate in that respect.

## PRACTICAL APPLICATION OF STATUTE

Essentially, 2C:21-4 deals with the falsification, destruction, removal, or concealing of any writing or record with the purpose to deceive anyone or to conceal wrongdoing. Subsection b. of the statute deals specifically with issuing false financial statements.

Here's an example of an offense under this statute. Let's say Maxwell Borscht had actually stayed in business for a while, somehow eluding the authorities and the Pellman Group as to his business's true nature. During this time, he submits false reports as to the fiscal condition of the company to banks or other corporate insurance agencies in order to obtain loans or insurance coverage. Here, Borscht would be guilty of a third degree crime under subsection b.(1) of this statute. Why? Because b.(1) makes it such an offense when "with purpose to deceive" a person knowingly submits an instrument purporting to describe the financial condition of a person or entity and the instrument is inaccurate in some substantial respect.

**2C:21-4.1.**      ### Destruction, alteration, falsification of records, crime of fourth degree

A person is guilty of a crime of the fourth degree if he purposefully destroys, alters or falsifies any record relating to the care of a medical or surgical or podiatric patient in order to deceive or mislead any person as to information, including, but not limited to, a diagnosis, test, medication, treatment or medical or psychological history, concerning the patient.

## PRACTICAL APPLICATION OF STATUTE

Per 2C:21-4.1, a defendant is guilty of a crime of the fourth degree if he purposefully destroys, alters, or falsifies any record relating to care of a medical patient for the purpose of deceiving a person as to such information.

Maxwell Borscht is guilty of a crime under this statute. Borscht assumed the identity of corporate executive Kalman Greenwald. After doing so, he obtained Greenwald's medical records and began to alter them. Specifically, Borscht changed a diagnosis made by Kalman Greenwald's cardiologist from "heart murmur" to "chronic heart disease . . . which necessited a heart transplant" for the purpose of soliciting funds to pay for bogus costs associated with the "heart transplant." Here, Borscht held the necessary *mens rea* of intent to deceive and certainly committed the *actus reus* by purposefully altering the medical record. Accordingly, he is guilty of the fourth degree crime set forth in 2C:21-4.1.

**2C:21-4.2.**      ### Definitions relative to health care claims fraud

As used in this act:

"Health care claims fraud" means making, or causing to be made, a false, fictitious, fraudulent, or misleading statement of material fact in, or omitting a material fact from, or causing a material fact to be omitted from, any record, bill, claim or other document, in writing, electronically or in any other form, that a person attempts to submit, submits, causes to be submitted, or attempts to cause to be submitted for payment or reimbursement for health care services.

"Practitioner" means a person licensed in this State to practice medicine and surgery, chiropractic, podiatry, dentistry, optometry, psychology, pharmacy, nursing, physical therapy, or law; any other person licensed, registered or certified by any State agency to practice a profession or occupation in the State of New Jersey or any person similarly licensed, registered, or certified in another jurisdiction.

**2C:21-4.3.**    **Health care claims fraud; degree of crime; prosecution guidelines**

a. A practitioner is guilty of a crime of the second degree if that person knowingly commits health care claims fraud in the course of providing professional services. In addition to all other criminal penalties allowed by law, a person convicted under this subsection may be subject to a fine of up to five times the pecuniary benefit obtained or sought to be obtained.

b. A practitioner is guilty of a crime of the third degree if that person recklessly commits health care claims fraud in the course of providing professional services. In addition to all other criminal penalties allowed by law, a person convicted under this subsection may be subject to a fine of up to five times the pecuniary benefit obtained or sought to be obtained.

c. A person, who is not a practitioner subject to the provisions of subsection a. or b. of this section, is guilty of a crime of the third degree if that person knowingly commits health care claims fraud. A person, who is not a practitioner subject to the provisions of subsection a. or b. of this section, is guilty of a crime of the second degree if that person knowingly commits five or more acts of health care claims fraud and the aggregate pecuniary benefit obtained or sought to be obtained is at least $1,000. In addition to all other criminal penalties allowed by law, a person convicted under this subsection may be subject to a fine of up to five times the pecuniary benefit obtained or sought to be obtained.

d. A person, who is not a practitioner subject to the provisions of subsection a. or b. of this section, is guilty of a crime of the fourth degree if that person recklessly commits health care claims fraud. In addition to all other criminal penalties allowed by law, a person convicted under this subsection may be subject to a fine of up to five times the pecuniary benefit obtained or sought to be obtained.

e. Each act of health care claims fraud shall constitute an additional, separate and distinct offense, except that five or more separate acts may be aggregated for the purpose of establishing liability pursuant to subsection c. of this section.

f. (1) The falsity, fictitiousness, fraudulence or misleading nature of a statement may be inferred by the trier of fact in the case of a practitioner who attempts to submit, submits, causes to be submitted, or attempts to cause to be submitted, any record, bill, claim or other document for treatment or procedure without the practitioner, or an associate of the practitioner, having performed an assessment of the physical or mental condition of the patient or client necessary to determine the appropriate course of treatment.

(2) The falsity, fictitiousness, fraudulence or misleading nature of a statement may be inferred by the trier of fact in the case of a person who attempts to submit, submits, causes to be submitted, or attempts to cause to be submitted any record, bill, claim or other document for more treatments or procedures than can be performed during the time in which the treatments or procedures were represented to have been performed.

(3) Proof that a practitioner has signed or initialed a record, bill, claim or other document gives rise to an inference that the practitioner has read and reviewed that record, bill, claim or other document.

g. In order to promote the uniform enforcement of this act, the Attorney General shall develop health care claims fraud prosecution guidelines and disseminate them to the county prosecutors within 120 days of the effective date of this act.

h. For the purposes of this section, a person acts recklessly with respect to a material element of an offense when he consciously disregards a substantial and unjustifiable risk that the material element exists or will result from his conduct. The risk must be of such a nature and degree that, considering the nature and purpose of the actor's conduct and the circumstances known to him, its disregard involves a gross deviation from the standard of conduct that a reasonable person would observe in the actor's situation.

i.  (1)  Nothing in this act shall preclude an indictment and conviction for any other offense defined by the laws of this State.

(2)  Nothing in this act shall preclude an assignment judge from dismissing a prosecution of health care claims fraud if the assignment judge determines, pursuant to N.J.S. 2C:2-11, the conduct charged to be a de minimis infraction.

## PRACTICAL APPLICATION OF STATUTE

Both Maxwell Borscht and Dr. Elias Williamson would be guilty of crimes under 2C:21-4.3. This statute generally makes it a crime of varying degrees to either "knowingly" or "recklessly" commit health care claims fraud as defined by 2C:21-4.2. In a nutshell, health care claims fraud means the making of any false or misleading statement for the purpose of obtaining some fiduciary benefit as a result of such statement. 2C:21-4.3 breaks down this sort of fraud into different degrees depending upon whether the defendant is a "practitioner" and whether the *mens rea* was "knowing" or "reckless."

Maxwell Borscht went to his friend, Dr. Williamson, and asked him to act as if he performed heart transplant surgery for Borscht. Of course, no such surgery was ever performed. Thereafter, Dr. Williamson submitted claims to the appropriate insurance company to cover the "surgery" costs; the proceeds of the insurance payments were split between the doctor and Borscht.

Our good doctor would be guilty of the most severe second degree crime of health care claims fraud because he qualifies as a "practitioner" (defined in 2C:21-4.2 generally as any person licensed in New Jersey to practice medicine or other qualified medical practice) and because he "knowingly" submitted the bogus claims to the insurance company. Had Dr. Williamson submitted the claim without making reasonable efforts to confirm its authenticity but without actually knowing the claim was false, he would have likely been found to be "reckless" under subsection b. of the statute and therefore guilty of the lesser third degree offense.

Since Borscht does not qualify as a "practitioner," his offense would fall under either subsection c. or d. of the statute. Given that he "knowingly" committed health care claims fraud, Borscht would be guilty of the third degree crime under subsection c. It is important to note that under this subsection, there is a provision that would increase this crime to the second degree if the "non-practitioner" was found to have "knowingly" committed five or more acts of health care claims fraud with an aggregate pecuniary benefit of $1,000 or more. Subsection d. makes the offense one of the fourth degree when the intent is merely "reckless," as opposed to "knowing."

It is interesting to note that the New Jersey legislature has included several "presumptions" favorable to the prosecution of health care claims fraud; these are found within subsection f. of the statute. The presumptions essentially list certain behaviors or acts that if shown at trial automatically create an inference of fraudulent intent by the defendant. In general, these activities include submission of claims without performing an assessment of the patient or submission of claims for more treatments or procedures than could be performed during the time in which the procedures were represented to have been performed. It may also be inferred by the trier of fact that any document signed or initialed by the practitioner has been read and reviewed by the practitioner.

**2C:21-5.**          **Bad checks**

A person who issues or passes a check or similar sight order for the payment of money, knowing that it will not be honored by the drawee, commits an offense as provided for in subsection c. of this section. For the purposes of this section as well as in any prosecution for theft committed by means of a bad check, an issuer is presumed to know that the check or money order (other than a post-dated check or order) would not be paid, if:

a. The issuer had no account with the drawee at the time the check or order was issued; or

b. Payment was refused by the drawee for lack of funds, or due to a closed account, after a deposit by the payee into a bank for collection or after presentation to the drawee within 46 days after issue, and the issuer failed to make good within 10 days after receiving notice of that refusal or after notice has been sent to the issuer's last known address. Notice of refusal may be given to the issuer orally or in writing in any reasonable manner by any person.

c. An offense under this section is:

(1) a crime of the second degree if the check or money order is $75,000.00 or more;

(2) a crime of the third degree if the check or money order is $1,000.00 or more but is less than $75,000.00;

(3) a crime of the fourth degree if the check or money order is $200.00 or more but is less than $1,000.00;

(4) a disorderly persons offense if the check or money order is less than $200.00.

## PRACTICAL APPLICATION OF STATUTE

2C:21-5 makes it an offense to write a check "knowing" that it will not be honored by the drawee (generally a bank) under one of two circumstances. Subsection a. applies to those issuing a check where the issuer has no account with the drawee at the time the check was issued. Subsection b. applies when after the check has been refused by the drawee for lack of funds, notice is given to the issuer and he fails to make good on the amount due within 10 days after receiving notice of the refusal.

Maxwell Borscht issued a check for $3,500 in exchange for various livestock that a farmer owned in Sussex County. Borscht "knew" his check was bad. (At the time he issued the check, he was aware that no bank account existed to cover it.) Accordingly, he is guilty of an offense under 2C:21-5a.

If there had been an active account but it did not hold sufficient funds to cover the check, Borscht probably would have been guilty under subsection b., since it is unlikely he would have responded to notice of the bank's refusal to pay. It is important to note that this statute only applies to those who know that the check will not clear for any of the above reasons; therefore, individuals who accidentally overdraft their account would not be guilty of an offense under this statute.

Subsection c. of the statute lays out the degrees of offense determined by the amount of the check or money order. The degrees/amounts are set forth as follows: second degree crime for amounts of $75,000 or more; third degree for amounts of $1,000 or more but less than $75,000; fourth degree for amounts of $200 or more but less than $1,000; and it is a disorderly persons offense if the check or money order is less than

$200. Given that Borscht's bad check to the farmer was for $3,500, he is guilty of a third degree crime.

---

**2C:21-6.**        **Credit cards**

a. **Definitions.** As used in this section:

(1) "Cardholder" means the person or organization named on the face of a credit card to whom or for whose benefit the credit card is issued by an issuer.

(2) "Credit card" means any tangible or intangible instrument or device issued with or without fee by an issuer that can be used, alone or in connection with another means of account access, in obtaining money, goods, services or anything else of value on credit, including credit cards, credit plates, account numbers, or any other means of account access.

(3) "Expired credit card" means a credit card which is no longer valid because the term shown either on it or on documentation provided to the cardholder by the issuer has elapsed.

(4) "Issuer" means the business organization or financial institution which issues a credit card or its duly authorized agent.

(5) "Receives" or "receiving" means acquiring possession or control or accepting a credit card as security for a loan.

(6) "Revoked credit card" means a credit card which is no longer valid because permission to use it has been suspended or terminated by the issuer.

b. **False statements made in procuring issuance of credit card.** A person who makes or causes to be made, either directly or indirectly, any false statement in writing, knowing it to be false and with intent that it be relied on, respecting his identity or that of any other person, firm or corporation, or his financial condition or that of any other person, firm or corporation, for the purpose of procuring the issuance of a credit card is guilty of a crime of the fourth degree.

c. **Credit card theft.**

(1) A person who takes or obtains a credit card from the person, possession, custody or control of another without the cardholder's consent or who, with knowledge that it has been so taken, receives the credit card with intent to use it or to sell it, or to transfer it to a person other than the issuer or the cardholder is guilty of a crime of the fourth degree. Taking a credit card without consent includes obtaining it by any conduct defined and prescribed in Chapter 20 of this title, Theft and Related Offenses.

   A person who has in his possession or under his control (a) credit cards issued in the names of two or more other persons or, (b) two or more stolen credit cards is presumed to have violated this paragraph

(2) A person who receives a credit card that he knows to have been lost, mislaid, or delivered under a mistake as to the identity or address of the cardholder, and who retains possession with intent to use it or to sell it or to transfer it to a person other than the issuer or the cardholder is guilty of a crime of the fourth degree.

(3) A person other than the issuer who sells a credit card or a person who buys a credit card from a person other than the issuer is guilty of a crime of the fourth degree.

(4) A person who, with intent to defraud the issuer, a person or organization providing money, goods, services or anything else of value, or any other person,

obtains control over a credit card as security for debt is guilty of a crime of the fourth degree.

(5) A person who, with intent to defraud a purported issuer, a person or organization providing money, goods, services or anything else of value, or any other person, falsely makes or falsely embosses a purported credit card or utters such a credit card is guilty of a third degree offense. A person other than the purported issuer who possesses two or more credit cards which are falsely made or falsely embossed is presumed to have violated this paragraph. A person "falsely makes" a credit card when he makes or draws, in whole or in part, a device or instrument which purports to be the credit card of a named issuer but which is not such a credit card because the issuer did not authorize the making or drawing, or alters a credit card which was validly issued. A person "falsely embosses" a credit card when, without the authorization of the named issuer, he completes a credit card by adding any of the matter, other than the signature of the cardholder, which an issuer requires to appear on the credit card before it can be used by a cardholder.

(6) A person other than the cardholder or a person authorized by him who, with intent to defraud the issuer, or a person or organization providing money, goods, services or anything else of value, or any other person, signs a credit card, is guilty of a crime of the fourth degree. A person who possesses two or more credit cards which are so signed is presumed to have violated this paragraph.

d. **Intent of cardholder to defraud; penalties; knowledge of revocation.** A person, who, with intent to defraud the issuer, a person or organization providing money, goods, services or anything else of value, or any other person, (1) uses for the purpose of obtaining money, goods, services or anything else of value a credit card obtained or retained in violation of subsection c. of this section or a credit card which he knows is forged, expired or revoked, or (2) obtains money, goods, services or anything else of value by representing without the consent of the cardholder that he is the holder of a specified card or by representing that he is the holder of a card and such card has not in fact been issued, is guilty of a crime of the third degree. Knowledge of revocation shall be presumed to have been received by a cardholder four days after it has been mailed to him at the address set forth on the credit card or at his last known address by registered or certified mail, return receipt requested, and, if the address is more than 500 miles from the place of mailing, by air mail. If the address is located outside the United States, Puerto Rico, the Virgin Islands, the Canal Zone and Canada, notice shall be presumed to have been received 10 days after mailing by registered or certified mail.

e. **Intent to defraud by person authorized to furnish money, goods, or services; penalties**

(1) A person who is authorized by an issuer to furnish money, goods, services or anything else of value upon presentation of a credit card by the cardholder, or any agent or employees of such person, who, with intent to defraud the issuer or the cardholder, furnishes money, goods, services or anything else of value upon presentation of a credit card obtained or retained in violation of subsection c. of this section or a credit card which he knows is forged, expired or revoked violates this paragraph and is guilty of a crime of the third degree.

(2) A person who is authorized by an issuer to furnish money, goods, services or anything else of value upon presentation of a credit card by the cardholder, fails to furnish money, goods, services or anything else of value which he represents in writing to the issuer that he has furnished is guilty of a crime of the fourth degree.

f. **Incomplete credit cards; intent to complete without consent.** A person other than the cardholder possessing two or more incomplete credit cards, with intent to complete them without the consent of the issuer or a person possessing, with knowledge of its character, machinery, plates or any other contrivance designed to reproduce instruments purporting to be the credit cards of an issuer who has not consented to the preparation of such credit cards, is guilty of a crime of the third degree. A credit card is "incomplete" if part of the matter other than the signature of the cardholder, which an issuer requires to appear on the credit card, before it can be used by a cardholder, has not yet been stamped, embossed, imprinted or written on it.

g. **Receiving anything of value knowing or believing that it was obtained in violation of subsection d. of N.J.S.2C:21-6.** A person who receives money, goods, services or anything else of value obtained in violation of subsection d. of this section, knowing or believing that it was so obtained is guilty of a crime of the fourth degree. A person who obtains, at a discount price a ticket issued by an airline, railroad, steamship or other transportation company which was acquired in violation of subsection d. of this section without reasonable inquiry to ascertain that the person from whom it was obtained had a legal right to possess it shall be presumed to know that such ticket was acquired under circumstances constituting a violation of subsection d. of this section.

h. **Fraudulent use of credit cards.** A person who knowingly uses any counterfeit, fictitious, altered, forged, lost, stolen or fraudulently obtained credit card to obtain money, goods or services, or anything else of value; or who, with unlawful or fraudulent intent, furnishes, acquires, or uses any actual or fictitious credit card, whether alone or together with names of credit cardholders, or other information pertaining to a credit card account in any form, is guilty of a crime of the third degree.

## PRACTICAL APPLICATION OF STATUTE

2C:21-6 is a long and complex statute dealing with credit card theft and fraudulent use of either unlawfully acquired credit cards or falsely made cards. In Maxwell Borscht's case, he could rightfully be found guilty of offenses under subsections b., c., and d. of this statute.

Subsection c. makes it a crime of the fourth degree to obtain a credit card from a person without the cardholder's consent, and with intent to use it. Obviously, when Borscht stole the two cards from the Cape May home of Kalman Greenwald, he did so "without the cardholder's consent." His intent to use them was clearly manifested when he later presented the cards to obtain cash advances. With these two elements met, Borscht could be convicted of a fourth degree crime as provided for in 2C:21-6c. However, his crime should probably be elevated to one of the third degree.

Subsection c., as discussed above, deals with the possession of credit cards "with intent to defraud." Once the defendant actually uses the cards for the purpose of obtaining money, goods, services, or anything else of value, he falls into subsection d. of the statute, which automatically makes such behavior a crime of the third degree. In our case, once Borscht maxed out the cards via cash advances, he moved from the fourth degree crime of mere possession with intent to defraud to the third degree offense of actually using them to defraud the issuer.

In addition to this offense, Borscht violated subsection b. when he used the stolen cards, along with his phony driver's license, to apply for additional credit cards in Kalman Greenwald's name. Under subsection b. of the statute, it is a crime of the fourth degree to make false statements for the purpose of procuring the issuance of a credit card.

2C:21-7.    **Deceptive business practices**

A person commits an offense if in the course of business he:
   a. Uses or possesses for use a false weight or measure, or any other device for falsely determining or recording any quality or quantity;
   b. Sells, offers or exposes for sale, or delivers less than the represented quantity of any commodity or service;
   c. Takes or attempts to take more than the represented quantity of any commodity or service when as buyer he furnishes the weight or measure;
   d. Sells, offers or exposes for sale adulterated or mislabeled commodities;
   e. Makes a false or misleading statement in any advertisement addressed to the public or to a substantial segment thereof for the purpose of promoting the purchase or sale of property or services;
   f. Deleted by Amendment (P.L.1981, c. 290).
   g. Deleted by Amendment (P.L.1981, c. 290).
   h. Makes a false or misleading written statement for the purpose of obtaining property or credit; or
   i. Makes a false or misleading written statement for the purpose of promoting the sale of securities, or omits information required by law to be disclosed in written documents relating to securities.

    The offense is a crime of the fourth degree if subsection h. or i. is violated. Otherwise it is a disorderly persons offense.

    It is an affirmative defense to prosecution under this section if the defendant proves by a preponderance of the evidence that his conduct was not knowingly or recklessly deceptive.

"Adulterated" means varying from the standard of composition or quality prescribed by or pursuant to any statute providing criminal penalties for such variance, or set by established commercial usage. "Mislabeled" means varying from the standard of truth or disclosure in labeling prescribed by or pursuant to any statute providing criminal penalties for such variance, or set by established commercial usage.

## PRACTICAL APPLICATION OF STATUTE

Perhaps it is only fitting that Maxwell Borscht became a victim of fraud at some point during his own series of deceptions. When Borshct actually paid for a large jar of "anti-aging" pills that were labeled as being made from rare coral found only off the coast of Australia, the merchant was in violation of 2C:21-7d. Why? Because it turned out that the merchant had actually produced the pills in his own basement from common household ingredients.

    2C:21-7d. makes it a disorderly persons offense to sell, offer, or expose for sale mislabeled commodities. The statute, in total, deals with various deceptive means of selling a falsely determined quality or quantity of any sort of commodity or service. While subsection d. qualifies as a disorderly persons offense, there are two subsections of 2C:21-7 that deal with offenses considered fourth degree crimes. These subsections, h. and i., make it a fourth degree crime to either make false or misleading written statements for the purpose of obtaining property or credit or make false or misleading written statements (or to omit information required by law to be disclosed) for the purpose of promoting the sale of securities.

In the case of the "anti-aging" pill merchant, he is guilty of 2C:21-7's lesser offense. He misrepresented where the pills' ingredients were derived from in order to facilitate sales; accordingly, he violated subsection d. of the statute and is guilty of a disorderly persons offense.

**2C:21-7.1.**   **Repealed**

**2C:21-7.2.**   **Definitions**

As used in this act:

a. "Advertise" means engaging in promotional activities including, but not limited to, newspaper, radio and television advertising; the distribution of fliers and circulars; and the display of window and interior signs.

b. "Food," "food product," or "food commodity" means any food, food product or food preparation, whether raw or prepared for human consumption, and whether in a solid or liquid state, including, but not limited to, any meat, meat product or meat preparation; any milk, milk product or milk preparation; and any alcoholic or non-alcoholic beverage.

c. "Food commodity in package form" means a food commodity put up or packaged in any manner in advance of sale in units suitable for retail sale and which is not intended for consumption at the point of manufacture.

d. "Kosher" means prepared under and maintained in strict compliance with the laws and customs of the Orthodox Jewish religion and includes foods prepared for the festival of Passover and represented to be "kosher for Passover."

**2C:21-7.3.**   **False representations**

a. A false representation prohibited by this act shall include any oral or written statement that directly or indirectly tends to deceive or otherwise lead a reasonable individual to believe that a non-kosher food or food product is kosher.

b. The presence of any non-kosher food or food product in any place of business that advertises or represents itself in any manner as selling, offering for sale, preparing or serving kosher food or food products only, is presumptive evidence that the person in possession offers the same for sale in violation of this act.

c. It shall be a complete defense to a prosecution under this act that the defendant relied in good faith upon the representations of a slaughterhouse, manufacturer, processor, packer or distributor, or any person or organization which certifies or represents any food or food product at issue to be kosher, kosher for Passover, or as having been prepared under or sanctioned by Orthodox Jewish religious requirements.

**2C:21-7.4.**   **Disorderly persons offense**

A person commits a disorderly persons offense if in the course of business he:

a. (1) Falsely represents any food sold, prepared, served or offered for sale to be kosher or kosher for Passover;

(2) Removes or destroys, or causes to be removed or destroyed, the original means of identification affixed to food commodities to indicate that same are kosher or kosher for Passover, except that this paragraph shall not be construed to prevent the removal of the identification if the commodity is offered for sale as non-kosher; or

(3) Sells, disposes of or has in his possession for the purpose of resale as kosher any food commodity to which a slaughterhouse plumba, mark, stamp, tag, brand, label or other means of identification has been fraudulently attached.

b.  (1) Labels or identifies a food commodity in package form to be kosher or kosher for Passover or possesses such labels or means of identification, unless he is the manufacturer or packer of the food commodity in package form;

(2) Labels or identifies an article of food not in package form to be kosher or kosher for Passover or possesses such labels or other means of identification, unless he is the manufacturer of the article of food;

(3) Falsely labels any food commodity in package form as kosher or kosher for Passover by having or permitting to be inscribed on it, in any language, the words "kosher" or "kosher for Passover," "parve," "glatt," or any other words or symbols which would tend to deceive or otherwise lead a reasonable individual to believe that the commodity is kosher or kosher for Passover; or

(4) Labels any food commodity in package form by having or permitting to be inscribed on it the words "kosher-style," "kosher-type," "Jewish," or "Jewish-style," unless the product label also displays the word "non-kosher" in letters at least as large and in close proximity.

c.  (1) Sells, offers for sale, prepares, or serves in or from the same place of business both unpackaged non-kosher food and unpackaged food he represents to be kosher unless he posts a window sign at the entrance of his establishment which states in block letters at least four inches in height: "Kosher and Non-Kosher Foods Sold Here," or "Kosher and Non-Kosher Foods Served Here," or a statement of similar import; or

(2) Employs any Hebrew word or symbol in any advertising of any food offered for sale or place of business in which food is prepared, whether for on-premises or off-premises consumption, unless the advertisement also sets forth in conjunction therewith and in English, the words "We Sell Kosher Food Only," "We Sell Both Kosher and Non-Kosher Foods," or words of similar import, in letters of at least the same size as the characters used in Hebrew. For the purpose of this paragraph, "Hebrew symbol" means any Hebrew word, or letter, or any symbol, emblem, sign, insignia, or other mark that simulates a Hebrew word or letter.

d.  (1) Displays for sale in the same show window or other location on or in his place of business, both unpackaged food represented to be kosher and unpackaged non-kosher food, unless he:

(a) displays over the kosher and non-kosher food signs that read, in clearly visible block letters, "kosher food" and "non-kosher food," respectively, or, as to the display of meat alone, "kosher meat" and "non-kosher meat," respectively;

(b) separates the kosher food products from the non-kosher food products by keeping the products in separate display cabinets, or by segregating kosher items from non-kosher items by use of clearly visible dividers; and

(c) slices or otherwise prepares the kosher food products for sale with utensils used solely for kosher food items;

(2) Prepares or serves any food as kosher whether for consumption in his place of business or elsewhere if in the same place of business he also prepares or serves non-kosher food, unless he:

(a) uses and maintains separate and distinctly labeled or marked dishes and utensils for each type of food; and

(b) includes in clearly visible block letters the statement "Kosher and Non-Kosher Foods Prepared and Sold Here" in each menu or sign used or posted on the premises or distributed or advertised off the premises;

(3) Sells or has in his possession for the purpose of resale as kosher any food commodity not having affixed thereto the original slaughterhouse plumba, mark, stamp, tag, brand, label or other means of identification employed to indicate that the food commodity is kosher or kosher for Passover; or

(4) Sells or offers for sale, as kosher, any fresh meat or poultry that is identified as "soaked and salted," unless (a) the product has in fact been soaked and salted in a manner which makes it kosher; and (b) the product is marked "soaked and salted" on the package label or, if the product is not packaged, on a sign prominently displayed in conjunction with the product. For the purpose of this paragraph, "fresh meat or poultry" shall mean meat and poultry that has not been processed except for salting and soaking.

## PRACTICAL APPLICATION OF STATUTE

2C:21-7.2, 2C:21-7.3, and 2C:21-7.4 work together to make it a disorderly persons offense to "knowingly" misrepresent non-kosher foods as being kosher or "kosher for Passover." 2C:21-7.2 contains the general definitions to be used in these related statutes, which are basically self-explanatory. 2C:21-7.3 contains some further definitional subsections, explaining that a "false representation" prohibited by the act constitutes any oral or written statement that either directly or indirectly leads a person to believe that non-kosher food or food products are kosher.

It is important to note, however, that subsection c. of 2C:21-7.3 provides a complete defense to any prosecution under the three statutes. If the defendant relied in good faith upon the representations of an organization, such as a slaughterhouse, which certified any food at issue to be kosher (or having been prepared under Orthodox Jewish religious requirements), then he has an affirmative defense.

The heart of these three statutes lies in 2C:21-7.4, which provides an extensive list of offenses, all considered disorderly persons offenses, dealing with the knowing misrepresentation of non-kosher foods as being kosher. Although the entire list boils down to the aforementioned knowing misrepresentation, the specifics include activities such as mislabeling or falsely labeling any food commodity as kosher and removing original means of identification indicating that foods are kosher. There are additional requirements mentioned, such as the use of separate utensils for serving or preparing kosher and non-kosher foods, but ultimately the bottom line is that one cannot falsely serve, label, prepare, display, or otherwise promote packaged or non-packaged food as kosher unless he has followed the strict Orthodox Jewish religious requirements. Failure to do so may result in a conviction of a disorderly persons offense.

**2C:21-8.**

### Misrepresentation of mileage of motor vehicle

A person commits a disorderly persons offense when he sells, exchanges, offers for sale or exchange or exposes for sale or exchange a used motor vehicle on which he has changed or disconnected the mileage registering instrument on the vehicle to show a lesser mileage reading than that actually recorded on the vehicle or on the instrument with purpose to misrepresent the mileage of the vehicle. This provision shall not prevent the servicing, repair or replacement of a mileage registering instrument which by reason of normal wear or through damage requires service, repair or replacement if the instrument is then set at zero or at the actual previously recorded mileage.

In addition to the penalty authorized for violation of this section, the Director of the Division of Motor Vehicles may, after notice and hearing, revoke the license of any motor vehicle dealer as defined in R.S. 39:1-1 so convicted.

## PRACTICAL APPLICATION OF STATUTE

Let us assume that Maxwell Borscht had come up with yet another scheme for raising start-up capital for his fraudulent business, Jackpot Entertainment Insurance. This time he happens to find several cars in Kalman Greenwald's garage and decides to modify the odometer on a few of them. He then sells them for more money than their fair market value would have yielded if the true mileage was presented. Here, Borscht would have committed a disorderly persons offense under 2C:21-8. This statute proscribes the sale or exchange, or offer for sale or exchange, of any used motor vehicle on which a person has changed the mileage on the vehicle—to show a lesser mileage than actually recorded on the vehicle. In order to be convicted under 2C:21-8, the defendant must act "with purpose to misrepresent the mileage of the vehicle." But why else would someone set back the mileage of a vehicle? Perhaps accidentally?

**2C:21-8.1.**        **Definition; determination of degree of offense**

a. As used in chapter 21, unless a different meaning plainly is required:

"Benefit derived" means the loss resulting from the offense or any gain or advantage to the actor, or coconspirators, or any person in whom the actor is interested, whichever is greater, whether loss, gain or advantage takes the form of money, property, commercial interests or anything else the primary significance of which is economic gain.

b. The benefit derived or resulting harm in violation of chapter 21 shall be determined by the trier of fact. The benefit derived or resulting harm pursuant to one scheme or course of conduct, whether in relation to the same person or several persons, may be aggregated in determining the degree of the offense.

**2C:21-9.**        **Misconduct by corporate official**

A person is guilty of a crime when:

a. Being a director of a corporation, he knowingly with purpose to defraud, concurs in any vote or act of the directors of such corporation, or any of them, which has the purpose of:

(1) Making a dividend except in the manner provided by law;

(2) Dividing, withdrawing or in any manner paying to any stockholder any part of the capital stock of the corporation except in the manner provided by law;

(3) Discounting or receiving any note or other evidence of debt in payment of an installment of capital stock actually called in and required to be paid, or with purpose of providing the means of making such payment;

(4) Receiving or discounting any note or other evidence of debt with purpose of enabling any stockholder to withdraw any part of the money paid in by him on his stock; or

(5) Applying any portion of the funds of such corporation, directly or indirectly, to the purchase of shares of its own stock, except in the manner provided by law; or

b. Being a director or officer of a corporation, he, with purpose to defraud:

(1) Issues, participates in issuing, or concurs in a vote to issue any increase of its capital stock beyond the amount of the capital stock thereof, duly authorized by or in pursuance of law; or

(2) Sells, or agrees to sell, or is directly interested in the sale of any share of stock of such corporation, or in any agreement to sell the same, unless at the time of such sale or agreement he is an actual owner of such share, provided that the foregoing shall not apply to a sale by or on behalf of an underwriter or dealer in connection with a bona fide public offering of shares of stock of such corporation.

c. He purposely or knowingly uses, controls or operates a corporation for the furtherance or promotion of any criminal object.

If the benefit derived from a violation of this section is $75,000.00, or more, the offender is guilty of a crime of the second degree. If the benefit derived exceeds $1,000.00, but is less than $75,000.00, the offender is guilty of a crime of the third degree. If the benefit derived is $1,000.00, or less, the offender is guilty of a crime of the fourth degree.

## Practical Application of Statute

Aside from the problems that Maxwell Borscht likely caused The Pellman Group, Sandi Ireland and the other board members of that company could be facing serious second degree criminal charges themselves for their arbitrary decision to issue a $150,000 "President's Day bonus" dividend to each other while knowing this was in violation of the corporation's bylaws.

2C:21-9a.(1) specifically proscribes the board members' actions by making it a crime for a director of a corporation to "knowingly with purpose to defraud" vote in his capacity as a director to issue a dividend. Only dividends issued in "the manner provided by law" are permissible per this statute. Because the board members were aware that this "President's Day bonus" was not allowed, they certainly had the requisite *mens rea*, "knowingly with purpose to defraud," necessary for conviction under this statute.

2C:21-9 breaks down these offenses into degree based upon the monetary benefit derived from the violation. Given that each board member voted for a bonus of $150,000 for each individual, they would fall into the most severe category, which makes it a second degree crime when the benefit derived is $75,000 or more. Amounts over $1,000 but less than $75,000 fall into the third degree category, and amounts of $1,000 or less are fourth degree crimes.

**2C:21-10.**     **Commercial bribery and breach of duty to act disinterestedly**

a. A person commits a crime if he solicits, accepts or agrees to accept any benefit as consideration for knowingly violating or agreeing to violate a duty of fidelity to which he is subject as

(1) An agent, partner or employee of another;

(2) A trustee, guardian, or other fiduciary;

(3) A lawyer, physician, accountant, appraiser, or other professional adviser or informant;

(4) An officer, director, manager or other participant in the direction of the affairs of an incorporated or unincorporated association;

(5) A labor official, including any duly appointed representative of a labor organization or any duly appointed trustee or representative of an employee welfare trust fund; or

(6) An arbitrator or other purportedly disinterested adjudicator or referee.

b. A person who holds himself out to the public as being engaged in the business of making disinterested selection, appraisal, or criticism of commodities, real properties or services commits a crime if he solicits, accepts or agrees to accept any benefit to influence his selection, appraisal or criticism.

c. A person commits a crime if he confers, or offers or agrees to confer, any benefit the acceptance of which would be criminal under this section.

d. If the benefit offered, conferred, agreed to be conferred, solicited, accepted or agreed to be accepted in violation of this section is $75,000.00 or more, the offender is guilty of a crime of the second degree. If the benefit exceeds $1,000.00, but is less than $75,000.00, the offender is guilty of a crime of the third degree. If the benefit is $1,000.00 or less, the offender is guilty of a crime of the fourth degree.

## PRACTICAL APPLICATION OF STATUTE

Sandi Ireland, one of The Pellman Group's board of directors, accepted $50,000 from Maxwell Borscht in return for granting the formation of a subsidiary company named Jackpot Entertainment Insurance. She knew that the creation of this subsidiary company could be detrimental to The Pellman Group and its shareholders. This act renders her guilty of a third degree crime.

2C:21-10 makes it a crime for a director, such as Ireland, to accept any benefit as consideration for "knowingly" violating a duty of fidelity to the company that she serves. Subsection a. lists various positions from which a duty of fidelity to another person or entity is implied. In Ireland's case, she falls within subsection a.(4) as a director of "an incorporated or unincorporated association," violating her fiduciary duty not only to The Pellman Group but to its shareholders as well. Her acceptance of $50,000 in return for the formation of the subsidiary without any sort of research into the proposed subsidiary or Borscht himself would probably constitute a breach of fiduciary duty. Given that Ireland "knew" what Borscht was up to—in creating a sham subsidiary, she certainly breached this fiduciary duty and committed a crime under 2C:21-10.

Similar to the previous statute, the degree of crime associated with a violation of 2C:21-10 is broken down by the dollar amount of the benefit offered, conferred, accepted, or agreed to. The most severe, second degree crime, is reserved for benefits of $75,000 or more. Amounts less than $75,000 but more than $1,000 are third degree crimes, and benefits of $1,000 or less are considered crimes of the fourth degree. Ireland's acceptance of $50,000 would place her within the third degree version of this crime.

**2C:21-11.**     **Rigging publicly exhibited contest**

a. A person commits a crime if, with purpose to prevent a publicly exhibited contest from being conducted in accordance with the rules and usages which govern it, he:

(1) Confers or offers or agrees to confer any benefit upon, or threatens any injury to a participant, official or other person associated with the contest or exhibition; or

(2) Tampers with any person, animal or thing.

b. **Soliciting or accepting benefit for rigging.** A person commits a crime if he knowingly solicits, accepts or agrees to accept any benefit the giving of which would be criminal under subsection a.

c. If the benefit offered, conferred, agreed to be conferred, solicited, accepted or agreed to be accepted in violation of subsections a. and b. of this section is $75,000.00 or more, the offender is guilty of a crime of the second degree. If the benefit exceeds $1,000.00, but is less than $75,000.00, the offender is guilty of a crime of the third degree. If the benefit is $1,000.00 or less, the offender is guilty of a crime of the fourth degree.

d. **Failure to report solicitation for rigging.** A person commits a disorderly persons offense if he fails to report, with reasonable promptness, a solicitation to accept any benefit or to do any tampering, the giving or doing of which would be criminal under subsection a.

e. **Participation in rigged contest.** A person commits a crime of the fourth degree if he knowingly engages in, sponsors, pr1oduces, judges, or otherwise participates in a publicly exhibited contest knowing that the contest is being conducted in violation of subsection a. of this section.

## PRACTICAL APPLICATION OF STATUTE

2C:21-11 makes it criminal, in varying degrees, to engage in activities involving the rigging of contests. Very simply, a person commits a crime if he attempts to either confer any benefit upon or threaten injury to a participant, official, or other person associated with the contest "with a purpose" to prevent the contest from being conducted in accordance with its rules. This applies to a number of situations, including anyone who would tamper with a person, animal, or thing in an attempt to alter the outcome. For instance, if a jockey was found to have used some sort of electrical shock system forbidden by the horse racing rules in order to get his horse to outperform the rest of the horses, he could be convicted of an offense under this statute. Dependent upon the amount of benefit offered, conferred, or agreed to, the offense would vary in degree from a second degree crime to a crime of the fourth degree. Amounts of $75,000 or more are second degree offenses, less than $75,000 but more than $1,000 are third degree crimes, and $1,000 or less are fourth degree crimes.

The statute also makes it a disorderly persons offense to fail to report solicitation for such rigging. If a person is solicited to accept any benefit or do any tampering that would constitute illegal tampering, he is required to report such solicitation with "reasonable promptness." Although the statute does not give a specific time line of what "reasonable promptness" is, it would be safe to assume that the solicitee would be required to report the solicitation at the earliest opportune moment given the facts and circumstances of the matter.

## 2C:21-12.    Defrauding secured creditors

A person is guilty of a crime of the fourth degree when he destroys, removes, conceals, encumbers, transfers or otherwise deals with property subject to a security interest with purpose to hinder enforcement of that interest.

## PRACTICAL APPLICATION OF STATUTE

Let's say Maxwell Borscht had rightful possession of a mortgaged truck which he used in his pizza business. If he, with the intent to defraud the mortgagee, removed the truck from the state when he fell behind in payments and received notice of repossession, he would be guilty of the fourth degree crime of defrauding secured creditors. 2C:21-12 makes it a crime to remove property subject to a security interest with the purpose to hinder enforcement of that interest. It is important to note that there must be an intent to defraud in order to be convicted under this statute. Therefore, if Borscht had simply been operating his truck in the tristate area as part of his normal course of business (and not to hinder the lawful repossession of it), his removal of the property from the state would not constitute a violation of this statute.

**2C:21-13.**    **Fraud in insolvency**

A person commits a crime if, knowing that proceedings have been or are about to be instituted for the appointment of a receiver or other person entitled to administer property for the benefit of creditors, or that any other composition or liquidation for the benefit of creditors has been or is about to be made, he:

a. Destroys, removes, conceals, encumbers, transfers, or otherwise deals with any property or obtains any substantial part of or interest in the debtor's estate with purpose to defeat or obstruct the claim of any creditor, or otherwise to obstruct the operation of any law relating to administration of property for the benefit of creditors;

b. Knowingly falsifies any writing or record relating to the property; or

c. Knowingly misrepresents or refuses to disclose to a receiver or other person entitled to administer property for the benefit of creditors, the existence, amount or location of the property, or any other information which the actor could be legally required to furnish in relation to such administration.

If the benefit derived from a violation of this section is $75,000.00, or more, the offender is guilty of a crime of the second degree. If the benefit derived exceeds $1,000.00, but is less than $75,000.00, the offender is guilty of a crime of the third degree. If the benefit derived is $1,000.00, or less, the offender is guilty of a crime of the fourth degree.

## PRACTICAL APPLICATION OF STATUTE

Returning to the pizza parlor example, let's say Maxwell Borscht had become insolvent and received notice that proceedings had been started for the repossession of the parlors and all his materials used in the business. The proceedings were initiated to repay creditors to which he owed money. Borscht, though, decides that he is not going to allow authorities to take his things. Instead, he destroys everything that he can't remove from the parlors and hides everything else in a warehouse that he secretly rented under another name. Here, he would have committed the crime of fraud in insolvency as defined in 2C:21-13.

Subsection a. of this statute makes it a crime when a person—"knowing" that proceedings have been instituted for repossession of property for the benefit of creditors—destroys, removes, conceals, encumbers, or transfers any property "with purpose to defeat or obstruct the claim of any creditor." Since this is exactly what Borscht did in the above example, he is guilty of violating subsection a. of 2C:21-13.

If the repossession team knew Borscht had hidden certain materials and he refused to disclose the location of such materials upon request, Borscht's behavior would fall within subsection c. of the statute. This subsection makes it a crime to knowingly misrepresent the existence, amount, or location of such property.

Given that the value of Borscht's materials that were either demolished or hidden would likely exceed $75,000, Borscht would be convicted of the second degree version of this crime. This statute follows many of the preceding statutes in determining the degree of the crime in association with the dollar amount of benefit derived: second degree for amounts over $75,000, third degree for amounts above $1,000 but less than $75,000, and fourth degree for amounts of $1,000 or less.

## 2C:21-14.    Receiving deposits in a failing financial institution

An officer, manager or other person directing or participating in the direction of a financial institution commits a crime of the fourth degree if he receives or permits the receipt of a deposit, premium payment or other investment in the institution knowing that:

a. Due to financial difficulties the institution is about to suspend operations or go into receivership or reorganization; and

b. The person making the deposit or other payment is unaware of the precarious situation of the institution.

## PRACTICAL APPLICATION OF STATUTE

This fairly straightforward statute makes it a crime of the fourth degree for a financial institution or authorized person thereof to accept deposits, premium payments, or other investments in the institution knowing that the institution is about to stop operations due to financial difficulties and knowing that the person making the deposit or other payment is unaware of the precarious situation of the institution. It is important to note that this crime requires the knowledge of both prongs of the offense. Therefore, regardless of the institution's financial problems, if the person making the deposit is aware of this "precarious situation" and still makes the deposit, the institution or its managers have not committed an offense under this statute. Obviously, a teller or other employee of the institution accepting deposits without the requisite knowledge of the institution's financial condition should not be found guilty of this crime.

## 2C:21-15.    Misapplication of entrusted property and property of government or financial institution

A person commits a crime if he applies or disposes of property that has been entrusted to him as a fiduciary, or property belonging to or required to be withheld for the benefit of the government or of a financial institution in a manner which he knows is unlawful and involves substantial risk of loss or detriment to the owner of the property or to a person for whose benefit the property was entrusted whether or not the actor has derived a pecuniary benefit. "Fiduciary" includes trustee, guardian, executor, administrator, receiver and any person carrying on fiduciary functions on behalf of a corporation or other organization which is a fiduciary.

If the benefit derived from a violation of this section is $75,000.00, or more, the offender is guilty of a crime of the second degree. If the benefit derived exceeds $1,000.00, but is less than $75,000.00, the offender is guilty of a crime of the third degree. If the benefit derived is $1,000.00, or less, the offender is guilty of a crime of the fourth degree.

For the purposes of this section, the term "benefit derived" shall include but shall not be limited to the amount of any tax avoided, evaded or otherwise unpaid or improperly retained or disposed of.

## Practical Application of Statute

Extending the facts of Maxwell Borscht's case can help explain this statute. Borscht hires a few employees for his bogus Jackpot Entertainment Insurance company. In an attempt to make the company appear as legitimate as possible, he institutes 401(k) plans for these employees. Instead of using the money contributed by the employees for the plan, though, he uses this money to cover his company's expenses. Here, Borscht could rightfully be found guilty of a crime under 2C:21-15.

This statute makes it criminal to apply or dispose of property that has been entrusted to a person as a fiduciary "in a manner which he knows is unlawful and involves substantial risk of loss or detriment to the owner of the property or to a person for whose benefit the property was entrusted." Clearly, Borscht, posing as the head of Jackpot Entertainment Insurance, would be considered a fiduciary in respect to the money given to him by the employees for the 401(k) plan. Obviously, Borscht knew that using this money for company expenses was unlawful and involved a substantial risk of loss and detriment to the employees. Acccordingly, he is guilty of violating 2C:21-15; in this case, the crime would probably be one of the second degree, as the amount involved likely would exceed $75,000.

Like many of the other statutes in Chapter 21, the offense is broken into degrees based upon the dollar amount of the benefit. Amounts of $75,000 or more are second degree offenses, less than $75,000 but more than $1,000 are third degree, and $1,000 or less are a fourth degree offense. As mentioned earlier, the failure to report solicitation for rigging is a disorderly persons offense.

**2C:21-16.**     ### Securing execution of documents by deception

A person commits a crime of the fourth degree if by deception as to the contents of the instrument, he causes or induces another to execute any instrument affecting, purporting to affect, or likely to affect the pecuniary interest of any person.

## Practical Application of Statute

This short statute makes it a fourth degree crime to cause another to execute any instrument affecting the pecuniary interest of any person by means of deception as to the contents of the instrument. If we return to The Hunk's "restructuring" of Rando's father's will (making Rando the sole beneficiary of his dad's estate), we can apply this statute by modifying the facts a bit.

Instead of dissolving the will's ink and replacing it, The Hunk creates a new will containing the language favorable to Rando. The Hunk then proceeds to Rando's father and convinces him that the document is merely a receipt, acknowledging the delivery of a package, that requires his signature. If the man signed the will, thinking it was merely a receipt, The Hunk would have violated this statute and could rightfully be charged with a fourth degree crime.

**2C:21-17.**      **Impersonation; Theft of Identity; crime**

a. A person is guilty of an offense if the person:

(1) Impersonates another or assumes a false identity and does an act in such assumed character or false identity for purpose of obtaining a benefit for himself or another or to injure or defraud another;

(2) Pretends to be a representative of some person or organization and does an act in such pretended capacity for the purpose of obtaining a benefit for himself or another or to injure or defraud another;

(3) Impersonates another, assumes a false identity or makes a false or misleading statement regarding the identity of any person, in an oral or written application for services, for the purpose of obtaining services; or

(4) Obtains any personal identifying information pertaining to another person and uses that information, or assists another person in using the information, in order to assume the identity of or represent themselves as another person, without that person's authorization and with the purpose to fraudulently obtain or attempt to obtain a benefit or services, or avoid the payment of debt or other legal obligation or avoid prosecution for a crime by using the name of the other person.

As used in this section:

"Benefit" means, but is not limited to, any property, any pecuniary amount, any services, any pecuniary amount sought to be avoided or any injury or harm perpetrated on another where there is no pecuniary value.

b. A person is guilty of an offense if, in the course of making an oral or written application for services, the person impersonates another, assumes a false identity or makes a false or misleading statement with the purpose of avoiding payment for prior services. Purpose to avoid payment for prior services may be presumed upon proof that the person has not made full payment for prior services and has impersonated another, assumed a false identity or made a false or misleading statement regarding the identity of any person in the course of making oral or written application for services.

c. (1) If the actor obtains a benefit or deprives another of a benefit in an amount less than $500 and the offense involves the identity of one victim, the actor shall be guilty of a crime of the fourth degree.

(2) For a second or subsequent offense, or if the actor obtains a benefit or deprives another of a benefit in an amount of at least $500 but less than $75,000, or the offense involves the identity of at least two but less than five victims, the actor shall be guilty of a crime of the third degree.

(3) If the actor obtains a benefit or deprives another of a benefit in the amount of $75,000 or more, or the offense involves the identity of more than five victims, the actor shall be guilty of a crime of the second degree.

d. A violation of R.S.33:1-81 or section 6 of P.L.1968, c.313 (C.33:1-81.7) for using the personal identifying information of another to illegally purchase an alcoholic beverage or for using the personal identifying information of another to misrepresent his age for the purpose of obtaining tobacco or other consumer product denied to persons under 18 years of age shall not constitute an offense under this section if the actor received only that benefit or service and did not perpetrate or attempt to perpetrate any additional injury or fraud on another.

e. The sentencing court shall issue such orders as are necessary to correct any public record that contains false information as a result of a theft of identity. The sentencing court may provide restitution to the victim in accordance with the provisions of section 4 of P.L.2002, c.85 (C.2C:21-17.1).

## Practical Application of Statute

After Maxwell Borscht stole Kalman Greenwald's credit cards and created a phony driver's license in Greenwald's name, he set out to visit several businesses in New Jersey. Pursuant to these visits, he obtained, through impersonation of Greenwald, several items on credit from merchants. The merchants were familiar with Greenwald's reputation but not his physical appearance. By carrying these acts through, Borscht could add to his list of offenses an offense under 2C:21-17, subsection a.(1).

This statute makes it a crime to impersonate another, or assume a false identity, and perform an act under such assumed character. The illicit act must be done for the "purpose of obtaining a benefit for himself or another or to injure or defraud another."

Borscht used Greenwald's identity to defraud merchants and obtain benefit. Specifically, the false pretense allowed him to obtain several items of value on invoice, including office furniture, equipment, and handmade suits. Borscht, as Greenwald, agreed to pay the vendors within 30 days. Payment, of course, was never remitted. With this being the case, Borscht is guilty of a crime under 2C:21-17a.(1).

The offenses defined in this statute are broken down by degree in accordance with the pecuniary amount involved or the number of false identities assumed. Amounts of $75,000 or more, or more than five false identities, are considered crimes in the second degree; amounts less than $75,000 but of $500 or more, or at least two but less than five false identities are crimes of the third degree. For amounts less than $500, or one false identity, the offender is guilty of a crime of the fourth degree.

It appears from the facts in Borscht's case that he would be guilty of at least the third degree version of this crime. Possibly, he could be guilty of a crime of the second degree, since it is feasible that the office equipment, furniture, and handmade suits could come to an amount over $75,000.

It should be noted that if the impersonation was merely for the purpose of obtaining a driver's license or motor vehicle registration, or to purchase alcohol underage, it will not be considered an offense under this section if the actor received only that benefit or service and did not perpetrate or attempt to perpetrate any additional injury or fraud on another. This type of behavior is addressed and proscribed in other statutes found in the code.

**2C:21-17.1.     Restitution to victim of unlawful use of personal identifying information**

Restitution to a victim of an offense under N.J.S.2C:21-1, section 1 of P.L.1983, c.565 (C.2C:21-2.1) or N.J.S. 2C:21-17 when the offense concerns personal identifying information may include costs incurred by the victim:

a. in clearing the credit history or credit rating of the victim; or

b. in connection with any civil or administrative proceeding to satisfy any debt, lien, or other obligation of the victim arising as a result of the actions of the defendant.

**2C:21-17.2.**     ### Use of personal identifying information of another, certain; second degree crime

a. A person is guilty of a crime of the second degree if, in obtaining or attempting to obtain a driver's license or other document issued by a governmental agency which could be used as a means of verifying a person's identity, age or any other personal identifying information, that person knowingly exhibits, displays or utters a document or other writing which falsely purports to be a driver's license or other document issued by a governmental agency or which belongs or pertains to a person other than the person who possesses the document.

b. Notwithstanding the provisions of N.J.S.2C:1-8 or any other law, a conviction under this section shall not merge with a conviction of any other criminal offense, nor shall such other conviction merge with a conviction under this section, and the court shall impose separate sentences upon each violation of this section and any other criminal offense.

c. A violation of R.S.33:1-81 or section 6 of P.L.1968, c.313 (C.33:1-81.7) for using the personal identifying information of another to illegally purchase an alcoholic beverage or for using the personal identifying information of another to misrepresent his age for the purpose of obtaining tobacco or other consumer product denied to persons under 18 years of age shall not constitute an offense under this section if the actor received only that benefit or service and did not perpetrate or attempt to perpetrate any additional injury or fraud on another.

## PRACTICAL APPLICATION OF STATUTE

This 2003-enacted statute apparently makes it a second degree crime to obtain or attempt to obtain a driver's license (or other government document that can be used as personal identification) by "knowingly" exhibiting a document "which falsely purports to be a driver's license or other document issued by a governmental agency or which belongs or pertains to a person other than the person who possesses the document." The case of Maxwell Borscht can help explain this statute.

Let's say Borscht appears at the New Jersey Division of Motor Vehicles and presents a fictitious Maryland driver's license in the name of Frank Malpone. Borscht claims to be Malpone and is now seeking a New Jersey driver's license in that name. Here, Borscht "knowingly" exhibited a government document that "falsely purported" to be a "driver's license" of another. He did this in an effort to fraudulently obtain a New Jersey driver's license. Accordingly, he is guilty of violating 2C:21-17.2.

### Exception for Alcohol and Tobacco Purchases

Subsection c. of 2C:21-17.2 carves out an exception wherein the statute shall not apply. A person may avoid conviction under 2C:21-17.2 if he:

1. uses the personal identifying information of another for the purpose of illegally purchasing alcohol; or

2. uses the personal identifying information of another "to misrepresent his age for the purpose of obtaining tobacco or other consumer product denied to persons under 18 years of age."

The aforementioned acts shall not constitute an offense under 2C:21-17.2 if the actor received *only* the above benefits or services and if the actor "did not perpetrate or attempt to perpetrate any additional injury or fraud on another."

**2C:21-17.3.**    **Trafficking in personal identifying information pertaining to another person, certain; crime degrees; terms defined**

    a.  A person who knowingly distributes, manufactures or possesses any item containing personal identifying information pertaining to another person, without that person's authorization, and with knowledge that the actor is facilitating a fraud or injury to be perpetrated by anyone is guilty of a crime of the fourth degree.

    b.  (1)  If the person distributes, manufactures or possesses 20 or more items containing personal identifying information pertaining to another person, or five or more items containing personal information pertaining to five or more separate persons, without authorization, and with knowledge that the actor is facilitating a fraud or injury to be perpetrated by anyone the person is guilty of a crime of the third degree.

        (2)  If the person distributes, manufactures or possesses 50 or more items containing personal identifying information pertaining to another person, or ten or more items containing personal identifying information pertaining to five or more separate persons, without authorization, and with knowledge that the actor is facilitating a fraud or injury to be perpetrated by anyone the person is guilty of a crime of the second degree.

    c.  Distribution, manufacture or possession of 20 or more items containing personal identifying information pertaining to another person or of items containing personal identifying information pertaining to five or more separate persons without authorization shall create an inference that the items were distributed, manufactured or possessed with knowledge that the actor is facilitating a fraud or injury to be perpetrated by anyone.

    d.  As used in this section:

        "Distribute" means, but is not limited to, any sale, purchase, transfer, gift, delivery, or provision to another, regardless of whether the distribution was for compensation.

        "Item" means a writing or document, whether issued by a governmental agency or made by any business or person, recorded by any method that contains personal identifying information. Item includes, but is not limited to, an access device, book, check, paper, card, instrument, or information stored in electronic form by way of e-mail or otherwise, on any computer, computer storage medium, computer program, computer software, computer equipment, computer system or computer network or any part thereof, or by other mechanical or electronic device such as cellular telephone, pager or other electronic device capable of storing information.

## PRACTICAL APPLICATION OF STATUTE

2C:21-17.3 was enacted in 2003 to combat the trafficking of individuals' personal identifying information. It prohibits the distribution, manufacture, or possession of "any item containing personal identifying information" of another person. To be convicted under this statute, the actor must commit the proscribed acts without the other person's authorization and "with knowledge that is facilitating a fraud or injury to be perpetrated by anyone." An example where 2C:21-17.3 can be implemented is set forth below.

    The Hunk, with knowledge that he is facilitating fraud, manufactures a birth certificate in the name of Selma Gonzalez. He does this without Gonzalez's authorization and sells the identifying document to Carmella Swiss. Here, The Hunk has committed a fourth degree crime per subsection a. of 2C:21-17.3.

The severity of this offense increases where the actor unlawfully distributes, manufactures, or possesses multiple items containing personal identifying information. Subsections b.(1) and b.(2) define where the offense increases to a third degree crime and a second degree crime, respectively.

---

**2C:21-17.4.     Action by person defrauded by unauthorized use of personal identifying information**

a. Any person who suffers any ascertainable loss of moneys or property, real or personal, as a result of the use of that person's personal identifying information, in violation of N.J.S.2C:21-1, section 1 of P.L.1983, c.565 (2C:21-2.1) or N.J.S.2C:21-17, may bring an action in any court of competent jurisdiction. In any action under this section the court shall, in addition to any other appropriate legal or equitable relief, award damages in an amount three times the value of all costs incurred by the victim as a result of the person's criminal activity. These costs may include, but are not limited to, those incurred by the victim in clearing his credit history or credit rating, or those incurred in connection with any civil or administrative proceeding to satisfy any debt, lien, or other obligation of the victim arising as a result of the actions of the defendant. The victim may also recover those costs incurred for attorneys' fees, court costs and any out-of-pocket losses. A financial institution, insurance company, bonding association or business that suffers direct financial loss as a result of the offense shall also be entitled to damages, but damages to natural persons shall be fully satisfied prior to any payment to a financial institution, insurance company, bonding association or business.

b. The standard of proof in actions brought under this section is a preponderance of the evidence, and the fact that a prosecution for a violation of N.J.S.2C:21-1, section 1 of P.L.1983, c.565 (2C:21-2.1) or N.J.S.2C:21-17 is not instituted or, where instituted, terminates without a conviction shall not preclude an action pursuant to this section. A final judgment rendered in favor of the State in any criminal proceeding shall estop the defendant from denying the same conduct in any civil action brought pursuant to this section.

c. The cause of action authorized by this section shall be in addition to and not in lieu of any forfeiture or any other action, injunctive relief or any other remedy available at law, except that where the defendant is convicted of a violation of this act, the court in the criminal action, upon the application of the Attorney General or the prosecutor, shall in addition to any other disposition authorized by this Title sentence the defendant to pay restitution in an amount equal to the costs incurred by the victim as a result of the defendant's criminal activity, regardless of whether a civil action has been instituted. These costs may include, but are not limited to those incurred by the victim in clearing his credit history or credit rating; those incurred in connection with any civil or administrative proceeding to satisfy any debt, lien, or other obligation of the victim arising as a result of the actions of the defendant; or those incurred for attorneys' fees, court costs and any out-of-pocket losses. A financial institution, insurance company, bonding association or business that suffers direct financial loss as a result of the offense shall also be entitled to restitution, but restitution to natural persons shall be fully satisfied prior to any payment to a financial institution, insurance company, bonding association or business.

**2C:21-17.5.     Deletion of certain items from victim's consumer reporting files**

a. On motion of a person who has been the victim of a violation of N.J.S.2C:21-1, section 1 of P.L.1983, c.565 (2C:21-2.1) or N.J.S.2C:21-17 or on its own motion, the court may, without a hearing, grant an order directing all consumer reporting agencies doing business within the State of New Jersey to delete those items of information from the victim's file that were the result of the unlawful use of the victim's personal identifying information. The consumer reporting agency shall thereafter, provide the victim with a copy of the corrected credit history report at no charge.

b. Following any deletion of information pursuant to this section, the consumer reporting agency shall, at the request of the victim, furnish notification that the item has been deleted, to any person specifically designated by the victim who has within two years prior thereto received a consumer report for employment purposes, or within one year prior thereto received a consumer report for any other purpose, which contained the deleted or disputed information.

## 2C:21-18.    Slugs

A person is guilty of a disorderly persons offense when, other than under such circumstances as would constitute a violation of any of the provisions of the "Casino Control Act" (P.L. 1977, c. 110):

a. He inserts or deposits a slug, key, tool, instrument, explosive or device in a coin, currency or credit card activated machine with purpose to defraud; or

b. He makes, possesses or disposes of a slug, key, tool, instrument, explosive or device or a drawing, print or mold of a key, tool, instrument, explosive or device with purpose to enable a person to insert or deposit it in a coin, currency or credit card activated machine.

"Slug" means an object or article which, by virtue of its size, shape or any other quality is capable of being inserted or deposited in a coin, currency or credit card activated machine as an improper substitute for money.

## PRACTICAL APPLICATION OF STATUTE

Simply put, it is a disorderly persons offense for a person to use any sort of slug (defined as any object that is capable of being inserted in a coin-, currency-, or credit card-activated machine as an improper substitute for money) in any machine meant to accept legal currency or credit cards. An example of this offense is a person inserting a round metal object that substitutes as a quarter into a vending machine. Please note that it is also a disorderly persons offense to possess any tool, instrument, or other paraphernalia that would enable a person to create or use a slug.

## 2C:21-19.    Wrongful credit practices and related offenses

a. **Criminal usury.** A person is guilty of criminal usury when not being authorized or permitted by law to do so, he:

(1) Loans or agrees to loan, directly or indirectly, any money or other property at a rate exceeding the maximum rate permitted by law; or

(2) Takes, agrees to take, or receives any money or other property as interest on the loan or on the forbearance of any money or other interest in excess of the maximum rate permitted by law.

For the purposes of this section and notwithstanding any law of this State which permits as a maximum interest rate a rate or rates agreed to by the parties of the transaction, any loan or forbearance with an interest rate which exceeds 30% per annum shall not be a rate authorized or permitted by law, except if the loan or forbearance is made to a corporation, limited liability company or limited liability partnership any rate not in excess of 50% per annum shall be a rate authorized or permitted by law.

Criminal usury is a crime of the second degree if the rate of interest on any loan made to any person exceeds 50% per annum or the equivalent rate for a longer or shorter period. It is a crime of the third degree if the interest rate on any loan made to any person except a corporation, limited liability company or limited liability partnership does not exceed 50% per annum but the amount of the loan or forbearance exceeds $1,000.00. Otherwise, making a loan to any person in violation of subsections a.(1) and a.(2) of this section is a disorderly persons offense.

b. **Business of criminal usury.** Any person who knowingly engages in the business of making loans or forbearances in violation of subsection a. of this section is guilty of a crime of the second degree and, notwithstanding the provisions of N.J.S. 2C:43-3, shall be subject to a fine of not more than $250,000.00 and any other appropriate disposition authorized by N.J.S. 2C:43-2b.

c. **Possession of usurious loan records.** A person is guilty of a crime of the third degree when, with knowledge of the nature thereof, he possesses any writing, paper instrument or article used to record criminally usurious transactions prohibited by subsection a. of this section.

d. **Unlawful collection practices.** A person is guilty of a disorderly persons offense when, with purpose to enforce a claim or judgment for money or property, he sends, mails or delivers to another person a notice, document or other instrument which has no judicial or official sanction and which in its format or appearance simulates a summons, complaint, court order or process or an insignia, seal or printed form of a federal, State or local government or an instrumentality thereof, or is otherwise calculated to induce a belief that such notice, document or instrument has a judicial or official sanction.

e. **Making a false statement of credit terms.** A person is guilty of a disorderly persons offense when he understates or fails to state the interest rate, or makes a false or inaccurate or incomplete statement of any other credit terms.

f. **Debt adjusters.** Any person who shall act or offer to act as a debt adjuster shall be guilty of a crime of the fourth degree.

"Debt adjuster" means a person who either (1) acts or offers to act for a consideration as an intermediary between a debtor and his creditors for the purpose of settling, compounding, or otherwise altering the terms of payment of any debts of the debtor, or (2) who, to that end, receives money or other property from the debtor, or on behalf of the debtor, for payment to, or distribution among, the creditors of the debtor. "Debtor" means an individual or two or more individuals who are jointly and severally, or jointly or severally indebted

The following persons shall not be deemed debt adjusters for the purposes of this section: an attorney at law of this State who is not principally engaged as a debt adjuster; a nonprofit social service or consumer credit counseling agency licensed pursuant to P.L.1979, c.16 (C.17:16G-1 et seq.); a person who is a regular, full-time employee of a debtor, and who acts as an adjuster of his employer's debts; a person acting pursuant to any order or judgment of court, or pursuant to authority conferred by any law of this State or of the United States; a person who is a creditor of the debtor, or an agent of one or more creditors of the debtor, and whose services in adjusting the debtor's debts are rendered without cost to the debtor; or a person who, at the request of the debtor, arranges for or makes a loan to the debtor, and who, at the authorization of the debtor, acts as an adjuster of the debtor's debts in the disbursement of the proceeds of the loan, without compensation for the services rendered in adjusting such debts.

## PRACTICAL APPLICATION OF STATUTE

Section 2C:21-19 proscribes all forms of criminal usury, more commonly know as loan-sharking. A person is guilty of criminal usury when, not being authorized by the law to do so, he loans or otherwise engages in the exchange of money or property as interest on a loan in excess of the maximum rates permitted by law. Anyone who makes loan-sharking his business or is even found to be in knowing possession of usurious loan records is also guilty of a crime. For the purposes of this statute, any loan with an interest rate over 30% per annum is in excess of the maximum rates permitted by law except if the loan is made to a corporation or other business entity, in which case any rate over 50% per annum is in excess of the maximum permitted by law.

The degree of offense varies from a crime of the second degree down to a disorderly persons offense, depending upon the nature of the activity. Pursuant to subsection a. of the statute, the highest second degree version applies to any person found guilty of making any loan to another person with an interest rate over 50% per year. Per subsection b., any person who "knowingly engages in the business of making loans or forbearances" is similarly guilty of a second degree crime.

Returning to subsection a., the third degree type applies when the loans are less than 50% but over 30% and the amount of the loan is more than $1,000. This provision, however, is not applicable if such a loan is made to a corporation, limited liability company, or limited liability partnership.

As subsection c. provides, it is a third degree crime to possess usurious loan records, provided that the defendant held the requisite knowledge of the nature of such records. All other loans in violation of this section are disorderly persons offenses; unlawful collection practices are disorderly persons offenses as well. Unlawful collection practices are basically the issuance of any sort of notice or document that has no actual judicial or official effect. Such a notice or document simulates a summons, court order, or other official instrument for the purpose of collecting a debt; as such, it makes the debtor believe that the notice has a valid judicial or official sanction.

**2C:21-20.**     **Unlicensed practice of medicine, crime of third degree**

A person is guilty of a crime of the third degree if he knowingly does not possess a license or permit to practice medicine and surgery or podiatry, or knowingly has had the license or permit suspended, revoked or otherwise limited by an order entered by the State Board of Medical Examiners, and he

a. engages in that practice;

b. exceeds the scope of practice permitted by the board order;

c. holds himself out to the public or any person as being eligible to engage in that practice;

d. engages in any activity for which such license or permit is a necessary prerequisite, including, but not limited to, the ordering of controlled dangerous substances or prescription legend drugs from a distributor or manufacturer;

e. practices medicine or surgery or podiatry under a false or assumed name or falsely impersonates another person licensed by the board.

# Practical Application of Statute

What if our buddy Maxwell Borscht had decided to get especially gutsy and had The Hulk forge a medical license and other documentation that allowed him to set up a bogus liposuction clinic in Jersey City? In that case, he could be convicted of a third degree crime per 2C:21-20.

Figuring he could score some quick and easy income by reading a few books on the subject and then sucking the cellulite and the cash out of some of the area's more wealthy and vain residents, Borscht sets up shop. However, he is busted when his first client gets suspicious of his "get tough," no-anesthesia approach and hastily reports him to the authorities.

Borscht would likely be able to add 2C:21-20 to his list of offenses if the above was true. Why? Because this statute makes it a third degree crime for a person, knowing he does not possess a license to practice medicine, surgery, or podiatry, or knowing that the license has been suspended or otherwise limited, to engage in any activity for which such license is required. Performing liposuction surgery without a valid license certainly violates this statute.

**2C:21-21.**    **Short title; definitions; offenses; punishment**

    a.  This act shall be known and may be cited as the "New Jersey Anti-Piracy Act."

    b.  As used in this act:

        (1)  "Sound recording" means any phonograph record, disc, tape, film, wire, cartridge, cassette, player piano roll or similar material object from which sounds can be reproduced either directly or with the aid of a machine.

        (2)  "Owner" means (a) the person who owns the sounds fixed in any master sound recording on which the original sounds were fixed and from which transferred recorded sounds are directly or indirectly derived; or (b) the person who owns the rights to record or authorize the recording of a live performance.

        (3)  "Audiovisual work" means any work that consists of a series of related images which are intrinsically intended to be shown by the use of machines or devices such as projectors, viewers, or electronic equipment, together with accompanying sounds, if any, regardless of the nature of the material object, such as film or tape, in which the work is embodied.

    c.  A person commits an offense who:

        (1)  Knowingly transfers, without the consent of the owner, any sounds recorded on a sound recording with intent to sell the sound recording onto which the sounds are transferred or to use the sound recording to promote the sale of any product, provided, however, that this paragraph shall only apply to sound recordings initially fixed prior to February 15, 1972.

        (2)  Knowingly transports, advertises, sells, resells, rents, or offers for rental, sale or resale, any sound recording or audiovisual work that the person knows has been produced in violation of this act.

        (3)  Knowingly manufactures or transfers, directly or indirectly by any means, or records or fixes a sound recording or audiovisual work, with the intent to sell or distribute for commercial advantage or private financial gain, a live performance with the knowledge that the live performance has been recorded or fixed without the consent of the owner of the live performance.

(4) For commercial advantage or private financial gain, knowingly advertises or offers for sale, resale or rental, or sells, resells, rents or transports, a sound recording or audiovisual work or possesses with intent to advertise, sell, resell, rent or transport any sound recording or audiovisual work, the label, cover, box or jacket of which does not clearly and conspicuously disclose the true name and address of the manufacturer, and, in the case of a sound recording, the name of the actual performer or group.

d. Notwithstanding the provisions of subsection b. of N.J.S.2C:43-3:

(1) Any offense set forth in this act which involves at least 1,000 unlawful sound recordings or at least 65 audiovisual works within any 180-day period shall be punishable as a crime of the third degree and a fine of up to $250,000 may be imposed.

(2) Any offense which involves more than 100 but less than 1,000 unlawful sound recordings or more than 7 but less than 65 unlawful audiovisual works within any 180-day period shall be punishable as a crime of the third degree and a fine of up to $150,000 may be imposed.

(3) Any offense punishable under the provisions of this act not described in paragraphs (1) or (2) of this subsection shall be punishable for the first offense as a crime of the fourth degree and a fine of up to $25,000 may be imposed. For a second and subsequent offense pursuant to this paragraph, a person shall be guilty of a crime of the third degree. A fine of up to $50,000 may be imposed for a second offense pursuant to this paragraph and a fine of up to $100,000 for a third and subsequent offense may be imposed.

e. All unlawful sound recordings and audiovisual works and any equipment or components used in violation of the provisions of this act shall be subject to forfeiture in accordance with the procedures set forth in chapter 64 of Title 2C of the New Jersey Statutes.

f. The provisions of this act shall not apply to:

(1) Any broadcaster who, in connection with or as part of a radio or television broadcast transmission, or for the purposes of archival preservation, transfers any sounds or images recorded on a sound recording or audiovisual work

(2) Any person who, in his own home, for his own personal use, and without deriving any profit, transfers any sounds or images recorded on a sound recording or audiovisual work.

## PRACTICAL APPLICATION OF STATUTE

This statute was enacted and has been amended in an attempt to keep up with the growing industry and technological advances associated with the unlawful taking and distribution of audiovisual recordings without the consent of the owners of such media. Aside from any separate federal copyright or trademark issues that could come into play with such an offense, 2C:21-21 makes it a crime of various degrees to knowingly, and with the intent to gain commercial advantage or private financial gain, transfer, record, transport, advertise, sell, rent, or offer for sale or rental any sound recording or audiovisual work without the consent of the rightful owner.

This statute also includes a "truth in labeling" provision which makes it a crime to sell, rent, possess, transport, or otherwise unlawfully deal in any sound recording or audiovisual work that does not clearly and conspicuously disclose the true name and address of the manufacturer, and, in the case of a sound recording, the name of the actual performer or group. It should be noted that there are exceptions to this statute which generally allow for any "fair use" of such materials. Therefore, the provisions of this statute do not apply to any person who records or transfers such materials for his own personal, nonprofit use, or any broadcaster who, in connection with a radio or television broadcast, or for archival preservation, transfers such sound or audiovisual works.

An example of an offense under this statute is as follows. Slick Timmy knows that Bobberino wants 100 different movies to start a video collection. Slick Timmy then hooks up two separate VCRs to his television set and records 100 different movies onto blank VHS tapes. He then sells the VHS copies he made to Bobberino for $500. The entirety of his work, from copying to sale, took two weeks. Slick Timmy did not have the consent of any of the movies' owners to perform such transfers or sales.

The number and type of offenses under this statute determine the degree of the crime. For instance, any offense under this statute that involves 1,000 or more unlawful sound recordings or at least 65 audiovisual works within any 180-day period will constitute a crime of the third degree. Slick Timmy, without the owners' consent, transferred and sold 100 audiovisual works (the movies) in a two-week period. Therefore, he is guilty of a third degree crime under 2C:21-21.

**2C:21-22.**     **Unauthorized practice of law, penalties**

    a. A person is guilty of a disorderly persons offense if the person knowingly engages in the unauthorized practice of law.

    b. A person is guilty of a crime of the fourth degree if the person knowingly engages in the unauthorized practice of law and

        (1) Creates or reinforces a false impression that the person is licensed to engage in the practice of law; or

        (2) Derives a benefit; or

        (3) In fact causes injury to another.

    c. For the purposes of this section, the phrase "in fact" indicates strict liability.

## PRACTICAL APPLICATION OF STATUTE

2C:21-22 makes it a disorderly persons offense for a person to knowingly engage in the unauthorized practice of law. The degree of the crime is increased to the fourth degree if, while engaging in this unauthorized practice, he derives a benefit, actually causes injury to another, or "creates or reinforces a false impression" that he is licensed to engage in the practice of law. But what is the difference between the disorderly persons offense of "unauthorized practice of law" and the fourth degree crime of the unauthorized practice of law where the person "creates or reinforces a false impression" that he is licensed to engage in the practice of law?

Here's an example. Bart, the aspiring law student, witnesses a car accident and approaches the driver of the vehicle who he feels is at fault. Bart tells the driver, Eddie, that although he is not a lawyer, he is an expert in law and advises Eddie that in order to escape liability for the accident, he should issue a ticket for speeding against the other driver. Bart then meets with Eddie the next day and drafts a civil complaint naming Eddie as the plaintiff and the other driver as the defendant. Eddie likes the complaint, so Bart sends it to the court for filing and mails a copy to the "defendant."

Bart obviously engaged in the "unauthorized practice of law." However, he didn't "create or reinforce a false impression" that he was *licensed* to engage in the practice of law. In fact, he advised that he was not a lawyer. Accordingly, as long as Bart didn't charge Eddie any money or derive any other benefit—and as long as no one was ultimately injured, financially or otherwise, by his actions—Bart would be guilty of the disorderly persons offense of engaging in the "unauthorized practice of law." His offense would be elevated to a crime of the fourth degree, though, if he had told Eddie that he was a lawyer or otherwise created such a false impression.

## 2C:21-22.1.     Definitions relative to use of runners; crime; sentencing

a. As used in this section: "Provider" means an attorney, a health care professional, an owner or operator of a health care practice or facility, any person who creates the impression that he or his practice or facility can provide legal or health care services, or any person employed or acting on behalf of any of the aforementioned persons.

"Public media" means telephone directories, professional directories, newspapers and other periodicals, radio and television, billboards and mailed or electronically transmitted written communications that do not involve in-person contact with a specific prospective client, patient or customer.

"Runner" means a person who, for a pecuniary benefit, procures or attempts to procure a client, patient or customer at the direction of, request of or in cooperation with a provider whose purpose is to seek to obtain benefits under a contract of insurance or assert a claim against an insured or an insurance carrier for providing services to the client, patient or customer. "Runner" shall not include a person who procures or attempts to procure clients, patients or customers for a provider through public media or a person who refers clients, patients or customers to a provider as otherwise authorized by law.

b. A person is guilty of a crime of the third degree if that person knowingly acts as a runner or uses, solicits, directs, hires or employs another to act as a runner.

c. Notwithstanding the provisions of subsection e. of N.J.S.2C:44-1, the court shall deal with a person who has been convicted of a violation of this section by imposing a sentence of imprisonment unless, having regard to the character and condition of the person, the court is of the opinion that imprisonment would be a serious injustice which overrides the need to deter such conduct by others. If the court imposes a noncustodial or probationary sentence, such sentence shall not become final for 10 days in order to permit the appeal of such sentence by the prosecution. Nothing in this section shall preclude an indictment and conviction for any other offense defined by the laws of this State.

## PRACTICAL APPLICATION OF STATUTE

Although this statute is primarily a definitional section, it is notable in its definition and prohibition of being a "runner." A person commits the third degree crime of being a "runner" if, for pecuniary benefit, he procures or attempts to procure a client, patient, or customer at the direction of any type of "provider" whose purpose is to obtain benefits under any type of insurance contract. A "provider" is basically defined in this section as any attorney or health care provider or owner/operator of such a facility. The "provider" also may be convicted of a third degree crime under this statute; that is, if the "provider" "uses, solicits, directs, hires, or employs to act as a runner."

It is important to note that the term "runner" does not include a person "who procures or attempts to procure clients, patients or customers for a provider through public media or a person who refers clients, patients or customers to a provider as otherwise authorized by law." Accordingly, persons who act in the aforementioned capacities are not violating the provisions of 2C:21-22.1.

---

**2C:21-23.**        **Findings, declarations**

The Legislature hereby finds and declares to be the public policy of this State, the following:

a. By enactment of the "Criminal Justice Act of 1970," P.L.1970, c.74 (C.52:17B-97 et seq.), the legislature recognized that the existence of organized crime and organized crime type activities present a serious threat to the political, social and economic institutions of this State.

b. By enactment of P.L.1981, c.167 (C.2C:41-1 et al.), the Legislature recognized the need to impose strict civil and criminal sanctions upon those whose activity is inimical to the general health, welfare and prosperity of this State, including, but not limited to, those who drain money from the economy by illegal conduct and then undertake the operation of otherwise legitimate businesses with the proceeds of illegal conduct.

c. By enactment of the "Comprehensive Drug Reform Act of 1987," P.L.1987, c.106 (C.2C:35-1 et seq.), the Legislature recognized the need to punish the more culpable drug offenders with strict, consistently imposed criminal sanctions. The Legislature intended a greater culpability for those who profit from the illegal trafficking of drugs and expressed an intent that such individuals be dealt with swiftly and sternly.

d. Despite the impressive efforts and gains of our law enforcement agencies, individuals still profit financially from illegal organized criminal activities and illegal trafficking of drugs, and they continue to pose a serious and pervasive threat to the health, safety and welfare of the citizens of this State while, at the same time, converting their illegally obtained profits into "legitimate" funds with the assistance of other individuals.

e. The increased trafficking in drugs and other organized criminal activities have strengthened the money laundering industry which takes illegally acquired income and makes that money appear to be legitimate. In order to safeguard the public interest and stop the conversion of ill-gotten criminal profits, effective criminal and civil sanctions are needed to deter and punish those who are converting the illegal profits, those who are providing a method of hiding the true source of the funds, and those who facilitate such activities. It is in the public interest to make such conduct subject to strict criminal and civil penalties because of a need to deter individuals and business entities from assisting in the "legitimizing" of proceeds of illegal activity. To allow individuals or business entities to avoid responsibility for their criminal assistance in money laundering is clearly inimical to the public good.

**2C:21-24.**        **Definitions**

As used in this act:

"Attorney General" includes the Attorney General of the State of New Jersey and the Attorney General's assistants and deputies. The term also shall include a county prosecutor or the county prosecutor's designated assistant prosecutor if a county prosecutor is expressly authorized in writing by the Attorney General pursuant to this act.

"Derived from" means obtained directly or indirectly from, maintained by or realized through.

"Person" means any corporation, unincorporated association or any other entity or enterprise, as defined in subsection q. of N.J.S.2C:20-1, which is capable of holding a legal or beneficial interest in property.

"Property" means anything of value, as defined in subsection g. of N.J.S.2C:20-1, and includes any benefit or interest without reduction for expenses incurred for acquisition, maintenance or any other purpose.

**2C:21-25.**     **Money laundering, illegal investment, crime**

A person is guilty of a crime if the person:

  a. transports or possesses property known or which a reasonable person would believe to be derived from criminal activity; or

  b. engages in a transaction involving property known or which a reasonable person would believe to be derived from criminal activity

    (1) with the intent to facilitate or promote the criminal activity; or

    (2) knowing that the transaction is designed in whole or in part:

      (a) to conceal or disguise the nature, location, source, ownership or control of the property derived from criminal activity; or

      (b) to avoid a transaction reporting requirement under the laws of this State or any other state or of the United States; or

  c. directs, organizes, finances, plans, manages, supervises, or controls the transportation of or transactions in property known or which a reasonable person would believe to be derived from criminal activity.

  d. For the purposes of this act, property is known to be derived from criminal activity if the person knows that the property involved represents proceeds from some form, though not necessarily which form, of criminal activity. Among the factors that the finder of fact may consider in determining that a transaction has been designed to avoid a transaction reporting requirement shall be whether the person, acting alone or with others, conducted one or more transactions in currency, in any amount, at one or more financial institutions, on one or more days, in any manner. The phrase "in any manner" includes the breaking down of a single sum of currency exceeding the transaction reporting requirement into smaller sums, including sums at or below the transaction reporting requirement, or the conduct of a transaction, or series of currency transactions, including transactions at or below the transaction reporting requirement. The transaction or transactions need not exceed the transaction reporting threshold at any single financial institution on any single day in order to demonstrate a violation of subparagraph (b) of paragraph (2) of subsection b. of this section.

  e. A person is guilty of a crime if, with the purpose to evade a transaction reporting requirement of this State or of 31 U.S.C. s.5311 et seq. or 31 C.F.R. s.103 et seq., or any rules or regulations adopted under those chapters and sections, he:

    (1) causes or attempts to cause a financial institution, including a foreign or domestic money transmitter or an authorized delegate thereof, casino, check casher, person engaged in a trade or business or any other individual or entity required by State or federal law to file a report regarding currency transactions or suspicious transactions to fail to file a report; or

(2) causes or attempts to cause a financial institution, including a foreign or domestic money transmitter or an authorized delegate thereof, casino, check casher, person engaged in a trade or business or any other individual or entity required by State or federal law to file a report regarding currency transactions or suspicious transactions to file a report that contains a material omission or misstatement of fact; or

(3) structures or assists in structuring, or attempts to structure or assist in structuring any transaction with one or more financial institutions, including foreign or domestic money transmitters or an authorized delegate thereof, casinos, check cashers, persons engaged in a trade or business or any other individuals or entities required by State or federal law to file a report regarding currency transactions or suspicious transactions. "Structure" or "structuring" means that a person, acting alone, or in conjunction with, or on behalf of, other persons, conducts or attempts to conduct one or more transactions in currency, in any amount, at one or more financial institutions, on one or more days, in any manner, for the purpose of evading currency transaction reporting requirements provided by State or federal law. "In any manner" includes, but is not limited to, the breaking down into smaller sums of a single sum of currency meeting or exceeding that which is necessary to trigger a currency reporting requirement or the conduct of a transaction, or series of currency transactions, at or below the reporting requirement. The transaction or transactions need not exceed the reporting threshold at any single financial institution on any single day in order to meet the definition of "structure" or "structuring" provided in this paragraph.

## PRACTICAL APPLICATION OF STATUTE

Topping off Maxwell Borscht's impressive résumé of violations under this statute was his act of money laundering. Sections 2C:21-25 through 2C:21-28 all deal with the crime and punishment of money laundering and any activities facilitating the act of this offense.

Prior to Borscht's Jackpot Insurance scam, he sold heroin. When he first arrived in New Jersey, he utilized pizza places to disguise the real manner in which he earned his funds. His goal was to act like the money was made legitimately via the restaurants, sending it through these businesses' records as if an enormous number of pizzas and calzones were sold. In reality, the money was being made from his illicit drug distribution.

Maxwell Borscht's above-referenced activity falls squarely within the prohibitions of 2C:21-25b.(2)(a). This subsection makes it a crime to engage in any transactions involving property derived from criminal activity while knowing that the transaction is designed to conceal the nature of the property derived from criminal activity.

Although the term "property" conjures up an image of some tangible object, the cash Borscht had made through his illegal heroin sales is considered property for the purposes of this statute. Making the money/property look as though it was made through the restaurants by sending it through their business records, Borscht knowingly conducted these transactions with the purpose to conceal the nature of where the money actually came from. Therefore, he is guilty of money laundering.

The gradation of money laundering offenses is found in 2C:21-27. Depending upon how lucrative Borscht's heroin racket was, he could face up to a first degree criminal charge. For the offenses defined in subsections a., b., and c. of 2C:21-25 (Borscht's offense falls under subsection b.), it is a crime of the first degree if the amount involved is $500,000 or more. If the amount is at least $75,000 but less than $500,000, the offense constitutes a crime of the second degree; for all other amounts, it is a crime of the third degree.

---

**2C:21-26.**     **Knowledge inferred**

For the purposes of section 3 of this act, the requisite knowledge may be inferred where the property is transported or possessed in a fashion inconsistent with the ordinary or usual means of transportation or possession of such property and where the property is discovered in the absence of any documentation or other indicia of legitimate origin or right to such property.

**2C:21-27.**     **Degrees of offense; penalties; nonmerger**

a. The offense defined in subsections a. b. and c. of section 3 of P.L.1994, c.121 (C.2C:21-25) constitutes a crime of the first degree if the amount involved is $500,000.00 or more. If the amount involved is at least $75,000.00 but less than $500,000.00 the offense constitutes a crime of the second degree; otherwise, the offense constitutes a crime of the third degree. The offense defined in subsection e. of section 3 of P.L.1994, c.121 (C.2C:21-25) constitutes a crime of the third degree. Notwithstanding the provisions of N.J.S.2C:43-3, the court may also impose a fine up to $500,000.00. The amount involved in a prosecution for violation of this section shall be determined by the trier of fact. Amounts involved in transactions conducted pursuant to one scheme or course of conduct may be aggregated in determining the degree of the offense. Notwithstanding the provisions of paragraph (1) of subsection a. of N.J.S.2C:43-6, a person convicted of a crime of the first degree pursuant to the provisions of this subsection shall be sentenced to a term of imprisonment that shall include the imposition of a minimum term which shall be fixed at, or between, one-third and one-half of the sentence imposed, during which time the defendant shall not be eligible for parole.

b. In addition to any other dispositions authorized by this Title, upon conviction of a violation of this section, the court may sentence the defendant to pay an amount as calculated pursuant to subsection a. of section 6 of P.L.1994, c.121 (C.2C:21-28).

c. Notwithstanding N.J.S.2C:1-8 or any other provision of law, a conviction of an offense defined in this section shall not merge with the conviction of any other offense constituting the criminal activity involved or from which the property was derived, and a conviction of any offense constituting the criminal activity involved or from which the property was derived shall not merge with a conviction of an offense defined in section 3 of P.L.1994, c.121 (C.2C:21-25), and the sentence imposed upon a conviction of any offense defined in section 3 of P.L.1994, c.121 (C.2C:21-25) shall be ordered to be served consecutively to that imposed for a conviction of any offense constituting the criminal activity involved or from which the property was derived. Nothing in P.L.1994, c.121 (C.2C:21-23 et seq.) shall be construed in any way to preclude or limit a prosecution or conviction for any other offense defined in this Title or any other criminal law of this State.

**2C:21-27.1.**     **Criteria for imposition of anti-money laundering profiteering penalty**

In addition to any other disposition authorized by this title, including but not limited to any fines which may be imposed pursuant to the provisions of N.J.S.2C:43-3, where a person has been convicted of a crime defined in P.L.1994, c.121 (C.2C:21-23 et seq.) or an attempt or conspiracy to commit such a crime, the court shall, upon the application of the prosecutor, sentence the person to pay a monetary penalty in an amount determined pursuant to section 9 of P.L.1999, c.25 (C.2C:21-27.2), provided the court finds at a hearing, which may occur at the time of sentencing, that the prosecutor has established by a preponderance of the evidence that the defendant was convicted of a violation of P.L.1994, c.121 (C.2C:21-23 et seq.).

**2C:21-27.2.**    **Calculation of anti-money laundering profiteering penalty**

Where, pursuant to section 8 of P.L.1999, c.25 (C.2C:21-27.1) the prosecutor has established by a preponderance of the evidence that the defendant was convicted of a violation of P.L.1994, c.121 (C.2C:21-23 et seq.), the court shall assess a monetary penalty as follows:

  a.  $500,000.00 in the case of a crime of the first degree; $250,000.00 in the case of a crime of the second degree; $75,000.00 in the case of a crime of the third degree; or

  b.  an amount equal to three times the value of any property involved in a money laundering activity in violation of P.L.1994, c.121 (C.2C:21-23 et seq.).

  c.  Where the prosecution requests that the court assess a penalty in an amount calculated pursuant to subsection b. of this section, the prosecutor shall have the burden of establishing by a preponderance of the evidence the appropriate amount of the penalty to be assessed pursuant to that subsection. In making its finding, the court shall take judicial notice of any evidence, testimony or information adduced at trial, plea hearing or other court proceedings and shall also consider the presentence report and other relevant information, including expert opinion in the form of live testimony or by affidavit. The court's findings shall be incorporated in the record, and such findings shall not be subject to modification by an appellate court except upon a showing that the finding was totally lacking support in the record or was arbitrary and capricious.

**2C:21-27.3.**    **Revocation or reduction of penalty assessment**

The court shall not revoke or reduce a penalty imposed pursuant to section 9 of P.L.1999, c.25 (C.2C:21-27.2). An anti-money laundering profiteering penalty imposed pursuant to section 9 of P.L.1999, c.25 (C.2C:21-27.2) shall not be deemed a fine for purposes of N.J.S.2C:46-3.

**2C:21-27.4.**    **Payment schedule**

The court may, for good cause shown, and subject to the provisions of this section, grant permission for the payment of an anti-money laundering profiteering penalty assessed pursuant to section 9 of P.L.1999, c.25 (C.2C:21-27.2) to be made within a specified period of time or in specified installments, provided however that the payment schedule fixed by the court shall require the defendant to pay the anti-money laundering profiteering penalty in the shortest period of time consistent with the nature and extent of his assets and his ability to pay, and further provided that the prosecutor shall be afforded the opportunity to present evidence or information concerning the nature, extent and location of the defendant's assets or interests in property which are or might be subject to levy and execution. In such event, the court may only grant permission for the payment to be made within a specified period of time or installments with respect to that portion of the assessed penalty which would not be satisfied by the liquidation of property which is or may be subject to levy and execution, unless the court finds that the immediate liquidation of such property would result in undue hardship to innocent persons. If no permission to make payment within a specified period of time or in installments is embodied in the sentence, the entire penalty shall be payable forthwith.

**2C:21-27.5.**    **Relation to other dispositions**

    a.  An anti-money laundering profiteering penalty assessed pursuant to section 9 of P.L.1999, c.25 (C.2C:21-27.2) shall be imposed and paid in addition to any penalty, fine, fee or order for restitution which may be imposed.

    b.  An anti-money laundering profiteering penalty imposed pursuant to section 9 of P.L.1999, c.25 (C.2C:21-27.2) shall be in addition to and not in lieu of any forfeiture or other cause of action instituted pursuant to chapter 41 or 64 of Title 2C of the New Jersey Statutes, and nothing in this chapter shall be construed in any way to preclude, preempt or limit any such cause of action. A defendant shall not be entitled to receive credit toward the payment of an anti-money laundering profiteering penalty imposed pursuant to section 9 of P.L.1999, c.25 (C.2C:21-27.2) for the value of property forfeited, or subject to forfeiture, pursuant to the provisions of chapter 41 or 64 of Title 2C of the New Jersey Statutes.

**2C:21-27.6.**    **Collection and distribution**

All anti-money laundering profiteering penalties assessed pursuant to section 9 of P.L.1999, c.25 (C.2C:21-27.2) shall be docketed and collected as provided for the collection of fines, penalties, fees and restitution in chapter 46 of Title 2C of the New Jersey Statutes. The Attorney General or prosecutor may prosecute an action to collect any anti-money laundering profiteering penalties imposed pursuant to section 9 of P.L.1999, c.25 (C.2C:21-27.2). All anti-money laundering profiteering penalties assessed pursuant to section 9 of P.L.1999, c.25 (C.2C:21-27.2) shall be disposed of, distributed, appropriated and used as if the collected penalties were the proceeds of property forfeited pursuant to chapter 64 of Title 2C of the New Jersey Statutes.

**2C:21-28.**    **Civil action for treble damages; allocation**

    a.  The Attorney General may institute a civil action against any person who violates section 3 of this act, and may recover a judgment against all persons who violate this section, jointly and severally, for damages in an amount equal to three times the value of all property involved in the criminal activity, together with costs incurred for resources and personnel used in the investigation and litigation of both criminal and civil proceedings. The standard of proof in actions brought under this subsection is a preponderance of the evidence, and the fact that a prosecution for a violation of this act is not instituted or, where instituted, terminates without a conviction shall not preclude an action pursuant to this subsection. A final judgment rendered in favor of the State in any criminal proceedings shall estop the defendant from denying the same conduct in any civil action brought pursuant to this subsection.

    b.  The cause of action authorized by this section shall be in addition to and not in lieu of any forfeiture or any other action, injunctive relief or any other remedy available at law, except that where the defendant is convicted of a violation of this act, the court in the criminal action, upon the application of the Attorney General or the prosecutor, may in addition to any other disposition authorized by this Title, sentence the defendant to pay an amount equal to the damages calculated pursuant to the provisions of this subsection, whether or not a civil action has been instituted.

    c.  Notwithstanding any other provision of law, all monies collected pursuant to any judgment recovered or order issued pursuant to this section shall first be allocated to the payment of any State tax, penalty and interest due and owing to the State as a result of the conduct which is the basis for the action. Monies collected shall be allocated next in accordance with the provisions of N.J.S.2C:64-6 as if collected pursuant to chapter 64 of Title 2C, in an amount equal to the amount of all property involved in the criminal activity plus the costs incurred for resources and personnel used in the investigation and litigation. The remainder of the monies collected shall be allocated to the General Fund of the State.

**2C:21-29.**     **Investigative interrogatives**

a. Whenever the Attorney General, by the Attorney General's own inquiry or as the result of a complaint, determines that there exists reasonable suspicion that a violation of this act is occurring, has occurred or is about to occur, or, whenever the Attorney General believes it to be in the public interest that an investigation be made, the Attorney General may, prior to the institution of any criminal or civil action, issue in writing and cause to be served upon any person investigative interrogatories requiring the person to answer and produce material for examination.

b. Any investigative interrogatories issued pursuant to this subsection and all procedures related to such interrogatories shall comply with the provisions of N.J.S.2C:41-5.

**2C:21-30.**     **Unlawful practice of dentistry; third degree crime**

A person is guilty of a crime of the third degree if he knowingly does not possess a license to practice dentistry or knowingly has had the license suspended, revoked or otherwise limited by an order entered by the New Jersey State Board of Dentistry, and he:

a. engages in that practice;

b. exceeds the scope of practice permitted by a board order;

c. holds himself out to the public or any person as being eligible to engage in that practice;

d. engages in any activity for which such license is a necessary prerequisite, including, but not limited to, the ordering of controlled dangerous substances or prescription legend drugs from a distributor or manufacturer; or

e. practices dentistry under a false or assumed name or falsely impersonates another person licensed by the board.

## PRACTICAL APPLICATION OF STATUTE

2C:21-30 simply proscribes the unlawful practice of dentistry. A violation under this statute is a third degree crime. Please note that 2C:21-30 requires that the defendant "knowingly" engage in the prohibited activities. This intent requirement would presumably prevent any sort of prosecution under circumstances where the individual had inadvertently been working under an expired license or otherwise believed in good faith that he was properly authorized.

**2C:21-31.**     **Unauthorized practice of immigration law; penalties**

a. As used in this section:

(1) "Immigration consultant" means any person rendering services for a fee, including the completion of forms and applications, to another person in furtherance of that person's desire to determine or modify his status in an immigration or naturalization matter under federal law.

(2) "Immigration or naturalization matter" means any matter which involves any law, action, filing or proceeding related to a person's immigration or citizenship status in the United States.

   (3) "Immigration-related document" means any birth certificate or marriage certificate; any document issued by the government of the United States, any foreign country, any state, or any other public entity relating to a person's immigration or naturalization status.

b. Any immigration consultant not licensed as an attorney or counselor at law who:

   (1) Engages in this State in the practice of law; or

   (2) Holds himself out to the public, either alone or together with, by or through another person, whether such other person is licensed as an attorney or counselor at law or not, as engaging in or entitled to engage in the practice of law, or as rendering legal service or advice, or as furnishing attorneys or counsel, in any immigration or naturalization matter; or

   (3) Assumes, uses or advertises the title of lawyer or attorney at law, or equivalent terms, in the English language or any other language, is guilty of a crime of the fourth degree.

c. Any person who knowingly retains possession of another person's immigration-related document for more than a reasonable time after the person who owns the document has submitted a written request for the document's return is guilty of a crime of the fourth degree.

d. Nothing in this section shall be construed to prohibit a person accredited as a representative by federal law pursuant to 8 CFR 292.2 from providing immigration services.

## PRACTICAL APPLICATION OF STATUTE

The primary purpose of this statute is to prohibit "immigration consultants" from practicing law unless they are indeed attorneys. The term "immigration consultant" is defined in subsection a. of 2C:21-31. A violation of this statute constitutes a fourth degree crime.

**2C:21-32.**     **Short title; definitions relative to counterfeit marks; offenses**

a. This act shall be known and may be cited as the "New Jersey Trademark Counterfeiting Act."

b. As used in this act:

   (1) "Counterfeit mark" means a spurious mark that is identical with or substantially indistinguishable from a genuine mark that is registered on the principal register in the United States Patent and Trademark Office or registered in the New Jersey Secretary of State's office or a spurious mark that is identical with or substantially indistinguishable from the words, names, symbols, emblems, signs, insignias or any combination thereof, of the United States Olympic Committee or the International Olympic Committee; and that is used or is intended to be used on, or in conjunction with, goods or services for which the genuine mark is registered and in use.

   (2) "Retail value" means the counterfeiter's regular selling price for the item or service bearing or identified by the counterfeit mark. In the case of items bearing a counterfeit mark which are components of a finished product, the retail value shall be the counterfeiter's regular selling price of the finished product on or in which the component would be utilized.

c. A person commits the offense of counterfeiting who, with the intent to deceive or defraud some other person, knowingly manufactures, uses, displays, advertises, distributes, offers for sale, sells, or possesses with intent to sell or distribute within, or in conjunction with commercial activities within New Jersey, any item, or services, bearing, or identified by, a counterfeit mark.

A person who has in his possession or under his control more than 25 items bearing a counterfeit mark shall be presumed to have violated this section.

d. (1) An offense set forth in this act shall be punishable as a crime of the fourth degree if:

the offense involves fewer than 100 items bearing a counterfeit mark;

the offense involves a total retail value of less than $1,000.00 for all items bearing, or services identified by, a counterfeit mark; or

the offense involves a first conviction under this act.

(2) An offense set forth in this act shall be punishable as a crime of the third degree if:

the offense involves 100 or more but fewer than 1,000 items bearing a counterfeit mark;

the offense involves a total retail value of $1,000.00 or more but less than $15,000.00 of all items bearing, or services identified by, a counterfeit mark; or

the offense involves a second conviction under this act.

(3) An offense set forth in this act shall be punishable as a crime of the second degree if:

the offense involves 1,000 or more items bearing a counterfeit mark;

the offense involves a total retail value of $15,000.00 or more of all items bearing, or services identified by a counterfeit mark; or

the offense involves a third or subsequent conviction under this act.

In addition, any person convicted under this act, notwithstanding the provisions of N.J.S.2C:43-3, shall be fined by the court an amount up to threefold the retail value of the items or services involved, providing that the fine imposed shall not exceed the following amounts: for a crime of the fourth degree, $100,000.00; for a crime of the third degree, $250,000.00; and for a crime of the second degree, $500,000.00.

e. All items bearing a counterfeit mark, and all personal property, including but not limited to, any items, objects, tools, machines, equipment, instrumentalities or vehicles of any kind, employed or used in connection with a violation of this act, shall be subject to forfeiture in accordance with the procedures set forth in chapter 64 of Title 2C of the New Jersey Statutes.

f. For purposes of this act:

(1) the quantity or retail value of items or services shall include the aggregate quantity or retail value of all items bearing, or services identified by, every counterfeit mark the defendant manufactures, uses, displays, advertises, distributes, offers for sale, sells or possesses;

(2) any State or federal certificate of registration of any intellectual property shall be prima facie evidence of the facts stated therein.

g. Conviction for an offense under this act does not preclude the defendant's liability for the civil remedy available pursuant to section 2 of P.L.1987, c.454 (C.56:3-13.16).

## PRACTICAL APPLICATION OF STATUTE

If Maxwell Borscht had decided to raise a little more capital by operating a small stand selling women's purses with the name and logo of a famous clothing designer while "knowing" that the purses were not actually produced with the authorization of this designer, Borscht would be in violation of 2C:21-32. This statute is more commonly known as the New Jersey Trademark Counterfeiting Act.

2C:21-32 makes it a crime to knowingly manufacture, use, display, advertise, distribute, or sell (or possess with intent to sell) any item or service identified by a counterfeit mark. In order to be guilty of an offense under this statute, the defendant must intend to "deceive or defraud" another.

Although 2C:21-32 does not necessarily make it a crime to possess one of these counterfeit items, any person who has possession of more than 25 items bearing a counterfeit mark is presumed to be in violation of this statute. The offenses range from the fourth degree to the second degree, depending upon the number and retail value of the prohibited items. See subsections d.(1), (2), and (3) for specifics in this respect.

**2C:21-33.**    **Electrical contracting without business permit, fourth degree crime**

   a. A person is guilty of a crime of the fourth degree if that person knowingly engages in the business of electrical contracting without having a business permit issued by the Board of Examiners of Electrical Contractors and:

   (1) Creates or reinforces a false impression that the person is licensed as an electrical contractor or possesses a business permit; or

   (2) Derives a benefit, the value of which is more than incidental; or

   (3) In fact causes injury to another.

   b. For the purposes of this section, the phrase "in fact" indicates strict liability.

## PRACTICAL APPLICATION OF STATUTE

Those engaging in the "business of electrical contracting without having a business permit issued by the Board of Examiners of Electrical Contractors" may be guilty of a fourth degree crime. This is the case if they do the aforementioned *and* cause injury to another or derive a significant benefit (e.g. monetary) from the work or create a "false impression" that they possess the appropriate license or permit.

**2C:21-34.**    **Penalty for false contract payment claims, representation, for a government contract; grading**

   a. A person commits a crime if the person knowingly submits to the government any claim for payment for performance of a government contract knowing such claim to be false, fictitious, or fraudulent. If the claim submitted is for $25,000.00 or above, the offender is guilty of a crime of the second degree. If the claim exceeds $2,500.00, but is less than $25,000.00, the offender is guilty of a crime of the third degree. If the claim is for $2,500.00 or less, the offender is guilty of a crime of the fourth degree.

   b. A person commits a crime if the person knowingly makes a material representation that is false in connection with the negotiation, award or performance of a government contract. If the contract amount is for $25,000.00 or above, the offender is guilty of a crime of the second degree. If the contract amount exceeds $2,500.00, but is less than $25,000.00, the offender is guilty of a crime of the third degree. If the contract amount is for $2,500.00 or less, the offender is guilty of a crime of the fourth degree.

## PRACTICAL APPLICATION OF STATUTE

Under 2C:21-34, a person commits a crime by either knowingly submitting a false claim for payment on a government contract or knowingly making a materially false representation in connection with the negotiation or award of a government contract. For example, this statute could apply to a construction company contracted by the government to build a new firehouse. If the company president submitted claims to the government containing charges for items that were never used or containing charges in excess of the actual cost of materials, then the company president is ripe for a charge under 2C:21-34. The crime is of the second degree for amounts of $25,000 or more. It is a third degree crime for amounts over $2,500 but less than $25,000 and a crime of the fourth degree for amounts of $2,500 or less.

# 22

# DISTURBING HUMAN REMAINS

**2C:22-1.**     **Disturbing, desecrating human remains; offenses**

a. A person commits a crime of the second degree if he:
   (1) Unlawfully disturbs, moves or conceals human remains;
   (2) Unlawfully desecrates, damages or destroys human remains; or
   (3) Commits an act of sexual penetration or sexual contact, as defined in N.J.S.2C:14-1, upon human remains.

b. A person commits a crime of the third degree if he purposely or knowingly fails to dispose of human remains in a manner required by law.

c. As used in this act, "human remains" means the body of a deceased person or the dismembered part of a body of a living person but does not include cremated remains.

d. Nothing in this section shall be construed to apply to any act performed in accordance with law, including but not limited to the "State Medical Examiner Act," P.L.1967, c.234 (C.52:17B-78 et al.); the "Mortuary Science Act," P.L.1952, c.340 (C.45:7-32 et seq.); the provisions of chapters 6 and 7 of Title 26 of the Revised Statutes concerning disposal of dead bodies and cremation; the "New Jersey Cemetery Act," N.J.S.8A:1-1 et seq.; a criminal investigation conducted by a law enforcement authority; or an order of a court of competent jurisdiction or other appropriate legal authority. Nothing in this section shall be construed to criminalize any good faith action involving interment or disinterment which disturbs, moves, conceals, desecrates, damages or destroys human remains.

## PRACTICAL APPLICATION OF STATUTE

Maxwell Borscht violated 2C:22-1 by disturbing the remains of an unnamed man buried in a Cherry Hill cemetery. This is a crime of the second degree.

Pursuant to subsection a. of 2C:22-1, a person commits a second degree crime if he unlawfully disturbs, moves, conceals, desecrates, damages, or destroys human remains. Similarly, he is guilty of a second degree crime if he commits an act of sexual penetration or sexual contact upon human remains. Per subsection b., a third degree crime has been committed where a person "purposely or knowingly" fails to dispose of human remains in a manner required by law.

Borscht is guilty of a second degree crime as provided for in subsection a. The gentleman believed a family myth that his great uncle was buried in an unmarked grave in Cherry Hill. The significance of the myth was that $5 million in gold bullion was buried with him.

Cranford Police Captain Christian Star had been searching for Borscht pursuant to a massive insurance scam that he had perpetrated. Relying on a tip from a witness, Star traveled to Cherry Hill and began visiting the town's cemeteries. As he approached his third graveyard, he did indeed find Borscht, shovel in hand, breaking open a pine box casket in an unmarked grave.

Borscht pulled the human remains from the box, tossed them aside, and threw up his hands. He then kicked the unfortunate, unnamed man's skeleton and cried, "Where's the bullion, you bony fool?" At this point, Star pointed his pistol at Borscht, dangling handcuffs from his free hand. Borscht was then appropriately arrested.

Given that Maxwell Borscht had no lawful reason to disturb and damage the human remains of the unnamed man, he is guilty of a second degree crime under 2C:22-1.

**Chapter 23—Reserved**

# 24

# OFFENSES AGAINST THE FAMILY, CHILDREN, AND INCOMPETENTS

## FACT PATTERN (PERTAINS TO CHAPTERS 24 AND 25)

Bridgewater Police Patrolman Ra Davis reported to an alleged domestic violence dispute at the home of Barbie Penn, a 38-year-old woman who lived with her 10-year-old daughter. Also living in the house were Barbie's 40-year-old mentally incompetent cousin and her 75-year-old mother. Barbie was paid by her late father's estate to care for her mother and cousin on a daily basis.

Once at the Penn residency, Patrolman Davis heard yelling through the front door. Although he could decipher a few words coming from a man's mouth, he was unable to understand the content. The officer rang the doorbell, hoping to interrupt; Barbie Penn answered within seconds.

Standing beside Barbie was Jerry Penn, her husband. Officer Davis immediately observed that Jerry was bleeding from the nose, and upon closer inspection of Barbie, he noted that a small bruise was beginning to form under her eye. Accordingly, he asked what had occurred. Jerry advised that he and Barbie had been separated for about ten months. Per court order, he was permitted to have visitation with their daughter, Suzie, twice a week. However, the daughter was to be picked up and dropped off by Jerry's mother, because the court had also issued a restraining order against Jerry whereby he was not to have any contact with Barbie. When Officer Davis inquired why Jerry was at the house in obvious violation of the restraining order, he only replied with, "Because I heard this lunatic was doing some very bad things in front of my daughter." Barbie then lunged at Jerry, punching him in the chin. As Officer Davis restrained her, she screamed, "And I'm not sorry I broke your nose. You deserved it because you're ugly." At that, Davis arrested both Jerry and Barbie. He thereafter called the appropriate state agencies to ensure proper care for Suzie and the other women living in the home.

Jerry Penn's statement irked the Bridgewater patrolman enough so that he contacted the department's Deputy Chief, who headed their detective unit. What unfolded pursuant to a one-month follow-up investigation didn't just provide validity to Jerry

Penn's words—it shocked the entire town of Bridgewater. The following offenses involving Barbie Penn were uncovered:

1. On three separate occasions, Barbie Penn engaged in numerous sexual acts with two men at the same time. These acts, which included sexual intercourse, were performed in the presence of her 10-year-old daughter, Suzie. The men, Frank Roberts and Fred Rodriguez, were not her boyfriends; they were both legally married to Barbie. This brought her total number of current marriages to three. Both Roberts and Rodriguez knew that Barbie was married to Jerry Penn when they took their vows to marry her.

2. Frank Roberts brought a video cameraman to Barbie's house for the purpose of shooting footage of 10-year-old Suzie. The video footage was of Suzie having sex with a 13-year-old boy. Barbie permitted the video photography, watching over the entire session. The cameraman, Willie Maxso, turned over the tapes to Roberts, who then sold copies of the same to several New Jersey residents, including a prominent state senator. In addition, Roberts posted the video on the Internet, charging any persons who logged onto his website. Roberts also paid the 13-year-old boy to steal Maxso's camera from him after the shooting was completed. The camera was valued at $1,000.

3. Barbie routinely maltreated and endangered her 75-year-old mother and mentally incompetent adult cousin. On one occasion, "for laughs" as Barbie later described it, she baked brownies laced with marijuana and fed them to her cousin. The Bridgewater Police also learned that Barbie once locked her elderly mother in her bedroom for 72 hours. The woman's only recourse for nutrition was tap water from the room's adjoining bathroom and two candy bars that she had stashed in her bureau. The mother's food deprivation caused her to be hospitalized.

At the conclusion of the Deputy Chief's investigation, Barbie Penn was arrested at her home. On the same day, Frank Roberts and Willie Maxso were picked up while they were commingling at a local bar. Frank Rodriguez was nabbed at his place of employment. The state senator turned himself in to police headquarters when he learned that a warrant had been issued for his arrest. All of these adults were charged accordingly, and bail was set.

---

**2C:24-1.** **Bigamy**

a. **Bigamy.** A married person is guilty of bigamy, a disorderly persons offense, if he contracts or purports to contract another marriage, unless at the time of the subsequent marriage:

    (1) The actor believes that the prior spouse is dead;

    (2) The actor and the prior spouse have been living apart for 5 consecutive years throughout which the prior spouse was not known by the actor to be alive;

    (3) A court has entered a judgment purporting to terminate or annul any prior disqualifying marriage, and the actor does not know that judgment to be invalid; or

    (4) The actor reasonably believes that he is legally eligible to remarry.

b. **Other party to bigamous marriage.** A person is guilty of bigamy if he contracts or purports to contract marriage with another knowing that the other is thereby committing bigamy.

## PRACTICAL APPLICATION OF STATUTE

### Bigamy

Pursuant to 2C:24-1, Barbie Penn was charged with two counts of bigamy for her marriages to Frank Roberts and Fred Rodriguez. Bigamy is a disorderly persons offense.

The statute basically provides that a married person who engages in another marriage is guilty of bigamy: you can't be married to two or three people at once. Because Barbie was only separated from her husband Jerry, and not legally divorced, her subsequent marriages to Frank and Fred make her guilty of bigamy.

It should be noted that under subsections a.(1) through a.(4), certain circumstances vitiate a bigamy offense. These exceptions are varied and include situations such as an actor's belief that the prior spouse is dead and that an erroneous court order had terminated the prior marriage. Barbie, however, does not have these defenses.

### Other Party to Bigamous Marriage

Frank Roberts and Fred Rodriguez should also be charged with bigamy as they knew they were marrying a married woman. At the time each man took his wedding vows, he was aware of Barbie's prior existing marriage to Jerry Penn. Accordingly, they are both guilty of this disorderly persons offense.

---

**2C:24-2,**  **Blank**
**2C:24-3.**

**2C:24-4.**  **Endangering welfare of children**

    a. Any person having a legal duty for the care of a child or who has assumed responsibility for the care of a child who engages in sexual conduct which would impair or debauch the morals of the child, or who causes the child harm that would make the child an abused or neglected child as defined in R.S.9:6-1, R.S.9:6-3 and P.L.1974, c.119, s.1 (C.9:6-8.21) is guilty of a crime of the second degree. Any other person who engages in conduct or who causes harm as described in this subsection to a child under the age of 16 is guilty of a crime of the third degree.

    b. (1) As used in this subsection:

      "Child" means any person under 16 years of age.

      "Internet" means the international computer network of both federal and non-federal interoperable packet switched data networks.

      "Prohibited sexual act" means

        (a) Sexual intercourse; or

        (b) Anal intercourse; or

        (c) Masturbation; or

        (d) Bestiality; or

        (e) Sadism; or

        (f) Masochism; or

        (g) Fellatio; or

        (h) Cunnilingus;

(i) Nudity, if depicted for the purpose of sexual stimulation or gratification of any person who may view such depiction; or

(j) Any act of sexual penetration or sexual contact as defined in N.J.S.2C:14-1. "Reproduction" means, but is not limited to, computer generated images.

(2) (Deleted by amendment, P.L.2001, c.291).

(3) A person commits a crime of the second degree if he causes or permits a child to engage in a prohibited sexual act or in the simulation of such an act if the person knows, has reason to know or intends that the prohibited act may be photographed, filmed, reproduced, or reconstructed in any manner, including on the Internet, or may be part of an exhibition or performance. If the person is a parent, guardian or other person legally charged with the care or custody of the child, the person shall be guilty of a crime of the first degree.

(4) Any person who photographs or films a child in a prohibited sexual act or in the simulation of such an act or who uses any device, including a computer, to reproduce or reconstruct the image of a child in a prohibited sexual act or in the simulation of such an act is guilty of a crime of the second degree.

(5) (a) Any person who knowingly receives for the purpose of selling or who knowingly sells, procures, manufactures, gives, provides, lends, trades, mails, delivers, transfers, publishes, distributes, circulates, disseminates, presents, exhibits, advertises, offers or agrees to offer, through any means, including the Internet, any photograph, film, videotape, computer program or file, video game or any other reproduction or reconstruction which depicts a child engaging in a prohibited sexual act or in the simulation of such an act, is guilty of a crime of the second degree.

(b) Any person who knowingly possesses or knowingly views any photograph, film, videotape, computer program or file, video game or any other reproduction or reconstruction which depicts a child engaging in a prohibited sexual act or in the simulation of such an act, including on the Internet, is guilty of a crime of the fourth degree.

(6) For purposes of this subsection, a person who is depicted as or presents the appearance of being under the age of 16 in any photograph, film, videotape, computer program or file, video game or any other reproduction or reconstruction shall be rebuttably presumed to be under the age of 16. If the child who is depicted as engaging in, or who is caused to engage in, a prohibited sexual act or simulation of a prohibited sexual act is under the age of 16, the actor shall be strictly liable and it shall not be a defense that the actor did not know that the child was under the age of 16, nor shall it be a defense that the actor believed that the child was 16 years of age or older, even if such a mistaken belief was reasonable.

## PRACTICAL APPLICATION OF STATUTE

### Endangering the Welfare of a Child—Debauching Morals

For engaging in sexual activity with two men in front of her 10-year-old daughter, Barbie Penn was appropriately charged with endangering the welfare of a child. Her legal duty to care for her daughter—as her mother—is the linchpin that makes this a second degree crime.

Per subsection a. of 2C:24-4, a person who has a "legal duty for the care of a child" (or who has assumed responsibility to care for the child) is guilty of a second degree crime if he engages in sexual conduct that would "impair" or "debauch" the child's morals. On three separate occasions, Barbie Penn engaged in numerous sexual acts, including sexual intercourse with two men, in front of her 10-year-old daughter, Suzie. This kind of conduct performed in the presence of such a young child reasonably would "impair" and/or "debauch" the juvenile's morals. Given that Barbie Penn had custody of Suzie and is the child's mother, she had a legal duty to care for her. With these two elements met, Penn is guilty of a second degree crime for endangering her daughter's welfare.

Frank Roberts and Fred Rodriguez should also be charged under subsection a. of the statute, as their sexual conduct similarly would be found to endanger Suzie's welfare. However, their actions, in being the two men having sex with Barbie Penn, only amount to a third degree crime. This is because they did not have a legal duty to care for the 10-year-old girl.

### Child Pornography—Permitting Act

Barbie Penn is guilty of a first degree crime for permitting her daughter Suzie to be filmed while having sex with a 13-year-old boy. This serious offense is grounded in subsection b. of the endangering welfare of children statute.

Under 2C:24-4b.(3), any person who "causes or permits" a child to engage in a "prohibited sexual act" while such act is photographed or filmed is guilty of a second degree crime. If the person is the child's parent or guardian, the crime is elevated to a first degree offense.

One of Penn's husbands, Frank Roberts, brought a cameraman to her home. Once there, he shot video footage of 10-year-old Suzie having sex with another minor. Not only did Penn allow this deviant act to occur, she actually stood by and watched. Accordingly, this mother is guilty of first degree endangering the welfare of a child.

It should be noted that a "simulated" sexual act—one that appears to be occurring—is prohibited under this statute as well. Also, still photography (or any kind of reproduction of a prohibited act) is illegal. In other words, if Penn had permitted still pictures of Suzie in a simulated sexual act to appear on the Internet, she would still be guilty of this first degree crime.

These additional matters apply not only for subsection b.(3) but also for subsections b.(4) and b.(5).

### Child Pornography—Photographing Act

Cameraman Willie Maxso is guilty of a second degree crime for videotaping 10-year-old Suzie having sex with a 13-year-old boy. Simply, subsection b.(4) makes it unlawful for anyone to photograph or film a child engaging in any prohibited sexual act.

### Child Pornography—The Seller

In selling the videotapes of the 10- and 13-year-old's sexual acts, Frank Roberts has endangered the welfare of these children. Under 2C:24-4b.(5)(a), Roberts is guilty of a second degree crime.

This subsection carefully enumerates the multiple manners of distribution of child pornography that will render an individual guilty of this offense. Unlawful distribution-type activities include activities such as selling, publishing, circulating, and advertising.

A person can be convicted under b.(5)(a) even if he has only "received" child pornography material, but only if the prosecution proves that he received it "for the purpose of selling" it.

### Child Pornography—The Buyer

One who "knowingly" possesses (or views) child pornography but is not in the business of selling it is guilty of a fourth degree crime. Accordingly, because the state senator purposely bought the illicit videotape of 10-year-old Suzie, he is guilty of this crime, which is set forth in subsection b.(5)(b) of the endangering welfare of children statute.

The "knowingly" mental state component of this subsection is particularly important. For example, had the state senator unwittingly entered a child porn website while surfing the Internet, he should not be charged with this crime. Likewise, if he attended a party where all of a sudden a guest popped a child porn tape into the VCR, he should not be convicted under this statute unless, of course, he stayed and watched.

## 2C:24-5. Willful nonsupport

A person commits a crime of the fourth degree if he willfully fails to provide support which he can provide and which he knows he is legally obliged to provide to a spouse, child or other dependent. In addition to the sentence authorized by the code, the court may proceed under section 2C:62-1.

## 2C:24-6. Unlawful adoptions

Unlawful adoptions shall be governed by the provisions of Title 9 of the Revised Statutes.

## 2C:24-7. Endangering the welfare of an incompetent person

A person is guilty of a disorderly persons offense when he knowingly acts in a manner likely to be injurious to the physical, mental or moral welfare of a person who is unable to care for himself because of mental disease or defect.

## PRACTICAL APPLICATION OF STATUTE

Barbie Penn should be charged with violating 2C:24-7 for feeding her adult cousin brownies laced with marijuana. Her action constitutes endangering the welfare of an incompetent person, which is a disorderly persons offense.

An individual who knowingly performs an act that likely will be injurious to the "physical, mental or moral welfare" of an incompetent person has violated 2C:24-7. Penn fed her cousin, a mentally incompetent woman, brownies with an illegal controlled dangerous substance, marijuana. This act, which she stated she did "for laughs," certainly was likely to be injurious to both the woman's "physical" and "mental" welfare. With this being the case, Penn is guilty of violating this statute.

## 2C:24-8. Abandonment, neglect of elderly person, disabled adult; third degree crime

a. A person having a legal duty to care for or who has assumed continuing responsibility for the care of a person 60 years of age or older or a disabled adult, who abandons the elderly person or disabled adult or unreasonably neglects to do or fails to permit to be done any act necessary for the physical or mental health of the elderly person or disabled adult, is guilty of a crime of the third degree. For purposes of this section "abandon" means the willful desertion or forsaking of an elderly person or disabled adult.

b. A person shall not be considered to commit an offense under this section for the sole reason that he provides or permits to be provided nonmedical remedial treatment by spiritual means through prayer alone in lieu of medical care, in accordance with the tenets and practices of the elderly person's or disabled adult's established religious tradition, to an elderly person or disabled adult to whom he has a legal duty to care for or has assumed responsibility for the care of.

c. Nothing in this section shall be construed to preclude or limit the prosecution or conviction for any other offense defined in this code or in any other law of this State.

## PRACTICAL APPLICATION OF STATUTE

Endangering the welfare of an elderly or disabled person is a crime of the third degree. Barbie Penn is guilty of this offense for locking her elderly mother in the bedroom for 72 hours straight.

In order to be convicted under this statute, the defendant must have a "legal duty" to care for an elderly (60 years or older) or disabled person. At minimum, the defendant must have assumed a continuing responsibility to provide such care. A violation has occurred where the care provider has abandoned or unreasonably neglected the above described person.

Barbie Penn was under a legal duty to care for her 75-year-old mother. She was paid by her late father's estate to handle the same on a daily basis. For some reason, Penn locked the elderly lady in her bedroom for 72 consecutive hours. The woman's only recourse for nutrition was tap water from the room's adjoining bathroom and two candy bars that she had stashed in her bureau. The tramautic event caused Penn's mother to be hospitalized for food deprivation.

Barbie Penn's neglect of her mother was clearly unreasonable. Not only did she fail to provide food for the woman, but she precluded her from all the normal activities of daily life—locking a 75-year-old woman in her bedroom is tantamount to imprisonment. Not to mention, Penn placed her mother in other considerable danger: if a medical emergency had arisen, who would know? Under these circumstances, Penn, an individual who had a legal duty to care for her elderly mother, is guilty of violating 2C:24-8 for endangering her welfare.

Penn probably also should be charged with false imprisonment or perhaps criminal restraint. After all, she did place her mother at risk of serious bodily injury by depriving her of food and general care. Subsection c. of 2C:24-8 provides a special provision, advising that a charge under this statute does not preclude prosecution under any other offense defined in the code. This should be no surprise, though, as any one incident may result in volations of a number of different offenses.

**2C:24-9.**     **Use of 17-year-old or younger to commit criminal offense; crime**

a. Except as provided in P.L.1991, c.81 (C.2C:20-17) and N.J.S.2C:35-6, any person who is at least 18 years of age who knowingly uses, solicits, directs, hires, employs or conspires with a person who is in fact 17 years of age or younger to commit a criminal offense is guilty of a crime.

b. An offense under this section constitutes a crime of the fourth degree if the underlying offense is a disorderly persons offense. Otherwise, an offense under this section shall be classified one degree higher than the underlying offense.

c. Notwithstanding the provisions of N.J.S.2C:1-8, a conviction under this section shall not merge with a conviction for the underlying offense. Nor shall a conviction for the underlying offense merge with a conviction under this section. Nothing contained in this act shall prohibit the court from imposing an extended term of imprisonment pursuant to 2C:43-7; nor shall this be construed to preclude or limit a prosecution or conviction of any person for conspiracy under N.J.S.2C:5-2, or any prosecution or conviction for any offense.

d. It shall be no defense to a prosecution under this act that the actor mistakenly believed that the person which the actor used, solicited, directed, hired or employed was 18 years of age or older, even if such mistaken belief was reasonable.

## PRACTICAL APPLICATION OF STATUTE

Frank Roberts is ripe for a charge under 2C:24-9 for paying a 13-year-old boy to steal Willie Maxso's camera. Given that the underlying theft offense is a third degree crime, Roberts's charge for criminally employing this juvenile is one of the second degree.

A person is guilty of an offense under 2C:24-9 where he "knowingly" solicits or employs or conspires with a juvenile (17 or younger) to commit a criminal offense. This type of activity is a fourth degree crime where the underlying offense is a disorderly persons offense. Otherwise, it is a crime one degree higher than the underlying offense.

Frank Roberts actively paid a 13-year-old boy to steal a camera. Accordingly, he should be charged with violating 2C:24-9 as he "knowingly" employed a juvenile to commit a criminal offense. The value of the camera was $1,000, which means the underlying theft offense is a third degree crime (thefts where the amount involved exceeds $500 but is less than $75,000 are third degree crimes). Therefore, because an offense under 2C:24-9 is one degree higher than the underlying offense, Roberts should here be charged with a second degree crime.

### No Defense Where Reasonable Belief Actor Is 18 or Older

Pursuant to subsection d., there is no defense available where the actor reasonably believed the juvenile employed was 18 years of age or older. If the juvenile used in the crime was in fact 17 or younger, the actor is automatically guilty of violating this statute.

# 25

# DOMESTIC VIOLENCE

**2C:25-1**            **Repealed**
**to 2C:25-16.**

**2C:25-17.**          **Short title**

This act shall be known and may be cited as the "Prevention of Domestic Violence Act of 1991."

**2C:25-18.**          **Findings, declarations**

The Legislature finds and declares that domestic violence is a serious crime against society; that there are thousands of persons in this State who are regularly beaten, tortured and in some cases even killed by their spouses or cohabitants; that a significant number of women who are assaulted are pregnant; that victims of domestic violence come from all social and economic backgrounds and ethnic groups; that there is a positive correlation between spousal abuse and child abuse; and that children, even when they are not themselves physically assaulted, suffer deep and lasting emotional effects from exposure to domestic violence. It is therefore, the intent of the Legislature to assure the victims of domestic violence the maximum protection from abuse the law can provide.

The Legislature further finds and declares that the health and welfare of some of its most vulnerable citizens, the elderly and disabled, are at risk because of incidents of reported and unreported domestic violence, abuse and neglect which are known to include acts which victimize the elderly and disabled emotionally, psychologically, physically and financially; because of age, disabilities or infirmities, this group of citizens frequently must rely on the aid and support of others; while the institutionalized elderly are protected under P.L.1977, c.239 (C.52:27G-1 et seq.), elderly and disabled adults in noninstitutionalized or community settings may find themselves victimized by family members or others upon whom they feel compelled to depend.

The Legislature further finds and declares that violence against the elderly and disabled, including criminal neglect of the elderly and disabled under section 1 of P.L.1989, c.23 (C.2C:24-8), must be recognized and addressed on an equal basis as violence against spouses and children in order to fulfill our responsibility as a society to protect those who are less able to protect themselves.

The Legislature further finds and declares that even though many of the existing criminal statutes are applicable to acts of domestic violence, previous societal attitudes concerning domestic violence have affected the response of our law enforcement and judicial systems, resulting in these acts receiving different treatment from similar crimes when they occur in a domestic context. The Legislature finds that battered adults presently experience substantial difficulty in gaining access to protection from the judicial system, particularly due to that system's inability to generate a prompt response in an emergency situation.

It is the intent of the Legislature to stress that the primary duty of a law enforcement officer when responding to a domestic violence call is to enforce the laws allegedly violated and to protect the victim. Further, it is the responsibility of the courts to protect victims of violence that occurs in a family or family-like setting by providing access to both emergent and long-term civil and criminal remedies and sanctions, and by ordering those remedies and sanctions that are available to assure the safety of the victims and the public. To that end, the Legislature encourages the training of all police and judicial personnel in the procedures and enforcement of this act, and about the social and psychological context in which domestic violence occurs; and it further encourages the broad application of the remedies available under this act in the civil and criminal courts of this State. It is further intended that the official response to domestic violence shall communicate the attitude that violent behavior will not be excused or tolerated, and shall make clear the fact that the existing criminal laws and civil remedies created under this act will be enforced without regard to the fact that the violence grows out of a domestic situation.

**2C:25-19.**        **Definitions**

As used in this act:

a. "Domestic violence" means the occurrence of one or more of the following acts inflicted upon a person protected under this act by an adult or an emancipated minor.

(1) Homicide N.J.S.2C:11-1 et seq.

(2) Assault N.J.S.2C:12-1

(3) Terroristic threats N.J.S.2C:12-3

(4) Kidnapping N.J.S.2C:13-1

(5) Criminal restraint N.J.S.2C:13-2

(6) False imprisonment N.J.S.2C:13-3

(7) Sexual assault N.J.S.2C:14-2

(8) Criminal sexual contact N.J.S.2C:14-3

(9) Lewdness N.J.S.2C:14-4

(10) Criminal mischief N.J.S.2C:17-3

(11) Burglary N.J.S.2C:18-2

(12) Criminal trespass N.J.S.2C:18-3

(13) Harassment N.J.S.2C:33-4

(14) Stalking P.L.1992, c.209 (C.2C:12-10)

When one or more of these acts is inflicted by an unemancipated minor upon a person protected under this act, the occurrence shall not constitute "domestic violence," but may be the basis for the filing of a petition or complaint pursuant to the provisions of section 11 of P.L.1982, c.77 (C.2A:4A-30).

b. "Law enforcement agency" means a department, division, bureau, commission, board or other authority of the State or of any political subdivision thereof which employs law enforcement officers.

c. "Law enforcement officer" means a person whose public duties include the power to act as an officer for the detection, apprehension, arrest and conviction of offenders against the laws of this State.

d. "Victim of domestic violence" means a person protected under this act and shall include any person who is 18 years of age or older or who is an emancipated minor and who has been subjected to domestic violence by a spouse, former spouse, or any other person who is a present or former household member. "Victim of domestic violence" also includes any person, regardless of age, who has been subjected to domestic violence by a person with whom the victim has a child in common, or with whom the victim anticipates having a child in common, if one of the parties is pregnant. "Victim of domestic violence" also includes any person who has been subjected to domestic violence by a person with whom the victim has had a dating relationship.

e. "Emancipated minor" means a person who is under 18 years of age but who has been married, has entered military service, has a child or is pregnant or has been previously declared by a court or an administrative agency to be emancipated.

**2C:25-20.**  **Development of training course; curriculum**

a.  (1)  The Division of Criminal Justice shall develop and approve a training course and curriculum on the handling, investigation and response procedures concerning reports of domestic violence and abuse and neglect of the elderly and disabled. This training course and curriculum shall be reviewed at least every two years and modified by the Division of Criminal Justice from time to time as need may require. The Division of Criminal Justice shall distribute the curriculum to all local police agencies.

(2)  The Attorney General shall be responsible for ensuring that all law enforcement officers attend initial training within 90 days of appointment or transfer and annual inservice training of at least four hours as described in this section.

b.  (1)  The Administrative Office of the Courts shall develop and approve a training course and a curriculum on the handling, investigation and response procedures concerning allegations of domestic violence. This training course shall be reviewed at least every two years and modified by the Administrative Office of the Courts from time to time as need may require.

(2)  The Administrative Director of the Courts shall be responsible for ensuring that all judges and judicial personnel attend initial training within 90 days of appointment or transfer and annual inservice training as described in this section.

(3)  The Division of Criminal Justice and the Administrative Office of the Courts shall provide that all training on the handling of domestic violence matters shall include information concerning the impact of domestic violence on society, the dynamics of domestic violence, the statutory and case law concerning domestic violence, the necessary elements of a protection order, policies and procedures as promulgated or ordered by the Attorney General or the Supreme Court, and the use of available community resources, support services, available sanctions and treatment options. Law enforcement agencies shall: (1) establish domestic crisis teams or participate in established domestic crisis teams, and (2) shall train individual officers in methods of dealing with domestic violence and neglect and abuse of the elderly and disabled. The teams may include social workers, clergy or other persons trained in counseling, crisis intervention or in the treatment of domestic violence and neglect and abuse of the elderly and disabled victims.

**2C:25-21.**  **Arrest of alleged attacker; seizure of weapons**

a.  When a person claims to be a victim of domestic violence, and where a law enforcement officer responding to the incident finds probable cause to believe that domestic violence has occurred, the law enforcement officer shall arrest the person who is alleged to be the person who subjected the victim to domestic violence and shall sign a criminal complaint if:

(1)  The victim exhibits signs of injury caused by an act of domestic violence;

(2)  A warrant is in effect;

(3) There is probable cause to believe that the person has violated N.J.S.2C:29-9, and there is probable cause to believe that the person has been served with the order alleged to have been violated. If the victim does not have a copy of a purported order, the officer may verify the existence of an order with the appropriate law enforcement agency; or

(4) There is probable cause to believe that a weapon as defined in N.J.S.2C:39-1 has been involved in the commission of an act of domestic violence.

b.  A law enforcement officer may arrest a person; or may sign a criminal complaint against that person, or may do both, where there is probable cause to believe that an act of domestic violence has been committed, but where none of the conditions in subsection a. of this section applies.

c.  (1) As used in this section, the word "exhibits" is to be liberally construed to mean any indication that a victim has suffered bodily injury, which shall include physical pain or any impairment of physical condition. Where the victim exhibits no visible sign of injury, but states that an injury has occurred, the officer should consider other relevant factors in determining whether there is probable cause to make an arrest.

(2) In determining which party in a domestic violence incident is the victim where both parties exhibit signs of injury, the officer should consider the comparative extent of the injuries, the history of domestic violence between the parties, if any, and any other relevant factors.

(3) No victim shall be denied relief or arrested or charged under this act with an offense because the victim used reasonable force in self defense against domestic violence by an attacker.

d.  (1) In addition to a law enforcement officer's authority to seize any weapon that is contraband, evidence or an instrumentality of crime, a law enforcement officer who has probable cause to believe that an act of domestic violence has been committed may:

(a) question persons present to determine whether there are weapons on the premises; and

(b) upon observing or learning that a weapon is present on the premises, seize any weapon that the officer reasonably believes would expose the victim to a risk of serious bodily injury.

(2) A law enforcement officer shall deliver all weapons seized pursuant to this section to the county prosecutor and shall append an inventory of all seized weapons to the domestic violence report.

(3) Weapons seized in accordance with the above shall be returned to the owner except upon order of the Superior Court. The prosecutor who has possession of the seized weapons may, upon notice to the owner, petition a judge of the Family Part of the Superior Court, Chancery Division, within 45 days of seizure, to obtain title to the seized weapons, or to revoke any and all permits, licenses and other authorizations for the use, possession, or ownership of such weapons pursuant to the law governing such use, possession, or ownership, or may object to the return of the weapons on such grounds as are provided for the initial rejection or later revocation of the authorizations, or on the grounds that the owner is unfit or that the owner poses a threat to the public in general or a person or persons in particular.

A hearing shall be held and a record made thereof within 15 days of the notice provided above. No formal pleading and no filing fee shall be required as a preliminary to such hearing. The hearing shall be summary in nature. Appeals from the results of the hearing shall be to the Superior Court, Appellate Division, in accordance with the law.

If the prosecutor does not institute an action within 45 days of seizure, the seized weapons shall be returned to the owner.

After the hearing the court shall order the return of the firearms, weapons and any authorization papers relating to the seized weapons to the owner if the complaint has been dismissed at the request of the complainant and the prosecutor determines that there is insufficient probable cause to indict; or if the defendant is found not guilty of the charges; or if the court determines that the domestic violence situation no longer exists.

Nothing in this act shall impair the right of the State to retain evidence pending a criminal prosecution. Nor shall any provision of this act be construed to limit the authority of the State or a law enforcement officer to seize, retain or forfeit property pursuant to chapter 64 of Title 2C of the New Jersey Statutes.

If, after the hearing, the court determines that the weapons are not to be returned to the owner, the court may:

(a) With respect to weapons other than firearms, order the prosecutor to dispose of the weapons if the owner does not arrange for the transfer or sale of the weapons to an appropriate person within 60 days; or

(b) Order the revocation of the owner's firearms purchaser identification card or any permit, license or authorization, in which case the court shall order the owner to surrender any firearm seized and all other firearms possessed to the prosecutor and shall order the prosecutor to dispose of the firearms if the owner does not arrange for the sale of the firearms to a registered dealer of the firearms within 60 days; or

(c) Order such other relief as it may deem appropriate. When the court orders the weapons forfeited to the State or the prosecutor is required to dispose of the weapons, the prosecutor shall dispose of the property as provided in N.J.S. 2C:64-6.

(4) A civil suit may be brought to enjoin a wrongful failure to return a seized firearm where the prosecutor refuses to return the weapon after receiving a written request to do so and notice of the owner's intent to bring a civil action pursuant to this section. Failure of the prosecutor to comply with the provisions of this act shall entitle the prevailing party in the civil suit to reasonable costs, including attorney's fees, provided that the court finds that the prosecutor failed to act in good faith in retaining the seized weapon.

(5) No law enforcement officer or agency shall be held liable in any civil action brought by any person for failing to learn of, locate or seize a weapon pursuant to this act, or for returning a seized weapon to its owner.

## PRACTICAL APPLICATION OF STATUTE

### Domestic Violence—Types of Offenses, Who Is a Victim, Probable Cause, and Required Arrests Generally

"Domestic violence" includes offenses ranging from homicide to assault to stalking to harassment (see 2C:25-19 for a complete list). A "victim of domestic violence" is defined as any person who is 18 years or older, or who is an emancipated minor, who has some type of close relationship with the perpetrator. Per 2C:25-19, relationships that qualify an individual to be protected under the Domestic Violence Act include where the perpetrator is a spouse, former spouse, any person who is a present or former household member, or any person who has ever dated the victim. Also, a person can be a "victim of domestic violence," regardless of his age, where the perpetrator is a person who has a child with the victim or who anticipates having a child with the victim, meaning that one of the parties is pregnant.

Where a law enforcement officer finds "probable cause" to believe that an act of domestic violence has occurred, he "can" arrest the person he believes committed the act. The officer "shall" or "must" arrest the suspect if one of the following circumstances exists in addition to his finding of probable cause: The victim has a visible sign of injury, a warrant is in effect, the suspect is in contempt of a court order, or a weapon was involved in the act of domestic violence. Probable cause—and nothing more—that the suspect utilized a weapon or is in contempt of a court order necessitates that the officer must arrest him. It should be noted that even where none of the aforementioned additional circumstances exist, an officer may still arrest an individual where he simply has probable cause to believe a domestic violence act has been committed.

### Arrest Required Due to Probable Cause, Visible Signs of Injuries, and Contempt of Court

Bridgewater Police Patrolman Ra Davis was in a situation where he "must" have arrested both Barbie Penn and Jerry Penn for committing acts of domestic violence. Officer Davis responded to a report of violence at the home of Barbie Penn. Upon his arrival at her house, he found Barbie with her husband, Jerry Penn. Davis immediately observed that Jerry was bleeding from his nose, and upon closer inspection of Barbie, he noted that a small bruise was beginning to form under her eye. Both parties admitted to physically fighting with each other. Barbie even stated, "And I'm not sorry I broke your nose. You deserved it because you're ugly." Jerry Penn advised that he was at the house even though there was a court order which forbade him from having contact with Barbie. He claimed, however, that he was there in an effort to protect his daughter from "bad things" being performed in front of her by Barbie.

Under the totality of the circumstances, Patrolman Davis was required to arrest both Jerry and Barbie Penn for committing acts of domestic violence. First, both parties qualify as "victims" as defined in 2C:25-19. Although separated, they are spouses. Even if divorced, however, they would qualify as former spouses or people who previously lived in the same household. Second, Officer Davis had probable cause to believe that both Jerry and Barbie had committed prohibited acts of domestic violence—simple assaults:

1. Both parties admitted to fighting with each other;
2. Barbie even admitted to breaking Jerry's nose;
3. Jerry was obviously upset that Barbie was doing something improper, or perhaps illegal, in front of their daughter, thus giving him a motive to act out violently;
4. Both individuals exhibited signs of injuries.

The visible signs of injuries are important. This factor, in addition to Davis's finding of probable cause that an act of domestic violence occurred, meant that he had to arrest both Barbie and Jerry. It is integral to note here, however, that had Davis found that either party had caused injuries to the other by using "reasonable force" to protect himself, then Davis should *not* arrest the person. 2C:25-21c.(3) sets forth an exception to a "must" arrest where a person has used reasonable force in self-defense from an attacker. For example, if Jerry had fought off Barbie (the aggressor who broke his nose because he was "ugly") then Davis should not arrest Jerry because of visible injuries he noted on Barbie. Officer Davis, though, had to arrest Jerry in any case. He was in contempt of a court order.

Jerry Penn admitted to Officer Davis that he was present at Barbie's home in face of a court order prohibiting his contact with her. This contempt violation, in addition to Davis's finding of probable cause that an act of domestic violence had been committed by Jerry, required Officer Davis to arrest him. The fact that Jerry claimed he was there in an effort to stop his estranged wife from doing "very bad things" in front of their child should not preclude Officer Davis from effectuating the arrest. Based on all of the above, Jerry Penn should be arrested as a domestic violence offender and charged with simple assault; he should further be charged under 2C:29-9 for contempt of court, as he violated the court's order to have no contact with his estranged wife. Barbie, too, should be arrested for committing an act of domestic violence, with a charge of simple assault filed against her. Thereafter, the courts will resolve the outcome of the charges.

### Seizure of Weapons

Where a law enforcement officer has probable cause to believe an act of domestic violence has occurred, he may seize any weapons that he reasonably believes would expose the victim to risk of serious bodily injury. This authority is set forth in subsection d. of 2C:25-21. This subsection also permits an officer to "question persons present to determine whether there are weapons on the premises." Upon seizure of any weapons, the officer must turn the same over to the county prosecutor's office.

## 2C:25-22.    Immunity from civil liability

A law enforcement officer or a member of a domestic crisis team or any person who, in good faith, reports a possible incident of domestic violence to the police shall not be held liable in any civil action brought by any party for an arrest based on probable cause, enforcement in good faith of a court order, or any other act or omission in good faith under this act.

## 2C:25-23.    Dissemination of notice to victim of domestic violence

A law enforcement officer shall disseminate and explain to the victim the following notice, which shall be written in both English and Spanish:

"You have the right to go to court to get an order called a temporary restraining order, also called a TRO, which may protect you from more abuse by your attacker. The officer who handed you this card can tell you how to get a TRO.

The kinds of things a judge can order in a TRO may include:

1. That your attacker is temporarily forbidden from entering the home you live in;
2. That your attacker is temporarily forbidden from having contact with you or your relatives;
3. That your attacker is temporarily forbidden from bothering you at work;
4. That your attacker has to pay temporary child support or support for you;
5. That you be given temporary custody of your children;
6. That your attacker pay you back any money you have to spend for medical treatment or repairs because of the violence. There are other things the court can order, and the court clerk will explain the procedure to you and will help you fill out the papers for a TRO.

You also have the right to file a criminal complaint against your attacker. The police officer who gave you this paper will tell you how to file a criminal complaint.

On weekends, holidays and other times when the courts are closed, you still have a right to get a TRO. The police officer who gave you this paper can help you get in touch with a judge who can give you a TRO."

**2C:25-24.**   **Domestic violence offense reports**

a. It shall be the duty of a law enforcement officer who responds to a domestic violence call to complete a domestic violence offense report. All information contained in the domestic violence offense report shall be forwarded to the appropriate county bureau of identification and to the State bureau of records and identification in the Division of State Police in the Department of Law and Public Safety. A copy of the domestic violence offense report shall be forwarded to the municipal court where the offense was committed unless the case has been transferred to the Superior Court.

b. The domestic violence offense report shall be on a form prescribed by the supervisor of the State bureau of records and identification which shall include, but not be limited to, the following information:

   (1) The relationship of the parties;

   (2) The sex of the parties;

   (3) The time and date of the incident;

   (4) The number of domestic violence calls investigated;

   (5) Whether children were involved, or whether the alleged act of domestic violence had been committed in the presence of children;

   (6) The type and extent of abuse;

   (7) The number and type of weapons involved;

   (8) The action taken by the law enforcement officer;

   (9) The existence of any prior court orders issued pursuant to this act concerning the parties;

   (10) The number of domestic violence calls alleging a violation of a domestic violence restraining order;

   (11) The number of arrests for a violation of a domestic violence order; and

   (12) Any other data that may be necessary for a complete analysis of all circumstances leading to the alleged incident of domestic violence.

c. It shall be the duty of the Superintendent of the State Police with the assistance of the Division of Systems and Communications in the Department of Law and Public Safety to compile and report annually to the Governor, the Legislature and the Advisory Council on Domestic Violence on the tabulated data from the domestic violence offense reports, classified by county.

**2C:25-25.**   **Criminal complaints; proceedings**

The court in a criminal complaint arising from a domestic violence incident:

a. Shall not dismiss any charge or delay disposition of a case because of concurrent dissolution of a marriage, other civil proceedings, or because the victim has left the residence to avoid further incidents of domestic violence;

b. Shall not require proof that either party is seeking a dissolution of a marriage prior to institution of criminal proceedings;

c. Shall waive any requirement that the victim's location be disclosed to any person.

**2C:25-26.**    **Release of defendant before trial; conditions**

    a. When a defendant charged with a crime or offense involving domestic violence is released from custody before trial on bail or personal recognizance, the court authorizing the release may as a condition of release issue an order prohibiting the defendant from having any contact with the victim including, but not limited to, restraining the defendant from entering the victim's residence, place of employment or business, or school, and from harassing or stalking the victim or victim's relatives in any way. The court may enter an order prohibiting the defendant from possessing any firearm or other weapon enumerated in subsection r. of N.J.S.2C:39-1 and ordering the search for and seizure of any such weapon at any location where the judge has reasonable cause to believe the weapon is located. The judge shall state with specificity the reasons for and scope of the search and seizure authorized by the order.

    b. The written court order releasing the defendant shall contain the court's directives specifically restricting the defendant's ability to have contact with the victim or the victim's friends, co-workers or relatives. The clerk of the court or other person designated by the court shall provide a copy of this order to the victim forthwith.

    c. The victim's location shall remain confidential and shall not appear on any documents or records to which the defendant has access.

    d. Before bail is set, the defendant's prior record shall be considered by the court. The court shall also conduct a search of the domestic violence central registry. Bail shall be set as soon as is feasible, but in all cases within 24 hours of arrest.

    e. Once bail is set it shall not be reduced without prior notice to the county prosecutor and the victim. Bail shall not be reduced by a judge other than the judge who originally ordered bail, unless the reasons for the amount of the original bail are available to the judge who reduces the bail and are set forth in the record.

    f. A victim shall not be prohibited from applying for, and a court shall not be prohibited from issuing, temporary restraints pursuant to this act because the victim has charged any person with commission of a criminal act.

**2C:25-26.1.**    **Notification of victim of release of defendant**

Notwithstanding any other provision of law to the contrary, whenever a defendant charged with a crime or an offense involving domestic violence is released from custody the prosecuting agency shall notify the victim.

**2C:25-27.**    **Conditions of sentencing of defendant found guilty of domestic violence**

When a defendant is found guilty of a crime or offense involving domestic violence and a condition of sentence restricts the defendant's ability to have contact with the victim, that condition shall be recorded in an order of the court and a written copy of that order shall be provided to the victim by the clerk of the court or other person designated by the court. In addition to restricting a defendant's ability to have contact with the victim, the court may require the defendant to receive professional counseling from either a private source or a source appointed by the court, and if the court so orders, the court shall require the defendant to provide documentation of attendance at the professional counseling. In any case where the court order contains a requirement that the defendant receive professional counseling, no application by the defendant to dissolve the restraining order shall be granted unless, in addition to any other provisions required by law or conditions ordered by the court, the defendant has completed all required attendance at such counseling.

**2C:25-28.        Filing complaint alleging domestic violence in Family Part; proceedings**

    a. A victim may file a complaint alleging the commission of an act of domestic violence with the Family Part of the Chancery Division of the Superior Court in conformity with the rules of court. The court shall not dismiss any complaint or delay disposition of a case because the victim has left the residence to avoid further incidents of domestic violence. Filing a complaint pursuant to this section shall not prevent the filing of a criminal complaint for the same act.

    On weekends, holidays and other times when the court is closed, a victim may file a complaint before a judge of the Family Part of the Chancery Division of the Superior Court or a municipal court judge who shall be assigned to accept complaints and issue emergency, ex parte relief in the form of temporary restraining orders pursuant to this act.

    A plaintiff may apply for relief under this section in a court having jurisdiction over the place where the alleged act of domestic violence occurred, where the defendant resides, or where the plaintiff resides or is sheltered, and the court shall follow the same procedures applicable to other emergency applications. Criminal complaints filed pursuant to this act shall be investigated and prosecuted in the jurisdiction where the offense is alleged to have occurred. Contempt complaints filed pursuant to N.J.S.2C:29-9 shall be prosecuted in the county where the contempt is alleged to have been committed and a copy of the contempt complaint shall be forwarded to the court that issued the order alleged to have been violated.

    b. The court shall waive any requirement that the petitioner's place of residence appear on the complaint.

    c. The clerk of the court, or other person designated by the court, shall assist the parties in completing any forms necessary for the filing of a summons, complaint, answer or other pleading.

    d. Summons and complaint forms shall be readily available at the clerk's office, at the municipal courts and at municipal and State police stations.

    e. As soon as the domestic violence complaint is filed, both the victim and the abuser shall be advised of any programs or services available for advice and counseling.

    f. A plaintiff may seek emergency, ex parte relief in the nature of a temporary restraining order. A municipal court judge or a judge of the Family Part of the Chancery Division of the Superior Court may enter an ex parte order when necessary to protect the life, health or well-being of a victim on whose behalf the relief is sought.

    g. If it appears that the plaintiff is in danger of domestic violence, the judge shall, upon consideration of the plaintiff's domestic violence complaint, order emergency ex parte relief, in the nature of a temporary restraining order. A decision shall be made by the judge regarding the emergency relief forthwith.

    h. A judge may issue a temporary restraining order upon sworn testimony or complaint of an applicant who is not physically present, pursuant to court rules, or by a person who represents a person who is physically or mentally incapable of filing personally. A temporary restraining order may be issued if the judge is satisfied that exigent circumstances exist sufficient to excuse the failure of the applicant to appear personally and that sufficient grounds for granting the application have been shown.

    i. An order for emergency, ex parte relief shall be granted upon good cause shown and shall remain in effect until a judge of the Family Part issues a further order. Any temporary order hereunder is immediately appealable for a plenary hearing de novo not on the record before any judge of the Family Part of the county in which the plaintiff resides or is sheltered if that judge issued the temporary order or has access to the reasons for the issuance of the temporary order and sets forth in the record the reasons for the modification or dissolution. The denial of a temporary restraining order by a municipal court judge and subsequent administrative dismissal of the complaint shall not bar the victim from refiling a complaint in the Family Part based on the same incident and receiving an emergency, exparte hearing de novo not on the record before a Family Part judge, and every denial of relief by a municipal court judge shall so state.

j.  Emergency relief may include forbidding the defendant from returning to the scene of the domestic violence, forbidding the defendant to possess any firearm or other weapon enumerated in subsection r. of N.J.S.2C:39-1, ordering the search for and seizure of any such weapon at any location where the judge has reasonable cause to believe the weapon is located and any other appropriate relief. The judge shall state with specificity the reasons for and scope of the search and seizure authorized by the order.

k.  The judge may permit the defendant to return to the scene of the domestic violence to pick up personal belongings and effects but shall, in the order granting relief, restrict the time and duration of such permission and provide for police supervision of such visit.

l.  An order granting emergency relief, together with the complaint or complaints, shall immediately be forwarded to the appropriate law enforcement agency for service on the defendant, and to the police of the municipality in which the plaintiff resides or is sheltered, and shall immediately be served upon the defendant by the police, except that an order issued during regular court hours may be forwarded to the sheriff for immediate service upon the defendant in accordance with the Rules of Court. If personal service cannot be effected upon the defendant, the court may order other appropriate substituted service. At no time shall the plaintiff be asked or required to serve any order on the defendant.

m.  (Deleted by amendment, P.L.1994, c.94.)

n.  Notice of temporary restraining orders issued pursuant to this section shall be sent by the clerk of the court or other person designated by the court to the appropriate chiefs of police, members of the State Police and any other appropriate law enforcement agency or court.

o.  (Deleted by amendment, P.L.1994, c.94.)

p.  Any temporary or permanent restraining order issued pursuant to this act shall be in effect throughout the State, and shall be enforced by all law enforcement officers.

q.  Prior to the issuance of any temporary or permanent restraining order issued pursuant to this section, the court shall order that a search be made of the domestic violence central registry with regard to the defendant's record.

## 2C:25-28.1.     In-house restraining order prohibited

Notwithstanding any provision of P.L.1991, c.261 (C.2C:25-17 et seq.) to the contrary, no order issued by the Family Part of the Chancery Division of the Superior Court pursuant to section 12 or section 13 of P.L.1991, c.261 (C.2C:25-28 or 2C:25-29) regarding emergency, temporary or final relief shall include an in-house restraining order which permits the victim and the defendant to occupy the same premises but limits the defendant's use of that premises.

## 2C:25-29.     Hearing procedure; relief

a.  A hearing shall be held in the Family Part of the Chancery Division of the Superior Court within 10 days of the filing of a complaint pursuant to section 12 of P.L.1991, c.261 (C.2C:25-28) in the county where the ex parte restraints were ordered, unless good cause is shown for the hearing to be held elsewhere. A copy of the complaint shall be served on the defendant in conformity with the Rules of Court. If a criminal complaint arising out of the same incident which is the subject matter of a complaint brought under P.L.1981, c.426 (C.2C:25-1 et seq.) or P.L.1991, c.261 (C.2C:25-17 et seq.) has been filed, testimony given by the plaintiff or defendant in the domestic violence matter shall not be used in the simultaneous or subsequent criminal proceeding against the defendant, other than domestic violence contempt matters and where it would otherwise be admissible hearsay under the rules of evidence that govern where a party is unavailable. At the hearing the standard for proving the allegations in the complaint shall be by a preponderance of the evidence. The court shall consider but not be limited to the following factors:

(1) The previous history of domestic violence between the plaintiff and defendant, including threats, harassment and physical abuse;

(2) The existence of immediate danger to person or property;

(3) The financial circumstances of the plaintiff and defendant;

(4) The best interests of the victim and any child;

(5) In determining custody and parenting time the protection of the victim's safety; and

(6) The existence of a verifiable order of protection from another jurisdiction.

An order issued under this act shall only restrain or provide damages payable from a person against whom a complaint has been filed under this act and only after a finding or an admission is made that an act of domestic violence was committed by that person. The issue of whether or not a violation of this act occurred, including an act of contempt under this act, shall not be subject to mediation or negotiation in any form. In addition, where a temporary or final order has been issued pursuant to this act, no party shall be ordered to participate in mediation on the issue of custody or parenting time.

b. In proceedings in which complaints for restraining orders have been filed, the court shall grant any relief necessary to prevent further abuse. At the hearing the judge of the Family Part of the Chancery Division of the Superior Court may issue an order granting any or all of the following relief:

(1) An order restraining the defendant from subjecting the victim to domestic violence, as defined in this act.

(2) An order granting exclusive possession to the plaintiff of the residence or household regardless of whether the residence or household is jointly or solely owned by the parties or jointly or solely leased by the parties. This order shall not in any manner affect title or interest to any real property held by either party or both jointly. If it is not possible for the victim to remain in the residence, the court may order the defendant to pay the victim's rent at a residence other than the one previously shared by the parties if the defendant is found to have a duty to support the victim and the victim requires alternative housing.

(3) An order providing for parenting time. The order shall protect the safety and well-being of the plaintiff and minor children and shall specify the place and frequency of parenting time. Parenting time arrangements shall not compromise any other remedy provided by the court by requiring or encouraging contact between the plaintiff and defendant. Orders for parenting time may include a designation of a place of parenting time away from the plaintiff, the participation of a third party, or supervised parenting time.

(a) The court shall consider a request by a custodial parent who has been subjected to domestic violence by a person with parenting time rights to a child in the parent's custody for an investigation or evaluation by the appropriate agency to assess the risk of harm to the child prior to the entry of a parenting time order. Any denial of such a request must be on the record and shall only be made if the judge finds the request to be arbitrary or capricious.

(b) The court shall consider suspension of the parenting time order and hold an emergency hearing upon an application made by the plaintiff certifying under oath that the defendant's access to the child pursuant to the parenting time order has threatened the safety and well-being of the child.

(4) An order requiring the defendant to pay to the victim monetary compensation for losses suffered as a direct result of the act of domestic violence. The order may require the defendant to pay the victim directly, to reimburse the Victims of Crime Compensation Board for any and all compensation paid by the Victims of Crime Compensation Board directly to or on behalf of the victim, and may require that the defendant reimburse any parties that may have compensated the victim, as the court may determine. Compensatory losses shall include, but not be limited to, loss of earnings or other support, including child or spousal support, out-of-pocket losses for injuries sustained, cost of repair or replacement of real or personal property damaged or destroyed or taken by the defendant, cost of counseling for the victim, moving or other travel expenses, reasonable attorney's fees, court costs, and compensation for pain and suffering. Where appropriate, punitive damages may be awarded in addition to compensatory damages.

(5) An order requiring the defendant to receive professional domestic violence counseling from either a private source or a source appointed by the court and, in that event, requiring the defendant to provide the court at specified intervals with documentation of attendance at the professional counseling. The court may order the defendant to pay for the professional counseling. No application by the defendant to dissolve a final order which contains a requirement for attendance at professional counseling pursuant to this paragraph shall be granted by the court unless, in addition to any other provisions required by law or conditions ordered by the court, the defendant has completed all required attendance at such counseling.

(6) An order restraining the defendant from entering the residence, property, school, or place of employment of the victim or of other family or household members of the victim and requiring the defendant to stay away from any specified place that is named in the order and is frequented regularly by the victim or other family or household members.

(7) An order restraining the defendant from making contact with the plaintiff or others, including an order forbidding the defendant from personally or through an agent initiating any communication likely to cause annoyance or alarm including, but not limited to, personal, written, or telephone contact with the victim or other family members, or their employers, employees, or fellow workers, or others with whom communication would be likely to cause annoyance or alarm to the victim.

(8) An order requiring that the defendant make or continue to make rent or mortgage payments on the residence occupied by the victim if the defendant is found to have a duty to support the victim or other dependent household members; provided that this issue has not been resolved or is not being litigated between the parties in another action.

(9) An order granting either party temporary possession of specified personal property, such as an automobile, checkbook, documentation of health insurance, an identification document, a key, and other personal effects.

(10) An order awarding emergency monetary relief, including emergency support for minor children, to the victim and other dependents, if any. An ongoing obligation of support shall be determined at a later date pursuant to applicable law.

(11) An order awarding temporary custody of a minor child. The court shall presume that the best interests of the child are served by an award of custody to the non-abusive parent.

(12) An order requiring that a law enforcement officer accompany either party to the residence or any shared business premises to supervise the removal of personal belongings

in order to ensure the personal safety of the plaintiff when a restraining order has been issued. This order shall be restricted in duration.

(13) (Deleted by amendment, P.L.1995, c.242).

(14) An order granting any other appropriate relief for the plaintiff and dependent children, provided that the plaintiff consents to such relief, including relief requested by the plaintiff at the final hearing, whether or not the plaintiff requested such relief at the time of the granting of the initial emergency order.

(15) An order that requires that the defendant report to the intake unit of the Family Part of the Chancery Division of the Superior Court for monitoring of any other provision of the order.

(16) An order prohibiting the defendant from possessing any firearm or other weapon enumerated in subsection r. of N.J.S.2C:39-1 and ordering the search for and seizure of any such weapon at any location where the judge has reasonable cause to believe the weapon is located. The judge shall state with specificity the reasons for and scope of the search and seizure authorized by the order.

(17) An order prohibiting the defendant from stalking or following, or threatening to harm, to stalk or to follow, the complainant or any other person named in the order in a manner that, taken in the context of past actions of the defendant, would put the complainant in reasonable fear that the defendant would cause the death or injury of the complainant or any other person. Behavior prohibited under this act includes, but is not limited to, behavior prohibited under the provisions of P.L.1992, c.209 (C.2C:12-10).

(18) An order requiring the defendant to undergo a psychiatric evaluation.

c. Notice of orders issued pursuant to this section shall be sent by the clerk of the Family Part of the Chancery Division of the Superior Court or other person designated by the court to the appropriate chiefs of police, members of the State Police and any other appropriate law enforcement agency.

d. Upon good cause shown, any final order may be dissolved or modified upon application to the Family Part of the Chancery Division of the Superior Court, but only if the judge who dissolves or modifies the order is the same judge who entered the order, or has available a complete record of the hearing or hearings on which the order was based.

e. Prior to the issuance of any order pursuant to this section, the court shall order that a search be made of the domestic violence central registry.

### 2C:25-29.1.        Civil penalty for certain domestic violence offenders

In addition to any other disposition, any person found by the court in a final hearing pursuant to section 13 of P.L.1991, c.261 (C.2C:25-29) to have committed an act of domestic violence shall be ordered by the court to pay a civil penalty of at least $50, but not to exceed $500. In imposing this civil penalty, the court shall take into consideration the nature and degree of injury suffered by the victim. The court may waive the penalty in cases of extreme financial hardship.

### 2C:25-29.2.        Collection, distribution of civil penalties collected

All civil penalties imposed pursuant to section 1 of P.L.2001, c.195 (C.2C:25-29.1) shall be collected as provided by the Rules of Court. All moneys collected shall be forwarded to the Domestic Violence Victims' Fund established pursuant to section 3 of P.L.2001, c.195 (C.30:14-15).

### 2C:25-29.3.        Rules of Court

The Supreme Court may promulgate Rules of Court to effectuate the purposes of this act.

**2C:25-29.4.** **Surcharge for domestic violence offender to find grants**

In addition to any other penalty, fine or charge imposed pursuant to law, a person convicted of an act of domestic violence, as that term is defined by subsection a. of section 3 of P.L.1991, c.261 (C.2C:25-19), shall be subject to a surcharge in the amount of $100 payable to the Treasurer of the State of New Jersey for use by the Department of Human Services to fund grants for domestic violence prevention, training and assessment.

**2C:25-30.** **Violations; penalties**

Except as provided below, a violation by the defendant of an order issued pursuant to this act shall constitute an offense under subsection b. of N.J.S.2C:29-9 and each order shall so state. All contempt proceedings conducted pursuant to N.J.S.2C:29-9 involving domestic violence orders, other than those constituting indictable offenses, shall be heard by the Family Part of the Chancery Division of the Superior Court. All contempt proceedings brought pursuant to P.L.1991, c.261 (C.2C:25-17 et seq.) shall be subject to any rules or guidelines established by the Supreme Court to guarantee the prompt disposition of criminal matters. Additionally, and notwithstanding the term of imprisonment provided in N.J.S.2C:43-8, any person convicted of a second or subsequent nonindictable domestic violence contempt offense shall serve a minimum term of not less than 30 days. Orders entered pursuant to paragraphs (3), (4), (5), (8) and (9) of subsection b. of section 13 of this act shall be excluded from enforcement under subsection b. of N.J.S.2C:29-9; however, violations of these orders may be enforced in a civil or criminal action initiated by the plaintiff or by the court, on its own motion, pursuant to applicable court rules.

**2C:25-31.** **Contempt, law enforcement procedures**

Where a law enforcement officer finds that there is probable cause that a defendant has committed contempt of an order entered pursuant to the provisions of P.L.1981, c.426 (C.2C:25-1 et seq.) or P.L.1991, c.261 (C.2C:25-17 et seq.), the defendant shall be arrested and taken into custody by a law enforcement officer. The law enforcement officer shall follow these procedures:

The law enforcement officer shall transport the defendant to the police station or such other place as the law enforcement officer shall determine is proper. The law enforcement officer shall:

a. Conduct a search of the domestic violence central registry and sign a complaint concerning the incident which gave rise to the contempt charge;

b. Telephone or communicate in person or by facsimile with the appropriate judge assigned pursuant to this act and request bail be set on the contempt charge;

c. If the defendant is unable to meet the bail set, take the necessary steps to insure that the defendant shall be incarcerated at police headquarters or at the county jail; and

d. During regular court hours, the defendant shall have bail set by a Superior Court judge that day. On weekends, holidays and other times when the court is closed, the officer shall arrange to have the clerk of the Family Part notified on the next working day of the new complaint, the amount of bail, the defendant's whereabouts and all other necessary details. In addition, if a municipal court judge set the bail, the arresting officer shall notify the clerk of that municipal court of this information.

**2C:25-32.** **Alleged contempt; complainant's procedure**

Where a person alleges that a defendant has committed contempt of an order entered pursuant to the provisions of P.L.1981, c.426 (C.2C:25-1 et seq.) or P.L.1991, c.261, but where a law enforcement officer has found that there is not probable cause sufficient to arrest the defendant, the law enforcement officer shall advise the complainant of the procedure for completing and signing a criminal complaint alleging a violation of N.J.S.2C:29-9. During regular court hours, the assistance of the clerk of the Family Part of the Chancery Division of the Superior Court shall be made available to such complainants. Nothing in this section shall be construed to prevent the court from granting any other emergency relief it deems necessary.

**2C:25-33.**        **Records of applications for relief; reports; confidentiality; forms**

a. The Administrative Office of the Courts shall, with the assistance of the Attorney General and the county prosecutors, maintain a uniform record of all applications for relief pursuant to sections 9, 10, 11, 12, and 13 of P.L.1991, c.261 (C.2C:25-25, C.2C:25-26, C.2C:25-27, C.2C:25-28, and C.2C:25-29). The record shall include the following information:

   (1) The number of criminal and civil complaints filed in all municipal courts and the Superior Court;

   (2) The sex of the parties;

   (3) The relationship of the parties;

   (4) The relief sought or the offense charged, or both;

   (5) The nature of the relief granted or penalty imposed, or both, including, but not limited to, the following:

      (a) custody;

      (b) child support;

      (c) the specific restraints ordered;

      (d) any requirements or conditions imposed pursuant to paragraphs (1) through (18) of subsection b. of section 13 of P.L.1991, c.261 (C.2C:25-29), including but not limited to professional counseling or psychiatric evaluations;

   (6) The effective date of each order issued; and

   (7) In the case of a civil action in which no permanent restraints are entered, or in the case of a criminal matter that does not proceed to trial, the reason or reasons for the disposition.

   It shall be the duty of the Director of the Administrative Office of the Courts to compile and report annually to the Governor, the Legislature and the Advisory Council on Domestic Violence on the data tabulated from the records of these orders.

   All records maintained pursuant to this act shall be confidential and shall not be made available to any individual or institution except as otherwise provided by law.

b. In addition to the provisions of subsection a. of this section, the Administrative Office of the Courts shall, with the assistance of the Attorney General and the county prosecutors, create and maintain uniform forms to record sentencing, bail conditions and dismissals. The forms shall be used by the Superior Court and by every municipal court to record any order in a case brought pursuant to this act. Such recording shall include but not be limited to, the specific restraints ordered, any requirements or conditions imposed on the defendant, and any conditions of bail.

**2C:25-34.**        **Domestic violence restraining orders; central registry**

The Administrative Office of the Courts shall establish and maintain a central registry of all persons who have had domestic violence restraining orders entered against them, all persons who have been charged with a crime or offense involving domestic violence, and all persons who have been charged with a violation of a court order involving domestic violence. All records made pursuant to this section shall be kept confidential and shall be released only to:

    a. A public agency authorized to investigate a report of domestic violence;

    b. A police or other law enforcement agency investigating a report of domestic violence, or conducting a background investigation involving a person's application for a firearm permit or employment as a police or law enforcement officer or for any other purpose authorized by law or the Supreme Court of the State of New Jersey; or

    c. A court, upon its finding that access to such records may be necessary for determination of an issue before the court.

Any individual, agency or court which receives from the Administrative Office of the Courts the records referred to in this section shall keep such records and reports, or parts thereof, confidential and shall not disseminate or disclose such records and reports, or parts thereof; provided that nothing in this section shall prohibit a receiving individual, agency or court from disclosing records and reports, or parts thereof, in a manner consistent with and in furtherance of the purpose for which the records and reports or parts thereof were received.

Any individual who disseminates or discloses a record or report, or parts thereof, of the central registry, for a purpose other than investigating a report of domestic violence, conducting a background investigation involving a person's application for a firearm permit or employment as a police or law enforcement officer, making a determination of an issue before the court, or for any other purpose other than that which is authorized by law or the Supreme Court of the State of New Jersey, shall be guilty of a crime of the fourth degree.

**2C:25-35.**      **Rules of Court concerning central registry for domestic violence**

The Supreme Court of New Jersey may adopt Rules of Court appropriate or necessary to effectuate the purposes of this act.

### Chapter 26—Reserved

# 27

# BRIBERY AND CORRUPT INFLUENCE

**FACT PATTERN (PERTAINS TO CHAPTERS 27 AND 28)**

Mercer County Prosecutor Hoyt Wilder called a special press conference at the gates of his office. Flanked by his chief of investigators and his first assistant prosecutor, Wilder announced that his office had just completed an investigation that resulted in the arrests and indictments of more than ten individuals, including a number of elected officials and public servants. Unrolling a papyrus-type scroll, he tapped the microphone in front of him and read aloud the names and facts pertaining to a number of the indictments.

## So You Want to Be the Police Director?

In Ewing Township, the mayor and certain town council members sought to pass legislation creating a police director position. Four affirmative votes of the council were necessary in order for the ordinance to pass. However, only three of the local legislators were publicly in favor of the new top cop job. In an attempt to swing the likely dissenting voters to his side, Mayor Packer Winstrol met individually with each councilperson. He was confident that at least one, Caroline Timborelli, would join his cause.

Mayor Winstrol met with Councilwoman Timborelli at her four-bedroom colonial home. After a light dinner, Francis Pinkerton joined them for tea cakes and various herbal teas. Pinkerton, owner of a local hotel and a number of township shops, was the leading candidate for the police director position. After he explained a detailed plan for the success of the Ewing police force under his leadership, Pinkerton passed the councilwoman an envelope and said, "I hope all of my offerings will secure your vote on the ordinance." Timborelli casually thumbed through the envelope's contents—$5,000 in 20 dollar bills—and replied, "I'm certain they have. You're a good man, Francis Pinkerton."

The ordinance passed the following Thursday, with Councilwoman Timborelli casting the deciding vote. A week later, Mayor Winstrol appointed Pinkerton to the police director post. One month after that, Prosecutor Wilder recorded Mayor Winstrol and Pinkerton in a conversation at one of his shops. During their discussion, the mayor stated to Pinkerton, "I assume you appreciate my appointment. Now how about helping your old friend out? I don't need any cash. Just put my kid up in your hotel for the next year for free . . . I want him out of the house. You promised you would do this if I ensured your appointment."

Prosecutor Wilder convened a grand jury to seek indictments against Mayor Winstrol, Councilwoman Timborelli, and Police Director Pinkerton. Somehow, Pinkerton learned that Timborelli was cooperating with Wilder's office and that she was going to provide testimony against him and Winstrol. The day before she was to appear at the grand jury, Pinkerton tracked down Timborelli in the driveway of her home. With an unidentified man, he wielded a baseball bat in front of her face and told her, "Testify tomorrow, and I will break your legs." Timborelli, frightened, simply nodded favorably. Pinkerton, then satisfied, fled with his friend.

The following day, not only did Timborelli unleash all of the payoff information to the grand jury, she also testified about Pinkerton's threats. Mayor Winstrol appeared next. He, however, gave testimony in direct contradiction to Timborelli. After taking the appropriate oath and swearing to tell the truth, Winstrol told the grand jurors that he was not present at Timborelli's home when she was allegedly paid $5,000 by Pinkerton. He then categorically denied every charge levied against him.

A week later, the grand jury handed down indictments against Mayor Winstrol, Councilwoman Timborelli, and Police Director Pinkerton. They were all arrested at the Ewing Township municipal complex during a council meeting.

### Does My Councilman Grow Marijuana?

In Trenton, three local officials and an 18-year-old high school cheerleader were indicted together in an unusual corruption conspiracy. Trenton High School senior Lacey Campbell appeared at a police precinct in the Chambersberg section of the city. She complained to the desk sergeant that one of the city's new council members, Mario Conti, was growing marijuana in his backyard. Upon some questioning, Campbell agreed to provide a written statement. Her statement was then turned over to the department's detective bureau and an investigation was initiated.

Arriving in a marked Trenton Police cruiser, two detectives met Councilman Conti on the street in front of his home. They asked the councilman for permission to check his backyard for marijuana plants. Conti, almost laughing, granted their request and led the detectives through the yard's gate. Next door, hidden in the brush, a tabloid photographer looked on with interest. He watched as the plainclothes officers went from plant to plant. They pulled up tomato vines, smelled basil leaves, closely inspected an oregano plant, and eyeballed several other forms of greenery. They finally came to a halt, though, at one particular large growth. Uprooting it from the ground, the detectives conducted a quick field test. It proved positive for marijuana. The photographer shot two rolls of film as the officers bagged the illegal drugs and handcuffed the shocked councilman.

The pictures and story of Conti's arrest became headlines in the morning edition of every local newspaper in the Trenton area. Conti's attorney, however, vehemently proclaimed his client's innocence and vowed that they would show that the newly elected public servant had been framed . . . and indeed they did. This is what happened.

An elderly woman, who resided in the house behind Conti's, came forward after she read of her neighbor's arrest. She told authorities that a young woman fitting Lacey Campbell's description had visited Conti's backyard a week earlier. The senior citizen advised that she saw the girl "planting something" but had dismissed the matter as an innocent botanical act.

The same detectives who arrested Conti questioned Campbell. She immediately folded and explained that she was dating a man much older than herself. Her boyfriend was Michael Stanowitz, chief of the Trenton Fire Department. Stanowitz and Conti were longtime adversaries, who most recently had butted heads over Conti's refusal to vote for an ordinance that would have appropriated over $100,000 toward two new fire engines. Stanowitz, in fact, was already under investigation for allegedly threatening to "ignite into flames" Conti's automobile if he failed to vote for the ordinance. When that didn't persuade the councilman to change his mind, he enlisted Campbell's aid to frame the man. Accordingly, two weeks after Conti and the council rejected the ordinance, Campbell appeared at the Chambersberg precinct and falsely incriminated the councilman of growing marijuana in his backyard.

With his illicit plot uncovered, Stanowitz was expeditiously arrested and appropriately charged along with his 18-year-old girlfriend. The charge against Councilman Conti was, of course, dismissed.

---

## 2C:27-1.         Definitions

In chapters 27 through 30, unless a different meaning plainly is required:

a. "Benefit" means gain or advantage, or anything regarded by the beneficiary as gain or advantage, including a pecuniary benefit or a benefit to any other person or entity in whose welfare he is interested;

b. "Government" includes any branch, subdivision or agency of the government of the State or any locality within it;

c. "Harm" means loss, disadvantage or injury, or anything so regarded by the person affected, including loss, disadvantage or injury to any other person or entity in whose welfare he is interested;

d. "Official proceeding" means a proceeding heard or which may be heard before any legislative, judicial, administrative or other governmental agency, arbitration proceeding, or official authorized to take evidence under oath, including any arbitrator, referee, hearing examiner, commissioner, notary or other person taking testimony or deposition in connection with any such proceeding;

e. "Party official" means a person who holds an elective or appointive post in a political party in the United States by virtue of which he directs or conducts, or participates in directing or conducting party affairs at any level of responsibility;

f. "Pecuniary benefit" is benefit in the form of money, property, commercial interests or anything else the primary significance of which is economic gain;

g. "Public servant" means any officer or employee of government, including legislators and judges, and any person participating as juror, advisor, consultant or otherwise, in performing a governmental function, but the term does not include witnesses;

h. "Administrative proceeding" means any proceeding, other than a judicial proceeding, the outcome of which is required to be based on a record or documentation prescribed by law, or in which law or regulation is particularized in application to individuals;

i. "Statement" means any representation, but includes a representation of opinion, belief or other state of mind only if the representation clearly relates to state of mind apart from or in addition to any facts which are the subject of the representation.

**2C:27-2.**          **Bribery in official and political matters**

A person is guilty of bribery if he directly or indirectly offers, confers or agrees to confer upon another, or solicits, accepts or agrees to accept from another

a. Any benefit as consideration for a decision, opinion, recommendation, vote or exercise of discretion of a public servant, party official or voter on any public issue or in any public election; or

b. Any benefit as consideration for a decision, vote, recommendation or exercise of official discretion in a judicial or administrative proceeding; or

c. Any benefit as consideration for a violation of an official duty of a public servant or party official; or

d. Any benefit as consideration for the performance of official duties.

For the purposes of this section "benefit as consideration" shall be deemed to mean any benefit not authorized by law.

It is no defense to prosecution under this section that a person whom the actor sought to influence was not qualified to act in the desired way whether because he had not yet assumed office, or lacked jurisdiction, or for any other reason.

In any prosecution under this section of an actor who offered, conferred or agreed to confer, or who solicited, accepted or agreed to accept a benefit, it is no defense that he did so as a result of conduct by another constituting theft by extortion or coercion or an attempt to commit either of those crimes.

Any offense proscribed by this section is a crime of the second degree. If the benefit offered, conferred, agreed to be conferred, solicited, accepted or agreed to be accepted is of the value of $200.00 or less, any offense proscribed by this section is a crime of the third degree.

## PRACTICAL APPLICATION OF STATUTE

Both Francis Pinkerton and Councilwoman Caroline Timborelli are guilty of bribery. 2C:27-2 makes it illegal for an individual to offer a bribe—and for an individual to accept a bribe. The Pinkerton-Timborelli bribe falls under subsection a. of the statute and is a second degree offense.

2C:27-2a. provides that the crime of bribery has occurred where a person has either offered or accepted "any benefit as consideration" for matters such as a "decision" or a "vote" of a "public servant" on any "public issue." It is not necessary that the bribe transaction actually be completed: "agreeing to confer" or "agreeing to accept" the benefit is sufficient for conviction.

Francis Pinkerton wanted a Ewing Township ordinance, creating a police director position, to be passed. In an effort to accomplish this goal, he ate tea cakes and drank herbal tea with Councilwoman Timborelli—and he also gave her an envelope with $5,000 cash. Pinkerton in fact stated to her, "I hope all of my offerings will secure your vote on the ordinance." The councilwoman replied, "I'm certain they have. . . ."

Here, an offer of money—which is the "benefit"—was "accepted" by Councilwoman Timborelli, a "public servant." The money was provided as "consideration" for her "vote" on a "public issue"—the creation of a police director position in Ewing Township. Accordingly, both Francis Pinkerton and Councilwoman Caroline Timborelli are guilty of second degree bribery.

It should be noted that 2C:27-2 makes it illegal to bribe any public servant for basically any violation of an official duty (see subsection c.) or for any "performance" of an official duty (see subsection d.). "Public servants" include elected officials, such as mayors, councilmen, state assemblymen, state senators, and the governor, as well as individuals such as board of education members, planning board members, and any other employees of the government. Bribery involving party officials (e.g., county chairmen) similarly falls under the prohibitions of the statute.

The offer or acceptance of a bribe by a judge likewise comes under the domain of 2C:27-2. Subsection b. specifically makes it illegal for a person to offer or accept a benefit in exchange for a decision in a judicial or administrative proceeding.

Bribery is a second degree crime unless the value of the benefit involved is $200 or less. In that case, it is a crime of the third degree.

---

**2C:27-3.**    **Threats and other improper influence in official and political matters**

    a. **Offenses defined.** A person commits an offense if he directly or indirectly:

        (1) Threatens unlawful harm to any person with purpose to influence a decision, opinion, recommendation, vote or exercise of discretion of a public servant, party official or voter on any public issue or in any public election; or

        (2) Threatens harm to any public servant with purpose to influence a decision, opinion, recommendation, vote or exercise of discretion in a judicial or administrative proceeding; or

        (3) Threatens harm to any public servant or party official with purpose to influence him to violate his official duty.

           It is no defense to prosecution under this section that a person whom the actor sought to influence was not qualified to act in the desired way, whether because he had not yet assumed office or lacked jurisdiction, or for any other reason.

    b. **Grading.** An offense under this section is a crime of the third degree.

## PRACTICAL APPLICATION OF STATUTE

Trenton Fire Chief Michael Stanowitz is guilty of violating 2C:27-3 for threatening Councilman Mario Conti. The crime is one of the third degree if the offense is directly related to Conti's position as a public servant.

2C:27-3a.(1) provides that an offense has been committed where a person threatens a public servant with unlawful harm in order to influence matters such as a decision or vote. Chief Stanowitz, a longtime adversary of Councilman Conti, threatened to "ignite into flames" the Councilman's automobile if he failed to vote for an ordinance which was designed to appropriate over $100,000 toward two new fire engines. Given that there was a threat of harm (arson) toward a public servant (a councilman) in an attempt to influence a vote (on an ordinance), Chief Stanowitz is guilty of this third degree crime.

---

**2C:27-4.**    **Unlawful benefits for official behavior; grading**

    a. A person commits a crime if the person, as a public servant:

        (1) directly or indirectly, knowingly solicits, accepts or agrees to accept any benefit from another for or because of any official act performed or to be performed by the person or for or because of a violation of official duty;

(2) directly or indirectly, knowingly receives any benefit from another who is or was in a position, different from that of a member of the general public, to benefit, directly or indirectly, from a violation of official duty or the performance of official duties; or

(3) directly or indirectly, knowingly receives any benefit from or by reason of a contract or agreement for goods, property or services if the contract or agreement is awarded, made or paid by the agency that employs the person or if the goods, property or services are provided to the government agency that employs the public servant.

b. A person commits a crime if the person offers, confers or agrees to confer a benefit, acceptance of which is prohibited by this section.

c. Any offense proscribed by this section is a crime of the second degree. If the benefit solicited, accepted, agreed to be accepted, offered, conferred or agreed to be conferred is of a value of $200.00 or less, any offense proscribed by this section is a crime of the third degree.

## PRACTICAL APPLICATION OF STATUTE

This statute is quite similar to bribery as defined in 2C:27-2. However, this one only appears to apply to "public servants," and each subsection has a particular type of act that it prohibits. Subsection a.(1), for instance, has language that specifically prohibits receipt of any benefit for *past* official behavior. This is the statute that best suits Prosecutor Wilder's needs in a case against Mayor Winstrol for his son's year-long housing in Francis Pinkerton's hotel.

2C:27-4a.(1) makes it illegal for a public servant to solicit or receive a benefit for any official act previously performed by him or to be performed in the future. Mayor Winstrol appointed Francis Pinkerton to be the police director. One month later, Prosecutor Wilder recorded a conversation between the two men. During this discussion, the mayor stated to Pinkerton, "I assume you appreciate my appointment. Now how about helping your old friend out? I don't need any cash. Just put my kid up in your hotel for the next year for free . . . I want him out of the house. You promised you would do this if I ensured your appointment." In this circumstance, Mayor Winstrol solicited a benefit—free housing for his son—in exchange for his previously performed official act of appointing Pinkerton to the post of police director. Accordingly, the mayor should be charged under 2C:27-4a.(1), which is a second degree offense.

### Benefit from People in Special Positions

Subsections a.(2) and a.(3) provide interesting, specific language. The latter sets forth that a public servant has committed a crime where he receives a benefit for doling out a *contract* (e.g., a mayor gives the city's sewer contract to a specific company in exchange for a Mercedes).

Per subsection a.(2), a public servant is guilty of a crime where he receives a benefit "from another who is or was in a position different from that of a member of the general public." What does this mean? The mayor of Jersey City's wife receives a speeding ticket in Hoboken. He approaches Hoboken's municipal court judge and says, "Do me a favor. Dismiss my wife's ticket. I have a spot for you in Jersey City next year." The Hoboken judge then dismisses Jersey City's First Lady's speeding ticket. Here, the Jersey

City mayor has received a "benefit"—the dismissal of his wife's ticket. The benefit came from a judge—someone who is in a position "different from that of a member of the general public." Therefore, the Jersey City mayor is ripe for a charge under 2C:27-4a.(2).

The grading of the mayor's offense is particularly challenging. It should probably be a third degree crime, because the fine for a speeding ticket is generally under $200. But is that really the value of the benefit received by the mayor? He and his wife most likely saved themselves at least a grand in insurance surcharges by the ticket's dismissal. Given that any offense under 2C:27-4 where the benefit solicited or received is over $200 is a second degree crime, perhaps that should be the degree of the mayor's charge.

## 2C:27-5.        Retaliation for past official action

A person commits a crime of the fourth degree if he harms another by any unlawful act with purpose to retaliate for or on account of the service of another as a public servant.

## PRACTICAL APPLICATION OF STATUTE

Prosecutor Wilder appropriately had Trenton Fire Chief Michael Stanowitz charged with violating 2C:27-5 for his retaliatory acts against Councilman Mario Conti. This is a fourth degree crime.

2C:27-5 makes it illegal for a person to retaliate against a public servant for a past official act performed by the official. In order for the retaliation to be a crime, it must be an "unlawful act." In Stanowitz's case, it was just that.

Chief Stanowitz was angered at Councilman Conti, a public servant, for voting against an ordinance that would have appropriated over $100,000 toward two new fire engines. In an effort to retaliate against Conti, Stanowitz conspired with his girlfriend to harm the councilman by engaging in the unlawful act of falsely incriminating him to the police—they attempted to frame Conti for growing marijuana in his backyard. Accordingly, Stanowitz should be charged with violating 2C:27-5 for retaliating unlawfully against the councilman.

## 2C:27-6.        Unlawful benefits acceptance

a. Except as provided in subsection d. of this section, a public servant commits a crime if the person, knowingly and under color of office, directly or indirectly solicits, accepts or agrees to accept any benefit for that person or another not allowed by law.

b. Except as provided in subsection d. of this section, a person commits a crime if the person, directly or indirectly, confers or agrees to confer any benefit not allowed by law to a public servant.

c. (Deleted by amendment, P.L.1999, c.440.)

d. This section shall not apply to:

(1) Fees prescribed by law to be received by a public servant, or any other benefit to which the public servant is otherwise legally entitled; or

(2) Gifts or other benefits conferred on account of kinship or other personal, professional or business relationship independent of the official status of the recipient; or

(3) Trivial benefits the receipt of which involve no risk that the public servant would perform official duties in a biased or partial manner.

e. An offense under this section is a crime of the third degree. If the gift or other benefit is of a value of $200.00 or less, any offense proscribed by this section is a crime of the fourth degree.

## PRACTICAL APPLICATION OF STATUTE

The "gifts to public servants" statute is basically another bribery statute. Public servants who solicit gifts (for illicit reasons) as well as those who offer/confer gifts (for illicit reasons) can be convicted of this offense, which is a third degree crime. If the value of the gift is under $200, it is a fourth degree crime.

Illicit gifts can range from vacation packages to a new house roof to sterling silver forks. If they are provided in an effort to influence the public servant in his duties, then the gifts are illegal. Where the gift is considered "trivial," no offense is deemed to be committed at all—this is because such gifts "involve no risk that the public servant would perform official duties in a biased or partial manner." Trivial gifts include items like a cup of coffee or a pen.

| | |
|---|---|
| **2C:27-7.** | **Repealed** |
| **2C:27-8.** | **Repealed** |
| **2C:27-9.** | **Unlawful official business transaction where interest is involved; grading; conditions** |

A public servant commits a crime of the fourth degree if, while performing his official functions on behalf of a governmental entity, the public servant knowingly transacts any business with himself, a member of his immediate family, or a business organization in which the public servant or an immediate family member has an interest. For purposes of this section, an interest in a business organization shall not include aggregate familial ownership or control of one percent or less of an interest in the capital or equity of the business organization. A public servant shall not be guilty of an offense under this section if the public servant's performance of official functions would not affect the public servant, family member or business organization differently than such performance would affect the public generally, or would not affect the public servant, family member or business organization, as a member of a business, profession, occupation or group, differently than such performance would affect any other member of such business, profession, occupation or group.

## PRACTICAL APPLICATION OF STATUTE

This is yet another bribery-type statute. 2C:27-9, though, sets forth specific language to prohibit circumstances where a public servant "transacts" with himself or members of his immediate family. This means that a mayor or board of education member or state assemblyman (or any other public servant) cannot provide public contracts to his own company or a company owned by people such as his wife, sister, or mother.

# 28

# PERJURY AND OTHER FALSIFICATION IN OFFICIAL MATTERS

**2C:28-1.**    **Perjury**

a. **Offense defined.** A person is guilty of perjury, a crime of the third degree, if in any official proceeding he makes a false statement under oath or equivalent affirmation, or swears or affirms the truth of a statement previously made, when the statement is material and he does not believe it to be true.

b. **Materiality.** Falsification is material, regardless of the admissibility of the statement under rules of evidence, if it could have affected the course or outcome of the proceeding or the disposition of the matter. It is no defense that the declarant mistakenly believed the falsification to be immaterial. Whether a falsification is material is a question of law.

c. **Irregularities no defense.** It is not a defense to prosecution under this section that the oath or affirmation was administered or taken in an irregular manner. A document purporting to be made upon oath or affirmation at any time when the actor presents it as being so verified shall be deemed to have been duly sworn or affirmed.

d. **Retraction.** It is an affirmative defense under this section that the actor retracted the falsification in the course of the proceeding or matter in which it was made prior to the termination of the proceeding or matter without having caused irreparable harm to any party.

e. **Corroboration.** No person shall be convicted of an offense under this section where proof of falsity rests solely upon contradiction by testimony of a single person other than the defendant.

## PRACTICAL APPLICATION OF STATUTE

### Perjury

Mayor Packer Winstrol is guilty of perjury, which is a third degree offense. The mayor's crime results from his willfully false testimony provided before the grand jury.

A person is guilty of perjury where he makes a false statement under oath and knows it not to be true. Also key to this offense is that the satement is "material," meaning that it is relevant, perhaps crucial, to the proceeding where the testimony is provided.

Basically, if the false statement can affect the outcome of the proceeding, it is "material." However, "materiality" is a question to be decided by the courts.

Mayor Winstrol was present at Councilwoman Timborelli's house when she received a $5,000 bribe from Francis Pinkerton. In fact, he set up the meeting. Winstrol also solicited a benefit from Pinkerton—to put up his son, for free, in Pinkerton's hotel. This benefit was requested in exchange for the mayor's past appointment of Pinkerton as the township police director. Mayor Winstrol then willfully lied at grand jury proceedings about these matters, grand jury proceedings that were specifically convened to ascertain the truth about the alleged aforementioned corrupt activities of the mayor, Councilwoman Timborelli, and Police Director Pinkerton. Accordingly, the mayor's false statements were obviously "material" as, if they were believed, they could have affected the outcome of the proceedings and vindicated the mayor and the others. With this being the case, Mayor Packer Winstrol is guilty of perjury.

### Retraction—Affirmative Defense

If a person retracts his false testimony during the course of the proceeding where it was made—and it hasn't caused "irreparable harm" to any party—he has an affirmative defense to perjury. This provision can be found under subsection d. of the statute.

Mayor Winstrol committed perjury when he testified in front of the grand jury. However, had he retracted his false testimony before the end of the grand jury proceedings, he would have had an affirmative defense to a perjury charge and could not be convicted of this offense. The only thing that would vitiate the affirmative defense, though, is if the false testimony had caused irreparable harm to the prosecution (e.g., the false testimony caused another key witness to jump bail and refuse to testify).

### No Conviction Where Testimony Contradicted by Just One Party

The prosecution would not be able to convict Mayor Winstrol of perjury if they only had one person to contradict his testimony. Subsection e. of the statute provides that a person cannot be convicted of perjury "where proof of falsity rests solely" upon one person's contradictory testimony. Accordingly, if the state could only produce Councilwoman Timborelli to contradict the mayor's false testimony, he could not be convicted of perjury. However, since Prosecutor Wilder possessed tape-recorded conversations of Mayor Winstrol, it is unlikely that the politician could avoid a perjury conviction.

---

**2C:28-2.**      **False swearing**

     a. **False swearing.** A person who makes a false statement under oath or equivalent affirmation, or swears or affirms the truth of such a statement previously made, when he does not believe the statement to be true, is guilty of a crime of the fourth degree.

     b. **Perjury provisions applicable.** Subsections c. and d. of section 2C:28-1 apply to the present section.

     c. **Inconsistent statements.** Where the defendant made inconsistent statements under oath or equivalent affirmation, both having been made within the period of the statute of limitations, the prosecution may proceed by setting forth the inconsistent statements in a single count alleging in the alternative that one or the other was false and not believed by the defendant. In such case it shall not be necessary for the prosecution to prove which statement was false but only that one or the other was false and not believed by the defendant to be true.

## PRACTICAL APPLICATION OF STATUTE

Whereas perjury is a third degree crime, false swearing is a fourth degree crime. The offenses are quite similar, with false swearing having the same retraction defense as found in the perjury statute. The difference lies in the lack of a requirement of materiality.

Basically, where a person makes a statement *under oath* and willfully gives false testimony, he can be convicted under 2C:28-2, instead of 2C:28-1, as long as the false statement was not material. Of course, in order for a conviction to result, the person must believe the statement is not true when he makes it.

**2C:28-3.**        **Unsworn falsification to authorities**

a. **Statements "Under Penalty."** A person commits a crime of the fourth degree if he makes a written false statement which he does not believe to be true, on or pursuant to a form bearing notice, authorized by law, to the effect that false statements made therein are punishable.

b. **In general.** A person commits a disorderly persons offense if, with purpose to mislead a public servant in performing his function, he:

(1) Makes any written false statement which he does not believe to be true;

(2) Purposely creates a false impression in a written application for any pecuniary or other benefit, by omitting information necessary to prevent statements therein from being misleading;

(3) Submits or invites reliance on any writing which he knows to be forged, altered or otherwise lacking in authenticity; or

(4) Submits or invites reliance on any sample, specimen, map, boundary-mark, or other object which he knows to be false.

c. **Perjury provisions applicable.** Subsections c. and d. of section 2C:28-1 and subsection c. of 2C:28-2 apply to the present section.

## PRACTICAL APPLICATION OF STATUTE

### Unsworn Falsification—Generally

This is another perjury-type statute, though the false statement does not need to be made "under oath" in order for a conviction to occur. Per subsection a. of 2C:28-3, a person commits a fourth degree crime if he makes a false statement—which he knows is not true—on a form bearing notice "authorized by law" that false statements made therein are punishable. What does this mean?

Lacey Campbell, the high school cheerleader and girlfriend of Fire Chief Stanowitz, appeared at the Trenton Police Department. There she spoke to officers, telling them that the councilman was growing marijuana in his backyard. Immediately after her oral recitation, Campbell provided a written statement to the officers, again stating that Councilman Conti was growing marijuana in his backyard. Although Campbell knew her written statement was false, she signed the statement. If this statement provided notice that false statements made within it were punishable under the authorization of state law, then Campbell could be convicted of a fourth degree unsworn falsification charge.

### No Notice That False Statements Are Punishable as Authorized by Law

If Campbell's statement did *not* contain any language that false statements are "punishable" as "authorized by law," then she should be charged with a disorderly persons offense. This is per subsection b. of the statute.

Per 2C:28-3b.(1), a person commits a disorderly persons offense where he makes a written false statement "with purpose to mislead a public servant." Campbell obviously purposely intended to mislead the Trenton Police when she provided her written statement to them—she lied, stating that Councilman Conti was growing marijuana when she in fact planted the illegal vegetation in his backyard. Accordingly, if her written statement did not contain a notice advising that false statements are "punishable" as "authorized by law," then she should be charged with a disorderly persons offense under subsection b. of the statute.

---

**2C:28-4.**        **False reports to law enforcement authorities**

a. **Falsely incriminating another.** A person who knowingly gives or causes to be given false information to any law enforcement officer with purpose to implicate another commits a crime of the fourth degree.

b. **Fictitious reports.** A person commits a disorderly persons offense if he:

(1) Reports or causes to be reported to law enforcement authorities an offense or other incident within their concern knowing that it did not occur; or

(2) Pretends to furnish or causes to be furnished such authorities with information relating to an offense or incident when he knows he has no information relating to such offense or incident.

## PRACTICAL APPLICATION OF STATUTE

### Falsely Incriminating Another

Lacey Campbell is guilty of violating 2C:28-4 for providing false information to the Trenton Police that implicated Councilman Conti of illegally growing marijuana. This is a crime of the fourth degree.

A person is guilty of violating this statute where he "knowingly" gives (or causes to be given) false information to any law enforcement officer "with purpose to implicate another." For a conviction to occur under this statute, the information does not need to be provided under oath or in a written statement.

Campbell appeared at the Trenton Police Department and told officers that City Councilman Mario Conti was growing marijuana in his backyard. She knew her statement was false, as she had planted the substance in his backyard without the man's permission. Since Campbell "knowingly" gave "false information" to police officers, with the purpose to implicate Councilman Conti of committing a crime, she is guilty of a fourth degree crime under 2C:28-4.

It is interesting to note that Campbell's older boyfriend, Trenton Fire Chief Michael Stanowitz, also would probably be convicted under 2C:28-4 for Campbell's false incrimination of Councilman Conti. How? As an accomplice in the commission of the offense. If the state can prove that Stanowitz solicited Campbell or aided her in some way in the commission of the false incrimination, then he also can be convicted of the crime.

## Fictitious Reports

A person can be convicted under 2C:28-4 for reporting fictitious information to law enforcement officers even where the false information does not incriminate another. These types of matters are disorderly persons offenses.

Under subsection b.(1) of the statute, if a person reports an offense that he knows did not occur, he is guilty of a disorderly persons offense (e.g., Bob tells police that someone broke into his house when no such offense occurred). Per b.(2), a person is guilty of a disorderly persons offense if he furnishes authorities with information relating to an offense when "he knows he has no information relating to such offense."

For an example, Karla's house falls victim to a burglar who enters the home by kicking down the front door. Frank tells police that he saw a woman in a yellow hat kick down the door. Frank's statement, though, is a lie, as he was in Montana when the burglary occurred. Accordingly, since Frank never saw a woman in a yellow hat and has no true information about the burglary of Karla's house, he is guilty of violating 2C:28-4b.(2) for providing a fictitious report.

---

**2C:28-5.**        **Tampering with witnesses and informants; retaliation against them**

a. **Tampering.** A person commits an offense if, believing that an official proceeding or investigation is pending or about to be instituted, he knowingly attempts to induce or otherwise cause a witness or informant to:

(1) Testify or inform falsely;

(2) Withhold any testimony, information, document or thing;

(3) Elude legal process summoning him to testify or supply evidence; or

(4) Absent himself from any proceeding or investigation to which he has been legally summoned.

The offense is a crime of the second degree if the actor employs force or threat of force. Otherwise it is a crime of the third degree. Privileged communications may not be used as evidence in any prosecution for violations of paragraph (2), (3) or (4).

b. **Retaliation against witness or informant.** A person commits a crime of the fourth degree if he harms another by an unlawful act with purpose to retaliate for or on account of the service of another as a witness or informant.

c. **Witness or informant taking bribe.** A person commits a crime of the third degree if he solicits, accepts or agrees to accept any benefit in consideration of his doing any of the things specified in subsection a. (1) through (4) of this section.

## PRACTICAL APPLICATION OF STATUTE

### Witness Tampering—Generally Third Degree Offense; Second Degree When Force Threatened

Ewing Township Police Director Francis Pinkerton is guilty of a second degree crime for threatening to break Councilwoman Timborelli's legs if she testified in front of the grand jury. Pinkerton's crime is one of the second degree because of his threat of force; otherwise, he would be guilty of a third degree offense.

Pursuant to 2C:28-5a., a person commits witness tampering if, believing that an official proceeding or investigation is pending, he knowingly attempts to induce a witness to withhold testimony or to testify falsely. Also, this subsection makes it illegal to attempt to induce a witness to evade legal process summoning him to testify, or to withhold any type of evidence.

Francis Pinkerton knew that Councilwoman Timborelli was scheduled to testify before a grand jury; even more so, he knew that she was going to provide testimony that would incriminate him. In an effort to persuade her to not testify, Pinkerton ambushed the councilwoman at her home. Standing in the doorway with an unidentified man, Pinkerton wielded a baseball bat in front of her face and told her, "Testify tomorrow, and I will break your legs." The councilwoman, frightened, simply nodded favorably. Pinkerton, then satisfied, fled with his friend.

Police Director Pinkerton's actions constitute witness tampering. Believing the grand jury—an official proceeding—was meeting the next day, Pinkerton knowingly attempted to induce Councilwoman Timborelli to not testify. His attempt to induce her was through wielding a baseball bat and threatening to break her legs. Normally, the police director would be guilty of a third degree crime for engaging in witness tampering. However, because he threatened Councilwoman Timborelli with force during his unlawful activities, his offense is elevated to a crime of the second degreee. It should be noted that this subsection, as well as the other subsections in 2C:28-5, apply to informants as well as witnesses.

### Retaliation Against Witness—Fourth Degree Offense

If Police Director Pinkerton had hit Councilwoman Timborelli with a baseball bat after she testified, he could be charged with a fourth degree crime under 2C:28-5b. This subsection makes it illegal for a person to harm another "by an unlawful act" in retaliation for the individual's service as a witness. Accordingly, had Pinkerton struck the councilwoman with a baseball bat because he was angered that she testified against him, he would be appropriately charged under this subsection. This charge obviously would be in addition to an aggravated assault charge under 2C:12-1b.

### Witness Taking a Bribe or Some Other Benefit—Third Degree Offense

If Police Director Pinkerton had persuaded Councilwoman Timborelli to not testify by providing her a monetary bribe, then she would be guilty of a third degree crime under 2C:28-5c.

Simply, subsection c. of the statute makes it illegal for a person to solicit or accept a bribe in exchange for withholding testimony or testifying falsely at an official proceeding. Accordingly, had the councilwoman accepted money or some other benefit (or even solicited it) in consideration for withholding her testimony at the grand jury, then she would be guilty of a third degree offense per this subsection.

**2C:28-5.1.**    **Witness, victim protective orders**

If a court having jurisdiction under any criminal matter finds that the defendant in that criminal action or any other person connected in any way with the action has violated or is likely to violate N.J.S. 2C:28-5, N.J.S. 2C:29-3 or N.J.S. 2C:29-4 in regard to the pending offense, or that the defendant or other person has injured or intimidated or is threatening to injure or intimidate any witness in the pending offense or member of the witness' family with purpose to affect the testimony of the witness, the court may issue a protective order providing:

   a. That the defendant or other person not violate any provision of N.J.S. 2C:28-5, N.J.S. 2C:29-3, or N.J.S. 2C:29-4;

   b. That the defendant or other person maintain a prescribed geographic distance from any specified witness or victim;

   c. That the defendant or other person have no communication with any specified witness or victim, except through an attorney under any reasonable restrictions which the court may impose.

**2C:28-5.2.**    **Penalties for violations**

Any person violating any order made pursuant to section 1 of this act may be subject to any of the following penalties:

   a. He may be charged with any substantive offense defined in N.J.S. 2C:28-5, N.J.S. 2C:29-3, or N.J.S. 2C:29-4 when violation of an order constitutes violation of any provision of those statutes;

   b. He may be charged with contempt of the court that made the order. No finding of contempt shall be a bar to prosecution for a substantive offense; and any sentence for a conviction of contempt may be served consecutively to any sentence imposed for the underlying substantive offense. If the court does not impose a consecutive sentence, the court shall state on the record the reason for not imposing a consecutive sentence.

**2C:28-5.3.**    **Moving parties**

A motion for an order as provided by section 1 of this act may be made by the prosecuting authority, the defendant, or by any witness.

**2C:28-5.4.**    **Standard for issuance**

No order may be issued under this act unless the court's findings are made upon a preponderance of evidence adduced at a hearing. The rules of evidence shall not be applicable to any such hearing.

**2C:28-5.5.**    **No interference with defense preparation**

No order shall be entered under this act which interferes with the preparation of the underlying criminal case by the defendant or by his attorney, if any.

**2C:28-6.**     **Tampering with or fabricating physical evidence**

A person commits a crime of the fourth degree if, believing that an official proceeding or investigation is pending or about to be instituted, he:

(1) Alters, destroys, conceals or removes any article, object, record, document or other thing of physical substance with purpose to impair its verity or availability in such proceeding or investigation; or

(2) Makes, devises, prepares, presents, offers or uses any article, object, record, document or other thing of physical substance knowing it to be false and with purpose to mislead a public servant who is engaged in such proceeding or investigation.

## PRACTICAL APPLICATION OF STATUTE

One who destroys, alters, or removes any type of evidence in effort to impair its accuracy or availability in an official proceeding is guilty of a fourth degree crime under subsection (1) of 2C:28-6. Examples of this include destroying a knife that was used in a stabbing, burning a diary in which a person admitted to committing a string of burglaries, and altering a photograph to make it appear that an individual was not in the picture when he really was in it.

**2C:28-7.**     **Tampering with public records or information**

a. **Offense defined.** A person commits an offense if he

(1) Knowingly makes a false entry in, or false alteration of, any record, document or thing belonging to, or received or kept by, the government for information or record, or required by law to be kept by others for information of the government;

(2) Makes, presents, offers for filing, or uses any record, document or thing knowing it to be false, and with purpose that it be taken as a genuine part of information or records referred to in paragraph (1); or

(3) Purposely and unlawfully destroys, conceals, removes, mutilates, or otherwise impairs the verity or availability of any such record, document or thing.

b. **Grading.** An offense under subsection a. is a disorderly persons offense unless the actor's purpose is to defraud or injure anyone, in which case the offense is a crime of the third degree.

c. A person commits a crime of the fourth degree if he purposely and unlawfully alters, destroys, conceals, removes or disables any camera or other monitoring device including any videotape, film or other medium used to record sound or images that is installed in a patrol vehicle.

## PRACTICAL APPLICATION OF STATUTE

Alfredo "The King" Minoso sneaks into the Wildwood Police Department. Once inside, he finds a speeding ticket issued against him by one of the town's officers. He then proceeds to change the ticket to read "40 in 35" instead of "70 in 35." The King's alteration of his speeding ticket constitutes an offense as provided for in 2C:28-7. Generally, such an offense would be graded as a disorderly persons offense; this is unless the act is found to "defraud or injure anyone," wherein it would be elevated to a crime of the third degree.

**2C:28-8.**        **Impersonating a public servant or law enforcement officer**

    a. Except as provided in subsection b. of this section, a person commits a disorderly persons offense if he falsely pretends to hold a position in the public service with purpose to induce another to submit to such pretended official authority or otherwise to act in reliance upon that pretense.

    b. A person commits a crime of the fourth degree if he falsely pretends to hold a position as an officer or member or employee or agent of any organization or association of law enforcement officers with purpose to induce another to submit to such pretended official authority or otherwise to act in reliance upon that pretense.

## PRACTICAL APPLICATION OF STATUTE

Under subsection a. of this statute, an individual is guilty of a disorderly persons offense if he impersonates a public servant such as mayor, state assemblyman, or board of education member. However, to be convicted of this offense, the defendant must do more than just pretend to be a public official. His false pretense must be "with purpose" to induce another to "submit to such pretended official authority." For instance, if Jerry Jamone impersonates the mayor of Newark in an effort to get city sanitation workers to pick up rubbish from an unsightly construction site located on the street where he resides, then he is guilty of a disorderly persons offense. However, if Jamone pretends to be the mayor of Newark at a party but does nothing in furtherance of his false representation, then he is not ripe for a conviction under this statute.

    Please note that per subsection b., the offense is upgraded to a fourth degree crime where a person impersonates a law enforcement officer. Accordingly, if Jamone, pretending to be a police officer, pulled over an operator of a motor vehicle for speeding, then he would be guilty of a fourth degree crime.

# 29

# OBSTRUCTING GOVERNMENTAL OPERATIONS: ESCAPES

## FACT PATTERN (PERTAINS TO CHAPTERS 29 AND 30)

While awaiting sentencing in the Ocean County Jail, two men formed an unlikely friendship and bond. Each man was a resident of Seaside Heights, and each previously held positions as public servants in the sandy shore town. The men, however, came from different sides of the political fence and actually had once run against each other for an open board of education seat.

Herman Diaz was a staunch conservative who advocated family values and decreased spending on the public schools. He wanted to see less tax dollars paid by his town's residents into what he called a "luxury vacation center for the town's children and educators." Mark Garner, on the other hand, called for increased budgetary outputs for the school system. He argued that with a better-funded, higher-rated school system, the residents' property values would actually increase. He also proclaimed that it was morally appropriate, and socially necessary, to provide the best education for Seaside Heights children.

Herman Diaz won the political race. He later became the president of the Seaside Heights Board of Education and then superintendent of the school system. Mark Garner moved on to become a patrolman in the town's police department and then a sergeant, who was cited by the department's chief for his strong leadership capabilities. Through their official capacities, though, both Garner and Diaz, independently, ultimately found their way into the county's jail population. There, they discussed their woes and collaborated on their plans for the future.

### A Swan, a Pumpkin, a Clementine . . . and Diaz

After two years as Seaside Heights Superintendent of Schools, Herman Diaz suddenly changed his stance on spending. He began advocating the hiring of several new teachers, ranging from elementary school positions to high school educators to specialized instructors. He also sought the purchase of high-tech computer hardware and upgraded equipment for all of the high school's athletic teams. In fact, he ordered monetary disbursements

**269**

which he knew exceeded the board's budget, and he duped the district's business administrator into cutting checks to pay for the new items and services.

A group of local residents who had formerly supported Diaz became outraged at
his spending spree. Their anger grew when they learned that three of the newly hired
teachers were family members of Diaz. The group also suspected impropriety in Diaz's
unusual push for Seaside's purchase of a stretch of land that was to be dedicated to
the high school as a new sports stadium. Privately, Diaz had strongly advocated for this
purchase when he was president of the board of eduction. In fact, he initiated a purchase
price, $1,000,000, for the land which was later approved by the town's residents via a
referendum vote. What appeared questionable to the group, though, was that prior to the
referendum being put on the ballot, a corporation purchased the land for $500,000.
Now, pursuant to the referendum victory, Seaside was buying the land for $1,000,000
from the corporation.

On the day the deal closed, the group learned that the corporation had only two
shareholders, Cecilia Swan and Carmine Mahob. Swan was one of the newly hired
teachers and Diaz's sister-in-law. Swan later advised authorities that Carmine Mahob
was the name of a deceased man and that 90% of the proceeds were actually going to
Diaz, who orchestrated the deal. Swan said that she agreed to be part of the scam in
exchange for her 10% share and the teacher position.

To strengthen their case against Superintendent Diaz, Ocean County Assistant
Prosecutor Marjorie Callahan negotiated a plea arrangement with Swan where she
would receive a lighter sentence if she agreed to wear a wire and speak to Diaz about
their deal. Swan, who was on parole for a prior drug distribution charge, however, fled
Seaside before her scheduled meeting with Diaz. Not knowing when, or if, authorities
would find Swan, Assistant Prosecutor Callahan ordered the arrest of Diaz. The superintendent was immediately arrested without incident.

Through a bizarre chain of events, Cecilia Swan was arrested the same day. Her
capture was about 85 miles north in the small Bergen County town of Hillsdale, resulting from a 9-1-1 call by an elderly woman stating that her son was just paid $1,000 to
not report a burglary of their neighbor's home. When police responded, the woman's
son, Strom Milton, admitted that he accepted the payment from a woman whose name
he did not know. As Milton was providing the woman's description, he suddenly
pointed across the street and said, "That's her!" The woman was Cecilia Swan.

Swan, noting the police presence, fled in her SUV. Two police cruisers, with
activated overhead lights and sirens, trailed her at a safe distance as she raced through
the town's narrow streets, running stop signs and red lights. They thought the pursuit
was finished, though, when Swan crashed into another moving vehicle. Swan, however,
had other plans, jumping a fence and running through backyards. One officer followed
her as the other tended to possible injured victims in the hit automobile. The chasing
officer was unable to catch her.

Hillsdale immediately contacted county police, and a search for Swan was initiated.
Canine units were employed in the manhunt, which proved to be a good choice. One
particular dog, Clementine, ranted and barked wildly at the foot of the town's only trailer
home. Clementine's partner, Officer Wil Frietag, in full police uniform, knocked on the
trailer's door, knowing he did not have a warrant. A man, Peter Pumpcano, answered.
Clementine continued to bark wildly as Officer Frietag inquired into whether Pumpcano
knew of Cecilia Swan or her whereabouts. When Pumpcano denied knowing Swan,

Officer Frietag politely thanked him and determined to leave to procure a warrant and call for backup. As Pumpcano went to shut the door, however, Clementine broke loose from his officer-partner and shot through the door.

Officer Frietag chased after the canine but heard a loud yelp before he could visually locate him. As he passed by Pumpcano, Frietag found Cecilia Swan viciously biting Clementine's neck. When she spotted the officer, Swan released the dog from her oral grasp, kicked the patrolman, and struggled with him, trying to avoid an arrest. Frietag continually advised her to submit as she was "under arrest." The officer was finally able to restrain Swan after about a 90-second struggle and then handcuffed her.

Pumpcano was arrested by a backup unit that arrived shortly thereafter. Upon questioning, Pumpcano again reiterated that his name was indeed "Peter Pumpcano," and he provided a New Jersey driver's license to that effect. However, a search of his trailer revealed a birth certificate and another New Jersey driver's license that had him named as "Peter Jasowitz." Police also found a blond wig, black lipstick, a handgun, and $5,000 in cash in a bag that was marked with a note that read "For my love, Cecilia." Pumpcano/Jasowitz was charged accordingly.

### Better Ways to Deal with a Toothache

The case against Sergeant Mark Garner began with an innocent toothache, although it was a painful oral matter. Aspirin had failed him. Soothing medicated liquid hadn't helped him. And he couldn't sleep it off. So the man began to drink, but not tea or coffee. Instead, he tried to comfort himself with bourbon, whiskey, and beer. When that didn't remedy the pain, Garner decided to visit a dentist, a wise decision it would seem. The problem, though, was that the dentist was his ex-wife, Cybil Carrington, who had a restraining order against him. The order forbade the officer from having contact with Carrington. The issuing of this court order had almost cost Garner his job with the Seaside Heights Police Department, but his promises that he would stay away from Cybil assuaged their concerns. The liquor and the toothache, however, quickly rekindled the matter.

Garner drove to his ex-wife's house in neighboring Lavallette, awakening the woman instantly as he crashed his private sedan into her garage door. When she arrived at the garage and saw the destruction he had caused, she ordered Garner to leave. Instead, he said to her, "Honey, I know we're not married anymore, but could you still be my dentist?" Cybil ignored him and began to walk away. As she did, she yelled back, "I'm calling the police." Realizing that he would lose his job, Garner suddenly became enraged, ran up to Cybil, and slapped her twice across the face. Cybil then ran in the house, locked the door, and phoned the Lavallette Police.

Garner made a tactical decision to leave. Still suffering from his toothache and yet to find a remedy, the sergeant drove his dented vehicle to a local drug dealer. There, he inquired about a cocaine purchase. The dealer, having sold to Garner before, advised his client that he did indeed have the substance available, but it would come for a price that was not monetary. He told Garner that he would provide the aching officer with a thousand dollars worth of coke and $10,000 in cash if he did the following: utilize his position as a Seaside Heights police officer to enter the department's evidence locker and heist fifty pounds of marijuana that had just been confiscated from a rival dealer. Garner, desperate for his drug of choice and believing that he was going to lose his job anyway, agreed to the task. Although the sergeant was successful in the theft, he was arrested a day later when the crime was detected and expeditiously solved.

Bail was set at $100,000 without a 10% option. Ironically, even though Cybil had notified the Lavallette Police of Garner's first unlawful act, she felt guilty and posted the bail. He returned her generosity by immediately fleeing the jurisdiction and failing to appear for his first court appearance. The bail was revoked and a manhunt commenced. Garner, however, apparently hadn't learned much from the crafty criminals he often dealt with as a police officer and was spotted at a dentist's office in Cape May.

The individual who picked Garner out was a rookie Cape May police officer, present for his six-month checkup. What he didn't know, though, was that his dentist, Dr. Sharise Witherspoon, was Garner's most recent lover. And when he identified himself as a police officer and attempted to effectuate the man's arrest, Witherspoon jumped in front of him, blocking his path to Garner. Her human barricade lasted just long enough for Garner to slip out of the office's back door. The rookie, a former high school football star, raced after Garner and caught him only two blocks away. The suspended sergeant was arrested along with his lover, Dr. Witherspoon.

### The Trials—A Little Help from Lovers Didn't Go a Long Way

Both Mark Garner and Herman Diaz were convicted at their respective trials. Each case was marked with sensation and intrigue. In Garner's case, Dr. Witherspoon attempted to influence a juror to acquit her boyfriend by providing the juror with $20,000 in cash. Another juror attempted to contract with a film production company to sell her knowledge of Garner's case—before the trial was even completed.

During Diaz's trial, his wife baked a cake and had it delivered to the former superintendent in his courtroom holding cell. The sheriff's officers, not suspecting the oldest trick in the book, gave the cake to Diaz. Inside the tasty dessert, wrapped in a plastic bag, was a powerful knockout chemical which Diaz was able to slip into the blue raspberry fruit punch being enjoyed by his jailers. As they passed out, he was able to snatch the keys to his cell. He unlocked it and escaped into the courtroom. There, however, he was recaptured by the court stenographer who tripped him with an umbrella as he attempted to make his way to freedom. She then dove atop Diaz and twisted him in a contorted grappling hold until law enforcement officers rallied to the scene and handcuffed the convict.

The two former public servants, Herman Diaz and Mark Garner, now sulked together in the Ocean County Jail. They awaited their lengthy prison sentences, being tape-recorded by jail officials as they plotted dream plans of escape.

---

**2C:29-1.**        **Obstructing administration of law or other governmental function**

a. A person commits an offense if he purposely obstructs, impairs or perverts the administration of law or other governmental function or prevents or attempts to prevent a public servant from lawfully performing an official function by means of flight, intimidation, force, violence, or physical interference or obstacle, or by means of any independently unlawful act. This section does not apply to failure to perform a legal duty other than an official duty, or any other means of avoiding compliance with law without affirmative interference with governmental functions.

b. An offense under this section is a crime of the fourth degree if the actor obstructs the detection or investigation of a crime or the prosecution of a person for a crime, otherwise it is a disorderly persons offense.

## PRACTICAL APPLICATION OF STATUTE

Dr. Sharise Witherspoon is guilty of obstructing the administration of law for jumping in front of a Cape May police officer who was attempting to arrest former Seaside Heights Police Officer Mark Garner. In Witherspoon's case, this is a crime of the fourth degree.

Pursuant to 2C:29-1a., a person is guilty of obstructing the administration of law where he purposely prevents (or attempts to prevent) a public servant from lawfully performing an official function by actions such as intimidation, force, and physical interference. The Cape May police officer attempted to arrest Mark Garner in Dr. Witherspoon's dentist office. As he attempted to effectuate the arrest, Witherspoon intentionally jumped in front of the officer, blocking his path to Garner. Here the doctor "purposely" prevented a "public servant"—the police officer—from performing the "official function" of an arrest. She prevented the officer from making the arrest by the "physical interference" of blocking his path. Accordingly, Dr. Witherspoon is guilty of obstructing the administration of law.

Subsection b. of the statute provides the grading of this offense. If the actor obstructs an official function pertaining to a crime, then the actor is guilty of a fourth degree offense. Otherwise, the actor is guilty of a disorderly persons offense. Because Dr. Witherspoon obstructed the arrest of Mark Garner—a person who was being sought for the crimes of contempt, official misconduct, and bail jumping—she is guilty of a fourth degree obstructing the administration of law.

2C:29-2. **Resisting arrest, eluding officer**

a. (1) Except as provided in paragraph (3), a person is guilty of a disorderly persons offense if he purposely prevents or attempts to prevent a law enforcement officer from effecting an arrest. (2) Except as provided in paragraph (3), a person is guilty of a crime of the fourth degree if he, by flight, purposely prevents or attempts to prevent a law enforcement officer from effecting an arrest. (3) An offense under paragraph (1) or (2) of subsection a. is a crime of the third degree if the person:

   (a) Uses or threatens to use physical force or violence against the law enforcement officer or another; or

   (b) Uses any other means to create a substantial risk of causing physical injury to the public servant or another.

   It is not a defense to a prosecution under this subsection that the law enforcement officer was acting unlawfully in making the arrest, provided he was acting under color of his official authority and provided the law enforcement officer announces his intention to arrest prior to the resistance.

b. Any person, while operating a motor vehicle on any street or highway in this State or any vessel, as defined pursuant to section 2 of P.L.1995, c.401 (C.12:7-71), on the waters of this State, who knowingly flees or attempts to elude any police or law enforcement officer after having received any signal from such officer to bring the vehicle or vessel to a full stop commits a crime of the third degree; except that, a person is guilty of a crime of the second degree if the flight or attempt to elude creates a risk of death or injury to any person. For purposes of this subsection, there shall be a permissive inference that the flight or attempt to elude creates a risk of death or injury to any person if the person's conduct involves a violation of chapter 4 of Title 39 or chapter 7 of Title 12 of the Revised Statutes. In addition to the penalty prescribed under this subsection or any other section of law, the court shall order the suspension of that person's driver's license, or privilege to operate a vessel, whichever is appropriate, for a period of not less than six months or more than two years.

In the case of a person who is at the time of the imposition of sentence less than 17 years of age, the period of the suspension of driving privileges authorized herein, including a suspension of the privilege of operating a motorized bicycle, shall commence on the day the sentence is imposed and shall run for a period as fixed by the court. If the driving or vessel operating privilege of any person is under revocation, suspension, or postponement for a violation of any provision of this Title or Title 39 of the Revised Statutes at the time of any conviction or adjudication of delinquency for a violation of any offense defined in this chapter or chapter 36 of this Title, the revocation, suspension, or postponement period imposed herein shall commence as of the date of termination of the existing revocation, suspension, or postponement.

Upon conviction the court shall collect forthwith the New Jersey driver's licenses of the person and forward such license or licenses to the Director of the Division of Motor Vehicles along with a report indicating the first and last day of the suspension or postponement period imposed by the court pursuant to this section. If the court is for any reason unable to collect the license or licenses of the person, the court shall cause a report of the conviction or adjudication of delinquency to be filed with the director. That report shall include the complete name, address, date of birth, eye color, and sex of the person and shall indicate the first and last day of the suspension or postponement period imposed by the court pursuant to this section. The court shall inform the person orally and in writing that if the person is convicted of personally operating a motor vehicle or a vessel, whichever is appropriate, during the period of license suspension or postponement imposed pursuant to this section the person shall, upon conviction, be subject to the penalties set forth in R.S.39:3-40 or section 14 of P.L.1995, c.401 (C.12:7-83), whichever is appropriate. A person shall be required to acknowledge receipt of the written notice in writing. Failure to receive a written notice or failure to acknowledge in writing the receipt of a written notice shall not be a defense to a subsequent charge of violation of R.S.39:3-40 or section 14 of P.L.1995, c.401 (C.12:7-83), whichever is appropriate. If the person is the holder of a driver's or vessel operator's license from another jurisdiction, the court shall not collect the license but shall notify the director who shall notify the appropriate officials in the licensing jurisdiction. The court shall, however, in accordance with the provisions of this section, revoke the person's non-resident driving or vessel operating privileges, whichever is appropriate, in this State.

For the purposes of this subsection, it shall be a rebuttable presumption that the owner of a vehicle or vessel was the operator of the vehicle or vessel at the time of the offense.

## PRACTICAL APPLICATION OF STATUTE

### Resisting Arrest

Per the provisions of 2C:29-2a., Cecilia Swan is guilty of resisting arrest for her attempt to prevent Bergen County Police Officer Wil Frietag from effecting an arrest of her. In this case, Swan is guilty of a third degree crime.

Normally, resisting arrest is a disorderly persons offense (see subsection a.(1)). It is elevated to a fourth degree crime where an actor's flight prevents a law enforcement officer from effecting an arrest (see a.(2)). Resisting arrest becomes a third degree offense if an actor uses or threatens physical force (see a.(3)(a.)) or creates any other kind of substantial risk of physical injury by his resisting actions (see a.(3)(b.)). It is important to note that the actor must "purposely" prevent or attempt to prevent the arrest in order to be guilty of this offense.

Cecilia Swan was a fugitive from justice, having fled Ocean County where she faced criminal charges. Once away from the shore area, she committed a multitude of other criminal offenses in the Bergen County town of Hillsdale. This resulted in a massive law enforcement search for her whereabouts. Officer Frietag located the fugitive at a trailer home owned by Peter Pumpcano. There, Frietag's canine partner, Clementine, chased Swan until the two tangled in a violent squabble wherein Swan viciously bit the dog. Frietag, in full police uniform, attempted to effectuate an arrest of Swan, announcing the same. However, he was kicked by the woman in an attempt to prevent the arrest from being executed. Finally, Frietag was able to control Swan's resisting and handcuffed her.

Cecilia Swan knew that she was a fugitive from justice and that police were actively searching for her. Moreover, she was confronted by Wil Frietag, a fully uniformed police officer, who announced that she was under arrest. Still, she "purposely" resisted his attempts to arrest her. Swan's resisting, however, was not limited to argument or even simple flight. She battled with the officer, using physical force in an attempt to prevent the arrest. Accordingly, Swan is guilty of a third degree resisting arrest offense, per subsection a.(3)(a), as she used force against the officer during his attempt to arrest her.

## Eluding While Operating a Motor Vehicle

Any person who "knowingly" flees from a law enforcement officer—in a motor vehicle—after having received a signal to stop is guilty of eluding. This is a third degree crime; it is elevated to a second degree crime if the eluding "creates a risk of death or injury to any person."

Cecilia Swan is guilty of second degree eluding. As a fugitive from Ocean County and an individual who had just committed a burglary in Bergen County, Swan fled in her automobile when she noted that Hillsdale police officers wanted to speak to her. The officers activated the overhead lights and sirens of their cruisers, clearly signaling Swan to stop. Swan ignored their commands and continued to flee. She was therefore "knowingly" eluding the officers.

As Swan fled, the Hillsdale officers trailed her at a safe distance. Still, she raced through the town's narrow streets, running stop signs and red lights. Eventually, she plowed into another moving motor vehicle. Given this type of reckless driving and the ultimate car crash, Swan obviously created a "risk of death or injury" to other individuals. Under these circumstances, she is guilty of a second degree eluding per 2C:29-2b.

---

**2C:29-3.**      **Hindering apprehension or prosecution**

a. A person commits an offense if, with purpose to hinder the detention, apprehension, investigation, prosecution, conviction or punishment of another for an offense or violation of

Title 39 of the New Jersey Statutes or a violation of chapter 33A of Title 17 of the Revised Statutes he:

(1) Harbors or conceals the other;

(2) Provides or aids in providing a weapon, money, transportation, disguise or other means of avoiding discovery or apprehension or effecting escape;

(3) Suppresses, by way of concealment or destruction, any evidence of the crime, or tampers with a witness, informant, document or other source of information, regardless of its admissibility in evidence, which might aid in the discovery or apprehension of such person or in the lodging of a charge against him;

(4) Warns the other of impending discovery or apprehension, except that this paragraph does not apply to a warning given in connection with an effort to bring another into compliance with law;

(5) Prevents or obstructs, by means of force, intimidation or deception, anyone from performing an act which might aid in the discovery or apprehension of such person or in the lodging of a charge against him;

(6) Aids such person to protect or expeditiously profit from an advantage derived from such crime; or

(7) Gives false information to a law enforcement officer or a civil State investigator assigned to the Office of the Insurance Fraud Prosecutor established by section 32 of P.L.1998, c.21 (C.17:33A-16).

The offense is a crime of the third degree if the conduct which the actor knows has been charged or is liable to be charged against the person aided would constitute a crime of the second degree or greater, unless the actor is a spouse, parent or child of the person aided, in which case the offense is a crime of the fourth degree. The offense is a crime of the fourth degree if such conduct would constitute a crime of the third degree. Otherwise it is a disorderly persons offense.

b. A person commits an offense if, with purpose to hinder his own detention, apprehension, investigation, prosecution, conviction or punishment for an offense or violation of Title 39 of the New Jersey Statutes or a violation of chapter 33A of Title 17 of the Revised Statutes, he:

(1) Suppresses, by way of concealment or destruction, any evidence of the crime or tampers with a document or other source of information, regardless of its admissibility in evidence, which might aid in his discovery or apprehension or in the lodging of a charge against him; or

(2) Prevents or obstructs by means of force or intimidation anyone from performing an act which might aid in his discovery or apprehension or in the lodging of a charge against him; or

(3) Prevents or obstructs by means of force, intimidation or deception any witness or informant from providing testimony or information, regardless of its admissibility, which might aid in his discovery or apprehension or in the lodging of a charge against him; or

(4) Gives false information to a law enforcement officer or a civil State investigator assigned to the Office of the Insurance Fraud Prosecutor established by section 32 of P.L.1998, c.21 (C.17:33A-16).

The offense is a crime of the third degree if the conduct which the actor knows has been charged or is liable to be charged against him would constitute a crime of the second degree or greater. The offense is a crime of the fourth degree if such conduct would constitute a crime of the third degree. Otherwise it is a disorderly persons offense.

## PRACTICAL APPLICATION OF STATUTE

### Hindering Another's Apprehension

Peter Pumpcano is guilty of hindering apprehension for harboring and concealing Cecilia Swan in his trailer home. His offense falls under subsection a. of the statute; this subsection covers hindering *another's* apprehension or prosecution.

2C:29-3a.(1) through (7) sets forth seven types of actions where a person can be convicted for hindering another's apprehension. These actions range from harboring/concealing someone to providing disguises or money to a fugitive to giving false information to a law enforcement officer. In all seven scenarios, the person can only be convicted if he is hindering the apprehension of another who is facing a criminal offense or other charges such as disorderly persons offenses or motor vehicle offenses.

Bergen County Police Officer Wil Frietag and his canine partner, Clementine, located fugitive Cecilia Swan at Peter Pumpcano's trailer home. The law enforcement team, however, did not find Swan via Pumpcano's cooperation. In fact, Pumpcano denied knowing Swan. The fugitive was only apprehended after a wildly barking Clementine broke from Officer Frietag's grasp and hunted down Swan in the trailer. The woman was ultimately arrested after a struggle. A subsequent search of Pumpcano's home revealed a bag that contained a blond wig, black lipstick, a handgun, and $5,000 cash. The bag was marked with a note that read "For my love, Cecilia."

Here, Peter Pumpcano is guilty of hindering apprehension under 2C:29-3a.(1), which prohibits the harboring or concealing of another. He is also guilty of this offense under 2C:29-3a.(2), which prohibits providing items such as disguises, money, and weapons to individuals sought by law enforcement. Cecilia Swan was a fugitive from justice who was facing charges in Ocean County; she had absconded from parole and had just committed several crimes in Hillsdale, including burglary and eluding. Pumpcano was obviously aware of her flight from the law. Yet he chose to lie to Officer Frietag about Swan's whereabouts and conceal her in his trailer home. This concealing of Swan warrants a charge under subsection a.(1) of the statute. Pumpcano's gift bag of disguises (the blond wig and black lipstick), handgun, and money subjects him to a charge under subsection a.(2) of the statute.

It is very important to note that the grading of a hindering apprehension charge under subsection a. depends upon two matters: (1) the seriousness of the underlying offense which the "other" is trying to avoid and (2) the relationship between the "aider" and the "other." The "aider" must also "know" the type of offense the "other" is facing.

If the aider "knows" that he is hindering the apprehension of another who is facing a first or second degree crime, then the aider is guilty of a third degree hindering apprehension. There is one caveat, though: if the aider is a "spouse," "parent," or "child" of the other, then it is a fourth degree hindering apprehension.

If the aider "knows" that he is hindering the apprehension of another who is facing a third degree crime, then the aider is guilty of a fourth degree hindering apprehension. All other matters are disorderly persons offenses.

In Pumpcano's case, his charge should probably be a third degree hindering apprehension. Cecilia Swan had committed several crimes, including a second degree eluding. If Pumpcano "knew" she had committed this serious crime, then he is guilty of a third degree hindering apprehension. Since Cecilia Swan was not Pumpcano's spouse, parent, or child, his charge should not be lowered to a fourth degree offense.

### Hindering One's Own Apprehension

For hindering his own apprehension, Peter Pumpcano should be charged with an offense under subsection b. of 2C:29-3. This charge arises out of Pumpcano's provision of a false name and driver's license to a Bergen County police officer.

Per subsection b.(4), a person is guilty of an offense when he "gives false information to a law enforcement officer" in an effort to hinder his own apprehension or prosecution. Peter Pumpcano was facing charges for hindering Cecilia Swan's apprehension. In an effort to avoid his own ultimate prosecution, he told the Bergen County police officer that his name was Peter Pumpcano, and he provided him with a New Jersey driver's license which stated the same. Police later searched Pumpcano's home and found a birth certificate and another New Jersey driver's license that named him as "Peter Jasowitz." For providing the law enforcement officers with the false name and driver's license, Pumpcano/Jasowitz should be charged with hindering his own apprehension.

The grading of an offense under subsection b. depends upon the underlying offense which the actor knows he has been charged with, or with which he is likely to be charged. If he is trying to avoid the prosecution of a first or second degree offense, he is guilty of a third degree hindering apprehension. If he is trying to avoid the prosecution of a third degree offense, he is guilty of a fourth degree hindering apprehension. All other matters are disorderly persons offenses.

With reference to Pumpcano's hindering his own apprehension, he should be charged with a fourth degree offense. Why? Pumpcano presented the false name in an attempt to avoid prosecution for hindering Cecilia Swan's apprehension. That underlying offense was a third degree crime. Accordingly, because he was trying to avoid the prosecution of a third degree crime, Pumpcano here should be charged with a fourth degree hindering apprehension.

---

**2C:29-3.1.**     **Animal owned, used by law enforcement agency, infliction of harm upon, interference with officer, degree of crime, penalties**

Any person who purposely kills a dog, horse or other animal owned or used by a law enforcement agency shall be guilty of a crime of the third degree. Any person who purposely maims or otherwise inflicts harm upon a dog, horse or other animal owned or used by a law enforcement agency shall be guilty of a crime of the fourth degree. Any person who interferes with any law enforcement officer using an animal in the performance of his official duties commits a disorderly persons offense, subject to a sentence of six months' imprisonment, some or all of which may be community service, restitution and a $1,000.00 fine.

### PRACTICAL APPLICATION OF STATUTE

In addition to all of her other offenses, Cecilia Swan is guilty of violating 2C:29-3.1 for viciously biting Bergen County Canine Unit, Clementine. In her case, this is a fourth degree crime.

Per this statute, any person who kills a dog or any other animal used by law enforcement is guilty of a third degree offense. Any person who maims or otherwise inflicts harm upon any of these animals is guilty of a fourth degree offense. Cecilia Swan, a fugitive from justice who was the subject of a Bergen County manhunt, was located by Clementine, a police dog. Either in an effort to thwart the dog's efforts or just to harm the innocent animal, Swan viciously bit Clementine's neck. The dog survived her attack after his partner, Officer Wil Frietag, interceded. Accordingly, Swan is guilty of a fourth degree crime.

**2C:29-4.**

### Compounding

A person commits a crime if he accepts or agrees to accept any pecuniary benefit in consideration of refraining from reporting to law enforcement authorities the commission or suspected commission of any offense or information relating to an offense or from seeking prosecution of an offense. A person commits a crime if he confers or agrees to confer any pecuniary benefit in consideration of the other person agreeing to refrain from any such reporting or seeking prosecution. It is an affirmative defense to prosecution under this section that the pecuniary benefit did not exceed an amount which the actor reasonably believed to be due as restitution or indemnification for harm caused by the offense. An offense proscribed by this section is a crime of the second degree. If the thing of value accepted, agreed to be accepted, conferred or agreed to be conferred is any benefit of $200.00 or less, an offense proscribed by this section is a crime of the third degree.

## PRACTICAL APPLICATION OF STATUTE

Compounding is a rarely invoked statute which makes it a crime for a person to accept money for refraining from reporting an offense to law enforcement. The statute also makes it a crime to offer money to another in exchange for agreeing to not report an offense. Strom Milton, a Hillsdale resident, is guilty of compounding, which is a second degree crime. Cecilia Swan, likewise, is guilty of this crime.

Cecilia Swan committed a burglary in the small Bergen County town of Hillsdale. In an effort to avoid being caught for her crime, she offered to pay Milton $1,000. (Milton, a neighbor of the burglarized home, had witnessed the crime.) Milton accepted her payment. This payoff situation renders both Milton and Swan guilty of a second degree compounding. Their charge could only be one of the third degree if the monetary benefit involved was of a value of $200 or less.

**2C:29-5.**

### Escape

a. **Escape.** A person commits an offense if he without lawful authority removes himself from official detention or fails to return to official detention following temporary leave granted for a specific purpose or limited period. "Official detention" means arrest, detention in any facility for custody of persons under charge or conviction of a crime or offense, or committed pursuant to chapter 4 of this Title, or alleged or found to be delinquent, detention for extradition or deportation, or any other detention for law enforcement purposes; but "official detention" does not include supervision of probation or parole, or constraint incidental to release on bail.

b. **Absconding from parole.** A person subject to parole commits a crime of the third degree if the person goes into hiding or leaves the State with a purpose of avoiding supervision. As used in this subsection, "parole" includes participation in the Intensive Supervision Program (ISP) established pursuant to the Rules Governing the Courts of the State of New Jersey. Abandoning a place of residence without the prior permission of or notice to the appropriate supervising authority shall constitute prima facie evidence that the person intended to avoid such supervision.

c. **Permitting or facilitating escape.** A public servant concerned in detention commits an offense if he knowingly or recklessly permits an escape. Any person who knowingly causes or facilitates an escape commits an offense.

d. **Effect of legal irregularity in detention.** Irregularity in bringing about or maintaining detention, or lack of jurisdiction of the committing or detaining authority, shall not be a defense to prosecution under this section if the escape is from a prison or other custodial facility or from detention pursuant to commitment by official proceedings. In the case of other detentions, irregularity or lack of jurisdiction shall be a defense only if:

(1) The escape involved no substantial risk of harm to the person or property of anyone other than the detainee; or

(2) The detaining authority did not act in good faith under color of law.

e. **Grading of offenses.** An offense under subsection a. or c. of this section is a crime of the second degree where the actor employs force, threat, deadly weapon or other dangerous instrumentality to effect the escape. Otherwise it is a crime of the third degree.

## PRACTICAL APPLICATION OF STATUTE

### Escape

Herman Diaz should be charged with escape. In his case, he is ripe for a second degree conviction.

Simply, a person is guilty of escape if he leaves an "official detention" (e.g., prison, jail, holding cell, or custodial arrest) or if he fails to return to official detention after being granted a temporary leave. If the escape involved "force, threat, deadly weapon or other dangerous instrumentality," it is a second degree crime. Otherwise, it is a third degree offense.

Former Seaside Heights Superintendent of Schools, Herman Diaz, was standing trial in Ocean County. During the trial, Diaz's wife baked a cake and had it delivered to him in his courtroom holding cell. Inside the dessert, wrapped in a plastic bag, was a powerful knockout chemical. Diaz slipped this drug into the blue raspberry fruit punch that was being enjoyed by his sheriff's officer jailers. As they passed out, the prisoner was able to snatch the cell keys and escape. Diaz, though, was later captured by a brave courtroom stenographer who tripped him with an umbrella and restrained him in a grappling hold.

Here, Diaz was in "official detention"—a courtroom holding cell. He unlawfully left the cell by stealing the cell's keys from the sheriff's officers who were watching over him. His escape involved the employment of "dangerous instrumentality," a powerful knockout chemical that was slipped into the officers' beverage. Accordingly, Diaz is guilty of second degree escape as provided for in subsection c. of the statute.

## Facilitating Escape

Pursuant to subsection c. of the escape statute, Herman Diaz's wife is guilty of facilitating an escape. This is a second degree crime for the same reason that her husband's escape is a second degree crime.

One who facilitates or permits an escape is just as criminally liable as the individual who actually escapes. A public official, such as a sheriff's officer or corrections officer, who aids or permits an escape is likewise guilty of a crime under 2C:29-5c. Similarly, any person at all who facilitates an escape is guilty of a crime under 2C:29-5c. It is important to note that where a public official "knowingly" or "recklessly" facilitates the escape, he is guilty of this offense. Any other person is guilty of this offense *only* if he "knowingly" facilitates the escape.

The above-mentioned "facilitators'" offenses are just as serious as the escapee's, meaning that if "force, threat, deadly weapon or other dangerous instrumentality" is employed in the escape, then the aiders are guilty of a second degree crime. Therefore, because Diaz's wife "knowingly" facilitated his escape by providing him the cake packed with the powerful knockout chemical—a "dangerous instrumentality"—she is guilty of a second degree crime per subsection c. of 2C:29-5.

## Absconding from Parole

Cecilia Swan is guilty of absconding from parole, a crime which is defined in subsection b. of 2C:29-5. This third degree offense occurs where a parolee either "goes into hiding" or "leaves the state" with a "purpose of avoiding supervision."

Cecilia Swan was on parole for a prior drug distribution conviction when she was arrested in Ocean County for her involvement in a real estate scam with her brother-in-law, Herman Diaz. With a purpose of avoiding her parole supervision (and her pending charges in Ocean County), Swan went "into hiding," trekking 85 miles to Hillsdale and concealing herself in the trailer home of Peter Pumpcano. This constitutes a violation of 2C:29-5b., for absconding from parole.

---

**2C:29-6.**     ## Implements for escape; other contraband

a. **Escape implements**

(1) A person commits an offense if he knowingly and unlawfully introduces within an institution for commitment of persons under N.J.S. 2C:4-8 or a detention facility, or knowingly and unlawfully provides an inmate with any weapon, tool, instrument, document or other thing which may be useful for escape. The offense is a crime of the second degree and shall be punished by a minimum term of imprisonment, which shall be fixed at no less than three years if the item is a weapon as defined by N.J.S. 2C:39-1(r). Otherwise it is a crime of the third degree.

(2) An inmate of an institution or facility defined by paragraph (1) of subsection a. of this section commits an offense if he knowingly and unlawfully procures, makes, or otherwise provides himself with, or has in his possession, any such implement of escape. The offense is a crime of the second degree and shall be punished by a minimum term of imprisonment, which shall be fixed at no less than three years if the item is a weapon as defined by N.J.S. 2C:39-1(r). Otherwise it is a crime of the third degree.

"Unlawfully" means surreptitiously or contrary to law, regulation or order of the detaining authority.

b. **Other contraband.** A person commits a petty disorderly persons offense if he provides an inmate with any other thing which the actor knows or should know it is unlawful for the inmate to possess.

## PRACTICAL APPLICATION OF STATUTE

### Escape Implements

Herman Diaz's wife is guilty of introducing an implement for escape into his detention facility. Her crime should be graded as a second degree offense.

Herman Diaz was incarcerated in a courtroom holding cell during his trial. While waiting there, Diaz's wife had a cake delivered to him; baked inside the cake was a powerful knockout chemical wrapped in a plastic bag. Diaz's wife planted the chemicals in the cake to assist her husband in escaping. Because subsection a. of the statute makes it illegal for anyone to "knowingly and unlawfully" provide an inmate with any item, such as a weapon, tool, or document, to aid in escape, she is guilty of violating this statute.

It is impotant to note that this is only a crime of the second degree where the escape implement involved is a "weapon as defined by N.J.S. 2C:39-1(r)." Weapons as defined by 2C:39-1(r) include "anything readily capable of lethal use or of inflicting serious bodily injury." Given that a powerful knockout chemical could likely inflict "serious bodily injury," Diaz's wife should be charged with a second degree crime under 2C:29-6a.(1). Otherwise, where the escape implement is not a weapon, this is a third degree crime.

Please also note that Herman Diaz should be charged with a second degree crime for possessing the knockout chemical. As an inmate, his offense is pursuant to a violation of subsection a.(2) of the statute.

### Providing Inmate with Other Contraband

Where an individual provides an inmate with contraband other than escape implements, he is guilty of a petty disorderly persons offense. In order for a conviction, though, the actor must "know" or "should know" that it is unlawful for an inmate to possess the contraband. For example, one who provides an inmate with a six-pack of beer should know that it is unlawful for the inmate to possess alcoholic beverages. Therefore, this person would probably be convicted of a petty disorderly persons offense per subsection b. of 2C:29-6.

**2C:29-7.**    ## Bail jumping; default in required appearance

A person set at liberty by court order, with or without bail, or who has been issued a summons, upon condition that he will subsequently appear at a specified time and place in connection with any offense or any violation of law punishable by a period of incarceration, commits an offense if, without lawful excuse, he fails to appear at that time and place. It is an affirmative defense for the defendant to prove, by a preponderance of evidence, that he did not knowingly fail to appear. The offense constitutes a crime of the third degree where the required appearance was to answer to a charge of a crime of the third degree or greater, or for disposition of any such charge and the actor took flight or went into hiding to avoid apprehension, trial or punishment. The offense constitutes a crime of the fourth degree where the required appearance was otherwise to answer to a charge of crime or for disposition of such charge. The offense constitutes a disorderly persons offense or a petty disorderly persons offense, respectively, when the required appearance was to answer a charge of such an offense or for disposition of any such charge. Where the bail imposed or summons issued is in connection with any other violation of law, the failure to appear shall be a disorderly persons offense.

This section does not apply to obligations to appear incident to release under suspended sentence or on probation or parole. Nothing herein shall interfere with or prevent the exercise by any court of this State of its power to punish for contempt.

## PRACTICAL APPLICATION OF STATUTE

Bail jumping is an offense that can range from a petty disorderly persons offense to a third degree crime. The degree of bail jumping depends upon the underlying offense that the actor is trying to avoid. If the underlying offense is a third degree crime (or greater), a person who jumps bail is guilty of a third degree crime; where the underlying offense is a fourth degree crime, the bail jumping is a crime of the fourth degree. A person who jumps bail on a disorderly persons offense is guilty of a bail jumping disorderly persons offense. In the same vein, where a person jumps bail on a petty disorderly persons offense, the bail jumping is a petty disorderly persons offense.

Mark Garner is guilty of the most serious bail jumping offense—a third degree crime. Garner, a Seaside Heights police officer, was arrested for committing a number of offenses, including official misconduct, a second degree crime. The police officer then jumped bail. Because one of his underlying offenses was a third degree crime (or greater), Garner is guilty of a third degree bail jumping.

**2C:29-8.**          ### Corrupting or influencing a jury

Any person who, directly or indirectly, corrupts, influences or attempts to corrupt or influence a jury or juror to be more favorable to the one side than to the other by promises, persuasions, entreaties, threats, letters, money, entertainment or other sinister means; or any person who employs any unfair or fraudulent practice, art or contrivance to obtain a verdict, or attempts to instruct a jury or juror beforehand at any place or time, or in any manner or way, except in open court at the trial of the cause, by the strength of the evidence, the arguments of the parties or their counsel, or the opinion or charge of the court is guilty of a crime. Corrupting or influencing a jury is a crime of the second degree if it is committed by means of violence or the threat of violence. Otherwise, it is a crime of the third degree, provided, however, that the presumption of nonimprisonment set forth in subsection e. of 2C:44-1 for persons who have not previously been convicted of an offense shall not apply.

## PRACTICAL APPLICATION OF STATUTE

Mark Garner's girlfriend, Dr. Sharise Witherspoon, is guilty of attempting to influence a juror. In her case, it is a crime of the third degree.

In situations where a person attempts to influence a juror's decision by violence, the person is guilty of a second degree crime. If a person attempts to influence a juror by any other means, he is guilty of a third degree crime.

Mark Garner was on trial for committing a number of crimes. Dr. Witherspoon, Garner's girlfriend, attempted to influence a juror to acquit him by providing the juror with $20,000 in cash. Her influence attempt did not involve violence; accordingly, she is guilty of a third degree crime.

## 2C:29-8.1. Prohibited juror contract

a. Any person impaneled as a petit or grand juror in any criminal action in this State who, before the rendering of a verdict, entry of a plea, or the termination of service as a grand juror, solicits, negotiates, accepts, or agrees to accept a contract for a movie, book, magazine article, other literary expression, recording, radio or television presentation, or live entertainment or presentation of any kind which would depict his service as a juror is guilty of a crime of the fourth degree.

b. Any person who offers, negotiates, confers, or agrees to confer a contract for a movie, book, magazine article, other literary expression, recording, radio or television presentation, or live entertainment or presentation of any kind which would depict the juror's service, to any person impaneled as a petit or grand juror in any criminal action in this State, during the term of service of the juror, is guilty of a crime of the fourth degree.

## PRACTICAL APPLICATION OF STATUTE

During Mark Garner's trial, a juror attempted to contract with a film production company to sell her knowledge of Garner's case. This is illegal per the provisions of 2C:29-8.1.

Any juror who solicits, or agrees to accept, a contract for any entertainment deal, such as a movie or book, during his service as a juror is guilty of a fourth degree crime. Similarly, one who offers such a contract to a juror is guilty of a fourth degree crime. The juror in Garner's case attempted to contract with a film production company concerning her knowledge of the case. Since she attempted this deal during the course of the trial, she is guilty of a fourth degree crime.

## 2C:29-9. Contempt

a. A person is guilty of a crime of the fourth degree if he purposely or knowingly disobeys a judicial order or hinders, obstructs or impedes the effectuation of a judicial order or the exercise of jurisdiction over any person, thing or controversy by a court, administrative body or investigative entity.

b. Except as provided below, a person is guilty of a crime of the fourth degree if that person purposely or knowingly violates any provision in an order entered under the provisions of the "Prevention of Domestic Violence Act of 1991," P.L.1991, c.261 (C.2C:25-17 et al.) when the conduct which constitutes the violation could also constitute a crime or a disorderly persons offense. In all other cases a person is guilty of a disorderly persons offense if that person knowingly violates an order entered under the provisions of this act. Orders entered pursuant to paragraphs (3), (4), (5), (8) and (9) of subsection b. of section 13 of P.L.1991, c.261 (C.2C:25-29) shall be excluded from the provisions of this subsection.

## PRACTICAL APPLICATION OF STATUTE

### Contempt—Fourth Degree Crime

For ignoring a court order forbidding him contact with his ex-wife, Mark Garner is guilty of contempt. Garner's contempt is a fourth degree crime.

Generally, any person who "purposely" or "knowingly" disobeys a judicial order is guilty of a fourth degree offense. This is per the language of subsection a. of 2C:29-9. Pursuant to the language of subsection b. of the statute, any person who "purposely" or "knowingly" violates a judicial order entered under the provisions of the Domestic Violence Act is guilty of a fourth degree crime, as long as "the conduct which constitutes the violation could also constitute a crime or disorderly persons offense." What does this mean? Mark Garner's case can explain it.

Seaside Heights Police Officer Mark Garner suffered a toothache. To remedy his discomfort, he decided to visit his dentist. A wise decision, it would seem. The problem, though, was that Garner's dentist was his ex-wife, Cybil Carrington. The woman had a restraining order against him, an order that was entered under the provisions of New Jersey's Domestic Violence Act. Still, Garner "purposely" violated this judicial order by driving to Carrington's house.

The police officer's conduct became even more violative of the law when he slapped his ex-wife in the face because she ordered him to leave. Here, the conduct which "constitutes the violation"—not only having contact with his wife, but slapping her in the face—also "constitutes a crime or a disorderly persons offense." By slapping Carrington in the face, Garner committed a simple assault, which is a disorderly persons offense. Accordingly, Garner is guilty of a fourth degree contempt of court.

### Contempt—Disorderly Persons Offense

It is important to note that even if Mark Garner did not commit a "crime or disorderly persons offense" when he violated his restraining order, he would still be guilty of a disorderly persons offense. If he simply showed up at his ex-wife's house, or "purposely" or "knowingly" made any contact with her whatsoever, Garner would still be guilty of contempt for violating the restraining order's general "no contact" provision. In this case, where no offense (such as simple assault) occurred in addition to the prohibited contact, Garner would be guilty of a disorderly persons offense for his contempt.

# 30

# MISCONDUCT IN OFFICE; ABUSE OF OFFICE

| | |
|---|---|
| **2C:30-1.** | **Repealed** |
| **2C:30-2.** | **Official misconduct** |

A public servant is guilty of official misconduct when, with purpose to obtain a benefit for himself or another or to injure or to deprive another of a benefit:

a. He commits an act relating to his office but constituting an unauthorized exercise of his official functions, knowing that such act is unauthorized or he is committing such act in an unauthorized manner; or

b. He knowingly refrains from performing a duty which is imposed upon him by law or is clearly inherent in the nature of his office.

Official misconduct is a crime of the second degree. If the benefit obtained or sought to be obtained, or of which another is deprived or sought to be deprived, is of a value of $200.00 or less, the offense of official misconduct is a crime of the third degree.

## PRACTICAL APPLICATION OF STATUTE

Seaside Heights Police Sergeant Mark Garner entered the evidence locker of his police department and stole 50 pounds of seized marijuana. This illicit behavior is violative of 2C:30-2, as it amounts to official misconduct. This is a crime of the second degree.

Official misconduct is a crime that only applies to public servants. Those in such positions of trust (e.g., elected officials, judges, police officers) who commit acts within their positions which they know are "unauthorized" in exchange for a "benefit" can be convicted of official misconduct. This is per subsection a. of the statute. Likewise, under subsection b., where a public servant "refrains from performing a duty" in exchange for a benefit, he is guilty of official misconduct. This statute also applies to those public servants who act illicitly in order "to injure or deprive another of a benefit."

Mark Garner's crime of official misconduct falls under the provisions set forth in subsection a. of 2C:30-2. The Seaside Heights police officer was desperate to remedy the physical pain of a toothache and the mental anguish he was suffering due to his ex-wife's refusal to see him. Garner's despair was exacerbated as he knew that he had just violated a restraining order which would affect his job. The sum total of his woes led Garner to a local drug dealer, where he inquired about a cocaine purchase. The dealer advised that he would indeed provide the aching officer with a thousand dollars worth of coke and ten thousand dollars in cash if Garner did the following: utilize his position as a Seaside Heights police officer to enter the department's evidence locker and heist fifty pounds of marijuana that had just been confiscated from a rival dealer. Garner agreed, performed the act, and was caught.

As a Seaside Heights police officer, Mark Garner was a public servant. With a purpose to benefit himself (obtaining cocaine and cash), Garner performed an "unauthorized" exercise of his official function as a police officer: He took marijuana from the evidence locker with the intent to turn it over to a drug dealer. Garner obviously knew that his heist was not only unauthorized but illegal. Accordingly, the Seaside Heights police officer is guilty of official misconduct, per the provisions of subsection a. of the statute. In this case, the official misconduct is a second degree crime, given that the value of the cocaine and cash was greater than $200. In situations where the "benefit" sought—or where the item "deprived"—is of a "value of $200 or less," the official misconduct is a third degree crime.

**2C:30-3.**

## Speculating or wagering on official action or information

A person commits a crime if, in contemplation of official action by himself or by a governmental unit with which he is or has been associated, or in reliance on information to which he has or has had access in an official capacity and which has not been made public, he:

  a. Acquires a pecuniary interest in any property, transaction or enterprise which may be affected by such information or official; or

  b. Speculates or wagers on the basis of such information or official action; or

  c. Aids another to do any of the foregoing, while in office or after leaving office with a purpose of using such information.

An offense proscribed by this section is a crime of the second degree. If the benefit acquired or sought to be acquired is of a value of $200.00 or less, an offense proscribed by this section is a crime of the third degree.

## PRACTICAL APPLICATION OF STATUTE

2C:30-3 is a statute that basically prohibits public servants from utilizing "inside information" in order to acquire a pecuniary interest in a property or otherwise obtain monetary gain. Herman Diaz did just this, using his position with the Seaside Heights Board of Education to manipulate a real estate purchase that netted him a sizable pecuniary profit. Similar to official misconduct, this is a second degree crime. It would only be lowered to a crime of the third degree if the value involved was $200 or less. In Diaz's case, though, the amount of money involved far exceeded a few hundred dollars.

In addition to acquiring a pecuniary interest, two elements are necessary for a conviction under 2C:20-3: (1) The person "contemplates" official action by himself; or (2) a governmental unit that he is associated with *and* the information involved "has not been made public." So, how is Herman Diaz guilty of a crime under this statute?

Diaz was the Seaside Heights Superintendent of Schools. Prior to this post, he was the president of the town's board of education. At that time, Diaz privately pushed for Seaside's purchase of a stretch of land that was to be dedicated to the high school as a new sports stadium. In fact, he initiated a purchase price—$1 million—for the land. In contemplation of this million dollar purchase by Seaside, Diaz secretly formed a corporation which bought the land from its owner for $500,000. Thereafter, Diaz's corporation sold the land to Seaside for the $1million prize, resulting in a $500,000 profit to his corporation. Diaz owned 90% of the corporation's shares.

Here, all the elements of the offense have been met. Diaz acquired a "pecuniary interest" in a property "in contemplation" of an official action (the land purchase) by a governmental unit (the board of education) with which he had been associated. The information about the land's pending purchase was not public at the time Diaz's corporation bought it from its original owner. The ultimate benefit he obtained was in the hundreds of thousands of dollars. Thus, he is guilty of a second degree crime under 2C:30-3.

## 2C:30-4.  Disbursing moneys, incurring obligations in excess of appropriations

A person or member of a board or body charged with or having the control of a State office, division, department or institution or a member of a county or municipal governing body or a member of a board of education, commits a crime of the fourth degree if he purposely and knowingly:

a. Disburses, orders or votes for the disbursement of public moneys, in excess of the appropriation for that office, division, department, institution, board or body; or

b. Incurs obligations in excess of the appropriation and limit of expenditure provided by law for that office, division, department, institution, board or body.

Nothing contained in this section shall be construed to prevent a board of education from keeping open the public schools.

## PRACTICAL APPLICATION OF STATUTE

Seaside Heights Superintendent of Schools Herman Diaz is guilty of violating 2C:30-4 for ordering monetary disbursements by the board of education that he knew exceeded the board's budget. This is a fourth degree crime.

Simply, this statute prohibits those having control over governing bodies, such as courts, freeholder boards, municipal governments, boards of education, from disbursing public moneys "in excess of the appropriation" for that body. Herman Diaz did just this.

In an effort to hire more teachers (some, his own family members) and to obtain high-tech computer hardware and upgraded athletic equipment, Diaz ordered monetary disbursements that he knew exceeded the board of education's budget. This improper commitment of public moneys renders Diaz guilty of a fourth degree crime.

## 2C:30-5.  Findings, declarations relative to deprivation of civil rights by public officials

The Legislature finds and declares that:

a. Public confidence in the institutions of government is undermined when an official engages in any form of misconduct involving the official's office.

b. Such misconduct, and the corresponding damage to the public confidence, impairs the ability of government to function properly, fosters mistrust and engenders disrespect for government and public servants.

c. A particular concern arises when a law enforcement official, duly entrusted to protect the public safety and impartially enforce the laws, abuses that trust by unlawfully depriving persons of their civil rights, especially in the context of racial profiling.

d. It is important to ensure that law enforcement officers are prohibited from using racial characteristics or color, either alone or in conjunction with other composite characteristics such as a generalized vehicle description or the age of the driver or passengers, as the basis for initiating an investigative stop.

e. Existing laws must be amended to provide a greater deterrent to this type of conduct, as well as to enhance other provisions of the law targeting official misconduct.

f. Accordingly, it is in the public interest to strengthen our laws that define and punish acts of official misconduct by members of law enforcement and other public servants.

## 2C:30-6. Crime of official deprivation of civil rights

a. A public servant acting or purporting to act in an official capacity commits the crime of official deprivation of civil rights if, knowing that his conduct is unlawful, and acting with the purpose to intimidate or discriminate against an individual or group of individuals because of race, color, religion, gender, handicap, sexual orientation or ethnicity, the public servant: (1) subjects another to unlawful arrest or detention, including, but not limited to, motor vehicle investigative stops, search, seizure, dispossession, assessment, lien or other infringement of personal or property rights; or (2) denies or impedes another in the lawful exercise or enjoyment of any right, privilege, power or immunity.

b. (1) Except as provided in paragraphs (2) and (3) of this subsection, a public servant who violates the provisions of subsection a. of this section is guilty of a crime of the third degree.

(2) If bodily injury results from depriving a person of a right or privilege in violation of subsection a. of this section, the public servant is guilty of a crime of the second degree.

(3) If, during the course of violating the provisions of this section, a public servant commits or attempts or conspires to commit murder, manslaughter, kidnapping or aggravated sexual assault against a person who is being deprived of a right or privilege in violation of subsection a. of this section, the public servant is guilty of a crime of the first degree.

c. Notwithstanding the provisions of N.J.S.2C:1-8 or any other law, a conviction of official deprivation of civil rights under this section shall not merge with a conviction of any other criminal offense, nor shall such other conviction merge with a conviction under this section, and the court shall impose separate sentences upon each violation of this section and any other criminal offense.

d. Proof that a public servant made a false statement, prepared a false report, or, if the agency that employs the public servant, the Attorney General or the county prosecutor having supervisory authority over the agency required a report to be prepared, failed to prepare a report concerning the conduct that is the subject of the prosecution, shall give rise to an inference that the actor knew his conduct was unlawful.

e. For purposes of this section, an act is unlawful if it violates the Constitution of the United States or the Constitution of this State, or if it constitutes a criminal offense under the laws of this State.

## PRACTICAL APPLICATION OF STATUTE

2C:30-6 was enacted in 2003 in an effort to prevent public servants from utilizing their authority to unlawfully discriminate against others based on "race, color, religion, gender, handicap, sexual orientation or ethnicity." In order for a public servant to be convicted under this statute, two threshold prongs must first be met:

1. the public servant must "know" that his conduct is unlawful; and
2. he must act "with the purpose to intimidate or discriminate" against an individual(s) because of his status in one of the protected classes (e.g., race, religion, etc.).

With the above state of mind established, the public servant can be prosecuted under 2C:30-6 if he:

1. subjects the victim(s) to an unlawful arrest or detention such as a motor vehicle stop or search; or
2. denies or impedes the victim(s) in the lawful exercise or enjoyment of any right, privilege, power or immunity.

Now, how does that work practically? Let's say Clint the Cop, during patrol, watches nine cars pass him by; some are speeding, others are driving within the speed limit. Clint does nothing but smile, wave, and play a handheld video game. A tenth car approaches, moving five miles per hour under the speed limit. At the wheel is Nicola Coppola; a bumper sticker on the back of his automobile reads "The Italian Prince." Clint puts down his video game, activates his overhead lights and sirens, and speeds after "The Italian Prince."

Coppola immediately pulls over. Clint orders Coppola out of the automobile and proceeds to search Coppola's person and vehicle. After coming up with no contraband, Clint issues Coppola a speeding ticket. When Coppola asks Clint why he was pulled over, searched, and issued a summons, Clint replies, "Why? Because you're an I-talian. A mobster. A sure criminal."

Here, Clint has committed the crime of official deprivation of civil rights, as all the elements of 2C:30-6 have been met. First, Clint, a police officer, is a "public servant." As a police officer, he surely "knew" that his "conduct" was "unlawful." He pulled Coppola over and searched him, knowing that he had no probable cause for the stop and the subsequent search; even more so, he issued a speeding summons when he knew that the man wasn't speeding. Next, Clint's unlawful conduct was obviously instituted "with the purpose" to "discriminate" against Coppola on the basis of his Italian "ethnicity." He told Coppola that he stopped, searched and ticketed him ". . . Because you're an I-talian. A mobster. A sure criminal." Finally, Clint's discriminatory practice manifested itself in the form of an "unlawful detention," a motor vehicle stop and search. With all these factors present, Clint is guilty of violating 2C:30-6, a third degree crime.

It is important to note that had Clint pulled over Coppola not because he was Italian, but because he was a Red Sox fan or because he was a lawyer, Clint would not be guilty of an offense under 2C:30-6. The police officer's stop, search, and speeding ticket would all still be unlawful and invalid, but they would not constitute the crime of "official deprivation of civil rights." A conviction of this offense can only occur if the unlawful conduct is rooted in a purpose to "discriminate" on the basis of "race, color, religion, gender, handicap, sexual orientation or ethnicity." Whereas "ethnicity" is one of the aforementioned protected classes, being a lawyer or Red Sox fan is not.

## Grading of Offense Elevated in Certain Circumstances

Generally a violation of 2C:30-6 is a third degree crime. However, per subsection b.(2), it is elevated to a crime of the second degree where "bodily injury results from depriving a person of a right or privilege." Per subsection b.(3), the offense becomes a crime of the first degree where the "public servant commits or attempts or conspires to commit" crimes such as murder and kidnapping while violating the provisions of the statute.

**2C:30-7.**     ### Crime of pattern of official misconduct

a. A person commits the crime of pattern of official misconduct if he commits two or more acts that violate the provisions of N.J.S.2C:30-2 or section 2 of P.L.2003, c.31 (C.2C:30-6). It shall not be a defense that the violations were not part of a common plan or scheme, or did not have similar methods of commission.

b. Pattern of official misconduct is a crime of the second degree if one of the acts committed by the defendant is a first or second degree crime; otherwise, it is a crime of the third degree, provided, however, that the presumption of nonimprisonment set forth in subsection e. of N.J.S.2C:44-1 for persons who have not previously been convicted of an offense shall not apply. Notwithstanding the provisions of N.J.S.2C:1-8 or any other law, a conviction of pattern of official misconduct shall not merge with a conviction of official misconduct, official deprivation of civil rights, or any other criminal offense, nor shall such other conviction merge with a conviction under this section, and the court shall impose separate sentences upon each violation of N.J.S.2C:30-2 and sections 2 and 3 of P.L.2003, c.31 (C.2C:30-6 and C.2C:30-7).

## PRACTICAL APPLICATION OF STATUTE

2C:30-7, just passed in 2003, is basically an extension of the "official misconduct" statute (2C:30-2). That statute's *practical application section* explains the elements of "official misconduct" and how a public servant can be convicted of that offense.

Per 2C:30-7, a "pattern of official misconduct" has been committed where a public servant "commits two or more acts that violate the provisions of 2C:30-2." So where does this apply?

Really, any time a public servant commits more than one act of official misconduct. For example, Sheriff's Officer Penelope smuggles ten pounds of cocaine into the jail where she works, in an effort to sell it to the jail population. In a separate incident, as an act of revenge, she falsely charges an inmate with prostitution. Here, even though these acts were completely unrelated and not part of a common plan or scheme, Officer Penelope is guilty of a "pattern of official misconduct."

Subsection b. of 2C:30-7 sets forth the grading of this offense. If one of the acts of official misconduct is a first or second degree crime, then a second degree offense has been committed under 2C:30-7. In all other cases, a "pattern of official misconduct" is a third degree crime.

**Chapters 31, 32—Reserved**

# 33

# RIOT, DISORDERLY CONDUCT, AND RELATED OFFENSES

## FACT PATTERN (PERTAINS TO CHAPTERS 33 AND 34)

Milo, Smiles, Bertha, Camille, Bambie, and Horatio formed North Jersey's toughest gang, The Bean-Bag Mean Team. Each gang member was required to wear a chili bean pin on the lapel of his shirt; during the commission of crimes, the pin was to be placed on the inside of the shirt. The gang initially was ruthless and did in fact commit numerous hard-core crimes, including over 50 carjackings in the previous two years. They also engaged in numerous robberies, burglaries, and aggravated assaults.

The Bean-Bag Mean Team, though, recently determined to change its course of business and social activities. After the gang had increased its New Jersey membership to over 1,000 members, it solicited one final member, Ned "The Brainiac" Shipman. The Brainiac was courted primarily by Bertha, who sought his induction into the gang with the purpose that he would plan and aid the carrying through of their future criminal events. The Brainiac was receptive and agreed that if he was indeed admitted to be a member, he would actively plot and engage in fresh criminal activities.

In order to become a member of The Bean-Bag Mean Team, the founding members demanded that each new recruit perform multiple acts to prove their dedication and worthiness. Even though The Brainiac was highly sought after, he was still required to conform to the leadership's demands. Accordingly, he completed the following acts:

Smiles owned a 1986 Chevy Cavalier that he no longer wanted. Since he knew that The Brainiac was a licensed used car dealer, he ordered The Brainiac to sell the automobile. There was a catch, though—the car had to be sold on a Sunday. The Brainiac complied and sold the Cavalier at his Clifton dealership on an early Sunday morning.

On the same day, Camille provided The Brainiac with a "laundry list" of tasks to complete by the end of the week. They included going to Newark's most renowned drug distribution area and purchasing a $10 bag of marijuana; calling the Kearny Fire Department and reporting that an explosion was about to occur at the library, even though he knew such was false, with a goal to cause an evacuation at the library; anonymously calling Camille's ex-boyfriend at 2:00 a.m. and screaming and cursing at him; lying down on a busy one-way street in East Newark, thereby preventing cars from passing; showing up at a Hackensack Library Board of Trustees meeting and locking them out of the library; going to "the rock" in Glen Rock and cutting out a piece of it with an electric saw; painting a swastika on the front door of a Jersey City councilman's home and writing "You're dead, pal" on the same; removing the doors from a Secaucus church and spray-painting "Kill you" on the wall; smoking on a public bus in Paterson; after exiting the bus, throwing eggs at it as it drives away; ripping down a railroad crossing safety gate in Glen Rock; and bringing a bottle of whiskey to Westwood High School and drinking the entire bottle with two students. The Brainiac diligently completed all of the aforementioned matters within three days.

At this point, Milo presented The Brainiac with his final demonstration of worthiness. The Brainiac was instructed to gather with nine members of The Bean-Bag Mean Team at the Willowbrook Mall in Wayne. Once there, The Brainiac and the others were to herd over 30 cows and bulls into the mall. As the animals paraded through the building, the group would scream and yell and pick fights with the mall's patrons. The purpose of the chaos was to distract mall security and merchants while The Brainiac snuck into an upscale jewelry store and heisted $50,000 in gold and silver.

The following day, The Brainiac performed as directed; he turned over the precious gems to Milo and became a bona fide member of The Bean-Bag Mean Team. The mall incident, though, resulted in four members of the gang being arrested for refusing to disperse from the scene when ordered to do so by police.

To celebrate his induction, The Brainiac went on a date with Bertha. Their first stop was at the Wood Chop Candy Shop in Butler, where The Brainiac sought to purchase green olives and seltzer water. As he impatiently waited in line, The Brainiac watched the clerk sell cigarettes to a 12-year-old boy. The clerk then turned to The Brainiac and said, "What brand would you like?" The Brainiac, now completely annoyed, responded by jumping on the counter, knocking over all the items on it, and screaming, "I don't smoke! I don't smoke! It's just olives and seltzer I want." He then smashed the olive bottle against the wall. Before leaving, he picked out a few of the pimentos and threw them at the clerk.

Bertha, who had been waiting in the car, closely listened to a "police radio system." She frantically waved The Brainiac back to the automobile as she heard information that particularly interested her. A Butler police dispatcher advised all units that an alleged heroin transaction was occurring directly across the street from where they were currently located. Realizing that the dealers would probably have significant amounts of cash and drugs on them, Bertha suggested that they run across the street and rob them. The pair then did just that—and Bertha was correct, as they left the site with nearly $5,000 in cash and heroin with a street value of about $10,000. As they drove away giggling, they monitored the police radio so as to avoid any law enforcement that might have been attempting to track them.

The two gang members next arrived at Stu's House of Chow where they intended to enjoy a hearty meal. Although the restaurant had no liquor license, the owner permitted The Brainiac and Bertha to drink scotch at a regular dining table. The owner usually charged diners with a "corkage fee" to consume alcohol in his restaurant but waived the fee for his gang member customers.

After dinner, The Brainiac had a special surprise for Bertha. He brought her to two businesses that he had developed for The Bean-Bag Mean Team. The first, Mack Daddy's, was located in Parsippany. Mack Daddy's was a private, 24-hour club purporting to hold an exclusive membership of checkers and jacks players. In reality, it was a "house of prostitution," where patrons paid adult women and men to have sex with them. Mack Daddy's was owned and managed by The Brainiac. On a daily basis, he oversaw and encouraged the individuals who worked there to have sexual relations with the club's many eager clients. Over 30 employees accepted cash in exchange for their services.

Not far down the highway from Mack Daddy's was The Brainiac's second entrepreneurial effort, Piper's Home of Love. This storefront business offered live performances where women danced in G-strings and bikini tops and routinely fondled themselves in the genital and breast areas. They also engaged in simulated acts of masturbation. Piper's Home of Love offered the use of enclosed booths to its patrons where "lap dances" were performed. Sexual activity many times occurred during these sessions.

After observing and engaging in a few lap dances, The Brainiac and Bertha proceeded to the building attached to Piper's Home of Love, which was known as The Annex. There they thumbed through multiple magazines, looking at hundreds of erotic and sexually explicit pictures. The couple looked on as an employee at The Annex sold two such magazines to a 14-year-old boy and five magazines to a 33-year-old woman. The Brainiac noted that the magazines were easily accessible to the customers, as they all were displayed on shelves less than five feet in height and without any blinders or coverings on them.

Once The Brainiac ended his tour of The Bean-Bag Mean Team's new businesses, he and Bertha headed to a cottage in Lavallette where they intended to spend the remainder of the evening. They stopped, though, in Newark and began roaming the streets, asking several different people where they could find a prostitute, as they wanted to "speak to one." Unfortunately for the gang members, however, an undercover police officer heard their discourse and arrested them on the spot.

The Brainiac and Bertha smirked at the arresting officer, minimizing what they considered an inconsequential matter. At headquarters, though, their tone changed when they learned that there were multiple outstanding arrest warrants arising out of The Brainiac's previous days' rampage. Someone had "dropped dime" and multiple charges were being levied.

## 2C:33-1.   Riot, failure to disperse

a. **Riot.** A person is guilty of riot if he participates with four or more others in a course of disorderly conduct as defined in section 2C:33-2a:

(1) With purpose to commit or facilitate the commission of a crime;

(2) With purpose to prevent or coerce official action; or

(3) When he or any other participant, known to him, uses or plans to use a firearm or other deadly weapon.

Riot if committed under circumstances set forth in paragraph (3) is a crime of the third degree. Otherwise riot is a crime of the fourth degree.

b. **Failure of disorderly persons to disperse upon official order.** Where five or more persons are participating in a course of disorderly conduct as defined in section 2C:33-2 a. likely to cause substantial harm, a peace officer or other public servant engaged in executing or enforcing the law may order the participants and others in the immediate vicinity to disperse. A person who refuses or knowingly fails to obey such an order commits a disorderly persons offense.

## PRACTICAL APPLICATION OF STATUTE

### Riot

Engaging in a riot can be a crime of the third degree or the fourth degree pursuant to 2C:33-1a. The Brainiac is guilty of fourth degree riot for his actions at the Willowbrook Mall in Wayne.

Riot is an interesting crime in that it encompasses a whole other offense—disorderly conduct as defined in 2C:33-2a.—as one of its elements. In other words, in order for an individual to be guilty of riot, he must have committed an act of disorderly conduct first. But there is more. To be convicted of riot, his disorderly conduct must be joined by at least four others who are also engaging in disorderly conduct. And then this entire group's course of disorderly conduct has to be accompanied by one of the following circumstances: a purpose to commit or facilitate a crime; a purpose to prevent or coerce official action; or carrying on while a participant "known" to him uses or plans to use a firearm or other deadly weapon. Got all that? Well, The Brainiac's antics at the Willowbrook Mall can help to make it understandable.

The Brainiac and nine members of the ruthless street gang, The Bean-Bag Mean Team, met at the Willowbrook Mall. Once there, they herded over 30 cows and bulls into the large shopping facility. As the animals paraded through the building, the group screamed and yelled wildly and picked fights with the mall's patrons. The purpose of this chaos was to distract mall security and merchants while The Brainiac snuck into an upscale jewelry store and heisted $50,000 in gold and silver.

In this case, all of the elements of riot have been met. First, The Brainiac was joined by nine other people in engaging in a course of disorderly conduct: The group engaged in the tumultuous and violent behavior of picking fights with mall patrons, screaming and yelling, and letting loose over 30 cows and bulls into the mall. Next, the purpose of the chaos was to facilitate the commission of a crime, namely the theft of the gold and silver. Accordingly, The Brainiac is guilty of riot. His offense is a fourth degree crime; it would only be elevated to a crime of the third degree if he, or one of the participants "known" to him, used or planned to use a firearm or other deadly weapon.

It is important to note that the nine other gang members who participated in the mall event with The Brainiac also could be convicted of riot. Even though they didn't actually carry out the heist, their purpose was to facilitate it. Therefore, they are equally as culpable.

### Failure to Disperse

Four of The Brainiac's counterparts at the Willowbrook Mall riot are guilty of failure to disperse. Per subsection b. of 2C:33-1, this is a disorderly persons offense.

In order to be convicted of failure to disperse, four elements must be met: (1) five or more people must be participating in a course of disorderly conduct; (2) said conduct must be "likely to cause substantial harm"; (3) a peace officer or public servant must order them to disperse from the vicinity; and (4) the defendant must refuse or knowingly fail to leave.

The four gang members engaged in a course of disorderly conduct at the Willowbrook Mall—the group engaged in the tumultuous and violent behavior of picking fights with mall patrons, screaming and yelling, and letting loose over 30 cows and bulls into the shopping facility. For obvious reasons, this behavior was "likely to cause substantial harm." Upon observing this chaos, police officers ordered them to disperse from the scene. They refused to do so. With all these elements in place, the four gang members are guilty of the disorderly persons offense, failure to disperse.

## 2C:33-2.        Disorderly conduct

a. **Improper behavior.** A person is guilty of a petty disorderly persons offense, if with purpose to cause public inconvenience, annoyance or alarm, or recklessly creating a risk thereof he

(1) Engages in fighting or threatening, or in violent or tumultuous behavior; or

(2) Creates a hazardous or physically dangerous condition by any act which serves no legitimate purpose of the actor.

b. **Offensive language.** A person is guilty of a petty disorderly persons offense if, in a public place, and with purpose to offend the sensibilities of a hearer or in reckless disregard of the probability of so doing, he addresses unreasonably loud and offensively coarse or abusive language, given the circumstances of the person present and the setting of the utterance, to any person present.

"Public" means affecting or likely to affect persons in a place to which the public or a substantial group has access; among the places included are highways, transport facilities, schools, prisons, apartment houses, places of business or amusement, or any neighborhood.

## PRACTICAL APPLICATION OF STATUTE

Whether "improper behavior" or "offensive language," disorderly conduct is a petty disorderly persons offense. The Brainiac is guilty of "improper behavior" per subsection a. of the disorderly conduct statute. The Wood Chop Candy Shop in Butler was the venue of his most salient offense.

A conviction for "improper behavior" requires a two-pronged test to be met: (1) the defendant must engage in matters such as a fight, violent act, or tumultuous behavior or create a dangerous condition which serves no legitimate purpose, *and* (2) this behavior has to be performed with an illicit purpose (e.g., to cause public inconvenience, annoyance, or alarm).

At the Wood Chop Candy Shop in Butler, The Brainiac impatiently waited in line for the store clerk to finish with a prior customer. Upon the clerk asking The Brainiac a question he apparently didn't like, The Brainiac jumped on the counter, knocking over all the items on it, and screamed, "I don't smoke! I don't smoke! It's just olives and seltzer I want." He then smashed a bottle of olives against the wall. Before leaving the store, he picked out a few pimentos and threw them at the clerk.

Here The Brainiac violated subsection a. of the disorderly conduct statute by acting with "improper behavior." By screaming, jumping on the counter, knocking over all the items, throwing a bottle against the wall, and throwing parts of olives at the store clerk, The Brainiac has acted tumultuously and violently. This behavior was certainly performed with a purpose to cause annoyance and alarm to the public—this was a place of business where several members of the public could be affected by his antics. Accordingly, The Brainiac is guilty of disorderly conduct, a petty disorderly persons offense.

## Offensive Language

Watch for First Amendment, free speech, issues. Subsection b. of 2C:33-2 provides for a petty disorderly persons offense where an individual speaks in a public place with "unreasonably loud and offensively coarse or abusive language." The subsection clearly sets out that the speech must be performed "with purpose to offend the sensibilities" of the person hearing it; the circumstances of the hearer and the setting are taken into account. Inevitably, however, free speech issues are likely to be evaluated by courts hearing "offensive language" cases—and the constitutional right to speak many times will override another's offended sensibilities.

---

**2C:33-2.1.**   **"Public place" defined; loitering to obtain or distribute CDS is a disorderly persons offense**

   a. As used in this section:
   "Public place" means any place to which the public has access, including but not limited to a public street, road, thoroughfare, sidewalk, bridge, alley, plaza, park, recreation or shopping area, public transportation facility, vehicle used for public transportation, parking lot, public library or any other public building, structure or area.

   b. A person, whether on foot or in a motor vehicle, commits a disorderly persons offense if (1) he wanders, remains or prowls in a public place with the purpose of unlawfully obtaining or distributing a controlled dangerous substance or controlled substance analog; and (2) engages in conduct that, under the circumstances, manifests a purpose to obtain or distribute a controlled dangerous substance or controlled substance analog.

   c. Conduct that may, where warranted under the circumstances, be deemed adequate to manifest a purpose to obtain or distribute a controlled dangerous substance or controlled substance analog includes, but is not limited to, conduct such as the following:

   (1) Repeatedly beckoning to or stopping pedestrians or motorists in a public place;

   (2) Repeatedly passing objects to or receiving objects from pedestrians or motorists in a public place;

   (3) Repeatedly circling in a public place in a motor vehicle and on one or more occasions passing any object to or receiving any object from a person in a public place.

   d. The element of the offense described in paragraph (1) of subsection b. of this section may not be established solely by proof that the actor engaged in the conduct that is used to satisfy the element described in paragraph (2) of subsection b. of this section.

## PRACTICAL APPLICATION OF STATUTE

As part of Camille's laundry list of gang initiation tasks, The Brainiac was required to purchase a $10 bag of marijuana in Newark's most renowned drug distribution area. His search to obtain the controlled dangerous substance (CDS) could cause him to face a disorderly persons offense under 2C:33-2.1.

This statute, in a quick summary, prohibits a person from "remaining" or "wandering," in public, in an effort to obtain or distribute controlled dangerous substances.

But how is it possible to prove that someone is "remaining" or "wandering" in a public place for the purpose of carrying out one of these illicit activities?

2C:33-2.1 provides that the defendant's "conduct" is the dispositive factor. Subsection c. goes as far as defining what "conduct" will "be deemed adequate to manifest a purpose to obtain or distribute a controlled dangerous substance." This "conduct" includes, but is not limited to: repeatedly stopping pedestrians or motorists; repeatedly passing objects to or receiving objects from pedestrians and motorists; and repeatedly circling in a motor vehicle and, on one or more occasions, passing any object to or receiving any object from a person.

Nothing in the statute requires that any actual evidence of the use, possession, purchase, or sale of any controlled dangerous substance be presented in order for a conviction under 2C:33-2.1 to occur. However, subsection d., when dissected, does set out that the above described "conduct" *alone cannot* solely establish that the defendant acted "with the purpose" to obtain or distribute a CDS. This implies that some other evidence, such as the odor of a drug or witness testimony identifying something that appeared to be a CDS, is necessary for a conviction.

Now what does all this mean for The Brainiac's Newark marijuana purchase? It means that even if law enforcement didn't apprehend him with marijuana, he could still be convicted of loitering for the purpose of possessing a controlled dangerous substance. If his "conduct" in the well-known drug distribution area manifested "a purpose to obtain" CDS's (e.g. he drove around in circles, then passed an object and received another), then the prosecution has the basis for a case under 2C:33-2.1. But remember, this "conduct" alone is not enough. The prosecution must present something additional, such as witness testimony, that he received a bag with a vegetation-like substance in it. If this evidence was put forward against The Brainiac, he could actually be convicted of a disorderly persons offense for loitering for the purpose of obtaining a controlled dangerous substance.

## 2C:33-3.     False public alarms

a. Except as provided in subsection b. or c. of this section, a person is guilty of a crime of the third degree if he initiates or circulates a report or warning of an impending fire, explosion, bombing, crime, catastrophe or emergency knowing that the report or warning is false or baseless and that it is likely to cause evacuation of a building, place of assembly, or facility of public transport, or to cause public inconvenience or alarm. A person is guilty of a crime of the third degree if he knowingly causes such false alarm to be transmitted to or within any organization, official or volunteer, for dealing with emergencies involving danger to life or property.

b. A person is guilty of a crime of the second degree if in addition to the report or warning initiated, circulated or transmitted under subsection a. of this section, he places or causes to be placed any false or facsimile bomb in a building, place of assembly, or facility of public transport or in a place likely to cause public inconvenience or alarm. A violation of this subsection is a crime of the first degree if it occurs during a declared period of national, State or county emergency.

c. A person is guilty of a crime of the second degree if a violation of subsection a. of this section in fact results in serious bodily injury to another person or occurs during a declared period of national, State or county emergency. A person is guilty of a crime of the first degree if a violation of subsection a. of this section in fact results in death.

d. For the purposes of this section, "in fact" means that strict liability is imposed. It shall not be a defense that the death or serious bodily injury was not a foreseeable consequence of the person's acts or that the death or serious bodily injury was caused by the actions of another person or by circumstances beyond the control of the actor. The actor shall be strictly liable upon proof that the crime occurred during a declared period of national, State or county emergency. It shall not be a defense that the actor did not know that there was a declared period of emergency at the time the crime occurred.

e. A person is guilty of a crime of the fourth degree if the person knowingly places a call to a 91-1 emergency telephone system without purpose of reporting the need for 9-1-1 service.

## PRACTICAL APPLICATION OF STATUTE

### False Report of Public Alarms

The Brainiac called the Kearny Fire Department and reported that an explosion was about to occur at the town's library, even though he knew that such was false. This false report warrants a charge for a third degree crime.

In order to be convicted of a crime under 2C:33-3a., two elements need to be met. First, the defendant must initiate or circulate "a report or warning of an impending fire, explosion, bombing, crime, catastrophe or emergency." Second, he must "know" that the report is false and that it is likely to cause evacuation of places such as buildings or is likely to cause public inconvenience or alarm. Generally, this is a crime of the third degree. Per subsection c., however, if "serious bodily injury" of another person or "death" does in fact occur, then it is a second degree crime.

In The Brainiac's case, he reported to the Kearny Fire Department that an explosion was about to occur at the town's library. He "knew" that the report was false—and did it with the purpose to cause the library to be evacuated. With these two elements met, he should be charged with a third degree crime. But how could this be elevated to a second degree crime? Let's say, in a frenzy, a person was trampled to death trying to exit the library; this would render The Brainiac guilty of a second degree crime. Similarly, if a fire truck crashed on the way to the library, causing serious bodily injury to a fireman, this would give rise to a second degree offense.

### False Bombs/Unnecessary 9-1-1 Calls

It should be noted that per subsection b. of 2C:33-3, a person is guilty of a third degree crime if in addition to a false emergency report (e.g., a bombing or explosion), he places a fake bomb in a structure such as a building. Also, where a person places a 9-1-1 call "without purpose of reporting the need for 9-1-1 service," he is guilty of a disorderly persons offense under subsection e. of this statute.

**2C:33-3.1.**　　**Penalties for juvenile violating N.J.S.2C:33-3**

a. In the case of a juvenile adjudicated delinquent for a violation of N.J.S. 2C:33-3 the court shall suspend or postpone the juvenile's right to operate a motor vehicle including a motorized bicycle for a period of six months, in addition to any other disposition ordered by the court under section 24 of P.L.1982, c.77 (C.2A:4A-43). In the case of a person who at the time of the disposition is less than 17 years of age, the period of the suspension of driving privileges authorized herein, including a suspension of the privilege of operating a motorized bicycle, shall commence on the day the disposition is imposed and shall run for a period of six months after the day the person reaches the age of 17 years.

b. In addition to any other sentence imposed by the court under this code, the court shall suspend or postpone a person's right to operate a motor vehicle including a motorized bicycle for any person who is convicted under N.J.S.2C:33-3 and is less than 21 years of age at the time of the conviction. The period of the suspension of driving privileges authorized herein, including a suspension of the privilege of operating a motorized bicycle, shall commence on the day the sentence is imposed and shall run for a period of six months.

c. If the driving privilege of any person is under revocation, suspension, or postponement for a violation of any provision of this Title or Title 39 of the Revised Statutes at the time of any adjudication of delinquency for a violation of N.J.S.2C:33-3 or a conviction under N.J.S.2C:33-3, the revocation, suspension, or postponement period imposed herein shall commence as of the date of termination of the existing revocation, suspension, or postponement.

d. The court before whom any person is convicted or adjudicated delinquent for a violation of N.J.S.2C:33-3 shall collect forthwith the New Jersey driver's license or licenses of the person and forward such license or licenses to the Director of the Division of Motor Vehicles along with a report indicating the first and last day of the suspension or postponement period imposed by the court pursuant to this section. If the court is for any reason unable to collect the license or licenses of the person, the court shall cause a report of the conviction or adjudication of delinquency to be filed with the director. That report shall include the complete name, address, date of birth, eye color, and sex of the person and shall indicate the first and last day of the suspension or postponement period imposed by the court pursuant to this section. The court shall inform the person orally and in writing that if the person is convicted of personally operating a motor vehicle during the period of license suspension or postponement imposed pursuant to this section the person shall, upon conviction, be subject to the penalties set forth in R.S.39:3-40. A person shall be required to acknowledge receipt of the written notice in writing. Failure to receive a written notice or failure to acknowledge in writing the receipt of a written notice shall not be a defense to a subsequent charge of violation of R.S.39:3-40. If the person is the holder of a driver's license from another jurisdiction, the court shall not collect the license but shall notify the director who shall notify the appropriate officials in the licensing jurisdiction. The court shall, however, in accordance with the provisions of this section, revoke the person's non-resident driving privileges in this State.

**2C:33-3.2.**

### Fines for violation of N.J.S. 2C:33-3

Any person who violates the provisions of N.J.S.2C:33-3 shall be liable for a civil penalty of not less than $2,000 or actual costs incurred by or resulting from the law enforcement and emergency services response to the false alarm, whichever is higher. Any monies collected pursuant to this section shall be made payable to the municipality or other entity providing the law enforcement or emergency services response to the false alarm. "Emergency services" includes, but is not limited to, paid or volunteer fire fighters, paramedics, members of an ambulance team, rescue squad or mobile intensive care unit.

**2C:33-4.**

### Harassment

Except as provided in subsection e., a person commits a petty disorderly persons offense if, with purpose to harass another, he:

a. Makes, or causes to be made, a communication or communications anonymously or at extremely inconvenient hours, or in offensively coarse language, or any other manner likely to cause annoyance or alarm;

b. Subjects another to striking, kicking, shoving, or other offensive touching, or threatens to do so; or

c. Engages in any other course of alarming conduct or of repeatedly committed acts with purpose to alarm or seriously annoy such other person.

> A communication under subsection a. may be deemed to have been made either at the place where it originated or at the place where it was received.

d. (Deleted by amendment, P.L.2001, c.443).

e. A person commits a crime of the fourth degree if, in committing an offense under this section, he was serving a term of imprisonment or was on parole or probation as the result of a conviction of any indictable offense under the laws of this State, any other state or the United States.

## PRACTICAL APPLICATION OF STATUTE

The Brainiac is guilty of harassment for anonymously calling Bean-Bag Mean Team gang member Camille's ex-boyfriend and screaming and cursing at him. This is a petty disorderly persons offense.

Pursuant to 2C:33-4, a person commits a petty disorderly persons offense if, "with purpose to harass another," he engages in one of three types of activities. These activities are found in subsections a. through c. of the statute and include: making anonymous communications, communicating at extremely inconvenient hours, or using offensively coarse language (see subsection a.); subjecting another to offensive touching such as striking or kicking (see subsection b.); and repeatedly committing acts with purpose to alarm or seriously annoy another (see subsection c.).

A conviction under this statute hinges on the language "with purpose to harass." In other words, a simple "late night" call does not necessarily rise to the level of harassment. The Brainiac's phone call, however, does.

Gang member Camille had an estranged relationship with her former boyfriend. In an effort to get back at him, she ordered The Brainiac to call him as part of his pledging duties to become a member of the gang. This was not a normal phone call, however. The Brainiac called the ex-lover at the extremely inconvenient hour of 2:00 a.m. His entire telephone dialogue consisted of screaming and cursing at the man. Here this call was made "with a purpose to harass," and accordingly The Brainiac is guilty of a petty disorderly persons offense under 2C:33-4.

Per subsection e., the offense could become a crime of the fourth degree, however. This is only if The Brainiac was "serving a term of imprisonment or was on parole or probation as the result of a conviction of any indictable offense" when the act of harassment was committed.

| | |
|---|---|
| **2C:33-5, 33-6.** | **Blank** |
| **2C:33-7.** | **Obstructing highways and other public passages** |

a. A person, who, having no legal privilege to do so, purposely or recklessly obstructs any highway or other public passage whether alone or with others, commits a petty disorderly persons offense. "Obstructs" means renders impassable without unreasonable inconvenience or hazard. No person shall be deemed guilty of recklessly obstructing in violation of this subsection solely because of a gathering of persons to hear him speak or otherwise communicate, or solely because of being a member of such a gathering.

   b. A person in a gathering commits a petty disorderly persons offense if he refuses to obey a reasonable official request or order to move:

     (1) To prevent obstruction of a highway or other public passage; or

     (2) To maintain public safety by dispersing those gathered in dangerous proximity to a fire or other hazard.

An order to move, addressed to a person whose speech or other lawful behavior attracts an obstructing audience, shall not be deemed reasonable if the obstruction can be readily remedied by police control of the size or location of the gathering.

## PRACTICAL APPLICATION OF STATUTE

In order to become a member of the ruthless gang, The Bean-Bag Mean Team, The Brainiac was provided a laundry list of "tasks" to complete. One of the "tasks" was to lie down on a busy one-way street in East Newark, thereby preventing automobiles from passing. This is an example of a petty disorderly persons offense as defined in 2C:33-7.

## 2C:33-8. Disrupting meetings and processions

A person commits a disorderly persons offense if, with purpose to prevent or disrupt a lawful meeting, procession or gathering, he does an act tending to obstruct or interfere with it physically.

## PRACTICAL APPLICATION OF STATUTE

The Brainiac showed up at a Hackensack Library Board of Trustees meeting and locked the members out of the building. Here, The Brainiac committed a disorderly persons offense under 2C:33-8 for purposely disrupting and preventing this lawful meeting.

## 2C:33-9. Desecration of venerated objects

A person commits a disorderly persons offense if he purposely desecrates any public monument, insignia, symbol, or structure, or place of worship or burial. "Desecrate" means defacing, damaging or polluting.

## PRACTICAL APPLICATION OF STATUTE

Arriving in the town of Glen Rock with a special electric saw, The Brainiac cut out a piece of the town's "rock." For this desecration of the town's defining monument, The Brainiac should face a disorderly persons offense per the provisions of 2C:33-9.

## 2C:33-10. Causing fear of unlawful bodily violence, crime of third degree; act of graffiti, additional penalty

A person is guilty of a crime of the third degree if he purposely, knowingly or recklessly puts or attempts to put another in fear of bodily violence by placing on private property of another a symbol, an object, a characterization, an appellation or graffiti that exposes another to threats of violence. A person shall not be guilty of an attempt unless his actions cause a serious and imminent likelihood of causing fear of unlawful bodily violence.

A person convicted of an offense under this section that involves an act of graffiti may, in addition to any other penalty imposed by the court, be required either to pay to the owner of the damaged property monetary restitution in the amount of the pecuniary damage caused by the act of graffiti or to perform community service, which shall include removing the graffiti from the property, if appropriate. If community service is ordered, it shall be for either not less than 20 days nor less than the number of days necessary to remove the graffiti from the property.

## Practical Application of Statute

In Jersey City, The Brainiac painted a swastika on the front door of a councilman's home. He also inscribed the words, "You're dead, pal" on the house. This constitutes a crime of the third degree.

2C:33-10 provides that a person who "purposely, knowingly or recklessly puts or attempts to put another in fear of bodily violence"—by placing items such as symbols or graffiti on private property—is guilty of a third degree crime. Anyone who writes "You're dead, pal" and paints a swastika on the door of another's home knows that he is going to put that other person "in fear of bodily violence." The Brainiac, therefore, is guilty of violating 2C:33-10 for his acts of graffiti at the Jersey City councilman's home.

**2C:33-11.**    ### Defacement of private property, crime of fourth degree; act of graffiti, additional penalty

A person is guilty of a crime of the fourth degree if he purposely defaces or damages, without authorization of the owner or tenant, any private premises or property primarily used for religious, educational, residential, memorial, charitable, or cemetery purposes, or for assembly by persons for purpose of exercising any right guaranteed by law or by the Constitution of this State or of the United States by placing thereon a symbol, an object, a characterization, an appellation, or graffiti that exposes another to threat of violence.

A person convicted of an offense under this section that involves an act of graffiti may, in addition to any other penalty imposed by the court, be required either to pay to the owner of the damaged property monetary restitution in the amount of pecuniary damage caused by the act of graffiti or to perform community service, which shall include removing the graffiti from the property, if appropriate. If community service is ordered, it shall be for either not less than 20 days or not less than the number of days necessary to remove the graffiti from the property.

## Practical Application of Statute

Without authorization, The Brainiac removed the doors from a Secaucus church and spray-painted the words "Kill you" on the wall. This is a violation of 2C:33-11 which sets out special prohibitions against defacing or damaging any private property primarily used for matters such as religious, educational, or cemetery purposes. If the defacement "exposes another to threat of violence," the actor is guilty of a fourth degree crime.

The Brainiac's damage to the church doors and graffiti verbiage "Kill you" certainly would expose the congregation to a threat of violence. Accordingly, per the dictates of 2C:33-11, The Brainiac is guilty of a fourth degree crime.

**2C:33-12.**     **Maintaining a nuisance**

A person is guilty of maintaining a nuisance when:

    a. By conduct either unlawful in itself or unreasonable under all the circumstances, he knowingly or recklessly creates or maintains a condition which endangers the safety or health of a considerable number of persons;

    b. He knowingly conducts or maintains any premises, place or resort where persons gather for purposes of engaging in unlawful conduct; or

    c. He knowingly conducts or maintains any premises, place or resort as a house of prostitution or as a place where obscene material, as defined in N.J.S. 2C:34-2 and N.J.S. 2C: 34-3, is sold, photographed, manufactured, exhibited or otherwise prepared or shown, in violation of N.J.S. 2C:34-2, N.J.S. 2C:34-3, and N.J.S. 2C:34-4.

A person is guilty of a disorderly persons offense if the person is convicted under subsection a. or b. of this section. A person is guilty of a crime of the fourth degree if the person is convicted under subsection c. of this section.

Upon conviction under this section, in addition to the sentence authorized by this code, the court may proceed as set forth in section 2C:33-12.1.

## PRACTICAL APPLICATION OF STATUTE

The Brainiac is guilty of maintaining a nuisance for the "house of prostitution" he conducted at Mack Daddy's in Parsippany. This is a fourth degree crime.

Per 2C:33-12, an individual can be convicted of maintaining a nuisance for maintaining a condition that endangers the safety of a considerable number of persons (see subsection a.), maintaining premises where persons gather to engage in unlawful conduct (see subsection b.), or for maintaining a "house of prostitution" or other place where "obscene material" is sold, photographed, manufactured, or exhibited (see subsection c.). A violation of subsection c. renders a defendant guilty of a fourth degree crime. A violation of the other two subsections is a disorderly persons offense.

The Brainiac maintained and operated Mack Daddy's, a private club purporting to hold an exclusive membership of checkers and jacks players. In reality, it was a club where patrons paid adult women and men to have sex with them. Accordingly, The Brainiac violated subsection c. of the statute for maintaining a "house of prostitution" and is guilty of a fourth degree crime.

**2C:33-12.1.**     **Abating nuisance**

    a. In addition to the penalty imposed in case of conviction under N.J.S.2C:33-12 or under section 2 of P.L.1995, c.167 (C.2C:33-12.2), the court may order the immediate abatement of the nuisance, and for that purpose may order the seizure and forfeiture or destruction of any chattels, liquors, obscene material or other personal property which may be found in such building or place, and which the court is satisfied from the evidence were possessed or used with a purpose of maintaining the nuisance. Any such forfeiture shall be in the name and to the use of the State of New Jersey, and the court shall direct the forfeited property to be sold at public sale, the proceeds to be paid to the treasurer of the county wherein conviction was had.

b.  If the owner of any building or place is found guilty of maintaining a nuisance, the court may order that the building or place where the nuisance was maintained be closed and not used for a period not exceeding one year from the date of the conviction.

**2C:33-12.2.**          **Sexually oriented business, nuisance; crime**

a.  As used in this act:

    (1) "Sexually oriented business" means:

        (a) A commercial establishment which as one of its principal business purposes offers for sale, rental, or display any of the following:

            Books, magazines, periodicals or other printed material, or photographs, films, motion pictures, video cassettes, slides or other visual representations which depict or describe a "specified sexual activity" or "specified anatomical area"; or still or motion picture machines, projectors or other image-producing devices which show images to one person per machine at any one time, and where the images so displayed are characterized by the depiction of a "specified sexual activity" or "specified anatomical area"; or instruments, devices, or paraphernalia which are designed for use in connection with a "specified sexual activity"; or

        (b) A commercial establishment which regularly features live performances characterized by the exposure of a "specified anatomical area" or by a "specified sexual activity," or which regularly shows films, motion pictures, video cassettes, slides, or other photographic representations which depict or describe a "specified sexual activity" or "specified anatomical area";

    (2) "Person" means an individual, proprietorship, partnership, corporation, association, or other legal entity.

    (3) "Specified anatomical area" means:

        (a) Less than completely and opaquely covered human genitals, pubic region, buttock or female breasts below a point immediately above the top of the areola; or

        (b) Human male genitals in a discernibly turgid state, even if covered.

    (4) "Specified sexual activity" means:

        (a) The fondling or other erotic touching of covered or uncovered human genitals, pubic region, buttock or female breast; or

        (b) Any actual or simulated act of human masturbation, sexual intercourse or deviate sexual intercourse.

b.  In addition to any activities proscribed by the provisions of N.J.S.2C:33-12, a person is guilty of maintaining a nuisance when the person owns or operates a sexually oriented business which offers for public use booths, screens, enclosures or other devices which facilitate sexual activity by patrons.

c.  Notwithstanding any other provision of law, a municipality shall have the power to determine restrictions, if any, on the hours of operation of sexually oriented businesses.

d.  A person who violates this act is guilty of a crime of the fourth degree.

## PRACTICAL APPLICATION OF STATUTE

The Brainiac is guilty of violating 2C:33-12.2 for offering patrons the use of enclosed booths at his "sexually oriented business," Piper's Home of Love. This is a fourth degree crime.

Any person who owns or operates a "sexually oriented business" that "offers for public use booths, screens, enclosures or other devices which facilitate sexual activity by patrons" is guilty of a fourth degree crime. "Sexually oriented business" is just what it sounds like: a business that sells items, such as books, magazines, or films, that depict sexual activity or a business that provides live nude or quasi-nude performances. The complete definition of "sexually oriented business" can be found in subsection a. of 2C:33-12.2.

Piper's Home of Love was a commercial establishment owned and operated by The Brainiac. This storefront business provided live performances where women danced in G-strings and bikini tops and routinely fondled themselves in the breast and genital areas. They also engaged in simulated acts of masturbation. Accordingly, Piper's Home of Love was a "sexually oriented business."

The Brainiac is guilty of violating 2C:33-12.2 not for simply operating this business, however. His offense arises out of the fact that this "sexually oriented business" offered patrons the use of enclosed booths where "lap dances" occurred; sexual activity many times resulted during these sessions. Given that the enclosed booths in Piper's Home of Love "facilitated sexual activity by patrons," The Brainiac is guilty of a fourth degree crime under 2C:33-12.2.

## 2C:33-13.     Smoking in public

a. Any person who smokes or carries lighted tobacco in or upon any bus or other public conveyance, except group charter buses, specially marked railroad smoking cars, limousines or livery services, and, when the driver is the only person in the vehicle, autocabs, is a petty disorderly person.

b. Any person who smokes or carries lighted tobacco in any public place, including but not limited to places of public accommodation, where such smoking is prohibited by municipal ordinance under authority of R.S. 40:48-1 and 40:48-2 or by the owner or person responsible for the operation of the public place, and when adequate notice of such prohibition has been conspicuously posted, is guilty of a petty disorderly persons offense. Notwithstanding the provisions of 2C:43-3, the maximum fine which can be imposed for violation of this section is $200.00.

c. The provisions of this section shall supersede any other statute and any rule or regulation adopted pursuant to law.

## PRACTICAL APPLICATION OF STATUTE

The Briainiac smoked a cigarette on a public bus in Paterson. This is an example of a petty disorderly persons offense as defined in 2C:33-13.

A cab driver, with no passengers in the vehicle, smokes a cigarette in the cab. This is an example where the statute does not apply. However, if the cab carries even one passenger, the driver is guilty of a petty disorderly persons offense for his smoking.

**2C:33-13.1.**     ### Sale of cigarettes to minors, petty disorderly persons offense

a. A person who sells or gives to a person under 18 years of age any cigarettes made of tobacco or of any other matter or substance which can be smoked, or any cigarette paper or tobacco in any form, including smokeless tobacco, shall be punished by a fine as provided for a petty disorderly persons offense. A person who has been previously punished under this section and who commits another offense under it may be punishable by a fine of twice that provided for a petty disorderly persons offense.

b. The establishment of all of the following shall constitute a defense to any prosecution brought pursuant to subsection a. of this section:

   (1) that the purchaser or recipient of the tobacco product falsely represented, by producing either a driver's license or non-driver identification card issued by the Division of Motor Vehicles in the Department of Transportation, a similar card issued pursuant to the laws of another state or the federal government of Canada, or a photographic identification card issued by a county clerk, that the purchaser or recipient was of legal age to purchase or receive the tobacco product;

   (2) that the appearance of the purchaser or recipient of the tobacco product was such that an ordinary prudent person would believe the purchaser or recipient to be of legal age to purchase or receive the tobacco product; and

   (3) that the sale or distribution of the tobacco product was made in good faith, relying upon the production of the identification set forth in paragraph (1) of this subsection, the appearance of the purchaser or recipient, and in the reasonable belief that the purchaser or recipient was of legal age to purchase or receive the tobacco product.

c. A penalty imposed pursuant to this section shall be in addition to any penalty that may be imposed pursuant to section 1 of P.L.2000, c.87 (C.2A:170-51.4).

## PRACTICAL APPLICATION OF STATUTE

An example of this statute's petty disorderly persons offense is the clerk's sale of cigarettes to a 12-year-old boy at the Wood Chop Candy Shop in Butler. Although subsection b. of 2C:33-13.1 provides an affirmative defense, it is unlikely to work in this case, as one of the elements the defendant needs to establish is that the purchaser's appearance "was such that an ordinary prudent person would believe the purchaser or recipient to be of legal age" to purchase tobacco. What 12-year-old boy looks like he is 18 or older?

**2C:33-14.**     ### Interference with transportation

a. Interference with Transportation. A person is guilty of interference with transportation if the person purposely or knowingly:

   (1) casts, shoots or throws anything at, against or into any vehicle, railroad car, trolley car, subway car, ferry, airplane, or other facility of transportation; or

   (2) casts, shoots, throws or otherwise places any stick, stone, object or other substance upon any street railway track, trolley track or railroad track; or

   (3) endangers or obstructs the safe operation of motor vehicles by casting, shooting, throwing or otherwise placing any stick, stone, object or other substance upon any highway or roadway; or

   (4) unlawfully climbs into or upon any railroad car, either in motion or standing on the track of any railroad company in this State; or

(5) unlawfully disrupts, delays or prevents the operation of any train, bus, jitney, trolley, subway, airplane or any other facility of transportation. The term "unlawfully disrupts, delays or prevents the operation of" does not include non-violent conduct growing out of a labor dispute as defined in N.J.S.2A:15-58.

b. Interference with transportation is a disorderly persons offense.

c. Interference with transportation is a crime of the fourth degree if the person purposely, knowingly or recklessly causes bodily injury to another person or causes pecuniary loss in excess of $500 but less than $2000.

d. Interference with transportation is a crime of the third degree if the person purposely, knowingly or recklessly causes significant bodily injury to another person or causes pecuniary loss of $2000 or more, or if the person purposely or knowingly creates a risk of significant bodily injury to another person.

e. Interference with transportation is a crime of the second degree if the person purposely, knowingly or recklessly causes serious bodily injury to another person.

## PRACTICAL APPLICATION OF STATUTE

The Brainiac threw eggs at a moving bus in Paterson. This is an example of an offense as defined in 2C:33-14. Under these circumstances, where no one was injured and no property damage occurred, this is a disorderly persons offense.

If "bodily injury" had occurred, or if "pecuniary loss in excess of $500 but less than $2,000" had occurred, then the offense would be a fourth degree crime. The offense is elevated to a third degree crime if "pecuniary loss of $2,000 or more" had resulted or if the defendant caused "significant bodily injury" to another—or even if he "purposely or knowingly" created a risk of "significant bodily injury" to another. Finally, The Brainiac would be guilty of a second degree crime if "serious bodily injury" had resulted from his reckless egg-throwing actions.

**2C:33-14.1.**    ### Vandalizing railroad crossing devices, property; grading of offenses; graffiti

a. Any person who purposely, knowingly or recklessly defaces, damages, obstructs, removes or otherwise impairs the operation of any railroad crossing warning signal or protection device, including, but not limited to safety gates, electric bell, electric sign or any other alarm or protection system authorized by the Commissioner of Transportation, which is required under the provisions of R.S.48:12-54 or R.S.48:2-29, or any other railroad property or equipment, other than administrative buildings, offices or equipment, shall, for a first offense, be guilty of a crime of the fourth degree; however, if the defacement, damage, obstruction, removal or impediment of the crossing warning signal or protection device, property or equipment recklessly causes bodily injury or pecuniary loss of $2000 or more, the actor is guilty of a crime of the third degree, or if it recklessly causes a death or serious bodily injury, the actor is guilty of a crime of the second degree.

b. A person convicted of a violation of this section that involves an act of graffiti may, in addition to any other penalty imposed by the court, be required to pay to the owner of the damaged property monetary restitution in the amount of the pecuniary damage caused by the act of graffiti and to perform community service, which shall include removing the graffiti from the property, if appropriate. If community service is ordered, it shall be for either not less than 20 days or not less than the number of days necessary to remove the graffiti from the property. As used in this section, "act of graffiti" means the drawing, painting or making of any mark or inscription on public or private real or personal property without the permission of the owner.

## PRACTICAL APPLICATION OF STATUTE

In Glen Rock, The Brainiac ripped down a railroad crossing safety gate. This is a fourth degree crime per 2C:33-14.1.

If this act had "recklessly" caused "bodily injury or pecuniary loss of $2,000 or more," then a third degree crime has been committed. If it recklessly caused "death or serious bodily injury," the offense is elevated to a crime of the second degree.

**2C:33-15.**  **Possession, consumption of alcoholic beverages by person under legal age; penalty**

a. Any person under the legal age to purchase alcoholic beverages who knowingly possesses without legal authority or who knowingly consumes any alcoholic beverage in any school, public conveyance, public place, or place of public assembly, or motor vehicle, is guilty of a disorderly persons offense, and shall be fined not less than $500.00.

b. Whenever this offense is committed in a motor vehicle, the court shall, in addition to the sentence authorized for the offense, suspend or postpone for six months the driving privilege of the defendant. Upon the conviction of any person under this section, the court shall forward a report to the Division of Motor Vehicles stating the first and last day of the suspension or postponement period imposed by the court pursuant to this section. If a person at the time of the imposition of a sentence is less than 17 years of age, the period of license postponement, including a suspension or postponement of the privilege of operating a motorized bicycle, shall commence on the day the sentence is imposed and shall run for a period of six months after the person reaches the age of 17 years.

   If a person at the time of the imposition of a sentence has a valid driver's license issued by this State, the court shall immediately collect the license and forward it to the division along with the report. If for any reason the license cannot be collected, the court shall include in the report the complete name, address, date of birth, eye color, and sex of the person as well as the first and last date of the license suspension period imposed by the court.

   The court shall inform the person orally and in writing that if the person is convicted of operating a motor vehicle during the period of license suspension or postponement, the person shall be subject to the penalties set forth in R.S.39:3-40. A person shall be required to acknowledge receipt of the written notice in writing. Failure to receive a written notice or failure to acknowledge in writing the receipt of a written notice shall not be a defense to a subsequent charge of a violation of R.S.39:3-40.

   If the person convicted under this section is not a New Jersey resident, the court shall suspend or postpone, as appropriate, the non-resident driving privilege of the person based on the age of the person and submit to the division the required report. The court shall not collect the license of a non-resident convicted under this section. Upon receipt of a report by the court, the division shall notify the appropriate officials in the licensing jurisdiction of the suspension or postponement.

c. In addition to the general penalty prescribed for a disorderly persons offense, the court may require any person who violates this act to participate in an alcohol education or treatment program, authorized by the Department of Health and Senior Services, for a period not to exceed the maximum period of confinement prescribed by law for the offense for which the individual has been convicted.

d. Nothing in this act shall apply to possession of alcoholic beverages by any such person while actually engaged in the performance of employment pursuant to an employment permit issued by the Director of the Division of Alcoholic Beverage Control, or for a bona fide hotel or restaurant, in accordance with the provisions of R.S.33:1-26, or while actively engaged in the preparation of food while enrolled in a culinary arts or hotel management program at a county vocational school or post secondary educational institution.

e. The provisions of section 3 of P.L.1991, c.169 (C.33:1-81.1a) shall apply to a parent, guardian or other person with legal custody of a person under 18 years of age who is found to be in violation of this section.

## PRACTICAL APPLICATION OF STATUTE

The Brainiac shared a bottle of whisky with two students at Westwood High School. The students, both under 21 years of age, are guilty of a disorderly persons offense per 2C:33-15.

Those under 21 commit a disorderly persons offense if they "knowingly" possess or consume alcohol in locations such as a school, motor vehicle, or any public place. An exception to this rule is set forth in subsection d. of 2C:33-15. Bartenders, cooks, and waitresses under the legal age can legally possess alcohol while performing their jobs or training for such occupations in schools.

The Westwood High School students are not exempt from the prohibitions set out in this statute. Accordingly, their underage consumption of whisky on school property renders them guilty of a disorderly persons offense.

## 2C:33-16.

### Alcoholic beverages; bringing or possession on school property by person of legal age; penalty

Any person of legal age to purchase alcoholic beverages, who knowingly and without the express written permission of the school board, its delegated authority, or any school principal, brings or possesses any alcoholic beverages on any property used for school purposes which is owned by any school or school board, is guilty of a disorderly persons offense.

## PRACTICAL APPLICATION OF STATUTE

The Brainiac is guilty of a disorderly persons offense for "knowingly" bringing a bottle of whisky onto the Westwood High School property. He is guilty of this offense as all the elements of 2C:33-16 were met in his case: He was of legal age to purchase alcohol; he "knowingly" brought the alcohol onto school property; and he did not have any appropriate school authority's written permission to do so.

## 2C:33-17.

### Avaliability of alcoholic beverages to underaged, offenses

a. Anyone who purposely or knowingly offers or serves or makes available an alcoholic beverage to a person under the legal age for consuming alcoholic beverages or entices or encourages that person to drink an alcoholic beverage is a disorderly person.

This subsection shall not apply to a parent or guardian of the person under legal age for consuming alcoholic beverages if the parent or guardian is of the legal age to consume alcoholic beverages or to a religious observance, ceremony or rite. This subsection shall also not apply to any person in his home who is of the legal age to consume alcoholic beverages who offers or serves or makes available an alcoholic beverage to a person under the legal age for consuming alcoholic beverages or entices that person to drink an alcoholic beverage in the presence of and with the permission of the parent or guardian of the person under the legal age for consuming alcoholic beverages if the parent or guardian is of the legal age to consume alcoholic beverages.

A person who makes real property owned, leased or managed by him available to, or leaves that property in the care of, another person with the purpose that alcoholic beverages will be made available for consumption by, or will be consumed by, persons who are under the legal age for consuming alcoholic beverages is guilty of a disorderly persons offense.

This subsection shall not apply if:

(1)  the real property is licensed or required to be licensed by the Division of Alcoholic Beverage Control in accordance with the provisions of R.S.33:1-1 et seq;

(2)  the person making the property available, or leaving it in the care of another person, is of the legal age to consume alcoholic beverages and is the parent or guardian of the person who consumes alcoholic beverages while under the legal age for consuming alcoholic beverages; or

(3)  the alcoholic beverages are consumed by a person under the legal age for consuming alcoholic beverages during a religious observance, ceremony or rite.

## PRACTICAL APPLICATION OF STATUTE

For offering whisky to the Westwood High School students, The Brainiac is guilty of a disorderly persons offense. Why? Simply because 2C:33-17 makes it an offense to "purposely or knowingly" offer, serve, make available, or encourage anyone under 21 to drink an alcoholic beverage.

It is intereting to note, however, that this statute does not apply to parents or guardians of those underage. The statute also does not apply to any person who "in his home" offers, serves, etc., alcohol to someone under 21—as long as the underage person's parent/guardian is present and gives permission to do so. In all these circumstances, the person making the alcohol offering (and the parent/guardian) must be "of the legal age to consume alcoholic beverages." Finally, this statute does not apply to a "religious observance, ceremony or rite."

2C:33-18.     **Repealed**

2C:33-19.     **Possession of remotely activated paging devices on school property, disorderly persons offense; exemptions**

No person enrolled as a student of an elementary or secondary school, knowingly and without the express written permission of the school board, its delegated authority, or any school principal, shall bring or possess any remotely activated paging device on any property used for school purposes, at any time and regardless of whether school is in session or other persons are present. A violation of this section shall be a disorderly persons offense. No permission to bring or possess any remotely activated paging device on school property shall be granted unless and until a student shall have established to the satisfaction of the school authorities a reasonable basis for the possession of the device on school property.

This section shall not apply to any student who is an active member in good standing of a volunteer fire company or first aid, ambulance or rescue squad provided that (1) the student is required to respond to an emergency and (2) a copy of the statement by the chief executive officer of the volunteer fire company or first aid, ambulance or rescue squad authorizing the possession of the paging device is in the possession of the student at all times while that student is in possession of the remotely activated paging device.

## PRACTICAL APPLICATION OF STATUTE

School students cannot bring a pager on school property unless they have written permission from an appropriate school authority. A violation of 2C:33-19 is a disorderly persons offense—really, that's what this statute provides.

2C:33-19 does set forth an exception for individuals who serve as members of a "volunteer fire company or first aid, ambulance or rescue squad." They, though, still need to present proof of their said membership; a written statement from the "chief executive officer" of the relevant squad is a necessity.

**2C:33-20.**    **Use of remotely activated paging device during commission of certain crimes is a crime of fourth degree**

A person is guilty of a crime of the fourth degree if he uses a remotely activated paging device while engaged in the commission of, or an attempt to commit, or flight after committing or attempting to commit any crime or offense enumerated in chapter 35 or 36 of Title 2C of the New Jersey Statutes.

## PRACTICAL APPLICATION OF STATUTE

"Bob the Drug Dealer" provides cocaine to "Ted the Addict." Druing this sale, Bob calls a pager to notify his partner, "Mike the Money Man," that the transaction has been completed. Mike then meets up with Ted to collect the money owed for the cocaine. The use of the pager device, under these circumstances, renders both Bob and Mike guilty of a fourth degree crime under 2C:33-20.

**2C:33-21.**    **Interception or use of official communications**

Any person who intercepts any message or transmission made on or over any police, fire or emergency medical communications system, or any person who is the recipient of information so intercepted, and who uses the information obtained thereby to facilitate the commission of or the attempt to commit a crime or a violation of any law of this State, or uses the same in a manner which interferes with the discharge of police or firefighting operations or provision of medical services by first aid, rescue or ambulance squad personnel, shall be guilty of a crime of the fourth degree.

## PRACTICAL APPLICATION OF STATUTE

Bean-Bag Mean Team gang member Bertha closely listened to a police radio system while she waited in an automobile for new gang member, The Brainiac. She heard a Butler police dispatcher advise all units that an alleged heroin transaction was occurring directly across the street from where their car was currently located.

Realizing that the dealers would probably have significant amounts of cash and drugs on them, Bertha frantically waved The Brainiac back to their car. Immediately upon his arrival, she suggested that they run across the street and rob them. The pair then did just that—and Bertha was correct, as they left the site with nearly $5,000 in cash and heroin with a street value of about $10,000.

Bertha used the information she intercepted from the "police communication system" to facilitate a crime—the drug dealer robbery. This misuse of information constitutes a fourth degree crime under 2C:33-21.

**2C:33-22.** **Possession of emergency communications receiver**

Any person who, while in the course of committing or attempting to commit a crime, including the immediate flight therefrom, possesses or controls a radio capable of receiving any message or transmission made on or over any police, fire or emergency medical communications system, shall be guilty of a crime of the fourth degree.

## PRACTICAL APPLICATION OF STATUTE

As Bertha and The Brainiac drove away from their drug dealer robbery, they monitored a "police radio system" so as to avoid any law enforcement that might be attempting to track them. This is an example of a fourth degree crime as set out in 2C:33-22.

**2C:33-23.** **Radar device not included**

For purposes of P.L.1991, c.432 (C.2C:33-21 et seq.), the term "police, fire or emergency medical communications system" shall not include radar devices used to monitor vehicular speed.

**2C:33-24.** **Definitions**

As used in this chapter:
   a. "Act of graffiti" means the drawing, painting or making any mark or inscription on public or private real or personal property without the permission of the owner.
   b. "Spray paint" means any paint or pigmented substance that is in an aerosol or similar spray container.

**2C:33-25.** **Warning sign required for sale of spray paint; violations, penalties**

No person shall knowingly sell or offer for sale to the general public any spray paint unless a sign is exhibited, either where the product is displayed or where it is paid for, warning that in New Jersey an act of graffiti committed by a juvenile may carry a penalty of a one-year driver's license suspension for a first offense and a two-year suspension for a second offense, and that an act of graffiti committed by either an adult or a juvenile may carry a penalty of restitution or 20 days' community service.

A person who knowingly violates this section shall be fined $50 for the first offense and $100 for a second or subsequent offense.

## PRACTICAL APPLICATION OF STATUTE

This statute is rarely invoked, but in a nutshell it provides that merchants selling spray paint must exhibit warning signs outlining penalties for using the spray paint to commit acts of graffiti. Failure to exhibit the signs required under this statute shall subject a violator to conviction of a petty disorderly persons offense.

**2C:33-26.**    **Sale of motor vehicle on Sunday**

A person who engages in the business of buying, selling or exchanging motor vehicles or who opens a place of business and attempts to engage in such conduct on a Sunday commits a disorderly persons offense. The first offense is punishable by a fine not to exceed $100.00 or imprisonment for a period of not more than 10 days or both; the second offense is punishable by a fine not to exceed $500 or imprisonment for a period of not more than 30 days or both; the third or each subsequent offense is punishable by a fine of $750.00 or imprisonment for a period of six months or both. If the person is a licensed dealer in new or used motor vehicles in this State, under the provisions of chapter 10, Title 39 of the Revised Statutes, the person shall also be subject to suspension or revocation of his dealer's license to engage in the business of buying, selling or exchanging in motor vehicles in this State as provided in Title 39, chapter 10, section 10, section 20, for violation of this statute.

## PRACTICAL APPLICATION OF STATUTE

The Brainiac, a licensed used car dealer, sold a 1986 Chevy Cavalier on a Sunday. Believe it or not, this Sunday car sale constitutes a disorderly persons offense under 2C:33-26.

**2C:33-27.**    **Consumption of alcohol in restaurants**

a. No person who owns or operates a restaurant, dining room or other public place where food or liquid refreshments are sold or served to the general public, and for which premises a license or permit authorizing the sale of alcoholic beverages for on-premises consumption has not been issued:

   (1) Shall allow the consumption of alcoholic beverages, other than wine or a malt alcoholic beverage, in a portion of the premises which is open to the public; or

   (2) Shall charge any admission fee or cover, corkage or service charge or advertise inside or outside of such premises that patrons may bring and consume their own wine or malt alcoholic beverages in a portion of the premises which is open to the public.

   (3) Shall allow the consumption of wine or malt alcoholic beverages at times or by persons to whom the service or consumption or alcoholic beverages on licensed premises is prohibited by State or municipal law or regulation.

b. Nothing in this act shall restrict the right of a municipality or an owner or operator of a restaurant, dining room or other public place where food or liquid refreshments are sold or served to the general public from prohibiting the consumption of alcoholic beverages on those premises.

c. A person who violates any provision of this act is a disorderly person, and the court, in addition to the sentence imposed for the disorderly person violation, may by its judgment bar the owner or operator from allowing consumption of wine or malt alcoholic beverages in his premises as authorized by this act.

## PRACTICAL APPLICATION OF STATUTE

Bean-Bag Mean Team gang members Bertha and The Brainiac enjoyed a hearty meal at Stu's House of Chow. Although the restaurant had no liquor license, the owner permitted the gang members to drink scotch at a regular dining table.

2C:33-27a.(1) prohibits a restaurant owner (who does not have a liquor license) from allowing "the consumption of alcoholic beverages, other than wine or a malt alcoholic beverage, in a portion of the premises which is open to the public." A violation of this provision constitutes a disorderly persons offense.

Scotch is not "wine" or a "malt beverage." Bertha and The Brainiac drank this liquor at a regular dining table, a table located in a portion of the restaurant that was open to the public. Accordingly, the owner of Stu's House of Chow is guilty of a disorderly persons offense for allowing Bertha and The Brainiac to drink scotch at this table.

**2C:33-28.**    **Solicitation, recruitment to join criminal street gang; crime, degrees**

  a. An actor who solicits or recruits another to join or actively participate in a criminal street gang with the knowledge or purpose that the person who is solicited or recruited will promote, further, assist, plan, aid, agree, or attempt to aid in the commission of criminal conduct by a member of a criminal street gang commits a crime of the fourth degree. For purposes of this section, the actor shall have the requisite knowledge or purpose if he knows that the person who is solicited or recruited will engage in some form, though not necessarily which form, of criminal activity. "Criminal street gang" shall have the meaning set forth in subsection h. of N.J.S.2C:44-3.

  b. An actor who, in the course of violating subsection a. of this section, threatens another with bodily injury on two or more separate occasions within a 30-day period commits a crime of the third degree.

  c. An actor who, in the course of violating subsection a. of this section, inflicts significant bodily injury upon another commits a crime of the second degree.

  d. Any defendant convicted of soliciting, recruiting, coercing or threatening a person under 18 years of age in violation of subsection a., b. or c. of this section shall be sentenced by the court to an extended term of imprisonment as set forth in subsection a. of N.J.S.2C:43-7. Notwithstanding the provisions of N.J.S.2C:1-8, N.J.S.2C:44-5 or any other provision of law, a conviction arising under this section shall not merge with a conviction for any criminal offense that the actor committed while involved in criminal street gang related activity, as defined in subsection h. of N.J.S.2C:44-3, nor shall the conviction for any such offense merge with a conviction pursuant to this section and the sentence imposed upon a violation of this section shall be ordered to be served consecutively to that imposed upon any other such conviction.

## PRACTICAL APPLICATION OF STATUTE

Bertha recruited The Brainiac to join the "criminal street gang," The Bean-Bag Mean Team. This is a crime of the fourth degree.

2C:33-28 sets forth the provisions that make it a crime to solicit or recruit another to join a "criminal street gang." This term is defined in 2C:44-3. Primarily, a "criminal street gang" exists where two prongs are met. First, three or more people must be "associated in fact" (i.e., having a common group name or identifying symbol, tattoo, or sign).

Second, within the preceding three years, gang members need to have committed "two or more offenses" of crimes such as carjacking, robbery, burglary, aggravated assault, and kidnapping.

Where the aforesaid solicitation or recruiting occurs "with the knowledge or purpose that the person who is solicited" will promote, assist, or otherwise aid a gang member in the commission of criminal conduct, the actor engaging in the recruitment is guilty of a fourth degree crime.

The offense is elevated to a third degree crime where, during the course of the recruiting, others are threatened with bodily injury "on two or more occasions within a 30-day period." It becomes a second degree crime if the actor violating this statute "inflicts significant bodily injury upon another."

The Bean-Bag Mean Team is a "criminal street gang." Milo, Smiles, Bertha, Camille, Bambie, and Horatio formed The Bean-Bag Mean Team. Each member was required to wear a chili bean pin on the lapel of his shirt; during the commission of crimes, the pin was to be placed on the inside of the shirt. The gang initially was ruthless and did in fact commit numerous hard-core crimes, including over 50 carjackings in the previous two years. They also engaged in numerous robberies, burglaries, and aggravated assaults. Recently, the membership had reached over 1,000 individuals. Given the number of gang members, the gang-signifying chili bean pin, and the quantity of carjackings committed by gang members in the preceding three years, The Bean-Bag Mean Team qualifies as a "criminal street gang."

Bertha solicited The Brainiac to be the gang's final member. She sought his induction into the gang with the purpose that he would plan and aid the carrying through of their future criminal events. The Brainiac was receptive to her advances and agreed that if he was indeed admitted to be a member, he would actively plot and engage in fresh criminal activities.

Since Bertha recruited The Brainiac to be part of her "criminal street gang" with the knowledge that The Brainiac would assist and aid in gang criminal conduct, she is guilty of a crime under 2C:33-28. Her crime would only be one of the fourth degree if neither threats of bodily injury nor actual significant bodily injury occurred in the course of her violating this statute. With "significant bodily injury" occurring, it would be elevated to a second degree crime.

# 34

# PUBLIC INDECENCY

**2C:34-1.**      **Prostitution and related offenses**

a.  As used in this section:

   (1) "Prostitution" is sexual activity with another person in exchange for something of economic value, or the offer or acceptance of an offer to engage in sexual activity in exchange for something of economic value.

   (2) "Sexual activity" includes, but is not limited to, sexual intercourse, including genital-genital, oral-genital, anal-genital, and oral-anal contact, whether between persons of the same or opposite sex; masturbation; touching of the genitals, buttocks, or female breasts; sadistic or masochistic abuse and other deviate sexual relations.

   (3) "House of prostitution" is any place where prostitution or promotion of prostitution is regularly carried on by one person under the control, management or supervision of another.

   (4) "Promoting prostitution" is:

      (a) Owning, controlling, managing, supervising or otherwise keeping, alone or in association with another, a house of prostitution or a prostitution business;

      (b) Procuring an inmate for a house of prostitution or place in a house of prostitution for one who would be an inmate;

      (c) Encouraging, inducing, or otherwise purposely causing another to become or remain a prostitute;

      (d) Soliciting a person to patronize a prostitute;

      (e) Procuring a prostitute for a patron;

      (f) Transporting a person into or within this State with purpose to promote that person's engaging in prostitution, or procuring or paying for transportation with that purpose; or

      (g) Leasing or otherwise permitting a place controlled by the actor, alone or in association with others, to be regularly used for prostitution or promotion of prostitution, or failure to make a reasonable effort to abate such use by ejecting the tenant, notifying law enforcement authorities, or other legally available means.

b.  A person commits an offense if:

   (1) The actor engages in prostitution;

   (2) The actor promotes prostitution;

   (3) The actor knowingly promotes prostitution of a child under 18 whether or not the actor mistakenly believed that the child was 18 years of age or older, even if such mistaken belief was reasonable;

**317**

(4) The actor knowingly promotes prostitution of the actor's child, ward, or any other person for whose care the actor is responsible;

(5) The actor compels another to engage in or promote prostitution;

(6) The actor promotes prostitution of the actor's spouse; or

(7) The actor knowingly engages in prostitution with a person under the age of 18, or if the actor enters into or remains in a house of prostitution for the purpose of engaging in sexual activity with a child under the age of 18, or if the actor solicits or requests a child under the age of 18 to engage in sexual activity. It shall be no defense to a prosecution under this paragraph that the actor mistakenly believed that the child was 18 years of age or older, even if such mistaken belief was reasonable.

c. Grading of offenses under subsection b.

(1) An offense under subsection b. constitutes a crime of the second degree if the offense falls within paragraph (3) or (4) of that subsection.

(2) An offense under subsection b. constitutes a crime of the third degree if the offense falls within paragraph (5), (6) or (7) of that subsection.

(3) An offense under paragraph (2) of subsection b. constitutes a crime of the third degree if the conduct falls within subparagraph (a), (b), or (c) of paragraph (4) of subsection a. Otherwise the offense is a crime of the fourth degree.

(4) An offense under subsection b. constitutes a disorderly persons offense if the offense falls within paragraph (1) of that subsection except that a second or subsequent conviction for such an offense constitutes a crime of the fourth degree. In addition, where a motor vehicle was used in the commission of any offense under paragraph (1) of subsection b. the court shall suspend for six months the driving privilege of any such offender who has a valid driver's license issued by this State. Upon conviction, the court shall immediately collect the offender's driver's license and shall forward it, along with a report stating the first and last day of the suspension imposed pursuant to this paragraph, to the Division of Motor Vehicles.

d. Presumption from living off prostitutes. A person, other than the prostitute or the prostitute's minor child or other legal dependent incapable of self-support, who is supported in whole or substantial part by the proceeds of prostitution is presumed to be knowingly promoting prostitution.

## PRACTICAL APPLICATION OF STATUTE

### Promoting Prostitution

The Brainiac is guilty of promoting prostitution for his ownership and management activities at Mack Daddy's in Parsippany. In his case, it is a third degree crime.

Per 2C:34-1, a person can be convicted of an offense for engaging in prostitution or promoting prostitution. The offenses are graded in subsection c. of the statute. Promoting prostitution can be a second, third, or fourth degree crime, depending upon the circumstances. Per subsection c.(1), promoting prostitution is a second degree crime where "the offense falls within paragraph (3) or (4)" of subsection b.

This means it is a second degree crime in circumstances such as where the actor knowingly promotes prostitution of the actor's own child (see b.(4)) and where the actor knowingly promotes prostitution of a child under 18 years of age (see b.(3)). It is interesting to note that per b.(3), it doesn't matter whether the actor "mistakenly believed" the child was 18 or older; in other words, even if the mistaken belief was reasonable, he could still be convicted of a second degree crime.

Subsection c.(3) states "an offense under paragraph (2) of subsection b. constitutes a crime of the third degree if the conduct falls within subparagraph (a), (b), or (c) of paragraph (4) of subsection a. Otherwise the offense is a crime of the fourth degree." Huh?! What?! This is clear, right? The case of The Brainiac will help to explain what this means.

After The Brainiac's celebration dinner with his gang member date, Bertha, The Brainiac brought Bertha to his Parsippany business, Mack Daddy's. This was a private, 24-hour club purporting to hold an exclusive membership of checkers and jacks players. In reality, Mack Daddy's was a "house of prostitution," where patrons paid adult women and men to have sex with them.

Mack Daddy's was owned and managed by The Brainiac on a daily basis. He oversaw and encouraged the individuals who worked there to have sexual relations with the club's many eager clients. Over 30 employees accepted cash in exchange for their services.

Now let's revisit the language of subsection c.(3): "an offense under paragraph (2) of subsection b. constitutes a crime of the third degree if the conduct falls within subparagraph (a), (b), or (c) of paragraph (4) of subsection a. Otherwise the offense is a crime of the fourth degreee." Now let's break down this language.

Paragraph (2) of subsection b. provides that a person commits an offense if the actor promotes prostitution. But how does a person "promote prostitution"? This is defined in subsection a.(4), which is further divided into subparagraphs (a) through (g). Persons who promote prostitution via actions defined in subparagraphs (a), (b) and (c) are those guilty of third degree crimes. "Otherwise," those who promote prostitution via actions defined in the remaining subparagraphs ((d) through (g)) are guilty of a fourth degree crime.

The Brainiac is guilty of a third degree promotion of prostitution offense. Why? Because he violated both subparagraphs (a) and (c) of subsection a.(4): He owned and managed a "house of prostitution" (which violates a.(4)(a)), and he "encouraged" others to remain prostitutes, which violates a.(4)(c).

It is important to note that subsection d. drops in a special provision that makes it an offense of promoting prostitution in situations where people are "living off prostitutes." The subsection provides that a person is "presumed" to be knowingly promoting prostitution where he is "supported in whole or substantial part by the proceeds of prostitution." Difficult to prove? Perhaps, but this is ultimately a matter to be decided in the courts.

### Engaging in Prostitution

The prostitutes who worked for The Brainiac at Mack Daddy's—and the "johns" who utilized their services—are guilty of "engaging in prostitution." This can be a third or fourth degree crime, or a disorderly persons offense, depending upon the circumstances.

As 2C:34-1c.(2) states, "engaging in prostitution" is a third degree crime where it falls within subsections b.(5) through b.(7) of 2C:34-1. This means that it is a third degree crime where the actor "compels another to engage" in prostitution (see b.(5)), where the actor "promotes prostitution of the actor's spouse" (see b.(6)) or where the actor "engages in prostitution with a person under the age of 18" (see b.(7)). The latter subsection is similarly violated if the actor remains in a house of prostitution with the purpose of engaging in sexual activity with a person under 18 or solicits/requests a child under 18 to have sexual relations with him. Under all these circumstances, it is no defense where the actor mistakenly believed that the child was 18 or older—even if the mistaken belief was reasonable.

"Engaging in prostitution," however, is generally a disorderly persons offense as per subsection c.(4). This means that two consenting adults who decide to engage in prostitution are both guilty of a disorderly persons offense and not a third degree crime. For example, in the case where John, 40, goes to Mack Daddy's and pays Wilma, 21, $50 to have sex with him, they are both guilty of a disorderly persons offense. Their offense can be elevated to a fourth degree crime, though, if they have been previously convicted of engaging in prostitution.

**2C:34-1.1.**    **Loitering for the purpose of engaging in prostitution**

   a. As used in this section, "public place" means any place to which the public has access, including but not limited to any public street, sidewalk, bridge, alley, plaza, park, boardwalk, driveway, parking lot or transportation facility, public library or the doorways and entrance ways to any building which fronts on any of the aforesaid places, or a motor vehicle in or on any such place.

   b. A person commits a disorderly persons offense if he:

      (1) wanders, remains or prowls in a public place with the purpose of engaging in prostitution or promoting prostitution as defined in N.J.S.2C:34-1; and

      (2) engages in conduct that, under the circumstances, manifests a purpose to engage in prostitution or promoting prostitution as defined in N.J.S.2C:34-1.

   c. Conduct that may, where warranted under the circumstances, be deemed adequate to manifest a purpose to engage in prostitution or promoting prostitution includes, but is not limited to, conduct such as the following:

      (1) Repeatedly beckoning to or stopping pedestrians or motorists in a public place;

      (2) Repeatedly attempting to stop, or repeatedly attempting to engage passers-by in conversation;

      (3) Repeatedly stopping or attempting to stop motor vehicles.

   d. The element described in paragraph (1) of subsection b. of this section may not be established solely by proof that the actor engaged in the conduct that is used to satisfy the element described in paragraph (2) of subsection b. of this section.

## PRACTICAL APPLICATION OF STATUTE

2C:34-1.1 makes it illegal for individuals to loiter for the "purpose of engaging in prostitution or promoting prostitution." The case of The Brainiac provides an example of how loiterers can be convicted of this disorderly persons offense.

This statute is nearly identical, in language and form, to 2C:33-2.1 (loitering for purpose of illegally using, possessing, or selling CDSs). Accordingly, it will be explained in the same manner. 2C:34-1.1, in a quick summary, prohibits a person from "wandering" or "remaining" in public with a purpose to engage in or promote prostitution. But how is it possible to prove that someone is "wandering" or "remaining" in a public place for the purpose of carrying out one of these illicit activities?

2C:34-1.1 provides that the defendant's "conduct" is the dispositive factor. Subsection c. goes as far as defining what "conduct" will be "deemed adequate to manifest a purpose to engage in prostitution or promoting prostitution." This conduct includes, but is not limited to, repeatedly stopping pedestrians or motorists and repeatedly engaging passers-by in conversations.

Nothing in this statute requires that any actual evidence of "promoting prostitution" or "engaging in prostitution" be presented in order for a conviction under 2C:34-1.1 to occur. However, subsection d., when dissected, does set out that the above described "conduct," *alone cannot* solely establish that the defendant acted "with the purpose" to "promote prostitution" or "engage in prostitution." This implies that some other evidence (e.g., statements by the defendants) is necessary for a conviction.

Now how does The Brainiac's case help explain the practical use of this statute? After celebrating his induction in the ruthless gang, The Bean-Bag Mean Team, The Brainiac took fellow gang member Bertha on a date. Their last stop of the evening was in Newark, where they roamed the streets, asking several different people where they could find a prostitute, as they wanted to "speak to one."

Here, the "conduct" of The Brainiac and Bertha could "be deemed adequate to manifest a purpose to engage in prostitution"—they repeatedly stopped several pedestrians and passers-by, engaging them in conversations. But remember, this "conduct" alone is not enough; the prosecution must present something additional for a conviction to occur. In The Brainiac's case, there is that something—he and Bertha asked the individuals they stopped where they could find a prostitute. Accordingly, with these combined factors existing, The Brainiac and Bertha could be convicted of "loitering for the purpose of engaging in prostitution."

---

**2C:34-2.**       **Obscenity for persons 18 years of age or older**

  a. Definitions for purpose of this section:

    (1) "Obscene material" means any description, narrative account, display, or depiction of sexual activity or anatomical area contained in, or consisting of, a picture or other representation, publication, sound recording, live performance, or film, which by means of posing, composition, format or animated sensual details:

      (a) Depicts or describes in a patently offensive way, ultimate sexual acts, normal or perverted, actual or simulated, masturbation, excretory functions, or lewd exhibition of the genitals,

      (b) Lacks serious literary, artistic, political, or scientific value, when taken as a whole, and

      (c) Is a part of a work, which to the average person applying contemporary community standards, has a dominant theme taken as a whole, which appeals to the prurient interest.

    (2) "Exhibit" means the sale of admission to view obscene material.

  b. A person who sells, distributes, rents or exhibits obscene material to a person 18 years of age or older commits a crime of the fourth degree. Sale of obscene material shall be deemed to include any form of transaction which results in the admission to a display or depiction of obscene material or temporary or permanent access to any obscene material.

Nothing contained herein or in section 3 of P.L.1995, c.230 (C.2C:34-7) shall be construed to prohibit a municipality from adopting as a part of its zoning ordinances an ordinance permitting the sale, distribution, rental or exhibition of obscene material in which event such sale, distribution, rental or exhibition shall be deemed legal.

## PRACTICAL APPLICATION OF STATUTE

At a store known as The Annex, Bean-Bag Mean Team members, The Brainiac and Bertha, thumbed through multiple magazines, looking at hundreds of erotic and sexually explicit pictures. They watched as the store clerk sold five of the magazines to a 33-year-old woman. For this sale, could the clerk be convicted of selling "obscene material," which is a fourth degree crime per 2C:34-2?

Subsection a. of this statute provides a definition for "obscene material." Basically, any magazine, video, etc., containing sexual activity or nudity—in any description, narrative account, display, or depiction—could be stretched to fall under this definition. Pursuant to subsection b., any person who "sells, distributes, rents or exhibits" any of this "obscene material" to any person 18 years of age or older commits a fourth degree crime.

Okay, so The Annex clerk technically could be convicted of a fourth degree crime for selling sexually explicit magazines to the 33-year-old woman. Does this sound right, though? If this is the case, how are the hundreds, if not thousands, of stores across the state of New Jersey selling sexually explicit magazines and videos? Well, according to the final paragraph of the statute, any municipality can adopt a municipal ordinance to legally permit the "sale, distribution, rental or exhibition of obscene material" to persons 18 or older. In the event that such an ordinance is adopted, the sale, etc., of "obscene material" to persons 18 or older is "deemed legal."

**2C:34-3.**     **Obscenity for persons under 18**

a. Definitions for purposes of this section:

(1) "Obscene material" means any description, narrative account, display, depiction of a specified anatomical area or specified sexual activity contained in, or consisting of, a picture or other representation, publication, sound recording, live performance or film, which by means of posing, composition, format or animated sensual details, emits sensuality with sufficient impact to concentrate prurient interest on the area or activity.

(2) "Obscene film" means any motion picture film or preview or trailer to a film, not including newsreels portraying actual current events or pictorial news of the day, in which a scene, taken by itself:

(a) Depicts a specified anatomical area or specified sexual activity, or the simulation of a specified sexual activity, or verbalization concerning a specified sexual activity; and

(b) Emits sensuality sufficient, in terms of the duration and impact of the depiction, to appeal to prurient interest.

(3) "Specified anatomical area" means:

(a) Less than completely and opaquely covered human genitals, pubic region, buttock or female breasts below a point immediately above the top of the areola; or

(b) Human male genitals in a discernibly turgid state, even if covered.

(4) "Specified sexual activity" means:

    (a) Human genitals in a state of sexual stimulation or arousal; or

    (b) Any act of human masturbation, sexual intercourse or deviate sexual intercourse; or

    (c) Fondling or other erotic touching of covered or uncovered human genitals, pubic region, buttock or female breast.

(5) "Knowingly" means:

    (a) Having knowledge of the character and content of the material or film described herein; or

    (b) Having failed to exercise reasonable inspection which would disclose its character and content.

(6) "Exhibit" means the sale of admission to view obscene material.

(7) "Show" means cause or allow to be seen.

b. **Promoting obscene material.**

    (1) A person who knowingly sells, distributes, rents or exhibits to a person under 18 years of age obscene material is guilty of a crime of the third degree.

    (2) A person who knowingly shows obscene material to a person under 18 years of age with the knowledge or purpose to arouse, gratify or stimulate himself or another is guilty of a crime of the third degree if the person showing the obscene material is at least four years older than the person under 18 years of age viewing the material.

c. **Admitting to exhibition of obscene film.**

    (1) Any person who knowingly admits a person under 18 years of age to a theatre then exhibiting an obscene film is guilty of a crime of the third degree.

    (2) A person who knowingly shows an obscene film to a person under 18 years of age with the knowledge or purpose to arouse, gratify or stimulate himself or another is guilty of a crime of the third degree if the person showing the obscene film is at least four years older than the person under 18 years of age viewing the film.

d. **Presumption of knowledge and age.** The requisite knowledge with regard to the character and content of the film or material and of the age of the person is presumed in the case of an actor who sells, distributes, rents, exhibits or shows obscene material to a person under 18 years of age or admits to a film obscene for a person under 18 years of age a person who is under 18 years of age.

e. **Defenses.**

    (1) It is an affirmative defense to a prosecution under subsections b. and c. which the defendant must prove by a preponderance of evidence that:

        (a) The person under age 18 falsely represented in or by writing that he was age 18 or over;

        (b) The person's appearance was such that an individual of ordinary prudence would believe him to be age 18 or over; and

        (c) The sale, distribution, rental, showing or exhibition to or admission of the person was made in good faith relying upon such written representation and appearance and in the reasonable belief that he was actually age 18 or over.

    (2) It is an affirmative defense to a prosecution under subsection c. that the defendant is an employee in a motion picture theatre who has no financial interest in that motion picture theatre other than his wages and has no decision-making authority or responsibility with respect to the selection of the motion picture show which is exhibited.

## Practical Application of Statute

The clerk of The Annex sold two sexually explicit magazines to a 14-year-old boy. This is a crime of the third degree.

While 2C:34-2 allows for municipalities to adopt an ordinance that permits the sale, etc., of "obscene material" to persons 18 or older, 2C:34-3 has no such provision. Why is this important? Because 2C:34-3 is the statute which governs the sale, distribution, rental, or exhibition of "obscene material" to persons *under* 18 years of age.

The definitions pertinent to "obscenity" for persons under 18 are set forth in subsection a. of the statute. The definition of "obscene material" in 2C:34-3a.(1) is even more narrow than the definition in its counterpart statute, 2C:34-2. Also, a person who violates the provisions of 2C:34-3 is guilty of a third degree crime, whereas a violator of 2C:34-2 is guilty of a crime of the fourth degree.

Not only is it a third degree crime to sell, etc., "obscene material" to persons under 18, it is also a third degree crime to "show" such material to minors. Subsection b.(2) sets out caveats to the latter prohibition, however. In order to be convicted of an offense for "showing obscene material" to someone under 18, the person must do it with the knowledge or purpose "to arouse, gratify or stimulate himself or another." In addition, for a conviction to occur here, the person "showing" the "obscene material" must be "at least four years older than the person under 18 years of age viewing the material."

The clerk at The Annex sold two sexually explicit magazines, containing pictures that are considered "obscene material" under 2C:34-3 to a 14-year-old boy. Accordingly, he is guilty of a third degree crime.

### "Knowingly" Requirement

It is important to note that 2C:34-3 provides that an individual such as the clerk must "knowingly" sell, etc., "obscene material" to a person under 18. "Knowingly," in a nutshell, means that he has knowledge that "obscene material" is within the items he is selling or that he failed to make a reasonable inspection of the material that would disclose its content. Obviously, The Annex clerk knew what he was selling to the 14-year-old—the entire product line in his store was erotic and sexually explicit material.

### Affirmative Defenses

It is also important to note that subsection e. of the statute provides affirmative defenses to the offenses in 2C:34-3. One of the defenses is that the juvenile falsely represented "in or by writing" that he was 18 or over. For this defense to succeed, however, the juvenile must appear 18 or older to an ordinary, prudent person. And the defendant must rely in good faith on this appearance and written repesentation, thereby actually believing the juvenile was over 18.

The Annex clerk is unlikely to prevail with this defense concerning his sale to the 14-year-old boy. No written representation was presented—and how many 14-year-old boys look 18 or older?

**Obscene Films**

As explained above, 2C:34-3 provides prohibitions against the sale, etc., of "obscene material" to persons under 18 years of age. The statute, via subsection c., also provides prohibitions against admitting persons under 18 to a theater exhibiting an "obscene film" and "showing" an "obscene film" to persons under 18 years of age. Both of these offenses are crimes of the third degree.

**2C:34-3.1.**          **Retailer defined**

"Retailer," as used in this act, means any person who operates a store, newsstand, booth, concession or similar business with unimpeded access for persons under 18 years old, who is in the business of making sales of periodicals or other publications at retail containing pictures, drawings or photographs.

**2C:34-3.2.**          **Display of obscene material**

A municipality may enact an ordinance making it a petty disorderly persons offense for a retailer to display or permit to be displayed at his business premises any obscene material as defined in N.J.S. 2C:34-3, at a height of less than 5 feet or without a blinder or other covering placed or printed on the front of the material displayed. Any such ordinance shall contain a provision stating that public display of the obscene material shall constitute presumptive evidence that the retailer knowingly made or permitted the display.

## PRACTICAL APPLICATION OF STATUTE

The owner of The Annex may be guilty of a petty disorderly persons offense for displaying "obscene material" (magazines) on shelves "at a height less than five feet" and without blinders or coverings on the front of the material.

The Annex owner, however, may be able to evade conviction under this statute. Why? Because the statute is only in effect in municipalities that have enacted an ordinance providing for the aforesaid provisions. If The Annex is located in a municipality that has failed to enact such an ordinance, the owner cannot be convicted of the petty disorderly persons offense defined in 2C:34-3.2.

**2C:34-3.**          **Repealed**

**2C:34-4.**          **Public communication of obscenity**

a. "Publicly communicate" means to display, post, exhibit, give away or vocalize material in such a way that its character and content may be readily and distinctly perceived by the public by normal unaided vision or hearing when viewing or hearing it in, on or from a public street, road, thoroughfare, recreation or shopping center or area, public transportation facility or vehicle used for public transportation.

b. A person who knowingly publicly communicates obscene material, as defined in section 2C:34-3 or causes or permits it to be publicly communicated on property he owns or leases or operates is guilty of a crime of the fourth degree.

c. Public communication of obscene material shall constitute presumptive evidence that the defendant made the communication or caused or permitted it to be made knowingly.

## PRACTICAL APPLICATION OF STATUTE

Land owners, lessees, and operators of property cannot "publicly communicate" "obscenity"; that is, "obscene material" as defined in 2C:34-3. Doing so constitutes a crime of the fourth degree.

But what does "publicly communicate" mean? Can a person talking in an obscene manner on his front porch be convicted of 2C:34-4's fourth degree crime? Probably not, as First Amendment rights would likely prevent a conviction. How about a person who puts up a theatrical screen on his front lawn and shows a pornographic movie? Would he be convicted of "publicly communicating" obscenity? In this case, probably yes.

"Publicly communicate" is defined in subsection a. of the statute. The definition primarily provides that "publicly communicate" means the exhibition or vocalization of "obscene material" that a person could readily and distinctly hear or see from areas such as public streets and shopping centers. Accordingly, in the case of the man exhibiting a pornographic movie on his front lawn, he is ripe for a fourth degree crime conviction in a situation where a passer-by or motorist could see or hear the film.

**2C:34-5.**     **Diseased person committing an act of sexual penetration**

    a. A person is guilty of a crime of the fourth degree who, knowing that he or she is infected with a venereal disease such as chancroid, gonorrhea, syphilis, herpes virus, or any of the varieties or stages of such diseases, commits an act of sexual penetration without the informed consent of the other person.

    b. A person is guilty of a crime of the third degree who, knowing that he or she is infected with human immune deficiency virus (HIV) or any other related virus identified as a probable causative agent of acquired immune deficiency syndrome (AIDS), commits an act of sexual penetration without the informed consent of the other person.

## PRACTICAL APPLICATION OF STATUTE

Per subsection a. of 2C:34-5, anyone who commits an act of sexual penetration while "knowing" that he is infected with a venereal disease is guilty of a fourth degree crime. Pursuant to subsection b., anyone who commits an act of sexual penetration while "knowing" that he is infected with HIV or AIDS is guilty of a third degree crime. There is one caveat, though. A person cannot be convicted under this statute if he has the "informed consent" of the person with whom he is having sex. In other words, if Bob's partner knows that Bob has AIDS or the venereal disease herpes and still consents to the act of penetration, Bob cannot be convicted of an offense under 2C:34-5.

**2C:34-6.**     **Definitions**

As used in sections 2 and 3 of this act:

    a. "Sexually oriented business" means:

        (1) A commercial establishment which as one of its principal business purposes offers for sale, rental, or display any of the following:

            Books, magazines, periodicals or other printed material, or photographs, films, motion pictures, video cassettes, slides or other visual representations which depict or describe a "specified sexual activity" or "specified anatomical area"; or still or motion picture machines, projectors or other image-producing devices which show images to one person per machine at any one time, and where the images so displayed are characterized by the depiction of a "specified sexual activity" or "specified anatomical area"; or instruments, devices, or paraphernalia which are designed for use in connection with a "specified sexual activity"; or

(2) A commercial establishment which regularly features live performances characterized by the exposure of a "specified anatomical area" or by a "specified sexual activity," or which regularly shows films, motion pictures, video cassettes, slides, or other photographic representations which depict or describe a "specified sexual activity" or "specified anatomical area."

b. "Person" means an individual, proprietorship, partnership, corporation, association, or other legal entity.

c. "Specified anatomical area" means:

(1) Less than completely and opaquely covered human genitals, pubic region, buttock or female breasts below a point immediately above the top of the areola; or

(2) Human male genitals in a discernibly turgid state, even if covered.

d. "Specified sexual activity" means:

(1) The fondling or other erotic touching of covered or uncovered human genitals, pubic region, buttock or female breast; or

(2) Any actual or simulated act of human masturbation, sexual intercourse or deviate sexual intercourse.

## 2C:34-7.    Sexually oriented business; location; building requirements; penalty

a. Except as provided in a municipal zoning ordinance adopted pursuant to N.J.S.2C:34-2, no person shall operate a sexually oriented business within 1,000 feet of any existing sexually oriented business, or any church, synagogue, temple or other place of public worship, or any elementary or secondary school or any school bus stop, or any municipal or county playground or place of public resort and recreation, or any hospital or any child care center, or within 1,000 feet of any area zoned for residential use. This subsection shall not apply to a sexually oriented business already lawfully operating on the effective date of this act where another sexually oriented business, an elementary or secondary school or school bus stop, or any municipal or county playground or place of public resort and recreation, or any hospital or any child care center, is subsequently established within 1,000 feet, or a residential district or residential lot is subsequently established within 1,000 feet.

b. Every sexually oriented business shall be surrounded by a perimeter buffer of at least 50 feet in width with plantings, fence, or other physical divider along the outside of the perimeter sufficient to impede the view of the interior of the premises in which the business is located. The municipality may, by ordinance, require the perimeter buffer to meet additional requirements or standards. This subsection shall not apply to a sexually oriented business already lawfully operating on the effective date of this act.

c. No sexually oriented business shall display more than two exterior signs, consisting of one identification sign and one sign giving notice that the premises are off limits to minors. The identification sign shall be no more than 40 square feet in size.

d. A person who violates this section is guilty of a crime of the fourth degree.

## PRACTICAL APPLICATION OF STATUTE

2C:34-7 provides a number of requirements that "sexually oriented businesses" must meet. For example, subsection a. sets out that no person shall operate a "sexually oriented business within 1,000 feet" of a number of locations such as churches, schools, school bus stops, hospitals, and other existing sexually oriented businesses. There are exceptions to this provision, though; for instance, if a municipal zoning ordinance provides otherwise. A violation of this subsection, or any subsection of 2C:34-7, constitutes a fourth degree crime. "Sexually oriented business," by the way, is defined in the previous statute, 2C:34-6.

# 35

# CONTROLLED DANGEROUS SUBSTANCES

## FACT PATTERN (PERTAINS TO CHAPTERS 35 AND 36)

Hawthorne, New Jersey, was the site of the year's largest drug bust. The event was sparked by an unlikely perceptive operative, the borough's mayor, Frank Castelleti. The ultimate seizure, however, was the result of careful planning and brave, raw police work carried out by Hawthorne's finest. The department's chief, Seamus Mallorin, orchestrated the monumental law enforcement maneuver with the head of his detective bureau, Captain Ryan O'Dashing.

Mayor Castelleti and his wife, Betty, finished an early supper at one of Hawthorne's quaint Italian eateries, Lancellotti's. As he prepared to pay the $100 bill plus his usual 25% gratuity, Castelleti overheard two out-of-towners discussing an unusual topic—a drug deal. The first man, who stood approximately six feet tall and sported a red beard, advised the other, "Step out to my pickup, and I'll drop you the eight-ball." The second man responded with, "How about a bunch of eight-balls." The red-bearded fellow nodded and said, "Fine."

Castelleti, understanding some drug lingo, knew that the red-bearded gentleman was referring to cocaine. Riled by this illegal intrusion upon Hawthorne, Castelleti immediately phoned the borough's police department and spoke directly to Captain O'Dashing.

A patrol unit, followed by O'Dashing in a detective vehicle, was at Lancellotti's within minutes, where they captured the two men amidst their parking lot CDS transfer, cash being exchanged for several packages of cocaine. A headquarters interrogation of the red-bearded man that followed not only caused O'Dashing to call his chief in from home but resulted in the creation of "Project Red Beard."

In the meantime, Red Beard's car was towed to the Hawthorne Police Department headquarters. There a routine inventory search of the automobile revealed the following: 29 individually wrapped packages of cocaine marked with the logo "Tuned-Up," which totaled 11 ounces in weight; 25 grams of marijuana in a plastic container; a pipe ordinarily used for smoking marijuana; a hypodermic needle; and $2,400 in cash.

Captain O'Dashing, Chief Mallorin, and two Hawthorne detectives positioned themselves in chairs, circling Red Beard, who was handcuffed to a pole in the center of the department's detective bureau. After Miranda warnings were read for a second time following the arrest, a flurry of questions were fired at the drug dealer. Where did he live? Where did he work? Was cocaine distribution his only business? Where did he obtain his cocaine? How about the marijuana? Who did he work with or for? How often did he deal in Hawthorne? Was this his main venue of operation or was he just passing through?

Red Beard was initially unfazed by the officers' questions, only advising that he did not reside in Hawthorne. However, his demeanor changed when Captain O'Dashing slapped a copy of the man's New Jersey driver's license against the pole.

"Where did you get that?" Red Beard demanded. "I don't carry any ID."

O'Dashing replied with a slight smile and then looked to Chief Mallorin who unleashed a twenty-page rap sheet. As the document unraveled from the top of the pole to the floor, Red Beard mumbled, "Okay, I'll talk."

Chief Mallorin responded with a third Miranda reading and inquired, "Are you sure you don't want an attorney present?" Red Beard looked at him and the rap sheet and answered, "Just get a prosecutor down here so we can cut a deal. I know I'm looking at a lot of time without a deal." An assistant prosecutor was then summoned from the Passaic County Prosecutor's Office. After her arrival, the cocaine dealer was promised a plea agreement, which provided for a reduced prison sentence in exchange for specifics about what Red Beard termed "a monumental drug bust." And yes, a monumental drug bust it would be.

Red Beard rolled—and rolled hard—on a close friend, Charlie Chaplowitz. Ironically, although the two men were both in the business of selling drugs, they kept their business dealings separate. Red Beard, currently a resident of Hunterdon County, was actually in Hawthorne on the day of his arrest to meet with Chaplowitz. The two had been friends since childhood and still shared each other's company to discuss their various business ventures and to play chess.

According to Red Beard, the men were quite different in their affairs and personalities. Chaplowitz was a quiet, well-dressed restauranteur who never used drugs. He also had never been arrested and was never suspected by law enforcement of any illegal activities whatsoever. Chaplowitz was a ten-year resident of Hawthorne.

Red Beard, on the other hand, was a traveler, never living in any one town for more than two years. He was a career drug dealer and hardly put up a front that he was involved in any legitimate businesses. He also regularly smoked marijuana and dabbled in other, more serious controlled dangerous substances such as heroin. That drug was one of the reasons why Red Beard liked to meet with Chaplowitz—because Chaplowitz provided him with his personal stash of heroin. Many times, though, Red Beard won his little packages of junk when he was the victor of their chess matches; Chaplowitz simply gave it to him. As the assistant prosecutor and the Hawthorne officers learned, Charlie Chaplowitz had plenty of heroin to spare.

Approximately one-half mile from Lancellotti's was another thriving Hawthorne restaurant, The Fire Down Under. Serving a variety of spicy entrees and unusual pasta dishes, The Fire Down Under also doubled as an upscale dance club on Friday and Saturday nights. Unusual about the restaurant was that although the building had a large lower level, it was never utilized for dining or dancing. Chaplowitz, the apparent owner of The Fire Down Under, held out that the space was reserved for "future plans." No one ever had a reason to suspect anything illicit about Chaplowitz, the restaurant, or the empty space, so his assertion about "future plans" went unquestioned. Chaplowitz's plans, however, were quite current—and the space was far from empty.

Located on the lower level of The Fire Down Under was a carefully plotted and controlled heroin manufacturing and distribution hub. Ten employees, working directly under Chaplowitz's command, prepared and packaged large quantities of heroin that were disseminated to multiple street dealers across New Jersey. Four other silent partners joined Chaplowitz as financiers of the network. The drug was never sold in small quantities, and it was never distributed in the restaurant. Buyers were strictly dealers who appeared in person at various highway locations to pick up weekly supplies of heroin. It was a cash-and-carry business.

Chief Mallorin assessed the situation with Captain O'Dashing and the assistant prosecutor. His first thought was to simply procure a search warrant based on Red Beard's information. However, O'Dashing, who had been searching tax records, advised that the restaurant and property were actually owned by a corporation whose principals did not include Chaplowitz. Without this direct ownership link to The Fire Down Under, he thought problems might arise when trying to legally tie Chaplowitz to the restuaruant and its lower level.

Mallorin needed a different plan to ensure an airtight case against Chaplowitz. The Chief wanted to act quickly because he feared that as more time passed it would become more likely that Chaplowitz would learn of Red Beard's arrest. With this in mind, he arranged for Red Beard to phone Chaplowitz and advise that he was delayed in reaching Hawthorne. Mallorin then made a tactical, but risky, decision.

Red Beard was suited with a wire and told to meet Chaplowitz at The Fire Down Under, as they had agreed in their phone conversation. Joining Red Beard, however, would be the newest addition to Hawthorne's police department, Cole Morrison. Although a recent arrival, Morrison was a ten-year law enforcement veteran, having transferred from the Essex County Sheriff's Department. He was a street-smart officer and personally physically equipped, able to bench-press well over 400 pounds. Chief Mallorin was confident in Morrison's abilities, but he knew Chaplowitz would be wary of his presence.

To counteract Chaplowitz's likely suspicions, Mallorin and O'Dashing formed a simple but important plan. Their goal was to make the drug kingpin comfortable with Morrison—comfortable enough to show him his heroin manufacturing center.

Red Beard and Morrison were to be cousins. Morrison was new to New Jersey, having arrived from California a month prior. In California, Morrison dealt in heroin, although only in small amounts. Because Red Beard limited his dealing to cocaine, Morrison would be a perfect street partner for him—someone he knew and trusted and someone who was accustomed to dealing that substance. Morrison was quickly schooled in Red Beard's background: his age, mother's and sister's names, the fact that his father was deceased, his delight in smoking marijuana, his abilities in chess, the type of vehicle he drove. Then the men were off to meet with Charlie Chaplowitz.

An hour later, a conversation unfolded where Morrison talked in passing about Aunt Carol and joked, much to Red Beard's chagrin, about how Cousin Cindy was "hot." The authenticity of their personal bantering was an instant sale. Chaplowitz, never suspecting that Red Beard would roll on him, invited the pair into the lower level to play chess and to inspect the operation and sample the product. Within minutes, half of the Hawthorne Police Department, accompanied by several prosecutor's office narcotics investigators, descended into the bowels of The Fire Down Under. They arrested Charlie Chaplowitz and seven of his employees—and confiscated over 500 pounds of pure heroin.

A subsequent, thorough search of the manufacturing center revealed that there was only one entrance/exit door to the lower level. The door was made of solid, thick steel and surrounded by an intricate, but cleverly hidden, alarm device. The alarm, it was later learned, only notified Chaplowitz and his direct underlings if it was activated. Beyond the steel door was a hallway, which led to a similar steel door and alarm device. This door not only required two keys for entrance but also a computerized security card. Once through this door, those entering would come into a dark, large empty room. There a flashlight was procured to lead the entering individuals to a special unmarked brick located in the center of a brick-walled fireplace. Upon pushing the brick, a secret passage opened up, which led the individuals down a flight of stairs and into the manufacturing center. Law enforcement personnel were not going to find Chaplowitz's operation unless he, or someone involved with him, led them to it. Unfortunately for him, he was duped by a disloyal friend and a few crafty, gutsy police officers.

## 2C:35-1.    Short title

This act shall be known and may be cited as the "Comprehensive Drug Reform Act of 1987."

## 2C:35-1.1.    Declaration of policy and legislative findings

The Legislature hereby finds and declares to be the public policy of this State, the following:

a. By enactment of the "New Jersey Code of Criminal Justice," N.J.S. 2C:1-1 et seq., the Legislature recognized the need for the comprehensive reevaluation, revision, consolidation and codification of our criminal laws, and the need to ensure a uniform, consistent and predictable system for the sentencing of convicted offenders, focusing principally on the seriousness and degree of dangerousness inherent in a particular offense. In enacting the sentencing provisions of the penal code, the Legislature recognized that the imposition of a uniform, consistent and predictable sentence for a given offense is an essential prerequisite to any rational deterrent scheme designed ultimately to reduce the incidence of crime.

b. Despite the impressive efforts and gains of our law enforcement agencies, the unlawful use, manufacture and distribution of controlled dangerous substances continues to pose a serious and pervasive threat to the health, safety and welfare of the citizens of this State. New Jersey continues to experience an unacceptably high rate of drug-related crime, and continues to serve as a conduit for the illegal trafficking of drugs to and from other jurisdictions. In addition to the harm suffered by the victims of drug abuse and drug-related crime, the incidence of such offenses is directly related to the rate of other violent and nonviolent crimes, including murder, assault, robbery, theft, burglary and organized criminal activities. For this reason, enhanced and coordinated efforts designed specifically to curtail drug-related offenses will lead inexorably to a reduction in the rate of crime generally, and is therefore decidedly in the public interest.

c. In order to be effective, the battle against drug abuse and drug-related crime must be waged aggressively at every level along the drug distribution chain, but in particular, our criminal laws must target for expedited prosecution and enhanced punishment those repeat drug offenders and upper echelon members of organized narcotics trafficking networks who pose the greatest danger to society. In order to ensure the most efficient and effective dedication of limited investigative, prosecutorial, judicial and correctional resources, it is the policy of this State to distinguish between drug offenders based on the seriousness of the offense, considering principally the nature, quantity and purity of the controlled substance involved, and the role of the actor in the overall drug distribution network. It is the intention of the Legislature to provide for the strict punishment, deterrence and incapacitation of the most culpable and dangerous drug offenders, and to facilitate where feasible the rehabilitation of drug dependent persons so as ultimately to reduce the demand for illegal controlled dangerous substances and the incidence of drug-related crime. It is also the policy of this State to afford special protection to children from the perils of drug trafficking, to ensure that all schools and areas adjacent to schools are kept free from drug distribution activities, and to provide especially stern punishment for those drug offenders who operate on or near schools and school buses, who distribute to juveniles, or who employ juveniles in a drug distribution scheme. In addition, our criminal laws and sentencing practices must be reexamined and amended so as to minimize pretrial delay, thereby to ensure the prompt disposition of all drug-related criminal charges and the prompt imposition of fair and certain punishment.

d. Under the current drug laws, there are inadequate sentencing guidelines with which consistently to identify the most serious offenders and offenses and to guard against sentencing disparity and the resulting depreciation of the deterrent thrust of the criminal law. In order to protect the public interest, and so as to deter, disrupt and eliminate the operation of organized drug trafficking networks, it is necessary to undertake a comprehensive reexamination of our controlled dangerous substances laws, procedures and sentencing practices. The transfer of the provisions of the "New Jersey Controlled Dangerous Substances Act," P.L. 1970, c. 226 (C. 24:21-1 et seq.) into the penal code which is accomplished herein, along with the amendments and supplements thereto, will better ensure that the most culpable drug offenders will be subject to swift prosecutions and strict, consistently imposed criminal sanctions.

## 2C:35-1.2.     Reference to Code of Criminal Justice

Whenever in any law, rule or regulation, reference is made to the "New Jersey Controlled Dangerous Substances Act," P.L. 1970, c. 226 (C. 24:21-1 et seq.) or any part thereof, the same shall mean and refer to the appropriate chapter, section or provision of the "New Jersey Code of Criminal Justice" as amended and supplemented herein. Similarly, any reference to chapter 35 or 36 in the "New Jersey Code of Criminal Justice" shall be deemed to incorporate P.L.1970, c.226 (C.24:21-1 et seq.) or any other predecessor statute.

## 2C:35-2.     Definitions

As used in this chapter:

"Administer" means the direct application of a controlled dangerous substance or controlled substance analog, whether by injection, inhalation, ingestion, or any other means, to the body of a patient or research subject by: (1) a practitioner (or, in his presence, by his lawfully authorized agent), or (2) the patient or research subject at the lawful direction and in the presence of the practitioner.

"Agent" means an authorized person who acts on behalf of or at the direction of a manufacturer, distributor, or dispenser but does not include a common or contract carrier, public warehouseman, or employee thereof.

"Controlled dangerous substance" means a drug, substance, or immediate precursor in Schedules I through V, any substance the distribution of which is specifically prohibited in N.J.S.2C:35-3, in section 3 of P.L.1997, c.194 (C.2C:35-5.2) or in section 5 of P.L.1997,c. 194 (C.2C:35-5.3) and any drug or substance which, when ingested, is metabolized or otherwise becomes a controlled dangerous substance in the human body. When any statute refers to controlled dangerous substances, or to a specific controlled dangerous substance, it shall also be deemed to refer to any drug or substance which, when ingested, is metabolized or otherwise becomes a controlled dangerous substance or the specific controlled dangerous substance, and to any substance that is an immediate precursor of a controlled dangerous substance or the specific controlled dangerous substance. The term shall not include distilled spirits, wine, malt beverages, as those terms are defined or used in R.S.33:1-1 et seq., or tobacco and tobacco products. The term, wherever it appears in any law or administrative regulation of this State, shall include controlled substance analogs.

"Controlled substance analog" means a substance that has a chemical structure substantially similar to that of a controlled dangerous substance and that was specifically designed to produce an effect substantially similar to that of a controlled dangerous substance. The term shall not include a substance manufactured or distributed in conformance with the provisions of an approved new drug application or an exemption for investigational use within the meaning of section 505 of the "Federal Food, Drug and Cosmetic Act," 52 Stat. 1052 (21 U.S.C. s. 355).

"Counterfeit substance" means a controlled dangerous substance or controlled substance analog which, or the container or labeling of which, without authorization, bears the trademark, trade name, or other identifying mark, imprint, number or device, or any likeness thereof, of a manufacturer, distributor, or dispenser other than the person or persons who in fact manufactured, distributed or dispensed such substance and which thereby falsely purports or is represented to be the product of, or to have been distributed by, such other manufacturer, distributor, or dispenser.

"Deliver" or "delivery" means the actual, constructive, or attempted transfer from one person to another of a controlled dangerous substance or controlled substance analog, whether or not there is an agency relationship.

"Dispense" means to deliver a controlled dangerous substance or controlled substance analog to an ultimate user or research subject by or pursuant to the lawful order of a practitioner, including the prescribing, administering, packaging, labeling, or compounding necessary to prepare the substance for that delivery. "Dispenser" means a practitioner who dispenses.

"Distribute" means to deliver other than by administering or dispensing a controlled dangerous substance or controlled substance analog. "Distributor" means a person who distributes.

"Drugs" means (a) substances recognized in the official United States Pharmacopoeia, official Homeopathic Pharmacopoeia of the United States, or official National Formulary, or any supplement to any of them; and (b) substances intended for use in the diagnosis, cure, mitigation, treatment, or prevention of disease in man or other animals; and (c) substances (other than food) intended to affect the structure or any function of the body of man or other animals; and (d) substances intended for use as a component of any article specified in subsections (a), (b) and (c) of this section; but does not include devices or their components, parts or accessories.

"Drug or alcohol dependent person" means a person who as a result of using a controlled dangerous substance or controlled substance analog or alcohol has been in a state of psychic or physical dependence, or both, arising from the use of that controlled dangerous substance or controlled substance analog or alcohol on a continuous or repetitive basis. Drug or alcohol dependence is characterized by behavioral and other responses, including but not limited to a strong compulsion to take the substance on a recurring basis in order to experience its psychic effects, or to avoid the discomfort of its absence.

"Hashish" means the resin extracted from any part of the plant Genus Cannabis L. and any compound, manufacture, salt, derivative, mixture, or preparation of such resin.

"Manufacture" means the production, preparation, propagation, compounding, conversion or processing of a controlled dangerous substance or controlled substance analog, either directly or by extraction from substances of natural origin, or independently by means of chemical synthesis, or by a combination of extraction and chemical synthesis, and includes any packaging or repackaging of the substance or labeling or relabeling of its container, except that this term does not include the preparation or compounding of a controlled dangerous substance or controlled substance analog by an individual for his own use or the preparation, compounding, packaging, or labeling of a controlled dangerous substance: (1) by a practitioner as an incident to his administering or dispensing of a controlled dangerous substance or controlled substance analog in the course of his professional practice, or (2) by a practitioner (or under his supervision) for the purpose of, or as an incident to, research, teaching, or chemical analysis and not for sale.

"Marijuana" means all parts of the plant Genus Cannabis L., whether growing or not; the seeds thereof, and every compound, manufacture, salt, derivative, mixture, or preparation of such plant or its seeds, except those containing resin extracted from such plant; but shall not include the mature stalks of such plant, fiber produced from such stalks, oil or cake made from the seeds of such plant, any other compound, manufacture, salt, derivative, mixture, or preparation of such mature stalks, fiber, oil, or cake, or the sterilized seed of such plant which is incapable of germination.

"Narcotic drug" means any of the following, whether produced directly or indirectly by extraction from substances of vegetable origin, or independently by means of chemical synthesis, or by a combination of extraction and chemical synthesis:

a. Opium, coca leaves, and opiates;

b. A compound, manufacture, salt, derivative, or preparation of opium, coca leaves, or opiates;

c. A substance (and any compound, manufacture, salt, derivative, or preparation thereof) which is chemically identical with any of the substances referred to in subsections (a) and (b), except that the words "narcotic drug" as used in this act shall not include decocainized coca leaves or extracts of coca leaves, which extracts do not contain cocaine or ecogine.

"Opiate" means any dangerous substance having an addiction-forming or addiction-sustaining liability similar to morphine or being capable of conversion into a drug having such addiction-forming or addiction-sustaining liability. It does not include, unless specifically designated as controlled pursuant to the provisions of section 3 of P.L.1970, c.226 (C.24:21-3), the dextrorotatory isomer of 3-methoxy-n-methylmorphinan and its salts (dextromethorphan). It does include its racemic and levorotatory forms.

"Opium poppy" means the plant of the species Papaver somniferum L., except the seeds thereof.

"Person" means any corporation, association, partnership, trust, other institution or entity or one or more individuals.

"Plant" means an organism having leaves and a readily observable root formation, including, but not limited to, a cutting having roots, a rootball or root hairs.

"Poppy straw" means all parts, except the seeds, of the opium poppy, after mowing.

"Practitioner" means a physician, dentist, veterinarian, scientific investigator, laboratory, pharmacy, hospital or other person licensed, registered, or otherwise permitted to distribute, dispense, conduct research with respect to, or administer a controlled dangerous substance or controlled substance analog in the course of professional practice or research in this State.

a. "Physician" means a physician authorized by law to practice medicine in this or any other state and any other person authorized by law to treat sick and injured human beings in this or any other state.

b. "Veterinarian" means a veterinarian authorized by law to practice veterinary medicine in this State.

c. "Dentist" means a dentist authorized by law to practice dentistry in this State.

d. "Hospital" means any federal institution, or any institution for the care and treatment of the sick and injured, operated or approved by the appropriate State department as proper to be entrusted with the custody and professional use of controlled dangerous substances or controlled substance analogs.

e. "Laboratory" means a laboratory to be entrusted with the custody of narcotic drugs and the use of controlled dangerous substances or controlled substance analogs for scientific, experimental and medical purposes and for purposes of instruction approved by the State Department of Health and Senior Services.

"Production" includes the manufacture, planting, cultivation, growing, or harvesting of a controlled dangerous substance or controlled substance analog.

"Immediate precursor" means a substance which the State Department of Health and Senior Services has found to be and by regulation designates as being the principal compound commonly used or produced primarily for use, and which is an immediate chemical intermediary used or likely to be used in the manufacture of a controlled dangerous substance or controlled substance analog, the control of which is necessary to prevent, curtail, or limit such manufacture.

"Residential treatment facility" means any facility licensed and approved by the Department of Health and Senior Services and which is approved by any county probation department for the inpatient treatment and rehabilitation of drug or alcohol dependent persons.

"Schedules I, II, III, IV, and V" are the schedules set forth in sections 5 through 8 of P.L.1970, c.226 (C.24:21-5 through 24:21-8) and in section 4 of P.L.1971, c.3 (C.24:21-8.1) and as modified by any regulations issued by the Commissioner of Health and Senior Services pursuant to his authority as provided in section 3 of P.L.1970, c.226 (C.24:21-3).

"State" means the State of New Jersey.

"Ultimate user" means a person who lawfully possesses a controlled dangerous substance or controlled substance analog for his own use or for the use of a member of his household or for administration to an animal owned by him or by a member of his household.

"Prescription legend drug" means any drug which under federal or State law requires dispensing by prescription or order of a licensed physician, veterinarian or dentist and is required to bear the statement "Caution: Federal law prohibits dispensing without a prescription" and is not a controlled dangerous substance or stramonium preparation.

"Stramonium preparation" means a substance prepared from any part of the stramonium plant in the form of a powder, pipe mixture, cigarette, or any other form with or without other ingredients.

"Stramonium plant" means the plant Datura Stramonium Linne, including Datura Tatula Linne.

**2C:35-3.        Leader of narcotics trafficking network**

As used in this section:

"Financier" means a person who, with the intent to derive a profit, provides money or credit or other thing of value in order to purchase a controlled dangerous substance or an immediate precursor, or otherwise to finance the operations of a drug trafficking network.

A person is a leader of a narcotics trafficking network if he conspires with two or more other persons in a scheme or course of conduct to unlawfully manufacture, distribute, dispense, bring into or transport in this State methamphetamine, lysergic acid diethylamide, phencyclidine, gamma hydroxybutyrate, flunitrazepam or any controlled dangerous substance classified in Schedule I or II, or any controlled substance analog thereof as a financier, or as an organizer, supervisor or manager of at least one other person.

Leader of narcotics trafficking network is a crime of the first degree and upon conviction thereof, except as may be provided by N.J.S.2C:35-12, a person shall be sentenced to an ordinary term of life imprisonment during which the person must serve 25 years before being eligible for parole. Notwithstanding the provisions of subsection a. of N.J.S.2C:43-3, the court may also impose a fine not to exceed $750,000.00 or five times the street value of the controlled dangerous substance, controlled substance analog, gamma hydroxybutyrate or flunitrazepam involved, whichever is greater.

Notwithstanding the provisions of N.J.S.2C:1-8, a conviction of leader of narcotics trafficking network shall not merge with the conviction for any offense which is the object of the conspiracy. Nothing contained in this section shall prohibit the court from imposing an extended term pursuant to N.J.S.2C:43-7; nor shall this section be construed in any way to preclude or limit the prosecution or conviction of any person for conspiracy under N.J.S.2C:5-2, or any prosecution or conviction under N.J.S.2C:35-4 (maintaining or operating a CDS production facility), N.J.S.2C:35-5 (manufacturing, distributing or dispensing), N.J.S.2C:35-6 (employing a juvenile in a drug distribution scheme), N.J.S.2C:35-9 (strict liability for drug induced death), N.J.S.2C:41-2 (racketeering activities) or subsection g. of N.J.S.2C:5-2 (leader of organized crime).

It shall not be necessary in any prosecution under this section for the State to prove that any intended profit was actually realized. The trier of fact may infer that a particular scheme or course of conduct was undertaken for profit from all of the attendant circumstances, including but not limited to the number of persons involved in the scheme or course of conduct, the actor's net worth and his expenditures in relation to his legitimate sources of income, the amount or purity of the specified controlled dangerous substance, controlled substance analog, gamma hydroxybutyrate or flunitrazepam involved, or the amount of cash or currency involved.

It shall not be a defense to a prosecution under this section that such controlled dangerous substance, controlled substance analog, gamma hydroxybutyrate or flunitrazepam was brought into or transported in this State solely for ultimate distribution or dispensing in another jurisdiction; nor shall it be a defense that any profit was intended to be made in another jurisdiction.

It shall not be a defense that the defendant was subject to the supervision or management of another, nor that another person or persons were also leaders of the narcotics trafficking network.

## PRACTICAL APPLICATION OF STATUTE

Charlie Chaplowitz should be prosecuted as a leader of a narcotics trafficking network for his operation headquartered at The Fire Down Under restaurant in Hawthorne. This is a crime of the first degree as stated in 2C:35-3.

A person is a leader of a narcotics trafficking network if two elements are met: (1) he conspires with two or more other persons in a scheme or course of conduct to unlawfully manufacture, distribute, dispense, or bring into the state one of a number of drugs; and (2) he has some sort of leadership position in the conspiracy, such as a financier or manager of at least one other person.

A person can only be charged under this statute if he is the leader of a drug dealing scheme that involves methamphetamine (speed), lysergic acid diethylamide (LSD), phencyclidine (PCP), gamma hydroxybutyrate (GHB), flunitrazepam (roofies), or any controlled dangerous substance classified in Schedule I or II. In other words, while the manufacture/distribution of a multitude of substances can result in a charge under 2C:35-5, there are several others (specifically, those classified in Schedules III, IV, and V) that do not warrant a charge. Please note here that a detailed discussion of the different substances found in Schedules I, II, III, IV, and V will be provided in the Practical Application section for 2C:35-5.

Charlie Chaplowitz ran The Fire Down Under restaurant in Hawthorne. However, while his patrons were dining and dancing in the upper level of the establishment, Chaplowitz was cooking up and packaging hundreds of pounds of heroin in the restaurant's lower level. Pursuant to a plan devised by Hawthorne top police brass, Chief Seamus Mallorin and Detective Captain Ryan O'Dashing, an undercover officer, aided by an informant, infiltrated the facility. Chaplowitz and several co-conspirators were then quickly arrested. Coinciding with the arrests was the seizure of over 500 pounds of heroin.

Hawthorne Police uncovered a massive drug dealing scheme that stretched across the entire Garden State. Charlie Chaplowitz, an unassuming restauranteur, headed a carefully plotted and controlled heroin manufacturing and distribution hub. Ten employees, working directly under Chaplowitz's command, prepared and packaged large quantities of heroin that were disseminated to multiple street dealers across New Jersey. The network was financed by Chaplowitz and four other silent partners.

Here, Chaplowitz should be charged as a leader of a narcotics trafficking network as all the elements of the offense have been met. First, Chaplowitz conspired with several individuals to manufacture and distribute heroin, a controlled dangerous substance classified in Schedule I. His co-conspirators included four silent partners who financed the scheme with him and the several employees that worked under his command. Chaplowitz's managerial role in the business, along with his position as a financier, ensures that the offense's second element has been met. Accordingly, Chaplowitz should be charged as the leader of a narcotics trafficking network.

### No Defense Under Management of Another or That Another Is Charged with the Offense

It is important to note that other members of Chaplowitz's narcotics trafficking scheme could also be charged under 2C:35-3. The statute provides that it shall not be a defense that a defendant was subject to the management of another nor that "another person or persons were also leaders of the narcotics trafficking network." In other words, if all the elements of the offense are met—the conspiracy, the financier/management component, and the right kind of drugs—then a number of individuals could conceivably be charged as a leader of one particular narcotics trafficking network. In Chaplowitz's case, it is very likely that his silent partners, as well as some of the employees that worked under him, would face this charge.

**2C:35-4.**     ### Maintaining or operating a controlled dangerous substance facility

Except as authorized by P.L.1970, c.226 (C.24:21-1 et seq.), any person who knowingly maintains or operates any premises, place or facility used for the manufacture of methamphetamine, lysergic acid diethylamide, phencyclidine, gamma hydroxybutyrate, flunitrazepam, marijuana in an amount greater than five pounds or ten plants or any substance listed in Schedule I or II, or the analog of any such substance, or any person who knowingly aids, promotes, finances or otherwise participates in the maintenance or operations of such premises, place or facility, is guilty of a crime of the first degree and shall, except as provided in N.J.S.2C:35-12, be sentenced to a term of imprisonment which shall include the imposition of a minimum term which shall be fixed at, or between, one-third and one-half of the sentence imposed, during which the defendant shall be ineligible for parole. Notwithstanding the provisions of subsection a. of N.J.S.2C:43-3, the court may also impose a fine not to exceed $750,000.00 or five times the street value of all controlled dangerous substances, controlled substance analogs, gamma hydroxybutyrate or flunitrazepam at any time manufactured or stored at such premises, place or facility, whichever is greater.

### PRACTICAL APPLICATION OF STATUTE

Maintaining or operating a controlled dangerous substance production facility is a crime of the first degree. Charlie Chaplowitz is guilty of this offense.

Anyone who maintains/operates—or aids, promotes, or finances—a facility used for the manufacture of serious controlled dangerous substances, such as heroin, LSD, GHB, and methamphetamine, is guilty of violating 2C:35-4. Other drugs that can give rise to a charge under this statute are PCP, flunitrazepam, marijuana (where the amount involved is greater than five pounds or ten plants), and any substance listed in Schedules I or II.

Charlie Chaplowitz is guilty of violating 2C:35-4, for he maintained and operated a facility that manufactured the Schedule I substance heroin. This facility, located at the lower level of his restaurant, The Fire Down Under, served as a major manufacturing and distribution center for this illegal drug; at the time it was infiltrated by police, in fact, 500 pounds of the substance was confiscated. Because Chaplowitz was the mastermind behind this huge drug dealing operation who actively maintained and operated the facility at The Fire Down Under, he is guilty of violating 2C:35-4.

## 2C:35-4.1.    Booby traps in manufacturing or distribution facilities; fortified premises

a. As used in this section:

   (1) "Booby trap" means any concealed or camouflaged device designed or reasonably likely to cause bodily injury when triggered by the action of a person entering a property or building or any portion thereof, or moving on the property or in the building, or by the action of another person. The term includes, but is not limited to, firearms, ammunition or destructive devices activated by a trip wire or other triggering mechanism, sharpened stakes, traps, and lines or wires with hooks, weights or other objects attached.

   (2) "Structure" means any building, room, ship, vessel or airplane and also means any place adapted for overnight accommodation of persons, or for carrying on business therein, whether or not the person is actually present.

b. Any person who knowingly assembles, maintains, places or causes to be placed a booby trap on property used for the manufacture, distribution, dispensing, or possession or control with intent to manufacture, distribute or dispense, controlled dangerous substances in violation of this chapter shall be guilty of a crime of the second degree. If the booby trap causes bodily injury to any person, the defendant shall be guilty of a crime of the first degree.

   It shall not be a defense that the device was inoperable or was not actually triggered, or that its existence or location was known to a law enforcement officer or another person.

c. Any person who fortifies or maintains in a fortified condition a structure for the manufacture, distribution, dispensing or possession or control with intent to manufacture, distribute or dispense, controlled dangerous substances, or who violates section 3, 4, 5, 6 or 7 of chapter 35 in a structure which he owns, leases, occupies or controls, and which has been fortified, is guilty of a crime of the third degree. A structure has been fortified if steel doors, wooden planking, cross bars, alarm systems, dogs, lookouts or any other means are employed to prevent, impede, delay or provide warning of the entry into a structure or any part of a structure by law enforcement officers.

d. A booby trap or fortification is maintained if it remains on property or in a structure while the property or structure is owned, occupied, controlled or used by the defendant.

e. Nothing herein shall be deemed to preclude, if the evidence so warrants, an indictment and conviction for a violation of chapters 11, 12, 17, and 39 of this title, or any other law. Notwithstanding the provisions of N.J.S.2C:1-8, N.J.S.2C:44-5 or any other provisions of law, a conviction arising under this section shall not merge with a conviction for a violation of any section of chapter 35 of Title 2C of the New Jersey Statutes, or for conspiring or attempting to violate any section of chapter 35 of Title 2C of the New Jersey Statutes, and the sentence imposed upon a violation of this section shall be ordered to be served consecutively to that imposed for any other conviction arising under any section of chapter 35 of Title 2C of the New Jersey Statutes or for conspiracy or attempt to violate any section of chapter 35 of Title 2C of the New Jersey Statutes, unless the court, in consideration of the character and circumstances of the defendant, finds that imposition of consecutive sentences would be a serious injustice which overrides the need to deter such conduct by others. If the court does not impose a consecutive sentence, the sentence shall not become final for 10 days in order to permit the appeal of such sentence by the prosecution.

## PRACTICAL APPLICATION OF STATUTE

### Booby Traps

If Charlie Chaplowitz had set up "booby traps" in his heroin manufacturing facility, he would have been guilty of a second degree crime. Booby traps are basically any "concealed or camouflaged" devices that are erected in an effort to cause bodily injury to any unwanted persons who enter a drug manufacturing house. Chaplowitz did not utilize booby traps at his facility at The Fire Down Under—but he did fortify the structure.

### Fortified Premises

One who "fortifies" a drug manufacturing facility is guilty of a third degree crime. A structure is considered to be fortified if items such as steel doors, wooden planking, or alarm systems are put in place in order to prevent, impede, or provide warning of the entrance by law enforcement officers into the facility. The use of dogs or lookouts is also prohibited under the statute.

Charlie Chaplowitz maintained a massive heroin manufacturing center in the lower level of his restaurant, The Fire Down Under. In an effort to prevent law enforcement officers (or any other uninvited guests) from entering the facility, Chaplowitz fortified the premises with two solid, thick steel doors, a computerized security card system, and a hidden alarm system. But his preventive measures didn't end there. After clearing the steel doors and security card and alarm systems, those entering had to find a special unmarked brick located in the center of a brick-walled fireplace. Upon pushing the brick, a secret passage opened up, which led the individuals down a flight of stairs and into the manufacturing center. This intricate fortification of his facility renders Chaplowitz guilty of a third degree crime.

**2C:35-5.**      **Manufacturing, distributing or dispensing**

a. Except as authorized by P.L.1970, c.226 (C.24:21-1 et seq.), it shall be unlawful for any person knowingly or purposely:

   (1) To manufacture, distribute or dispense, or to possess or have under his control with intent to manufacture, distribute or dispense, a controlled dangerous substance or controlled substance analog; or

   (2) To create, distribute, or possess or have under his control with intent to distribute, a counterfeit controlled dangerous substance.

b. Any person who violates subsection a. with respect to:

   (1) Heroin, or its analog, or coca leaves and any salt, compound, derivative, or preparation of coca leaves, and any salt, compound, derivative, or preparation thereof which is chemically equivalent or identical with any of these substances, or analogs, except that the substances shall not include decocainized coca leaves or extractions which do not contain cocaine or ecogine, or or 3,4-methylenedioxymethamphetamine or 3,4-methylenedioxyamphetamine, in a quantity of five ounces or more including any adulterants or dilutants is guilty of a crime of the first degree. The defendant shall, except as provided in N.J.S.2C:35-12, be sentenced to a term of imprisonment by the court. The term of imprisonment shall include the imposition of a minimum term which shall be fixed at, or between, one-third and one-half of the sentence imposed, during which the defendant shall be ineligible for parole. Notwithstanding the provisions of subsection a. of N.J.S.2C:43-3, a fine of up to $500,000.00 may be imposed;

   (2) A substance referred to in paragraph (1) of this subsection, in a quantity of one-half ounce or more but less than five ounces, including any adulterants or dilutants is guilty of a crime of the second degree;

   (3) A substance referred to in paragraph (1) of this subsection in a quantity less than one-half ounce including any adulterants or dilutants is guilty of a crime of the third degree except that, notwithstanding the provisions of subsection b. of N.J.S.2C:43-3, a fine of up to $75,000.00 may be imposed;

   (4) A substance classified as a narcotic drug in Schedule I or II other than those specifically covered in this section, or the analog of any such substance, in a quantity of one ounce or more including any adulterants or dilutants is guilty of a crime of the second degree;

   (5) A substance classified as a narcotic drug in Schedule I or II other than those specifically covered in this section, or the analog of any such substance, in a quantity of less than one ounce including any adulterants or dilutants is guilty of a crime of the third degree except that, notwithstanding the provisions of subsection b. of N.J.S.2C:43-3, a fine of up to $75,000.00 may be imposed;

   (6) Lysergic acid diethylamide, or its analog, in a quantity of 100 milligrams or more including any adulterants or dilutants, or phencyclidine, or its analog, in a quantity of 10 grams or more including any adulterants or dilutants, is guilty of a crime of the first degree. Except as provided in N.J.S.2C:35-12, the court shall impose a term of imprisonment which shall include the imposition of a minimum term, fixed at, or between, one-third and one-half of the sentence imposed by the court, during which the defendant shall be ineligible for parole. Notwithstanding the provisions of subsection a. of N.J.S.2C:43-3, a fine of up to $500,000.00 may be imposed;

   (7) Lysergic acid diethylamide, or its analog, in a quantity of less than 100 milligrams including any adulterants or dilutants, or where the amount is undetermined, or phencyclidine, or its analog, in a quantity of less than 10 grams including any adulterants or dilutants, or where the amount is undetermined, is guilty of a crime of the second degree;

   (8) Methamphetamine, or its analog, or phenyl-2-propanone (P2P), in a quantity of five ounces or more including any adulterants or dilutants is guilty of a crime of the first degree. Notwithstanding the provisions of subsection a. of N.J.S.2C:43-3, a fine of up to $300,000.00 may be imposed;

   (9) (a) Methamphetamine, or its analog, or phenyl-2-propanone (P2P), in a quantity of one-half ounce or more but less than five ounces including any adulterants or dilutants is guilty of a crime of the second degree;

(b) Methamphetamine, or its analog, or phenyl-2-propanone (P2P), in a quantity of less than one-half ounce including any adulterants or dilutants is guilty of a crime of the third degree except that notwithstanding the provisions of subsection b. of N.J.S.2C:43-3, a fine of up to $75,000.00 may be imposed;

(10) (a) Marijuana in a quantity of 25 pounds or more including any adulterants or dilutants, or 50 or more marijuana plants, regardless of weight, or hashish in a quantity of five pounds or more including any adulterants or dilutants, is guilty of a crime of the first degree. Notwithstanding the provisions of subsection a. of N.J.S.2C:43-3, a fine of up to $300,000.00 may be imposed;

(b) Marijuana in a quantity of five pounds or more but less than 25 pounds including any adulterants or dilutants, or 10 or more but fewer than 50 marijuana plants, regardless of weight, or hashish in a quantity of one pound or more but less than five pounds, including any adulterants and dilutants, is guilty of a crime of the second degree;

(11) Marijuana in a quantity of one ounce or more but less than five pounds including any adulterants or dilutants, or hashish in a quantity of five grams or more but less than one pound including any adulterants or dilutants, is guilty of a crime of the third degree except that, notwithstanding the provisions of subsection b. of N.J.S.2C:43-3, a fine of up to $25,000.00 may be imposed;

(12) Marijuana in a quantity of less than one ounce including any adulterants or dilutants, or hashish in a quantity of less than five grams including any adulterants or dilutants, is guilty of a crime of the fourth degree;

(13) Any other controlled dangerous substance classified in Schedule I, II, III or IV, or its analog, is guilty of a crime of the third degree, except that, notwithstanding the provisions of subsection b. of N.J.S.2C:43-3, a fine of up to $25,000.00 may be imposed; or

(14) Any Schedule V substance, or its analog, is guilty of a crime of the fourth degree except that, notwithstanding the provisions of subsection b. of N.J.S.2C:43-3, a fine of up to $25,000.00 may be imposed.

c. Where the degree of the offense for violation of this section depends on the quantity of the substance, the quantity involved shall be determined by the trier of fact. Where the indictment or accusation so provides, the quantity involved in individual acts of manufacturing, distribution, dispensing or possessing with intent to distribute may be aggregated in determining the grade of the offense, whether distribution or dispensing is to the same person or several persons, provided that each individual act of manufacturing, distribution, dispensing or possession with intent to distribute was committed within the applicable statute of limitations.

## PRACTICAL APPLICATION OF STATUTE

### Schedule I, II, III, IV, and V Substances—Unlawful Distribution Prohibited

2C:35-5 is the statute that prohibits the unlawful manufacturing, distributing, and dispensing of all substances (or their analogs) classified in Schedules I, II, III, IV, and V. The only exceptions for the manufacturing, dispensing, or distributing of these substances (e.g., by medical doctors) are found in P.L. 1970, c. 226 (c. 24:21-1 et seq.). Please note that one who "intends" to manufacture, distribute, or dispense any of these substances is equally culpable under 2C:35-5.

But what exactly are Schedule I, II, III, IV, and V substances? Pursuant to the definitions found in 2C:35-2, the schedules are set forth in sections 5 through 8 of

P.L. 1970, c. 226 (c. 24:21-5 through 24:21-8) and in section 4 of P.L. 1971, c. 3 (c. 24:21-8.1). Okay; now what *are* these substances?

Per 24:21-5, a Schedule I substance is a substance that "(1) has high potential for abuse; and (2) has no accepted medical use in treatment in the United States; or lacks accepted safety for use in treatment under medical supervision." Schedule I substances include opiates, narcotics, and hallucinogenic substances. Examples of Schedule I opiates are acetylmethadol, betameprodine, ketobemidone, and trimeperidine. Heroin, morphine methylbromide, and codeine-n-oxide are some of the narcotics found in Schedule I. Hallucinogens listed in this schedule include LSD, mescaline, and peyote.

A Schedule II substance is defined in 24:21-6 as a substance that "(1) has high abuse potential; (2) has currently accepted medical use in treatment in the United States, or currently accepted medical use with severe restrictions; and (3) abuse may lead to severe psychic or physical dependence." Schedule II substances include cocaine, anileridine, and piminodine.

Per 24:21-7, a Schedule III substance is one that "(1) has a potential for abuse less than the substances listed in Schedules I and II; (2) has currently accepted medical use in treatment in the United States; and (3) abuse may lead to moderate or low physical dependence or high psychological dependence." Examples of Schedule III substances are amphetamine, chlorhexadol, and sulfunethylmethone.

As defined in 24:21-8, a substance is classified in Schedule IV if it "(1) has low potential for abuse relative to the substances listed in Schedule III; (2) has currently accepted medical use in treatment in the United States; and (3) may lead to limited physical dependence or psychological dependence relative to the substances listed in Schedule III." Schedule IV substances include barbital, chloral betaine, and methohexital.

Finally, pursuant to 24:21-8.1, a Schedule V substance is defined as a substance that "(1) has low potential for abuse relative to the substances listed in Schedule IV; (2) has currently accepted medical use in treatment in the United States; and (3) has limited physical dependence or psychological dependence liability relative to substances listed in Schedule IV."

Schedule V substances are primarily compounds or mixtures that contain limited quantities of narcotic drugs within them—but these mixtures contain "one or more nonnarcotic active medicinal ingredients in sufficient proportion to confer upon the mixture, valuable medicinal qualities other than those possessed by the narcotic drug alone." An example of a Schedule V substance is one that contains "not more than 200 milligrams of codeine or any of its salts per 100 milliliters or per 100 grams."

### Specific Drugs Itemized; Quantity of CDS Determines Degree of Offense in Many Categories

While 2C:35-5 prohibits the manufacturing, distributing, and dispensing of all substances classified in Schedules I, II, III, IV, and V, it sets forth specific subsections for heroin, cocaine, LSD, marijuana, hashish, and methamphetamine.

These subsections generally define the degree of the offense based on the *quantity* of the substance involved. For example, 2C:35-5b.(10)(a) provides that a person who distributes marijuana in a "quantity of 25 pounds or more" is guilty of a first degree crime. 2C:35-5b.(10)(b), on the other hand, provides that a second degree crime has been committed where a person distributes marijuana in a quantity of "five pounds or more but less than 25 pounds."

It is interesting to note that the weight of all substances discussed in 2C:35-5 includes "any adulterants or dilutants." However, at the end of the day, as subsection c. of the statute states, the ultimate quantity involved "shall be determined by the trier of fact." This means the jury or judge.

### Heroin and Cocaine Distribution

Red Beard should be charged with a first degree crime for possession of cocaine with the intent to distribute it. Likewise, Charlie Chaplowitz should be charged with a first degree CDS distribution offense arising out of his intent to sell heroin. In both cases, these men face the most serious degree offense—one of the first degree—based on the quantity of drugs that they had in their control and possession.

Per 2C:35-5b.(1), the distribution of heroin in a quantity of five ounces or more is a first degree crime. Likewise, the distribution of powder or crack cocaine (products of coca leaves) in a quantity of five ounces or more is a first degree crime. If the weight of the heroin/cocaine distributed is more than one-half ounce but less than five ounces, the appropriate charge is a second degree crime (see b.(2)). Where the amount involved is less than one-half ounce, a third degree crime has been committed (see b.(3)). Please remember that one can be convicted of all of the above (or for violating any of the subsections found in 2C:35-5) for manufacturing, distributing, dispensing, or *possessing with intent* to manufacture, distribute, or dispense these prohibited drugs. To make things simple, these various activities will be collectively referred to as "distributing" in this Practical Application section.

Mayor Frank Castelleti overheard Red Beard engaging in conversation about a pending cocaine drug deal. In an effort to thwart it, he contacted the Hawthorne Police Department, who immediately responded to the scene. There Red Beard was captured in the process of effectuating a cocaine sale. He was arrested with various drugs in his possession, including 11 ounces of cocaine which had been divided into 29 individually wrapped packages marked with the logo "Tuned-Up."

Clearly, Red Beard was in the business of selling cocaine—the 29 individual packages were not for his personal use. Even more so, he was caught in a transaction, actually distributing the illicit substance for a cash payment. The facts accordingly merit a drug distribution charge rather than simple possession. Given that the ultimate weight of the cocaine confiscated was 11 ounces, exceeding the 5-ounce minimum necessary for a first degree charge, Red Beard is guilty of a first degree cocaine distribution offense.

Charlie Chaplowitz, the drug kingpin handed to Hawthorne Police by Red Beard, similarly is guilty of a first degree drug distribution offense. Simply, Chaplowitz was caught at his CDS manufacturing warehouse with over 500 pounds of heroin, all of which was being prepared and packaged for the purpose of being distributed to buyers. Therefore, Chaplowitz is guilty of first degree heroin distribution.

### Distribution of LSD and PCP

Had Red Beard been caught distributing lysergic acid diethylamide, commonly known as LSD, in an amount of 100 milligrams or more, he would be guilty of a first degree crime pursuant to 2C:35-5b.(6). This same subsection similarly makes it a first degree crime to distribute 10 grams or more of phencyclidine, which is better known as PCP or "angel dust."

Per subsection b.(7), if a person distributes LSD in a quantity of less than 100 milligrams—or where the amount is undetermined—he is guilty of a second degree crime. Likewise, where a person distributes PCP in a quantity of less than ten grams, or where it is undetermined, he is guilty of a second degree offense.

### Marijuana Distribution

Marijuana distribution offenses are graded according to pounds and ounces—and sometimes by the number of plants involved. Under 2C:35-5b.(10)(a), where an individual distributes marijuana in a "quantity of 25 pounds or more," he is guilty of a first degree crime. He is also guilty of a first degree crime if he is busted with 50 or more marijuana plants, possessed for the purpose of distribution; here, weight is not a factor.

Per subsection b.(10)(b), the distributor is guilty of a second degree crime where the quantity of marijuana is "five pounds or more but less than 25 pounds." A second degree crime has also been committed if he is caught with between ten and 50 marijuana plants, possessed for the purpose of distribution. Again, weight is not a factor.

Per subsection b.(11), a person is guilty of a third degree crime if he distributes marijuana in a "quantity of one ounce or more but less than five pounds." Finally, under subsection b.(12), he is guilty of a fourth degree crime where he distributes less than one ounce of marijuana.

### Hashish, Speed, Ecstasy, and Other CDS Distribution

The terms defining the gradation of hashish distribution offenses are found in the same subsections for marijuana distribution, subsections b.(1) through b.(12). Methamphetamine, commonly known as "speed," and P2P distribution offenses are set forth in b.(8) and b.(9). Included within the heroin and cocaine subsections (b.(1) through b.(3)) are the provisions outlawing distribution of 3,4-methylenedioxymethamphetamine and 3,4-methylenedioxyamphetamine, best known as "ecstacy."

Subsections b.(4) and b.(5) provide the different gradations of offenses for distributing any *narcotic* drug in Schedule I or II "other than those specifically covered" in 2C:35-5. Subsection b.(13) sets forth that distribution of "any other controlled dangerous substance classified in Schedule I, II, III or IV" is a third degree offense. This means any CDS in those schedules other than those specifically itemized in the previous subsections. And finally, b.(14) provides that distributing "any Schedule V substance" will result in conviction of a fourth degree crime.

### Distribution of Counterfeit Controlled Dangerous Substances

Pursuant to 2C:35-5a.(2), it is equally illegal to distribute a "counterfeit" version of all the controlled dangerous substances referred to in the statute. Per the definitions set forth in 2C:35-1.2, a counterfeit controlled dangerous substance is basically a CDS that is distributed via false representation that it is legal. For example, a dealer may package a drug, without authorization, in a container that bears a legitimate manufacturer's trademark or trade name, thereby purporting the substance to be distributed by that legitimate company. This, however, is illegal drug distribution to the same extent as any other drug distribution that is prohibited by 2C:35-5.

**2C:35-5.1.    Repealed**

**2C:35-5.2.    Manufacturing, etc. gamma hydroxybutyrate; penalties**

a. Except as authorized by P.L.1970, c.226 (C.24:21-1 et seq.), it shall be a crime of the second degree for any person knowingly or purposely to manufacture, distribute or dispense, or to possess or have under his control with intent to manufacture, distribute or dispense gamma hydroxybutyrate.

b. Notwithstanding the provisions of N.J.S.2C:43-3 or any other law, a fine of up to $150,000.00 may be imposed upon a person who violates this section.

## PRACTICAL APPLICATION OF STATUTE

It is a crime of the second degree for any individual to manufacture, distribute, or possess with the intent to distribute gamma hydroxybutyrate, commonly known as GHB. The statute apparently does not differentiate among quantities of GHD. Accordingly, had Red Beard attempted to sell packages of GHB rather than cocaine, he would be guilty of a second degree crime, regardless of the amount of GHB that he was intending to distribute.

**2C:35-5.3.    Manufacturing, etc. flunitrazepam; penalties**

a. Except as authorized by P.L.1970, c.226 (C.24:21-1 et seq.), it is unlawful for any person knowingly or purposely to manufacture, distribute or dispense, or to possess or have under his control with intent to manufacture, distribute or dispense flunitrazepam.

b. A person who violates subsection a. of this section with respect to flunitrazepam in a quantity of one gram or more is guilty of a crime of the first degree and, notwithstanding the provisions of N.J.S.2C:43-3 or any other law, a fine of up to $250,000.00 may be imposed upon the person.

c. A person who violates subsection a. of this section with respect to flunitrazepam in a quantity of less than one gram is guilty of a crime of the second degree and, notwithstanding the provisions of N.J.S.2C:43-3 or any other law, a fine of up to $150,000.00 may be imposed upon the person.

## PRACTICAL APPLICATION OF STATUTE

Flunitrazepam is known on the streets as "roofies." Per subsection b. of the statute, anyone who distributes this drug in a "quantity of one gram or more" is guilty of a first degree crime. Under subsection c., a person has committed a crime of the second degree if he distributes "less than one gram" of this substance.

**2C:35-5.4.    Short title**

This act shall be known and may be cited as the "Drug Offender Restraining Order Act of 1999."

**2C:35-5.5.    Findings, declarations relative to removal, restraint of certain drug offenders**

The Legislature hereby finds and declares to be the public policy of this State, the following:

a. By the enactment of the "Comprehensive Drug Reform Act of 1987," N.J.S.2C:35-1 et seq., the Legislature recognized that the unlawful manufacture, distribution, possession and use of controlled dangerous substances poses a serious and pervasive threat to the health, safety and welfare of the citizens of this State.

b. In particular, the unlawful manufacture and distribution of controlled dangerous substances can undermine the quality of life enjoyed by all persons who live or work in a neighborhood where such unlawful activity occurs.

c. Persons who engage in unlawful drug activity serve as negative role models for the young, enlist others to join in illicit enterprises, attract violent criminals who prey upon the innocent, and drive away law-abiding citizens, thus having an adverse impact upon legitimate businesses.

d. Displacing those who engage in the unlawful manufacture and distribution of controlled dangerous substances from the situs of their offenses will disrupt drug trafficking by forcing offenders to abandon familiar and comfortable surroundings and requiring them to rely on more cumbersome techniques for conducting street-level transactions. Restraining orders will also protect the public by separating drug offenders from their known markets for sales and purchases of controlled dangerous substances.

## 2C:35-5.6. Definitions relative to removal, restraint of certain offenders

As used in this act:

a. "Person" means any person charged with or convicted of a criminal offense or any juvenile charged with delinquency or adjudicated delinquent for an act which, if committed by an adult, would be a criminal offense.

b. "Place" includes any premises, residence, business establishment, location or specified area including all buildings and all appurtenant land, in which or at which a criminal offense occurred or is alleged to have occurred or is affected by the criminal offense with which the person is charged. "Place" does not include public rail, bus or air transportation lines or limited access highways which do not allow pedestrian access.

c. "Criminal offense" means:

(1) any of the following: N.J.S.2C:35-3, N.J.S.2C:35-4, N.J.S.2C:35-5, N.J.S.2C:35-6, N.J.S.2C:35-8, N.J.S.2C:35-9, P.L.1997, c.185 (C.2C:35-4.1), sections 3 or 5 of P.L.1997, c.194 (C.2C:35-5.2 or C.2C:35-5.3), P.L.1987, c.101 (C.2C:35-7) or P.L.1997, c.327 (C.2C:35-7.1), or

(2) the unlawful possession or use of an assault firearm as defined in subsection w. of N.J.S.2C:39-1.

## 2C:35-5.7. Issuance of order by court

a. When a person is charged with a criminal offense on a warrant and the person is released from custody before trial on bail or personal recognizance, the court, upon application of a law enforcement officer or prosecuting attorney pursuant to section 3 of P.L. 2001, c.365 (C.2C:35-5.9) and except as provided in subsection e. of this section, shall as a condition of release issue an order prohibiting the person from entering any place defined by subsection b. of section 3 of P.L.1999, c.334 (C.2C:35-5.6), including a buffer zone surrounding the place or modifications as provided by subsection f. of this section.

b. When a person is charged with a criminal offense on a summons, the court, upon application of a law enforcement officer or prosecuting attorney pursuant to section 3 of P.L. 2001, c.365 (C.2C:35-5.9) and except as provided in subsection e. of this section, shall, at the time of the defendant's first appearance, issue an order prohibiting the person from entering any place defined by subsection b. of section 3 of P.L.1999, c.334 (C.2C:35-5.6), including a buffer zone surrounding the place or modifications as provided by subsection f. of this section.

c. When a person is charged with a criminal offense on a juvenile delinquency complaint and is released from custody at a detention hearing pursuant to section 19 of P.L.1982, c.77 (C.2A:4A-38), the court, upon application of a law enforcement officer or prosecuting attorney pursuant to section 3 of P.L. 2001, c.365 (C.2C:35-5.9) and except as provided in subsection e. of this section, shall issue an order prohibiting the person from entering any place defined by subsection b. of section 3 of P.L.1999, c.334 (C.2C:35-5.6), including a buffer zone surrounding the place or modifications as provided by subsection f. of this section.

d. When a person is charged with a criminal offense on a juvenile delinquency complaint and is released without being detained pursuant to section 15 or 16 of P.L.1982, c.77 (C.2A:4A:34 or C.2A:4A-35), the law enforcement officer or prosecuting attorney shall prepare an application pursuant to section 3 of P.L. 2001, c.365 (C.2C:35-5.9) for filing on the next court day.

The law enforcement officer releasing the juvenile shall serve the juvenile and his parent or guardian with written notice that an order shall be issued by the Family Part of the Superior Court on the next court day prohibiting the juvenile from entering any place defined by subsection b. of section 3 of P.L.1999, c.334 (C.2C:35-5.6), including a buffer zone surrounding the place or modifications as provided by subsection f. of this section.

The court shall issue such order on the first court day following the release of the juvenile. If the restraints contained in the court order differ from the restraints contained in the notice, the order shall not be effective until the third court day following the issuance of the order. The juvenile may apply to the court to stay or modify the order on the grounds set forth in subsection e. of this section.

e. The court may forego issuing a restraining order for which application has been made pursuant to section 3 of P.L. 2001, c.365 (C.2C:35-5.9) only if the defendant establishes by clear and convincing evidence that:

(1) the defendant lawfully resides at or has legitimate business on or near the place, or otherwise legitimately needs to enter the place. In such an event, the court shall not issue an order pursuant to this section unless the court is clearly convinced that the need to bar the person from the place in order to protect the public safety and the rights, safety and health of the residents and persons working in the place outweighs the person's interest in returning to the place. If the balance of the interests of the person and the public so warrants, the court may issue an order imposing conditions upon the person's entry at, upon or near the place; or

(2) the issuance of an order would cause undue hardship to innocent persons and would constitute a serious injustice which overrides the need to protect the rights, safety and health of persons residing in or having business in the place.

f. A restraining order issued pursuant to subsection a., b., c., d. or h. of this section shall describe the place from which the person has been barred and any conditions upon the person's entry into the place, with sufficient specificity to enable the person to guide his conduct accordingly and to enable a law enforcement officer to enforce the order. The order shall also prohibit the person from entering an area of up to 500 feet surrounding the place, unless the court rules that a different buffer zone would better effectuate the purposes of this act. In the discretion of the court, the order may contain modifications to permit the person to enter the area during specified times for specified purposes, such as attending school during regular school hours. When appropriate, the court may append to the order a map depicting the place. The person shall be given a copy of the restraining order and any appended map and shall acknowledge in writing the receipt thereof.

g. (1) The court shall provide notice of the restraining order to the local law enforcement agency where the arrest occurred and to the county prosecutor.

(2) Notwithstanding the provisions of section 1 of P.L.1982, c.79 (C.2A:4A-60), prior to the person's conviction or adjudication of delinquency for a criminal offense, the local law enforcement agency may post a copy of any orders issued pursuant to this section, or an equivalent notice containing the terms of the order, upon one or more of the principal entrances of the place or in any other conspicuous location. Such posting shall be for the purpose of informing the public, and the failure to post a copy of the order shall in no way excuse any violation of the order.

(3) Notwithstanding the provisions of section 1 of P.L.1982, c.79 (C.2A:4A-60), prior to the person's conviction or adjudication of delinquency for a criminal offense, any law enforcement agency may publish a copy of any orders issued pursuant to this section, or an equivalent notice containing the terms of the order, in a newspaper circulating in the area of the restraining order. Such publication shall be for the purpose of informing the public, and the failure to publish a copy of the order shall in no way excuse any violation of the order.

(4) Notwithstanding the provisions of section 1 of P.L.1982, c.79 (C.2A:4A-60), prior to the person's conviction or adjudication of delinquency for a criminal offense, any law enforcement agency may distribute copies of any orders issued pursuant to this section, or an equivalent notice containing the terms of the order, to residents or businesses located within the area delineated in the order or, in the case of a school or any government-owned property, to the appropriate administrator, or to any tenant association representing the residents of the affected area. Such distribution shall be for the purpose of informing the public, and the failure to publish a copy of the order shall in no way excuse any violation of the order.

h. When a person is convicted of or adjudicated delinquent for any criminal offense, the court, upon application of a law enforcement officer or prosecuting attorney pursuant to section 3 of P.L. 2001, c.365 (C.2C:35-5.9) and except as provided in subsection e. of this section, shall, by separate order or within the judgment of conviction, issue an order prohibiting the person from entering any place defined by subsection b. of section 3 of P.L.1999, c.334 (C.2C:35-5.6), including a buffer zone surrounding the place or modifications as provided by subsection f. of this section. Upon the person's conviction or adjudication of delinquency for a criminal offense, a law enforcement agency, in addition to posting, publishing, and distributing the order or an equivalent notice pursuant to paragraphs (2), (3) and (4) of subsection g. of this section, may also post, publish and distribute a photograph of the person.

i. When a juvenile has been adjudicated delinquent for an act which, if committed by an adult, would be a criminal offense, in addition to an order required by subsection h. of this section or any other disposition authorized by law, the court may order the juvenile and any parent, guardian or any family member over whom the court has jurisdiction to take such actions or obey such restraints as may be necessary to facilitate the rehabilitation of the juvenile or to protect public safety or to safeguard or enforce the rights of residents of the place. The court may commit the juvenile to the care of the Department of Human Services under the responsibility of the Division of Youth and Family Services until such time as the juvenile reaches the age of 18 or until the order of removal and restraint expires, whichever first occurs, or to such alternative residential placement as is practicable.

j. An order issued pursuant to subsection a., b., c. or d. of this section shall remain in effect until the case has been adjudicated or dismissed, or for not less than two years, whichever is less. An order issued pursuant to subsection h. of this section shall remain in effect for such period of time as shall be fixed by the court but not longer than the maximum term of imprisonment or incarceration allowed by law for the underlying offense or offenses. When the court issues a restraining order pursuant to subsection h. of this section and the person is also sentenced to any form of probationary supervision or participation in the Intensive Supervision Program, the court shall make continuing compliance with the order an express condition of probation or the Intensive Supervision Program. When the person has been sentenced to a term of incarceration, continuing compliance with the terms and conditions of the order shall be made an express condition of the person's release from confinement or incarceration on parole. At the time of sentencing or, in the case of a juvenile, at the time of disposition of the juvenile case, the court shall advise the defendant that the restraining order shall include a fixed time period in accordance with this subsection and shall include that provision in the judgment of conviction, dispositional order, separate order or order vacating an existing restraining order, to the law enforcement agency that made the arrest and to the county prosecutor.

k.  All applications to stay or modify an order issued pursuant to this act, including an order originally issued in municipal court, shall be made in the Superior Court. The court shall immediately notify the county prosecutor in writing whenever an application is made to stay or modify an order issued pursuant to this act. If the court does not issue a restraining order, the sentence imposed by the court for a criminal offense as defined in subsection b. of this section shall not become final for ten days in order to permit the appeal of the court's findings by the prosecution.

l.  Nothing in this section shall be construed in any way to limit the authority of the court to take such other actions or to issue such orders as may be necessary to protect the public safety or to safeguard or enforce the rights of others with respect to the place.

m.  Notwithstanding any other provision of this section, the court may permit the person to return to the place to obtain personal belongings and effects and, by court order, may restrict the time and duration and provide for police supervision of such a visit.

## 2C:35-5.8.    Violations, penalties

Violation of any order issued pursuant to this act shall subject the person to civil contempt, criminal contempt, revocation of bail, probation or parole, or any combination of these sanctions and any other sanctions authorized by law. A law enforcement officer may arrest an adult or take into custody a juvenile when an officer has probable cause to believe that the person has violated the terms of any removal and restraining order issued pursuant to section 4 of P.L.1999, c.334 (C.2C:35-5.7).

## 2C:35-5.9.    Certification of offense location

The court shall issue a restraining order pursuant to P.L.1999, c.334 (C.2C:35-5.4 et seq.) only upon request by a law enforcement officer or prosecuting attorney and submission of a certification describing the location of the offense.

## 2C:35-5.10.    Discretion to not seek restraining order

A law enforcement officer or prosecuting attorney shall have discretion to not seek a restraining order pursuant to P.L.1999, c.334 (C.2C:35-5.4 et seq.) if the defendant is charged with an offense resulting from the stop of a motor vehicle, if the defendant was using public transportation, or if the provisions of paragraph (1) or (2) of subsection e. of section 4 of P.L.1999, c.334 (C.2C:35-5.7) are applicable.

## 2C:35-5.11.    Drug enforcement and demand reduction penalty doubled for certain offenses

Any person who possesses, distributes, dispenses or has under his control with intent to distribute or dispense 3,4-methylenedioxymethamphetamine, 3,4-methylenedioxyamphetamine, gammabutyrolactone, gamma hydroxybutyrate or flunitrazepam, or a controlled substance analog of any of these substances, shall, notwithstanding the provisions of any other law, be subject to a drug enforcement and demand reduction penalty of twice the amount otherwise applicable to the offense.

**2C:35-6.**

## Employing a juvenile in a drug distribution scheme

Any person being at least 18 years of age who knowingly uses, solicits, directs, hires or employs a person 17 years of age or younger to violate N.J.S.2C:35-4 or subsection a. of N.J.S.2C:35-5, is guilty of a crime of the second degree and shall, except as provided in N.J.S.2C:35-12, be sentenced to a term of imprisonment which shall include the imposition of a minimum term which shall be fixed at, or between, one-third and one-half of the sentence imposed, or five years, whichever is greater, during which the defendant shall be ineligible for parole. Notwithstanding the provisions of subsection a. of N.J.S.2C:43-3, the court may also impose a fine not to exceed $500,000.00 or five times the street value of the controlled dangerous substance or controlled substance analog involved, whichever is greater.

It shall be no defense to a prosecution under this section that the actor mistakenly believed that the person which the actor used, solicited, directed, hired or employed was 18 years of age or older, even if such mistaken belief was reasonable.

Nothing in this section shall be construed to preclude or limit a prosecution or conviction for a violation of any offense defined in this chapter pursuant to N.J.S.2C:2-6 or any other provision of law governing an actor's liability for the conduct of another, and, notwithstanding the provisions of N.J.S.2C:1-8 or any other provision of law, a conviction arising under this section shall not merge with a conviction for a violation of N.J.S.2C:35-3 (leader of narcotics trafficking network), N.J.S.2C:35-4 (maintaining or operating a CDS production facility), N.J.S.2C:35-5 (manufacturing, distributing or dispensing), or N.J.S.2C:35-9 (strict liability for drug induced death).

## PRACTICAL APPLICATION OF STATUTE

If any one of Charlie Chaplowitz's employees at his heroin manufacturing center was 17 years old or younger, Chaplowitz would be guilty of a second degree crime under 2C:35-6. This is basically a strict liability offense.

2C:35-6 provides that anyone at least 18 years of age who solicits or employs a juvenile (someone 17 or younger) to violate 2C:35-4 (maintain/operate a drug manufacturing center) or 2C:35-5 (distribute CDSs) is guilty of a second degree crime. The statute also provides that it is not a defense if the defendant mistakenly believed that the individual he solicited or employed was 18 or older. Accordingly, Chaplowitz would be strictly liable for violating 2C:35-6 if any of the individuals he employed in his drug distribution operation was under 18 years of age.

**2C:35-7.**

## Distribution on or within 1,000 feet of school property

Any person who violates subsection a. of N.J.S.2C:35-5 by distributing, dispensing or possessing with intent to distribute a controlled dangerous substance or controlled substance analog while on any school property used for school purposes which is owned by or leased to any elementary or secondary school or school board, or within 1,000 feet of such school property or a school bus, or while on any school bus, is guilty of a crime of the third degree and shall, except as provided in N.J.S.2C:35-12, be sentenced by the court to a term of imprisonment. Where the violation involves less than one ounce of marijuana, the term of imprisonment shall include the imposition of a minimum term which shall be fixed at, or between, one-third and one-half of the sentence imposed, or one year, whichever is greater, during which the defendant shall be ineligible for parole. In all other cases, the term of imprisonment shall include the imposition of a minimum term which shall be fixed at, or between, one-third and one-half of the sentence imposed, or three years, whichever is greater, during which the defendant shall be ineligible for parole. Notwithstanding the provisions of subsection b. of N.J.S.2C:43-3, a fine of up to $150,000.00 may also be imposed upon any conviction for a violation of this section.

Notwithstanding the provisions of N.J.S.2C:1-8 or any other provisions of law, a conviction arising under this section shall not merge with a conviction for a violation of subsection a. of N.J.S.2C:35-5 (manufacturing, distributing or dispensing) or N.J.S.2C:35-6 (employing a juvenile in a drug distribution scheme).

It shall be no defense to a prosecution for a violation of this section that the actor was unaware that the prohibited conduct took place while on or within 1,000 feet of any school property. Nor shall it be a defense to a prosecution under this section, or under any other provision of this title, that no juveniles were present on the school property at the time of the offense or that the school was not in session.

It is an affirmative defense to prosecution for a violation of this section that the prohibited conduct took place entirely within a private residence, that no person 17 years of age or younger was present in such private residence at any time during the commission of the offense, and that the prohibited conduct did not involve distributing, dispensing or possessing with the intent to distribute or dispense any controlled dangerous substance or controlled substance analog for profit. The affirmative defense established in this section shall be proved by the defendant by a preponderance of the evidence. Nothing herein shall be construed to establish an affirmative defense with respect to a prosecution for an offense defined in any other section of this chapter.

In a prosecution under this section, a map produced or reproduced by any municipal or county engineer for the purpose of depicting the location and boundaries of the area on or within 1,000 feet of any property used for school purposes which is owned by or leased to any elementary or secondary school or school board, or a true copy of such a map, shall, upon proper authentication, be admissible and shall constitute prima facie evidence of the location and boundaries of those areas, provided that the governing body of the municipality or county has adopted a resolution or ordinance approving the map as official finding and record of the location and boundaries of the area or areas on or within 1,000 feet of the school property. Any map approved pursuant to this section may be changed from time to time by the governing body of the municipality or county. The original of every map approved or revised pursuant to this section, or a true copy thereof, shall be filed with the clerk of the municipality or county, and shall be maintained as an official record of the municipality or county. Nothing in this section shall be construed to preclude the prosecution from introducing or relying upon any other evidence or testimony to establish any element of this offense; nor shall this section be construed to preclude the use or admissibility of any map or diagram other than one which has been approved by the governing body of a municipality or county, provided that the map or diagram is otherwise admissible pursuant to the Rules of Evidence.

## PRACTICAL APPLICATION OF STATUTE

A drug dealer who distributes a controlled dangerous substance (or its analog) or a counterfeit controlled dangerous substance within 1,000 feet of school property or a school bus is guilty of a third degree crime. School property is defined as "any school property used for school purposes which is owned by or leased to any elementary or secondary school or school board." Accordingly, this would include any public or private grammar school or high school, but not colleges or universities.

A "1,000 feet" offense is in addition to any offense the dealer has committed under 23:35-5 (manufacturing, distributing, or dispensing CDSs). A survey of Red Beard's case can serve as an example of how this statute works.

Red Beard exited the Italian restaurant, Lancellotti's, with another man. They walked directly to his pickup truck where the man handed Red Beard cash in exchange for several packages of cocaine. Upon a tip from Hawthorne's mayor, police immediately responded to the scene, arrested Red Beard, and confiscated 11 ounces of cocaine from him.

Here Red Beard is guilty of violating 2C:35-5 for distributing cocaine. Because the quantity of cocaine seized from him was over five ounces, he is guilty of a first degree crime under that statute. However, he may also be guilty of an additional third degree crime pursuant to the provisions of 2C:35-7; that is, if his drug distribution was within 1,000 feet of school property or a school bus.

It should be noted that a drug dealer has no defense that he was unaware that his distribution occurred within 1,000 feet of school property or a school bus. Also, it is no defense that "no juveniles were present on the school property at the time of the offense or that the school was not in session."

---

**2C:35-7.1.**     **Violations of N.J.S.2C:35-5, certain locations; degree of crime; terms defined**

   a. Any person who violates subsection a. of N.J.S.2C:35-5 by distributing, dispensing or possessing with intent to distribute a controlled dangerous substance or controlled substance analog while in, on or within 500 feet of the real property comprising a public housing facility, a public park, or a public building is guilty of a crime of the second degree, except that it is a crime of the third degree if the violation involved less than one ounce of marijuana.

   b. It shall be no defense to a prosecution for violation of this section that the actor was unaware that the prohibited conduct took place while on or within 500 feet of a public housing facility, a public park, or a public building.

   c. Notwithstanding the provisions of N.J.S.2C:1-8 or any other provisions of law, a conviction arising under this section shall not merge with a conviction for a violation of subsection a. of N.J.S.2C:35-5 (manufacturing, distributing or dispensing) or N.J.S.2C:35-6 (employing a juvenile in a drug distribution scheme). Nothing in this section shall be construed to preclude or limit a prosecution or conviction for a violation of N.J.S.2C:35-7 or any other offense defined in this chapter.

   d. It is an affirmative defense to prosecution for a violation of this section that the prohibited conduct did not involve distributing, dispensing or possessing with the intent to distribute or dispense any controlled dangerous substance or controlled substance analog for profit, and that the prohibited conduct did not involve distribution to a person 17 years of age or younger. The affirmative defense established in this section shall be proved by the defendant by a preponderance of the evidence. Nothing herein shall be construed to establish an affirmative defense with respect to a prosecution for an offense defined in any other section of this chapter.

   e. In a prosecution under this section, a map produced or reproduced by any municipal or county engineer for the purpose of depicting the location and boundaries of the area on or within 500 feet of a public housing facility which is owned by or leased to a housing authority according to the "Local Redevelopment and Housing Law," P.L.1992, c.79 (C.40A:12A-1 et seq.), the area in or within 500 feet of a public park, or the area in or within 500 feet of a public building, or a true copy of such a map, shall, upon proper authentication, be admissible and shall constitute prima facie evidence of the location and boundaries of those areas, provided that the governing body of the municipality or county has adopted a resolution or ordinance approving the map as official finding and record of the location and boundaries of the area or areas on or within 500 feet of a public housing facility, a public park, or a public building. Any map approved pursuant to this section may be changed from time to time by the governing body of the municipality or county. The original of every map approved or revised pursuant to this section, or a true copy thereof, shall be filed with the clerk of the municipality or county, and shall be maintained as an official record of the municipality or county. Nothing in this section shall be construed to preclude the prosecution from introducing or relying upon any other evidence or testimony to establish any element of this offense; nor shall this section be construed to preclude the use or admissibility of any map or diagram other than one which has been approved by the governing body of a municipality or county, provided that the map or diagram is otherwise admissible pursuant to the Rules of Evidence.

f.   As used in this act:

"Public housing facility" means any dwelling, complex of dwellings, accommodation, building, structure or facility and real property of any nature appurtenant thereto and used in connection therewith, which is owned by or leased to a local housing authority in accordance with the "Local Redevelopment and Housing Law," P.L.1992, c.79 (C.40A:12A-1 et seq.) for the purpose of providing living accommodations to persons of low income.

"Public park" means a park, recreation facility or area or playground owned or controlled by a State, county or local government unit.

"Public building" means any publicly owned or leased library or museum.

## PRACTICAL APPLICATION OF STATUTE

Similar to the language of 2C:35-7 (the "1,000 feet" offense), 2C:35-7.1 provides that an additional crime has been committed when drug distribution has occurred "on or within 500 feet" of a public housing facility, public park, or public building. Like the "1,000 feet" statute, there is no defense available where the actor was unaware that he was within 500 feet of these public areas. A "500 feet" offense is a crime of the second degree except if the violation involved "less than one ounce of marijuana"; in that case, it is a third degree crime.

Accordingly, had Red Beard's cocaine distribution occurred within 500 feet of a public housing facilitiy, a public park, or a public building, he would be guilty of a second degree crime under 2C:35-7.1. This would be in addition to his drug distribution charge under 2C:35-5.

While the statute's definition of "public housing facility" and "public park" are quite broad, its definition of "public building" is rather narrow. It is confined to any publicly owned or leased "library or museum." "Public housing facility" includes any property "owned by or leased to a local housing authority," and "public park" means any "park, recreation facility or area or playground controlled by a State, county or local government unit."

## 2C:35-8.     Distribution to persons under age 18; enhanced punishment

Upon the application of the prosecuting attorney, any person being at least 18 years of age who has been convicted for violating subsection a. of N.J.S. 2C:35-5 or section 1 of P.L. 1987, c. 101 (C. 2C:35-7) by distributing a controlled dangerous substance or controlled substance analog to a pregnant female or a person 17 years of age or younger shall, except as provided in N.J.S.

2C:35-12, be subject to twice the term of imprisonment, fine and penalty, including twice the term of parole ineligibility, if any, authorized or required to be imposed by subsection b. of N.J.S. 2C:35-5 or section 1 of P.L. 1987, c. 101 (C. 2C:35-7) or any other provision of this title. In addition, the presumption of non-imprisonment for certain offenders set forth in subsection e. of N.J.S. 2C:44-1 shall not apply to any person subject to enhanced punishment pursuant to this section.

The court shall not impose more than one enhanced sentence pursuant to this section. If the defendant is convicted of more than one offense which is otherwise subject to enhanced punishment pursuant to this section, the court shall impose enhanced punishment based upon the most serious such offense for which the defendant was convicted, or, where applicable, the offense which mandates the imposition of the longest term of parole ineligibility. Notwithstanding the provisions of paragraph (2) of subsection a. of 2C:44-5, nothing herein shall prevent the court from also imposing an extended term pursuant to subsection f. of N.J.S. 2C:43-6. The court shall not impose an enhanced sentence pursuant to this section unless the prosecutor has established the ground therefor by a preponderance of the evidence at a hearing, which may occur at the time of sentencing. In making its finding, the court shall take judicial notice of any evidence, testimony or information adduced at the trial, plea hearing or other court proceedings, and shall also consider the presentence report and any other relevant information. It shall not be relevant to the imposition of enhanced punishment pursuant to this section that the defendant mistakenly believed that the recipient of the substance was 18 years of age or older, even if the mistaken belief was reasonable. Nor shall it be relevant to the imposition of enhanced punishment pursuant to this section that the defendant did not know that the recipient was pregnant.

**2C:35-9.** **Strict liability for drug-induced deaths**

    a. Any person who manufactures, distributes or dispenses methamphetamine, lysergic acid diethylamide, phencyclidine or any other controlled dangerous substance classified in Schedules I or II, or any controlled substance analog thereof, in violation of subsection a. of N.J.S. 2C:35-5, is strictly liable for a death which results from the injection, inhalation or ingestion of that substance, and is guilty of a crime of the first degree.

    b. The provisions of N.J.S. 2C:2-3 (governing the causal relationship between conduct and result) shall not apply in a prosecution under this section. For purposes of this offense, the defendant's act of manufacturing, distributing or dispensing a substance is the cause of a death when:

      (1) The injection, inhalation or ingestion of the substance is an antecedent but for which the death would not have occurred; and

      (2) The death was not:

        (a) too remote in its occurrence as to have a just bearing on the defendant's liability; or

        (b) too dependent upon conduct of another person which was unrelated to the injection, inhalation or ingestion of the substance or its effect as to have a just bearing on the defendant's liability.

    c. It shall not be a defense to a prosecution under this section that the decedent contributed to his own death by his purposeful, knowing, reckless or negligent injection, inhalation or ingestion of the substance, or by his consenting to the administration of the substance by another.

    d. Nothing in this section shall be construed to preclude or limit any prosecution for homicide. Notwithstanding the provisions of N.J.S. 2C:1-8 or any other provision of law, a conviction arising under this section shall not merge with a conviction for leader of narcotics trafficking network, maintaining or operating a controlled dangerous substance production facility, or for unlawfully manufacturing, distributing, dispensing or possessing with intent to manufacture, distribute or dispense the controlled dangerous substance or controlled substance analog which resulted in the death.

## PRACTICAL APPLICATION OF STATUTE

Technically, 2C:35-9 is not a homicide statute—although its provisions basically amount to one. The elements of this offense are rather confusing, but in sum total they primarily provide that an individual who distributes certain drugs to another is "strictly liable" for that person's death if that other person dies from using the drugs. Huh? Let's look at Red Beard's case for a detailed explanation.

Red Beard attempted to sell cocaine to another man in a restaurant parking lot in Hawthorne. His drug dealing efforts, though, were thwarted when Hawthorne Police arrested him. But what if the deal had been consummated and the buyer went on his jolly way with the cocaine—and then snorted it all up and died? Well, then, Red Beard would most likely be liable for his purchaser's death under 2C:35-9, facing a first degree crime.

Subsection a. of the statute enumerates the drugs whose distribution can give rise to a strict liability death charge. They include methamphetamine, LSD, PCP, and all CDSs classified in Schedules I and II. If a person manufactures one of these substances, but another injects, inhales, or ingests it—and dies—then that manufacturer is guilty of a first degree crime. If a person distributes one of these substances to another, who in turn takes it and dies, then that distributor is guilty of a first degree crime. If a person dispenses one of these substances to another, and that other individual dies after taking it, then the one who dispensed it is guilty of a first degree crime. Please keep in mind that the manufacturer, distributor, or dispenser is only liable if he performs these activities illegally, in violation of 2C:35-5.

Subsection b. specifically sets forth that the provisions of 2C:2-3 (governing the causal relationship between conduct and result) "shall not apply in a prosecution under this section." The subsection then goes on to set forth exactly when a manufacturer/distributor/dispenser's actions will be considered the "cause" of someone's death. Per b.(1), a death is deemed to be caused if the person would not have died "but for" the taking of the drug. However, pursuant to b.(2), the taking of the drug will *not* be considered the cause of death if the death was "too remote" in time from the taking of the drug or if the death was "too dependent upon conduct of another person which was unrelated" to the taking of the drug (see b.(2)(b)). So what does all this mean? Let's go back to Red Beard.

Red Beard's buyer inhales the massive quantities of cocaine dealt to him and then dies. If the man had never taken the illegal substance, he would not have died; In other words, "but for" his use of the cocaine, his death would not have occurred. Accordingly, Red Beard's cocaine distribution is deemed to be the "cause" of the man's death under 2C:35-9. Now what if he ingested all the cocaine and then died 18 months later? Are Red Beard's distribution activities the cause of the man's death? No, per subsection b.(2)(a)—because his death would be "too remote" in its occurrence to have a just bearing on the defendant's liability. What exactly is "too remote" is a matter of law to be decided in the courts.

What if the man snorted the cocaine, then went to a bar, got into a fistfight, and was killed during the fight? Does the fact that the man inhaled Red Beard's cocaine directly before his death make Red Beard liable for his demise? No, not per subsection b.(2)(b) because the man's death was "too dependent" upon another's conduct (the other fighter) to have a just bearing on Red Beard's liability.

Even though the statute carves out the above-mentioned situations where a person's drug dealing actions will not be deemed the "cause" of a user's death, in most scenarios the dealer will be held strictly liable. Accordingly, if Red Beard's purchaser inhaled the cocaine (a Schedule II substance), laid down in his bed, and then died as the result of the drug's intake, Red Beard would be held strictly liable for the man's death. And Red Beard cannot escape conviction of this first degree crime even if the user is found to have contributed to his death through his own purposeful, knowing, reckless, or negligent taking of the illegal drug.

---

**2C:35-10.**       **Possession, use or being under the influence, or failure to make lawful disposition**

a. It is unlawful for any person, knowingly or purposely, to obtain, or to possess, actually or constructively, a controlled dangerous substance or controlled substance analog, unless the substance was obtained directly, or pursuant to a valid prescription or order form from a practitioner, while acting in the course of his professional practice, or except as otherwise authorized by P.L.1970, c.226 (C.24:21-1 et seq.). Any person who violates this section with respect to:

   (1) A controlled dangerous substance, or its analog, classified in Schedule I, II, III or IV other than those specifically covered in this section, is guilty of a crime of the third degree except that, notwithstanding the provisions of subsection b. of N.J.S.2C:43-3, a fine of up to $35,000.00 may be imposed;

   (2) Any controlled dangerous substance, or its analog, classified in Schedule V, is guilty of a crime of the fourth degree except that, notwithstanding the provisions of subsection b. of N.J.S.2C:43-3, a fine of up to $15,000.00 may be imposed;

   (3) Possession of more than 50 grams of marijuana, including any adulterants or dilutants, or more than five grams of hashish is guilty of a crime of the fourth degree, except that, notwithstanding the provisions of subsection b. of N.J.S.2C:43-3, a fine of up to $25,000.00 may be imposed; or

   (4) Possession of 50 grams or less of marijuana, including any adulterants or dilutants, or five grams or less of hashish is a disorderly person.

   Any person who commits any offense defined in this section while on any property used for school purposes which is owned by or leased to any elementary or secondary school or school board, or within 1,000 feet of any such school property or a school bus, or while on any school bus, and who is not sentenced to a term of imprisonment, shall, in addition to any other sentence which the court may impose, be required to perform not less than 100 hours of community service.

b. Any person who uses or who is under the influence of any controlled dangerous substance, or its analog, for a purpose other than the treatment of sickness or injury as lawfully prescribed or administered by a physician is a disorderly person.

   In a prosecution under this subsection, it shall not be necessary for the State to prove that the accused did use or was under the influence of any specific drug, but it shall be sufficient for a conviction under this subsection for the State to prove that the accused did use or was under the influence of some controlled dangerous substance, counterfeit controlled dangerous substance, or controlled substance analog, by proving that the accused did manifest physical and physiological symptoms or reactions caused by the use of any controlled dangerous substance or controlled substance analog.

c. Any person who knowingly obtains or possesses a controlled dangerous substance or controlled substance analog in violation of subsection a. of this section and who fails to voluntarily deliver the substance to the nearest law enforcement officer is guilty of a disorderly persons offense. Nothing in this subsection shall be construed to preclude a prosecution or conviction for any other offense defined in this title or any other statute.

## PRACTICAL APPLICATION OF STATUTE

### Possession of CDS

Red Beard is guilty of violating 2C:35-10 for possessing marijuana. Given that the quantity he was caught with was less than 50 grams, he is guilty of a disorderly persons offense.

A person has not committed an offense if he possesses a controlled dangerous substance pursuant to a valid prescription from a practitioner who is acting in his professional capacity. However, generally, the possession of these substances is a third degree crime. Subsection a.(1) of the statute states that when a person possesses a "controlled dangerous substance, or its analog, classified in Schedule I, II, III or IV other than those specifically covered in this section," he is guilty of a crime of the third degree. Subsections a.(2) through a.(4) set forth the specific cases where CDS possession is a fourth degree crime or a disorderly persons offense. Per a.(2), a person is guilty of a fourth degree crime where he possesses any CDS or its analog classified in Schedule V. Similarly, under a.(3), a fourth degree crime has been committed where a person possesses "more than 50 grams of marijuana, including any adulterants or dilutants, or more than five grams of hashish." Please note, however, that an individual who possesses significant quantities of marijuana (or any CDS, for that matter) very likely will be charged under 2C:35-5 for possessing it "with intent to distribute" rather than just for simply possessing the substance.

Subsection a.(4) lowers CDS possession to a disorderly persons offense, but only in circumstances where the defendant possesses 50 grams or less of marijuana or five grams or less of hashish. Since Red Beard possessed only 25 grams of marijuana, he is guilty of a disorderly persons offense.

### Under the Influence of CDS

Simply, per 2C:35-10b., one who "uses" or is "under the influence" of any controlled dangerous substance (or its analog) is guilty of a disorderly persons offense. The only exception is if the use of the CDS was for treatment of sickness or injury as lawfully prescribed or administered by a physician.

Not so simple, though, is the statutory language of this subsection which provides that the State need not prove that a defendant was under the influence of any specific drug. Even more so, the subsection provides that a conviction can be sustained "by proving that the accused did manifest physical and physiological symptoms or reactions caused by the use of any controlled dangerous substance" or analog. What does this mean? It basically means that someone can be convicted of a disorderly persons offense if he appears to be under the influence of any illegal drug.

However, in order for the State to prove, beyond a reasonable doubt, that a person was actually under the influence of a CDS, expert testimony is necessary. In any case, it is a matter that ultimately must be decided in the courts by the trier of fact.

### Failure to Make Proper Disposition

Red Beard could be convicted of a disorderly persons offense under 2C:35-10c. for failing to "voluntarily" turn over his 25 grams of marijuana to a law enforcement officer. This conviction could be in addition to a CDS possession conviction under subsection a. of the statute.

Subsection c. of 2C:35-10 makes it a disorderly persons offense where a person fails to voluntarily turn over to the "nearest law enforcement officer" any controlled dangerous substances he illegally possesses. This means that if a person buys marijuana or cocaine, he should immediately go to the nearest police officer and give it to him or he can be charged with an offense under this subsection. And, this charge can be in addition to a CDS possession charge or any other appropriate charges. Accordingly, because Red Beard did not voluntarily turn over his stash of marijuana to any law enforcement officer, he is guilty of violating 2C:35-10c.

**2C:35-10.1.    Repealed**

**2C:35-10.2.    Possession, etc. of gamma hydroxybutyrate; penalties**

    a. It is a crime of the third degree for any person, knowingly or purposely, to obtain, or to possess, gamma hydroxybutyrate unless the substance was obtained directly, or pursuant to a valid prescription or order form from a practitioner, while acting in the course of his professional practice, or except as otherwise authorized by P.L.1970, c.226 (C.24:21-1 et seq.).

    b. Notwithstanding the provisions of N.J.S.2C:43-3 or any other law, a fine of up to $100,000.00 may be imposed upon a person who violates this section.

## PRACTICAL APPLICATION OF STATUTE

Simple possession of GHB—without a valid prescription—is a crime of the third degree. Accordingly, if Red Beard had a personal stash of GHB rather than marijuana, he would be guilty of a third degree crime.

**2C:35-10.3.    Possession, etc. of flunitrazepam; penalties**

    a. It is a crime of the third degree for any person, knowingly or purposely, to obtain, or to possess, flunitrazepam, unless the substance was obtained directly, or pursuant to a valid prescription or order form from a practitioner, while acting in the course of his professional practice, or except as otherwise authorized by P.L.1970, c.226 (C.24:21-1 et seq.).

    b. Notwithstanding the provisions of N.J.S.2C:43-3 or any other law, a fine of up to $100,000.00 may be imposed upon a person who violates this section.

## PRACTICAL APPLICATION OF STATUTE

Like possession of GHB, possession of flunitrazepam ("roofies") is a third degree crime. As per the other CDS possession statutes, a crime has not been committed if possession of the substance was pursuant to a valid prescription.

**2C:35-10.4.        Toxic chemicals**

a.  As used in this section the term "toxic chemical" means any chemical having the property of releasing toxic fumes and includes the following chemicals: acetone, acetate, benzene, butyl alcohol, ethyl alcohol, ethylene dichloride, isopropyl alcohol, methyl alcohol, methyl ethyl ketone, pentachlorophenol, petroleum ether, toluol, or toluene.

b.  A person commits a disorderly persons offense if the person:

(1)  inhales the fumes of any toxic chemical for the purpose of causing a condition of intoxication; or

(2)  possesses any toxic chemical for the purpose of causing a condition of intoxication.

c.  A person commits a fourth degree offense if the persons sells, or offers to sell, any substance containing a toxic chemical knowing that the intended use of the product is to cause a condition of intoxication, or knowing that the product does not include an additive required by the Commissioner of the State Department of Health and Senior Services to discourage the inhalation of vapors of toxic chemicals for the purpose of causing a condition of intoxication. This subsection does not apply to adhesives manufactured only for industrial application.

## PRACTICAL APPLICATION OF STATUTE

Per 2C:35-10.4, one who inhales (see subsection b.(1)) or possesses (see subsection b.(2)) any "toxic chemical" is guilty of a disorderly persons offense. Pursuant to subsection c., a person who sells any "toxic chemical" is guilty of a fourth degree crime. What constitutes a "toxic chemical" can be easily found in subsection a. of this statute.

**2C:35-10.5.        Prescription legend drugs**

a.  Except as authorized by sections 9 through 15 of P.L.1970, c.226 (C.24:21-9 through 24:21-15) a person who knowingly distributes a prescription legend drug or stramonium preparation unless lawfully prescribed or administered by a licensed physician, veterinarian or dentist is a disorderly person.

b.  A person who uses any prescription legend drug or stramonium preparation for a purpose other than treatment of sickness or injury as lawfully prescribed or administered by a licensed physician is a disorderly person.

c.  A defendant may be convicted for a violation of subsection b. if the State proves that the defendant manifested symptoms or reactions caused by the use of prescription legend drugs or stramonium preparation. The State need not prove which specific prescription legend drug or stramonium preparation defendant used.

d.  A person who obtains or attempts to obtain possession of a prescription legend drug or stramonium preparation by forgery or deception is a disorderly person. Nothing in this section shall be deemed to preclude or limit a prosecution for theft as defined in chapter 20 of Title 2C of the New Jersey Statutes.

## PRACTICAL APPLICATION OF STATUTE

### Drugs Generally

This statute enumerates offenses for possessing, distributing, and being under the influence of "prescription legend" drugs and "stramonium preparation." Per the definitions set forth in 2C:35-2, "prescription legend" drugs include steroids, cough syrup with codeine, and any other "drug which under Federal or State law requires dispensing by prescription or order of a licensed physician, veterinarian or dentist and is required to bear the statement 'Caution: Federal law prohibits dispensing without a prescription' and is not a controlled dangerous substance or stramonium preparation." "Stramonium preparation" is defined as "a substance prepared from any part of the stramonium plant in the form of a powder, pipe mixture, cigarette, or any other form with or without other ingredients." All violations of this statute are disorderly persons offenses.

### Distribution

A person who unlawfully distributes a "prescription legend drug" or "stramonium preparation" has violated subsection a. of 2C:35-10.5 and is guilty of a disorderly persons offense. Distribution of either matter is only legal where it is "lawfully prescribed or administered by a licensed physician, veterinarian or dentist."

### Possession/Under the Influence

One who uses a "prescription legend drug" or "stramonium preparation"—other than for a purpose of "treatment of sickness or injury as lawfully prescribed or administered by a licensed physician"—is guilty of a disorderly persons offense under subsection b. of the statute.

Subsection c. of 2C:35-10.5, in a vein similar to the provisions of the CDS "under the influence" statute (2C:35-10b.), sets out how a person can be convicted of unlawfully using a "prescription legend drug" or "stramonium preparation." The State need only prove that the "defendant manifested symptoms or reactions caused by the use of prescription legend drugs or stramonium preparation." The State, though, does not need to prove which specific substance the defendant used.

### Obtaining by Forgery

Subsection d. of this statute makes it a separate offense to obtain a prescription legend drug or stramonium preparation by forgery or deception. For instance, if a person created a false prescription and brought it to a pharmacist, he could be convicted of a disorderly persons offense pursuant to 2C:35-10.5d. Similarly, if he lifted a prescription pad from a medical doctor and thereafter used one of the pages to obtain a drug, he is ripe for a charge under this subsection, not to mention a charge of theft under 2C:20-3.

2C:35-11.          **Imitation controlled dangerous substances; distribution, possession, manufacture, etc; penalties**

a. It is unlawful for any person to distribute or to possess or have under his control with intent to distribute any substance which is not a controlled dangerous substance or controlled substance analog:

(1) Upon the express or implied representation to the recipient that the substance is a controlled dangerous substance or controlled substance analog; or

(2) Upon the express or implied representation to the recipient that the substance is of such nature, appearance or effect that the recipient will be able to distribute or use the substance as a controlled dangerous substance or controlled substance analog; or

(3) Under circumstances which would lead a reasonable person to believe that the substance is a controlled dangerous substance or controlled substance analog.

Any of the following shall constitute prima facie evidence of such circumstances:

(a) The substance was packaged in a manner normally used for the unlawful distribution of controlled dangerous substances or controlled substance analogs.

(b) The distribution or attempted distribution of the substance was accompanied by an exchange of or demand for money or other thing as consideration for the substance, and the value of the consideration exceeded the reasonable value of the substance.

(c) The physical appearance of the substance is substantially the same as that of a specific controlled dangerous substance or controlled substance analog.

b. It is unlawful for any person to manufacture, compound, encapsulate, package or imprint any substance which is not a controlled dangerous substance, controlled substance analog or any combination of such substances, other than a prescription drug, with the purpose that it resemble or duplicate the physical appearance of the finished form, package, label or imprint of a controlled dangerous substance or controlled substance analog.

c. In any prosecution under this section, it shall not be a defense that the defendant mistakenly believed a substance to be a controlled dangerous substance or controlled substance analog.

d. A violation of this section is a crime of the third degree, except that, notwithstanding the provisions of subsection b. of N.J.S.2C:43-3, a fine of up to $200,000.00 may be imposed.

e. The provisions of this section shall not be applicable to (1) practitioners or agents, servants and employees of practitioners dispensing or administering noncontrolled substances to patients on behalf of practitioners in the normal course of their business or professional practice; and (2) persons who manufacture, process, package, distribute or sell noncontrolled substances to practitioners for use as placebos in the normal course of their business, professional practice or research or for use in Federal Food and Drug Administration investigational new drug trials.

## Practical Application of Statute

Not only is the sale of controlled dangerous substances illegal, but the sale of imitation controlled dangerous substances is also illegal. Remember the case of Red Beard? He was caught selling cocaine to a man in a restaurant parking lot. If this substance had turned out to be flour, however, he still would be guilty of a crime. The violation: distributing imitation cocaine, which is a third degree offense.

2C:35-11, in a nutshell, makes it a crime for someone to represent to another that a substance that he is selling is a CDS. This representation may be expressed or implied. The statute, in fact, enumerates three types of circumstances where a person's actions constitute *prima facie* evidence of attempting to hold out a phony product as an actual CDS. These actions include when the substance is "packaged in a manner normally used for the unlawful distribution" of CDSs (see subsection a.(3)(a)); where the distribution is accompanied by an exchange of money and the amount of money "exceeded the reasonable value of the substance" (see subsection a.(3)(b)); and "the physical appearance of the substance is substantially the same as that of a specific" CDS (see subsection a.(3)(c)).

Subsection c. of the statute provides that it is not a defense that the defendant mistakenly believed the substance he was distributing was actually a controlled dangerous substance. The statute also does not utilize weight to differentiate among degrees of crimes. Simply, per subsection d., a violation of the statute is a third degree crime.

Now back to Red Beard. In the restaurant parking lot, Hawthorne Police caught Red Beard with 29 individually wrapped packages of cocaine marked with the logo "Tuned-Up," which totaled 11 ounces in weight. Prior to the sale, Hawthorne Mayor Frank Castelleti overheard Red Beard tell his potential buyer, "Step out to my pick up, and I'll drop you the eight-ball." This statement constituted an express representation by Red Beard that he was offering to sell cocaine, as "eight-ball" is street lingo for cocaine. In addition, there is separate *prima facie* evidence that he was representing the substance to be cocaine—it was wrapped in 29 individual packages and marked with the logo "Tuned-Up." This type of packaging is consistent with the packaging of a CDS that is unlawfully distributed. Accordingly, even if the substance turned out to be flour rather than cocaine, Red Beard would still be guilty of a third degree crime. As noted earlier, the quantity involved does not affect the degree of the crime under 2C:35-11. Thus Red Beard would face a third degree charge whether he attempted to sell one ounce, three ounces, 11 ounces, or 75 ounces of the substance.

It is interesting to note, though, that with the substance *actually* being cocaine, Red Beard would be guilty of a first degree distribution offense under 2C:35-5. Pursuant to that statute, distribution of cocaine in the amount of five ounces or more is a first degree crime. This means that because the quantity of cocaine involved was 11 ounces (exceeding five ounces), Red Beard would face a first degree charge for distribution of the real McCoy.

## 2C:35-12.  Waiver of mandatory minimum and extended terms

Whenever an offense defined in this chapter specifies a mandatory sentence of imprisonment which includes a minimum term during which the defendant shall be ineligible for parole, a mandatory extended term which includes a period of parole ineligibility, or an anti-drug profiteering penalty pursuant to section 2 of P.L.1997, c.187 (N.J.S.2C:35A-1 et seq.), the court upon conviction shall impose the mandatory sentence or anti-drug profiteering penalty unless the defendant has pleaded guilty pursuant to a negotiated agreement or, in cases resulting in trial, the defendant and the prosecution have entered into a post-conviction agreement, which provides for a lesser sentence, period of parole ineligibility or anti-drug profiteering penalty. The negotiated plea or post-conviction agreement may provide for a specified term of imprisonment within the range of ordinary or extended sentences authorized by law, a specified period of parole ineligibility, a specified fine, a specified anti-drug profiteering penalty, or other disposition. In that event, the court at sentencing shall not impose a lesser term of imprisonment, lesser period of parole ineligibility, lesser fine or lesser anti-drug profiteering penalty than that expressly provided for under the terms of the plea or post-conviction agreement.

## 2C:35-13.  Obtaining by fraud

It shall be unlawful for any person to acquire or obtain possession of a controlled dangerous substance or controlled substance analog by misrepresentation, fraud, forgery, deception or subterfuge. It shall be unlawful for any person to acquire or obtain possession of a forged or fraudulent certificate of destruction required pursuant to N.J.S.2C:35-21. A violation of this section shall be a crime of the third degree except that, notwithstanding the provisions of subsection b. of N.J.S.2C:43-3, a fine of up to $50,000.00 may be imposed. Nothing in this section shall be deemed to preclude or limit a prosecution for theft as defined in chapter 20 of this title.

## PRACTICAL APPLICATION OF STATUTE

A person can be convicted of a third degree crime under 2C:35-13 for obtaining a CDS by deceptive matters such as fraud or misrepresentation. Also, per this statute, a person can be convicted of a third degree crime for obtaining "possession of a forged or fraudulent certificate of destruction required pursuant to N.J.S.2C:35-21." What does that mean?

2C:35-21 sets forth what is required in order for forensic laboratories to destroy controlled dangerous substances. Specifically, that statute provides that the laboratory "shall file with the court a certificate under oath attesting to the date on which the substance was destroyed, the quantity of the substance destroyed, and the method used to destroy the substance."

So under what circumstances can a person face a charge under 2C:35-13? Let's say that after Red Beard's 11 ounces of cocaine were seized by Hawthorne Police, the state sought to have it destroyed. Thereafter, a colleague of Red Beard's, who worked in a state forensic laboratory, filed a "certificate of destruction" attesting to the date and method of destruction of the cocaine. The lab tech, however, never actually destroyed the drug but instead returned it to Red Beard who was out on bail. In this case, the lab tech would have presented a fraudulent "certificate of destruction" to the court and is therefore guilty of a third degree crime under 2C:35-13. Also, if Red Beard was part of this scheme, he similarly would be guilty of a third degree crime, as he would have "re-obtained" his cocaine via a deceptive act.

---

**2C:35-14.**    **Rehabilitation program for drug and alcohol dependent persons; criteria for imposing special probation; ineligible offenders; prosecutorial objections; mandatory commitment to residential treatment facilities; presumption of revocation; brief incarceration in lieu of permanent revocation**

    a. Notwithstanding the presumption of incarceration pursuant to the provisions of subsection d. of N.J.S.2C:44-1, and except as provided in subsection c. of this section, whenever a drug or alcohol dependent person is convicted of or adjudicated delinquent for an offense, other than one described in subsection b. of this section, the court, upon notice to the prosecutor, may, on motion of the person, or on the court's own motion, place the person on special probation, which shall be for a term of five years, provided that the court finds on the record that:

        (1) the person has undergone a professional diagnostic assessment to determine whether and to what extent the person is drug or alcohol dependent and would benefit from treatment; and

        (2) the person is a drug or alcohol dependent person within the meaning of N.J.S.2C:35-2 and was drug or alcohol dependent at the time of the commission of the present offense; and

        (3) the present offense was committed while the person was under the influence of a controlled dangerous substance, controlled substance analog or alcohol or was committed to acquire property or monies in order to support the person's drug or alcohol dependency; and

        (4) substance abuse treatment and monitoring will serve to benefit the person by addressing his drug or alcohol dependency and will thereby reduce the likelihood that the person will thereafter commit another offense; and

        (5) the person did not possess a firearm at the time of the present offense and did not possess a firearm at the time of any pending criminal charge; and

(6) the person has not been previously convicted on two or more separate occasions of crimes of the first, second or third degree, other than crimes defined in N.J.S. 2C:35-10; and

(7) the person has not been previously convicted or adjudicated delinquent for, and does not have a pending charge of murder, aggravated manslaughter, manslaughter, robbery, kidnapping, aggravated assault, aggravated sexual assault or sexual assault, or a similar crime under the laws of any other state or the United States; and

(8) a suitable treatment facility licensed and approved by the Department of Health and Senior Services is able and has agreed to provide appropriate treatment services in accordance with the requirements of this section; and

(9) no danger to the community will result from the person being placed on special probation pursuant to this section.

In determining whether to sentence the person pursuant to this section, the court shall consider all relevant circumstances, and shall take judicial notice of any evidence, testimony or information adduced at the trial, plea hearing or other court proceedings, and shall also consider the presentence report and the results of the professional diagnostic assessment to determine whether and to what extent the person is drug or alcohol dependent and would benefit from treatment.

As a condition of special probation, the court shall order the person to enter a treatment program at a facility licensed and approved by the Department of Health and Senior Services, to comply with program rules and the requirements of the course of treatment, to cooperate fully with the treatment provider, and to comply with such other reasonable terms and conditions as may be required by the court or by law, pursuant to N.J.S.2C:45-1, and which shall include periodic urine testing for drug or alcohol usage throughout the period of special probation. Subject to the requirements of subsection d. of this section, the conditions of special probation may include different methods and levels of community-based or residential supervision.

b. A person shall not be eligible for special probation pursuant to this section if the person is convicted of or adjudicated delinquent for:

(1) a crime of the first degree;

(2) a crime of the first or second degree enumerated in subsection d. of N.J.S.2C:43-7.2;

(3) a crime, other than that defined in N.J.S.2C:35-7, for which a mandatory minimum period of incarceration is prescribed under chapter 35 of this Title or any other law; or

(4) an offense that involved the distribution or the conspiracy or attempt to distribute a controlled dangerous substance or controlled substance analog to a juvenile near or on school property.

c. A person convicted of or adjudicated delinquent for an offense under section 1 of P.L.1987, c.101 (C.2C:35-7), subsection b. of section 1 of P.L.1997, c.185 (C.2C:35-4.1), or any crime for which there exists a presumption of imprisonment pursuant to subsection d. of N.J.S.2C:44-1 or any other statute, or who has been previously convicted of an offense under subsection a. of N.J.S.2C:35-5 or a similar offense under any other law of this State, any other state or the United States, shall not be eligible for sentence in accordance with this section if the prosecutor objects to the person being placed on special probation. The court shall not place a person on special probation over the prosecutor's objection except upon a finding by the court of a gross and patent abuse of prosecutorial discretion. If the court makes a finding of a gross and patent abuse of prosecutorial discretion and imposes a sentence of special probation notwithstanding the objection of the prosecutor, the sentence of special probation imposed pursuant to this section shall not become final for 10 days in order to permit the appeal of such sentence by the prosecution.

d. A person convicted of or adjudicated delinquent for a crime of the second degree or of a violation of section 1 of P.L.1987, c.101 (C.2C:35-7), or who previously has been convicted of or adjudicated delinquent for an offense under subsection a. of N.J.S.2C:35-5 or a similar offense under any other law of this State, any other state or the United States, who is placed on special probation under this section shall be committed to the custody of a residential treatment facility licensed and approved by the Department of Health and Senior Services, whether or not residential treatment was recommended by the person conducting the diagnostic assessment. The person shall be committed to the residential treatment facility immediately, unless the facility cannot accommodate the person, in which case the person shall be incarcerated to await commitment to the residential treatment facility. The term of such commitment shall be for a minimum of six months, or until the court, upon recommendation of the treatment provider, determines that the person has successfully completed the residential treatment program, whichever is later, except that no person shall remain in the custody of a residential treatment facility pursuant to this section for a period in excess of five years. Upon successful completion of the required residential treatment program, the person shall complete the period of special probation, as authorized by subsection a. of this section, with credit for time served for any imprisonment served as a condition of probation and credit for each day during which the person satisfactorily complied with the terms and conditions of special probation while committed pursuant to this section to a residential treatment facility. The person shall not be eligible for early discharge of special probation pursuant to N.J.S.2C:45-2, or any other provision of the law. The court, in determining the number of credits for time spent in residential treatment, shall consider the recommendations of the treatment provider. A person placed into a residential treatment facility pursuant to this section shall be deemed to be subject to official detention for the purposes of N.J.S.2C:29-5 (escape).

e. The probation department or other appropriate agency designated by the court to monitor or supervise the person's special probation shall report periodically to the court as to the person's progress in treatment and compliance with court-imposed terms and conditions. The treatment provider shall promptly report to the probation department or other appropriate agency all significant failures by the person to comply with any court imposed term or condition of special probation or any requirements of the course of treatment, including but not limited to a positive drug or alcohol test or the unexcused failure to attend any session or activity, and shall immediately report any act that would constitute an escape. The probation department or other appropriate agency shall immediately notify the court and the prosecutor in the event that the person refuses to submit to a periodic drug or alcohol test or for any reason terminates his participation in the course of treatment, or commits any act that would constitute an escape.

f. (1) Upon a first violation of any term or condition of the special probation authorized by this section or of any requirements of the course of treatment, the court in its discretion may permanently revoke the person's special probation.

    (2) Upon a second or subsequent violation of any term or condition of the special probation authorized by this section or of any requirements of the course of treatment, the court shall, subject only to the provisions of subsection g. of this section, permanently revoke the person's special probation unless the court finds on the record that there is a substantial likelihood that the person will successfully complete the treatment program if permitted to continue on special probation, and the court is clearly convinced, considering the nature and seriousness of the violations, that no danger to the community will result from permitting the person to continue on special probation pursuant to this section. The court's determination to permit the person to continue on special probation following a second or subsequent violation pursuant to this paragraph may be appealed by the prosecution.

(3) In making its determination whether to revoke special probation, and whether to overcome the presumption of revocation established in paragraph (2) of this subsection, the court shall consider the nature and seriousness of the present infraction and any past infractions in relation to the person's overall progress in the course of treatment, and shall also consider the recommendations of the treatment provider. The court shall give added weight to the treatment provider's recommendation that the person's special probation be permanently revoked, or to the treatment provider's opinion that the person is not amenable to treatment or is not likely to complete the treatment program successfully.

(4) If the court permanently revokes the person's special probation pursuant to this subsection, the court shall impose any sentence that might have been imposed, or that would have been required to be imposed, originally for the offense for which the person was convicted or adjudicated delinquent. The court shall conduct a de novo review of any aggravating and mitigating factors present at the time of both original sentencing and resentencing. If the court determines or is required pursuant to any other provision of this chapter or any other law to impose a term of imprisonment, the person shall receive credit for any time served in custody pursuant to N.J.S.2C:45-1 or while awaiting placement in a treatment facility pursuant to this section, and for each day during which the person satisfactorily complied with the terms and conditions of special probation while committed pursuant to this section to a residential treatment facility. The court, in determining the number of credits for time spent in a residential treatment facility, shall consider the recommendations of the treatment provider.

(5) Following a violation, if the court permits the person to continue on special probation pursuant to this section, the court shall order the person to comply with such additional terms and conditions, including but not limited to more frequent drug or alcohol testing, as are necessary to deter and promptly detect any further violation.

(6) Notwithstanding any other provision of this subsection, if the person at any time refuses to undergo urine testing for drug or alcohol usage as provided in subsection a. of this section, the court shall, subject only to the provisions of subsection g. of this section, permanently revoke the person's special probation. Notwithstanding any other provision of this section, if the person at any time while committed to the custody of a residential treatment facility pursuant to this section commits an act that would constitute an escape, the court shall forthwith permanently revoke the person's special probation.

(7) An action for a violation under this section may be brought by a probation officer or prosecutor or on the court's own motion. Failure to complete successfully the required treatment program shall constitute a violation of the person's special probation. A person who fails to comply with the terms of his special probation pursuant to this section and is thereafter sentenced to imprisonment in accordance with this subsection shall thereafter be ineligible for entry into the Intensive Supervision Program.

g. When a person on special probation is subject to a presumption of revocation on a second or subsequent violation pursuant to paragraph (2) of subsection f. of this section, or when the person refuses to undergo drug or alcohol testing pursuant to paragraph (6) of subsection f. of this section, the court may, in lieu of permanently revoking the person's special probation, impose a term of incarceration for a period of not less than 30 days nor more than six months, after which the person's term of special probation pursuant to this section may be reinstated. In determining whether to order a period of incarceration in lieu of permanent revocation pursuant to this subsection, the court shall consider the recommendations of the treatment provider with respect to the likelihood that such confinement would serve to motivate the person to make satisfactory progress in treatment once special probation is reinstated. This disposition may occur only once with respect to any person unless the court is clearly convinced that there are compelling and extraordinary reasons to justify reimposing this disposition with respect to the person. Any such determination by the court to reimpose this disposition may be appealed by the prosecution. Nothing in this subsection shall be construed to limit the authority of the court at any time during the period of special probation to order a person on special probation who is not subject to a presumption of revocation pursuant to paragraph (2) of subsection f. of this section to be incarcerated over the course of a weekend, or for any other reasonable period of time, when the court in its discretion determines that such incarceration would help to motivate the person to make satisfactory progress in treatment.

h. The court, as a condition of its order, and after considering the person's financial resources, shall require the person to pay that portion of the costs associated with his participation in any rehabilitation program or period of residential treatment imposed pursuant to this section which, in the opinion of the court, is consistent with the person's ability to pay, taking into account the court's authority to order payment or reimbursement to be made over time and in installments.

i. The court shall impose, as a condition of the special probation, any fine, penalty, fee or restitution applicable to the offense for which the person was convicted or adjudicated delinquent.

**2C:35-15.      Mandatory drug enforcement and demand reduction penalties; collection; disposition; suspension**

a. In addition to any disposition authorized by this title, the provisions of section 24 of P.L.1982, c.77 (C.2A:4A-43), or any other statute indicating the dispositions that can be ordered for an adjudication of delinquency, every person convicted of or adjudicated delinquent for a violation of any offense defined in this chapter or chapter 36 of this title shall be assessed for each such offense a penalty fixed at:

   (1) $3,000.00 in the case of a crime of the first degree;

   (2) $2,000.00 in the case of a crime of the second degree;

   (3) $1,000.00 in the case of a crime of the third degree;

   (4) $750.00 in the case of a crime of the fourth degree;

   (5) $500.00 in the case of a disorderly persons or petty disorderly persons offense.

   Every person placed in supervisory treatment pursuant to the provisions of N.J.S.2C:36A-1 or N.J.S.2C:43-12 for a violation of any offense defined in this chapter or chapter 36 of this title shall be assessed the penalty prescribed herein and applicable to the degree of the offense charged, except that the court shall not impose more than one such penalty regardless of the number of offenses charged. If the person is charged with more than one offense, the court shall impose as a condition of supervisory treatment the penalty applicable to the highest degree offense for which the person is charged.

   All penalties provided for in this section shall be in addition to and not in lieu of any fine authorized by law or required to be imposed pursuant to the provisions of N.J.S.2C:35-12.

b. All penalties provided for in this section shall be collected as provided for collection of fines and restitutions in section 3 of P.L.1979, c.396 (C.2C:46-4), and shall be forwarded to the Department of the Treasury as provided in subsection c. of this section.

c. All moneys collected pursuant to this section shall be forwarded to the Department of the Treasury to be deposited in a nonlapsing revolving fund to be known as the "Drug Enforcement and Demand Reduction Fund." Moneys in the fund shall be appropriated by the Legislature on an annual basis for the purposes of funding in the following order of priority: (1) the Alliance to Prevent Alcoholism and Drug Abuse and its administration by the Governor's Council on Alcoholism and Drug Abuse; (2) the "Alcoholism and Drug Abuse Program for the Deaf, Hard of Hearing and Disabled" established pursuant to section 2 of P.L.1995, c.318 (C.26:2B-37); (3) the "Partnership for a Drug Free New Jersey," the State affiliate of the "Partnership for a Drug Free America"; and (4) other alcohol and drug abuse programs.

Moneys appropriated for the purpose of funding the "Alcoholism and Drug Abuse Program for the Deaf, Hard of Hearing and Disabled" shall not be used to supplant moneys that are available to the Department of Health and Senior Services as of the effective date of P.L.1995, c.318 (C.26:2B-36 et al.), and that would otherwise have been made available to provide alcoholism and drug abuse services for the deaf, hard of hearing and disabled, nor shall the moneys be used for the administrative costs of the program.

d. (Deleted by amendment, P.L.1991, c.329).

e. The court may suspend the collection of a penalty imposed pursuant to this section; provided the person is ordered by the court to participate in a drug or alcohol rehabilitation program approved by the court; and further provided that the person agrees to pay for all or some portion of the costs associated with the rehabilitation program. In this case, the collection of a penalty imposed pursuant to this section shall be suspended during the person's participation in the approved, court-ordered rehabilitation program. Upon successful completion of the program, as determined by the court upon the recommendation of the treatment provider, the person may apply to the court to reduce the penalty imposed pursuant to this section by any amount actually paid by the person for his participation in the program. The court shall not reduce the penalty pursuant to this subsection unless the person establishes to the satisfaction of the court that he has successfully completed the rehabilitation program. If the person's participation is for any reason terminated before his successful completion of the rehabilitation program, collection of the entire penalty imposed pursuant to this section shall be enforced. Nothing in this section shall be deemed to affect or suspend any other criminal sanctions imposed pursuant to this chapter or chapter 36 of this title.

## 2C:35-16.  Mandatory forfetiure or postponement of driving privileges

In addition to any disposition authorized by this title, the provisions of section 24 of P.L. 1982, c. 77 (C. 2A:4A-43), or any other statute indicating the dispositions that can be ordered for an adjudication of delinquency, and notwithstanding the provisions of subsection c. of N.J.S. 2C:43-2 every person convicted of or adjudicated delinquent for a violation of any offense defined in this chapter or chapter 36 of this title shall forthwith forfeit his right to operate a motor vehicle over the highways of this State for a period to be fixed by the court at not less than six months or more than two years which shall commence on the day the sentence is imposed. In the case of any person who at the time of the imposition of sentence is less than 17 years of age, the period of the suspension of driving privileges authorized herein, including a suspension of the privilege of operating a motorized bicycle, shall commence on the day the sentence is imposed and shall run for a period as fixed by the court of not less than six months or more than two years after the day the person reaches the age of 17 years. If the driving privilege of any person is under revocation, suspension, or postponement for a violation of any provision of this title or Title 39 of the Revised Statutes at the time of any conviction or adjudication of delinquency for a violation of any offense defined in this chapter or chapter 36 of this title, the revocation, suspension, or postponement period imposed herein shall commence as of the date of termination of the existing revocation, suspension, or postponement.

The court before whom any person is convicted of or adjudicated delinquent for a violation of any offense defined in this chapter or chapter 36 of this title shall collect forthwith the New Jersey driver's license or licenses of the person and forward such license or licenses to the Director of the Division of Motor Vehicles along with a report indicating the first and last day of the suspension or postponement period imposed by the court pursuant to this section. If the court is for any reason unable to collect the license or licenses of the person, the court shall cause a report of the conviction or adjudication of delinquency to be filed with the Director. That report shall include the complete name, address, date of birth, eye color, and sex of the person and shall indicate the first and last day of the suspension or postponement period imposed by the court pursuant to this section. The court shall inform the person orally and in writing that if the person is convicted of personally operating a motor vehicle during the period of license suspension or postponement imposed pursuant to this section, the person shall, upon conviction, be subject to the penalties set forth in R.S. 39:3-40. A person shall be required to acknowledge receipt of the written notice in writing. Failure to receive a written notice or failure to acknowledge in writing the receipt of a written notice shall not be a defense to a subsequent charge of a violation of R.S. 39:3-40. If the person is the holder of a driver's license from another jurisdiction, the court shall not collect the license but shall notify forthwith the Director who shall notify the appropriate officials in the licensing jurisdiction. The court shall, however, in accordance with the provisions of this section, revoke the person's non-resident driving privilege in this State.

In addition to any other condition imposed, a court may in its discretion suspend, revoke or postpone in accordance with the provisions of this section the driving privileges of a person admitted to supervisory treatment under N.J.S. 2C:36A-1 or N.J.S. 2C:43-12 without a plea of guilty or finding of guilt.

**2C:35-16.1.    Notification to landlord of offenses committed by tenant under "Comprehensive Drug Reform Act of 1987"**

The court in which any conviction is had or any plea of guilty entered to a charge of an offense under the "Comprehensive Drug Reform Act of 1987," N.J.S.2C:35-1 et al., involving the use, possession, manufacture, dispensing or distribution of a controlled dangerous substance, controlled dangerous substance analog or drug paraphernalia, or in which any adjudication of juvenile delinquency is made on the basis of an act which if committed by an adult would constitute such an offense, shall ascertain whether the offense or act took place upon leased residential premises in which the defendant was a resident at the time of the offense or act, and upon ascertaining that it did so occur shall cause notice of the conviction, plea or adjudication to be forthwith transmitted to the owner of those premises or his appropriate agent.

**2C:35-17.    Exception to physician-patient privilege**

Information communicated to a practitioner in an effort unlawfully to obtain or procure the administration of a controlled dangerous substance or controlled substance analog shall not be a privileged communication.

**2C:35-18.    Exemption; burden of proof**

a. If conduct is authorized by the provisions of P.L. 1970, c. 226 (C. 24:21-1 et seq.), that authorization shall, subject to the provisions of this section, constitute an exemption from criminal liability under this chapter or chapter 36, and the absence of such authorization shall not be construed to be an element of any offense in this chapter or chapter 36. It is an affirmative defense to any criminal action arising under this chapter or chapter 36 that the defendant is the authorized holder of an appropriate registration or order form or is otherwise exempted or excepted from criminal liability by virtue of any provision of P.L. 1970, c. 226 (C. 24:21-1 et seq.). The affirmative defense established herein shall be proved by the defendant by a preponderance of the evidence. It shall not be necessary for the State to negate any exemption set forth in this act or in any provision of Title 24 of the Revised Statutes in any complaint, information, indictment or other pleading or in any trial, hearing or other proceeding under this act.

b. No liability shall be imposed by virtue of this chapter or chapter 36 upon any duly authorized State officer, engaged in the enforcement of any law or municipal ordinance relating to controlled dangerous substances or controlled substance analogs.

**2C:35-19.**     **Laboratory certificates; use; admission into evidence; objections**

a. The Attorney General of New Jersey may designate State Forensic Laboratories. These laboratories shall be staffed by employees of this State or any of the State's political subdivisions. In a proceeding for a violation of the provisions of chapters 35 and 36 of this title or any other statute concerning controlled dangerous substances or controlled dangerous substance analogs, a law enforcement agency may submit to one of these laboratories any substance, including, but not limited to, any substance believed to be a controlled dangerous substance or controlled substance analog thereof, or any poisons, drugs or medicines or human body tissues or fluids. The laboratory shall analyze these substances.

b. Upon the request of any law enforcement agency, the laboratory employee performing the analysis shall prepare a certificate. This employee shall sign the certificate under oath and shall include in the certificate an attestation as to the result of the analysis. The presentation of this certificate to a court by any party to a proceeding shall be evidence that all of the requirements and provisions of this section have been complied with. This certificate shall be sworn to before a notary public or other person empowered by law to take oaths and shall contain a statement establishing the following: the type of analysis performed; the result achieved; any conclusions reached based upon that result; that the subscriber is the person who performed the analysis and made the conclusions; the subscriber's training or experience to perform the analysis; and the nature and condition of the equipment used. When properly executed, the certificate shall, subject to subsection c. of this section and notwithstanding any other provision of law, be admissible evidence of the composition, quality, and quantity of the substance submitted to the laboratory for analysis, and the court shall take judicial notice of the signature of the person performing the analysis and of the fact that he is that person.

c. Whenever a party intends to proffer in a criminal or quasi-criminal proceeding, a certificate executed pursuant to this section, notice of an intent to proffer that certificate and all reports relating to the analysis in question, including a copy of the certificate, shall be conveyed to the opposing party or parties at least 20 days before the proceeding begins. An opposing party who intends to object to the admission into evidence of a certificate shall give notice of objection and the grounds for the objection within 10 days upon receiving the adversary's notice of intent to proffer the certificate. Whenever a notice of objection is filed, admissibility of the certificate shall be determined not later than two days before the beginning of the trial. A proffered certificate shall be admitted in evidence unless it appears from the notice of objection and specific grounds for that objection that the composition, quality, or quantity of the substance submitted to the laboratory for analysis will be contested at trial. A failure to comply with the time limitations regarding the notice of objection required by this section shall constitute a waiver of any objections to the admission of the certificate. The time limitations set forth in this section shall not be relaxed except upon a showing of good cause.

**2C:35-20.          Forensic laboratory fees**

a. In addition to any disposition made pursuant to the provisions of N.J.S. 2C:43-2, any person convicted of an offense under this chapter shall be assessed a criminal laboratory analysis fee of $50.00 for each offense for which he was convicted. Any person who is placed in supervisory treatment pursuant to N.J.S.2C:36A-1 or N.J.S.2 C:43-12 shall be assessed a criminal laboratory analysis fee of $50.00 for each such offense for which he was charged.

b. In addition to any other disposition made pursuant to the provisions of section 24 of P.L.1982, c.77 (C.2A:4A-43) or any other statute indicating the dispositions that can be ordered for adjudications of delinquency, any juvenile adjudicated delinquent for a violation of this chapter shall be assessed a laboratory analysis fee of $25.00 for each adjudication.

c. All criminal laboratory analysis fees provided for in this section shall be collected as provided for the collection of fines and restitutions in section 3 of P.L.1979, c.396 (C.2C:46-4), and shall be forwarded to the appropriate forensic laboratory fund as provided in subsection d. of this section.

d. Forensic laboratory funds shall be established as follows:

(1) Any county or municipality which maintains a publicly funded forensic laboratory that regularly employs at least one forensic chemist or scientist engaged in the analysis of controlled dangerous substances may establish a forensic laboratory fund within the office of the county or municipal treasurer.

(2) Any other county or municipality which has agreed by contract to pay or reimburse the entire salary of at least one forensic chemist or scientist employed by a laboratory designated as a State Forensic Laboratory pursuant to N.J.S.2C:35-19, may establish a forensic laboratory fund within the office of the county or municipal treasurer.

(3) A separate account shall be established in the State Treasury and shall be designated the "State Forensic Laboratory Fund."

e. The analysis fee provided for in subsections a. and b. of this section shall be forwarded to the office of the treasurer of the county or municipality that performed the laboratory analysis if that county or municipality has established a forensic laboratory fund or, to the State forensic laboratory fund if the analysis was performed by a laboratory operated by the State. If the county or municipality has not established a forensic laboratory fund, then the analysis fee shall be forwarded to the State forensic laboratory fund within the State Treasury. If the analysis was performed by a forensic chemist or scientist whose salary was paid or reimbursed by a county or municipality pursuant to a contract, the analysis fee shall be forwarded to the appropriate forensic laboratory fund established pursuant to paragraph (2) of subsection d. of this section unless the contract provides for a different means of allocating and distributing forensic laboratory fees, in which event the terms of the contract may determine the amounts to be forwarded to each forensic laboratory fund. The county or municipal treasurer and State Treasurer may retain an amount of the total of all collected analysis fees equal to the administrative costs incurred pursuant to carrying out their respective responsibilities under this section.

f. Moneys deposited in the county or municipal forensic laboratory fund created pursuant to paragraph (1) of subsection d. of this section shall be in addition to any allocations pursuant to existing law and shall be designated for the exclusive use of the county or municipal forensic laboratory. These uses may include, but are not limited to, the following:

(1) costs incurred in providing analyses for controlled substances in connection with criminal investigations conducted within this State;

(2) purchase and maintenance of equipment for use in performing analyses; and

(3) continuing education, training and scientific development of forensic scientists regularly employed by these laboratories.

g. Moneys deposited in the State forensic laboratory fund created pursuant to paragraph (3) of subsection d. of this section shall be used by State forensic laboratories that the Attorney General designates pursuant to N. J.S. 2C:35-19 and the Division of State Police in the Department of Law and Public Safety. These moneys shall be in addition to any allocations pursuant to existing law and shall be designated for the exclusive use of State forensic facilities. These uses may include those enumerated in subsection f. of this section.

**2C:35-21.**    **Seizure in violation of chapter; pretrial destruction of bulk seizures of controlled dangerous substances**

Any controlled dangerous substance or controlled substance analog seized in violation of this chapter shall be subject to the forfeiture provisions of chapter 64 of this title. In any case involving a bulk seizure of a controlled dangerous substance or a controlled substance analog, a prosecuting authority, upon notice to defense counsel, may apply to the trial court for an order to destroy all or some portion of the seized substance. The State, county or municipal forensic laboratory that analyzes the substance shall make a photographic record thereof.

In the event that the defendant objects to the application to destroy all or some portion of the controlled dangerous substance or controlled substance analog, defense counsel shall within 20 days of receiving notice from the prosecuting authority serve notice of objection upon the trial judge and the prosecuting authority. The notice of objection shall include the reasons therefor. Failure to comply with the time limitations regarding the notice of objection required by this section shall constitute a waiver of any objections to the destruction of all or some portion of the substance.

The decision to order the destruction of the substance shall be vested in the sound discretion of the trial court. Prior to the issuance of any order authorizing the destruction of all or some portion of the controlled dangerous substance or controlled substance analog, and subject to reasonable supervision by laboratory or agency personnel, defense counsel shall be afforded an opportunity to inspect or test the substance.

The State, county or municipal forensic laboratory authorized to destroy all or some portion of the controlled dangerous substance or controlled substance analog shall file with the court a certificate under oath attesting to the date on which the substance was destroyed, the quantity of the substance destroyed, and the method used to destroy the substance.

Notwithstanding any other provision of law, the photographic record made in accordance with the provisions of this section, upon proper authentication, may be introduced as evidence in any court.

**2C:35-22.**    **Severability**

If any one or more sections, clauses, sentences or parts of this chapter shall for any reason be questioned in any court, and shall be adjudged unconstitutional or invalid, the judgment shall not affect, impair or invalidate the remaining provisions thereof, but shall be confined in its operation to the specific provisions so held unconstitutional or invalid.

**2C:35-23.**    **Pending cases**

a. Except as provided in subsections b. and c. of this section, any violation of a provision of P.L. 1970, c. 226 (C. 24:21-1 et seq.) which is amended or deleted by this act, and which violation was committed prior to the effective date of this chapter, shall be governed by the prior law, which is continued in effect for that purpose, as if this act were not in force.

b. Any offense defined in this act and committed on or after the effective date shall be governed by the provisions of this act. For the purposes of this section, an offense was committed after the effective date of this act if any of the elements of the offense occurred subsequent thereto.

c. In any case pending on or initiated after the effective date of this act involving an offense defined herein and committed prior to such date:

(1) N.J.S. 2C:35-19 and N.J.S. 2C:35-21 shall govern, insofar as they are justly applicable and their application does not introduce confusion or delay;

(2) The court, with the consent of the defendant, may impose sentence under the provisions of this chapter applicable to the offense and the offender;

(3) A defendant who, on the effective date of this act, has not made application for supervisory treatment under section 27 of P.L. 1970, c. 226 (C. 24:21-27) shall not be eligible for supervisory treatment except pursuant to the provisions of 2C:43-12 and as provided in Chapter 36A of this title.

## 2C:35-24.     Possession of certain prescription drugs

A person who possesses a controlled dangerous substance that was prescribed or dispensed lawfully may possess it only in the container in which it was dispensed; except that the person may possess no more than a 10-day supply in other than the original container if the person produces, upon the request of a law enforcement officer, the name and address of the practitioner who prescribed the substance or the pharmacist who dispensed it. A person who violates this section is a disorderly person.

## PRACTICAL APPLICATION OF STATUTE

At times, an individual may lawfully possess a controlled dangerous substance. This legal possession of a CDS can only occur via a valid prescription from a practitioner such as a medical doctor.

Per 2C:35-24, an individual who lawfully possesses a controlled dangerous substance must keep it in the container in which it was originally dispensed. The only exception to this rule is that the person "may possess no more than a 10-day supply" in a different container. If a person violates the provisions of this statute, he is guilty of a disorderly persons offense.

# 35A

# ANTI-DRUG PROFITEERING

**2C:35A-1.**     **Short Title**

This act shall be known and may be cited as the "Anti-Drug Profiteering Act."

**2C:35A-2.**     **Declaration of policy and legislative findings**

The Legislature hereby finds and declares the following:

    a. Persons who engage in drug trafficking activities for profit are a form of professional criminal, and deserve enhanced punishment that is specially adapted to remove the economic incentives inherent in such criminal activities.

    b. It shall be the overriding objective of the provisions of this chapter to eliminate to the greatest extent possible the economic incentives inherent in commercial drug distribution activities at all levels within the drug distribution chain. In order to accomplish this objective, it is appropriate to impose stern economic sanctions in the form of monetary penalties against certain convicted drug offenders. So as to ensure that such economic sanctions are specially adapted and proportionate to the true nature, extent and profitability of the specific criminal activities involved, such monetary penalties should in appropriate cases be based upon a multiple of the street level value of all the illicit substances involved. The use of such a mechanism for calculating an appropriate monetary penalty will help to offset and overcome the perception of some drug offenders, and especially those who are well insulated within a drug trafficking network, that they face only a comparatively low risk of immediate detection and punishment. The Legislature, by adoption of the "Comprehensive Drug Reform Act," N.J.S.2C:35-1 et al., recognized the utility of such a mechanism by providing for the imposition of discretionary cash fines which may be based upon three, or in some cases five, times the street value of the illicit drugs involved.

    c. The imposition of monetary penalties pursuant to this act is intended to serve as an adjunct to forfeiture actions, which are designed to deprive offenders of the proceeds of their criminal activities and of all property used in furtherance of or to facilitate such illegal activities. While the seizure and forfeiture of property in accordance with the provisions of chapters 41 and 64 of this Title and P.L.1994, c.121 (money laundering) remain a critically important means by which to reduce the economic incentive inherent in drug trafficking activities, in many instances, given the efforts undertaken by offenders to conceal and disguise assets and to resort to complex financial transactions and money laundering schemes, it has become increasingly difficult for law enforcement agencies to establish to the required degree of certainty that a given asset or interest in property is subject to forfeiture.

Accordingly, it is necessary and appropriate to impose an in personam debt against the defendant which may be satisfied by proceeding against any asset or interest in property belonging to the defendant, whether or not such property can be directly or indirectly linked to criminal activity.

d. In order to ensure the maximum deterrent effect of imposing such specially adapted economic sanctions as are required pursuant to the provisions of this act, it shall be the policy of this State to enforce the judgment and to collect the entire debt, or the greatest possible portion thereof, as soon as is feasible following the imposition of the penalty, taking full advantage, where necessary, of this State's long arm jurisdiction and the full faith and credit clause of the Constitution of the United States.

## 2C:35A-3.    Criteria for imposition of anti-drug profiteering penalty

a. In addition to any other disposition authorized by this title, including but not limited to any fines which may be imposed pursuant to the provisions of N.J.S. 2C:43-3 and except as may be provided by section 5 of this chapter, where a person has been convicted of a crime defined in chapter 35 or 36 of this Title or any crime involving criminal street gang related activity as defined in subsection h. of N.J.S. 2C:44-3 or an attempt or conspiracy to commit such a crime, the court shall, upon the application of the prosecutor, sentence the person to pay a monetary penalty in an amount determined pursuant to section 4 of this chapter, provided the court finds at a hearing, which may occur at the time of sentencing, that the prosecutor has established by a preponderance of the evidence one or more of the grounds specified in this section. The findings of the court shall be incorporated in the record, and in making its findings, the court shall take judicial notice of any evidence, testimony or information adduced at the trial, plea hearing or other court proceedings and shall also consider the presentence report and any other relevant information.

b. Any of the following shall constitute grounds for imposing an Anti-Drug Profiteering Penalty:

   (1) The defendant was convicted of: (a) a violation of N.J.S. 2C:35-3 (leader of narcotics trafficking network), or (b) a violation of subsection g. of N.J.S. 2C:5-2 (leader of organized crime), or (c) an offense defined in chapter 41 of this Title (racketeering) which involved the manufacture, distribution, possession with intent to distribute or transportation of any controlled dangerous substance or controlled substance analog.

   (2) The defendant is a drug profiteer. A defendant is a drug profiteer when the conduct constituting the crime shows that the person has knowingly engaged in the illegal manufacture, distribution or transportation of any controlled dangerous substance, controlled substance analog or drug paraphernalia as a substantial source of livelihood. In making its determination, the court may consider all of the attending circumstances, including but not limited to the defendant's role in the criminal activity, the nature, amount and purity of the substance involved, the amount of cash or currency involved, the extent and accumulation of the defendant's assets during the course of the criminal activity and the defendant's net worth and his expenditures in relation to his legitimate sources of income.

   (3) The defendant is a wholesale drug distributor.

      (a) A defendant is a wholesale drug distributor when the conduct constituting the crime involves the manufacture, distribution or intended or attempted distribution of a controlled dangerous substance or controlled substance analog to any other person for pecuniary gain, knowing, believing, or under circumstances where it reasonably could be assumed that such other person would in turn distribute the substance to another or others for pecuniary gain. It shall not be necessary for the prosecution to establish to whom the substance was distributed or intended or attempted to be distributed, and the court may draw all reasonable inferences from the nature of the defendant's conduct and the substance involved that such other person, while not specifically identified, would in turn distribute the substance to another or others for pecuniary gain. In making its determination, the court shall consider all of the attending circumstances, including but not limited to the defendant's role in the criminal activity, the nature, amount and purity of the substance involved, and the likelihood that a substance of such purity would be intended to be distributed directly to the ultimate consumer of the substance.

(b) Notwithstanding that the prosecutor has established that the defendant is a wholesale drug distributor within the meaning of this paragraph, the court shall not impose an anti-drug profiteering penalty on that ground if the defendant establishes by a preponderance of the evidence at the hearing that his participation in the conduct constituting the crime was limited solely to operating a conveyance used to transport a controlled dangerous substance or controlled substance analog, or loading or unloading the substance into such a conveyance or storage facility. Nothing in this paragraph shall be construed to establish a basis for not imposing a penalty where the prosecutor has established any other ground or grounds specified in this section for the imposition of an anti-drug profiteering penalty.

(4) The defendant is a professional drug distributor. A professional drug distributor is a person who has at any time, for pecuniary gain, unlawfully distributed a controlled dangerous substance, controlled substance analog or drug paraphernalia to three or more different persons, or on five or more separate occasions regardless of the number of persons to whom the substance or paraphernalia was distributed.

(5) The defendant was involved in criminal street gang related activity.

c. In making its determination, the court may rely upon expert opinion in the form of live testimony or by affidavit, or by such other means as the court deems appropriate.

d. For the purposes of this chapter, an act is undertaken for pecuniary gain if it involves or contemplates the transfer of anything of value in exchange for a controlled dangerous substance, controlled substance analog or drug paraphernalia, provided that the thing of value received or intended to be received in exchange for the substance or paraphernalia is or was reasonably believed to be of a higher value than that expended by the defendant or by any other person with whom the actor is acting in concert, to acquire or manufacture the substance or paraphernalia. It shall also include any act which would constitute a violation of subsection a. of N.J.S. 2C:35-5, N.J.S. 2C:35-11, N.J.S. 2C:36-3 or any other crime for which the actor was paid or expected to be paid in return for performing such act, or from which the actor received a benefit for himself or another or injured another or deprived another of a benefit. There shall be a rebuttable presumption at the hearing that any manufacturing, distribution or possession with intent to distribute which contemplates or involves the payment or exchange of anything of value constitutes an act undertaken for pecuniary gain. It shall not be necessary for the prosecution to establish that any intended profit or payment was actually received; nor shall it be relevant that the act, payment in return for such act or the transfer of anything of value in exchange for the substance or paraphernalia, occurred or was intended to occur in another jurisdiction.

**2C:35A-4.        Calculation of anti-drug profiteering penalty**

    a. Where the prosecutor has established one or more grounds for imposing an Anti-Drug Profiteering Penalty pursuant to section 3 of this chapter, the court shall assess a monetary penalty as follows:

        (1) $200,000.00 in the case of a crime of the first degree; $100,000.00 in the case of a crime of the second degree; $50,000.00 in the case of a crime of the third degree; $25,000.00 in the case of a crime of the fourth degree;

        (2) an amount equal to three times the street value of all controlled dangerous substances or controlled substance analogs involved, or three times the market value of all drug paraphernalia involved, if this amount is greater than that provided in paragraph (1) of this subsection; or

        (3) an amount equal to three times the value of any benefit illegally obtained by the actor for himself or another, or any injury to or benefit deprived of

    b. When the court is for any reason unable to determine the amount of the penalty pursuant to paragraph (2) of subsection a., the court shall assess a penalty in the amount appropriate to the degree of the offense as provided in paragraph (1) of subsection a.

    c. In determining the street value of the substance involved or the market value of drug paraphernalia involved, the court shall take into account all amounts of the substance or paraphernalia reasonably believed to have been involved in the course of the criminal activity in which the defendant knowingly participated, and it shall not be relevant for the purposes of this section that some of those amounts or paraphernalia were involved in acts or transactions which occurred, or which were intended to occur, in another jurisdiction.

    d. Where the prosecution requests that the court assess a penalty in an amount calculated pursuant to paragraph (2) or (3) of subsection a., the prosecutor shall have the burden of establishing by a preponderance of the evidence the appropriate amount of the penalty to be assessed pursuant to that paragraph. In making its finding, the court shall take judicial notice of any evidence, testimony or information adduced at trial, plea hearing or other court proceedings and shall also consider the presentence report and other relevant information, including expert opinion in the form of live testimony or by affidavit. The court's findings shall be incorporated in the record, and such findings shall not be subject to modification by an appellate court except upon a showing that the finding was totally lacking support in the record or was arbitrary and capricious.

**2C:35A-5.        Revocation or reduction of penalty assessment**

The court shall not revoke or reduce a penalty imposed pursuant to this chapter except in accordance with the provisions of N.J.S. 2C:35-12. An anti-drug profiteering penalty imposed pursuant to this chapter shall not be deemed a fine for purposes of N.J.S. 2C:46-3.

**2C:35A-6.        Payment schedule**

The court may, for good cause shown, and subject to the provisions of this section, grant permission for the payment of a penalty assessed pursuant to this chapter to be made within a specified period of time or in specified installments, provided however that the payment schedule fixed by the court shall require the defendant to pay the penalty in the shortest period of time consistent with the nature and extent of his assets and his ability to pay, and further provided that the prosecutor shall be afforded the opportunity to present evidence or information concerning the nature, extent and location of the defendant's assets or interests in property which are or might be subject to levy and execution. In such event, the court may only grant permission for the payment to be made within a specified period of time or installments with respect to that portion of the assessed penalty which would not be satisfied by the liquidation of property which is or may be subject to levy and execution, unless the court finds that the immediate liquidation of such property would result in undue hardship to innocent persons. If no permission to make payment within a specified period of time or in installments is embodied in the sentence, the entire penalty shall be payable forthwith.

**2C:35A-7.**     **Relation to other dispositions**

a.  An anti-drug profiteering penalty assessed pursuant to this chapter shall be imposed and paid in addition to any penalty required to be imposed pursuant to N.J.S. 2C:35-15 and N.J.S. 2C:43-3.1, any fee required to be imposed pursuant to N.J.S. 2C:35-20, and any other fine, penalty, fee or order for restitution which may be imposed.

b.  An anti-drug profiteering penalty imposed pursuant to this chapter shall be in addition to and not in lieu of any forfeiture or other cause of action instituted pursuant to chapter 41 or 64 of this Title, and nothing in this chapter shall be construed in any way to preclude, preempt or limit any such cause of action. A defendant shall not be entitled to receive credit toward the payment of a penalty imposed pursuant to this chapter for the value of property forfeited, or subject to forfeiture, pursuant to the provisions of chapters 41 and 64 of this Title.

**2C:35A-8.**     **Collection and distribution**

All penalties assessed pursuant to this chapter shall be docketed and collected as provided for collection of fines, penalties and restitution in chapter 46 of this Title. The Attorney General or prosecutor may prosecute an action to collect penalties imposed pursuant to this chapter. All penalties assessed pursuant to this chapter shall be disposed of, distributed, appropriated and used as if the collected penalties were the proceeds of property forfeited pursuant to chapter 64 of this Title.

# 35B

# DRUG DEALER LIABILITY

**2C:35B-1.**      **Short title**

This act shall be known and may be cited as the "Drug Dealer Liability Act."

**2C:35B-2.**      **Findings, declarations regarding civil actions against drug dealers**

The Legislature finds and declares:

     a. Although the criminal justice system is an important weapon in the battle against controlled dangerous substances, the civil justice system can and must also be used. The civil justice system can provide an avenue of compensation for those who have suffered harm as a result of the marketing and distribution of controlled dangerous substances. The persons who have joined the marketing of controlled dangerous substances should bear the cost of the harm caused by that market in the community.

     b. The threat of liability under this act serves as an additional deterrent to a recognizable segment of the network for marketing controlled dangerous substances. Because of this threat, a person who has assets unrelated to the sale of controlled dangerous substances, who markets controlled dangerous substances at the workplace, who encourages friends to become users, is likely to decide that the added cost of entering the market is not worth the benefit. This is particularly true for a first-time, casual dealer who has not yet made substantial profits.

     c. This act is intended to provide a mechanism whereby the costs of the injuries caused by illegal drug use will be borne by those who benefit from illegal drug dealing.

     d. This act imposes liability against all participants in the marketing of controlled dangerous substances, including small dealers, particularly those in the workplace, who are not usually the focus of criminal investigations. Small dealers increase the number of users and ultimately are the people who become large dealers. It is these small dealers who are most likely to be deterred by the threat of liability.

**2C:35B-3.**      **Definitions regarding civil actions against drug dealers**

As used in this act:

     a. "Marketing of controlled dangerous substances" means the illegal distributing, dispensing, or possessing with intent to distribute, a specified controlled dangerous substance.

     b. "Individual user of controlled dangerous substance" means the individual whose illegal use of a specified controlled dangerous substance is the basis of an action brought under this act.

     c. "Level 1 offense" means:

         (1) possessing with intent to distribute less than four ounces of a specified controlled dangerous substance as defined in this section;

    (2) distributing or dispensing less than one ounce of a specified controlled dangerous substance as defined in this section;

    (3) possessing with intent to distribute 25 or more but less than 50 marijuana plants;

    (4) possessing with intent to distribute less than four pounds of marijuana, or

    (5) distributing or dispensing more than 28.5 grams of marijuana.

d. "Level 2 offense" means:

    (1) possessing with intent to distribute four ounces or more but less than eight ounces of a specified controlled dangerous substance as defined in this section;

    (2) distributing or dispensing one ounce or more but less than two ounces of a specified controlled dangerous substance as defined in this section;

    (3) possessing with intent to distribute 50 or more but less than 75 marijuana plants;

    (4) possessing with intent to distribute four pounds or more but less than eight pounds of marijuana, or

    (5) distributing or dispensing more than one pound but less than five pounds of marijuana.

e. "Level 3 offense" means:

    (1) possessing with intent to distribute eight ounces or more but less than 16 ounces of a specified controlled dangerous substance as defined in this section;

    (2) distributing or dispensing two ounces or more but less than four ounces of a specified controlled dangerous substance as defined in this section;

    (3) possessing with intent to distribute 75 or more but less than 100 marijuana plants;

    (4) possessing with intent to distribute eight pounds or more but less than 16 pounds of marijuana, or

    (5) distributing or dispensing more than five pounds but less than ten pounds of marijuana.

f. "Level 4 offense" means:

    (1) possessing with intent to distribute 16 ounces or more of a specified controlled dangerous substance as defined in this section;

    (2) distributing or dispensing four ounces or more of a specified controlled dangerous substance as defined in this section;

    (3) possessing with intent to distribute 100 or more marijuana plants;

    (4) possessing with intent to distribute 16 pounds or more of marijuana, or

    (5) distributing or dispensing more than 10 pounds of marijuana.

g. "Participate in the illegal marketing of controlled dangerous substances" means to transport, import into this State, distribute, dispense, sell, possess with intent to distribute, or offer to distribute a controlled dangerous substance, in violation of any of the provisions of chapter 35 of Title 2C of the New Jersey Statutes. "Participate in the marketing of controlled dangerous substances" does not include the purchase or receipt of a controlled dangerous substance for personal use only.

h. "Person" means any natural person, association, partnership, corporation or other entity.

i. "Period of illegal use" means, in relation to the individual user of a controlled dangerous substance, the time of the individual's first illegal use of a controlled dangerous substance to the accrual of the cause of action.

j. "Place of illegal activity" means, in relation to the individual user of a specified controlled dangerous substance, each county in which the individual illegally possess or uses a specified controlled dangerous substance.

k. "Place of participation" means, in relation to a defendant in an action brought under this act, each county in which the defendant participates in the marketing of controlled dangerous substances.

l. "Specified controlled dangerous substance" means heroin, cocaine, lysergic acid diethylamide, phencyclidine, methamphetamine, phenyl-2-propanone (P2P) and any other controlled dangerous substance specified under the provisions of N.J.S.2C:35-5 as being unlawful to manufacture, distribute, or dispense, or to possess or have under a person's control with intent to manufacture, distribute or dispense.

## 2C:35B-4.        Liability of illegal marketer of controlled dangerous substances

A person who knowingly participates in the illegal marketing of controlled dangerous substances within this State is liable for damages, as provided in this act, for injury resulting from an individual's illegal use of a controlled dangerous substance.

## 2C:35B-5.        Actions for damages; plaintiffs; offenses

a. Any of the following persons may bring an action for damages caused by an individual's illegal use of a controlled dangerous substance:

  (1) A parent, legal guardian, child, spouse, or sibling of the controlled dangerous substance user.

  (2) An individual who was exposed to a controlled dangerous substance in utero.

  (3) An employer of the controlled dangerous substance user.

  (4) A medical facility, insurer, employer, or other nongovernmental entity that funded a drug treatment program or employee assistance program for the controlled dangerous substance user or that otherwise expended money on behalf of the controlled dangerous substance user.

  (5) A person injured as a result of the reckless or negligent actions of an individual user of a controlled dangerous substance.

       No public entity, and no public agency other than a public hospital, shall have a cause of action under this act.

b. A person entitled to bring an action under this act may seek damages against:

  (1) A person who illegally distributed or dispensed a controlled dangerous substance to the individual user of the controlled dangerous substance; or

  (2) A person who knowingly participated in the illegal marketing of controlled dangerous substances, if all of the following apply:

    (a) The defendant's place of participation is situated in the same county as the individual user's place of illegal activity;

    (b) The defendant participated in the marketing of the same type of controlled dangerous substances as those used by the individual user;

    (c) The defendant was previously convicted of an offense in the State of New Jersey for that type of controlled dangerous substance; and

    (d) The defendant participated in the marketing of controlled dangerous substances at any time during the period the individual user unlawfully used the controlled dangerous substance.

c. A person entitled to bring an action under this section may recover all of the following damages:

(1) Economic damages, including, but not limited to, the cost of treatment and rehabilitation, medical expenses, loss of economic or educational potential, loss of productivity, absenteeism, support expenses, accidents or injury, and any other pecuniary loss proximately caused by the use of a controlled dangerous substance.

(2) Noneconomic damages, including but not limited to physical and emotional pain, suffering, physical impairment, physical impairment, emotional distress, disfigurement, loss of enjoyment, loss of companionship, services and consortium, and other nonpecuniary losses proximately caused by an individual's use of a controlled dangerous substance.

(3) Punitive damages.

(4) Reasonable attorney fees.

(5) Costs of suit, including, but not limited to, reasonable expenses for expert testimony.

**2C:35B-6.** **Controlled dangerous substance individual user; conditions to bring an action**

a. An individual user of a controlled dangerous substance may bring an action for damages caused by the use of a controlled dangerous substance only if all of the following conditions are met:

(1) The individual personally discloses to narcotics enforcement authorities all of the information known to the individual regarding all that individual's sources of controlled dangerous substances.

(2) The individual has not used a controlled dangerous substance within the 30 days before filing the action.

(3) The individual continues to remain free of the use of an illegal controlled substance throughout the pendency of the action.

b. An individual user entitled to bring an action under this section may seek damages only from a person who transported, imported into this State, distributed, dispensed, sold, possessed with intent to distribute, or offered to distribute, in violation of any of the provisions of chapter 35 of Title 2C of the New Jersey Statutes, the controlled dangerous substance actually used by the individual user of a controlled dangerous substance.

c. An individual user entitled to bring an action under this section may recover only the following damages:

(1) Economic damages, including, but not limited to, the cost of treatment, rehabilitation and medical expenses, loss of economic or educational potential, loss of productivity, absenteeism, accidents or injury, and any other pecuniary loss proximately caused by the person's use of a controlled dangerous substance.

(2) Reasonable attorney fees.

(3) Costs of suit, including, but not limited to, reasonable expenses for expert testimony.

**2C:35B-7.** **No third party damage payments; assignment of cause of action restricted**

a. A third party shall not pay damages awarded under this act, or provide a defense or money for a defense, on behalf of an insured under a contract of insurance or indemnification.

b. A cause of action authorized pursuant to this act may not be assigned, either expressly, by subrogation, or by any other means, directly or indirectly, to any public or publicly funded agency or institution.

**2C:35B-8.        Damage table**

A person whose participation in the marketing of controlled dangerous substances is grounds for liability pursuant to this act shall be rebuttably presumed to be liable for damages incurred by the plaintiff in the following percentages:

    a.  For a level 1 offense, 25 percent of the damages;

    b.  For a level 2 offense, 50 percent of the damages;

    c.  For a level 3 offense, 75 percent of the damages; and

    d.  For a level 4 offense, 100 percent of the damages.

**2C:35B-9.        Joint actions**

    a.  Two or more persons may join in one action under this act as plaintiffs if their respective actions have at least one market for controlled dangerous substances in common and if any portion of the period of use of a controlled dangerous substance overlaps with the period of use of a controlled dangerous substance for every other plaintiff.

    b.  Two or more persons may be joined in one action under this act as defendants if those persons are liable to at least one plaintiff.

**2C:35B-10.        Comparative responsibility governing action**

    a.  An action by an individual user of a controlled dangerous substance is governed by the principles of comparative responsibility. Comparative responsibility attributed to an individual user does not bar the user's recovery but diminishes the award of damages proportionately, according to the measure of responsibility attributed to the user. The burden of proving comparative responsibility is on the defendant, who shall prove comparative responsibility by clear and convincing evidence.

    b.  Comparative responsibility shall not be attributed to a plaintiff who is not an individual user of a controlled substance, unless that plaintiff knowingly gave the individual user money for the purchase of the controlled dangerous substance.

**2C:35B-11.        Right of action for contribution**

A person subject to liability under this act has a right of action for contribution against another person subject to liability under this act. Contribution may be enforced either in the original action or by a separate action brought for that purpose. A plaintiff may seek recovery in accordance with this act and other laws against a person whom a defendant has asserted a right of contribution.

**2C:35B-12.        Proof of liability; prima facie evidence**

    a.  Proof of liability in an action brought under this act shall be shown by clear and convincing evidence.

    b.  A person against whom recovery is sought who has been convicted of a violation of N.J.S.2C:35-5, Manufacturing, Distributing or Dispensing, or an equivalent offense under federal law or the law of any other state, is estopped from denying illegal participation in the market for controlled dangerous substances. If such conviction was based upon the same type of controlled dangerous substance as that used by the individual user, the conviction also constitutes prima facie evidence of the person's participation in the marketing of controlled dangerous substance user pursuant to this act.

c. The absence of a criminal conviction for a violation of N.J.S.2C:35-5 or an equivalent offense under federal law or the law of any other state does not bar recovery by a plaintiff bringing suit pursuant to subsection b. of section 5 of this act.

## 2C:35B-13. Ex parte prejudgment attachment order

A plaintiff under this act may request an ex parte prejudgment attachment order from the court against all assets of a defendant sufficient to satisfy a potential award. Any claim of the State authorized pursuant to chapter 35A and 64 of Title 2C of the New Jersey Statutes shall have priority over an order issued pursuant to this section.

## 2C:35B-14. Cause of action; accrual; statute of limitations on claim

a. A cause of action accrues under this act when a person has reason to know of the harm from use of a controlled dangerous substance that is the basis for the cause of action and has reason to know that the use of a controlled dangerous substance is the cause of the harm.

b. Except as provided in subsection a. of this section, a claim under this act shall not be brought more than one year after the defendant distributes, dispenses, or possesses with intent to distribute, the controlled dangerous substance or more than one year after the defendant is convicted of a crime involving controlled dangerous substances, whichever is the later.

## 2C:35B-15. Stay of action pending criminal action

On motion by a governmental agency involved in an investigation or prosecution involving a controlled dangerous substance, an action brought under this act shall be stayed until the completion of any underlying criminal investigation or prosecution.

## 2C:35B-16. Satisfaction of judgment after other fines, penalties, etc.

Any judgment resulting from a cause of action brought pursuant to this act shall be satisfied only after the satisfaction of any assessment, fine, fee, penalty or restitution imposed by law and enumerated in section 13 of P.L. 1991, c. 329 (C.2C:46-4.1).

## 2C:35B-17. Nonapplicability of act

No cause of action shall arise based on any act by a defendant which occurred prior to the effective date of this act.

# 36

# DRUG PARAPHERNALIA

**2C:36-1.**     **Drug paraphernalia; defined; determination**

As used in this act, "drug paraphernalia" means all equipment, products and materials of any kind which are used or intended for use in planting, propagating, cultivating, growing, harvesting, manufacturing, compounding, converting, producing, processing, preparing, testing, analyzing, packaging, repackaging, storing, containing, concealing, ingesting, inhaling, or otherwise introducing into the human body a controlled dangerous substance or controlled substance analog in violation of the provisions of chapter 35 of this title. It shall include, but not be limited to: a. kits used or intended for use in planting, propagating, cultivating, growing or harvesting of any species of plant which is a controlled dangerous substance or from which a controlled dangerous substance can be derived; b. kits used or intended for use in manufacturing, compounding, converting, producing, processing, or preparing controlled dangerous substances or controlled substance analogs; c. isomerization devices used or intended for use in increasing the potency of any species of plant which is a controlled dangerous substance; d. testing equipment used or intended for use identifying, or in analyzing the strength, effectiveness or purity of controlled dangerous substances or controlled substance analogs; e. scales and balances used or intended for use in weighing or measuring controlled dangerous substances or controlled substance analogs; f. dilutants and adulterants, such as quinine hydrochloride, mannitol, mannite, dextrose and lactose, used or intended for use in cutting controlled dangerous substances or controlled substance analogs; g. separation gins and sifters used or intended for use in removing twigs and seeds from, or in otherwise cleaning or refining, marihuana; h. blenders, bowls, containers, spoons and mixing devices used or intended for use in compounding controlled dangerous substances or controlled substance analogs; i. capsules, balloons, envelopes and other containers used or intended for use in packaging small quantities of controlled dangerous substances or controlled substance analogs; j. containers and other objects used or intended for use in storing or concealing controlled dangerous substances or controlled substance analogs; k. objects used or intended for use in ingesting, inhaling, or otherwise introducing marihuana, cocaine, hashish, or hashish oil into the human body, such as (1) metal, wooden, acrylic, glass, stone, plastic, or ceramic pipes with or without screens, permanent screens, hashish heads, or punctured metal bowls; (2) water pipes; (3) carburetion tubes and devices; (4) smoking and carburetion masks; (5) roach clips, meaning objects used to hold burning material, such as a marihuana cigarette, that has become too small or too short to be held in the hand; (6) miniature cocaine spoons, and cocaine vials; (7) chamber pipes; (8) carburetor pipes; (9) electric pipes; (10) air-driven pipes; (11) chillums; (12) bongs; and (13) ice pipes or chillers.

In determining whether or not an object is drug paraphernalia, the trier of fact, in addition to or as part of the proofs, may consider the following factors: a. statements by an owner or by anyone in control of the object concerning its use; b. the proximity of the object of illegally possessed controlled dangerous substances or controlled substance analogs; c. the existence of any residue of illegally possessed controlled dangerous substances or controlled substance analogs on the object; d. direct or circumstantial evidence of the intent of an owner, or of anyone in control of the object, to deliver it to persons whom he knows intend to use the object to facilitate a violation of this act; the innocence of an owner, or of anyone in control of the object, as to a direct violation of this act shall not prevent a finding that the object is intended for use as drug paraphernalia; e. instructions, oral or written, provided with the object concerning its use; f. descriptive materials accompanying the object which explain or depict its use; g. national or local advertising whose purpose the person knows or should know is to promote the sale of objects intended for use as drug paraphernalia; h. the manner in which the object is displayed for sale; i. the existence and scope of legitimate uses for the object in the community; and j. expert testimony concerning its use.

## 2C:36-2.          Use or possession with intent to use; disorderly persons offense

It shall be unlawful for any person to use, or to possess with intent to use, drug paraphernalia to plant, propagate, cultivate, grow, harvest, manufacture, compound, convert, produce, process, prepare, test, analyze, pack, repack, store, contain, conceal, ingest, inhale, or otherwise introduce into the human body a controlled dangerous substance or controlled substance analog in violation of the provisions of chapter 35 of this title. Any person who violates this section is guilty of a disorderly persons offense.

## PRACTICAL APPLICATION OF STATUTE

Red Beard is guilty of violating 2C:36-2 for possessing a pipe ordinarily used for smoking marijuana. This is a disorderly persons offense.

2C:36-2 is the statute that prohibits the possession or use of any drug paraphernalia. Drug paraphernalia are not just items such as pipes, bongs, and straws that are used for intake of controlled dangerous substances into the human body. Prohibited paraphernalia also include objects such as indoor gardening lamps and devices that are used for planting and cultivating CDSs. In addition, possession of "cow patties" and tropinine are violative of the statute, as they are used to manufacture psychedelic mushrooms and cocaine, respectively. Glass containers, bags, and vials can be considered drug paraphernalia as well, because drugs are often packaged and contained in them. In sum, this statute makes it illegal to possess a wide range of items—basically anything that is connected to the manufacture, distribution, and use of CDSs.

Red Beard was caught by the Hawthorne Police amidst a rather large illegal cocaine transaction. At the time of his arrest, cocaine and marijuana were confiscated from his person and automobile. Also confiscated was a pipe ordinarily used for smoking marijuana. Red Beard's possession of this item of drug paraphernalia renders him guilty of a disorderly persons offense under 2C:36-2.

## 2C:36-3.          Distribute, dispense or possession with intent to distribute or manufacture; crime of fourth degree

It shall be unlawful for any person to distribute or dispense, or possess with intent to distribute or dispense, or manufacture with intent to distribute or dispense, drug paraphernalia, knowing that it will be used to plant, propagate, cultivate, grow, harvest, manufacture, compound, convert, produce, process, prepare, test, analyze, pack, repack, store, contain, conceal, ingest, inhale or otherwise introduce into the human body a controlled dangerous substance or controlled substance analog in violation of the provisions of chapter 35 of this title. Any person who violates this section commits a crime of the fourth degree.

## PRACTICAL APPLICATION OF STATUTE

Whereas it is a disorderly persons offense to use or possess drug paraphernalia, it is a fourth degree crime to distribute it. Here the mental state of "knowledge" is key. One must "know" that the items he is distributing to another will be used as drug paraphernalia (i.e., used to cultivate, grow, manufacture, package, ingest, etc., a CDS).

**2C:36-4.**  **Advertising to promote sale; crime of fourth degree**

It shall be unlawful for any person to place in any newspaper, magazine, handbill, or other publication any advertisement, knowing that the purpose of the advertisement in whole or in part, is to promote the sale of objects intended for use as drug paraphernalia. Any person who violates this section commits a crime of the fourth degree.

## PRACTICAL APPLICATION OF STATUTE

It is a fourth degree crime to advertise in any publication the sale of any objects intended for use as drug paraphernalia. Again, "knowledge" is important. The defendant must "know" that the purpose of the ad is to promote the sale of drug paraphernalia. In other words, a person cannot be convicted under this statute if his total purpose of advertising a particular object was to promote the sale of the object for a lawful use (e.g., advertising in a medical magazine the sale of vials to hold blood).

**2C:36-5.**  **Delivering drug paraphernalia to person under 18 years of age; crime of third degreee**

Any person 18 years of age or over who violates N.J.S. 2C:36-3 by delivering drug paraphernalia to a person under 18 years of age commits a crime of the third degree.

## PRACTICAL APPLICATION OF STATUTE

This statute is an offshoot of 2C:36-3. Simply, a person who distributes drug paraphernalia to a minor is guilty of a third degree crime rather than a fourth degree crime.

**2C:36-6.**  **Possession or distribution of hypodermic syringe or needle**

   a. Except as authorized by subsection b., c. or other law, it shall be unlawful for a person to have under his control or possess with intent to use a hypodermic syringe, hypodermic needle or any other instrument adapted for the use of a controlled dangerous substance or a controlled substance analog as defined in chapter 35 of Title 2C of the New Jersey Statutes or to sell, furnish or give to any person such syringe, needle or instrument. Any person who violates this section is guilty of a disorderly persons offense.

b. A person is authorized to possess and use a hypodermic needle or hypodermic syringe if the person obtains the hypodermic syringe or hypodermic needle by a valid prescription issued by a licensed physician, dentist or veterinarian and uses it for its authorized purpose.

    No prescription for a hypodermic syringe, hypodermic needle or any other instrument adapted for the use of controlled dangerous substances by subcutaneous injections shall be valid for more than one year from the date of issuance.

c. Subsection a. does not apply to a duly licensed physician, dentist, veterinarian, undertaker, nurse, podiatrist, registered pharmacist, or a hospital, sanitarium, clinical laboratory or any other medical institution, or a state or a governmental agency, or a regular dealer in medical, dental or surgical supplies, or a resident physician or intern of a hospital, sanitarium or other medical institution.

## PRACTICAL APPLICATION OF STATUTE

Generally, any person who possesses a hypodermic needle or syringe is guilty of a disorderly persons offense. Following Red Beard's arrest for cocaine distribution, he was caught with a hypodermic syringe and should be convicted under this statute.

    Subsections b. and c. provide exceptions where individuals may lawfully possess hypodermic needles and syringes. Examples include licensed physicians, dentists, veterinarians, undertakers, nurses (see subsection c.), and individuals who are validly prescribed the objects by licensed physicians, dentists, and veterinarians (see subsection b.). Since Red Beard does not fall within any of these categories, he should be convicted of a disorderly persons offense under 2C:36-6. He had a hypodermic needle under his control—but no lawful reason for the same.

**2C:36-6.1.**      **Discarding hypodermic needle or syringe**

a. A person commits a petty disorderly persons offense if

    (1) the person discards, in a place accessible to other persons, a hypodermic needle or syringe without destroying the hypodermic needle or syringe; or

    (2) he is the owner, lessee or person in control of real property and, knowing that needles and syringes in an intact condition have been discarded or abandoned on his real property, allows them to remain.

b. A hypodermic needle is destroyed if the needle is broken from the hub or mangled. A syringe is destroyed if the nipple of the barrel is broken from the barrel, or the plunger and barrel are melted. Alternatively, a hypodermic needle or syringe is destroyed if it is discarded as a single unit, without recapping, into a rigid container and the container is destroyed by grinding or crushing in a compactor, or by burning in an incinerator approved by the Department of Environmental Protection, or by another method approved by the Department of Health and Senior Services.

## PRACTICAL APPLICATION OF STATUTE

Per 2C:36-6.1a.(1), a person who discards a hypodermic needle or syringe without destroying it is guilty of a petty disorderly persons offense—unless it is in a place not accessible to other persons. Likewise, under 2C:36-6.1a.(2), a person in control of real estate property (e.g., owner, lessee) who "knowingly" permits discarded, not destroyed, hypodermic needles to remain on the property is guilty of a petty disorderly persons offense. Subsection b. of the statute defines what constitutes "destroyed" needles and syringes.

**2C:36-7.**     **Seizure in violation of Chapter**

Any drug paraphernalia, hypodermic syringe or needle seized in violation of this chapter shall be subject to the forfeiture provisions of Chapter 64 of this title.

**2C:36-8.**     **Severability**

If any provision of this chapter or the application thereof to any person or circumstance are held invalid, the invalidity shall not affect other provisions or applications of the sections which can be given effect without the invalid provision or application, and to this end the provisions of this chapter are severable.

**2C:36-9.**     **Pending cases**

Notwithstanding any other provision of this act, the provisions of P.L. 1970, c. 226 (C. 24:21-1 et seq.) shall remain in full force and effect as to any offense committed prior to the effective date of this act.

**2C:36-10.**     **Definition of "defraud the administration of a drug test;" crime, grading**

    a. As used in this act, "defraud the administration of a drug test" means to submit a substance that purports to be from a person other than its actual source, or purports to have been excreted or collected at a time other than when it was actually excreted or collected, or to otherwise engage in conduct intended to produce a false or misleading outcome of a test for the presence of a chemical, drug or controlled dangerous substance, or a metabolite of a drug or controlled dangerous substance, in the human body. It shall specifically include, but shall not be limited to, the furnishing of urine with the purpose that the urine be submitted for urinalysis as a true specimen of a person.

    b. Any person who offers for sale or rental, or who manufactures, sells, transfers, or gives to any person, any instrument, tool, device or substance adapted, designed or commonly used to defraud the administration of a drug test, is guilty of a crime of the third degree.

    c. Any person who knowingly defrauds the administration of a drug test that is administered as a condition of employment or continued employment as a law enforcement officer, corrections officer, school bus driver, operator of a motorbus, employee of a rail passenger service, firefighter, provider of emergency first-aid or medical services, or any other occupation that requires the administration of a drug test as a condition of employment or continued employment by law, rule or regulation of the State or a local agency, public authority, or the federal government, is guilty of a crime of the third degree.

    d. Any person who knowingly defrauds the administration of a drug test that is administered as a condition of monitoring a person on bail, in custody or on parole, probation or pretrial intervention, or any other form of supervision administered in connection with a criminal offense or juvenile delinquency matter, is guilty of a crime of the third degree.

    e. Any person who knowingly possesses any instrument, product, tool, device or substance adapted, designed or commonly used to defraud the administration of a drug test is guilty of a crime of the fourth degree.

    f. Any person who knowingly defrauds the administration of a drug test which is administered as a condition of any employment or continued employment not specified in subsection c. of this section is guilty of a crime of the fourth degree.

# 36A

# CONDITIONAL DISCHARGE FOR CERTAIN FIRST OFFENDERS

**2C:36A-1.**    **Conditional discharge for certain first offenders; expunging of records**

a. Whenever any person who has not previously been convicted of any offense under section 20 of P.L.1970, c. 226 (C.24:21-20), or a disorderly persons or petty disorderly persons offense defined in chapter 35 or 36 of this title or, subsequent to the effective date of this title, under any law of the United States, this State or any other state relating to marijuana, or stimulant, depressant, or hallucinogenic drugs, is charged with or convicted of any disorderly persons offense or petty disorderly persons offense under chapter 35 or 36 of this title, the court upon notice to the prosecutor and subject to subsection c. of this section, may on motion of the defendant or the court:

(1) Suspend further proceedings and with the consent of the person after reference to the State Bureau of Identification criminal history record information files, place him under supervisory treatment upon such reasonable terms and conditions as it may require; or

(2) After plea of guilty or finding of guilty, and without entering a judgment of conviction, and with the consent of the person after proper reference to the State Bureau of Identification criminal history record information files, place him on supervisory treatment upon reasonable terms and conditions as it may require, or as otherwise provided by law.

b. In no event shall the court require as a term or condition of supervisory treatment under this section, referral to any residential treatment facility for a period exceeding the maximum period of confinement prescribed by law for the offense for which the individual has been charged or convicted, nor shall any term of supervisory treatment imposed under this subsection exceed a period of three years. If a person is placed under supervisory treatment under this section after a plea of guilty or finding of guilt, the court as a term and condition of supervisory treatment shall suspend the person's driving privileges for a period to be fixed by the court at not less than six months or more than two years. In the case of a person who at the time of placement under supervisory treatment under this section is less than 17 years of age, the period of suspension of driving privileges authorized herein, including a suspension of the privilege of operating a motorized bicycle, shall commence on the day the person is placed on supervisory treatment and shall run for a period as fixed by the court of not less than six months or more than two years after the day the person reaches the age of 17 years.

If the driving privilege of a person is under revocation, suspension, or postponement for a violation of this title or Title 39 of the Revised Statutes at the time of the person's placement on supervisory treatment under this section, the revocation, suspension or postponement period imposed herein shall commence as of the date of the termination of the existing revocation, suspension or postponement. The court which places a person on supervisory treatment under this section shall collect and forward the person's driver's license to the Division of Motor Vehicles and file an appropriate report with the division in accordance with the procedure set forth in N.J.S.2C:35-16. The court shall also inform the person of the penalties for operating a motor vehicle during the period of license suspension or postponement as required in N.J.S.2C:35-16.

Upon violation of a term or condition of supervisory treatment the court may enter a judgment of conviction and proceed as otherwise provided, or where there has been no plea of guilty or finding of guilty, resume proceedings. Upon fulfillment of the terms and conditions of supervisory treatment the court shall terminate the supervisory treatment and dismiss the proceedings against him. Termination of supervisory treatment and dismissal under this section shall be without court adjudication of guilt and shall not be deemed a conviction for purposes of disqualifications or disabilities, if any, imposed by law upon conviction of a crime or disorderly persons offense but shall be reported by the clerk of the court to the State Bureau of Identification criminal history record information files. Termination of supervisory treatment and dismissal under this section may occur only once with respect to any person. Imposition of supervisory treatment under this section shall not be deemed a conviction for the purposes of determining whether a second or subsequent offense has occurred under section 29 of P.L.1970, c. 226 (C.24:21-29), chapter 35 or 36 of this title or any law of this State.

c.  Proceedings under this section shall not be available to any defendant unless the court in its discretion concludes that:

   (1) The defendant's continued presence in the community, or in a civil treatment center or program, will not pose a danger to the community; or

   (2) That the terms and conditions of supervisory treatment will be adequate to protect the public and will benefit the defendant by serving to correct any dependence on or use of controlled substances which he may manifest; and

   (3) The person has not previously received supervisory treatment under section 27 of P.L.1970, c. 226 (C.24:21-27), N.J.S. 2C:43-12, or the provisions of this chapter.

d.  A person seeking conditional discharge pursuant to this section shall pay to the court a fee of $75.00. The court shall forward all money collected under this subsection to the treasurer of the county in which the court is located. This money shall be used to defray the cost of juror compensation within that county. A person may apply for a waiver of this fee, by reason of poverty, pursuant to the Rules Governing the Courts of the State of New Jersey. Of the moneys collected under this subsection, $30.00 of each fee shall be deposited in the temporary reserve fund created by section 25 of P.L.1993, c. 275. After December 31, 1994, the $75.00 fee shall be paid to the court, for use by the State.

# 37

# GAMBLING OFFENSES

## FACT PATTERN

Every Wednesday evening, for as long as he could remember, Earl "The Smart Man" Jackey held a poker game in his modest three-bedroom Morristown home. Invited to the game were Bobby "Small Teeth" Smith, James "The Hyena" Lamonti, and Stan "Knuckles" Malfowitz. Usually, The Smart Man's games lasted through the middle of the night and sometimes to early the next morning. The stakes were high—the gentlemen bet with the various vegetables that they cultivated in their respective home gardens. Small Teeth might lay out a few hundred tomatoes a night, while Knuckles was known to drop dozens upon dozens of eggplants. The Hyena's favorite betting vegetable was the carrot. The Smart Man was partial to corn on the cob. Indeed, both men, without fail, came to the table with baskets of each.

Now just because each player had his preferred stock, it didn't mean that other vegetables weren't part of the mix. String beans, parsley, cabbage, lettuce, zucchini, and squash were always valued commodities thrown out in a confident bet, daring bluff, or calculated gamble. Yes, the homegrown vegetables tossed around at The Smart Man's Wednesday night games were always interesting—always interesting, too, to a Morris County law enforcement task force which had been monitoring the games for nearly six months. Why? Becaue The Smart Man, Small Teeth, The Hyena, and Knuckles were the heads of the largest gambling ring ever operated in Morris County. The men felt comfortable in The Smart Man's house, which was often swept for bugs. They gambled and talked and gambled and talked through the late night and early morning hours. Unfortunately for these crime bosses, however, The Smart Man's countersurveillance tactics were not smart enough. The task force, through multiple, hidden mini-microphones, captured each and every word they said. Aside from various meatless recipes, this is what they uncovered.

Small Teeth was the lowest man on the totem pole. He acquired the various locations where the group's bookmaking activities occurred, and he solicited clients who placed bets with the group. Most recently, the task force recorded him bragging that his work "netted over 500 bets in the last week which totaled more than a million dollars."

Knuckles was the chief enforcer. He went out to personally collect money from losers who didn't come to him. On a weekly basis, he would receive seven figures in cash pursuant to the bettors' understanding that they had to pay up when they lost.

The Hyena actually manned the facilities where incoming bets were laid. Working under him were several other persons who answered phone calls, recording the code names and monetary figures of all those betting. The Hyena also ran a separate "after-hours" club, The Purple Mule, where gamblers played illegal games of poker, blackjack, craps, and roulette. On a nightly basis, The Hyena received significant amounts of cash and sometimes other items of substantial value, such as jewelry, automobiles, and property deeds—all from people who lost in their respective games.

The Smart Man oversaw the entire operation. At the end of each business day, all proceeds were personally turned over to him. Later, he divvied them up among the group. He also held all pertinent records in his possession.

Pursuant to the information learned by the Morris County task force, search warrants were procured. Members of the Morris County prosecutor's office, the Morris County Sheriff's Department, and the Morristown Police Department raided the various locations where bets were placed, the personal homes of the gang, and The Purple Mule.

At the betting locations, numerous phones and computers were confiscated. Also found in these offices were thousands of blank sheets of water-soluble paper. Coincidentally, the same water-soluble paper was found in the basement of The Smart Man's home—except there, the paper recovered contained over a thousand different coded bets valued in excess of $3 million. The task force estimated that several million dollars of additional bets were recorded on other such paper, but when they arrived at The Smart Man's home, he was in the process of spraying a fire hose all about his basement floor. Also confiscated from The Smart Man's bedroom was nearly $5 million in cash, which was stuffed in corn husks, green peppers, and hollowed-out large eggplants.

Upon executing the search warrant of The Purple Mule, law enforcement personnel confiscated five roulette boards, dozens of playing card decks, three craps tables, and various other objects related to the club's gambling activities. Other than cash, nothing else was seized at the personal homes of The Hyena, Small Teeth, and Knuckles. All three men, however, were arrested along with The Smart Man. They were charged accordingly.

---

**2C:37-1.**        **Definitions**

The following definitions apply to this chapter and to chapter 64:

   a. "Contest of chance" means any contest, game, pool, gaming scheme or gaming device in which the outcome depends in a material degree upon an element of chance, notwith-standing that skill of the contestants or some other persons may also be a factor therein.

   b. "Gambling" means staking or risking something of value upon the outcome of a contest of chance or a future contingent event not under the actor's control or influence, upon an agreement or understanding that he will receive something of value in the event of a certain outcome.

   c. "Player" means a person who engages in any form of gambling solely as a contestant or bettor, without receiving or becoming entitled to receive any profit therefrom other than personal gambling winnings, and without otherwise rendering any material assistance to the establishment, conduct or operation of the particular gambling activity. A person who gambles at a social game of chance on equal terms with the other participants therein does not thereby render material assistance to the establishment, conduct or operation of such game if he performs, without fee or remuneration, acts directed toward the arrangement or facilitation of the game, such as inviting persons to play, permitting the use of premises therefor or supplying cards or other equipment used therein. A person who engages in "bookmaking" as defined in this section is not a "player."

d. "Something of value" means any money or property, any token, object or article exchangeable for money or property, or any form of credit or promise directly or indirectly contemplating transfer of money or property or of any interest therein, or involving extension of a service, entertainment or a privilege of playing at a game or scheme without charge. This definition, however, does not include any form of promise involving extension of a privilege of playing at a game without charge on a mechanical or electronic amusement device, other than a slot machine as an award for the attainment of a certain score on that device.

e. "Gambling device" means any device, machine, paraphernalia or equipment which is used or usable in the playing phases of any gambling activity, whether such activity consists of gambling between persons or gambling by a person involving the playing of a machine. Notwithstanding the foregoing, lottery tickets, policy slips and other items used in the playing phases of lottery and policy schemes are not gambling devices.

f. "Slot machine" means any mechanical, electrical or other device, contrivance or machine which, upon insertion of a coin, token or similar object therein, or upon payment of any consideration whatsoever, is available to play or operate, the play or operation of which, whether by reason of the skill of the operator or application of the element of chance, or both, may deliver or entitle the person playing or operating the machine to receive cash or tokens to be exchanged for cash, whether the payoff is made automatically from the machine or in any other manner whatsoever. A device so constructed, or readily adaptable or convertible to such use, is no less a slot machine because it is not in working order or because some mechanical act of manipulation or repair is required to accomplish its adaptation, conversion or workability.

g. "Bookmaking" means advancing gambling activity by unlawfully accepting bets from members of the public upon the outcome of future contingent events as a business.

h. "Lottery" means an unlawful gambling scheme in which (a) the players pay or agree to pay something of value for chances, represented and differentiated by numbers or by combinations of numbers or by some other media, one or more of which chances are to be designated the winning ones; and (b) the winning chances are to be determined by a drawing or by some other method based upon the element of chance; and (c) the holders of the winning chances are to receive something of value.

i. "Policy" or "the numbers game" means a form of lottery in which the winning chances or plays are not determined upon the basis of a drawing or other act on the part of persons conducting or connected with the scheme, but upon the basis of the outcome or outcomes of a future contingent event or events otherwise unrelated to the particular scheme.

j. "Gambling resort" means a place to which persons may resort for engaging in gambling activity.

k. "Unlawful" means not specifically authorized by law.

## 2C:37-2.      Promoting gambling

a. Promoting Gambling Defined. A person is guilty of promoting gambling when he knowingly:

(1) Accepts or receives money or other property, pursuant to an agreement or understanding with any person whereby he participates or will participate in the proceeds of gambling activity; or

(2) Engages in conduct, which materially aids any form of gambling activity. Such conduct includes but is not limited to conduct directed toward the creation or establishment of the particular game, contest, scheme, device or activity involved, toward the acquisition or maintenance of premises, paraphernalia,

equipment or apparatus therefor, toward the solicitation or inducement of persons to participate therein, toward the actual conduct of the playing phases thereof, toward the arrangement of any of its financial or recording phases, or toward any other phase of its operation.

b.  Grading. A person who violates the provisions of subsection a. by:

(1)  Engaging in bookmaking to the extent he receives or accepts in any one day more than five bets totaling more than $1,000.00; or

(2)  Receiving, in connection with a lottery or policy scheme or enterprise (a) money or written records from a person other than a player whose chances or plays are represented by such money or records, or (b) more than $100.00 in any one day of money played in such scheme or enterprise, is guilty of a crime of the third degree and notwithstanding the provisions of section 2C:43-3 shall be subject to a fine of not more than $35,000.00 and any other appropriate disposition authorized by N.J.S.2C:43-2 b.

A person who violates the provisions of subsection a. by engaging in book-making to the extent he receives or accepts three or more bets in any two-week period is guilty of a crime of the fourth degree and notwithstanding the provisions of section 2C:43-3 shall be subject to a fine of not more than $25,000.00 and any other appropriate disposition authorized by N.J.S. 2C:43-2b. Otherwise, promoting gambling is a disorderly persons offense and notwithstanding the provisions of section 2C:43-3 shall be subject to a fine of not more than $10,000.00 and any other appropriate disposition authorized by N.J.S. 2C:43-2b.

c.  It is a defense to a prosecution under subsection a. that the person participated only as a player. It shall be the burden of the defendant to prove by clear and convincing evidence his status as such player.

## PRACTICAL APPLICATION OF STATUTE

All members of The Smart Man's gang are guilty of promoting gambling per the provisions of 2C:37-2. For particular examples, however, Knuckles is guilty of violating subsection a.(1) for his weekly collection work, and Small Teeth is guilty of violating subsection a.(2) for acquiring the various locations where the group's bookmaking activities occurred and for soliciting clients who placed bets.

### Promoting Gambling Under Subsection a.(1)

In a nutshell, per 2C:37-2a.(1), a person who accepts or receives money (or other property), pursuant to gambling activity, is guilty of promoting gambling. To be convicted, the person must "participate in the proceeds of the gambling activity." Per subsection b. of the statute, this is a third degree crime where "he receives or accepts in any one day more than five bets totaling more than $1,000." It is a fourth degree crime where "he receives or accepts three or more bets in any two-week period." Otherwise, it is a disorderly persons offense.

Knuckles was the chief enforcer of the gang. He went out to personally collect money from losers who didn't come to him. On a weekly basis, he would receive seven figures in cash pursuant to the bettors' understanding that they had to pay up when they lost. Knuckles personally profited from the proceeds of this gambling activity. Accordingly, his actions render him guilty of promoting gambling under subsection a.(1) of the statute. His offense is a third degree crime, given that his weekly seven figures collection obviously involved "more than five bets totaling more than $1,000" in any one day.

### Promoting Gambling Under Subsection a.(2)

A person is guilty of promoting gambling under subsection a.(2) where he "engages in conduct, which materially aids any form of gambling activity." Such conduct ranges from acquiring premises to obtaining gambling paraphernalia to soliciting gamblers. The grading of an offense under a.(2) is the same as it is under subsection a.(1).

Small Teeth acquired the various locations where the group's bookmaking activities occurred, and he solicited clients who placed bets with them. The Morris County task force investigating the gang actually recorded him bragging that his work "netted over 500 bets in the last week which totaled more than a million dollars." Small Teeth's conduct in acquiring locations and bringing in gamblers clearly materially aided the gang's gambling activity. Therefore, he is guilty of promoting gambling per the provisions of subsection a.(2) of the statute. This is a third degree crime—over 500 bets totaling more than a million dollars in a week surely exceeds the "five bets/$1,000 in a day" requirement necessary for this statute's highest degree offense.

### Player Defense

As is common throughout the gambling offenses, 2C:37-2 provides a defense for the bettors. Subsection c. of the statute states that a person has a defense to prosecution where he "participated only as a player."

---

**2C:37-3.**        **Possession of gambling records**

   a. A person is guilty of possession of gambling records when, with knowledge of the contents thereof, he possesses any writing, paper, instrument or article:

   (1) Of a kind commonly used in the operation or promotion of a bookmaking scheme or enterprise, including any paper or paper product in sheet form chemically converted to nitrocellulose having explosive characteristics as well as any water soluble paper or paper derivative in sheet form; or

   (2) Of a kind commonly used in the operation, promotion or playing of a lottery or policy scheme or enterprise.

   b. Defenses.

   (1) It is a defense to a prosecution under subsection a. (2) which must be proven by the defendant by clear and convincing evidence that the writing, paper, instrument or article possessed by the defendant constituted, reflected or represented plays, bets or chances of the defendant himself in a number not exceeding 10.

   (2) It is a defense to a prosecution under subsection a. which must be proven by the defendant by clear and convincing evidence that the writing, paper, instrument or article possessed by the defendant was neither used nor intended to be used in the operation or promotion of a bookmaking scheme or enterprise, or in the operation, promotion or playing of a lottery or policy scheme or enterprise.

   c. Grading. Possession of gambling records is a crime of the third degree and notwithstanding the provisions of section 2C:43-3 shall be subject to a fine of not more than $35,000.00 and any other appropriate disposition authorized by N.J.S. 2C:43-2b. when the writing, paper, instrument or article:

    (1)  In a bookmaking scheme or enterprise, constitute, reflect or represent more than five bets totaling more than $1,000.00; or

    (2)  In the case of a lottery or policy scheme or enterprise, constitute, reflect or represent more than one hundred plays or chances therein.

Otherwise, possession of gambling records is a disorderly persons offense and notwithstanding the provisions of section 2C:43-3 shall be subject to a fine of not more than $20,000.00 and any other appropriate disposition authorized by N.J.S. 2C:43-2b.

## PRACTICAL APPLICATION OF STATUTE

The Smart Man is guilty of possessing gambling records. In his case, it is a crime of the third degree.

A person who possesses items such as papers or instruments that are commonly used in promoting gambling activities may be convicted of an offense under 2C:37-3. However, as subsection a. of the statute provides, he must have "knowledge" that the items he possesses are actually records of gambling activities.

The Smart Man's personal home was raided by a Morris County task force armed with a search warrant. There they found The Smart Man spraying a fire hose all about his basement floor. He was attempting to destroy thousands of sheets of "water-soluble" paper that contained thousands of coded bets valued in the millions of dollars. The task force, however, was able to thwart The Smart Man's efforts to the extent that they recoverd sheets that contained over a thousand different bets valued in excess of $3 million.

"Water-soluble" paper is commonly used in gambling activities for the obvious reason that it is easy to destroy. This particular water-soluble paper supply contained thousands of coded bets which were worth millions of dollars. Thus, the sheets of paper are gambling records as defined in 2C:37-3. The question is, though, did The Smart Man have "knowledge" of the paper's illicit contents? Of course he did. The Smart Man was the individual who oversaw the gang's entire operation. The task force had evidence that at the end of each business day, all gambling proceeds were turned over to him. Not to mention he was furiously spraying water all over the paper in an effort to destroy it. The Smart Man, accordingly, is guilty of possessing gambling records.

Subsection c. of 2C:37-3 sets forth the grading for possession of gambling records. With reference to a bookmaking scheme, it is a third degree offense where the records "represent more than five bets totaling more than $1,000.00." Otherwise, it is a disorderly persons offense. Because The Smart Man's confiscated "water-soluble" paper contained over a thousand bets valued in excess of $3 million, he is guilty of a third degree gambling records offense.

### Defenses

Subsection b. creates defenses to prosecution under the statute. Of particular note is the language of b.(2) that allows a defendant to avoid prosecution where his records represent "plays, bets or chances of the defendant himself in a number not exceeding 10."

This again is a provision that protects players. In other words, if a gambler jots down on a piece of paper $500 on the Yankees, $500 on the Braves, $250 on the Cardinals, and $250 on the Mariners, he cannot be convicted of possessing gambling records.

**2C:37-4.     Maintenance of a gambling resort**

a.  A person is guilty of a crime of the fourth degree if, having substantial proprietary or other authoritative control over premises which are being used with his knowledge for purposes of activities prohibited by N.J.S. 2C:37-2 and N.J.S. 2C:37-3, he permits such to occur or continue or makes no effort to prevent its occurrence or continuation and he accepts or receives money or other property pursuant to an agreement or understanding with any person whereby he participates or will participate in the proceeds of such gambling activity on such premises and notwithstanding the provisions of section 2C:43-3 shall be subject to a fine of not more than $25,000.00 and any other appropriate disposition authorized by N.J.S. 2C:43-2b.

b.  A person is guilty of a crime of the fourth degree if, having substantial proprietary or other authoritative control over premises open to the general public which are being used with his knowledge for purposes of gambling activity, he permits such to occur or continue or makes no effort to prevent its occurrence or continuation and notwithstanding the provisions of section 2C:43-3 shall be subject to a fine of not more than $25,000.00 and any other appropriate disposition authorized by N.J.S.2C:43-2b.

## PRACTICAL APPLICATION OF STATUTE

The Hyena is guilty of maintaining a gambling resort for running The Purple Mule, an "after-hours" club where patrons gambled on a nightly basis. This is a crime of the fourth degree.

Basically, a person is guilty of maintaining a gambling resort where he permits gambling to occur on premises that he owns or has authoritative control over. In order to be convicted of this offense, the person must "know" that the gambling is happening. He also must accept or receive something of value (e.g., money) pursuant to an agreement (e.g., a bet), and he must "participate in the proceeds of such gambling activity."

The Hyena had authoritative control over the "after-hours" club, The Purple Mule—he ran it. At this club, people played illegal games of poker, blackjack, craps, and roulette. The Hyena not only "knew" that the illicit gambling was happening at The Purple Mule, he encouraged it to continue and participated in it. At the end of each evening, he received significant amounts of cash and sometimes other items of substantial monetary value, such as jewelry, automobiles, and property deeds—all from people who lost in their respective games. And The Hyena personally profited from the proceeds of the gambling at The Purple Mule, as it was split up among him and his partners. With all of the aforesaid elements occurring, The Hyena is guilty of the fourth degree crime of maintaining a gambling resort.

**2C:37-4.1.     Shipboard gambling; crime; grading; exception**

a.  A person is guilty of shipboard gambling when the person:

(1)  knowingly causes, engages in or permits any gambling activity prohibited under N.J.S.2C:37-2, 2C:37-3 or 2C:37-4 to be conducted on a vessel that embarks from any point within the State, and disembarks at the same or another point

within the State, whether the gambling activity is conducted within or without the waters of the State; or

(2) manages, supervises, controls, operates or owns any vessel that embarks from any point within the State, and disembarks at the same or another point within the State, during which time the person knowingly causes or permits any gambling activity prohibited under this chapter, whether the gambling activity is conducted within or without the waters of the State.

b. Any person who violates the provisions of subsection a. of this section is guilty of a crime of the same degree as the most serious crime that was committed in violation of N.J.S.2C:37-2, 2C:37-3 or 2C:37-4, as appropriate.

c. This section shall not apply to gambling activity conducted on United States-flagged or foreign-flagged vessels during travel from a foreign nation or another state or possession of the United States up to the point of first entry into New Jersey waters or during travel to a foreign nation or another state or possession of the United States from the point of departure from New Jersey waters, provided that nothing herein shall preclude prosecution for any other offense under this chapter.

## PRACTICAL APPLICATION OF STATUTE

This statute primarily prohibits any illegal gambling—as defined in 2C:37-2 (promoting gambling), 2C:37-3 (possessing gambling records), and 2C:37-4 (maintaining a gambling resort)—from occurring on a ship. A person is only guilty of an offense under this statute if the ship both embarks from a point in the state of New Jersey and disembarks at a point within the state. If these factors are met, it is irrelevant "whether the gambling activity is conducted within or without the waters" of the State of New Jersey.

Follow this example: A ship leaves Port Liberty in Jersey City. It travels to waters in New York wherein an illegal blackjack game is commenced by the ship's personnel. The personnel act as dealers while guests on the ship place bets. The gambling stops before the ship leaves the New York waters. The ship then turns around and heads to Point Pleasant, where it eventually docks. The ship personnel who "promoted gambling" as defined in 2C:37-2 are guilty of an offense under 2C:37-4.1—even though the actual gambling occurred in New York waters. Why? Because the ship both embarked and disembarked at points in New Jersey.

Subsection b. provides that any person who violates this statute "is guilty of a crime of the same degree as the most serious crime that was committed in violation of N.J.S. 2C:37-2, 2C:37-3 or 2C:37-4." Accordingly, if the shipboard gambling offenses included actions that would constitute a fourth degree maintenance of a gambling resort offense and a third degree promoting gambling offense, then the person would be guilty of a third degree crime under 2C:37-4.1. This is because the third degree promoting gambling offense was the most serious offense committed.

2C:37-5.    **Gambling offenses; presumption**

In any prosecution under this article in which it is necessary to prove the occurrence of a sporting event, a published report of its occurrence in any daily newspaper, magazine or other periodically printed publication of general circulation shall be admissible in evidence and shall constitute presumptive proof of the occurrence of such event.

**2C:37-6.**  **Lottery offenses; no defense**

Any offense defined in this article which consists of the commission of acts relating to a lottery is no less criminal because the lottery itself is drawn or conducted without the State. This section shall not apply to any person who has in his possession or custody any paper, document, slip or memorandum of a lottery which is authorized, sponsored and operated by any state of the United States, provided that the paper, document, slip or memorandum was purchased by the holder thereof in the State wherein such lottery was authorized, sponsored and operated.

**2C:37-6.1.**  **Lottery equipment or advice for out of state utilization; manufacture, sale and transport; inapplicability of law providing penalty or disability**

No law providing any penalty or disability for the sale of lottery tickets or any acts done in connection with a lottery shall apply to the rendering of consultation or advice in connection with a lottery, or the manufacturing, processing, selling, possessing or transporting of equipment, tickets or materials, for use or designed for use in a lottery, if such lottery is (a) conducted by a state of the United States and such equipment, tickets or materials are for shipment out of this State to addresses within such state, or (b) not violative of the laws of a foreign country in which it is conducted or intended to be conducted and such equipment, tickets or materials are for shipment to foreign countries to persons or entities that can lawfully use such materials. For purposes of this section, "foreign country" means any empire, country, dominion, colony or protectorate, or any subdivision or subdivisions thereof (other than the United States and its possessions).

**2C:37-7.**  **Possession of a gambling device**

A person except a player is guilty of possession of a gambling device when, with knowledge of the character thereof, he manufactures, sells, transports, places or possesses, or conducts or negotiates any transaction affecting or designed to affect ownership, custody or use of:

    a. A slot machine; or

    b. Any other gambling device, believing that the same is to be used in the advancement of unlawful gambling activity.

    Possession of a gambling device other than under such circumstances as would constitute a violation of section 116 of the "Casino Control Act" (P.L.1977, c. 110; C. 5:12-1 et seq.) is a disorderly persons offense; provided, however, that possession of not more than one gambling device other than a slot machine for social use within the home shall not be an offense under this section; and provided further, however that possession of one or more antique slot machines shall not be an offense under this section or under section 116 of the "Casino Control Act" (P.L.1977, c. 110; C. 5:12-1 et seq.). As used in this section, "antique slot machine" means a slot machine which was manufactured prior to 1941. Nothing herein contained shall be construed to authorize the use of an antique slot machine for any unlawful purpose or for gaming.

## PRACTICAL APPLICATION OF STATUTE

Members of the Morris County task force confiscated five roulette boards, dozens of playing card decks, and three craps tables at The Purple Mule. Pursuant to this seizure, The Hyena is guilty of possessing gambling devices, which is a disorderly persons offense.

    A person—except a player—is guilty of possessing a gambling device if he "believes that the same is to be used in the advancement of unlawful gambling activity." If the aforementioned elements are met, a person can be convicted of possessing a gambling device whether he simply possesses it, manufactures it, sells it, or even transports it.

The Hyena ran the "after-hours" club The Purple Mule, where gamblers played illegal games of poker, blackjack, craps, and roulette. He knew the gambling devices involved—the roulette boards, craps tables, and playing cards—were "used in the advancement of unlawful gambling activity." Accordingly, he has violated the provisions of 2C:37-7.

It is interesting to note that "possession of not more than one gambling device" does not constitute a violation of the statute. Also, a person can apparently possess any number of slot machines "for social use within the home" and not be guilty of an offense under 2C:37-7. Similarly, possession of "antique slot machines" is not unlawful—obviously, as long as they are not used for unlawful gambling purposes.

**2C:37-8.**    **Gambling offenses; jurisdiction**

All offenses under this chapter shall be prosecuted in the Superior Court.

**2C:37-9.**    **Nonapplicability**

Nothing in this chapter shall be construed to prohibit any activity authorized by the "Casino Control Act" (P.L.1977, c. 110; C. 5:12-1 et seq.), or to supersede any provision of said act.

# 38

# TERRORISM

## FACT PATTERN (PERTAINS TO CHAPTERS 38 TO 41)

State Police Captain Manny Tamro arrested brothers George and Alex Evile after a daring, and often grotesque, trek through Jersey City's underground sewer system. The Evile brothers had been the subject of a two-year arson and terrorism investigation that ended when George detonated a briefcase bomb at the Sharpese Hotel in New Brunswick.

George Evile was the founder and pastor of MIFA, a radical religious cult that consistently disrupted political activities through various disorderly behaviors. Several of the cult's members also had previously been arrested for an array of violent crimes. Evile, in an effort to instantly put MIFA on the national map, plotted and carried through the cult's ultimate act of infamy.

Posing as a lobbyist for a prestigious New Jersey firm, Evile arrived at the Sharpese Hotel on an otherwise uncelebrated Friday evening. He entered the hotel's lobby carrying an oversized briefcase. His destination was a convention of political lobbyists, who were assembled to hear one of the industry's top personnel speak on multiple domestic and international issues. Evile sat with the other lobbyists, mixing in with the men and women. Thereafter, he left his briefcase in the middle of the meeting room. The briefcase, however, did not include the usual materials retained by a lobbyist. Instead, it held a massive exploding device that contained the nerve agent Sarin. The bomb exploded five minutes after Evile's departure from the hotel. Fourteen people were killed by the explosion; another 75 were injured.

Evile stated his reason for the murders was "to exact revenge for New Jersey's unfair policies toward MIFA." He was specifically upset that the government required MIFA members to pay past due state income taxes. He also demanded that the state turn over Jersey City to MIFA, wherein the cult would run it as its own separate state. Evile warned that more devastation would occur if his demands were not met.

One week to the day of the bombing, Captain Tamro, off-duty, spotted an individual who appeared to be George Evile. Although the man was wearing a hard hat and sunglasses, the State Police Captain recognized the unmistakable cleft chin and unibrow that marked the master criminal's face. As Tamro approached, the suspect was descending into a manhole on a busy Jersey City street. Tamro withdrew his off-duty pistol and ordered the man to "freeze." Instead, the man scurried down the manhole; Tamro heard him yell, "Alex, move. It's 5-0." Tamro immediately followed—and the rat race commenced.

Thundering down the manhole ladder, Tamro could make out two shadowy figures streaming into the Jersey City sewer system. A former Olympic qualifier in the 1500 meter, Tamro utilized his long, terrific strides to catch up to the men within moments. He tackled the individual that was closest to him, forcing the man's nostrils and mouth into the sewer mush located on the ground beneath their feet—it was Alex Evile.

Tamro immediately knocked Alex unconscious and proceeded after George, who had left his younger brother in the dust. The former track star turned up the heat, accelerating to a speed that most could only accomplish in an automobile. Soon another human being was in his path. This time it was George Evile. Tamro again ordered the man to stop. Suddenly, Evile did, but instead of surrendering, he fired two quick rounds at his law enforcement pursuer. Tamro, unharmed, fired back, striking Evile in the leg and arm. The terrorist crumbled to the ground, crying and whimpering in pain. Backup soon arrived, and the Evile brothers were carted away to jail.

Subsequent to their arrests, both brothers, with the presence of legal counsel, provided statements to the state police. Their own words confirmed most of Captain Tamro's suspicions—the men brazenly admitted a variety of crimes.

Alex Evile was the president of a supposedly legitimate charitable organization, The Lady Dove Society, which purported to raise and distribute funds for a selection of endangered bird species. Evile, though, admitted that The Lady Dove Society was actually a front for MIFA. The majority of the funds raised via Evile's efforts were diverted to support the terrorist activities of MIFA; specifically, Alex Evile transferred over $500,000 to MIFA so his brother could carry out the bombing at the Sharpese Hotel.

In a separate MIFA fund-raising campaign, George Evile engaged in a multitude of activities involving firearms and other dangerous weapons. As his first order of business, Evile set up a machine gun manufacturing shop in Jersey City wherein he produced and sold in excess of 1,000 machine guns. Over 200 distinct transactions to nearly 150 separate buyers occurred over an eight-year period, the first occurring in 1995.

At this shop, Evile also routinely defaced firearms, such as automatic rifles and handguns. By removing these weapons' serial numbers, he could more readily sell them. Evile closely monitored his firearms shop, visiting the establishment on a daily basis and barking orders and directives to the dozens of employees that worked for him. When George couldn't make it to the shop, his brother Alex operated the business in his stead.

Outside of the gun shop, George Evile also personally committed a number of crimes where he employed the use of his firearms. Wielding an automatic rifle, he held up a candy shop in Weehawken; there he sported a body vest and shot the clerk in the leg just before fleeing the store. In Hoboken, Evile sold a kilogram of cocaine to a pawnbroker. To protect himself during the deal, Evile carried a machine gun and a .22-caliber pistol. During this same transaction, Evile sold the pawnbroker five handguns and ten daggers, which the pawnbroker re-sold to a college student later that day. The pawnbroker's last sale of the business day was three pairs of handcuffs and a combat knife with an eight-inch blade to a 15-year-old high school freshman. His overall day, though, ended when Evile appeared at his home and personally instructed the pawnbroker how to manufacture machine guns in exchange for a $20,000 cash payment. Evile did this, knowing that the pawnbroker was intending to manufacture machine guns, not for his usual sale activities but to use them in the commission of a string of planned armored car robberies.

Subsequent to the Evile brothers' confessions, Captain Tamro procured a search warrant to search their homes and businesses. At the machine gun shop, nearly 300 machine guns were seized along with several automatic rifles. At George Evile's home, the police confiscated a .22-caliber handgun and a handgun silencer. The search of Alex Evile's house netted a sawed-off shotgun, a 12-inch switchblade, and 500 hollow nose bullets. This search also resulted in the the arrest of Alice B. Mackerel. The reason: when the police arrived, she put up her hands and said, "Okay. You got me. I hid Alex's brother, George, in my basement after he bombed the Sharpese Hotel. I'm sorry . . . Does anyone have a cigarette?"

Back at the trooper barracks, Captain Tamro signed the complaints for the numerous charges filed against the Evile brothers, Alice B. Mackerel, and the pawnbroker, who was picked up on an arrest warrant. Criminal case histories were secured on each individual. Two had prior records. Alex Evile was convicted of arson when he was 33 years old; at 21, he also had faced a charge resulting from his paddling of three young men who were pledging his college fraternity.

The pawnbroker, though, boasted a lengthy rap sheet. He once was convicted of an offense for maintaining an uncovered abandoned cesspool on his property. In the same year, he was nabbed for selling portable, oil-burning heating devices which had never been inspected by any appropriate agency and which failed to be equipped with a feature that eliminated fire hazards in the event of tip-over. One year later, the pawnbroker was arrested at a supermarket for opening a package of cupcakes, spitting on the baked goods, and resealing the package. A month after that incident, he was arrested for his act of taking down a stop sign that was located at a busy Union City intersection. On the same day that he removed the sign, an unassuming motorist crossed though the intersection, without stopping, and crashed into another motor vehicle. A passenger in one of the cars was killed.

Several years later, the pawnbroker was charged with a number of offenses involving employees of his pawnshop business. He required two workers to submit to lie detector tests before he hired them. After they passed the tests to his satisfaction, he signed written contracts with them to pay each a wage of $1,000 per week. The pawnbroker, though, refused to pay the employees, even though they performed their work duties. In addition, he fired one of them because the employee's earnings were subject to garnishment. These offenses concluded the pawnbroker's criminal history.

---

## 2C:38-1.  Short title

Sections 1 through 5 of this act shall be known and may be cited as the "September 11th, 2001 Anti-Terrorism Act."

## 2C:38-2.  Crime of terrorism; definitions

a. A person is guilty of the crime of terrorism if he commits or attempts, conspires or threatens to commit any crime enumerated in subsection c. of this section with the purpose:

   (1)  to promote an act of terror; or

   (2)  to terrorize five or more persons; or

   (3)  to influence the policy or affect the conduct of government by terror; or

(4) to cause by an act of terror the impairment or interruption of public communications, public transportation, public or private buildings, common carriers, public utilities or other public services.

b. Terrorism is a crime of the first degree.

(1) Notwithstanding any other provision of law to the contrary, any person convicted under this section shall be sentenced to a term of 30 years, during which the person shall not be eligible for parole, or to a specific term of years which shall be between 30 years and life imprisonment, of which the person shall serve not less than 30 years before being eligible for parole.

(2) If a violation of this section results in death, the person shall be sentenced to a term of life imprisonment, during which time the person shall not be eligible for parole.

c. The crimes encompassed by this section are: murder pursuant to N.J.S. 2C:11-3; aggravated manslaughter or manslaughter pursuant to N.J.S. 2C:11-4; vehicular homicide pursuant to N.J.S. 2C:11-5; aggravated assault pursuant to subsection b. of N.J.S. 2C:12-1; disarming a law enforcement officer pursuant to section 1 of P.L.1996, c. 14 (C.2C:12-11); kidnapping pursuant to N.J.S. 2C:13-1; criminal restraint pursuant to N.J.S. 2C:13-2; robbery pursuant to N.J.S. 2C:15-1; carjacking pursuant to section 1 of P.L.1993, c. 221 (C.2C:15-2); aggravated arson or arson pursuant to N.J.S. 2C:17-1; causing or risking widespread injury or damage pursuant to N.J.S. 2C:17-2; damage to nuclear plant with the purpose to cause or threat to cause release of radiation pursuant to section 1 of P.L.1983, c. 480 (C.2C:17-7); damage to nuclear plant resulting in death by radiation pursuant to section 2 of P.L.1983, c. 480 (C.2C:17-8); damage to nuclear plant resulting in injury by radiation pursuant to section 3 of P.L.1983, c. 480 (C.2C:17-9); producing or possessing chemical weapons, biological agents or nuclear or radiological devices pursuant to section 3 of P.L.2002, c. 26 (C.2C:38-3); burglary pursuant to N.J.S. 2C:18-2; possession of prohibited weapons and devices pursuant to N.J.S. 2C:39-3; possession of weapons for unlawful purposes pursuant to N.J.S. 2C:39-4; unlawful possession of weapons pursuant to N.J.S. 2C:39-5; weapons training for illegal activities pursuant to section 1 of P.L.1983, c. 229 (C.2C:39-14); racketeering pursuant to N.J.S. 2C:41-1 et seq.; and any other crime involving a risk of death or serious bodily injury to any person.

d. Definitions. For the purposes of this section:

"Government" means the United States, any state, county, municipality, or other political unit, or any department, agency or subdivision of any of the foregoing, or any corporation or other association carrying out the functions of government.

"Serious bodily injury" means bodily injury which creates a substantial risk of death or which causes serious, permanent disfigurement, or protracted loss or impairment of the function of any bodily member or organ.

"Terror" means the menace or fear of death or serious bodily injury.

"Terrorize" means to convey the menace or fear of death or serious bodily injury by words or actions.

e. A prosecution pursuant to this section may be brought by the Attorney General, his assistants and deputies within the Division of Criminal Justice, or by a county prosecutor or a designated assistant prosecutor if the county prosecutor is expressly authorized in writing by the Attorney General to prosecute a violation of this section.

f. Notwithstanding the provisions of N.J.S. 2C:1-8 or any other provision of law, a conviction of terrorism under this section shall not merge with a conviction of any other offense, nor shall such other conviction merge with a conviction under this section, and the court shall impose separate sentences upon each violation of this section and any other offense.

g. Nothing contained in this section shall be deemed to preclude, if the evidence so warrants, an indictment and conviction for murder under the provisions of N.J.S. 2C:11-3 or any other offense.

## PRACTICAL APPLICATION OF STATUTE

George Evile is guilty of terrorism for murdering 14 individuals at the Sharpese Hotel. This is a crime of the first degree, and it is in addition to the separate offenses of murder that he is guilty of committing.

In order for a person to be convicted of terrorism, he must commit, attempt, conspire, or threaten to commit one of several offenses enumerated in subsection c. of 2C:38-2. The offenses found in subsection c. range from murder to aggravated assault to carjacking to racketeering to arson and include a number of others. In addition to being involved in one of these crimes, a defendant must act with the purpose "to promote an act of terror," "to terrorize five or more persons," or "to influence the policy or affect the conduct of government by terror." A defendant can also be convicted of terrorism if, in addition to being involved in one of the enumerated crimes, he causes "by an act of terror" the impairment of matters such as public transportation, public or private buildings, or public utilities.

"Terror" is defined in subsection d. of the statute as "the menace or fear of death or serious bodily injury." "Terrorize," per subsection d., means "to convey the menace or fear of death or serious bodily injury by words or actions."

George Evile entered the Sharpese Hotel carrying an oversized briefcase. His destination was a convention of political lobbyists, who were assembled to hear one of the industry's top personnel speak on various domestic and international issues. Evile sat with the lobbyists, mixing in with the men and women. Thereafter, he left his briefcase in the middle of the meeting room. The briefcase, however, did not contain the ususal materials retained by a lobbyist. Instead, it held a massive explosive device containing the nerve agent Sarin. The bomb exploded five minutes after Evile's departure from the hotel. Fourteen people were killed by the explosion; another 75 were injured.

George Evile stated his reason for the murders was "to exact revenge for New Jersey's unfair policies toward MIFA," his religious group, which failed to pay state taxes. He demanded that the government not only agree to relieve MIFA of its past due taxes but also must provide it Jersey City, where it would set up a separate state. He warned that more devastation would occur if his demands were not met.

George Evile is guilty of terrorism under 2C:38-2, as all of the elements of the statute were met through his mass murder at the Sharpese Hotel. First, Evile committed one of the crimes enumerated in subsection c.: He murdered 14 people and injured 75 others. He murdered these innocent people with the purpose "to influence the policy or affect the conduct of the government"—his goal was to avoid tax payments for his religious group, MIFA, and to obtain Jersey City as their own separate state. With these elements met, George Evile has committed the first degree crime of terrorism. He also has committed murder and aggravated assault and should be convicted under those statutes as well.

**2C:38-3.**     **Producing or possessing chemical weapons, biological agents or nuclear or radiological devices; definitions**

a. A person who, purposely or knowingly, unlawfully develops, produces, otherwise acquires, transfers, receives, stockpiles, retains, owns, possesses or uses, or threatens to use, any chemical weapon, biological agent, toxin, vector or delivery system for use as a weapon, or nuclear or radiological device commits a crime of the first degree, except that:

(1) Notwithstanding any other provision of law to the contrary, any person convicted under this subsection shall be sentenced to a term of 30 years, during which the person shall not be eligible for parole, or to a specific term of years which shall be between 30 years and life imprisonment, of which the person shall serve not less than 30 years before being eligible for parole.

(2) If a violation of this section results in death, the person shall be sentenced to a term of life imprisonment, during which time the person shall not be eligible for parole.

b. Any manufacturer, distributor, transferor, possessor or user of any toxic chemical, biological agent, toxin or vector, or radioactive material that is related to a lawful industrial, agricultural, research, medical, pharmaceutical or other activity, who recklessly allows an unauthorized individual to obtain access to the toxic chemical or biological agent, toxin or vector or radioactive material, commits a crime of the second degree and, notwithstanding the provisions of subsection a. of N.J.S. 2C:43-3, shall be subject to a fine of up to $250,000 for each violation.

c. For the purposes of this section:

(1) "Chemical weapon" means:

(a) a toxic chemical and its precursors, except where intended for a lawful purpose as long as the type and quantity is consistent with such a purpose. "Chemical weapon" shall include, but not be limited to:

(i) nerve agents, including GA (Tabun) cyanide irreversible inhibitor, Sarin (GB), GB (Soman) fluorine, reversible "slow aging," GF, and VX sulfur, irreversible;

(ii) choking agents, including Phosgene (CG) and Diphosgene (DP);

(iii) blood agents, including Hydrogen Cyanide (AC), Cyanogen Chloride (CK), and Arsine (SA); and

(iv) blister agents, including mustards (H, HD {sulfur mustard}, HN-1, HN-2, HN-3 {nitrogen mustard}), arsenicals, such as Lewisite (L), and urticants, including CX; and

(v) incapacitating agents, including BZ; or

(b) a munition or device specifically designed to cause death or other harm through the toxic properties of those chemical weapons defined in subparagraph (a) of paragraph (1) of subsection c. of this section, which would be released as a result of the employment of such munition or device; or

(c) any equipment specifically designed for use directly in connection with the employment of munitions or devices specified in subparagraph (b) of paragraph (1) of subsection c. of this section.

(2) "Biological agent" means any microorganism, virus, bacteria, rickettsiae, fungi, toxin, infectious substance or biological product that may be engineered as a result of biotechnology, or any naturally occurring or bioengineered component of any such

microorganism, virus, bacteria, rickettsiae, fungi, infectious substance or biological product, capable of causing:

(a) death, disease, or other biological malfunction in a human, an animal, a plant, or another living organism; or

(b) deterioration of food, water, equipment, supplies, or material of any kind; or

(c) deleterious alteration of the environment.

"Biological agent" shall include, but not be limited to: viruses, including Crimean-Congo hemorrhagic fever virus, eastern equine encephalitis virus, ebola viruses, equine morbilli virus, lassa fever virus, Marburg virus, Rift Valley fever virus, South American hemorrhagic fever viruses (Junin, Machupo, Sabia, Flexal, Guanarito), tick-borne encephalitis complex viruses, variola major virus (smallpox virus), Venezuelan equine encephalitis virus, viruses causing hantavirus pulmonary syndrome, and yellow fever virus; bacteria including Bacillus anthracis (commonly known as anthrax), Brucella abortus, Brucella melitensis, Brucella suis, Burkholderia (pseudomonas) mallei, Burkholderia (pseudomonas) pseudomallei, Clostridium botulinum, Francisella tularensis, Yersinia pestis (commonly known as plague); rickettsiae, including Coxiella burnetii, Rickettsia prowazekii and Rickettsia rickettsii; Coccidioides immitis fungus; and toxins, including abrin, aflatoxins, Botulinum toxins, Clostridium perringes epsilon toxin, conotoxins, diacetoxyscirpenol, ricin, saxitoxin, shiga-toxin, Staphylococcal enterotoxins, tetrodotoxins and T-2 toxin.

(3) "Toxin" means the toxic material of plants, animals, microorganisms, viruses, fungi, or infectious substances, or a recombinant molecule, whatever its origin or method of production, including:

(a) any poisonous substance or biological product that may be engineered as a result of biotechnology or produced by a living organism; or

(b) any poisonous isomer or biological product, homolog, or derivative of such a substance.

(4) "Vector" means a living organism or molecule, including a recombinant molecule, or biological product that may be engineered as a result of biotechnology, capable of carrying a biological agent or toxin to a host.

(5) "Nuclear or radiological device" includes: (a) any nuclear device which is an explosive device designed to cause a nuclear yield; (b) a radiological dispersal device which is an explosive device used to spread radioactive material; or (c) a simple radiological dispersal device which is any act, container or any other device used to release radiological material for use as a weapon.

(6) "Delivery system" means any apparatus, equipment, device, or means of delivery specifically designed to deliver or disseminate a biological agent, toxin or vector.

(7) "For use as a weapon" means all situations in which the circumstances indicate that the person intended to employ an item's ready capacity of lethal use or of inflicting serious bodily injury.

d. This section shall not apply to the development, production, acquisition, transfer, receipt, possession or use of any toxic chemical, biological agent, toxin or vector that is related to a lawful industrial, agricultural, research, medical, pharmaceutical, or other activity.

e. This section shall not apply to any device whose possession is otherwise lawful pursuant to N.J.S.2C:39-6.

f. Nothing contained in this section shall be deemed to preclude, if the evidence so warrants, an indictment and conviction for murder under the provisions of N.J.S.2C:11-3 or any other offense.

## PRACTICAL APPLICATION OF STATUTE

2C:38-3 provides that it is a first degree crime to possess any chemical weapons, biological agents, or nuclear or radiological devices. George Evile utilized the nerve agent sarin in his deadly bombing at the Sharpese Hotel and therefore is guilty of violating this statute.

Chemical weapons inclulde nerve agents (e.g., Sarin), choking agents (e.g., Phosgene), blood agents (e.g., Hydrogen Cyanide), blistering agents (e.g., sulfur mustard gas), and incapacitating agents (e.g., BZ). Biological agents are matters such as microorganisms, viruses, bacterias, and toxins that can cause death or disease to living organisms or deteriorate necessities such as food and water. Examples of biological agents that can be used as weapons are the smallpox virus, the plague, anthrax, and T-2 toxin.

Per subsection a. of the statute, it is not only an offense to possess a chemical weapon, biological agent, or nuclear or radiological device, a person is also obviously guilty of this crime for developing, acquiring, transferring, and using these items. He is even guilty of a first degree crime if he threatens to use any of them as a weapon.

George Evile did actually use the nerve agent Sarin as a chemical weapon. He left a briefcase in the middle of a conference room filled with political lobbyists at the Sharpese Hotel. This briefcase, however, did not include the usual materials retained by a lobbyist. Instead, it held a massive explosive device that contained Sarin. After Evile departed the room, the briefcase exploded, killing 14 people. For Evile's possession of the nerve agent Sarin, which he used as a chemical weapon, he is guilty of a first degree crime under 2C:38-3.

### Manufacturer/Distributor Recklessly Allowing Access to Chemical/Biological Agents/Radioactive Material

Even those who are permitted by law to manufacture, possess, and transfer matters such as toxic chemicals, biological agents, and radioactive material may be guilty of a crime. In certain circumstances, it is lawful to possess the aforementioned deadly items, for example, in agricultural research or medical activities. However, if someone involved in any of these activities (e.g., a manufacturer or distributor) "recklessly" allows an unauthorized individual to obtain access to any of the deadly matters, then that person is guilty of a second degree crime.

Here's an example. Jarrod Mashington is an employee of a medical research facility which is currently performing research on anthrax. Marty Ponroe approaches Mashington and advises that he will pay Mashington $5,000 to "sneak" him into the building. Ponroe tells Mashington that he wants to get into the building because the facility's president has a safe with over $100,000 cash stored in it. He further tells Mashington that he will provide him with an additional $15,000 once the money heist has been completed. Believing all this, Mashington sneaks Ponroe into the facility. Thereafter, Ponroe steals quantities of anthrax, his true target.

Jarrod Mashington should be convicted of a second degree crime under subsection b. of 2C:38-3. Although he didn't "purposely" or "knowingly" permit Ponroe, an unauthorized individual, access to the anthrax, he certainly did so "recklessly." His greed to obtain a cash reward in exchange for Ponroe's improper entrance into the facility more than carelessly opened the gateway for Ponroe to steal the deadly biological agent. Accordingly, Mashington is guilty of this second degree offense.

**2C:38-4.**  **Hindering apprehension or prosecution for terrorism**

a. A person commits a crime if, with the purpose to hinder the detention, apprehension, investigation, prosecution, conviction or punishment of another for the crime of terrorism, he:

(1) Harbors or conceals the other;

(2) Provides or aids in providing a weapon, money, transportation, disguise or other means of avoiding discovery or apprehension or effecting escape;

(3) Suppresses, by way of concealment or destruction, any evidence of the crime, or tampers with a witness, informant, document or other source of information, regardless of its admissibility in evidence, which might aid in the discovery or apprehension of such person or in the lodging of a charge against him;

(4) Warns the other of impending discovery or apprehension, except that this paragraph does not apply to a warning given in connection with an effort to bring another into compliance with law;

(5) Prevents or obstructs, by means of force, intimidation or deception, anyone from performing an act which might aid in the discovery or apprehension of such person or in the lodging of a charge against him;

(6) Aids such person to protect or expeditiously profit from an advantage derived from such crime; or

(7) Gives false information to a law enforcement officer.

b. violation of subsection a. of this section is a crime of the first degree if the crime of terrorism resulted in death. Otherwise, it is a crime of the second degree.

## PRACTICAL APPLICATION OF STATUTE

Alice B. Mackerel is guilty of violating the special hindering apprehension offense set forth in 2C:38-4. In her case, this is a crime of the first degree.

Normally, a person who hinders the apprehension of another will be charged under 2C:29-3. However, with the introduction of Chapter 38, which covers activities involving terrorism, 2C:38-4 was created to specifically address those who hinder the apprehension of terrorists.

Subsections a.(1) through a.(7) delineate the various manners in which a person can illegally hinder the apprehension of a terrorist suspect. These range from harboring the suspect to providing a disguise or transportation to him to giving false information to a law enforcement officer.

When the State Police conducted the search of Alex Evile's home, Alice B. Mackerel approached them and proclaimed, "Okay. You got me. I hid Alex's brother, George, in my basement after he bombed the Sharpese Hotel. I'm sorry . . . Does anyone have a cigarette?" Because Mackerel harbored the terrorist suspect George Evile, she is guilty of an offense under 2C:38-4. Her crime is one of the first degree because death had resulted from Evile's terrorist bombing. If death had not occurred, Mackerel would instead be guilty of a second degree offense under this statute.

**2C:38-5.    Soliciting or providing material support or resources for terrorism; definitions**

a. As used in this section:

"Charitable organization" means: (1) any person determined by the federal Internal Revenue Service to be a tax exempt organization pursuant to section 501(c)(3) of the Internal Revenue Code of 1986, 26 U.S.C. s.501(c)(3); or

(2) any person who is, or holds himself out to be, established for any benevolent, philanthropic, humane, social welfare, public health, or other eleemosynary purpose, or for the benefit of law enforcement personnel, firefighters or other persons who protect the public safety, or any person who in any manner employs a charitable appeal as the basis of any solicitation, or an appeal which has a tendency to suggest there is a charitable purpose to any such solicitation.

"Charitable purpose" means: (1) any purpose described in section 501 (c)(3)of the Internal Revenue Code of 1986, 26 U.S.C. s.501(c)(3); or (2) any benevolent, philanthropic, humane, social welfare, public health, or other eleemosynary objective, or an objective that benefits law enforcement personnel, firefighters, or other persons who protect the public safety.

"Material support or resources" means: (1) services or assistance with knowledge or purpose that the services or assistance will be used in preparing for or carrying out an act of terrorism in violation of section 2 of P.L.2002, c. 26 (C.2C:38-2);

(2) currency, financial securities or other monetary instruments, financial services, lodging, training, safehouses, false documentation or identification, communications equipment, facilities, weapons, lethal substances, explosives, personnel, transportation and other physical assets or anything of value; or

(3) any chemical weapon, or any biological agent, toxin, vector or delivery system for use as a weapon, or any nuclear or radiological device, as defined in subsection c. of section 3 of P.L.2002, c. 26 (C.2C:38-3).

"Professional fund raiser" means any person who for compensation performs for a charitable organization any service in connection with which contributions are or will be solicited in this State by that compensated person or by any compensated person he employs, procures, or engages, directly or indirectly to solicit contributions. A bona fide salaried officer, employee, or volunteer of a charitable organization shall not be deemed to be a professional fund raiser. No attorney, accountant or banker who advises a person to make a charitable contribution during the course of rendering professional services to that person shall be deemed, as a result of that advice, to be a professional fund raiser.

b. (1) It shall be unlawful for any person, charitable organization or professional fund raiser to solicit, transport or otherwise provide material support or resources with the purpose or knowledge that such material support or resources will be used, in whole or in part, to aid, plan, prepare or carry out an act of terrorism in violation of section 2 of P.L.2002, c. 26 (C.2C:38-2) or with the purpose or knowledge that such material support or resources are to be given, in whole or in part, to a person or an organization that has committed or has the purpose to commit or has threatened to commit an act of terrorism in violation of section 2 of P.L.2002, c.26 (C.2C:38-2).

(2) It shall be unlawful for any person, charitable organization or professional fund raiser to solicit, transport or otherwise provide material support or resources to or on behalf of a person or an organization that is designated as a foreign terrorist organization by the United States Secretary of State pursuant to 8 U.S.C. s.1189. It shall not be a defense to a prosecution for a violation of this section that the actor did not know that the person or organization is designated as a foreign terrorist organization.

c. A person who violates the provisions of subsection b. of this section shall be guilty of a crime of the first degree if the act of terrorism in violation of section 2 of P.L.2002, c. 26 (C.2C:38-2) results in death. Otherwise, it is a crime of the second degree.

## PRACTICAL APPLICATION OF STATUTE

Alex Evile's solicitation of funds for the supposedly legitimate charitable organization, The Lady Dove Society, violated 2C:38-5. His fund-raising activities render him guilty of a first degree crime. Why? Because his efforts were designed to not actually raise money for a charitable purpose, but to divert the funds to his brother's terrorist organization, MIFA.

In a nutshell, 2C:38-5 makes it unlawful for any charitable organization, professional fund-raiser—or any person whatsoever—to raise funds or provide material support or resources to any individual or organization that is involved in terrorist activities. It is irrelevant if the funds raised, or the resources provided, will be used in "whole" or "in part" for terrorist activities. However, in order for a conviction to be substantiated under the statute, the defendant must have at least "knowledge" that his funds or resources will be used in the advancement of terrorist activities.

Alex Evile was the president of a supposedly legitimate charitable organization, The Lady Dove Society, which purported to raise and distribute funds for a selection of endangered bird species. Evile, though, admitted that The Lady Dove Society was actually a front for MIFA. The majority of the funds raised via Evile's efforts were diverted to support the terrorist activities of MIFA. Specifically, Alex Evile transferred over $500,000 to MIFA so his brother could carry out the bombing at the Sharpese Hotel, which resulted in the death of 14 innocent people.

Given that Alex Evile "knew" his fund-raising efforts were performed to materially support the terrorist activities, he is guilty of violating 2C:38-5. Per subsection c. of the statute, a defendant has committed a first degree crime if the act of terrorism results in death. Otherwise, it is a crime of the second degree. Since the beneficiary of Alex Evile's fund-raising efforts, MIFA, carried out terrorist activities that resulted in death (i.e., the Sharpese Hotel bombing), Alex Evile is guilty of a first degree crime.

# 39

# FIREARMS, OTHER DANGEROUS WEAPONS, AND INSTRUMENTS OF CRIME

**2C:39-1.**     **Definitions**

Definitions. The following definitions apply to this chapter and to chapter 58:

a. "Antique firearm" means any rifle or shotgun and "antique cannon" means a destructive device defined in paragraph (3) of subsection c. of this section, if the rifle, shotgun or destructive device, as the case may be, is incapable of being fired or discharged, or which does not fire fixed ammunition, regardless of date of manufacture, or was manufactured before 1898 for which cartridge ammunition is not commercially available, and is possessed as a curiosity or ornament or for its historical significance or value.

b. "Deface" means to remove, deface, cover, alter or destroy the name of the maker, model designation, manufacturer's serial number or any other distinguishing identification mark or number on any firearm.

c. "Destructive device" means any device, instrument or object designed to explode or produce uncontrolled combustion, including (1) any explosive or incendiary bomb, mine or grenade; (2) any rocket having a propellant charge of more than four ounces or any missile having an explosive or incendiary charge of more than one-quarter of an ounce; (3) any weapon capable of firing a projectile of a caliber greater than 60 caliber, except a shotgun or shotgun ammunition generally recognized as suitable for sporting purposes; (4) any Molotov cocktail or other device consisting of a breakable container containing flammable liquid and having a wick or similar device capable of being ignited. The term does not include any device manufactured for the purpose of illumination, distress signaling, line-throwing, safety or similar purposes.

d. "Dispose of" means to give, give away, lease, loan, keep for sale, offer, offer for sale, sell, transfer, or otherwise transfer possession.

e. "Explosive" means any chemical compound or mixture that is commonly used or is possessed for the purpose of producing an explosion and which contains any oxidizing and combustible materials or other ingredients in such proportions, quantities or packing that an ignition by fire, by friction, by concussion or by detonation of any part of the compound or mixture may cause such a sudden generation of highly heated gases that the resultant gaseous pressures are capable of producing destructive effects on contiguous objects. The term shall not include small arms ammunition, or explosives in the form prescribed by the official United States Pharmacopoeia.

f. "Firearm" means any handgun, rifle, shotgun, machine gun, automatic or semi-automatic rifle, or any gun, device or instrument in the nature of a weapon from which may be fired or ejected any solid projectable ball, slug, pellet, missile or bullet, or any gas, vapor or other noxious thing, by means of a cartridge or shell or by the action of an explosive or the igniting of flammable or explosive substances. It shall also include, without limitation, any firearm which is in the nature of an air gun, spring gun or pistol or other weapon of a similar nature in which the propelling force is a spring, elastic band, carbon dioxide, compressed or other gas or vapor, air or compressed air, or is ignited by compressed air, and ejecting a bullet or missile smaller than three-eighths of an inch in diameter, with sufficient force to injure a person.

g. "Firearm silencer" means any instrument, attachment, weapon or appliance for causing the firing of any gun, revolver, pistol or other firearm to be silent, or intended to lessen or muffle the noise of the firing of any gun, revolver, pistol or other firearm.

h. "Gravity knife" means any knife which has a blade which is released from the handle or sheath thereof by the force of gravity or the application of centrifugal force.

i. "Machine gun" means any firearm, mechanism or instrument not requiring that the trigger be pressed for each shot and having a reservoir, belt or other means of storing and carrying ammunition which can be loaded into the firearm, mechanism or instrument and fired therefrom.

j. "Manufacturer" means any person who receives or obtains raw materials or parts and processes them into firearms or finished parts of firearms, except a person who exclusively processes grips, stocks and other nonmetal parts of firearms. The term does not include a person who repairs existing firearms or receives new and used raw materials or parts solely for the repair of existing firearms.

k. "Handgun" means any pistol, revolver or other firearm originally designed or manufactured to be fired by the use of a single hand.

l. "Retail dealer" means any person including a gunsmith, except a manufacturer or a wholesale dealer, who sells, transfers or assigns for a fee or profit any firearm or parts of firearms or ammunition which he has purchased or obtained with the intention, or for the purpose, of reselling or reassigning to persons who are reasonably understood to be the ultimate consumers, and includes any person who is engaged in the business of repairing firearms or who sells any firearm to satisfy a debt secured by the pledge of a firearm.

m. "Rifle" means any firearm designed to be fired from the shoulder and using the energy of the explosive in a fixed metallic cartridge to fire a single projectile through a rifled bore for each single pull of the trigger.

n. "Shotgun" means any firearm designed to be fired from the shoulder and using the energy of the explosive in a fixed shotgun shell to fire through a smooth bore either a number of ball shots or a single projectile for each pull of the trigger, or any firearm designed to be fired from the shoulder which does not fire fixed ammunition.

o. "Sawed-off shotgun" means any shotgun having a barrel or barrels of less than 18 inches in length measured from the breech to the muzzle, or a rifle having a barrel or barrels of less than 16 inches in length measured from the breech to the muzzle, or any firearm made from a rifle or a shotgun, whether by alteration, or otherwise, if such firearm as modified has an overall length of less than 26 inches.

p. "Switchblade knife" means any knife or similar device which has a blade which opens automatically by hand pressure applied to a button, spring or other device in the handle of the knife.

q. "Superintendent" means the Superintendent of the State Police.

r. "Weapon" means anything readily capable of lethal use or of inflicting serious bodily injury. The term includes, but is not limited to, all (1) firearms, even though not loaded or lacking a clip or other component to render them immediately operable; (2) components which can be readily assembled into a weapon; (3) gravity knives, switchblade knives, daggers, dirks, stilettos, or other dangerous knives, billies, blackjacks, bludgeons, metal knuckles, sandclubs, slingshots, cesti or similar leather bands studded with metal filings or razor blades imbedded in wood; and (4) stun guns; and any weapon or other device which projects, releases, or emits tear gas or any other substance intended to produce temporary physical discomfort or permanent injury through being vaporized or otherwise dispensed in the air.

s. "Wholesale dealer" means any person, except a manufacturer, who sells, transfers, or assigns firearms, or parts of firearms, to persons who are reasonably understood not to be the ultimate consumers, and includes persons who receive finished parts of firearms and assemble them into completed or partially completed firearms, in furtherance of such purpose, except that it shall not include those persons dealing exclusively in grips, stocks and other nonmetal parts of firearms.

t. "Stun gun" means any weapon or other device which emits an electrical charge or current intended to temporarily or permanently disable a person.

u. "Ballistic knife" means any weapon or other device capable of lethal use and which can propel a knife blade.

v. "Imitation firearm" means an object or device reasonably capable of being mistaken for a firearm.

w. "Assault firearm" means:

   (1) The following firearms:

   Algimec AGM1 type

   Any shotgun with a revolving cylinder such as the "Street Sweeper" or "Striker 12"

   Armalite AR-180 type

   Australian Automatic Arms SAR

   Avtomat Kalashnikov type semi-automatic firearms

   Beretta AR-70 and BM59 semi-automatic firearms

   Bushmaster Assault Rifle

   Calico M-900 Assault carbine and M-900

   CETME G3

   Chartered Industries of Singapore SR-88 type

   Colt AR-15 and CAR-15 series

   Daewoo K-1, K-2, Max 1 and Max 2, AR 100 types

   Demro TAC-1 carbine type

   Encom MP-9 and MP-45 carbine types

   FAMAS MAS223 types

   FN-FAL, FN-LAR, or FN-FNC type semi-automatic firearms

   Franchi SPAS 12 and LAW 12 shotguns

   G3SA type

   Galil type Heckler and Koch HK91, HK93, HK94, MP5, PSG-1

   Intratec TEC 9 and 22 semi-automatic firearms

   M1 carbine type

M14S type

MAC 10, MAC 11, MAC 11–9mm carbine type firearms

PJK M-68 carbine type

Plainfield Machine Company Carbine

Ruger K-Mini-14/5F and Mini-14/5RF

SIG AMT, SIG 550SP, SIG 551SP, SIG PE-57 types

SKS with detachable magazine type

Spectre Auto carbine type

Springfield Armory BM59 and SAR-48 type

Sterling MK-6, MK-7 and SAR types

Steyr A.U.G. semi-automatic firearms

USAS 12 semi-automatic type shotgun

Uzi type semi-automatic firearms

Valmet M62, M71S, M76, or M78 type semi-automatic firearms

Weaver Arm Nighthawk.

(2) Any firearm manufactured under any designation which is substantially identical to any of the firearms listed above.

(3) A semi-automatic shotgun with either a magazine capacity exceeding six rounds, a pistol grip, or a folding stock.

(4) A semi-automatic rifle with a fixed magazine capacity exceeding 15 rounds.

(5) A part or combination of parts designed or intended to convert a firearm into an assault firearm, or any combination of parts from which an assault firearm may be readily assembled if those parts are in the possession or under the control of the same person.

x. "Semi-automatic" means a firearm which fires a single projectile for each single pull of the trigger and is self-reloading or automatically chambers a round, cartridge, or bullet.

y. "Large capacity ammunition magazine" means a box, drum, tube or other container which is capable of holding more than 15 rounds of ammunition to be fed continuously and directly therefrom into a semi-automatic firearm.

z. "Pistol grip" means a well-defined handle, similar to that found on a handgun, that protrudes conspicuously beneath the action of the weapon, and which permits the shotgun to be held and fired with one hand.

aa. "Antique handgun" means a handgun manufactured before 1898, or a replica thereof, which is recognized as being historical in nature or of historical significance and either (1) utilizes a match, friction, flint, or percussion ignition, or which utilizes a pin-fire cartridge in which the pin is part of the cartridge or (2) does not fire fixed ammunition or for which cartridge ammunition is not commercially available.

bb. "Trigger lock" means a commercially available device approved by the Superintendent of State Police which is operated with a key or combination lock that prevents a firearm from being discharged while the device is attached to the firearm. It may include, but need not be limited to, devices that obstruct the barrel or cylinder of the firearm, as well as devices that immobilize the trigger.

cc. "Trigger locking device" means a device that, if installed on a firearm and secured by means of a key or mechanically, electronically or electromechanically operated combination lock, prevents the firearm from being discharged without first deactivating or removing the device by means of a key or mechanically, electronically or electromechanically operated combination lock.

dd. "Personalized handgun" means a handgun which incorporates within its design, and as part of its original manufacture, technology which automatically limits its operational use and which cannot be readily deactivated, so that it may only be fired by an authorized or recognized user. The technology limiting the handgun's operational use may include, but not be limited to: radio frequency tagging, touch memory, remote control, fingerprint, magnetic encoding and other automatic user identification systems utilizing biometric, mechanical or electronic systems. No make or model of a handgun shall be deemed to be a "personalized handgun" unless the Attorney General has determined, through testing or other reasonable means, that the handgun meets any reliability standards that the manufacturer may require for its commercially available handguns that are not personalized or, if the manufacturer has no such reliability standards, the handgun meets the reliability standards generally used in the industry for commercially available handguns.

## 2C:39-2.        Presumptions

a. Possession of firearms, weapons, destructive devices, silencers, or explosives in a vehicle. When a firearm, weapon, destructive device, silencer, or explosive described in this chapter is found in a vehicle, it is presumed to be in the possession of the occupant if there is but one. If there is more than one occupant in the vehicle, it shall be presumed to be in the possession of all, except under the following circumstances:

(1) When it is found upon the person of one of the occupants, it shall be presumed to be in the possession of that occupant alone;

(2) When the vehicle is not a stolen one and the weapon or other instrument is found out of view in a glove compartment, trunk or other enclosed customary depository, it shall be presumed to be in the possession of the occupant or occupants who own or have authority to operate the vehicle; and

(3) When the vehicle is a taxicab and a weapon or other instrument is found in the passenger's portion of the vehicle, it shall be presumed to be in the possession of all the passengers, if there are any, and if not, in the possession of the driver.

b. Licenses and permits. When the legality of a person's conduct under this chapter depends on his possession of a license or permit or on his having registered with or given notice to a particular person or agency, it shall be presumed that he does not possess such a license or permit or has not registered or given the required notice, until he establishes the contrary.

## 2C:39-3.        Prohibited weapons and devices

a. Destructive devices. Any person who knowingly has in his possession any destructive device is guilty of a crime of the third degree.

b. Sawed-off shotguns. Any person who knowingly has in his possession any sawed-off shotgun is guilty of a crime of the third degree.

c. Silencers. Any person who knowingly has in his possession any firearm silencer is guilty of a crime of the fourth degree.

d. Defaced firearms. Any person who knowingly has in his possession any firearm which has been defaced, except an antique firearm or an antique handgun, is guilty of a crime of the fourth degree.

e. Certain weapons. Any person who knowingly has in his possession any gravity knife, switchblade knife, dagger, dirk, stiletto, billy, blackjack, metal knuckle, sandclub, slingshot, cestus or similar leather band studded with metal filings or razor blades imbedded in wood, ballistic knife, without any explainable lawful purpose, is guilty of a crime of the fourth degree.

f. Dum-dum or body armor penetrating bullets. (1) Any person, other than a law enforcement officer or persons engaged in activities pursuant to subsection f. of N.J.S.2C:39-6, who knowingly has in his possession any hollow nose or dum-dum bullet, or (2) any person, other than a collector of firearms or ammunition as curios or relics as defined in Title 18, United States Code, section 921 (a) (13) and has in his possession a valid Collector of Curios and Relics License issued by the Bureau of Alcohol, Tobacco and Firearms, who knowingly has in his possession any body armor breaching or penetrating ammunition, which means: (a) ammunition primarily designed for use in a handgun, and (b) which is comprised of a bullet whose core or jacket, if the jacket is thicker than .025 of an inch, is made of tungsten carbide, or hard bronze, or other material which is harder than a rating of 72 or greater on the Rockwell B. Hardness Scale, and (c) is therefore capable of breaching or penetrating body armor, is guilty of a crime of the fourth degree. For purposes of this section, a collector may possess not more than three examples of each distinctive variation of the ammunition described above. A distinctive variation includes a different head stamp, composition, design, or color.

g. Exceptions.

(1) Nothing in subsection a., b., c., d., e., f., j. or k. of this section shall apply to any member of the Armed Forces of the United States or the National Guard, or except as otherwise provided, to any law enforcement officer while actually on duty or traveling to or from an authorized place of duty, provided that his possession of the prohibited weapon or device has been duly authorized under the applicable laws, regulations or military or law enforcement orders. Nothing in subsection h. of this section shall apply to any law enforcement officer who is exempted from the provisions of that subsection by the Attorney General. Nothing in this section shall apply to the possession of any weapon or device by a law enforcement officer who has confiscated, seized or otherwise taken possession of said weapon or device as evidence of the commission of a crime or because he believed it to be possessed illegally by the person from whom it was taken, provided that said law enforcement officer promptly notifies his superiors of his possession of such prohibited weapon or device.

(2) Nothing in subsection f. (1) shall be construed to prevent a person from keeping such ammunition at his dwelling, premises or other land owned or possessed by him, or from carrying such ammunition from the place of purchase to said dwelling or land, nor shall subsection f. (1) be construed to prevent any licensed retail or wholesale firearms dealer from possessing such ammunition at its licensed premises, provided that the seller of any such ammunition shall maintain a record of the name, age and place of residence of any purchaser who is not a licensed dealer, together with the date of sale and quantity of ammunition sold.

(3) Nothing in paragraph (2) of subsection f. or in subsection j. shall be construed to prevent any licensed retail or wholesale firearms dealer from possessing that ammunition or large capacity ammunition magazine at its licensed premises for sale or disposition to another licensed dealer, the Armed Forces of the United States or the National Guard, or to a law enforcement agency, provided that the seller maintains a record of any sale or disposition to a law enforcement agency. The record shall include the name of the purchasing agency, together with written authorization of the chief of police or highest ranking official of the agency, the name and rank of the purchasing law enforcement officer, if applicable, and the date, time and amount of ammunition sold or otherwise disposed. A copy of this record shall be forwarded by the seller to the Superintendent of the Division of State Police within 48 hours of the sale or disposition.

(4) Nothing in subsection a. of this section shall be construed to apply to antique cannons as exempted in subsection d. of N.J.S.2C:39-6.

(5) Nothing in subsection c. of this section shall be construed to apply to any person who is specifically identified in a special deer management permit issued by the Division of Fish and Wildlife to utilize a firearm silencer as part of an alternative deer control method implemented in accordance with a special deer management permit issued pursuant to section 4 of P.L.2000, c.46 (C.23:4-42.6), while the person is in the actual performance of the permitted alternative deer control method and while going to and from the place where the permitted alternative deer control method is being utilized. This exception shall not, however, otherwise apply to any person to authorize the purchase or possession of a firearm silencer.

h. Stun guns. Any person who knowingly has in his possession any stun gun is guilty of a crime of the fourth degree.

i. Nothing in subsection e. of this section shall be construed to prevent any guard in the employ of a private security company, who is licensed to carry a firearm, from the possession of a nightstick when in the actual performance of his official duties, provided that he has satisfactorily completed a training course approved by the Police Training Commission in the use of a nightstick.

j. Any person who knowingly has in his possession a large capacity ammunition magazine is guilty of a crime of the fourth degree unless the person has registered an assault firearm pursuant to section 11 of P.L.1990, c.32 (C.2C:58-12) and the magazine is maintained and used in connection with participation in competitive shooting matches sanctioned by the Director of Civilian Marksmanship of the United States Department of the Army.

k. Handcuffs. Any person who knowingly has in his possession handcuffs as defined in P.L.1991, c.437 (C.2C:39-9.2), under circumstances not manifestly appropriate for such lawful uses as handcuffs may have, is guilty of a disorderly persons offense. A law enforcement officer shall confiscate handcuffs possessed in violation of the law.

## PRACTICAL APPLICATION OF STATUTE

Alex Evile is guilty of a third degree crime for his possession of a sawed-off shotgun. He is also guilty of a fourth degree crime for possessing a 12-inch switchblade and a fourth degree crime for possessing hollow nose bullets. Alex's brother, George, is guilty of a crime of the fourth degree for possessing a handgun silencer. All of these offenses fall under the prohibitions set forth in 2C:39-3.

This statute provides that it is illegal for unauthorized persons to possess weapons ranging from sawed-off shotguns (see subsection b.) to defaced firearms (see subsection d.) to gravity knives, switchblades, blackjacks, metal knuckles, and slingshots (see subsection e.). Per subsection c., firearm silencers are prohibited. Subsection f. prohibits the possession of dum-dum, hollow nose, and body armor–penetrating bullets. Subsections h., j., and k. set out the prohibitions surrounding the possession of stun guns, large-capacity ammunitions magazines, and handcuffs, respectively. Finally, subsection a. makes it illegal to possess any "destructive device"—any device designed to explode or produce uncontrolled combustion. Each subsection clearly defines what degree of offense has occurred when the subsection's particular weapons or devices are possessed.

Accordingly, because subsection b. provides that it is a third degree crime to possess a sawed-off shotgun, Alex Evile is guilty of a third degree crime for the sawed-off shotgun that the State Police confiscated at his home. In the same vein, he is guilty of fourth degree crimes for his possession of a switchblade and hollow-nose bullets, as they are defined offenses in subsections e. and f., respectively. Possessing a firearm silencer is deemed a fourth degree crime per the tenets of subsection c. Therefore, George Evile is guilty of this degree offense for the silencer found in his home.

It is extremely important to note that 2C:39-3 sets forth a number of exceptions to the prohibited possession of weapons and devices, as defined in the statute. For example, subsection g. begins by stating that "nothing in subsections a., b., c., d., e., f., j., or k. of this section shall apply to any member of the Armed Forces of the United States or the National Guard." Other exceptions are obviously provided for as well. Although a trier of fact may ultimately determine if a particular defendant was legally authorized to possess a weapon or device prohibited under 2C:39-3, it is important to consider the exceptions carved out in the statute.

| 2C:39-4. | **Possession of weapons for unlawful purposes** |

a. Firearms. Any person who has in his possession any firearm with a purpose to use it unlawfully against the person or property of another is guilty of a crime of the second degree.

b. Explosives. Any person who has in his possession or carries any explosive substance with a purpose to use it unlawfully against the person or property of another is guilty of a crime of the second degree.

c. Destructive devices. Any person who has in his possession any destructive device with a purpose to use it unlawfully against the person or property of another is guilty of a crime of the second degree.

d. Other weapons. Any person who has in his possession any weapon, except a firearm, with a purpose to use it unlawfully against the person or property of another is guilty of a crime of the third degree.

e. Imitation firearms. Any person who has in his possession an imitation firearm under circumstances that would lead an observer to reasonably believe that it is possessed for an unlawful purpose is guilty of a crime of the fourth degree.

## PRACTICAL APPLICATION OF STATUTE

Any person who possesses firearms, explosives, or destructive devices for an unlawful purpose is guilty of a second degree crime. A person who possesses any weapon—other than a firearm—for an unlawful purpose is guilty of a third degree crime. And a person who possesses an imitation firearm for an unlawful purpose is guilty of a fourth degree crime. But what is an "unlawful purpose"? How can a person get convicted under this statute? A case involving George Evile can help to answer these questions.

Wielding an automatic rifle, George Evile held up a candy shop in Weehawken. During the stick-up, he shot the store's clerk in the leg. Here Evile is not just guilty of simple unlawful possession of the automatic rifle—he is guilty of unlawfully possessing this firearm for an "unlawful purpose." Evile's "unlawful purpose" was to utilize the firearm "against the person and property of another" in the commission of the crimes of robbery and aggravated assault. Accordingly, George Evile is guilty of a second degree crime under 2C:39-4.

**2C:39-4.1.**     **Weapons; controlled dangerous substances and other offenses, penalties**

a. Any person who has in his possession any firearm while in the course of committing, attempting to commit, or conspiring to commit a violation of N.J.S.2C:35-3, N.J.S. 2C:35-4, N.J.S.2C:35-5, section 3 or section 5 of P.L.1997, c.194 (C.2C:35-5.2 or 2C:35-5.3), N.J.S.2C:35-6, section 1 of P.L.1987, c.101 (C.2C:35-7), section 1 of P.L.1997, c.327 (C.2C:35-7.1), N.J.S.2C:35-11 or N.J.S.2C:16-1 is guilty of a crime of the second degree.

b. Any person who has in his possession any weapon, except a firearm, with a purpose to use such weapon unlawfully against the person or property of another, while in the course of committing, attempting to commit, or conspiring to commit a violation of N.J.S.2C:35-3, N.J.S.2C:35-4, N.J.S.2C:35-5, section 3 or 5 of P.L.1997, c.194 (C.2C:35-5.2 or 2C:35-5.3), N.J.S.2C:35-6, section 1 of P.L.1987, c.101 (C.2C:35-7), section 1 of P.L.1997, c.327 (C.2C:35-7.1), N.J.S.2C:35-11 or N.J.S.2C:16-1 is guilty of a crime of the second degree.

c. Any person who has in his possession any weapon, except a firearm, under circumstances not manifestly appropriate for such lawful uses as the weapon may have, while in the course of committing, attempting to commit, or conspiring to commit a violation of N.J.S.2C:35-3, N.J.S.2C:35-4, N.J.S.2C:35-5, section 3 or section 5 of P.L. 1997, c.194 (C.2C:35-5.2 or 2C:35-5.3), N.J.S.2C:35-6, section 1 of P.L.1987, c.101 (C.2C:35-7), section 1 of P.L.1997,c.327(C.2C:35-7.1), N.J.S.2C:35-11 or N.J.S.2C:16-1 is guilty of a crime of the second degree.

d. Notwithstanding the provisions of N.J.S.2C:1-8 or any other provision of law, a conviction arising under this section shall not merge with a conviction for a violation of any of the sections of chapter 35 or chapter 16 referred to in this section nor shall any conviction under those sections merge with a conviction under this section. Notwithstanding the provisions of N.J.S.2C:44-5 or any other provision of law, the sentence imposed upon a violation of this section shall be ordered to be served consecutively to that imposed for any conviction for a violation of any of the sections of chapter 35 or chapter 16 referred to in this section or a conviction for conspiracy or attempt to violate any of those sections.

e. Nothing herein shall be deemed to preclude, if the evidence so warrants, an indictment and conviction for a violation of N.J.S.2C:39-4 or N.J.S.2C:39-5 or any other provision of law.

f. Nothing herein shall prevent the court from also imposing enhanced punishments, pursuant to N.J.S.2C:35-8, section 2 of P.L.1997, c.117 (C.2C:43-7.2), or any other provision of law, or an extended term.

## PRACTICAL APPLICATION OF STATUTE

In Hoboken, George Evile sold a kilogram of cocaine to a pawnbroker. During the drug deal, Evile carried a .22-caliber pistol and a machine gun. For simply possessing these weapons during this CDS transaction, Evile is guilty of a second degree crime.

2C:39-4.1 is basically an extension of 2C:39-4. This statute, in subsection a., specifically provides that it is a second degree crime to possess a firearm while "committing, attempting to commit, or conspiring to commit" any one of a number of drug offenses (e.g., distributing a CDS per 2C:35-5, maintaining a CDS production facility per 2C:35-4, leading a narcotics trafficking network per 2C:35-3).

The firearm need not be possessed with a purpose to use it unlawfully against a person or property in order for a conviction to be sustained under this statute: simple possession during the commission of any of the drug offenses is enough. Accordingly, because Evile possessed a .22-caliber pistol and a machine gun during his cocaine transaction with the pawnbroker, he is guilty of a second degree offense as set forth in 2C:39-4.1.

Please note that 2C:39-4.1 also makes it a second degree crime for a person to possess any weapon—other than a firearm—during the enumerated drug offenses. However, simple possession of these "other" weapons will not be enough for a conviction under 2C:39-4.1. A conviction can only be sustained if the person possesses the weapon "with a purpose to use such weapon unlawfully against the person or property of another" (see subsection b.) or if the person possesses the weapon "under circumstances not manifestly appropriate for such lawful uses as the weapon may have" (see subsection c.). The moral of the story is, very often a person will face a higher degree crime if he possesses a weapon during the commission of a drug offense than if he simply possessed the weapon in other circumstances.

**2C:39-5.**    **Unlawful possession of weapons**

    a. Machine guns. Any person who knowingly has in his possession a machine gun or any instrument or device adaptable for use as a machine gun, without being licensed to do so as provided in N.J.S.2C:58-5, is guilty of a crime of the third degree.

    b. Handguns. Any person who knowingly has in his possession any handgun, including any antique handgun without first having obtained a permit to carry the same as provided in N.J.S.2C:58-4, is guilty of a crime of the third degree.

    c. Rifles and shotguns.

        (1) Any person who knowingly has in his possession any rifle or shotgun without having first obtained a firearms purchaser identification card in accordance with the provisions of N.J.S.2C:58-3, is guilty of a crime of the third degree.

        (2) Unless otherwise permitted by law, any person who knowingly has in his possession any loaded rifle or shotgun is guilty of a crime of the third degree.

    d. Other weapons. Any person who knowingly has in his possession any other weapon under circumstances not manifestly appropriate for such lawful uses as it may have is guilty of a crime of the fourth degree.

    e. Firearms or other weapons in educational institutions.

        (1) Any person who knowingly has in his possession any firearm in or upon any part of the buildings or grounds of any school, college, university or other educational institution, without the written authorization of the governing officer of the institution, is guilty of a crime of the third degree, irrespective of whether he possesses a valid permit to carry the firearm or a valid firearms purchaser identification card.

        (2) Any person who knowingly possesses any weapon enumerated in paragraphs (3) and (4) of subsection r. of N.J.S.2C:39-1 or any components which can readily be assembled into a firearm or other weapon enumerated in subsection r. of N.J.S.2C:39-1 or any other weapon under circumstances not manifestly appropriate for such lawful use as it may have, while in or upon any part of the buildings or grounds of any school, college, university or other educational institution without the written authorization of the governing officer of the institution is guilty of a crime of the fourth degree.

        (3) Any person who knowingly has in his possession any imitation firearm in or upon any part of the buildings or grounds of any school, college, university or other educational institution, without the written authorization of the governing officer of the institution, or while on any school bus is a disorderly person, irrespective of

whether he possesses a valid permit to carry a firearm or a valid firearms purchaser identification card.

f.  Assault firearms. Any person who knowingly has in his possession an assault firearm is guilty of a crime of the third degree except if the assault firearm is licensed pursuant to N.J.S.2C:58-5; registered pursuant to section 11 of P.L.1990, c.32 (C.2C:58-12) or rendered inoperable pursuant to section 12 of P.L.1990, c.32 (C.2C:58-13).

g.  (1)  The temporary possession of a handgun, rifle or shotgun by a person receiving, possessing, carrying or using the handgun, rifle, or shotgun under the provisions of section 1 of P.L.1992, c.74 (C.2C:58-3.1) shall not be considered unlawful possession under the provisions of subsection b. or c. of this section.

(2)  The temporary possession of a firearm by a person receiving, possessing, carrying or using the firearm under the provisions of section 1 of P.L.1997, c.375 (C.2C:58-3.2) shall not be considered unlawful possession under the provisions of this section.

## PRACTICAL APPLICATION OF STATUTE

Similar to 2C:39-3, 2C:39-5 makes it illegal for individuals to simply possess certain weapons. Pursuant to this statute, it is an offense to possess weapons such as machine guns, handguns, rifles, and shotguns. These crimes are all of the third degree and are found in subsections a. through c. Under subsection f., a person is guilty of a third degree crime for unlawfully possessing an assault firearm. Pursuant to subsection d., it is a fourth degree crime to possess "any other weapon under circumstances not manifestly appropriate for such lawful uses as it may have" (e.g., possessing a steak knife or a baseball bat "just in case a fight breaks out").

George Evile is guilty of a third degree crime under 2C:39-5 for the .22-caliber handgun confiscated at his home. This offense should be differentiated from his use of the .22-caliber gun during the Weehawken candy store robbery; pursuant to that incident, he should appropriately face the greater second degree charge of possession of a firearm for an unlawful purpose.

It is important to note that there are multiple exceptions and exemptions to the unlawful possession of weapons offenses located in 2C:39-5. For example, subsection g. of this statute provides exceptions to the unlawful possession of handguns, rifles, and shotguns. The entirety of 2C:39-6 sets forth exemptions where 2C:39-5 does not apply to individuals. When charging individuals under 2C:39-5, law enforcement should take special note of these exemptions.

### Weapons in Educational Institutions

Subsection e. of 2C:39-5 provides special provisions for individuals who possess weapons in educational institutions. For instance, under e.(1), a person is guilty of a third degree crime if he possesses a firearm "in or upon any part of the buildings or grounds of any . . . educational institution." A defendant is guilty of this offense even if "he possesses a valid permit" or a "valid firearms purchaser identification card"—unless he has "written authorization of the governing officer of the institution." In other words, if a private detective licensed to carry a handgun enters an academic building of Rutgers University carrying his pistol, he can be convicted of a third degree crime under subsection e. of 2C:39-5—unless the president of Rutgers gave him written authorization to carry the gun in the building.

**2C:39-6.**     **Exemptions**

a. Provided a person complies with the requirements of subsection j. of this section, N.J.S.2C:39-5 does not apply to:

(1) Members of the Armed Forces of the United States or of the National Guard while actually on duty, or while traveling between places of duty and carrying authorized weapons in the manner prescribed by the appropriate military authorities;

(2) Federal law enforcement officers, and any other federal officers and employees required to carry firearms in the performance of their official duties;

(3) Members of the State Police and, under conditions prescribed by the superintendent, members of the Marine Law Enforcement Bureau of the Division of State Police;

(4) A sheriff, undersheriff, sheriff's officer, county prosecutor, assistant prosecutor, prosecutor's detective or investigator, deputy attorney general or State investigator employed by the Division of Criminal Justice of the Department of Law and Public Safety, investigator employed by the State Commission of Investigation, inspector of the Alcoholic Beverage Control Enforcement Bureau of the Division of State Police in the Department of Law and Public Safety authorized to carry such weapons by the Superintendent of State Police, State park ranger, or State conservation officer;

(5) A prison or jail warden of any penal institution in this State or his deputies, or an employee of the Department of Corrections engaged in the interstate transportation of convicted offenders, while in the performance of his duties, and when required to possess the weapon by his superior officer, or a correction officer or keeper of a penal institution in this State at all times while in the State of New Jersey, provided he annually passes an examination approved by the superintendent testing his proficiency in the handling of firearms;

(6) A civilian employee of the United States Government under the supervision of the commanding officer of any post, camp, station, base or other military or naval installation located in this State who is required, in the performance of his official duties, to carry firearms, and who is authorized to carry such firearms by said commanding officer, while in the actual performance of his official duties;

(7) (a) A regularly employed member, including a detective, of the police department of any county or municipality, or of any State, interstate, municipal or county park police force or boulevard police force, at all times while in the State of New Jersey;

(b) A special law enforcement officer authorized to carry a weapon as provided in subsection b. of section 7 of P.L.1985, c.439 (C.40A:14-146.14);

(c) An airport security officer or a special law enforcement officer appointed by the governing body of any county or municipality, except as provided in subsection b. of this section, or by the commission, board or other body having control of a county park or airport or boulevard police force, while engaged in the actual performance of his official duties and when specifically authorized by the governing body to carry weapons;

(8) A full-time, paid member of a paid or part-paid fire department or force of any municipality who is assigned full-time or part-time to an arson investigation unit created pursuant to section 1 of P.L.1981, c.409 (C.40A:14-7.1) or to the county arson investigation unit in the county prosecutor's office, while either engaged in the actual performance of arson investigation duties or while actually on call to perform arson investigation duties and when specifically authorized by the governing body or the county prosecutor, as the case may be, to carry weapons. Prior to being

permitted to carry a firearm, such a member shall take and successfully complete a firearms training course administered by the Police Training Commission pursuant to P.L.1961, c.56 (C.52:17B-66 et seq.), and shall annually qualify in the use of a revolver or similar weapon prior to being permitted to carry a firearm;

(9)  A juvenile corrections officer in the employment of the Juvenile Justice Commission established pursuant to section 2 of P.L.1995, c.284 (C.52:17B-170) subject to the regulations promulgated by the commission.

b.  Subsections a., b. and c. of N.J.S.2C:39-5 do not apply to:

(1)  A law enforcement officer employed by a governmental agency outside of the State of New Jersey while actually engaged in his official duties, provided, however, that he has first notified the superintendent or the chief law enforcement officer of the municipality or the prosecutor of the county in which he is engaged; or

(2)  A licensed dealer in firearms and his registered employees during the course of their normal business while traveling to and from their place of business and other places for the purpose of demonstration, exhibition or delivery in connection with a sale, provided, however, that the weapon is carried in the manner specified in subsection g. of this section.

c.  Provided a person complies with the requirements of subsection j. of this section, subsections b. and c. of N.J.S.2C:39-5 do not apply to:

(1)  A special agent of the Division of Taxation who has passed an examination in an approved police training program testing proficiency in the handling of any firearm which he may be required to carry, while in the actual performance of his official duties and while going to or from his place of duty, or any other police officer, while in the actual performance of his official duties;

(2)  A State deputy conservation officer or a full-time employee of the Division of Parks and Forestry having the power of arrest and authorized to carry weapons, while in the actual performance of his official duties;

(3)  (Deleted by amendment, P.L.1986, c.150.)

(4)  A court attendant serving as such under appointment by the sheriff of the county or by the judge of any municipal court or other court of this State, while in the actual performance of his official duties;

(5)  A guard in the employ of any railway express company, banking or building and loan or savings and loan institution of this State, while in the actual performance of his official duties;

(6)  A member of a legally recognized military organization while actually under orders or while going to or from the prescribed place of meeting and carrying the weapons prescribed for drill, exercise or parade;

(7)  An officer of the Society for the Prevention of Cruelty to Animals, while in the actual performance of his duties;

(8)  An employee of a public utilities corporation actually engaged in the transportation of explosives;

(9)  A railway policeman, except a transit police officer of the New Jersey Transit Police Department, at all times while in the State of New Jersey, provided that he has passed an approved police academy training program consisting of at least 280 hours. The training program shall include, but need not be limited to, the handling of firearms, community relations, and juvenile relations;

(10)  A campus police officer appointed under P.L.1970, c.211 (C.18A:6-4.2 et seq.) at all times. Prior to being permitted to carry a firearm, a campus police officer shall take

and successfully complete a firearms training course administered by the Police Training Commission, pursuant to P.L.1961, c.56 (C.52:17B-66 et seq.), and shall annually qualify in the use of a revolver or similar weapon prior to being permitted to carry a firearm;

(11) A person who has not been convicted of a crime under the laws of this State or under the laws of another state or the United States, and who is employed as a full-time security guard for a nuclear power plant under the license of the Nuclear Regulatory Commission, while in the actual performance of his official duties;

(12) A transit police officer of the New Jersey Transit Police Department, at all times while in the State of New Jersey, provided the officer has satisfied the training requirements of the Police Training Commission, pursuant to subsection c. of section 2 of P.L.1989, c.291 (C.27:25-15.1);

(13) A parole officer employed by the State Parole Board at all times. Prior to being permitted to carry a firearm, a parole officer shall take and successfully complete a basic course for regular police officer training administered by the Police Training Commission, pursuant to P.L.1961, c.56 (C.52:17B-66 et seq.), and shall annually qualify in the use of a revolver or similar weapon prior to being permitted to carry a firearm;

(14) A Human Services police officer at all times while in the State of New Jersey, as authorized by the Commissioner of Human Services;

(15) A person or employee of any person who, pursuant to and as required by a contract with a governmental entity, supervises or transports persons charged with or convicted of an offense;

(16) A housing authority police officer appointed under P.L.1997, c.210 (C.40A:14-146.19 et al.) at all times while in the State of New Jersey; or

(17) A probation officer assigned to the "Probation Officer Community Safety Unit" created by section 2 of P.L.2001, c.362 (C.2B:10A-2) while in the actual performance of the probation officer's official duties. Prior to being permitted to carry a firearm, a probation officer shall take and successfully complete a basic course for regular police officer training administered by the Police Training Commission, pursuant to P.L.1961, c.56 (C.52:17B-66 et seq.), and shall annually qualify in the use of a revolver or similar weapon prior to being permitted to carry a firearm.

d.   (1) Subsections c. and d. of N.J.S.2C:39-5 do not apply to antique firearms, provided that such antique firearms are unloaded or are being fired for the purposes of exhibition or demonstration at an authorized target range or in such other manner as has been approved in writing by the chief law enforcement officer of the municipality in which the exhibition or demonstration is held, or if not held on property under the control of a particular municipality, the superintendent.

(2) Subsection a. of N.J.S.2C:39-3 and subsection d. of N.J.S.2C:39-5 do not apply to an antique cannon that is capable of being fired but that is unloaded and immobile, provided that the antique cannon is possessed by (a) a scholastic institution, a museum, a municipality, a county or the State, or (b) a person who obtained a firearms purchaser identification card as specified in N.J.S.2C:58-3.

(3) Subsection a. of N.J.S.2C:39-3 and subsection d. of N.J.S.2C:39-5 do not apply to an unloaded antique cannon that is being transported by one eligible to possess it, in compliance with regulations the superintendent may promulgate, between its permanent location and place of purchase or repair.

(4) Subsection a. of N.J.S.2C:39-3 and subsection d. of N.J.S.2C:39-5 do not apply to antique cannons that are being loaded or fired by one eligible to possess an antique

cannon, for purposes of exhibition or demonstration at an authorized target range or in the manner as has been approved in writing by the chief law enforcement officer of the municipality in which the exhibition or demonstration is held, or if not held on property under the control of a particular municipality, the superintendent, provided that performer has given at least 30 days' notice to the superintendent.

(5) Subsection a. of N.J.S.2C:39-3 and subsection d. of N.J.S.2C:39-5 do not apply to the transportation of unloaded antique cannons directly to or from exhibitions or demonstrations authorized under paragraph (4) of subsection d. of this section, provided that the transportation is in compliance with safety regulations the superintendent may promulgate. Nor do those subsections apply to transportation directly to or from exhibitions or demonstrations authorized under the law of another jurisdiction, provided that the superintendent has been given 30 days' notice and that the transportation is in compliance with safety regulations the superintendent may promulgate.

e. Nothing in subsections b., c. and d. of N.J.S.2C:39-5 shall be construed to prevent a person keeping or carrying about his place of business, residence, premises or other land owned or possessed by him, any firearm, or from carrying the same, in the manner specified in subsection g. of this section, from any place of purchase to his residence or place of business, between his dwelling and his place of business, between one place of business or residence and another when moving, or between his dwelling or place of business and place where such firearms are repaired, for the purpose of repair. For the purposes of this section, a place of business shall be deemed to be a fixed location.

f. Nothing in subsections b., c. and d. of N.J.S.2C:39-5 shall be construed to prevent:

(1) A member of any rifle or pistol club organized in accordance with the rules prescribed by the National Board for the Promotion of Rifle Practice, in going to or from a place of target practice, carrying such firearms as are necessary for said target practice, provided that the club has filed a copy of its charter with the superintendent and annually submits a list of its members to the superintendent and provided further that the firearms are carried in the manner specified in subsection g. of this section;

(2) A person carrying a firearm or knife in the woods or fields or upon the waters of this State for the purpose of hunting, target practice or fishing, provided that the firearm or knife is legal and appropriate for hunting or fishing purposes in this State and he has in his possession a valid hunting license, or, with respect to fresh water fishing, a valid fishing license;

(3) A person transporting any firearm or knife while traveling:

(a) Directly to or from any place for the purpose of hunting or fishing, provided the person has in his possession a valid hunting or fishing license; or

(b) Directly to or from any target range, or other authorized place for the purpose of practice, match, target, trap or skeet shooting exhibitions, provided in all cases that during the course of the travel all firearms are carried in the manner specified in subsection g. of this section and the person has complied with all the provisions and requirements of Title 23 of the Revised Statutes and any amendments thereto and all rules and regulations promulgated thereunder; or

(c) In the case of a firearm, directly to or from any exhibition or display of firearms which is sponsored by any law enforcement agency, any rifle or pistol club, or any firearms collectors club, for the purpose of displaying the firearms to the public or to the members of the organization or club, provided, however, that not less than 30 days prior to the exhibition or display, notice of the exhibition or display shall be given to the Superintendent of the State Police by the sponsoring organization or club, and the sponsor has complied with such reasonable safety regulations as the superintendent may promulgate. Any firearms transported pursuant to this section shall be transported in the manner specified in subsection g. of this section;

(4) A person from keeping or carrying about a private or commercial aircraft or any boat, or from transporting to or from such vessel for the purpose of installation or repair a visual distress signalling device approved by the United States Coast Guard.

g. All weapons being transported under paragraph (2) of subsection b., subsection e., or paragraph (1) or (3) of subsection f. of this section shall be carried unloaded and contained in a closed and fastened case, gunbox, securely tied package, or locked in the trunk of the automobile in which it is being transported, and in the course of travel shall include only such deviations as are reasonably necessary under the circumstances.

h. Nothing in subsection d. of N.J.S.2C:39-5 shall be construed to prevent any employee of a public utility, as defined in R.S.48:2-13, doing business in this State or any United States Postal Service employee, while in the actual performance of duties which specifically require regular and frequent visits to private premises, from possessing, carrying or using any device which projects, releases or emits any substance specified as being noninjurious to canines or other animals by the Commissioner of Health and Senior Services and which immobilizes only on a temporary basis and produces only temporary physical discomfort through being vaporized or otherwise dispensed in the air for the sole purpose of repelling canine or other animal attacks.

The device shall be used solely to repel only those canine or other animal attacks when the canines or other animals are not restrained in a fashion sufficient to allow the employee to properly perform his duties.

Any device used pursuant to this act shall be selected from a list of products, which consist of active and inert ingredients, permitted by the Commissioner of Health and Senior Services.

i. Nothing in N.J.S.2C:39-5 shall be construed to prevent any person who is 18 years of age or older and who has not been convicted of a felony, from possession for the purpose of personal self-defense of one pocket-sized device which contains and releases not more than three-quarters of an ounce of chemical substance not ordinarily capable of lethal use or of inflicting serious bodily injury, but rather, is intended to produce temporary physical discomfort or disability through being vaporized or otherwise dispensed in the air. Any person in possession of any device in violation of this subsection shall be deemed and adjudged to be a disorderly person, and upon conviction thereof, shall be punished by a fine of not less than $100.00.

j. A person shall qualify for an exemption from the provisions of N.J.S.2C:39-5, as specified under subsections a. and c. of this section, if the person has satisfactorily completed a firearms training course approved by the Police Training Commission.

Such exempt person shall not possess or carry a firearm until the person has satisfactorily completed a firearms training course and shall annually qualify in the use of a revolver or similar weapon. For purposes of this subsection, a "firearms training course" means a course of instruction in the safe use, maintenance and storage of firearms which is approved by the Police Training Commission. The commission shall approve a firearms training course if the requirements of the course are substantially equivalent to the requirements for firearms training provided by police training courses which are certified under section 6 of P.L.1961, c.56 (C.52:17B-71). A person who is specified in paragraph (1), (2), (3) or (6) of subsection a. of this section shall be exempt from the requirements of this subsection.

k.  Nothing in subsection d. of N.J.S.2C:39-5 shall be construed to prevent any financial institution, or any duly authorized personnel of the institution, from possessing, carrying or using for the protection of money or property, any device which projects, releases or emits tear gas or other substances intended to produce temporary physical discomfort or temporary identification.

l.  Nothing in subsection b. of N.J.S.2C:39-5 shall be construed to prevent a law enforcement officer who retired in good standing, including a retirement because of a disability pursuant to section 6 of P.L.1944, c.255 (C.43:16A-6), section 7 of P.L.1944, c.255 (C.43:16A-7), section 1 of P.L.1989, c.103 (C.43:16A-6.1) or any substantially similar statute governing the disability retirement of federal law enforcement officers, provided the officer was a regularly employed, full-time law enforcement officer for an aggregate of five or more years prior to his disability retirement and further provided that the disability which constituted the basis for the officer's retirement did not involve a certification that the officer was mentally incapacitated for the performance of his usual law enforcement duties and any other available duty in the department which his employer was willing to assign to him or does not subject that retired officer to any of the disabilities set forth in subsection c. of N.J.S.2C:58-3 which would disqualify the retired officer from possessing or carrying a firearm, who semi-annually qualifies in the use of the handgun he is permitted to carry in accordance with the requirements and procedures established by the Attorney General pursuant to subsection j. of this section and pays the actual costs associated with those semi-annual qualifications, who is less than 70 years of age, and who was regularly employed as a full-time member of the State Police; a full-time member of an interstate police force; a full-time member of a county or municipal police department in this State; a full-time member of a State law enforcement agency; a full-time sheriff, undersheriff or sheriff's officer of a county of this State; a full-time State or county corrections officer; a full-time county park police officer; a full-time county prosecutor's detective or investigator; or a full-time federal law enforcement officer from carrying a handgun in the same manner as law enforcement officers exempted under paragraph (7) of subsection a. of this section under the conditions provided herein:

(1)  The retired law enforcement officer, within six months after retirement, shall make application in writing to the Superintendent of State Police for approval to carry a handgun for one year. An application for annual renewal shall be submitted in the same manner.

(2)  Upon receipt of the written application of the retired law enforcement officer, the superintendent shall request a verification of service from the chief law enforcement officer of the organization in which the retired officer was last regularly employed as a full-time law enforcement officer prior to retiring. The verification of service shall include:

(a)  The name and address of the retired officer;

(b)  The date that the retired officer was hired and the date that the officer retired;

(c)  A list of all handguns known to be registered to that officer;

(d)  A statement that, to the reasonable knowledge of the chief law enforcement officer, the retired officer is not subject to any of the restrictions set forth in subsection c. of N.J.S.2C:58-3; and

(e)  A statement that the officer retired in good standing.

(3)  If the superintendent approves a retired officer's application or reapplication to carry a handgun pursuant to the provisions of this subsection, the superintendent shall

notify in writing the chief law enforcement officer of the municipality wherein that retired officer resides. In the event the retired officer resides in a municipality which has no chief law enforcement officer or law enforcement agency, the superintendent shall maintain a record of the approval.

(4) The superintendent shall issue to an approved retired officer an identification card permitting the retired officer to carry a handgun pursuant to this subsection. This identification card shall be valid for one year from the date of issuance and shall be valid throughout the State. The identification card shall not be transferable to any other person. The identification card shall be carried at all times on the person of the retired officer while the retired officer is carrying a handgun. The retired officer shall produce the identification card for review on the demand of any law enforcement officer or authority.

(5) Any person aggrieved by the denial of the superintendent of approval for a permit to carry a handgun pursuant to this subsection may request a hearing in the Superior Court of New Jersey in the county in which he resides by filing a written request for such a hearing within 30 days of the denial. Copies of the request shall be served upon the superintendent and the county prosecutor. The hearing shall be held within 30 days of the filing of the request, and no formal pleading or filing fee shall be required. Appeals from the determination of such a hearing shall be in accordance with law and the rules governing the courts of this State.

(6) A judge of the Superior Court may revoke a retired officer's privilege to carry a handgun pursuant to this subsection for good cause shown on the application of any interested person. A person who becomes subject to any of the disabilities set forth in subsection c. of N.J.S.2C:58-3 shall surrender, as prescribed by the superintendent, his identification card issued under paragraph (4) of this subsection to the chief law enforcement officer of the municipality wherein he resides or the superintendent, and shall be permanently disqualified to carry a handgun under this subsection.

(7) The superintendent may charge a reasonable application fee to retired officers to offset any costs associated with administering the application process set forth in this subsection.

m. Nothing in subsection d. of N.J.S.2C:39-5 shall be construed to prevent duly authorized personnel of the New Jersey Division of Fish, Game and Wildlife, while in the actual performance of duties, from possessing, transporting or using any device that projects, releases or emits any substance specified as being non-injurious to wildlife by the Director of the Division of Animal Health in the Department of Agriculture, and which may immobilize wildlife and produces only temporary physical discomfort through being vaporized or otherwise dispensed in the air for the purpose of repelling bear or other animal attacks or for the aversive conditioning of wildlife.

n. Nothing in subsection b., c., d. or e. of N.J.S.2C:39-5 shall be construed to prevent duly authorized personnel of the New Jersey Division of Fish, Game and Wildlife, while in the actual performance of duties, from possessing, transporting or using hand held pistol-like devices, rifles or shotguns that launch pyrotechnic missiles for the sole purpose of frightening, hazing or aversive conditioning of nuisance or depredating wildlife; from possessing, transporting or using rifles, pistols or similar devices for the sole purpose of chemically immobilizing wild or non-domestic animals; or, provided the duly authorized person complies with the requirements of subsection j. of this section, from possessing, transporting or using rifles or shotguns, upon completion of a Police Training Commission approved training course, in order to dispatch injured or dangerous animals or for non-lethal use for the purpose of frightening, hazing or aversive conditioning of nuisance or depredating wildlife.

**2C:39-6.1.**      **Certain retired law enforcement officers, application for permit to carry handgun**

Any retired law enforcement officer who meets all of the requirements set forth in subsection l. of N.J.S.2C:39-6, but retired prior to the effective date of P.L.1997, c.67, may apply to carry a handgun. The application shall be in the manner as provided in that subsection and the applicant, if approved, shall be subject to all the requirements set forth therein.

**2C:39-7.**      **Certain persons not to have weapons**

a. Except as provided in subsection b. of this section, any person, having been convicted in this State or elsewhere of the crime of aggravated assault, arson, burglary, escape, extortion, homicide, kidnapping, robbery, aggravated sexual assault, sexual assault, bias intimidation in violation of N.J.S.2C:16-1 or endangering the welfare of a child pursuant to N.J.S.2C:24-4, whether or not armed with or having in his possession any weapon enumerated in subsection r. of N.J.S.2C:39-1, or any person convicted of a crime pursuant to the provisions of N.J.S.2C:39-3, N.J.S.2C:39-4 or N.J.S.2C:39-9, or any person who has ever been committed for a mental disorder to any hospital, mental institution or sanitarium unless he possesses a certificate of a medical doctor or psychiatrist licensed to practice in New Jersey or other satisfactory proof that he is no longer suffering from a mental disorder which interferes with or handicaps him in the handling of a firearm, or any person who has been convicted of other than a disorderly persons or petty disorderly persons offense for the unlawful use, possession or sale of a controlled dangerous substance as defined in N.J.S.2C:35-2 who purchases, owns, possesses or controls any of the said weapons is guilty of a crime of the fourth degree.

b. A person having been convicted in this State or elsewhere of the crime of aggravated assault, arson, burglary, escape, extortion, homicide, kidnapping, robbery, aggravated sexual assault, sexual assault, bias intimidation in violation of N.J.S.2C:16-1 or endangering the welfare of a child pursuant to N.J.S.2C:24-4, whether or not armed with or having in his possession a weapon enumerated in subsection r. of N.J.S.2C:39-1, or a person having been convicted of a crime pursuant to the provisions of N.J.S.2C:35-3 through N.J.S.2C:35-6, inclusive; section 1 of P.L.1987, c.101 (C.2C:35-7); N.J.S.2C:35-11; N.J.S.2C:39-3; N.J.S.2C:39-4; or N.J.S.2C:39-9 who purchases, owns, possesses or controls a firearm is guilty of a crime of the second degree and upon conviction thereof, the person shall be sentenced to a term of imprisonment by the court. The term of imprisonment shall include the imposition of a minimum term, which shall be fixed at five years, during which the defendant shall be ineligible for parole. If the defendant is sentenced to an extended term of imprisonment pursuant to N.J.S. 2C:43-7, the extended term of imprisonment shall include the imposition of a minimum term, which shall be fixed at, or between, one-third and one-half of the sentence imposed by the court or five years, whichever is greater, during which the defendant shall be ineligible for parole.

c. Whenever any person shall have been convicted in another state, territory, commonwealth or other jurisdiction of the United States, or any country in the world, in a court of competent jurisdiction, of a crime which in said other jurisdiction or country is comparable to one of the crimes enumerated in subsection a. or b. of this section, then that person shall be subject to the provisions of this section.

## PRACTICAL APPLICATION OF STATUTE

2C:39-7a., in a lot of words, provides that certain persons who possess any weapons listed in subsection r. of 2C:39-1 are guilty of a fourth degree crime. This is in addition to any other applicable weapons offenses. Who are these certain persons? They range from people who have been "committed for a mental disorder" to people previously convicted of felonies such as homicide, kidnapping, burglary, arson, possession of a weapon for an unlawful purpose, and CDS distribution.

Subsection b. elaborates on subsection a. by making it a second degree crime—for persons convicted of the enumerated felonies only—for possessing a firearm. Interestingly, as subsection c. clarifies, a charge under 2C:39-7 is valid for any person who has been convicted anywhere in the United States (or anywhere in the world) "of a crime which in said other jurisdiction or country is comparable to one of the crimes enumerated in subsection a. or b. of this section."

Alex Evile is guilty of a second degree crime under 2C:39-7b. and a fourth degree crime under 2C:39-7a. Why? A sawed-off shotgun, a firearm, was found in his home. This constitutes the second degree charge under subsection b. of the statute. Also found in his home was a switchblade. This weapon possession renders him guilty of a fourth degree crime per subsection a. of the statute.

**2C:39-8.**    **Repealed**

**2C:39-9.**    **Manufacture, transport, disposition and defacement of weapons and dangerous instruments and appliances**

    a. Machine guns. Any person who manufactures, causes to be manufactured, transports, ships, sells or disposes of any machine gun without being registered or licensed to do so as provided in chapter 58 is guilty of a crime of the third degree.

    b. Sawed-off shotguns. Any person who manufactures, causes to be manufactured, transports, ships, sells or disposes of any sawed-off shotgun is guilty of a crime of the third degree.

    c. Firearm silencers. Any person who manufactures, causes to be manufactured, transports, ships, sells or disposes of any firearm silencer is guilty of a crime of the fourth degree.

    d. Weapons. Any person who manufactures, causes to be manufactured, transports, ships, sells or disposes of any weapon, including gravity knives, switchblade knives, ballistic knives, daggers, dirks, stilettos, billies, blackjacks, metal knuckles, sandclubs, slingshots, cesti or similar leather bands studded with metal filings, or in the case of firearms if he is not licensed or registered to do so as provided in chapter 58, is guilty of a crime of the fourth degree. Any person who manufactures, causes to be manufactured, transports, ships, sells or disposes of any weapon or other device which projects, releases or emits tear gas or other substances intended to produce temporary physical discomfort or permanent injury through being vaporized or otherwise dispensed in the air, which is intended to be used for any purpose other than for authorized military or law enforcement purposes by duly authorized military or law enforcement personnel or the device is for the purpose of personal self-defense, is pocket-sized and contains not more than three-quarters of an ounce of chemical substance not ordinarily capable of lethal use or of inflicting serious bodily injury, or other than to be used by any person permitted to possess such weapon or device under the provisions of subsection d. of N.J.S.2C:39-5, which is intended for use by financial and other business institutions as part of an integrated security system, placed at fixed locations, for the protection of money and property, by the duly authorized personnel of those institutions, is guilty of a crime of the fourth degree.

e.  Defaced firearms. Any person who defaces any firearm is guilty of a crime of the third degree. Any person who knowingly buys, receives, disposes of or conceals a defaced firearm, except an antique firearm or an antique handgun, is guilty of a crime of the fourth degree.

f.  (1)  Any person who manufactures, causes to be manufactured, transports, ships, sells, or disposes of any bullet, which is primarily designed for use in a handgun, and which is comprised of a bullet whose core or jacket, if the jacket is thicker than .025 of an inch, is made of tungsten carbide, or hard bronze, or other material which is harder than a rating of 72 or greater on the Rockwell B. Hardness Scale, and is therefore capable of breaching or penetrating body armor and which is intended to be used for any purpose other than for authorized military or law enforcement purposes by duly authorized military or law enforcement personnel, is guilty of a crime of the fourth degree.

  (2)  Nothing in this subsection shall be construed to prevent a licensed collector of ammunition as defined in paragraph (2) of subsection f. of N.J.S.2C:39-3 from transporting the bullets defined in paragraph (1) of this subsection from (a) any licensed retail or wholesale firearms dealer's place of business to the collector's dwelling, premises, or other land owned or possessed by him, or (b) to or from the collector's dwelling, premises or other land owned or possessed by him to any gun show for the purposes of display, sale, trade, or transfer between collectors, or (c) to or from the collector's dwelling, premises or other land owned or possessed by him to any rifle or pistol club organized in accordance with the rules prescribed by the National Board for the Promotion of Rifle Practice; provided that the club has filed a copy of its charter with the superintendent of the State Police and annually submits a list of its members to the superintendent, and provided further that the ammunition being transported shall be carried not loaded in any firearm and contained in a closed and fastened case, gun box, or locked in the trunk of the automobile in which it is being transported, and the course of travel shall include only such deviations as are reasonably necessary under the circumstances.

g.  Assault firearms. Any person who manufactures, causes to be manufactured, transports, ships, sells or disposes of an assault firearm without being registered or licensed to do so pursuant to N.J.S.2C:58-1 et seq. is guilty of a crime of the third degree.

h.  Large capacity ammunition magazines. Any person who manufactures, causes to be manufactured, transports, ships, sells or disposes of a large capacity ammunition magazine which is intended to be used for any purpose other than for authorized military or law enforcement purposes by duly authorized military or law enforcement personnel is guilty of a crime of the fourth degree.

## PRACTICAL APPLICATION OF STATUTE

George Evile is guilty of a third degree crime for manufacturing machine guns at his shop in Jersey City. He is also guilty of a third degree crime for defacing automatic rifles and handguns at this same location.

Pursuant to the tenets of 2C:39-9, it is a third degree crime to "manufacture, cause to manufacture, transport, ship, sell or dispose of" (herein, collectively "manufacture") machine guns (subsection a.), sawed-off shotguns (subsection b.), and assault firearms (subsection g.). Any person who manufactures bullets (subsection f.), firearm silencers (subsection c.), or large-capacity ammunition magazines (subsection h.) is guilty of a fourth degree crime.

Per subsection e. of the statute, a person who defaces any firearm is guilty of a third degree offense, whereas a person who "knowingly buys, receives, disposes of or conceals" a defaced firearm—other than an antique unit—is guilty of a fourth degree offense.

Subsection d. handles the statute's prohibitions against manufacturing weapons such as gravity knives, switchblades, billies, and blackjacks. It is a fourth degree offense to manufacture any of these items. This subsection also provides that it is a fourth degree offense to manufacture weapons or devices that emit tear gas or other injurious substances dispensed through the air such as mace. Obviously, anyone who is legally authorized to manufacture any of the weapons or items prohibited in 2C:39-9 is exempt from prosecution.

George Evile was not a licensed manufacturer of machine guns, and he would never be legally permitted to deface automatic rifles and handguns. Accordingly, he is guilty of third degree crimes for manufacturing machine guns (subsection a.) and defacing firearms (subsection e.) at his Jersey City shop.

**2C:39-9.1.**     **Sale of weapon to minor; crime of the fourth degree; exceptions**

A person who sells any hunting, fishing, combat or survival knife having a blade length of five inches or more or an overall length of 10 inches or more to a person under 18 years of age commits a crime of the fourth degree; except that the establishment by a preponderance of the evidence of all of the following facts by a person making the sale shall constitute an affirmative defense to any prosecution therefor: a. that the purchaser falsely represented his age by producing a driver's license bearing a photograph of the licensee, or by producing a photographic identification card issued pursuant to section 1 of P.L. 1968, c. 313 (C. 33:1-81.2) or by producing a similar card purporting to be a valid identification card indicating that he was 18 years of age or older, and b. that the appearance of the purchaser was such that an ordinary prudent person would believe him to be 18 years of age or older, and c. that the sale was made in good faith relying upon the indicators of age listed in a. and b. above.

## PRACTICAL APPLICATION OF STATUTE

The pawnbroker sold a combat knife with an eight-inch blade to a 15-year-old high school freshman. This is a fourth degree crime.

2C:39-9.1 provides that it is illegal to sell any hunting, fishing, combat, or survival knife to anyone under 18 years of age. The knife, though, must have a blade of five inches or more or have an overall length of ten inches.

Certain circumstances will afford a seller an affirmative defense to prosecution under 2C:39-9.1. If the seller can show that the minor provided him a card, such as a driver's license, that purported to be a valid identification card, he has met the first element to an affirmative defense. If he further can show that the appearance of the purchaser "was such that an ordinary person would believe him to be 18 years of age or older" and that the sale was made in good faith based on the indicators of age, then the seller has his affirmative defense.

The pawnbroker sold a combat knife to a 15-year-old high school student. The blade exceeded five inches in length, as it was eight inches. The student never presented any identification whatsoever to the pawnbroker indicating that he was 18 or older. Given all these facts, he is guilty of a fourth degree crime.

---

**2C:39-9.2.**    **Sale of handcuffs to minors, penalties**

A person who sells handcuffs to a person under 18 years of age is guilty of a disorderly persons offense. A law enforcement officer shall confiscate handcuffs sold in violation of the law. As used in this section, "handcuffs" mean a device, conventionally used for law enforcement purposes, that can be tightened and locked about the wrists for the purpose of restraining a person's movement.

## PRACTICAL APPLICATION OF STATUTE

The pawnbroker sold three pairs of handcuffs to a 15-year-old high school freshman. Simply, under 2C:39-9.2, he is guilty of a disorderly persons offense for this act.

---

**2C:39-10.**    **Violation of the regulatory provisions relating to firearms; false representation in applications**

a.  (1) Except as otherwise provided in paragraph (2) of this subsection, any person who knowingly violates the regulatory provisions relating to manufacturing or wholesaling of firearms (section 2C:58-1), retailing of firearms (section 2C:58-2), permits to purchase certain firearms (section 2C:58-3), permits to carry certain firearms (section 2C:58-4), licenses to procure machine guns or assault firearms (section 2C:58-5), or incendiary or tracer ammunition (section 2C:58-10), except acts which are punishable under section 2C:39-5 or section 2C:39-9, is guilty of a crime of the fourth degree.

   (2) A licensed dealer who knowingly violates the provisions of subparagraph (d) of paragraph (5) of subsection a. of N.J.S.2C:58-2 is a disorderly person.

b.  Any person who knowingly violates the regulatory provisions relating to notifying the authorities of possessing certain items of explosives (section 2C:58-7), or of certain wounds (section 2C:58-8) is a disorderly person.

c.  Any person who gives or causes to be given any false information, or signs a fictitious name or address, in applying for a firearms purchaser identification card, a permit to purchase a handgun, a permit to carry a handgun, a permit to possess a machine gun, a permit to possess an assault firearm, or in completing the certificate or any other instrument required by law in purchasing or otherwise acquiring delivery of any rifle, shotgun, handgun, machine gun, or assault firearm or any other firearm, is guilty of a crime of the third degree.

d.  Any person who gives or causes to be given any false information in registering an assault firearm pursuant to section 11 of P.L.1990, c.32 (C.2C:58-12) or in certifying that an assault firearm was rendered inoperable pursuant to section 12 of P.L.1990, c.32 (C.2C:58-13) commits a crime of the fourth degree.

e.  Any person who knowingly sells, gives, transfers, assigns or otherwise disposes of a firearm to a person who is under the age of 18 years, except as permitted in section 14 of P.L.1979, c.179 (C.2C:58-6.1), is guilty of a crime of the third degree. Notwithstanding any other provision of law to the contrary, the sentence imposed for a conviction under this subsection shall include a mandatory minimum three-year term of imprisonment, during which the defendant shall be ineligible for parole.

f.  Unless the recipient is authorized to possess the handgun in connection with the performance of official duties under the provisions of N.J.S.2C:39-6, any person who knowingly sells, gives, transfers, assigns or otherwise disposes of a handgun to a person who is under the age of 21 years, except as permitted in section 14 of P.L.1979, c.179 (C.2C:58-6.1), is guilty of a crime of the third degree.

## PRACTICAL APPLICATION OF STATUTE

### Generally

2C:39-10 sets forth various offenses for violating regulatory provisions relating to firearms (see subsections a. and b.). The statute also provides certain prohibitions against the transfer of firearms to minors (see subsection e.) and the transfer of handguns to those under 21 (see subsection f.). In addition, subsections c. and d. lay out the offenses for giving false information in matters such as applying for a handgun permit and registering an assault firearm. Following is more of an explanation of the subsections that set out the offenses for violating regulatory provisions.

### Violations of Regulatory Provisions Relating to Firearms

Chapter 58 of the codebook, in part, provides regulatory provisions pertaining to firearms (e.g., regarding manufacturing or wholesaling firearms, or regarding permits to purchase firearms). 2C:39-10, in subsection a.(1), makes it a fourth degree offense to "knowingly" violate any of these regulatory provisions. For example, Art Campos fills out an application with the state to manufacture assault rifles. "Knowing" the application is still pending, Campos decides to begin manufacturing the rifles anyway. Because his application had not yet been approved, Campos is guilty of a fourth degree offense for manufacturing the rifles without a permit as is required in Chapter 58.

### Delivering a Handgun Without a Trigger Lock or in a Locked Box

Subsection a.(2) makes it a disorderly persons offense for any licensed dealer to knowingly violate the "provisions of subparagraph (d) of paragraph (5) of subsection a. of N.J.S.2C:58-2." That's fine, but what is subparagraph (d) of paragraph (5) of subsection a. of N.J.S.2C:58-2? Simply, N.J.S.2C:58-2a.(5)(d) provides that a person cannot deliver a handgun to another unless "the handgun is accompanied by a trigger lock or a locked case, gun box, container or other secure facility." Accordingly, if Art Campos "knowingly" gave his friend Mike Bimino a handgun that neither was in a secure, locked box or had a trigger lock on it, he could face a disorderly persons offense. This would also seem to be the case even if the gun was sold legally.

### Possessing Explosives/Reporting Wounds

Subsection b. of 2C:39-10 references 2C:58-7 and 2C:58-8. Why? 2C:58-7 provides that any person who possesses explosives or destructive devices must notify the police that he possesses these items within 15 days of his receipt of them. If he fails to do this, he is guilty of a disorderly persons offense under 2C:39-10b.

2C:58-8, in a nutshell, requires that in every case where a person is treated at a hospital (or other similar institution) for any wound caused by a "firearm, destructive device, explosive or weapon," said wound must be reported to the police. If it is not, the physician consulted or the person in charge of the institution may be charged with a disorderly persons offense under 2C:39-10b.

## 2C:39-11.        Pawnbrokers; loaning on firearms

a. Any pawnbroker who sells, offers to sell or to lend or to give away any weapon, destructive device or explosive is guilty of a crime of the third degree.

b. Any person who loans money, the security for which is any handgun, rifle or shotgun is guilty of a disorderly persons offense.

## PRACTICAL APPLICATION OF STATUTE

The pawnbroker is guilty of a third degree crime under 2C:39-11. Under subsection a. of this statute, a pawnbroker who sells—or even gives away—any weapon, destructive device, or explosive is guilty of a crime of the third degree.

George Evile sold the pawnbroker cocaine and weapons. After their deal was completed, the pawnbroker re-sold a number of the items to a college student. Specifically, he sold the handguns and ten daggers to the young man. This illegal transaction renders the pawnbroker guilty of a third degree crime under 2C:39-11.

## 2C:39-12.        Voluntary surrender

No person shall be convicted of an offense under this chapter for possessing any firearms, weapons, destructive devices, silencers or explosives, if after giving written notice of his intention to do so, including the proposed date and time of surrender, he voluntarily surrendered the weapon, device, instrument or substance in question to the superintendent or to the chief of police in the municipality in which he resides, provided that the required notice is received by the superintendent or chief of police before any charges have been made or complaints filed against such person for the unlawful possession of the weapon, device, instrument or substance in question and before any investigation has been commenced by any law enforcement agency concerning the unlawful possession. Nothing in this section shall be construed as granting immunity from prosecution for any crime or offense except that of the unlawful possession of such weapons, devices, instruments or substances surrendered as herein provided.

## 2C:39-13.        Unlawful use of body vests

A person is guilty of a crime if he uses or wears a body vest while engaged in the commission of, or an attempt to commit, or flight after committing or attempting to commit murder, manslaughter, robbery, sexual assault, burglary, kidnaping, criminal escape or assault under N.J.S.2C:12-1b. Use or wearing a body vest while engaged in the commission of, or an attempt to commit, or flight after committing or attempting to commit a crime of the first degree is a crime of the second degree. Otherwise it is a crime of the third degree.

As used in this section, "body vest" means bullet-resistant body armor which is intended to provide ballistic and trauma protection.

## PRACTICAL APPLICATION OF STATUTE

George Evile wore a body vest when he robbed a candy store in Weehawken. This act warrants a second degree charge pursuant to 2C:39-13.

In addition to other appropriate charges, a person will face either a second or third degree charge if he wears a body vest during the commission of or flight from one of a number of serious crimes. The crimes that act as a springboard for the body vest charge under 2C:39-13 include offenses such as burglary, robbery, sexual assault, and murder. If the underlying offense is a crime of the first degree, the body vest charge will be one of the second degree. Otherwise, it will be a third degree crime.

Wielding an automatic rifle, George Evile held up a candy store in Weehawken. There, he sported a body vest and shot the clerk in the leg just before fleeing the store. Robbery and aggravated assault are among the crimes Evile committed at the candy store. In this case, the robbery is a crime of the first degree. Given the first degree nature of this underlying offense, Evile is guilty of a second degree crime for wearing a body vest during their commission.

**2C:39-14.**    **Training, practice or instruction in use, application of making of firearms or explosive devices**

a. Any person who teaches or demonstrates to any other person the use, application, or making of any firearm, explosive or destructive device, or technique capable of causing injury or death to a person, knowing or having reason to know or intending that it will be employed for use in, or in furtherance of, an illegal activity is guilty of a crime of the second degree.

b. Any person who assembles with one or more persons for the purpose of training with, practicing with, or being instructed in the use of any firearm, explosive or destructive device, or technique capable of causing injury or death to a person, intending to unlawfully employ it for use in, or in furtherance of, an illegal activity is guilty of a crime of the second degree.

## PRACTICAL APPLICATION OF STATUTE

For teaching the pawnbroker how to manufacture machine guns, George Evile is guilty of a second degree crime. Evile's "knowledge" that the pawnbroker was planning to utilize the machine guns for future robberies is the linchpin for a conviction under this statute.

Per subsection a. of 2C:39-14, a person who teaches another how to make "any firearm, explosive or destructive device, or technique capable of causing injury or death" can be convicted of a crime of the second degree. The statute further provides, though, that the teacher must perform the instruction "knowing or having reason to know or intending" that the devices or techniques will be "employed for use in, or in furtherance of, an illegal activity."

George Evile's instruction meets all of the elements of this offense. Evile appeared at the pawnbroker's home and personally instructed him how to manufacture firearms, specifically machine guns. Evile did this "knowing" that the pawnbroker was intending to manufacture the guns for use in the "illegal activity" of armored car robberies. Accordingly, George Evile should be convicted of a second degree crime as provided for in 2C:39-14.

## 2C:39-15.  Gun advertising requirement

Any person who offers to sell a machine gun, semi-automatic rifle, or assault firearm by means of an advertisement published in a newspaper circulating within this State, which advertisement does not specify that the purchaser shall hold a valid license to purchase and possess a machine gun or assault firearm, or a valid firearms identification card to purchase and possess an automatic or semi-automatic rifle, is a disorderly person.

## PRACTICAL APPLICATION OF STATUTE

Licensed dealers may advertise in New Jersey newspapers the sale of machine guns, semi-automatic rifles, or assault firearms. However, dealers can be convicted of a disorderly persons offense per 2C:39-15 if their advertisements fail to specify certain language in the case of machine guns and assault firearms. The advertisements must state that the purchaser must "hold a valid license" to purchase and possess such items; in the case of automatic and semi-automatic rifles, the ad must specify that the purchaser must possess "a valid firearms identification card."

## 2C:39-16.  "Leader of a firearms trafficking network" defined; first degree crime; fines; sentencing

A person is a leader of a firearms trafficking network if he conspires with others as an organizer, supervisor, financier or manager, to engage for profit in a scheme or course of conduct to unlawfully manufacture, transport, ship, sell or dispose of any firearm. Leader of firearms trafficking network is a crime of the first degree.

As used in this section: "leader of a firearms trafficking network" means a person who occupies a position of authority or control over other persons in a scheme or organization of illegal firearms manufacturing, transporting, shipping or selling and who exercises that authority or control over others involved in the scheme or organization.

Notwithstanding the provisions of subsection a. of N.J.S.2C:43-3, the court may also impose a fine not to exceed $500,000.00 or five times the value of the firearms involved, whichever is greater.

Notwithstanding the provisions of N.J.S.2C:1-8, a conviction of leader of firearms trafficking network shall not merge with the conviction for any offense which is the object of the conspiracy. Nothing contained in this section shall prohibit the court from imposing an extended term pursuant to N.J.S.2C:43-7; nor shall this section be construed in any way to preclude or limit the prosecution or conviction of any person for conspiracy under N.J.S.2C:5-2, or any prosecution or conviction for weapons offenses under the provisions of chapter 39 of Title 2C of the New Jersey Statutes, N.J.S.2C:41-2 (racketeering activities) or subsection g. of N.J.S.2C:5-2 (leader of organized crime).

It shall not be necessary in any prosecution under this section for the State to prove that any intended profit was actually realized. The trier of fact may infer that a particular scheme or course of conduct was undertaken for profit from all of the attendant circumstances, including but not limited to the number of persons involved in the scheme or course of conduct, the actor's net worth and his expenditures in relation to his legitimate sources of income, the amount of firearms involved, or the amount of cash or currency involved.

It shall not be a defense to a prosecution under this section that the firearms were brought into or transported in this State solely for ultimate distribution or dispensing in another jurisdiction; nor shall it be a defense that any profit was intended to be made in another jurisdiction.

## PRACTICAL APPLICATION OF STATUTE

George Evile is guilty of being the leader of a firearms trafficking network. This is a crime of the first degree.

In order to be convicted of being the leader of a firearms trafficking network, the defendant must "conspire with others" to "unlawfully manufacture, transport, ship, sell or dispose of any firearm." The work of the network must be performed in order to earn "profit," and the defendant must be an "organizer, supervisor, financier or manager" of the scheme.

George Evile set up a machine gun manufacturing shop in Jersey City wherein he produced and sold in excess of 1,000 machine guns. The shop was created by Evile for the purpose of raising funds for his terrorist group, MIFA. Evile closely monitored the manufacturing house, visiting the establishment on a daily basis and barking orders and directives to the dozens of employees that worked for him.

In this case, Evile "conspired with others" to "unlawfully manufacture" machine guns: Several people worked under him and they did not have a license to produce the firearms. The work of the group was performed in order to earn "profit": They were raising money for Evile's terrorist conglomerate, MIFA. And Evile was the "organizer" and "supervisor" of the operation: He set up the shop in Jersey City and barked orders and directives to his dozens of employees on a daily basis. With all of the aforementioned elements met, George Evile is guilty of being a leader of a firearms trafficking network. Pursuant to 2C:39-16, this is a first degree crime.

# 40

# OTHER OFFENSES RELATING TO PUBLIC SAFETY

**2C:40-1.**  **Creating a hazard**

A person is guilty of a disorderly persons offense when:

    a. He maintains, stores or displays unattended in a place other than a permanently enclosed building or discards in any public or private place, including any junkyard, where it might attract children, a container which has a compartment of more than one and one-half cubic feet capacity and a door or lid which locks or fastens automatically when closed and which cannot easily be opened from the inside, he fails to remove the door, lid, locking or fastening device;

    b. Being the owner or otherwise having possession of property upon which an abandoned well or cesspool is located, he fails to cover the same with suitable protective construction; or

    c. He discards or abandons in any public or private place accessible to children, whether or not such children are trespassers, any intact television picture tube, or being the owner, lessee or manager of such place, knowingly permits such abandoned or discarded television picture tube to remain there in such condition.

## PRACTICAL APPLICATION OF STATUTE

Pursuant to 2C:40-1, a person can be convicted of a disorderly persons offense for manufacturing items such as inoperable refrigerators (see subsection a.), abandoned cesspools (see subsection b.), and abandoned television picture tubes (see subsection c.). These items are potentially hazardous to children who may come upon them. For example, a child who climbs into a discarded refrigerator may have the door shut on him, and thereby faces peril.

    The pawnbroker was once convicted under this statute. Why? Because he kept an abandoned cesspool on property he owned. As long as the pawnbroker failed to "cover the same with suitable protective construction," as subsection b. provides, his disorderly persons offense conviction was proper.

**2C:40-2.**  **Refusing to yield a party line**

A person is guilty of a disorderly persons offense when, being informed that a party line is needed for an emergency call, he refuses immediately to relinquish such line.

"Party line" means a subscriber's line telephone circuit, consisting of two or more main telephone stations connected therewith, each station with a distinctive ring or telephone number.

"Emergency call" means a telephone call to a police or fire department or for medical aid or ambulance service, necessitated by a situation in which human life or property is in jeopardy and prompt summoning of aid is essential.

## PRACTICAL APPLICATION OF STATUTE

Hang up the phone or be convicted of a disorderly persons offense. Is that possible? Under 2C:40-2, it is. Here's an example.

Jack is on the phone, in his own house, with his girlfriend Melanie. The doorbell rings; Jack answers the door, holding his phone, and is met by a frantic man he does not know. The man tells him that he just got into an automobile accident and the driver of the other vehicle is bleeding from his head. The man tells Jack, "Please give me your phone to call the police!" Jack, however, slams the door closed and continues speaking to Melanie.

Here Jack is guilty of a disorderly persons offense. 2C:40-2 requires a person to give up a "party line"—the phone—if he is informed that the line is needed for an "emergency call." An "emergency call" is defined in the statute as meaning calls to "a police or fire department or for medical aid or ambulance service" for situations where "human life or property is in jeopardy and prompt summoning of aid is essential." Jack was advised that an automobile accident had occurred and that a human being was bleeding from the head. His failure to relinquish the telephone in that emergency circumstance renders him guilty of a disorderly persons offense per the tenets of 2C:40-2.

**2C:40-3.**    **Hazing; aggravated hazing**

   a. A person is guilty of hazing, a disorderly persons offense, if, in connection with initiation of applicants to or members of a student or fraternal organization, he knowingly or recklessly organizes, promotes, facilitates or engages in any conduct, other than competitive athletic events, which places or may place another person in danger of bodily injury.

   b. A person is guilty of aggravated hazing, a crime of the fourth degree, if he commits an act prohibited in subsection a. which results in serious bodily injury to another person.

## PRACTICAL APPLICATION OF STATUTE

Delta Delta Delta fraternity, located at a college in New Jersey, organized its final spring semester event for its newest pledge class. At the completion of this day's activities, each pledge would become a bona fide "brother" in the fraternity.

The majority of the morning and afternoon was marked by the pledges cleaning the fraternity house—mopping floors, washing dishes, vacuuming, dusting, and scrubbing the bathroom to a sparkling finish. During the twilight hours, the young men were ordered to take tests on fraternity history and to repeatedly enunciate and spell each brother's full name. The evening, though, yielded a different chain of events, specifically two separate and distinct activities.

First, every pledge was slapped ten times on the backside by Delta Delta Delta brothers Sam Concord and Michael Diaz. Next, brothers Tony Tangemi and Leroy Manning led the pledges to the fourth floor which was otherwise known as "the office." Once there, they were ordered to climb out a window and onto the house's roof. They were then told to jump from the roof into an in-ground pool below. All the pledges complied; all landed safely except for Pledge Karl, who broke his leg in three places.

In this case, brothers Sam Concord and Michael Diaz are guilty of hazing, a disorderly persons offense, as provided for in subsection a. of 2C:40-3. Brothers Tony Tangemi and Leroy Manning are guilty of aggravated hazing under subsection b. of the statute. Aggravated hazing is a fourth degree crime.

For a person to be convicted of hazing, he must "knowingly" or "recklessly" organize, promote, or facilitate an activity that places (or may place) another in danger of "bodily injury." However, there is an additional provision: this activity must be in connection with the initiation of applicants, such as pledges becoming members of a student or fraternal organization. Hazing is elevated to aggravated hazing if the said activity "results in serious bodily injury" to another.

The Delta Delta Delta fraternity is a fraternal organization located at a New Jersey college. In an organized ritual to allow their pledges to become brothers in the fraternity, they paddled the pledges and had them jump from a fourth-story roof into a pool. The brothers involved in these initiation practices at least "recklessly," if not "knowingly," promoted activities that placed the pledges in danger of bodily injury. Paddling someone certainly subjects that person to personal "bodily injuries" such as bruises and abrasions. Accordingly, Sam Concord and Michael Diaz are guilty of hazing, under subsection a. of the statute. Given that one of the pledges suffered the "serious bodily injury" of a broken leg when he jumped from the fraternity house roof, brothers Tony Tangemi and Leroy Manning are guilty of the fourth degree crime of aggravated hazing for their roles in that dangerous event.

It is important to note that a person (i.e., a fraternity member) cannot be prosecuted under 2C:40-3 in circumstances where he has pledges engage in competitive athletic events. Also interesting, per 2C:40-4, a pledge's "consent" to involve himself in any type of hazing activity shall not be a defense to prosecution under 2C:40-3.

### 2C:40-4.     Consent not available as defense to hazing

Notwithstanding any other provision of Title 2C of the New Jersey Statutes to the contrary, consent shall not be available as a defense to a prosecution under this Act.

### 2C:40-5.     Conduct constituting offense may be prosecuted under other provisions of Title 2C

Conduct constituting an offense under this Act may, at the discretion of the prosecuting attorney, be prosecuted under any other applicable provision of Title 2C of the New Jersey Statutes.

### 2C:40-6.     Definitions

As used in this act:
  a. "Portable, oil-burning heating device" means any self-contained, self-supporting, oil-fueled heater not connected to a flue, equipped with an integral reservoir, and designed to be carried from one location to another.

b. "Oil" means any liquid fuel with a flash point of greater than 100 degrees Fahrenheit, including but not limited to kerosene.

**2C:40-7.**    **Portable, oil-burning heating devices; certificate of evaluation by test of safety prior to sale, offer for sale or use**

A portable, oil-burning heating device shall not be sold, offered for sale, or used in this State unless a nationally recognized testing or inspection agency, such as but not limited to Underwriters' Laboratory, Inc.:

a. Has evaluated the portable, oil-burning heating device with respect to reasonably foreseeable hazards to life and property that it might cause;

b. Has found the portable, oil-burning heating device to be reasonably safe for its specific purpose;

c. Has shown the particular model of the portable, oil-burning heating device on a list of devices that have been evaluated according to the requirements of subsection a. of this section and found to be safe according to the requirements of subsection b. of this section;

d. Has accompanied the portable, oil-burning heating device with a certificate or with the mark, name, or symbol of the agency as an indication that it has been evaluated according to the requirements of subsection a. of this section, found safe according to the requirements of subsection b. of this section, and listed according to the requirements of subsection c. of this section. The certificate or the mark, name, or symbol of the agency must accompany the portable, oil-burning heating device at all times when it is sold, offered for sale, or used in this State.

**2C:40-8.**    **Label cautioning and informing user**

A portable, oil-burning heating device shall not be sold, offered for sale, or used in this State unless a label is affixed to the device cautioning and informing the user concerning:

a. The amount and source of ventilation that is adequate when the device is in operation;

b. The type of fuel that should be used in the device;

c. The steps that should be followed in order to refuel the device safely;

d. The proper placement and handling of the device when it is in operation to prevent fire, burns, and other safety hazards;

e. The proper procedures for lighting the device and regulating and extinguishing the flame.

**2C:40-9.**    **Inclusion of instructions concerning proper and safe maintenance and operation**

No portable, oil-burning heating device shall be sold or offered for sale in this State unless it is accompanied by instructions concerning its proper and safe maintenance and operation.

**2C:40-10.**    **Construction requirements**

No portable, oil-burning heating device shall be sold, offered for sale, or used in this State unless it is constructed with a low center of gravity and a minimum tipping angle of 33 degrees from the vertical with an empty reservoir.

**2C:40-11.**    **Automatic safety shut-off device or design feature to eliminate fire hazard in event of tipover**

No portable, oil-burning heating device shall be sold, offered for sale, or used in this State unless equipped with an automatic safety shut-off device or inherent design feature that eliminates fire hazards in the event of tipover.

**2C:40-12.          Carbon monoxide limitations**

No portable, oil-burning heating device which, when operated according to the instructions that must accompany the heater as required by section 4 of this act, produces carbon monoxide at a rate that creates a hazard shall be sold, offered for sale, or used in this State.

**2C:40-13.          Posting of sign at point of sale or display of prohibition of use in multiple dwellings or in residences in certain municipalities**

No portable, oil-burning heating device shall be sold or offered for sale in this State unless a conspicuous sign is posted at the point of sale and the point of display notifying a purchaser or potential purchaser that portable, oil-burning heating devices are prohibited for use in multiple dwellings in the State by regulations adopted pursuant to the "Hotel and Multiple Dwelling Law," P.L.1967, c. 76 (C. 55:13A-1 et seq.) and that certain municipalities in the State have adopted housing codes prohibiting the use of portable, oil-burning heating devices in residences within the municipality.

**2C:40-14.          Regulations**

Pursuant to the "Administrative Procedure Act," P.L.1968, c. 410 (C. 52:14B-1 et seq.), the Commissioner of the Department of Community Affairs shall adopt regulations for the implementation and enforcement of this act.

**2C:40-15.          Violations; petty disorderly persons offense**

Any person who sells, offers for sale or uses any portable kerosene-burning heating device in violation of the provisions of this act is guilty of a petty disorderly persons offense. Each sale of a heater in violation of this act constitutes a separate offense.

## PRACTICAL APPLICATION OF STATUTE

Statutes 2C:40-7 and 2C:40-10 set forth various offenses concerning safety issues surrounding the use and sale of portable, oil-burning heating devices. A violation under any of these statutes can result in petty disorderly persons offense conviction.

The pawnbroker violated 2C:40-7 for selling portable, oil-burning heating devices that had never been inspected by any appropriate testing agency. He also violated 2C:40-11 for selling the devices even though they failed to be equipped with "an automatic safety shut-off device or inherent design feature that eliminates fire hazards in the event of tipover." Given these sales activities, the pawnbroker is guilty of a few petty disorderly persons offenses.

Please note that a conviction under these statutes, like some others, may require the testimony of an expert witness. For example, 2C:40-12 provides that no portable, oil-burning heating device can be sold if it "produces carbon monoxide at a rate that creates a hazard." Obviously, an expert should be employed in order to advise what exactly is a "rate that creates a hazard." Those charging pursuant to these statutes should be guided accordingly.

**2C:40-16.          Definitions**

As used in this act:
  a. "Cosmetic" means any substance or other device which is used for the treatment of the skin, hair or nails.

b. "Drug" means any over-the-counter or prescribed medicine.

c. "Food product" means anything sold for human consumption, and includes tobacco products.

d. "Tamper" means to adulterate a cosmetic, drug or food product by adding any poisonous, deleterious or noxious substance which may be injurious or detrimental to a person's health.

## 2C:40-17. Fourth degree crime

A person who tampers with a cosmetic, drug or food product is guilty of a crime of the fourth degree, except that nothing herein shall be deemed to preclude a charge for a greater crime under any other provision of Title 2C of the New Jersey Statutes.

### PRACTICAL APPLICATION OF STATUTE

The pawnbroker was arrested at a supermarket for opening a package of cupcakes, spitting on the baked goods, and resealing the package. This is a fourth degree crime under 2C:40-17, as this statute prohibits a person from tampering with a "cosmetic, drug or food."

## 2C:40-18. Violation of law intended to protect public health and safety; grading

a. A person is guilty of a crime of the second degree if the person knowingly violates a law intended to protect the public health and safety or knowingly fails to perform a duty imposed by a law intended to protect the public health and safety and recklessly causes death.

b. A person is guilty of a crime of the third degree if the person knowingly violates a law intended to protect the public health and safety or knowingly fails to perform a duty imposed by a law intended to protect the public health and safety and recklessly causes serious bodily injury.

c. A person is guilty of a crime of the fourth degree if the person knowingly violates a law intended to protect the public health and safety or knowingly fails to perform a duty imposed by a law intended to protect the public health and safety and recklessly causes significant bodily injury.

### PRACTICAL APPLICATION OF STATUTE

2C:40-18a. makes it a second degree crime where a person "knowingly" violates a law (or fails to perform a duty) intended to protect the public health and safety—and "recklessly" causes "death." Under subsection b., this same type of behavior is a third degree crime where it "recklessly" causes "serious bodily injury." Per subsection c., it is a fourth degree crime if it "recklessly" causes "significant bodily injury." But where is this statute applicable? A review of another incident involving the pawnbroker can answer this question.

For some reason, the pawnbroker decided to remove a stop sign at a busy Union City intersection. On the same day, an unassuming motorist crossed through the intersection, without stopping, and crashed into another motor vehicle. A passenger in one of the cars was killed. Here the pawnbroker "knowingly" violated a law intended to protect the public health and safety: he committed an act of criminal mischief by taking down a stop sign. The stop sign was obviously in place to prevent the ill that did in fact occur—a motor vehicle accident. His action was certainly "reckless" in that any person could reasonably foresee that a motor vehicle accident could occur as a result of removing a stop sign at a busy intersection. Since his unlawful act "recklessly" resulted in death, the pawnbroker is guilty of a second degree crime as provided in subsection a. of 2C:40-18.

**2C:40-19.**  **Consumer products; unauthorized writing; offense**

a. Except as provided in subsection b. of this section, any person who stamps, prints, places or inserts any writing in or on a consumer product offered for sale or the box, package or other container containing the product is guilty of a disorderly persons offense.

b. This act shall not apply in any case where the owner or manager of the premises where the product is stored or sold; the product manufacturer; the authorized distributor or the retailer of the product consents to the placing or inserting of the writing.

c. As used in this act:

(1) "Writing" means any form of representation or communication, including handbills, notices or advertising, that contains letters, words or pictorial representations;

(2) "Consumer product" includes but is not limited to any cosmetic, drug or food product as defined in section 1 of P.L.1987, c.421 (C.2C:40-16) or any article, product or commodity which is customarily produced or distributed for use by individuals.

## PRACTICAL APPLICATION OF STATUTE

Manuk, a car dealer, enters a supermarket and stamps the following on every box of pasta in the store: "For the best car deals, come to Manuk's, in Freehold." This act renders Manuk guilty of a disorderly persons offense under 2C:40-19. Why? Because this statute makes it illegal to stamp, print, place, or insert any writing (e.g., advertisements, notices) on any "consumer product offered for sale or the box, package or other container containing the product." In the case where any authorized person (such as the store owner or the product manufacturer) consents to the placing or inserting of the writing, this statute does not apply.

**2C:40-20.**  **Use of certain cable, wire devices; fourth degree crime**

A person who uses any type of device, including but not limited to wire or cable, that is not a fence but is installed at a height under 10 feet from the ground, to indicate boundary lines or otherwise to divide, partition or segregate portions of real property, if the device is not readily visible or marked in such a way as to make it readily visible to persons who are pedestrians, equestrians, bicyclists or drivers of off-the-road vehicles and poses a risk of causing significant bodily injury to such persons, shall be guilty of a crime of the fourth degree. However, this section is not intended to apply to markers set by a licensed land surveyor, pursuant to existing statute.

## PRACTICAL APPLICATION OF STATUTE

Perry encircles his Jefferson Township ranch with a clear, heavyweight cable. The cable is approximately five feet from the ground, and during the night it is nearly impossible to see. Even during daylight hours it is difficult to see. On a late weekend evening, Marty decided to cut through Perry's yard in an effort to more quickly reach a home located behind Perry's house. Unfortunately for Marty, he was "clothes-lined" by the cable, running directly into it neck-high. Marty hit the ground with considerable force and broke his arm.

In the aforementioned matter, Perry is guilty of a fourth degree crime pursuant to the provisions laid out in 2C:40-20. This statute makes it such an offense where a person uses any type of device, such as cable or wire, that is "installed at a height under 10 feet from the ground" in order to indicate boundary lines or to otherwise separate portions of real property. However, in order for a conviction to occur under this statute, the device must not be readily visible and it must pose "a risk of causing significant bodily injury."

Perry's cable was five feet off the ground and it was not readily visible to people coming upon it. It obviously posed "a risk of causing significant bodily injury." Marty could not see it, was "clothes-lined," crashed to the ground, and broke his arm. Accordingly, the danger imposed by Perry renders him guilty of a fourth degree crime under 2C:40-20.

**2C:40-21.**     **Tattooing of a minor; parental permission required**

A person commits a disorderly persons offense if he knowingly tattoos or engages in body piercing of a minor under the age of 18 years without first having obtained the written permission of the minor's parent or legal guardian or, if neither exists, a person who stands in place of a parent.

## PRACTICAL APPLICATION OF STATUTE

A body piercer or tattoo artist must obtain written permission from a minor's parent or guardian before engaging in a body piercing or tattooing of the minor. If he does not, he can be convicted of a disorderly persons offense per 2C:40-21. Please note, the person performing the tattooing or piercing may have a defense if he did not "know" that the individual was under 18—the statute provides that he must perform the acts "knowingly."

**2C:40-22.**     **Penalty for causing death or injury while driving in violation of R.S.39:3-40**

   a. A person who, while operating a motor vehicle in violation of R.S.39:3-40, is involved in an accident resulting in the death of another person, shall be guilty of a crime of the third degree, in addition to any other penalties applicable under R.S.39:3-40. The person's driver's license shall be suspended for an additional period of one year, in addition to any suspension applicable under R.S.39:3-40. The additional period of suspension shall commence upon the completion of any term of imprisonment.

   b. A person who, while operating a motor vehicle in violation of R.S.39:3-40, is involved in an accident resulting in serious bodily injury, as defined in N.J.S.2C:11-1, to another person shall be guilty of a crime of the fourth degree, in addition to any other penalties applicable under R.S.39:3-40. The person's driver's license shall be suspended for an additional period of one year, in addition to any suspension applicable under R.S.39:3-40. The additional period of suspension shall commence upon the completion of any term of imprisonment.

   c. The provisions of N.J.S.2C:2-3 governing the causal relationship between conduct and result shall not apply in a prosecution under this section. For purposes of this offense, the defendant's act of operating a motor vehicle while his driver's license or reciprocity privilege has been suspended or revoked or who operates a motor vehicle without being licensed to do so is the cause of death or injury when:

(1) The operation of the motor vehicle is an antecedent but for which the death or injury would not have occurred; and

(2) The death or injury was not:

(a) too remote in its occurrence as to have a just bearing on the defendant's liability; or

(b) too dependent upon the conduct of another person which was unrelated to the defendant's operation of a motor vehicle as to have a just bearing on the defendant's liability.

d. It shall not be a defense to a prosecution under this section that the decedent contributed to his own death or injury by reckless or negligent conduct or operation of a motor vehicle.

e. Nothing in this section shall be construed to preclude or limit any prosecution for homicide.

## PRACTICAL APPLICATION OF STATUTE

Marquis, while driving on the revoked list, gets into an automobile accident. The accident results in the death of the driver of the other motor vehicle. Here Marquis is guilty of a third degree crime.

Under 2C:40-22, a person can be convicted of a crime if he drives in violation of 39:3-40, the motor vehicle statute that makes it unlawful to drive "while on the revoked list." Under subsection a. of 2C:40-22, a person who, while driving on the revoked list, gets into an accident that results in "the death of another," is guilty of a third degree crime. If these same circumstances are present but "serious bodily injury" occurs rather than death, then the defendant is guilty of a fourth degree crime.

In Marquis' case, he was driving on the revoked list. Unfortunately, he got into an accident where another person was killed. Accordingly, he is guilty of a third degree crime under subsection a. of 2C:40-22.

Please note that, pursuant to subsection d. of the statute, it is not a defense where the decedent contributed to his own death or injury—even if the decedent acted negligently or recklessly. Simply, if a person drives while on the revoked list and gets into an accident where another person is killed or seriously injured, he is guilty of violating 2C:40-22.

# 40A

# Miscellaneous

**2C:40A-1.**    **Employer requiring lie detector test**

Any person who as an employer shall influence, request or require an employee or prospective employee to take or submit to a lie detector test as a condition of employment or continued employment, commits a disorderly persons offense. The provisions of this section shall not apply if: (1) the employer is authorized to manufacture, distribute or dispense controlled dangerous substances pursuant to the provisions of the "New Jersey Controlled Dangerous Substances Act," P.L.1970, c.226 (C. 24:21-1 et seq.); (2) the employee or prospective employee is or will be directly involved in the manufacture, distribution, or dispensing of, or has or will have access to, legally distributed controlled dangerous substances; and (3) the test, which shall cover a period of time no greater than 5 years preceding the test, and except as provided in this section, shall be limited to the work of the employee or prospective employee and the individual's improper handling, use or illegal sale of legally distributed controlled dangerous substances. The test may include standard baseline questions necessary and for the sole purpose of establishing a normal test pattern. Any employee or prospective employee who is required to take a lie detector test as a precondition of employment or continued employment shall have the right to be represented by legal counsel. A copy of the report containing the results of a lie detector test shall be in writing and be provided, upon request, to the individual who has taken the test. Information obtained from the test shall not be released to any other employer or person. The employee or prospective employee shall be informed of his right to present to the employer the results of an independently administered second lie detector examination prior to any personnel decision being made in his behalf by the employer.

## Practical Application of Statute

The pawnbroker required two employees to submit to lie detector tests before hiring them. This renders him guilty of a disorderly persons offense.

2C:40A-1 provides that an employer who influences, requests, or requires an employee or prospective employee to take or submit to a lie detector test "as a condition of employment or continued employment" is guilty of a disorderly persons offense. The statute does provide for exceptions, though: in a nutshell, for businesses involved in the legal manufacturing of controlled dangerous substances (CDS).

In the pawnbroker's case, his company had nothing to do with lawful CDS manufacturing; his business was simply as a pawnbroker. Accordingly, he is guilty of a disorderly persons offense for requiring his employees to submit to a lie detector test as a condition of their employment.

**2C:40A-2.**        **Violation of contract to pay employees**

Violation of contract to pay employees.

    a. An employer who has agreed with an employee or with a bargaining agent for employees to pay wages, compensation or benefits to or for the benefit of employees commits a disorderly persons offense if the employer:

      (1) fails to pay wages when due; or

      (2) fails to pay compensation or benefits within 30 days after due.

    b. If a corporate employer violates subsection a., any officer or employee of the corporation who is responsible for the violation commits a disorderly persons offense.

## PRACTICAL APPLICATION OF STATUTE

Employers who fail to pay wages when due may be guilty of a disorderly persons offense. In the case of the pawnbroker, this is true.

Per 2C:40A-2, an employer who "has agreed with an employee . . . to pay wages" is guilty of a disorderly persons offense if he fails to pay the money when due. The statute also covers the failure of employers to pay compensation or benefits—they must be paid within 30 days after due.

The pawnbroker signed written contracts with two employees to pay each a wage of $1,000 per week. However, when it was time to pay, he refused to remit their funds—even though they had performed their work duties. While courts generally would consider such a failure to meet contractual obligations as a civil matter, an employer could be convicted of a disorderly persons offense under 2C:40A-2 for the withholding. The pawnbroker, therefore, could have been found guilty of violating this statute for refusing to pay his two employees as he had promised.

**2C:40A-3.**        **Wrongful discharge of employee**

Wrongful discharge of employee.

    a. An employer who discharges an employee or takes any other disciplinary action against the employee because the employee's earnings have been subjected to garnishment commits a disorderly persons offense.

    b. An employer who discharges an employee or takes any other disciplinary action in violation of this section shall re-employ any employee discharged, and shall compensate any employee for any damages resulting from the discharge or disciplinary action.

    c. The term "earnings" means any form of compensation payable for personal services, regardless of whether the payment is denominated as wages, salary, commission, bonus, income from trust funds, profits, or otherwise, and includes periodic payments pursuant to a pension or retirement program.

## PRACTICAL APPLICATION OF STATUTE

An employer is guilty of a disorderly persons offense if he discharges an employee or takes any disciplinary action against an employee "because the employee's earnings have been subjected to garnishment." The pawnbroker fired one of his workers for just this. Accordingly, he is guilty of a disorderly persons offense as provided for in 2C:40A-3.

**2C:40A-4.**   **Solicitation of professional employment, certain; regulated; terms defined; grade of offense**

a.  No person shall solicit professional employment from an accident or disaster victim or an accident or disaster victim's relative concerning an action for personal injury or wrongful death involving that accident or disaster victim for a period of 30 days after the date on which the accident or disaster occurred.

b.  Subsection a. of this section shall not apply if the accident or disaster victim, or his relative, as the case may be, had a previous professional business relationship with the professional.

c.  Subsection a. of this section shall not apply to recommendations or referrals by past or present clients or patients, friends, relatives or other individuals relying on the reputation of the professional, provided the recommendation or referral is not made for value.

d.  Subsection a. of this section shall not apply to any solicitation through advertising which is not directed to the victim or victims of a specific accident or disaster.

e.  Subsection a. of this section shall not apply to emergency medical care.

f.  For the purposes of this section:

"Professional employment" means services rendered by a physician, chiropractor or other health care professional.

"Solicit" means to contact a person with a request or plea, which is made in person, by telephone or other electronic medium.

g.  A person who violates the provisions of this section, and who acts with intent to accept money or something of value for his services, shall be guilty of a crime of the third degree.

## PRACTICAL APPLICATION OF STATUTE

Physicians beware. Pursuant to 2C:40A-4, certain professionals, including medical doctors who solicit "professional employment from an accident or disaster victim" or their relatives, concerning an action for personal injury or wrongful death, may be guilty of a third degree crime. However, for a conviction to occur, the solicitation must occur within 30 days after the date on which the accident or disaster occurred. Also, as subsection g. states, the person must act "with intent to accept money or something of value for his services."

It is interesting to note that prosecution under this statute appears to be limited to individuals in the health care profession. Subsection f. defines "professional employment" as "services rendered by a physician, chiropractor or other health care professional." 2C:40A-4, however, does provide several circumstances where the prohibitions do not apply (see subsections b. through e.).

**2C:40A-5.**   **Additional penalty for attorneys; grade of offense**

In addition to any other sanction that may be imposed by the Supreme Court, an attorney who violates the Rules of Professional Conduct promulgated by the Supreme Court of New Jersey by contacting an accident or disaster victim or an accident or disaster victim's relative, using means other than written communication, to solicit professional employment on the attorney's own behalf, and who acts with intent to accept money or something of value for his services, shall be guilty of a crime of the third degree.

## PRACTICAL APPLICATION OF STATUTE

This statute basically prohibits the same conduct prohibited in 2C:40A-4 except 2C:40A-5 applies to attorneys. In a nutshell, any attorney who violates the "Rules of Professional Conduct promulgated by the Supreme Court of New Jersey" by contacting an accident or disaster victim or their relatives—using means other than written communication—is guilty of a third degree crime. This, of course, is if the purpose of the attorney's contact is "to solicit professional employment" with the "intent to accept money or something of value for his services."

# 41

# RACKETEERING

**2C:41-1.**      **Definitions**

For purposes of this section and N.J.S.2C:41-2 through N.J.S.2C:41-6:

a. "Racketeering activity" means

(1) any of the following crimes which are crimes under the laws of New Jersey or are equivalent crimes under the laws of any other jurisdiction:

(a) murder

(b) kidnapping

(c) gambling

(d) promoting prostitution

(e) obscenity

(f) robbery

(g) bribery

(h) extortion

(i) criminal usury

(j) violations of Title 33 of the Revised Statutes

(k) violations of Title 54A of the New Jersey Statutes and Title 54 of the Revised Statutes

(l) arson

(m) burglary

(n) theft and all crimes defined in chapter 20 of Title 2C of the New Jersey Statutes

(o) forgery and fraudulent practices and all crimes defined in chapter 21 of Title 2C of the New Jersey Statutes

(p) fraud in the offering, sale or purchase of securities

(q) alteration of motor vehicle identification numbers

(r) unlawful manufacture, purchase, use or transfer of firearms

(s) unlawful possession or use of destructive devices or explosives

(t) violation of sections 112 through 116 inclusive of the "Casino Control Act," P.L.1977, c.110 (C.5:12-112 through 5:12-116)

(u) violation of N.J.S.2C:35-4, N.J.S.2C:35-5 or N.J.S.2C:35-6 and all crimes involving illegal distribution of a controlled dangerous substance or controlled substance analog, except possession of less than one ounce of marijuana

(v) violation of subsection b. of N.J.S.2C:24-4 except for subparagraph (b) of paragraph (5) of subsection b.

(w) violation of section 1 of P.L.1995, c.405 (C.2C:39-16), leader of firearms trafficking network

(x) violation of section 1 of P.L.1983, c.229 (C.2C:39-14), weapons training for illegal activities

(y) violation of section 2 of P.L.2002, c.26 (C.2C:38-2), terrorism.

(2) any conduct defined as "racketeering activity" under Title 18, U.S.C.s.1961(1)(A), (B) and (D).

b. "Person" includes any individual or entity or enterprise as defined herein holding or capable of holding a legal or beneficial interest in property.

c. "Enterprise" includes any individual, sole proprietorship, partnership, corporation, business or charitable trust, association, or other legal entity, any union or group of individuals associated in fact although not a legal entity, and it includes illicit as well as licit enterprises and governmental as well as other entities.

d. "Pattern of racketeering activity" requires

(1) Engaging in at least two incidents of racketeering conduct one of which shall have occurred after the effective date of this act and the last of which shall have occurred within 10 years (excluding any period of imprisonment) after a prior incident of racketeering activity; and

(2) A showing that the incidents of racketeering activity embrace criminal conduct that has either the same or similar purposes, results, participants or victims or methods of commission or are otherwise interrelated by distinguishing characteristics and are not isolated incidents.

e. "Unlawful debt" means a debt

(1) Which was incurred or contracted in gambling activity which was in violation of the law of the United States, a state or political subdivision thereof; or

(2) Which is unenforceable under state or federal law in whole or in part as to principal or interest because of the laws relating to usury.

f. "Documentary material" includes any book, paper, document, writing, drawing, graph, chart, photograph, phonorecord, magnetic or recording or video tape, computer printout, other data compilation from which information can be obtained or from which information can be translated into useable form or other tangible item.

g. "Attorney General" includes the Attorney General of New Jersey, his assistants and deputies. The term shall also include a county prosecutor or his designated assistant prosecutor if a county prosecutor is expressly authorized in writing by the Attorney General to carry out the powers conferred on the Attorney General by this chapter.

h. "Trade or commerce" shall include all economic activity involving or relating to any commodity or service.

## 2C:41-1.1.    Declaration of policy and legislative findings

The Legislature hereby finds and declares to be the public policy of this State, the following:

a. By enactment of the "Criminal Justice Act of 1970," P.L.1970, c. 74 (C. 52:17B-97 et seq.), the Legislature recognized that the existence of organized crime and organized crime type activities presents a serious threat to the political, social and economic institutions of this State.

b. Despite the impressive gains of our law enforcement agencies, organized crime and similar activities in this State are still a highly sophisticated, diversified and widespread activity that annually drains millions of dollars from this State's economy by unlawful conduct and the illegal use of force, fraud and corruption. In recent years, that organized crime and organized criminal type activity has spread to the operation of otherwise legitimate businesses.

c. In order to safeguard the public interest, effective criminal and civil sanctions are needed to prevent, disrupt and eliminate the infiltration of organized crime type activities which are substantial in nature into the legitimate trade or commerce of this State. It is, therefore, in the public interest to provide that activity which is inimical to the general health, welfare and prosperity of the State and its inhabitants be made subject to strict civil and criminal sanctions.

## 2C:41-2.    Prohibited activities

a. It shall be unlawful for any person who has received any income derived, directly or indirectly, from a pattern of racketeering activity or through collection of an unlawful debt in which he has participated as a principal within the meaning of N.J.S. 2C:2-6 to use or invest, directly or indirectly, any part of the income, or the proceeds of the income, in acquisition of any interest in, or the establishment or operation of any enterprise which is engaged in or the activities of which affect trade or commerce. A purchase of securities on the open market for purposes of investment, and without the intention of controlling or participating in the control of the issuer or of assisting another to do so, shall not be unlawful under this section, provided that the sum total of the securities of the issuer held by the purchaser, the members of his family, and his or their accomplices in any pattern of racketeering activity or in the collection of an unlawful debt does not amount in the aggregate to 1% of the outstanding securities of any one class, or does not, either in law or in fact, empower the holders thereof to elect one or more directors of the issuer, provided further, that if, in any proceeding involving an alleged investment in violation of this section, it is established that over half of the defendant's aggregate income for a period of 2 or more years immediately preceding the investment was derived from a pattern of racketeering activity, a rebuttable presumption shall arise that the investment included income derived from a pattern of racketeering activity.

b. It shall be unlawful for any person through a pattern of racketeering activity or through collection of an unlawful debt to acquire or maintain, directly or indirectly, any interest in or control of any enterprise which is engaged in or activities of which affect trade or commerce.

c. It shall be unlawful for any person employed by or associated with any enterprise engaged in or activities of which affect trade or commerce to conduct or participate, directly or indirectly, in the conduct of the enterprise's affairs through a pattern of racketeering activity or collection of unlawful debt.

d. It shall be unlawful for any person to conspire as defined by N.J.S. 2C:5-2, to violate any of the provisions of this section.

## PRACTICAL APPLICATION OF STATUTE

George and Alex Evile could be convicted of a first degree crime for violating 2C:41-2 by engaging in a "pattern of racketeering activity" in manufacturing machine guns. But what exactly is "racketeering?" What really constitutes an offense under 2C:41-2? Let's evaluate subsection a. to better understand this statute.

In a quick summary, 2C:41-2a. makes it unlawful for a person to use or invest any income that he derived from a "pattern of racketeering activity" (or from the collection of an "unlawful debt") to acquire any interest in an "enterprise" whose activites "affect trade or commerce." Okay. Now what does that mean?

First, what is "racketeering activity?" "Racketeering activity" and all the definitions pertinent to 2C:41-2 are defined in 2C:41-1. "Racketeering activity" basically means engaging in any one of numerous serious crimes, including but not limited to murder, kidnapping, gambling, unlawful manufacture of firearms, and usury.

A "pattern of racketeering activity" requires two elements: (1) engaging in at least two incidents of racketeering within a *specified time period* and (2) that the racketeering incidents embrace a pattern of criminal conduct, including matters such as similar purposes, results, participants, victims, or methods of commission.

The specified time period means that the first incident of racketeering must have occurred "after the effective date of this act," which is June 15, 1981. The last incident "shall have occurred within 10 years (excluding any period of imprisonment) after a prior incident of racketeering." Accordingly, if there are only two incidents of racketeering and the first incident happened in 1992, the last incident must happen by 2002—in order for a "pattern of racketeering activity" to occur.

How about an "unlawful debt"? What's that? It's a debt that was incurred through unlawful gambling activity or a debt which is unenforceable because of laws related to usury.

Now, let's revisit what 2C:41-2a. provides: any income derived from a "pattern of racketeering activity" or the collection of an "unlawful debt" violates the statute when it is used to acquire any interest in an "enterprise" whose activities "affect trade or commerce." Now, let's keep explaining the terms. What constitutes "enterprise" is simple. Basically, it's any business or entity, whether illicit or licit.

But how does one know if an enterprise's activities "affect trade or commerce?" 2C:41-1 provides that "trade or commerce shall include all economic activity involving or relating to any commodity or service." Well, what business's activities don't affect trade or commerce? For example, a shipping company has trucks and planes that carry packages across the country. Money is exchanged for the shipment of the packages; trucks and planes travel across roadways and the air. Accordingly, trade and commerce are affected by the enterprise's existence. Another example is a pizza parlor. Money is exchanged for the pizza, strombolis, and sodas. Food supplies, napkins, and cups are delivered to the pizza place; the delivery of these supplies requires trucks to travel to and from the restaurant. Accordingly, the existence of this pizza parlor "affects trade and commerce."

## The Evile Brothers—Guilty of Racketeering

George Evile set up an unlawful machine gun manufacturing shop in Jersey City wherein he provided and sold in excess of 1,000 machine guns. Evile's purpose in creating the shop was to sell the machine guns in order to raise funds for his terrorist group, MIFA.

Over 200 distinct transactions to nearly 150 separate buyers occurred over an eight-year period, the first occurring in 1995. Evile closely monitored his firearms shop, visiting the establishment on a daily basis and barking orders and directives to the dozens of employees that worked for him. When George couldn't make it to the shop, his brother Alex operated the business in his stead. The Evile brothers are obviously guilty of illegally manufacturing machine guns. But how can they be convicted of a "racketeering" offense under 2C:41-2a.?

First, they did in fact engage in "racketeering activity." The unlawful manufacturing of firearms is one of the many crimes which are considered "racketeering activity" as defined in 2C:41-1.

The men engaged in a "pattern of racketeering activity" given that both elements of that term have been met. First, they engaged in not just two incidents of racketeering but over 200. Remember, they engaged in over 200 distinct machine gun transactions to nearly 150 separate buyers. The incidents began in 1995, and all happened within eight years of each other, thereby occurring within the required time period outlined in 2C:41-1's definition of "pattern of racketeering activity."

The second element was met in that the racketeering incidents embraced a pattern of conduct that had similar purposes, participants, and methods of commission. The similar "purpose" was that each machine gun manufactured and sold was executed in an effort to raise funds for Evile's terrorist group, MIFA. The "participants" were similar—George Evile, Alex Evile, a consistent employee base, and repeat buyers. The "method of commission" was similar in that the machine guns were manufactured in a uniform manner and then sold to waiting buyers.

Engaging in a "pattern of racketeering activity" alone, however, is not sufficient for a conviction under 2C:41-2a. The Evile brothers must use or invest income derived from the "pattern of racketeering activity"—to acquire an interest in an "enterprise" whose activities "affect trade or commerce."

Let's say George and Alex Evile pull $100,000 from the proceeds of their machine gun sales to purchase and take over a fruit stand in Hoboken. Here they have used income derived from their "pattern of racketeering activity" to acquire an "enterprise," the fruit stand. This "enterprise's" activities—just like nearly all others—"affect trade or commerce." The fruit is purchased and delivered to the stand; money is paid to the "enterprise" when consumers buy the fruit.

With all of the aforementioned elements present, George and Alex Evile can be convicted of a "racketeering" offense under 2C:41-2a. In their case, it is a crime of the first degree. Why? 2C:41-3 provides that anyone who violates 2C:41-2 "in connection with a pattern of racketeering activity which involves a crime of violence, a crime of the first degree or the use of firearms" shall be guilty of a first degree crime. All other violations of 2C:41-2 are second degree crimes.

The Evile brothers' offense was in connection of a "pattern of racketeering activity" which involved firearms and at least one crime of the first degree. As leaders of a firearms trafficking network, they committed a first degree crime. Accordingly, their offense under 2C:41-2a. is a crime of the first degree.

---

**2C:41-3.**     ## Criminal penalties

a. Any person who violates any provision of N.J.S.2C:41-2 in connection with a pattern of racketeering activity which involves a crime of violence, a crime of the first degree or the use of firearms shall be guilty of a crime of the first degree. All other violations of N.J.S.2C:41-2 shall be crimes of the second degree.

b. In addition, such persons shall forfeit to the entity funding the prosecuting agency involved the following:

   (1) Any interest including money or anything of value he has acquired or maintained in violation of this chapter and

(2) Any interest in, security of, claim against, or property or contractual right of any kind affording a source of influence over any enterprise which he has established, acquired, maintained, operated, controlled, conducted, or participated in the conduct of, in violation of this chapter.

c.  In any action brought by the Attorney General under this section, the Superior Court shall have jurisdiction to enter such restraining orders or prohibitions, or to take such other actions, including, but not limited to, the acceptance of satisfactory performance bonds, in connection with any property or other interests subject to forfeiture under this section, as it shall deem proper.

d.  Upon conviction of a person under this section, the court shall authorize the Attorney General to seize all property or other interest declared forfeited under this section, subject to the rights of innocent persons such as any prior lienholders or other valid lienholders, upon such other terms and conditions as the court shall deem proper. If a property right or other interest is not exercisable or transferable for value by the Attorney General, it shall expire, and shall not revert to the convicted person.

e.  The Attorney General shall dispose of all such property as soon as commercially feasible, making due provision for the rights of innocent persons.

f.  When an offense charged may result in a criminal forfeiture, the indictment shall allege the extent of the interest or property subject to forfeiture. If the indictment alleges that an interest or property is subject to criminal forfeiture, a special verdict shall be returned as to the extent of the interest or property subject to forfeiture, if any.

**2C:41-4.        Civil remedies**

a.  The Superior Court, making due provision for the rights of innocent persons, shall have jurisdiction to prevent and restrain the acts or conduct which constitute violations of N.J.S.2C:41-2, by issuing appropriate orders, including, but not limited to:

(1) Ordering any person to divest himself of any interest, direct or indirect, in any enterprise;

(2) Imposing reasonable restrictions on the future activities or investments of any person, including but not limited to, prohibiting any person from engaging in the same type of endeavor as the enterprise found to be in violation of N.J.S. 2C:41-2;

(3) Ordering the dissolution or reorganization of any enterprise;

(4) Ordering the denial, suspension or revocation of the charter of any corporation organized under the laws of this State and to deny, suspend or revoke the license of any foreign corporation authorized to do business in the State of New Jersey;

(5) Ordering the denial, suspension or revocation of the license or permit granted to any enterprise by any department or agency of the State of New Jersey;

(6) Entering a cease and desist order which specifies the acts or conduct which is to be discontinued, altered or implemented by any person;

(7) Ordering the restitution of any moneys or property unlawfully obtained or retained by any person found to be in violation of N.J.S.2C:41-2;

(8) Assessing civil monetary penalties against any person who has violated N.J.S. 2C:41-2 to deter future violations, provided that the court shall, upon making a finding on the record as to the gain any such person has acquired or maintained through the violation, assess such penalties in an amount not to exceed three times the amount of the gain; and

(9) Ordering any person to forfeit to the State any interest he has acquired or maintained in violation of this chapter and any interest in, security of, claim against, or

property or contractual right of any kind affording a source of influence over any enterprises he has established, operated, controlled, conducted, or participated in the conduct of, in violation of this chapter. Forfeiture under this subsection shall be in accordance with chapter 64 of Title 2C of the New Jersey Statutes. The interest which shall be subject to forfeiture shall be as defined by this section and as defined by N.J.S. 2C:64-1a.;

(10) Imposing any or all of the foregoing sanctions in combination with each other.

b. The Attorney General may institute proceedings in Superior Court for violations of N.J.S. 2C:41-2. In any action brought under this section, the court shall proceed as soon as practicable to the hearing and determination thereof. Pending final determination thereof, the court may at any time enter restraining orders or prohibitions, or take other actions, including the acceptance of satisfactory performance bonds, as it shall deem proper.

c. Any person damaged in his business or property by reason of a violation of N.J.S.2C:41-2 may sue therefor in any appropriate court and shall recover threefold any damages he sustains and the cost of the suit, including a reasonable attorney's fee, costs of investigation and litigation.

d. A final judgment rendered in favor of the State in any criminal proceeding brought under this chapter shall estop the defendant from denying the essential allegations of the criminal offense in any subsequent civil proceeding.

## 2C:41-5.          Investigative interrogatories

a. Whenever the Attorney General determines that there exists a reasonable suspicion that any person or enterprise may have information or be in possession, custody, or control of any documentary materials relevant to an investigation under this chapter, or whenever the Attorney General believes it to be in the public interest that an investigation be made pursuant to this chapter, he may, prior to the institution of a civil or criminal proceeding thereon, issue in writing, and cause to be served upon the person, an investigative interrogatory requiring him to answer and produce material for examination.

b. Each interrogatory shall:

(1) State the nature of the conduct constituting the alleged violation which is under investigation and the provision of law applicable thereto;

(2) Advise the person that he has the right to discuss the interrogatory with legal counsel prior to returning it to the Attorney General or prior to making material available as provided hereinafter in subsection f. and that he has the right to file in Superior Court a petition to modify or set aside the interrogatory pursuant to subsection j. hereinafter;

(3) Describe the class or classes of documentary material to be produced thereunder with such specificity and certainty as to permit the material to be fairly identified;

(4) Prescribe a return date which will provide a reasonable period of time within which answers may be made and material so demanded may be assembled and made available for inspection and copying or reproduction as provided hereinafter in subsection f.

c. No interrogatory shall:

(1) Contain any requirement which would be held to be unreasonable if contained in a subpena duces tecum issued in aid of a grand jury investigation; or

(2) Require the production of any documentary evidence which would be otherwise privileged from disclosure if demanded by a subpena duces tecum issued in aid of a grand jury investigation.

d. Service of any interrogatory filed under this section may be made upon a person by:

   (1) Delivering a duly executed copy thereof to any partner, executive officer, managing agent, or general agent thereof, or to any agent thereof authorized by appointment or by law to receive service of process on behalf of the person, or upon any individual person; or

   (2) Delivering a duly executed copy thereof to the principal office or place of business of the person to be served; or

   (3) Depositing a copy in the United States mail, by registered or certified mail duly addressed to the person at his principal office or place of business.

e. A verified return by the individual serving any interrogatory, setting forth the manner of service shall be prima facie proof of service. In the case of service by registered or certified mail, the return shall be accompanied by the return post office receipt of delivery of the interrogatory.

f. Any person upon whom any interrogatory issued under this section has been duly served which requires the production of materials shall make the material available for inspection and copying or reproduction to the Attorney General at the principal place of business of that person in the State of New Jersey or at such other place as the Attorney General and the person thereafter may agree and prescribe in writing, on the return date specified in the interrogatory or on a later date as the Attorney General may prescribe in writing. Upon written agreement between the person and the Attorney General, copies may be substituted for all or any part of the original materials. The Attorney General may cause the preparation of any copies of documentary material as may be required for official use by the Attorney General.

   No material produced pursuant to this section shall be available for examination, without the consent of the person who produced the material, by an individual other than the Attorney General or any person retained by the Attorney General in connection with the enforcement of this act. Under reasonable terms and conditions as the Attorney General shall prescribe, documentary material while in his possession shall be available for examination by the person who produced the material or any duly authorized representatives of the person.

   In any case or proceeding involving any alleged violation of this chapter, the Attorney General may present before any court or Grand Jury, any such documentary material in his possession pursuant to this section subject to any protective order deemed proper by the Superior Court.

   Any person who shall disclose to any person other than the Attorney General or a person retained by the Attorney General as set forth above, the name of any person who receives an investigative interrogatory or any information obtained pursuant thereto, except in proceedings involving an alleged violation of this chapter and except as so directed by the Attorney General shall be guilty of a crime of the fourth degree.

g. Upon completion of:

   (1) The review and investigation for which any documentary material was produced under this section, and

   (2) Any case or proceeding arising from the investigation, the Attorney General shall return to the person who produced the material all the material other than copies thereof made by the Attorney General pursuant to this section which has not passed into the control of any court or grand jury through the introduction thereof into the record of the case or proceeding.

h. When any documentary material has been produced by any person under this section for use in any racketeering investigation, and no case or proceeding arising therefrom has been instituted within 2 years after completion of the examination and analysis of all evidence assembled in the course of the investigation, the person shall be entitled, upon written demand made upon the Attorney General, to the return of all documentary material other than copies thereof made pursuant to this section so produced by the person.

i. Whenever any person fails to comply with any investigative interrogatory duly served upon him under this section or whenever satisfactory copying or reproduction of any material cannot be done and the person refuses to surrender the material, the Attorney General may file in the Superior Court a petition for an order of the court for the enforcement of this section.

j. At any time before the return date specified in the interrogatory, such person may file in the Superior Court a petition for an order modifying or setting aside the interrogatory. The time allowed for compliance of the interrogatory, in whole or in part as deemed proper and ordered by the court, shall not run during the pendency of such petition in the court. The petition shall specify each ground upon which the petitioner relies in seeking relief, and may be based upon any failure of the interrogatory to comply with the provisions of this section or upon any constitutional or other legal right or privilege of the petitioner. In such proceeding the Attorney General shall establish the existence of an investigation pursuant to this chapter and the nature and subject matter of the investigation.

## 2C:41-6.     Liberal construction

The provisions of subsections a., c., d., e., and h. of 2C:41-1; 2C:41-2; subsections b., c., d., e., and f. of 2C:41-3; and 2C:41-4 shall be liberally construed to effectuate the remedial purposes of this chapter.

## 2C:41-6.1.     Remedies cumulative

The remedies provided in this act shall be cumulative with each other and other remedies at law.

## 2C:41-6.2.     Severability

If any one or more sections, clauses, sentences or parts of this act shall for any reason be questioned in any court, and shall be adjudged unconstitutional or invalid, such judgment shall not affect, impair or invalidate the remaining provisions thereof, but shall be confined in its operation to the specific provisions so held unconstitutional or invalid.

## Chapter 42—Reserved

# 43

# AUTHORIZED DISPOSITION OF OFFENDERS

**2C:43-1.**      **Degrees of crimes**

a. Crimes defined by this code are classified, for the purpose of sentence, into four degrees, as follows:

    (1)  Crimes of the first degree;

    (2)  Crimes of the second degree;

    (3)  Crimes of the third degree; and

    (4)  Crimes of the fourth degree.

        A crime is of the first, second, third or fourth degree when it is so designated by the code. An offense, declared to be a crime, without specification of degree, is of the fourth degree.

b. Notwithstanding any other provision of law, a crime defined by any statute of this State other than this code and designated as a high misdemeanor shall constitute for the purpose of sentence a crime of the third degree. Except as provided in sections 2C:1-4c. and 2C:1-5b. and notwithstanding any other provision of law, a crime defined by any statute of this State other than this code and designated as a misdemeanor shall constitute for the purpose of sentence a crime of the fourth degree.

**2C:43-2.**      **Sentence in accordance with code; authorized dispositions**

a. Except as otherwise provided by this code, all persons convicted of an offense or offenses shall be sentenced in accordance with this chapter.

b. Except as provided in subsection a. of this section and subject to the applicable provisions of the code, the court may suspend the imposition of sentence on a person who has been convicted of an offense, or may sentence him as follows:

    (1)  To pay a fine or make restitution authorized by N.J.S.2C:43-3 or P.L.1997, c.253 (C.2C:43-3.4 et al.); or

    (2)  To be placed on probation and, in the case of a person convicted of a crime, to imprisonment for a term fixed by the court not exceeding 364 days to be served as a condition of probation, or in the case of a person convicted of a disorderly persons offense, to imprisonment for a term fixed by the court not exceeding 90 days to be served as a condition of probation; or

    (3)  To imprisonment for a term authorized by sections 2C:11-3, 2C:43-5, 2C:43-6, 2C:43-7, and 2C:43-8 or 2C:44-5; or

(4) To pay a fine, make restitution and probation, or fine, restitution and imprisonment; or

(5) To release under supervision in the community or to require the performance of community-related service; or

(6) To a halfway house or other residential facility in the community, including agencies which are not operated by the Department of Human Services; or

(7) To imprisonment at night or on weekends with liberty to work or to participate in training or educational programs.

c. Instead of or in addition to any disposition made according to this section, the court may postpone, suspend, or revoke for a period not to exceed two years the driver's license, registration certificate, or both of any person convicted of a crime, disorderly persons offense, or petty disorderly persons offense in the course of which a motor vehicle was used. In imposing this disposition and in deciding the duration of the postponement, suspension, or revocation, the court shall consider the severity of the crime or offense and the potential effect of the loss of driving privileges on the person's ability to be rehabilitated. Any postponement, suspension, or revocation shall be imposed consecutively with any custodial sentence.

d. This chapter does not deprive the court of any authority conferred by law to decree a forfeiture of property, suspend or cancel a license, remove a person from office, or impose any other civil penalty. Such a judgment or order may be included in the sentence.

e. The court shall state on the record the reasons for imposing the sentence, including its findings pursuant to the criteria for withholding or imposing imprisonment or fines under sections 2C:44-1 to 2C:44-3, where imprisonment is imposed, consideration of the defendant's eligibility for release under the law governing parole and the factual basis supporting its findings of particular aggravating or mitigating factors affecting sentence.

f. The court shall explain the parole laws as they apply to the sentence and shall state:

(1) the approximate period of time in years and months the defendant will serve in custody before parole eligibility;

(2) the jail credits or the amount of time the defendant has already served;

(3) that the defendant may be entitled to good time and work credits; and

(4) that the defendant may be eligible for participation in the Intensive Supervision Program

## 2C:43-2.1. Motor vehicle theft or unlawful taking; restitution

A person who is convicted of an offense involving the theft or unlawful taking of a motor vehicle, in addition to any other fine, penalty, or restitution which may be imposed by law, is liable to the owner of the motor vehicle for any reasonable and necessary expense incurred by the owner in recovering the motor vehicle and for any damage to the motor vehicle prior to its recovery by the owner. In the sentencing proceedings on the offense, the owner may submit evidence of expenses incurred and damages sustained. The court shall make a finding of the amount of expenses incurred and damages sustained, and if the record does not contain sufficient evidence to support such a finding, the court may conduct a hearing upon the issue. The court shall order the person convicted of the offense to make restitution to the owner in the amount of the expenses and damages found by the court. The court shall file a copy of the order with the clerk of the Superior Court who shall enter upon his record of docketed judgments the name of the convicted person as judgment debtor, and of the owner as judgment creditor, a statement that the restitution is ordered under this section, the amount of the restitution, and the date of the order. This entry shall have the same force as a judgment docketed in the Superior Court.

**2C:43-2.2.          Issuance of court order requiring serological tests**

a. In addition to any other disposition made pursuant to law, a court shall order a person convicted of, indicted for or formally charged with, or a juvenile charged with delinquency or adjudicated delinquent for an act which if committed by an adult would constitute, aggravated sexual assault or sexual assault as defined in subsection a. or c. of N.J.S.2C:14-2 to submit to an approved serological test for acquired immune deficiency syndrome (AIDS) or infection with the human immunodeficiency virus (HIV) or any other related virus identified as a probable causative agent of AIDS. The court shall issue such an order only upon the request of the victim and upon application of the prosecutor made at the time of indictment, charge, conviction or adjudication of delinquency. The person or juvenile shall be ordered by the court to submit to such repeat or confirmatory tests as may be medically necessary.

As used in this section, "formal charge" includes a proceeding by accusation in the event that the defendant has waived the right to an indictment.

b. A court order issued pursuant to subsection a. of this section shall require testing to be performed as soon as practicable by the Commissioner of the Department of Corrections pursuant to authority granted to the commissioner by sections 6 and 10 of P.L.1976, c.98 (C.30:1B-6 and 30:1B-10), by a provider of health care, at a health facility licensed pursuant to section 12 of P.L.1971, c.136 (C.26:2H-12) or the Juvenile Justice Commission established pursuant to section 2 of P.L.1995, c.284 (C.52:17B-170). The order shall also require that the results of the test be reported to the offender and to the appropriate Office of Victim-Witness Advocacy.

c. The Office of Victim-Witness Advocacy, established pursuant to section 5 of P.L.1985, c.404 (C.52:4B-43), shall reimburse the Department of Corrections, Department of Health or the Juvenile Justice Commission for the direct costs incurred by these departments for any tests ordered by a court pursuant to subsection a. of this section. Reimbursement shall be made following a request from the department.

d. In addition to any other disposition authorized, a court may order an offender at the time of sentencing to reimburse the State for the costs of the tests ordered by subsection a. of this section.

e. Upon receipt of the result of a test ordered pursuant to subsection a. of this section, the Office of Victim-Witness Advocacy shall provide the victim with appropriate counseling, referral for counseling and if appropriate, referral for health care. The office shall notify the victim or make appropriate arrangements for the victim to be notified of the test result.

f. The result of a test ordered pursuant to subsection a. of this section shall be confidential and employees of the Department of Corrections, the Juvenile Justice Commission, the Office of Victim-Witness Advocacy, a health care provider, health care facility or counseling service shall not disclose the result of a test performed pursuant to this section except as authorized herein or as otherwise authorized by law or court order. The provisions of this section shall not be deemed to prohibit disclosure of a test result to the person tested.

g. Persons who perform tests ordered pursuant to subsection a. of this section in accordance with accepted medical standards for the performance of such tests shall be immune from civil and criminal liability arising from their conduct.

h. This section shall not be construed to preclude or limit any other testing for acquired immune deficiency syndrome (AIDS) or infection with the human immunodeficiency virus (HIV) or any other related virus identified as a probable causative agent of AIDS which is otherwise permitted by statute, court rule or common law.

**2C:43-2.3.**        **Orders for certain serological testing required under certain circumstances**

a. In addition to any other disposition made pursuant to law, a court shall order a person convicted of, indicted for or formally charged with a criminal offense, a disorderly persons offense or a petty disorderly persons offense, to submit to an approved serological test for acquired immune deficiency syndrome (AIDS) or infection with the human immunodeficiency virus (HIV) or any other related virus identified as a probable causative agent of AIDS if:

   (1) in the course of the commission of the offense, including the immediate flight thereafter or during any investigation or arrest related to that offense, a law enforcement officer, the victim or other person suffered a prick from a hypodermic needle, provided there is probable cause to believe that the defendant is an intravenous user of controlled dangerous substances; or

   (2) in the course of the commission of the offense, including the immediate flight thereafter or during any investigation or arrest related to that offense, a law enforcement officer, the victim or other person had contact with the defendant which involved or was likely to involve the transmission of bodily fluids.

   The court may order a person to submit to an approved serological test for AIDS or infection with the HIV or any other related virus identified as a probable causative agent of AIDS if in the course of the performance of any other law enforcement duties, a law enforcement officer suffers a prick from a hypodermic needle, provided that there is probable cause to believe that the defendant is an intravenous user of controlled dangerous substances, or had contact with the defendant which involved or was likely to involve the transmission of bodily fluids. The court shall issue such an order only upon the request of the law enforcement officer, victim of the offense or other affected person made at the time of indictment, charge or conviction. If a county prosecutor declines to make such an application within 72 hours of being requested to do so by the law enforcement officer, the law enforcement officer may appeal to the Division of Criminal Justice in the Department of Law and Public Safety for that officer to bring the application. The person shall be ordered by the court to submit to such repeat or confirmatory tests as may be medically necessary.

   As used in this section, "formal charge" includes a proceeding by accusation in the event that the defendant has waived the right to an indictment.

b. A court order issued pursuant to subsection a. of this section shall require testing to be performed as soon as practicable by the Commissioner of the Department of Corrections pursuant to authority granted to the commissioner by sections 6 and 10 of P.L.1976, c.98 (C.30:1B-6 and 30:1B-10) or by a provider of health care or at a health care facility licensed pursuant to section 12 of P.L.1971, c.136 (C.26:2H-12). The order shall also require that the results of the test be reported to the offender, the appropriate Office of Victim-Witness Advocacy if a victim of an offense is tested, and the affected law enforcement officer. Upon receipt of the result of a test ordered pursuant to subsection a. of this section, the Office of Victim-Witness Advocacy shall provide the victim with appropriate counseling, referral for counseling and if appropriate, referral for health care. The office shall notify the victim or make appropriate arrangements for the victim to be notified of the test result.

c. In addition to any other disposition authorized, a court may order an offender at the time of sentencing to reimburse the State for the costs of the tests ordered pursuant to subsection a. of this section.

d. The result of a test ordered pursuant to subsection a. of this section shall be confidential and health care providers and employees of the Department of Corrections, the Office of

Victim-Witness Advocacy, a health care facility or counseling service shall not disclose the result of a test performed pursuant to this section except as authorized herein or as otherwise authorized by law or court order. The provisions of this section shall not be deemed to prohibit disclosure of a test result to the person tested.

e. Persons who perform tests ordered pursuant to subsection a. of this section in accordance with accepted medical standards for the performance of such tests shall be immune from civil and criminal liability arising from their conduct.

f. This section shall not be construed to preclude or limit any other testing for AIDS or infection with the HIV or any other related virus identified as a probable causative agent of AIDS which is otherwise permitted by statute, court rule or common law.

## 2C:43-3. Fines and restitutions

A person who has been convicted of an offense may be sentenced to pay a fine, to make restitution, or both, such fine not to exceed:

a.  (1) $200,000.00 when the conviction is of a crime of the first degree;

   (2) $150,000.00 when the conviction is of a crime of the second degree;

b.  (1) $15,000.00 when the conviction is of a crime of the third degree;

   (2) $10,000.00 when the conviction is of a crime of the fourth degree;

c.  $1,000.00, when the conviction is of a disorderly persons offense;

d.  $500.00, when the conviction is of a petty disorderly persons offense;

e.  Any higher amount equal to double the pecuniary gain to the offender or loss to the victim caused by the conduct constituting the offense by the offender. In such case the court shall make a finding as to the amount of the gain or loss, and if the record does not contain sufficient evidence to support such a finding the court may conduct a hearing upon the issue. For purposes of this section the term "gain" means the amount of money or the value of property derived by the offender and "loss" means the amount of value separated from the victim or the amount of any payment owed to the victim and avoided or evaded and includes any reasonable and necessary expense incurred by the owner in recovering or replacing lost, stolen or damaged property, or recovering any payment avoided or evaded, and, with respect to property of a research facility, includes the cost of repeating an interrupted or invalidated experiment or loss of profits. The term "victim" shall mean a person who suffers a personal physical or psychological injury or death or incurs loss of or injury to personal or real property as a result of a crime committed against that person, or in the case of a homicide, the nearest relative of the victim. The terms "gain" and "loss" shall also mean, where appropriate, the amount of any tax, fee, penalty and interest avoided, evaded, or otherwise unpaid or improperly retained or disposed of;

f.  Any higher amount specifically authorized by another section of this code or any other statute;

g.  Up to twice the amounts authorized in subsection a., b., c. or d. of this section, in the case of a second or subsequent conviction of any tax offense defined in Title 54 of the Revised Statutes or Title 54A of the New Jersey Statutes, as amended and supplemented, or of any offense defined in chapter 20 or 21 of this code;

h.  In the case of violations of chapter 35, any higher amount equal to three times the street value of the controlled dangerous substance or controlled substance analog. The street value for purposes of this section shall be determined pursuant to subsection e. of N.J.S.2C:44-2.

The restitution ordered paid to the victim shall not exceed the victim's loss, except that in any case involving the failure to pay any State tax, the amount of restitution to the

State shall be the full amount of the tax avoided or evaded, including full civil penalties and interest as provided by law. In any case where the victim of the offense is any department or division of State government, the court shall order restitution to the victim. Any restitution imposed on a person shall be in addition to any fine which may be imposed pursuant to this section.

**2C:43-3.1.** **Victim, witness, criminal disposition, and collection funds**

a. (1) In addition to any disposition made pursuant to the provisions of N.J.S.2C:43-2, any person convicted of a crime of violence, theft of an automobile pursuant to N.J.S.2C:20-2, eluding a law enforcement officer pursuant to subsection b. of N.J.S.2C:29-2 or unlawful taking of a motor vehicle pursuant to subsection b., c. or d. of N.J.S.2C:20-10 shall be assessed at least $100.00, but not to exceed $10,000.00 for each such crime for which he was convicted which resulted in the injury or death of another person. In imposing this assessment, the court shall consider factors such as the severity of the crime, the defendant's criminal record, defendant's ability to pay and the economic impact of the assessment on the defendant's dependents.

(2) (a) In addition to any other disposition made pursuant to the provisions of N.J.S.2C:43-2 or any other statute imposing sentences for crimes, any person convicted of any disorderly persons offense, any petty disorderly persons offense, or any crime not resulting in the injury or death of any other person shall be assessed $50.00 for each such offense or crime for which he was convicted.

(b) In addition to any other disposition made pursuant to the provisions of section 24 of P.L.1982, c.77 (C.2A:4A-43) or any other statute indicating the dispositions that can be ordered for adjudications of delinquency, any juvenile adjudicated delinquent, according to the definition of "delinquency" established in section 4 of P.L.1982, c.77 (C.2A:4A-23), shall be assessed at least $30.00 for each such adjudication, but not to exceed the amount which could be assessed pursuant to paragraph (1) or paragraph (2) (a) of subsection a. of this section if the offense was committed by an adult.

(c) In addition to any other assessment imposed pursuant to the provisions of R.S.39:4-50, the provisions of section 12 of P.L.1990, c.103 (C.39:3-10.20) relating to a violation of section 5 of P.L.1990, c.103 (C.39:3-10.13), the provisions of section 19 of P.L.1954, c.236 (C.12:7-34.19) or the provisions of section 3 of P.L.1952, c.157 (C.12:7-46), any person convicted of operating a motor vehicle, commercial motor vehicle or vessel while under the influence of liquor or drugs shall be assessed $50.00.

(d) In addition to any term or condition that may be included in an agreement for supervisory treatment pursuant to N.J.S.2C:43-13 or imposed as a term or condition of conditional discharge pursuant to N.J.S.2C:36A-1, a participant in either program shall be required to pay an assessment of $50.00.

(3) All assessments provided for in this section shall be collected as provided in section 3 of P.L.1979, c.396 (C.2C:46-4) and the court shall so order at the time of sentencing. When a defendant who is sentenced to incarceration in a State correctional facility has not, at the time of sentencing, paid an assessment for the crime for which he is being sentenced or an assessment imposed for a previous crime, the court shall specifically order the Department of Corrections to collect the assessment during the period of incarceration and to deduct the assessment from any income the inmate receives as

a result of labor performed at the institution or on any work release program or from any personal account established in the institution for the benefit of the inmate. All moneys collected, whether in part or in full payment of any assessment imposed pursuant to this section, shall be forwarded monthly by the parties responsible for collection, together with a monthly accounting on forms prescribed by the Victims of Crime Compensation Board pursuant to section 19 of P.L.1991, c.329 (C.52:4B-8.1), to the Victims of Crime Compensation Board.

(4) The Victims of Crime Compensation Board shall forward monthly all moneys received from assessments collected pursuant to this section to the State Treasury for deposit as follows:

    (a) Of moneys collected on assessments imposed pursuant to paragraph a. (1):

        (i) the first $72.00 collected for deposit in the Victims of Crime Compensation Board Account,

        (ii) the next $3.00 collected for deposit in the Criminal Disposition and Revenue Collection Fund,

        (iii) the next $25.00 collected for deposit in the Victim Witness Advocacy Fund, and

        (iv) moneys collected in excess of $100.00 for deposit in the Victims of Crime Compensation Board Account;

    (b) Of moneys collected on assessments imposed pursuant to paragraph a. (2) (a), (c) or (d):

        (i) the first $39.00 collected for deposit in the Victims of Crime Compensation Board Account,

        (ii) the next $3.00 collected for deposit in the Criminal Disposition and Revenue Collection Fund, and

        (iii) the next $8.00 collected for deposit in the Victim and Witness Advocacy Fund;

    (c) Of moneys collected on assessments imposed pursuant to paragraph a. (2) (b):

        (i) the first $17.00 for deposit in the Victims of Crime Compensation Board Account, and

        (ii) the next $3.00 collected for deposit in the Criminal Disposition and Revenue Collection Fund, and

        (iii) the next $10.00 for deposit in the Victim and Witness Advocacy Fund, and

        (iv) moneys collected in excess of $30.00 for deposit in the Victims of Crime Compensation Board Account.

(5) The Victims of Crime Compensation Board shall provide the Attorney General with a monthly accounting of moneys received, deposited and identified as receivable, on forms prescribed pursuant to section 19 of P.L.1991, c.329 (C.52:4B-8.1).

(6) (a) The Victims of Crime Compensation Board Account shall be a separate, nonlapsing, revolving account that shall be administered by the Victims of Crime Compensation Board. All moneys deposited in that Account shall be used in satisfying claims pursuant to the provisions of the "Criminal Injuries Compensation Act of 1971," P.L.1971, c.317 (C.52:4B-1 et seq.) and for related administrative costs.

    (b) The Criminal Disposition and Revenue Collection Fund shall be a separate, nonlapsing, revolving account that shall be administered by the Victims of Crime Compensation Board. All moneys deposited in that Fund shall be used as provided in section 19 of P.L.1991, c.329 (C.52:4B-8.1).

(c) The Victim and Witness Advocacy Fund shall be a separate, nonlapsing, revolving fund and shall be administered by the Division of Criminal Justice, Department of Law and Public Safety and all moneys deposited in that Fund pursuant to this section shall be used for the benefit of victims and witnesses of crime as provided in section 20 of P.L.1991, c.329 (C.52:4B-43.1) and for related administrative costs.

b. (Deleted by amendment, P.L.1991, c.329).

c. (Deleted by amendment, P.L.1991, c.329).

d. (Deleted by amendment, P.L.1991, c.329).

**2C:43-3.2.**        **Assessments for Safe Neighborhoods Services Fund**

a. (1) In addition to any other fine, fee or assessment imposed, any person convicted of a crime, disorderly or petty disorderly persons offense or violation of R.S.39:4-50 shall be assessed $75 for each conviction.

(2) In addition to any term or condition that may be included in an agreement for supervisory treatment pursuant to N.J.S.2C:43-13 or imposed as a term or condition of conditional discharge pursuant to section 3 of P.L.1987, c.106 (C.2C:36A-1), a participant in either program shall be required to pay an assessment of $75.

b. All assessments provided for in this section shall be collected as provided for collection of fines and restitutions in section 3 of P.L.1979, c.396 (C.2C:46-4) and shall be forwarded to the Department of the Treasury as provided in subsection c. of this section.

c. All money collected pursuant to this section shall be forwarded to the Department of the Treasury to be deposited into the Safe Neighborhoods Services Fund created by section 5 of this act.

**2C:43-3.3.**        **Additional penalties for persons convicted of crime deposited in "Law Enforcement Officers Training and Equipment Fund"**

a. In addition to any disposition made pursuant to the provisions of Title 2C of the New Jersey Statutes, any person convicted of a crime shall be assessed a penalty of $30.

b. In addition to any other disposition made pursuant to the provisions of section 24 of P.L.1982, c.77 (C.2A:4A-43) or any other statute indicating the dispositions that may be ordered for adjudications of delinquency, a juvenile adjudicated delinquent for an offense which if committed by an adult would be a crime shall be assessed a penalty of $15.

c. The penalties assessed under subsections a. and b. of this section shall be collected as provided for the collection of fines and restitution in section 3 of P.L.1979, c.396 (C.2C:46-4) and forwarded to the State Treasury for deposit in a separate account to be known as the "Law Enforcement Officers Training and Equipment Fund." The penalty assessed in this section shall be collected only after a penalty assessed in section 2 of P.L.1979, c.396 (C.2C:43-3.1) and any restitution ordered is collected.

The fund shall be used to support the development and provision of basic and in-service training courses for law enforcement officers by police training schools approved pursuant to P.L.1961, c.56 (C.52:17B-66 et seq.). In addition, the fund shall also be used to enable police training schools to purchase equipment needed for the training of law enforcement officers. Distributions from the fund shall only be made directly to such approved schools.

d. The Police Training Commission in the Department of Law and Public Safety shall be responsible for the administration and distribution of the fund pursuant to its authority under section 6 of P.L.1961, c.56 (C.52:17B-71).

e. An adult prisoner of a State correctional institution who does not pay the penalty imposed pursuant to this section shall have the penalty deducted from any income the inmate receives as a result of labor performed at the institution or any type of work release program. If any person, including an inmate, fails to pay the penalty imposed pursuant to this section, the court may order the suspension of the person's driver's license or nonresident reciprocity privilege, or prohibit the person from receiving or obtaining a license until the assessment is paid. The court shall notify the Director of the Division of Motor Vehicles of such an action. Prior to any action being taken pursuant to this subsection, the person shall be given notice and a hearing before the court to contest the charge of the failure to pay the assessment.

## 2C:43-3.4.    Restitution for extradition costs

In addition to any fine or restitution authorized by N.J.S.2C:43-3, the court may sentence a defendant to make restitution for costs incurred by any law enforcement entity in extraditing the defendant from another jurisdiction if the court finds that, at the time of the extradition, the defendant was located in the other jurisdiction in order to avoid prosecution for a crime committed in this State or service of a criminal sentence imposed by a court of this State.

## 2C:43-3.5.    Additional penalty for certain offenses

a. In addition to any term or condition that may be included in an agreement for supervisory treatment pursuant to N.J.S.2C:43-13 or imposed as a term or condition of conditional discharge pursuant to N.J.S.2C:36A-1 for a violation of any offense defined in chapter 35 or 36 of Title 2C of the New Jersey Statutes, each participant shall be assessed a penalty of $50 for each adjudication or conviction.

b. All penalties provided by this section shall be collected as provided for collection of fines and restitutions in section 3 of P.L.1979, c.396 (C.2C:46-4) and shall be forwarded to the Department of the Treasury as provided in subsection c. of this section.

c. All monies collected pursuant to this section shall be forwarded to the Department of the Treasury to be deposited in the " Drug Abuse Education Fund" established pursuant to section 1 of P.L.1999, c.12 (C.54A:9-25.12).

d. Monies in the fund shall be appropriated by the Legislature on an annual basis in the manner and for the purposes prescribed by section 2 of P.L.1999, c.12 (C.54A:9-25.13).

## 2C:43-3.6.    Additional penalty for sex offense for deposit in Sexual Assault Nurse Examiner Program Fund

a. In addition to any fine, fee, assessment or penalty authorized under the provisions of Title 2C of the New Jersey Statutes, a person convicted of a sex offense, as defined in section 2 of P.L.1994, c. 133 (C.2C:7-2), shall be assessed a penalty of $800 for each such offense.

b. All penalties provided for in this section, collected as provided for the collection of fines and restitutions in section 3 of P.L.1979, c.396 (C.2C:46-4), shall be forwarded to the Department of the Treasury to be deposited in the "Statewide Sexual Assault Nurse Examiner Program Fund" established pursuant to section 12 of P.L.2001, c.81 (C.52:4B-59).

## 2C:43-3.7.    Surcharge for certain sexual offenders to fund grants, programs, certain

In addition to any other penalty, fine or charge imposed pursuant to law, a person convicted of an act of aggravated sexual assault or sexual assault under N.J.S.2C:14-2, or aggravated criminal sexual contact or criminal sexual contact under N.J.S.2C:14-3, shall be subject to a surcharge in the amount of $100 payable to the Treasurer of the State of New Jersey for use by the

Department of Community Affairs to fund programs and grants for the prevention of violence against women.

**2C:43-4.    Penalties against corporations; forfeiture of corporate charter or revocation of certificate authorizing foreign corporation to do business in the state**

    a. The court may suspend the imposition of sentence of a corporation which has been convicted of an offense or may sentence it to pay a fine of up to three times the fine provided for in N.J.S.2C:43-3 in addition to any restitution required by N.J.S.2C:44-2.

    b. When a corporation is convicted of an offense or a high managerial agent of a corporation, as defined in N.J.S.2C:2-7 is convicted of an offense committed in conducting the affairs of the corporation, the court may request the Attorney General to institute appropriate proceedings to dissolve the corporation, forfeit its charter, revoke any franchises held by it, or to revoke the certificate authorizing the corporation to conduct business in this State.

**2C:43-5.    Young adult offenders**

Any person who, at the time of sentencing, is less than 26 years of age and who has been convicted of a crime may be sentenced to an indeterminate term at the Youth Correctional Institution Complex, in accordance with R.S. 30:4-146 et seq., in the case of men, and to the Correctional Institution for Women, in accordance with R.S. 30:4-153 et seq., in the case of women, instead of the sentences otherwise authorized by the code. This section shall not apply to any person less than 26 years of age at the time of sentencing who qualifies for a mandatory minimum term of imprisonment without eligibility for parole, pursuant to subsection c. of N.J.S. 2C:43-6; however, notwithstanding the provisions of subsection c. of N.J.S. 2C:43-6, the mandatory minimum term may be served at the Youth Correctional Institution Complex or the Correctional Institution for Women.

**2C:43-6.    Sentence of imprisonment for crime; ordinary terms; mandatory terms**

    a. Except as otherwise provided, a person who has been convicted of a crime may be sentenced to imprisonment, as follows:

        (1) In the case of a crime of the first degree, for a specific term of years which shall be fixed by the court and shall be between 10 years and 20 years;

        (2) In the case of a crime of the second degree, for a specific term of years which shall be fixed by the court and shall be between five years and 10 years;

        (3) In the case of a crime of the third degree, for a specific term of years which shall be fixed by the court and shall be between three years and five years;

        (4) In the case of a crime of the fourth degree, for a specific term which shall be fixed by the court and shall not exceed 18 months.

    b. As part of a sentence for any crime, where the court is clearly convinced that the aggravating factors substantially outweigh the mitigating factors, as set forth in subsections a. and b. of 2C:44-1, the court may fix a minimum term not to exceed one-half of the term set pursuant to subsection a., or one-half of the term set pursuant to a maximum period of incarceration for a crime set forth in any statute other than this code, during which the defendant shall not be eligible for parole; provided that no defendant shall be eligible for parole at a date earlier than otherwise provided by the law governing parole.

    c. A person who has been convicted under 2C:39-4a. of possession of a firearm with intent to use it against the person of another, or of a crime under any of the following sections: 2C:11-3, 2C:11-4, 2C:12-1b., 2C:13-1, 2C:14-2a., 2C:14-3a., 2C:15-1, 2C:18-2, 2C:29-5, who, while in the course of committing or attempting to commit the crime, including the immediate flight therefrom, used or was in possession of a firearm as defined in 2C:39-1f., shall be sentenced to a term of imprisonment by the court. The term of imprisonment shall include the imposition of a minimum term. The minimum term shall be fixed at, or between, one-third and one-half of the sentence imposed by the court or three years, whichever is greater, or 18 months in the case of a fourth degree crime, during which the defendant shall be ineligible for parole.

The minimum terms established by this section shall not prevent the court from imposing presumptive terms of imprisonment pursuant to 2C:44-1f. (1) except in cases of crimes of the fourth degree.

A person who has been convicted of an offense enumerated by this subsection and who used or possessed a firearm during its commission, attempted commission or flight therefrom and who has been previously convicted of an offense involving the use or possession of a firearm as defined in 2C:44-3d., shall be sentenced by the court to an extended term as authorized by 2C:43-7c., notwithstanding that extended terms are ordinarily discretionary with the court.

d. The court shall not impose a mandatory sentence pursuant to subsection c. of this section, 2C:43-7c. or 2C:44-3d., unless the ground therefor has been established at a hearing. At the hearing, which may occur at the time of sentencing, the prosecutor shall establish by a preponderance of the evidence that the weapon used or possessed was a firearm. In making its finding, the court shall take judicial notice of any evidence, testimony or information adduced at the trial, plea hearing, or other court proceedings and shall also consider the presentence report and any other relevant information.

e. A person convicted of a third or subsequent offense involving State taxes under N.J.S.2C:20-9, N.J.S.2C:21-15, any other provision of this code, or under any of the provisions of Title 54 of the Revised Statutes, or Title 54A of the New Jersey Statutes, as amended and supplemented, shall be sentenced to a term of imprisonment by the court. This shall not preclude an application for and imposition of an extended term of imprisonment under N.J.S.2C:44-3 if the provisions of that section are applicable to the offender.

f. A person convicted of manufacturing, distributing, dispensing or possessing with intent to distribute any dangerous substance or controlled substance analog under N.J.S.2C:35-5, of maintaining or operating a controlled dangerous substance production facility under N.J.S.2C:35-4, of employing a juvenile in a drug distribution scheme under N.J.S.2C:35-6, leader of a narcotics trafficking network under N.J.S.2C:35-3, or of distributing, dispensing or possessing with intent to distribute on or near school property or buses under section 1 of P.L.1987, c.101 (C.2C:35-7), who has been previously convicted of manufacturing, distributing, dispensing or possessing with intent to distribute a controlled dangerous substance or controlled substance analog, shall upon application of the prosecuting attorney be sentenced by the court to an extended term as authorized by subsection c. of N.J.S.2C:43-7, notwithstanding that extended terms are ordinarily discretionary with the court. The term of imprisonment shall, except as may be provided in N.J.S.2C:35-12, include the imposition of a minimum term. The minimum term shall be fixed at, or between, one-third and one-half of the sentence imposed by the court or three years, whichever is greater, not less than seven years if the person is convicted of a violation of N.J.S.2C:35-6, or 18 months in the case of a fourth degree crime, during which the defendant shall be ineligible for parole.

The court shall not impose an extended term pursuant to this subsection unless the ground therefor has been established at a hearing. At the hearing, which may occur at the time of sentencing, the prosecutor shall establish the ground therefor by a preponderance of the evidence. In making its finding, the court shall take judicial notice of any evidence, testimony or information adduced at the trial, plea hearing, or other court proceedings and shall also consider the presentence report and any other relevant information.

For the purpose of this subsection, a previous conviction exists where the actor has at any time been convicted under chapter 35 of this title or Title 24 of the Revised Statutes or under any similar statute of the United States, this State, or any other state for an offense that is substantially equivalent to N.J.S.2C:35-3, N.J.S.2C:35-4, N.J.S.2C:35-5, N.J.S.2C:35-6 or section 1 of P.L.1987, c.101 (C.2C:35-7).

g. Any person who has been convicted under subsection a. of N.J.S.2C:39-4 of possessing a machine gun or assault firearm with intent to use it against the person of another, or of a crime under any of the following sections: N.J.S.2C:11-3, N.J.S.2C:11-4, N.J.S.2C:12-1b., N.J.S.2C:13-1, N.J.S.2C:14-2a., N.J.S.2C:14-3a., N.J.S.2C:15-1, N.J.S.2C:18-2, N.J.S.2C:29-5, N.J.S.2C:35-5, who, while in the course of committing or attempting to commit the crime, including the immediate flight therefrom, used or was in possession of a machine gun or assault firearm shall be sentenced to a term of imprisonment by the court. The term of imprisonment shall include the imposition of a minimum term. The minimum term shall be fixed at 10 years for a crime of the first or second degree, five years for a crime of the third degree, or 18 months in the case of a fourth degree crime, during which the defendant shall be ineligible for parole.

The minimum terms established by this section shall not prevent the court from imposing presumptive terms of imprisonment pursuant to paragraph (1) of subsection f. of N.J.S.2C:44-1 for crimes of the first degree.

A person who has been convicted of an offense enumerated in this subsection and who used or possessed a machine gun or assault firearm during its commission, attempted commission or flight therefrom and who has been previously convicted of an offense involving the use or possession of any firearm as defined in subsection d. of N.J.S.2C:44-3, shall be sentenced by the court to an extended term as authorized by subsection d. of N.J.S.2C:43-7, notwithstanding that extended terms are ordinarily discretionary with the court.

h. The court shall not impose a mandatory sentence pursuant to subsection g. of this section, subsections d. of N.J.S.2C:43-7 or N.J.S.2C:44-3, unless the ground therefor has been established at a hearing. At the hearing, which may occur at the time of sentencing, the prosecutor shall establish by a preponderance of the evidence that the weapon used or possessed was a machine gun or assault firearm. In making its finding, the court shall take judicial notice of any evidence, testimony or information adduced at the trial, plea hearing, or other court proceedings and shall also consider the presentence report and any other relevant information.

i. A person who has been convicted under paragraph (6) of subsection b. of 2C:12-1 of causing bodily injury while eluding shall be sentenced to a term of imprisonment by the court. The term of imprisonment shall include the imposition of a minimum term. The minimum term shall be fixed at, or between one-third and one-half of the sentence imposed by the court. The minimum term established by this subsection shall not prevent the court from imposing a presumptive term of imprisonment pursuant to paragraph (1) of subsection f. of 2C:44-1.

**2C:43-6.1.          Person under minimum mandatory sentence for possession of firearm with intent to use against property of another; review of sentence; imposition of other sentence**

Any person who, on the effective date of this amendatory and supplementary act, is serving a minimum mandatory sentence as provided for by N.J.S. 2C:43-6c. solely as a result of his conviction under subsection a. of N.J.S. 2C:39-4 for the possession of a firearm with intent to use it against the property of another, and has not had his sentence suspended or been paroled or discharged, may move to have his sentence reviewed by the sentencing court. For good cause shown, the court may impose any sentence which would have otherwise been available for such person.

## 2C:43-6.2.          Probation; reduction of mandatory minimum term

On a motion by the prosecutor made to the assignment judge that the imposition of a mandatory minimum term of imprisonment under (a) subsection c. of N.J.S.2C:43-6 for a defendant who has not previously been convicted of an offense under that subsection, or (b) subsection e. of N.J.S.2C:39-10 for a defendant who has not previously been convicted of an offense under chapter 39 of Title 2C of the New Jersey Statutes, does not serve the interests of justice, the assignment judge shall place the defendant on probation pursuant to paragraph (2) of subsection b. of N.J.S.2C:43-2 or reduce to one year the mandatory minimum term of imprisonment during which the defendant will be ineligible for parole. The sentencing court may also refer a case of a defendant who has not previously been convicted of an offense under that subsection to the assignment judge, with the approval of the prosecutor, if the sentencing court believes that the interests of justice would not be served by the imposition of a mandatory minimum term.

## 2C:43-6.3.          Review of sentence

Any person who, on the effective date of this act, is serving a mandatory minimum sentence as provided for by subsection c. of N.J.S.2C:43-6, who has not been previously convicted under that subsection, and has not had his sentence suspended or been paroled or discharged, may move to have his sentence reviewed by the assignment judge for the sentencing court. If the prosecutor agrees that the sentence under review does not serve the interests of justice, the judge shall reduce the mandatory minimum term of imprisonment without parole eligibility to one year or place the person on probation pursuant to paragraph (2) of subsection b. of N.J.S.2C:43-2.

## 2C:43-6.4.          Special sentence of community supervision for life

a. Notwithstanding any provision of law to the contrary, a court imposing sentence on a person who has been convicted of aggravated sexual assault, sexual assault, aggravated criminal sexual contact, kidnapping pursuant to paragraph (2) of subsection c. of N.J.S.2C:13-1, endangering the welfare of a child by engaging in sexual conduct which would impair or debauch the morals of the child pursuant to subsection a. of N.J.S.2C:24-4, luring or an attempt to commit any such offense shall include, in addition to any sentence authorized by this Code, a special sentence of community supervision for life.

b. The special sentence of community supervision required by this section shall commence upon completion of the sentence imposed pursuant to other applicable provisions of the Code of Criminal Justice. Persons serving a special sentence of community supervision shall be supervised as if on parole and subject to conditions appropriate to protect the public and foster rehabilitation.

c. A person sentenced to a term of community supervision for life may petition the Superior Court for release from community supervision. The court shall grant a petition for release from a special sentence of community supervision only upon proof that the person has not committed a crime for 15 years since the last conviction or release from incarceration, whichever is later, and that the person is not likely to pose a threat to the safety of others if released from supervision.

d. A person who violates a condition of a special sentence of community supervision without good cause is guilty of a crime of the fourth degree.

e. (1) A person serving a special sentence of community supervision imposed pursuant this section who commits a violation of 2C:11-3, 2C:11-4, section b. of 2C:12-1, 2C:13-1, 2C:13-6, 2C:14-2, 2C:14-3, 2C:24-4, a crime of the second degree under 2C:18-2 or subsection a. of 2C:39-4, shall be sentenced to an extended term of imprisonment.

(2) The court shall not impose a sentence of imprisonment pursuant to this subsection unless the ground therefor has been established at a hearing after the conviction of the defendant and on written notice to the defendant of the ground proposed. The defendant shall have the right to hear and controvert the evidence against him and to offer evidence upon the issue.

**2C:43-7.     Sentence of imprisonment for crime; extended terms**

a. In the cases designated in section 2C:44-3, a person who has been convicted of a crime may be sentenced, and in the cases designated in subsection e. of section 2 of P.L.1994, c.130 (C.2C:43-6.4), in subsection b. of section 2 of P.L.1995, c.126 (C.2C:43-7.1) and in the cases designated in section 1 of P.L.1997, c.410 (C.2C:44-5.1), a person who has been convicted of a crime shall be sentenced, to an extended term of imprisonment, as follows:

   (1) In case of aggravated manslaughter sentenced under subsection c. of N.J.S.2C:11-4; or kidnapping when sentenced as a crime of the first degree under paragraph (1) of subsection c. of 2C:13-1; or aggravated sexual assault if the person is eligible for an extended term pursuant to the provisions of subsection g. of N.J.S.2C:44-3 for a specific term of years which shall be between 30 years and life imprisonment;

   (2) Except for the crime of murder and except as provided in paragraph (1) of this subsection, in the case of a crime of the first degree, for a specific term of years which shall be fixed by the court and shall be between 20 years and life imprisonment;

   (3) In the case of a crime of the second degree, for a term which shall be fixed by the court between 10 and 20 years;

   (4) In the case of a crime of the third degree, for a term which shall be fixed by the court between five and 10 years;

   (5) In the case of a crime of the fourth degree pursuant to 2C:43-6c. and 2C:44-3d. for a term of five years, and in the case of a crime of the fourth degree pursuant to 2C:43-6f. and 2C:43-6g. for a term which shall be fixed by the court between three and five years;

   (6) In the case of the crime of murder, for a specific term of years which shall be fixed by the court between 35 years and life imprisonment, of which the defendant shall serve 35 years before being eligible for parole;

   (7) In the case of kidnapping under paragraph (2) of subsection c. of 2C:13-1, for a specific term of years which shall be fixed by the court between 30 years and life imprisonment, of which the defendant shall serve 30 years before being eligible for parole.

b. As part of a sentence for an extended term and notwithstanding the provisions of 2C:43-9, the court may fix a minimum term not to exceed one-half of the term set pursuant to subsection a. during which the defendant shall not be eligible for parole or a term of 25 years during which time the defendant shall not be eligible for parole where the sentence imposed was life imprisonment; provided that no defendant shall be eligible for parole at a date earlier than otherwise provided by the law governing parole.

c. In the case of a person sentenced to an extended term pursuant to 2C:43-6c., 2C:43-6f. and 2C:44-3d., the court shall impose a sentence within the ranges permitted by 2C:43-7a.(2), (3), (4) or (5) according to the degree or nature of the crime for which the defendant is being sentenced, which sentence shall include a minimum term which shall, except as may be specifically provided by N.J.S.2C:43-6f., be fixed at or between one-third and one-half of the sentence imposed by the court or five years, whichever is greater, during which the defendant shall not be eligible for parole. Where the sentence imposed is life imprisonment, the court shall impose a minimum term of 25 years during which the defendant shall not be eligible for parole, except that where the term of life imprisonment is imposed on a person convicted for a violation of N.J.S.2C:35-3, the term of parole ineligibility shall be 30 years.

d. In the case of a person sentenced to an extended term pursuant to N.J.S.2C:43-6g., the court shall impose a sentence within the ranges permitted by N.J.S.2C:43-7a(2), (3), (4) or (5) according to the degree or nature of the crime for which the defendant is being sentenced, which sentence shall include a minimum term which shall be fixed at 15 years for a crime of the first or second degree, eight years for a crime of the third degree, or five years for a crime of the fourth degree during which the defendant shall not be eligible for parole. Where the sentence imposed is life imprisonment, the court shall impose a minimum term of 25 years during which the defendant shall not be eligible for parole, except that where the term of life imprisonment is imposed on a person convicted of a violation of N.J.S.2C:35-3, the term of parole eligibility shall be 30 years.

## 2C:43-7.1.     Life imprisonment without parole

a. **Life imprisonment without parole.** A person convicted of a crime under any of the following: N.J.S.2C:11-3; subsection a. of N.J.S.2C:11-4; a crime of the first degree under N.J.S.2C:13-1, paragraphs (3) through (6) of subsection a. of N.J.S.2C:14-2; N.J.S.2C:15-1; or section 1 of P.L.1993, c.221 (C.2C:15-2), who has been convicted of two or more crimes that were committed on prior and separate occasions, regardless of the dates of the convictions, under any of the foregoing sections or under any similar statute of the United States, this State, or any other state for a crime that is substantially equivalent to a crime under any of the foregoing sections, shall be sentenced to a term of life imprisonment by the court, with no eligibility for parole.

b. **Extended term for repeat violent offenders.** A person shall be sentenced to an extended term of imprisonment pursuant to N.J.S.2C:43-7 if:

   (1) The person is convicted of any of the following crimes: a crime of the second degree under N.J.S.2C:11-4; a crime of the second or third degree under subsection b. of N.J.S.2C:12-1; a crime of the second degree under N.J.S.2C:13-1; a crime under N.J.S.2C:14-3 for aggravated criminal sexual contact under any of the circumstances set forth in paragraphs (3) through (6) of subsection a. of N.J.S.2C:14-2; a crime of the second degree under N.J.S.2C:15-1; a crime of the second degree under N.J.S.2C:18-2; or a crime of the second degree under N.J.S.2C:39-4 for possession of a weapon with the purpose of using it unlawfully against the person of another, and the person has been convicted of any of the foregoing crimes or any of the crimes enumerated in subsection a. of this section or under any similar statute of the United States, this State, or any other state for a crime that is substantially equivalent to a crime enumerated in this subsection or in subsection a. of this section committed on two or more prior and separate occasions regardless of the dates of the convictions, or

   (2) The person is convicted of a crime enumerated in subsection a. of this section, does not have two or more prior convictions that require sentencing under subsection a. and has two or more prior convictions that would require sentencing under paragraph (1) of this subsection if the person had been convicted of a crime enumerated in paragraph (1).

c. The provisions of this section shall not apply unless the prior convictions are for crimes committed on separate occasions and unless the crime for which the defendant is being sentenced was committed either within 10 years of the date of the defendant's last release from confinement for commission of any crime or within 10 years of the date of the commission of the most recent of the crimes for which the defendant has a prior conviction.

d. The court shall not impose a sentence of imprisonment pursuant to this section, unless the ground therefor has been established at a hearing after the conviction of the defendant and on written notice to the defendant of the ground proposed. The defendant shall have the right to hear and controvert the evidence against him and to offer evidence upon the issue. Prior convictions shall be defined and proven in accordance with N.J.S.2C:44-4.

e. For purposes of this section, a term of life shall mean the natural life of a person sentenced pursuant to this section. Except that a defendant who is at least 70 years of age and who has served at least 35 years in prison pursuant to a sentence imposed under this section shall be released on parole if the full Parole Board determines that the defendant is not a danger to the safety of any other person or the community.

**2C:43-7.2.**          **Mandatory service of 85% of sentence for certain offenses**

a. A court imposing a sentence of incarceration for a crime of the first or second degree enumerated in subsection d. of this section shall fix a minimum term of 85% of the sentence imposed, during which the defendant shall not be eligible for parole.

b. The minimum term required by subsection a. of this section shall be fixed as a part of every sentence of incarceration imposed upon every conviction of a crime enumerated in subsection d. of this section, whether the sentence of incarceration is determined pursuant to N.J.S.2C:43-6, N.J.S.2C:43-7, N.J.S.2C:11-3 or any other provision of law, and shall be calculated based upon the sentence of incarceration actually imposed. The provisions of subsection a. of this section shall not be construed or applied to reduce the time that must be served before eligibility for parole by an inmate sentenced to a mandatory minimum period of incarceration. Solely for the purpose of calculating the minimum term of parole ineligibility pursuant to subsection a. of this section, a sentence of life imprisonment shall be deemed to be 75 years.

c. Notwithstanding any other provision of law to the contrary and in addition to any other sentence imposed, a court imposing a minimum period of parole ineligibility of 85 percent of the sentence pursuant to this section shall also impose a five-year term of parole supervision if the defendant is being sentenced for a crime of the first degree, or a three-year term of parole supervision if the defendant is being sentenced for a crime of the second degree. The term of parole supervision shall commence upon the completion of the sentence of incarceration imposed by the court pursuant to subsection a. of this section unless the defendant is serving a sentence of incarceration for another crime at the time he completes the sentence of incarceration imposed pursuant to subsection a., in which case the term of parole supervision shall commence immediately upon the defendant's release from incarceration. During the term of parole supervision the defendant shall remain in release status in the community in the legal custody of the Commissioner of the Department of Corrections and shall be supervised by the State Parole Board as if on parole and shall be subject to the provisions and conditions of section 3 of P.L.1997, c.117 (C.30:4-123.51b).

d. The court shall impose sentence pursuant to subsection a. of this section upon conviction of the following crimes or an attempt or conspiracy to commit any of these crimes:

(1) N.J.S.2C:11-3, murder;

(2) N.J.S.2C:11-4, aggravated manslaughter or manslaughter;

(3) N.J.S.2C:11-5, vehicular homicide;

(4) subsection b. of N.J.S.2C:12-1, aggravated assault;

(5) subsection b. of N.J.S.2C:12-11, disarming a law enforcement officer;

      (6) N.J.S.2C:13-1, kidnapping;

      (7) subsection a. of N.J.S.2C:14-2, aggravated sexual assault;

      (8) subsection b. of N.J.S.2C:14-2 and paragraph (1) of subsection c. of N.J.S.2C:14-2, sexual assault;

      (9) N.J.S.2C:15-1, robbery;

      (10) section 1 of P.L.1993, c.221 (C.2C:15-2), carjacking;

      (11) paragraph (1) of subsection a. of N.J.S.2C:17-1, aggravated arson;

      (12) N.J.S.2C:18-2, burglary;

      (13) subsection a. of N.J.S.2C:20-5, extortion;

      (14) subsection b. of section 1 of P.L.1997, c.185 (C.2C:35-4.1), booby traps in manufacturing or distribution facilities; or

      (15) N.J.S.2C:35-9, strict liability for drug induced deaths.

      (16) section 2 of P.L.2002, c.26 (C.2C:38-2), terrorism; or

      (17) section 3 of P.L.2002, c.26 (C.2C:38-3), producing or possessing chemical weapons, biological agents or nuclear or radiological devices.

   e. (Deleted by amendment, P.L.2001, c.129.)

## 2C:43-8. Sentence of imprisonment for disorderly persons offenses and petty disorderly persons offenses

A person who has been convicted of a disorderly persons offense or a petty disorderly persons offense may be sentenced to imprisonment for a definite term which shall be fixed by the court and shall not exceed 6 months in the case of a disorderly persons offense or 30 days in the case of a petty disorderly persons offense.

## 2C:43-8.1. Seasonally leased premises; termination of right to occupy, visit

In addition to any other disposition authorized by law, if a person is convicted of a disorderly persons offense, a petty disorderly persons offense or a violation of a municipal ordinance and the offense or violation occurred at or involved the use of a seasonally leased premises, the court may order the termination of that person's right to occupy or visit the seasonally leased premises for a period not to exceed 125 days.

As used in this section, "seasonally leased premises" means premises leased as a residence for a period of less than 125 consecutive days. The term "seasonally leased premises" shall not include any structure provided by an employer on the employer's property which is used as living quarters for seasonal, temporary or migrant workers nor shall it include any premises used as the principal residence of a tenant pursuant to the terms of a month to month or week to week lease.

## 2C:43-9. Release of all offenders; length of recommitment and reparole after revocation of parole

Release of offenders on parole, recommitment and reparole after revocation shall be governed by the "Parole Act of 1979," P.L.1979, c. 441 (C. 30:4-123.45 et seq.).

## 2C:43-10. Place of imprisonment; beginning sentences; transfers

   a. **Sentences for terms of 1 year or longer.** Except as provided in section 2C:43-5 and in subsection b. of this section, when a person is sentenced to imprisonment for any term of 1 year or greater, the court shall commit him to the custody of the Commissioner of the

Department of Corrections for the term of his sentence and until released in accordance with law.

b. **County institution.** In any county in which a county penitentiary or a county workhouse is located, a person sentenced to imprisonment for a return not exceeding 18 months may be committed to the penitentiary or workhouse of such county.

c. **Sentences for terms of less than 1 year.** When a person is sentenced to imprisonment for a term of less than 1 year, the court shall commit him either to the common jail of the county, the county workhouse or the county penitentiary for the term of his sentence and until released in accordance with law. In counties of the first class having a workhouse or penitentiary, however, no sentence exceeding 6 months shall be to the common jail of the county.

d. Aggregation of sentences when a person is sentenced to more than one term of imprisonment, and the sentences are to be consecutive, the terms shall be aggregated for the purpose of determining the place of imprisonment under subsections a., b. or c. of this section.

e. **Duties of sheriff and keeper on sentence to State Prison.** In all cases where the defendant, upon conviction, is sentenced by the court to imprisonment, for any term of 1 year or greater, the sheriff of the county or his lawful deputy shall, within 15 days transport him to the State Prison and there deliver him into the custody of the Commissioner of the Department of Corrections together with a copy of the sentence of the court ordering such imprisonment certified by the clerk of the court where the conviction was had, a copy of the court's statement of reasons for the sentence, and a copy of the presentence report or any presentence information used by the judge in determining sentence.

In every case at least 48 hours, exclusive of Sundays and legal holidays, shall elapse between the time of sentence and removal to the State Prison.

f. **Beginning sentences in county institutions.** Every person sentenced to the county workhouse or penitentiary shall be transferred to and confined therein within 10 days after the sentence.

g. **Transfer of persons sentenced to county jail, penitentiary or workhouse from one to another thereof.** Every person sentenced to imprisonment in a county jail, penitentiary or workhouse may upon the application of the board of chosen freeholders of such county and by order of the Superior Court, be transferred from any one of such county penal institutions to any other thereof. No such transfer or retransfer shall in any way affect the term of the original sentence of the person so transferred or retransferred

**2C:43-11.**        **Program of intensive supervision, eligibility**

a. No custodial sentence imposed pursuant to Chapters 43, 44 or 45 of Title 2C shall be changed to permit entry into any program of intensive supervision established pursuant to the Rules Governing the Courts of the State of New Jersey if the inmate:

  (1) Is serving a sentence for a conviction of any crime of the first degree; or

  (2) Is serving a sentence for a conviction of any offense in which the sentencing court found that there is a substantial likelihood that the defendant is involved in organized criminal activity pursuant to N.J.S. 2C:44-1a(5); or

  (3) Is serving any statutorily mandated parole ineligibility, or any parole ineligibility imposed by the court pursuant to subsection b. of N.J.S. 2C:43-6; or

  (4) Has previously completed a program of intensive supervision established pursuant to the Rules Governing the Courts of the State of New Jersey; or

      (5) Has previously been convicted of a crime of the first degree, or of any offense in any other jurisdiction which, if committed in New Jersey, would constitute a crime of the first degree and the inmate was released from incarceration on the first degree offense within five years of the commission of the offense for which the inmate is applying for intensive supervision.

        Nothing in this subsection shall be construed to preclude the program of intensive supervision from imposing more restrictive standards for admission.

b. Unless the inmate is within nine months of parole eligibility and has served at least six months of the sentence, no custodial sentence of an inmate serving a sentence for conviction of any crime of the second degree shall be changed to permit entry into any program of intensive supervision established pursuant to the Rules Governing the Courts of the State of New Jersey, if, within 20 days of receipt of notice of the inmate's application, the county prosecutor or Attorney General objects in writing.

c. If an inmate's application for a change of custodial sentence to permit entry into any program of intensive supervision established pursuant to the Rules Governing the Courts of the State of New Jersey is granted over the objection of the county prosecutor or the Attorney General, the order shall not become final for 20 days or until reconsideration by the Intensive Supervision Resentencing Panel in order to permit the county prosecutor or the Attorney General to appear personally or in writing, with notice to defense counsel, to request reconsideration of the application approval.

d. A victim of the offense for which the inmate was sentenced shall have the right to make a written statement or to appear at a proceeding regarding the application for a change of custodial sentence imposed pursuant to Chapters 43, 44 or 45 of Title 2C for entry into any program of intensive supervision established pursuant to the Rules Governing the Courts of the State of New Jersey.

## 2C:43-12.   Supervisory treatment—pretrial intervention

a. **Public policy.** The purpose of sections 2C:43-12 through 2C:43-22 of this chapter is to effectuate a Statewide program of Pretrial Intervention. It is the policy of the State of New Jersey that supervisory treatment should ordinarily be limited to persons who have not previously been convicted of any criminal offense under the laws of New Jersey, or under any criminal law of the United States, or any other state when supervisory treatment would:

      (1) Provide applicants, on an equal basis, with opportunities to avoid ordinary prosecution by receiving early rehabilitative services or supervision, when such services or supervision can reasonably be expected to deter future criminal behavior by an applicant, and when there is apparent causal connection between the offense charged and the rehabilitative or supervisory need, without which cause both the alleged offense and the need to prosecute might not have occurred; or

      (2) Provide an alternative to prosecution for applicants who might be harmed by the imposition of criminal sanctions as presently administered, when such an alternative can be expected to serve as sufficient sanction to deter criminal conduct; or

      (3) Provide a mechanism for permitting the least burdensome form of prosecution possible for defendants charged with "victimless" offenses; or

      (4) Provide assistance to criminal calendars in order to focus expenditure of criminal justice resources on matters involving serious criminality and severe correctional problems; or

      (5) Provide deterrence of future criminal or disorderly behavior by an applicant in a program of supervisory treatment.

b. Admission of an applicant into a program of supervisory treatment shall be measured according to the applicant's amenability to correction, responsiveness to rehabilitation and the nature of the offense.

c. The decision and reasons therefor made by the designated judges (or assignment judges), prosecutors and program directors in granting or denying applications for supervisory treatment, in recommending and ordering termination from the program or dismissal of charges, in all cases shall be reduced to writing and disclosed to the applicant.

d. If an applicant desires to challenge the decision of the prosecutor or program director not to recommend enrollment in a program of supervisory treatment the proceedings prescribed under section 14 shall be followed.

e. **Referral.** At any time prior to trial but after the filing of a criminal complaint, or the filing of an accusation or the return of an indictment, with the consent of the prosecutor and upon written recommendation of the program director, the assignment judge or a judge designated by him may postpone all further proceedings against an applicant and refer said applicant to a program of supervisory treatment approved by the Supreme Court. Prosecutors and program directors shall consider in formulating their recommendation of an applicant's participation in a supervisory treatment program, among others, the following criteria:

    (1) The nature of the offense;

    (2) The facts of the case;

    (3) The motivation and age of the defendant;

    (4) The desire of the complainant or victim to forego prosecution;

    (5) The existence of personal problems and character traits which may be related to the applicant's crime and for which services are unavailable within the criminal justice system, or which may be provided more effectively through supervisory treatment and the probability that the causes of criminal behavior can be controlled by proper treatment;

    (6) The likelihood that the applicant's crime is related to a condition or situation that would be conducive to change through his participation in supervisory treatment;

    (7) The needs and interests of the victim and society;

    (8) The extent to which the applicant's crime constitutes part of a continuing pattern of anti-social behavior;

    (9) The applicant's record of criminal and penal violations and the extent to which he may present a substantial danger to others;

    (10) Whether or not the crime is of an assaultive or violent nature, whether in the criminal act itself or in the possible injurious consequences of such behavior;

    (11) Consideration of whether or not prosecution would exacerbate the social problem that led to the applicant's criminal act;

    (12) The history of the use of physical violence toward others;

    (13) Any involvement of the applicant with organized crime;

    (14) Whether or not the crime is of such a nature that the value of supervisory treatment would be outweighed by the public need for prosecution;

    (15) Whether or not the applicant's involvement with other people in the crime charged or in other crime is such that the interest of the State would be best served by processing his case through traditional criminal justice system procedures;

    (16) Whether or not the applicant's participation in pretrial intervention will adversely affect the prosecution of codefendants; and

(17) Whether or not the harm done to society by abandoning criminal prosecution would outweigh the benefits to society from channeling an offender into a supervisory treatment program.

f. **Review of supervisory treatment applications; procedure upon denial.** Each applicant for supervisory treatment shall be entitled to full and fair consideration of his application. If an application is denied, the program director or the prosecutor shall precisely state his findings and conclusion which shall include the facts upon which the application is based and the reasons offered for the denial. If the applicant desires to challenge the decision of a program director not to recommend, or of a prosecutor not to consent to, enrollment into a supervisory treatment program, a motion shall be filed before the designated judge (or assignment judge) authorized pursuant to the rules of court to enter orders.

g. **Limitations.** Supervisory treatment may occur only once with respect to any defendant and any person who has previously received supervisory treatment under section 27 of P.L.1970, c.226 (C.24:21-27), shall not be eligible for supervisory treatment under this section. However, supervisory treatment, as provided herein, shall be available to a defendant irrespective of whether the defendant contests his guilt of the charge or charges against him.

h. **Termination.** Termination of supervisory treatment under this section shall be immediately reported to the assignment judge of the county who shall forward such information to the Administrative Director of the Courts.

i. **Appointment of program directors; authorized referrals.** Programs of supervisory treatment and appointment of the program directors require approval by the Supreme Court with the consent of the assignment judge and prosecutor. Referrals of participants from supervisory treatment programs may be to any public or private office or agency, including but not limited to, programs within the probation service of the court, offering counseling or any other social service likely to aid in the rehabilitation of the participant and to deter the commission of other offenses.

j. **Health care professional licensing board notification.** The program director shall promptly notify the State Board of Medical Examiners when a State licensed physician or podiatrist has been enrolled in a supervisory treatment program after he has been charged with an offense involving drugs or alcohol.

**2C:43-13.**       **Supervisory treatment procedure**

a. **Agreement.** The terms and duration of the supervisory treatment shall be set forth in writing, signed by the prosecutor and agreed to and signed by the participant. Payment of the assessment required by section 2 of P.L.1979, c.396 (C.2C:43-3.1) shall be included as a term of the agreement. If the participant is represented by counsel, defense counsel shall also sign the agreement. Each order of supervisory treatment shall be filed with the county clerk.

b. **Charges.** During a period of supervisory treatment the charge or charges on which the participant is undergoing supervisory treatment shall be held in an inactive status pending termination of the supervisory treatment pursuant to subsection d. or e. of this section.

c. **Period of treatment.** Supervisory treatment may be for such period, as determined by the designated judge or the assignment judge, not to exceed three years, provided, however, that the period of supervisory treatment may be shortened or terminated as the program director may determine with the consent of the prosecutor and the approval of the court.

d. **Dismissal.** Upon completion of supervisory treatment, and with the consent of the prosecutor, the complaint, indictment or accusation against the participant may be dismissed with prejudice.

e. **Violation of conditions.** Upon violation of the conditions of supervisory treatment, the court shall determine, after summary hearing, whether said violation warrants the participant's dismissal from the supervisory treatment program or modification of the conditions of continued participation in that or another supervisory treatment program. Upon dismissal of the participant from the supervisory treatment program, the charges against the participant may be reactivated and the prosecutor may proceed as though no supervisory treatment had been commenced.

f. **Evidence.** No statement or other disclosure by a participant undergoing supervisory treatment made or disclosed to the person designated to provide such supervisory treatment shall be disclosed, at any time, to the prosecutor in connection with the charge or charges against the participant, nor shall any such statement or disclosure be admitted as evidence in any civil or criminal proceeding against the participant. Nothing provided herein, however, shall prevent the person providing supervisory treatment from informing the prosecutor, or the court, upon request or otherwise as to whether or not the participant is satisfactorily responding to supervisory treatment.

g. **Delay.** No participant agreeing to undergo supervisory treatment shall be permitted to complain of a lack of speedy trial for any delay caused by the commencement of supervisory treatment.

A person applying for admission to a program of supervisory treatment shall pay to the court a fee of $75.00. The court shall forward all money collected under this subsection to the treasurer of the county in which the court is located. This money shall be used to defray the cost of juror compensation within that county. A person may apply for a waiver of this fee, by reason of poverty, pursuant to the Rules Governing the Courts of the State of New Jersey. Of the moneys collected under this subsection, $30.00 of each application fee shall be deposited in the temporary reserve fund created by section 25 of P.L.1993, c.275. After December 31, 1994, the $75.00 fee shall be paid to the court, for use by the State.

## 2C:43-14.    Authority of Supreme Court

The Supreme Court may adopt rules dealing with Supervisory Treatment in accordance with procedures herein set forth.

## 2C:43-15.    Presentation of proposed rules at judicial conference

The subject matter and a tentative draft of a rule or rules proposed to be adopted pursuant to this chapter shall be entered upon the agenda and discussed at a Judicial Conference whose membership shall at least include delegates from the Supreme Court, the Appellate Division of the Superior Court, the judges of the Superior Court, the judges of the municipal courts, the surrogates, the State Bar Association, the county bar associations, the Senate and General Assembly, the Attorney General, the county prosecutors, the law schools of this State, and members of the public.

## 2C:43-16.    Public announcement of proposed rules; delivery of copies

The proposed rule or rules shall be publicly announced by the Supreme Court on September 15 next following such Judicial Conference (or, if such day be a Saturday, Sunday or legal holiday, on the first day thereafter that is not), and the court shall, on the same day, cause true copies thereof to be delivered to the President of the Senate, the Speaker of the General Assembly, and the Governor.

## 2C:43-17.    Effective date of rules; rules subject to cancellation by joint resolution

The rule or rules so announced and delivered shall take effect on July 1 next following; provided, however, that all such rules shall remain subject to cancellation at any time up to such effective date by joint resolution to that effect adopted by the Senate and General Assembly and signed by the Governor.

**2C:43-18.     Change or cancellation of rules by statute or adoption of subsequent rules**

Any rule or rules so proposed or adopted shall be subject to change or cancellation at any time by statute or by a subsequent rule adopted pursuant to this chapter.

**2C:43-19.     Adoption of rules at such time, or with such effective date, or without presentation at judicial conference, as may be provided in joint resolution**

By joint resolution adopted by the Senate and General Assembly and signed by the Governor with respect to a particular rule or rules therein specified the Supreme Court may adopt such rule or rules at such time or times, or with such effective date, or without presentation at a Judicial Conference, as may be provided in the joint resolution.

**2C:43-20.     Reduction or elimination of time during which rules may be canceled by joint resolution**

By joint resolution adopted by the Senate and General Assembly and signed by the Governor with respect to a particular rule or rules therein specified, the period of time as provided in 2C:43-17 during which the same may be canceled by joint resolution may be reduced or eliminated.

**2C:43-21.     Index and reports**

a. **Index.** The Administrative Director of the Courts shall establish and maintain an index of cases in which applications for supervisory treatment have been made and such index shall indicate the dispositions of those applications.

b. **Reports.** At the termination of the year in which this chapter takes effect and at the termination of each calendar year thereafter, for a period of 5 years, the assignment judge for each county shall report the results of the rehabilitative effort prescribed in this act to the Administrative Director of the Courts. The report shall include a description of offenses for which supervisory treatment was prescribed, the type of treatment to which defendants were assigned, the number and types of criminal acts, if any, committed by persons during their period of supervisory treatment, the number of persons successfully completing supervisory treatment and against whom charges were dismissed, and, where possible, the number and types of criminal acts, if any, committed by such persons subsequent to successful completion of supervisory treatment.

c. **Evaluation.** The Administrative Director of the Courts shall, from time to time as he deems necessary, or upon request from the Legislature, evaluate the program of supervisory treatment on the basis of reports made to him by county and municipal prosecutors. He shall submit his evaluation, together with special findings and recommendations to the Legislature.

d. No order of expungement or sealing shall affect any entry in the index or any registry of such information established by the Administrative Office of the Courts.

**2C:43-22.     Disclaimer**

Nothing contained in this act is intended to supersede, repeal or modify the authority granted and procedure prescribed under section 27 of P.L.1970, c. 226 (C. 24:21-27).

# 44

# AUTHORITY OF COURT IN SENTENCING

**2C:44-1.** **Criteria for withholding or imposing sentence of imprisonment**

a. In determining the appropriate sentence to be imposed on a person who has been convicted of an offense, the court shall consider the following aggravating circumstances:

(1) The nature and circumstances of the offense, and the role of the actor therein, including whether or not it was committed in an especially heinous, cruel, or depraved manner;

(2) The gravity and seriousness of harm inflicted on the victim, including whether or not the defendant knew or reasonably should have known that the victim of the offense was particularly vulnerable or incapable of resistance due to advanced age, ill-health, or extreme youth, or was for any other reason substantially incapable of exercising normal physical or mental power of resistance;

(3) The risk that the defendant will commit another offense;

(4) A lesser sentence will depreciate the seriousness of the defendant's offense because it involved a breach of the public trust under chapters 27 and 30, or the defendant took advantage of a position of trust or confidence to commit the offense;

(5) There is a substantial likelihood that the defendant is involved in organized criminal activity;

(6) The extent of the defendant's prior criminal record and the seriousness of the offenses of which he has been convicted;

(7) The defendant committed the offense pursuant to an agreement that he either pay or be paid for the commission of the offense and the pecuniary incentive was beyond that inherent in the offense itself;

(8) The defendant committed the offense against a police or other law enforcement officer, correctional employee or fireman, acting in the performance of his duties while in uniform or exhibiting evidence of his authority; the defendant committed the offense because of the status of the victim as a public servant; or the defendant committed the offense against a sports official, athletic coach or manager, acting in or immediately following the performance of his duties or because of the person's status as a sports official, coach or manager;

(9) The need for deterring the defendant and others from violating the law;

(10) The offense involved fraudulent or deceptive practices committed against any department or division of State government;

(11) The imposition of a fine, penalty or order of restitution without also imposing a term of imprisonment would be perceived by the defendant or others merely as part of the cost of doing business, or as an acceptable contingent business or operating expense associated with the initial decision to resort to unlawful practices;

(12) The defendant committed the offense against a person who he knew or should have known was 60 years of age or older, or disabled;

(13) The defendant, while in the course of committing or attempting to commit the crime, including the immediate flight therefrom, used or was in possession of a stolen motor vehicle.

b.  In determining the appropriate sentence to be imposed on a person who has been convicted of an offense, the court may properly consider the following mitigating circumstances:

(1) The defendant's conduct neither caused nor threatened serious harm;

(2) The defendant did not contemplate that his conduct would cause or threaten serious harm;

(3) The defendant acted under a strong provocation;

(4) There were substantial grounds tending to excuse or justify the defendant's conduct, though failing to establish a defense;

(5) The victim of the defendant's conduct induced or facilitated its commission;

(6) The defendant has compensated or will compensate the victim of his conduct for the damage or injury that he sustained, or will participate in a program of community service;

(7) The defendant has no history of prior delinquency or criminal activity or has led a law-abiding life for a substantial period of time before the commission of the present offense;

(8) The defendant's conduct was the result of circumstances unlikely to recur;

(9) The character and attitude of the defendant indicate that he is unlikely to commit another offense;

(10) The defendant is particularly likely to respond affirmatively to probationary treatment;

(11) The imprisonment of the defendant would entail excessive hardship to himself or his dependents;

(12) The willingness of the defendant to cooperate with law enforcement authorities;

(13) The conduct of a youthful defendant was substantially influenced by another person more mature than the defendant.

c.  (1) A plea of guilty by a defendant or failure to so plead shall not be considered in withholding or imposing a sentence of imprisonment.

(2) When imposing a sentence of imprisonment the court shall consider the defendant's eligibility for release under the law governing parole, including time credits awarded pursuant to Title 30 of the Revised Statutes, in determining the appropriate term of imprisonment.

d.  **Presumption of imprisonment.** The court shall deal with a person who has been convicted of a crime of the first or second degree by imposing a sentence of imprisonment unless, having regard to the character and condition of the defendant, it is of the opinion that his imprisonment would be a serious injustice which overrides the need to deter such conduct by others. Notwithstanding the provisions of subsection e. of this section, the court shall deal with a person who has been convicted of theft of a motor vehicle or of the unlawful taking of a motor vehicle and who has previously been convicted of either offense by imposing a sentence of imprisonment unless, having regard to the character and condition of the defendant, it is of the opinion that his imprisonment would be a serious injustice which overrides the need to deter such conduct by others.

e. The court shall deal with a person convicted of an offense other than a crime of the first or second degree, who has not previously been convicted of an offense, without imposing sentence of imprisonment unless, having regard to the nature and circumstances of the offense and the history, character and condition of the defendant, it is of the opinion that his imprisonment is necessary for the protection of the public under the criteria set forth in subsection a., except that this subsection shall not apply if the person is convicted of any of the following crimes of the third degree: theft of a motor vehicle; unlawful taking of a motor vehicle; or eluding; or if the person is convicted of a crime of the third or fourth degree constituting bias intimidation in violation of N.J.S.2C:16-1.

f. **Presumptive sentences.**

(1) Except for the crime of murder, unless the preponderance of aggravating or mitigating factors, as set forth in subsections a. and b., weighs in favor of a higher or lower term within the limits provided in N.J.S.2C:43-6, when a court determines that a sentence of imprisonment is warranted, it shall impose sentence as follows:

(a) To a term of 20 years for aggravated manslaughter or kidnapping pursuant to paragraph (1) of subsection c. of N.J.S.2C:13-1 when the offense constitutes a crime of the first degree;

(b) Except as provided in paragraph (a) of this subsection to a term of 15 years for a crime of the first degree;

(c) To a term of seven years for a crime of the second degree;

(d) To a term of four years for a crime of the third degree; and

(e) To a term of nine months for a crime of the fourth degree.

In imposing a minimum term pursuant to 2C:43-6b., the sentencing court shall specifically place on the record the aggravating factors set forth in this section which justify the imposition of a minimum term.

Unless the preponderance of mitigating factors set forth in subsection b. weighs in favor of a lower term within the limits authorized, sentences imposed pursuant to 2C:43-7a.(1) shall have a presumptive term of life imprisonment. Unless the preponderance of aggravating and mitigating factors set forth in subsections a. and b. weighs in favor of a higher or lower term within the limits authorized, sentences imposed pursuant to 2C:43-7a.(2) shall have a presumptive term of 50 years' imprisonment; sentences imposed pursuant to 2C:43-7a.(3) shall have a presumptive term of 15 years' imprisonment; and sentences imposed pursuant to 2C:43-7a.(4) shall have a presumptive term of seven years' imprisonment.

In imposing a minimum term pursuant to 2C:43-7b., the sentencing court shall specifically place on the record the aggravating factors set forth in this section which justify the imposition of a minimum term.

(2) In cases of convictions for crimes of the first or second degree where the court is clearly convinced that the mitigating factors substantially outweigh the aggravating factors and where the interest of justice demands, the court may sentence the defendant to a term appropriate to a crime of one degree lower than that of the crime for which he was convicted. If the court does impose sentence pursuant to this paragraph, or if the court imposes a noncustodial or probationary sentence upon conviction for a crime of the first or second degree, such sentence shall not become final for 10 days in order to permit the appeal of such sentence by the prosecution.

g. **Imposition of Noncustodial Sentences in Certain Cases.** If the court, in considering the aggravating factors set forth in subsection a., finds the aggravating factor in paragraph a.(2) or a.(12) and does not impose a custodial sentence, the court shall specifically place on the record the mitigating factors which justify the imposition of a noncustodial sentence.

h. Except as provided in section 2 of P.L.1993, c.123 (C.2C:43-11), the presumption of imprisonment as provided in subsection d. of this section shall not preclude the admission of a person to the Intensive Supervision Program, established pursuant to the Rules Governing the Courts of the State of New Jersey.

**2C:44-2.**        **Criteria for imposing fines and restitutions**

a. The court may sentence a defendant to pay a fine in addition to a sentence of imprisonment or probation if:

   (1) The defendant has derived a pecuniary gain from the offense or the court is of opinion that a fine is specially adapted to deterrence of the type of offense involved or to the correction of the offender;

   (2) The defendant is able, or given a fair opportunity to do so, will be able to pay the fine; and

   (3) The fine will not prevent the defendant from making restitution to the victim of the offense.

b. The court shall sentence a defendant to pay restitution in addition to a sentence of imprisonment or probation that may be imposed if:

   (1) The victim, or in the case of a homicide, the nearest relative of the victim, suffered a loss; and

   (2) The defendant is able to pay or, given a fair opportunity, will be able to pay restitution.

c. (1) In determining the amount and method of payment of a fine, the court shall take into account the financial resources of the defendant and the nature of the burden that its payment will impose.

   (2) In determining the amount and method of payment of restitution, the court shall take into account all financial resources of the defendant, including the defendant's likely future earnings, and shall set the amount of restitution so as to provide the victim with the fullest compensation for loss that is consistent with the defendant's ability to pay. The court shall not reduce a restitution award by any amount that the victim has received from the Violent Crimes Compensation Board, but shall order the defendant to pay any restitution ordered for a loss previously compensated by the Board to the Violent Crimes Compensation Board. If restitution to more than one person is set at the same time, the court shall set priorities of payment.

d. **Nonpayment.** When a defendant is sentenced to pay a fine or make restitution, or both, the court shall not impose at the same time an alternative sentence to be served in the event that the fine or restitution is not paid. The response of the court to nonpayment shall be determined only after the fine or restitution has not been paid, as provided in section 2C:46-2.

e. Whenever the maximum potential fine which may be imposed on a conviction for an offense defined in the "Comprehensive Drug Reform Act of 1986," N.J.S. 2C:35-1 et al. depends on the street value of the controlled dangerous substance or controlled substance analog involved and the court intends to impose a fine in excess of the maximum ordinary fine applicable to the offense for which defendant was convicted, and where the fine has not been agreed to pursuant to the provisions of N.J.S.2C:35-12, the court at the time of sentence shall determine the street value at the time and place of the offense based on the amount and purity of the controlled dangerous substance or controlled substance analog involved. The sentencing court's finding as to the street value may be based on expert opinion in the form of live testimony or by affidavit, or by such other means as the court deems appropriate. The court's finding as to street value shall not be subject to modification by an appellate court except upon a showing that the finding was totally lacking in support on the record or was arbitrary or capricious.

f. The ordering of restitution pursuant to this section shall not operate as a bar to the seeking of civil recovery by the victim based on the incident underlying the criminal conviction. Restitution ordered under this section is to be in addition to any civil remedy which a victim may possess, but any amount due the victim under any civil remedy shall be reduced by the amount ordered under this section to the extent necessary to avoid double compensation for the same loss, and the initial restitution judgment shall remain in full force and effect.

## 2C:44-3.        Criteria for sentence of extended term of imprisonment

The court may, upon application of the prosecuting attorney, sentence a person who has been convicted of a crime of the first, second or third degree to an extended term of imprisonment if it finds one or more of the grounds specified in subsection a., b., c., or f. of this section. If the grounds specified in subsection d. are found, and the person is being sentenced for commission of any of the offenses enumerated in N.J.S.2C:43-6c. or N.J.S.2C:43-6g., the court shall sentence the defendant to an extended term as required by N.J.S.2C:43-6c. or N.J.S.2C:43-6g., and application by the prosecutor shall not be required. The court shall, upon application of the prosecuting attorney, sentence a person who has been convicted of a crime under N.J.S.2C:14-2 or N.J.S.2C:14-3 to an extended term of imprisonment if the grounds specified in subsection g. of this section are found. The court shall, upon application of the prosecuting attorney, sentence a person who has been convicted of a crime to an extended term of imprisonment if the grounds specified in subsection h. of this section are found. The court shall, upon application of the prosecuting attorney, sentence a person to an extended term if the imposition of such term is required pursuant to the provisions of section 2 of P.L.1994, c.130 (C.2C:43-6.4). The finding of the court shall be incorporated in the record.

a. The defendant has been convicted of a crime of the first, second or third degree and is a persistent offender. A persistent offender is a person who at the time of the commission of the crime is 21 years of age or over, who has been previously convicted on at least two separate occasions of two crimes, committed at different times, when he was at least 18 years of age, if the latest in time of these crimes or the date of the defendant's last release from confinement, whichever is later, is within 10 years of the date of the crime for which the defendant is being sentenced.

b. The defendant has been convicted of a crime of the first, second or third degree and is a professional criminal. A professional criminal is a person who committed a crime as part of a continuing criminal activity in concert with two or more persons, and the circumstances of the crime show he has knowingly devoted himself to criminal activity as a major source of livelihood.

c. The defendant has been convicted of a crime of the first, second or third degree and committed the crime as consideration for the receipt, or in expectation of the receipt, of anything of pecuniary value the amount of which was unrelated to the proceeds of the crime or he procured the commission of the offense by payment or promise of payment of anything of pecuniary value.

d. **Second offender with a firearm.** The defendant is at least 18 years of age and has been previously convicted of any of the following crimes: 2C:11-3, 2C:11-4, 2C:12-1b., 2C:13-1, 2C:14-2a., 2C:14-3a., 2C:15-1, 2C:18-2, 2C:29-5, 2C:39-4a., or has been previously convicted of an offense under Title 2A of the New Jersey Statutes or under any statute of the United States or any other state which is substantially equivalent to the offenses enumerated in this subsection and he used or possessed a firearm, as defined in 2C:39-1f., in the course of committing or attempting to commit any of these crimes, including the immediate flight therefrom.

e. (Deleted by amendment, P.L.2001, c.443.)

f. The defendant has been convicted of a crime under any of the following sections: N.J.S.2C:11-4, N.J.S.2C:12-1b., N.J.S.2C:13-1, N.J.S.2C:14-2a., N.J.S.2C:14-3a., N.J.S.2C:15-1, N.J.S.2C:18-2, N.J.S.2C:29-2b., N.J.S.2C:29-5, N.J.S.2C:35-5, and in the course of committing or attempting to commit the crime, including the immediate flight therefrom, the defendant used or was in possession of a stolen motor vehicle.

g. The defendant has been convicted of a crime under N.J.S.2C:14-2 or N.J.S.2C:14-3 involving violence or the threat of violence and the victim of the crime was 16 years of age or less.

For purposes of this subsection, a crime involves violence or the threat of violence if the victim sustains serious bodily injury as defined in subsection b. of N.J.S.2C:11-1, or the actor is armed with and uses a deadly weapon or threatens by word or gesture to use a deadly weapon as defined in subsection c. of N.J.S.2C:11-1, or threatens to inflict serious bodily injury.

h. The crime was committed while the defendant was knowingly involved in criminal street gang related activity. A crime is committed while the defendant was involved in criminal street gang related activity if the crime was committed for the benefit of, at the direction of, or in association with a criminal street gang. "Criminal street gang" means three or more persons associated in fact. Individuals are associated in fact if (1) they have in common a group name or identifying sign, symbol, tattoo or other physical marking, style of dress or use of hand signs or other indicia of association or common leadership, and (2) individually or in combination with other members of a criminal street gang, while engaging in gang related activity, have committed, conspired or attempted to commit, within the preceding three years, two or more offenses of robbery, carjacking, aggravated assault, assault, aggravated sexual assault, sexual assault, arson, burglary, kidnapping, extortion, or a violation of chapter 11, section 3, 4, 5, 6 or 7 of chapter 35 or chapter 39 of Title 2C of the New Jersey Statutes regardless of whether the prior offenses have resulted in convictions.

The court shall not impose a sentence pursuant to this subsection unless the ground therefore has been established by a preponderance of the evidence established at a hearing, which may occur at the time of sentencing. In making its finding, the court shall take judicial notice of any testimony or information adduced at the trial, plea hearing or other court proceedings and also shall consider the presentence report and any other relevant information.

**2C:44-4.**        **Definition of prior conviction; conviction in another jurisdiction; proof of prior conviction**

a. **Prior conviction of an offense.** An adjudication by a court of competent jurisdiction that the defendant committed an offense constitutes a prior conviction.

b. **Prior conviction of a crime.** An adjudication by a court of competent jurisdiction that the defendant committed a crime constitutes a prior conviction, although sentence or the execution thereof was suspended, provided that the time to appeal has expired and that the defendant was not pardoned on the ground of innocence.

c. **Prior conviction in another jurisdiction.** A conviction in another jurisdiction shall constitute a prior conviction of a crime if a sentence of imprisonment in excess of 6 months was authorized under the law of the other jurisdiction.

d. **Proof of prior conviction.** Any prior conviction may be proved by any evidence, including fingerprint records made in connection with arrest, conviction or imprisonment, that reasonably satisfies the court that the defendant was convicted.

**2C:44-5.**        **Multiple sentences; concurrent and consecutive terms**

a. **Sentences of imprisonment for more than one offense.** When multiple sentences of imprisonment are imposed on a defendant for more than one offense, including an offense for which a previous suspended sentence or sentence of probation has been revoked, such multiple sentences shall run concurrently or consecutively as the court determines at the time of sentence, except that:

(1) The aggregate of consecutive terms to a county institution shall not exceed 18 months; and

(2) Not more than one sentence for an extended term shall be imposed.
There shall be no overall outer limit on the cumulation of consecutive sentences for multiple offenses.

b. **Sentences of imprisonment imposed at different times.** When a defendant who has previously been sentenced to imprisonment is subsequently sentenced to another term for an offense committed prior to the former sentence, other than an offense committed while in custody:

(1) The multiple sentences imposed shall so far as possible conform to subsection a. of this section; and

(2) Whether the court determines that the terms shall run concurrently or consecutively, the defendant shall be credited with time served in imprisonment on the prior sentence in determining the permissible aggregate length of the term or terms remaining to be served; and

(3) When a new sentence is imposed on a prisoner who is on parole, the balance of the parole term on the former sentence shall not be deemed to run during the period of the new imprisonment unless the court determines otherwise at the time of sentencing.

c. **Sentence of imprisonment for offense committed while on parole.** When a defendant is sentenced to imprisonment for an offense committed while on parole in this State, such term of imprisonment and any period of reimprisonment that the parole board may require the defendant to serve upon the revocation of his parole shall run consecutively unless the court orders these sentences to run concurrently.

d. **Multiple sentences of imprisonment in other cases.** Except as otherwise provided in this section, multiple terms of imprisonment shall run concurrently or consecutively as the court determines when the second or subsequent sentence is imposed.

e. **Calculation of concurrent and consecutive terms of imprisonment.**

(1) When terms of imprisonment run concurrently, the shorter terms merge in and are satisfied by discharge of the longest term.

(2) When terms of imprisonment run consecutively, the terms are added to arrive at an aggregate term to be served equal to the sum of all terms.

f. **Suspension of sentence or probation and imprisonment; multiple terms of suspension and probation.** When a defendant is sentenced for more than one offense or a defendant already under sentence is sentenced for another offense committed prior to the former sentence:

(1) The court shall not sentence to probation a defendant who is under sentence of imprisonment, except as authorized by paragraph (2) of subsection b. of N.J.S.2C:43-2;

(2) Multiple periods of suspension or probation shall run consecutively, unless the court orders these sentences to run concurrently from the date of the first such disposition;

(3) When a sentence of imprisonment in excess of one year is imposed, the service of such sentence shall satisfy a suspended sentence on another count or prior

suspended sentence or sentence to probation, unless the suspended sentence or probation has been violated in which case any imprisonment for the violation shall run consecutively; and

(4) When a sentence of imprisonment of one year or less is imposed, the period of a suspended sentence on another count or a prior suspended sentence or sentence to probation shall run during the period of such imprisonment, unless the suspended sentence or probation has been violated in which case any imprisonment for the violation shall run consecutively.

g. **Offense committed while under suspension of sentence or probation.** When a defendant is convicted of an offense committed while under suspension of sentence or on probation and such suspension or probation is not revoked:

(1) If the defendant is sentenced to imprisonment in excess of one year, the service of such sentence shall not satisfy the prior suspended sentence or sentence to probation, unless the court determines otherwise at the time of sentencing;

(2) If the defendant is sentenced to imprisonment of one year or less, the period of the suspension or probation shall not run during the period of such imprisonment; and

(3) If sentence is suspended or the defendant is sentenced to probation, the period of such suspension or probation shall run concurrently with or consecutively to the remainder of the prior periods, as the court determines at the time of sentence.

h. **Offense committed while released pending disposition of a previous offense.** When a defendant is sentenced to imprisonment for an offense committed while released, with or without bail, pending disposition of a previous offense, the term of imprisonment shall run consecutively to any sentence of imprisonment imposed for the previous offense, unless the court, in consideration of the character and conditions of the defendant, finds that imposition of consecutive sentences would be a serious injustice which overrides the need to deter such conduct by others.

i. **Sentence of imprisonment for assault on corrections employee.** Any term of imprisonment imposed on an inmate of a State or county correctional facility for an assault on a Department of Corrections employee, an employee of a county correctional facility, an employee of a State juvenile facility or a county juvenile detention facility, county sheriff's department employee or any State, county or municipal law enforcement officer while in the performance of his duties shall run consecutively to any term of imprisonment currently being served and to any other term imposed for any other offense committed at the time of the assault.

**2C:44-5.1.     Penalties for committing certain offenses while released on bail, own recognizance increased.**

a. A person who has been convicted under subsection a. of N.J.S.2C:39-4 of possession of a firearm with intent to use it unlawfully against the person of another; or a crime under N.J.S.2C:11-3; N.J.S.2C:11-4; N.J.S.2C:13-1; subsection a. of N.J.S.2C:14-2; subsection a. of N.J.S.2C:14-3; N.J.S.2C:15-1; N.J.S.2C:18-2 if the burglary is a crime of the second degree or the structure was adapted for overnight accommodation of persons; or a crime of the first, second or third degree under subsection b. of N.J.S.2C:12-1; shall be sentenced to an extended term of imprisonment pursuant to the provisions of N.J.S.2C:43-7 and shall be subject to double the fine authorized for that crime under the provisions of N.J.S.2C:43-3 if, at the time of the commission of the crime, the defendant was released on bail or on his own recognizance for one of the enumerated crimes and was convicted of that crime.

b. The court shall not impose a sentence of imprisonment pursuant to this section unless the ground therefor has been established at a hearing after the conviction of the defendant and on written notice to the defendant of the ground proposed. The defendant shall have the right to hear and controvert the evidence against the defendant and to offer evidence upon the issue.

**2C:44-6.**          **Procedure on sentence; presentence investigation and report**

a. The court shall not impose sentence without first ordering a presentence investigation of the defendant and according due consideration to a written report of such investigation when required by the Rules of Court. The court may order a presentence investigation in any other case.

b. The presentence investigation shall include an analysis of the circumstances attending the commission of the offense, the defendant's history of delinquency or criminality, family situation, financial resources, including whether or not the defendant is an enrollee or covered person under a health insurance contract, policy or plan, debts, including any amount owed for a fine, assessment or restitution ordered in accordance with the provisions of Title 2C, employment history, personal habits, the disposition of any charge made against any codefendants, the defendant's history of civil commitment, any disposition which arose out of charges suspended pursuant to N.J.S.2C:4-6 including the records of the disposition of those charges and any acquittal by reason of insanity pursuant to N.J.S.2C:4-1, and any other matters that the probation officer deems relevant or the court directs to be included. The defendant shall disclose any information concerning any history of civil commitment. The report shall also include a medical history of the defendant and a complete psychological evaluation of the defendant in any case in which the defendant is being sentenced for a first or second degree crime involving violence and:

(1)  the defendant has a prior acquittal by reason of insanity pursuant to N.J.S.2C:4-1 or had charges suspended pursuant to N.J.S.2C:4-6; or

(2)  the defendant has a prior conviction for murder pursuant to N.J.S.2C:11-3, aggravated sexual assault or sexual assault pursuant to N.J.S.2C:14-2, kidnapping pursuant to N.J.S.2C:13-1, endangering the welfare of a child which would constitute a crime of the second degree pursuant to N.J.S.2C:24-4, or stalking which would constitute a crime of the third degree pursuant to P.L.1992, c.209 (C.2C:12-10); or

(3)  the defendant has a prior diagnosis of psychosis.

The court, in its discretion and considering all the appropriate circumstances, may waive the medical history and psychological examination in any case in which a term of imprisonment including a period of parole ineligibility is imposed. In any case involving a conviction of N.J.S.2C:24-4, endangering the welfare of a child; N.J.S.2C:18-3, criminal trespass, where the trespass was committed in a school building or on school property; section 1 of P.L.1993, c.291 (C.2C:13-6), attempting to lure or entice a child with purpose to commit a criminal offense; section 1 of P.L.1992, c.209 (C.2C:12-10), stalking; or N.J.S.2C:13-1, kidnapping, where the victim of the offense is a child under the age of 18, the investigation shall include a report on the defendant's mental condition.

The presentence report shall also include a report on any compensation paid by the Victims of Crime Compensation Board as a result of the commission of the offense and, in any case where the victim chooses to provide one, a statement by the victim of the offense for which the defendant is being sentenced. The statement may include the nature and extent of any physical harm or psychological or emotional harm or trauma suffered by the victim, the extent of any loss to include loss of earnings or ability to work suffered by the victim and the effect of the crime upon the victim's family. The probation department shall notify the victim or nearest relative of a homicide victim of his right to make a statement for inclusion in the presentence report if the victim or relative so desires. Any such statement shall be made within 20 days of notification by the probation department.

The presentence report shall specifically include an assessment of the gravity and seriousness of harm inflicted on the victim, including whether or not the defendant knew or reasonably should have known that the victim of the offense was particularly vulnerable or incapable of resistance due to advanced age, disability, ill-health, or extreme youth, or was for any other reason substantially incapable of exercising normal physical or mental power of resistance.

c. If, after the presentence investigation, the court desires additional information concerning an offender convicted of an offense before imposing sentence, it may order any additional psychological or medical testing of the defendant.

d. Disclosure of any presentence investigation report or psychiatric examination report shall be in accordance with law and the Rules of Court, except that information concerning the defendant's financial resources shall be made available upon request to the Victims of Crime Compensation Board or to any officer authorized under the provisions of section 3 of P.L.1979, c.396 (C.2C:46-4) to collect payment on an assessment, restitution or fine and that information concerning the defendant's coverage under any health insurance contract, policy or plan shall be made available, as appropriate to the Commissioner of the Department of Corrections and to the chief administrative officer of a county jail in accordance with the provisions of P.L.1995, c.254 (C.30:7E-1 et al.).

e. The court shall not impose a sentence of imprisonment for an extended term unless the ground therefor has been established at a hearing after the conviction of the defendant and on written notice to him of the ground proposed. The defendant shall have the right to hear and controvert the evidence against him and to offer evidence upon the issue.

f. (Deleted by amendment, P.L.1986, c.85.)

**2C:44-6.1.      Defendant liable for cost of psychological evaluation; rules, regulations**

a. A defendant who is required to submit to a psychological evaluation pursuant to the provisions of N.J.S.2C:44-6 shall be liable for the cost of such evaluation. If the defendant is an enrollee or a covered person under a health insurance contract, policy or plan, the Administrative Office of the Courts shall file a claim with the health insurance contract, policy or plan for a reimbursement of the costs of the psychological evaluation. The claim shall be filed in accordance with the rules and regulations promulgated pursuant to subsection b. of this section. The reimbursement authorized under this section shall be payable to the Administrative Office of the Courts and shall be used exclusively for the purpose of defraying the costs incurred for the psychological evaluation.

b. The Commissioner of the Department of Banking and Insurance, in accordance with the provisions of the "Administrative Procedure Act," P.L.1968, c.410 (C.52:14B-1 et seq.), shall promulgate rules and regulations to effectuate the purposes of this section.

c. In the event that a defendant is not covered under a health insurance contract, policy or plan, or if the defendant's insurance contract, policy or plan does not fully cover the costs of the psychological evaluation, a lien may be filed for any unpaid amounts due and payable on any and all property and income to which the defendant shall have or may acquire an interest. Any lien filed shall be in accordance with the rules and regulations promulgated pursuant to subsection b. of this section.

**2C:44-7.**        **Appellate review of actions of sentencing court**

Any action taken by the court in imposing sentence shall be subject to review by an appellate court. The court shall specifically have the authority to review findings of fact by the sentencing court in support of its findings of aggravating and mitigating circumstances and to modify the defendant's sentence upon his application where such findings are not fairly supported on the record before the trial court.

**2C:44-8.**        **Blank**

# 45

# SUSPENSION OF SENTENCE; PROBATION

**2C:45-1.**     **Conditions of suspension or probation**

a. When the court suspends the imposition of sentence on a person who has been convicted of an offense or sentences him to be placed on probation, it shall attach such reasonable conditions, authorized by this section, as it deems necessary to insure that he will lead a law-abiding life or is likely to assist him to do so. These conditions may be set forth in a set of standardized conditions promulgated by the county probation department and approved by the court.

b. The court, as a condition of its order, may require the defendant:

    (1) To support his dependents and meet his family responsibilities;

    (2) To find and continue in gainful employment;

    (3) To undergo available medical or psychiatric treatment and to enter and remain in a specified institution, when required for that purpose;

    (4) To pursue a prescribed secular course of study or vocational training;

    (5) To attend or reside in a facility established for the instruction, recreation or residence of persons on probation;

    (6) To refrain from frequenting unlawful or disreputable places or consorting with disreputable persons;

    (7) Not to have in his possession any firearm or other dangerous weapon unless granted written permission;

    (8) (Deleted by amendment, P.L.1991, c.329);

    (9) To remain within the jurisdiction of the court and to notify the court or the probation officer of any change in his address or his employment;

    (10) To report as directed to the court or the probation officer, to permit the officer to visit his home, and to answer all reasonable inquiries by the probation officer;

    (11) To pay a fine;

    (12) To satisfy any other conditions reasonably related to the rehabilitation of the defendant and not unduly restrictive of his liberty or incompatible with his freedom of conscience;

    (13) To require the performance of community-related service.

c. The court, as a condition of its order, shall require the defendant to pay any assessments required by section 2 of P.L.1979, c.396 (C.2C:43-3.1) and shall, consistent with the applicable provisions of N.J.S.2C:43-3, N.J.S.2C:43-4 and N.J.S.2C:44-2 or section 1 of P.L. 1983, c.411 (C.2C:43-2.1) require the defendant to make restitution.

d.  In addition to any condition imposed pursuant to subsection b. or c., the court shall order a person placed on probation to pay a fee, not exceeding $25.00 per month for the probationary term, to probation services for use by the State, except as provided in subsection g. of this section. This fee may be waived in cases of indigency upon application by the chief probation officer to the sentencing court.

e.  When the court sentences a person who has been convicted of a crime to be placed on probation, it may require him to serve a term of imprisonment not exceeding 364 days as an additional condition of its order. When the court sentences a person convicted of a disorderly persons offense to be placed on probation, it may require him to serve a term of imprisonment not exceeding 90 days as an additional condition of its order. In imposing a term of imprisonment pursuant to this subsection, the sentencing court shall specifically place on the record the reasons which justify the sentence imposed. The term of imprisonment imposed hereunder shall be treated as part of the sentence, and in the event of a sentence of imprisonment upon the revocation of probation, the term of imprisonment served hereunder shall be credited toward service of such subsequent sentence. A term of imprisonment imposed under this section shall be governed by the "Parole Act of 1979," P.L.1979, c.441 (C.30:4-123.45 et al.).

   Whenever a person is serving a term of parole as a result of a sentence of incarceration imposed as a condition of probation, supervision over that person shall be maintained pursuant to the provisions of the law governing parole. Upon termination of the period of parole supervision provided by law, the county probation department shall assume responsibility for supervision of the person under sentence of probation. Nothing contained in this section shall prevent the sentencing court from at any time proceeding under the provisions of this chapter against any person for a violation of probation.

f.  The defendant shall be given a copy of the terms of his probation or suspension of sentence and any requirements imposed pursuant to this section, stated with sufficient specificity to enable him to guide himself accordingly. The defendant shall acknowledge, in writing, his receipt of these documents and his consent to their terms.

g.  Of the moneys collected under the provisions of subsection d. of this section, $15.00 of each monthly fee collected before January 1, 1995 shall be deposited in the temporary reserve fund created by section 25 of P.L.1993, c.275, and $10.00 of each shall be deposited into a "Community Service Supervision Fund" which shall be established by each county. The moneys in the "Community Service Supervision Fund" shall be expended only in accordance with the provisions of State law as shall be enacted to provide for expenditures from this fund for the purpose of supervising and monitoring probationers performing community service to ensure, by whatever means necessary and appropriate, that probationers are performing the community service ordered by the court and that the performance is in the manner and under the terms ordered by the court.

**2C:45-2.**          **Period of suspension or probation; modification of conditions; discharge of defendant**

a.  When the court has suspended imposition of sentence or has sentenced a defendant to be placed on probation, the period of the suspension shall be fixed by the court at not to exceed the maximum term which could have been imposed or more than 5 years whichever is lesser. The period of probation shall be fixed by the court at not less than 1 year nor more than 5 years. The court, on application of a probation officer or of the defendant, or on its own motion, may discharge the defendant at any time.

b.  During the period of the suspension or probation, the court, on application of a probation officer or of the defendant, or on its own motion, may (1) modify the requirements imposed on the defendants; or (2) add further requirements authorized by N.J.S.2C:45-1. The court shall eliminate any requirement that imposes an unreasonable burden on the defendant.

c. Upon the termination of the period of suspension or probation or the earlier discharge of the defendant, the defendant shall be relieved of any obligations imposed by the order of the court and shall have satisfied his sentence for the offense unless the defendant has failed:

(1) to fulfill conditions imposed pursuant to paragraph b. (11) of N.J.S.2C:45-1, in which event the court may order that the probationary period be extended for an additional period not to exceed that authorized by subsection a. of this section; or

(2) to fulfill the conditions imposed pursuant to subsection c. of N.J.S.2C:45-1, in which event the court shall order that the probationary period be extended for an additional period not to exceed that authorized by subsection a. of this section.

The extension may be entered by the court without the defendant's personal appearance if the defendant agrees to the extension.

**2C:45-3.**     **Summons or arrest of defendant under suspended sentence or on probation; commitment without bail; revocation and resentence**

a. At any time before the discharge of the defendant or the termination of the period of suspension or probation:

(1) The court may summon the defendant to appear before it or may issue a warrant for his arrest;

(2) A probation officer or peace officer, upon request of the chief probation officer or otherwise having probable cause to believe that the defendant has failed to comply with a requirement imposed as a condition of the order or that he has committed another offense, may arrest him without a warrant;

(3) The court, if there is probable cause to believe that the defendant has committed another offense or if he has been held to answer therefor, may commit him without bail, pending a determination of the charge by the court having jurisdiction thereof;

(4) The court, if satisfied that the defendant has inexcusably failed to comply with a substantial requirement imposed as a condition of the order or if he has been convicted of another offense, may revoke the suspension or probation and sentence or resentence the defendant, as provided in this section. No revocation of suspension or probation shall be based on failure to pay a fine or make restitution, unless the failure was willful.

b. When the court revokes a suspension or probation, it may impose on the defendant any sentence that might have been imposed originally for the offense of which he was convicted.

c. The commencement of a probation revocation proceeding shall toll the probationary period until termination of such proceedings. In the event that the court does not find a violation of probation, this subsection shall not operate to toll the probationary period.

**2C:45-4.**     **Notice and hearing on revocation or modification of conditions of suspension or probation**

The court shall not revoke a suspension of sentence or probation or delete, add or modify conditions of probation except after a hearing upon written notice to the defendant of the grounds on which such action is proposed. The defendant shall have the right to hear and controvert the evidence against him, to offer evidence in his defense, and to be represented by counsel.

# 46

# FINES AND RESTITUTIONS

**2C:46-1.**   **Time and method of payment; disposition of funds**

a.  When a defendant is sentenced to pay an assessment pursuant to section 2 of P.L.1979, c.396 (C.2C:43-3.1), a fine, a penalty imposed pursuant to N.J.S.2C:35-15, a forensic laboratory fee imposed pursuant to N.J.S.2C:35-20, a penalty imposed pursuant to section 1 of P.L.1999, c.295 (C.2C:43-3.5), a penalty imposed pursuant to section 11 of P.L.2001, c.81 (C.2C:43-3.6), or to make restitution, the court may grant permission for the payment to be made within a specified period of time or in specified installments. If no such permission is embodied in the sentence, the assessment, fine, penalty, fee or restitution shall be payable forthwith, and the court shall file a copy of the judgment of conviction with the Clerk of the Superior Court who shall enter the following information upon the record of docketed judgments:

   (1)  the name of the convicted person as judgment debtor;

   (2)  the amount of the assessment imposed pursuant to section 2 of P.L.1979, c.396 (C.2C:43-3.1) and the Violent Crimes Compensation Board as a judgment creditor in that amount;

   (3)  the amount of any restitution ordered and the name of any persons entitled to receive payment as judgment creditors in the amount and according to the priority set by the court;

   (4)  the amount of any fine and the governmental entity entitled to receive payment pursuant to N.J.S.2C:46-4;

   (5)  the amount of the mandatory Drug Enforcement and Demand Reduction penalty imposed;

   (6)  the amount of the forensic laboratory fee imposed;

   (7)  the amount of the penalty imposed pursuant to section 1 of P.L.1999, c.295 (C.2C:43-3.5);

   (8)  the date of the order; and

   (9)  the amount of the penalty imposed pursuant to section 11 of P.L.2001, c.81 (C.2C:43-3.6).

b.  (1)  When a defendant sentenced to pay an assessment imposed pursuant to section 2 of P.L.1979, c.396 (C.2C:43-3.1), a fine, a penalty imposed pursuant to N.J.S.2C:35-15, a forensic laboratory fee imposed pursuant to N.J.S.2C:35-20, a penalty imposed pursuant to section 1 of P.L.1999, c.295 (C.2C:43-3.5), a penalty imposed pursuant to section 11 of P.L.2001, c.81 (C.2C:43-3.6), or to make restitution is also sentenced to probation, the court shall make continuing payment of installments on the assessment and restitution a condition of probation, and may make continuing payment of

**501**

installments on the fine, the mandatory Drug Enforcement and Demand Reduction penalty, the mandatory penalty pursuant to section 1 of P.L.1999, c.295 (C.2C:43-3.5), the penalty pursuant to section 11 of P.L.2001, c.81 (C.2C:43-3.6), or the forensic laboratory fee a condition of probation.

(2) When a defendant sentenced to pay an assessment imposed pursuant to section 2 of P.L.1979, c.396 (C.2C:43-3.1), a fine, a penalty imposed pursuant to N.J.S.2C:35-15, a forensic laboratory fee imposed pursuant to N.J.S.2C:35-20, a penalty imposed pursuant to section 1 of P.L.1999, c.295 (C.2C:43-3.5), a penalty imposed pursuant to section 11 of P.L.2001, c.81 (C.2C:43-3.6), or to make restitution is also sentenced to a custodial term in a State correctional facility, the court may require the defendant to pay installments on the assessment, penalty, fee, fine and restitution.

c. The defendant shall pay an assessment imposed pursuant to section 2 of P.L.1979, c.396 (C.2C:43-3.1), restitution, penalty, fee or fine or any installment thereof to the officer entitled by law to collect the payment. In the event of default in payment, such agency shall take appropriate action for its collection.

d. (1) When, in connection with a sentence of probation, a defendant is sentenced to pay an assessment imposed pursuant to section 2 of P.L.1979, c.396 (C.2C:43-3.1), a fine, a penalty imposed pursuant to N.J.S.2C:35-15, a forensic laboratory fee imposed pursuant to N.J.S.2C:35-20, a penalty imposed pursuant to section 1 of P.L.1999, c.295 (C.2C:43-3.5), a penalty imposed pursuant to section 11 of P.L.2001, c.81 (C.2C:43-3.6), or to make restitution, the defendant, in addition, shall be sentenced to pay a transaction fee on each occasion that the defendant makes a payment or an installment payment, until the defendant has paid the full amount he is sentenced to pay. All other individuals making payments on court ordered financial obligations through the probation division shall also pay a transaction fee on each payment or installment payment. The Administrative Office of the Courts shall promulgate a transaction fee schedule for use in connection with installment payments made pursuant to this paragraph; provided, however, the transaction fee on an installment payment shall not exceed $2.00.

(2) When, in connection with a custodial sentence in a State correctional institution, a defendant is sentenced to pay an assessment imposed pursuant to section 2 of P.L.1979, c.396 (C.2C:43-3.1), a fine, a penalty imposed pursuant to N.J.S.2C:35-15, a forensic laboratory fee imposed pursuant to N.J.S.2C:35-20, a penalty imposed pursuant to section 1 of P.L.1999, c.295 (C.2C:43-3.5), a penalty imposed pursuant to section 11 of P.L.2001, c.81 (C.2C:43-3.6), or to make restitution, the defendant, in addition, shall be sentenced to pay a transaction fee on each occasion that the defendant makes a payment or an installment payment until the defendant has paid the full amount he is sentenced to pay. The Department of Corrections shall promulgate a transaction fee schedule for use in connection with installment payments made pursuant to this paragraph; provided, however, the transaction fee on an installment payment shall not exceed $1.00.

## 2C:46-1.1.     Computerized collection fund

a. Transaction fees collected pursuant to paragraph (1) of subsection d. of N.J.S.2C:46-1 shall be deposited in the Courts Computerized Collection Fund, which is hereby established as a separate fund in the General Fund, to be administered by the Administrative Office of the Courts and dedicated to the development, establishment, operation and maintenance of a computerized system for use by the Administrative Office of the Courts in developing, implementing, operating and improving the judiciary's component of the uniform system for tracking and collecting assessments, restitutions, penalties, fees and fines imposed in accordance with the provisions of Title 2C of the New Jersey Statutes, as required by section 19 of P.L.1991, c.329 (C.52:4B-8.1).

b. Transaction fees collected pursuant to paragraph (2) of subsection d. of N.J.S.2C:46-1 shall be deposited in the Corrections Computerized Collection Fund, which is hereby established as a separate fund in the General Fund, to be administered by the Department of Corrections and dedicated to the development, establishment, operation and maintenance of a computerized system for use by the Department of Corrections in developing, implementing, operating and improving the Department's component of the uniform system for tracking and collecting assessments, restitutions, penalties, fees and fines imposed in accordance with the provisions of Title 2C of the New Jersey Statutes, as required by section 19 of P.L.1991, c.329 (C.52:4B-8.1).

## 2C:46-1.2. Rules, regulations

a. The Supreme Court of New Jersey may issue Rules of Court to effectuate the purposes of this act.

b. The Commissioner of the Department of Corrections shall promulgate rules and regulations, pursuant to the "Administrative Procedures Act," P.L.1968, c.410 (C.52:14B-1 et seq.), necessary to effectuate the purposes of this act.

## 2C:46-2. Consequences of nonpayment; summary collection

a. When a defendant sentenced to pay an assessment imposed pursuant to section 2 of P.L.1979, c.396 (C.2C:43-3.1), a penalty imposed pursuant to section 11 of P.L.2001, c.81 (C.2C:43-3.6), monthly probation fee, fine, a penalty imposed pursuant to section 1 of P.L.1999, c.295 (C.2C:43-3.5), other court imposed financial penalties or to make restitution defaults in the payment thereof or of any installment, upon the motion of the person authorized by law to collect the payment, the motion of the prosecutor, the motion of the victim entitled to payment of restitution, the motion of the Violent Crimes Compensation Board, the motion of the State or county Office of Victim and Witness Advocacy or upon its own motion, the court shall recall him, or issue a summons or a warrant of arrest for his appearance. The court shall afford the person notice and an opportunity to be heard on the issue of default. Failure to make any payment when due shall be considered a default. The standard of proof shall be by a preponderance of the evidence, and the burden of establishing good cause for a default shall be on the person who has defaulted.

    (1) If the court finds that the person has defaulted without good cause, the court shall:

        (a) Order the suspension of the driver's license or the nonresident reciprocity driving privilege of the person; and

        (b) Prohibit the person from obtaining a driver's license or exercising reciprocity driving privileges until the person has made all past due payments; and

        (c) Notify the Director of the Division of Motor Vehicles of the action taken; and

        (d) Take such other actions as may be authorized by law.

    (2) If the court finds that the person defaulted on payment of a court imposed financial obligation without good cause and finds that the default was willful, the court may, in addition to the action required by paragraph (1) of this subsection a., impose a term of imprisonment or participation in a labor assistance program or enforced community service to achieve the objective of the court imposed financial obligation. These options shall not reduce the amount owed by the person in default. The term of imprisonment or enforced community service or participation in a labor assistance

program in such case shall be specified in the order of commitment. It need not be equated with any particular dollar amount but, in the case of a fine it shall not exceed one day for each $20.00 of the fine nor 40 days if the fine was imposed upon conviction of a disorderly persons offense nor 25 days for a petty disorderly persons offense nor one year in any other case, whichever is the shorter period. In no case shall the total period of imprisonment in the case of a disorderly persons offense for both the sentence of imprisonment and for failure to pay a fine exceed six months.

(3) Except where incarceration is ordered pursuant to paragraph (2) of this subsection a., if the court finds that the person has defaulted the court shall take appropriate action to modify or establish a reasonable schedule for payment, and, in the case of a fine, if the court finds that the circumstances that warranted the fine have changed or that it would be unjust to require payment, the court may revoke or suspend the fine or the unpaid portion of the fine.

(4) When failure to pay an assessment imposed pursuant to section 2 of P.L.1979, c.396 (C.2C:43-3.1), monthly probation fee, restitution, a penalty imposed pursuant to section 1 of P.L.1999, c.295 (C.2C:43-3.5), a penalty imposed pursuant to section 11 of P.L.2001, c.81 (C.2C:43-3.6), or other financial penalties or to perform enforced community service or to participate in a labor assistance program is determined to be willful, the failure to do so shall be considered to be contumacious.

(5) When a fine, assessment imposed pursuant to section 2 of P.L.1979, c.396 (C.2C:43-3.1), other financial penalty or restitution is imposed on a corporation, it is the duty of the person or persons authorized to make disbursements from the assets of the corporation or association to pay it from such assets and their failure so to do may be held to be contumacious.

b. Upon any default in the payment of a fine, assessment imposed pursuant to section 2 of P.L.1979, c.396 (C.2C:43-3.1), monthly probation fee, a penalty imposed pursuant to section 1 of P.L.1999, c.295 (C.2C:43-3.5), a penalty imposed pursuant to section 11 of P.L.2001, c.81 (C.2C:43-3.6), other financial penalties, restitution, or any installment thereof, execution may be levied and such other measures may be taken for collection of it or the unpaid balance thereof as are authorized for the collection of an unpaid civil judgment entered against the defendant in an action on a debt.

c. Upon any default in the payment of restitution or any installment thereof, the victim entitled to the payment may institute summary collection proceedings authorized by subsection b. of this section.

d. Upon any default in the payment of an assessment imposed pursuant to section 2 of P.L.1979, c.396 (C.2C:43-3.1) or any installment thereof, the Violent Crimes Compensation Board or the party responsible for collection may institute summary collection proceedings authorized by subsection b. of this section.

e. When a defendant sentenced to make restitution to a public entity other than the Violent Crimes Compensation Board, defaults in the payment thereof or any installment, the court may, in lieu of other modification of the sentence, order the defendant to perform work in a labor assistance program or enforced community service program.

f. If a defendant ordered to participate in a labor assistance program or enforced community service program fails to report for work or to perform the assigned work, the comprehensive enforcement hearing officer may revoke the work order and impose any sentence permitted as a consequence of the original conviction.

g. If a defendant ordered to participate in a labor assistance program or an enforced community service program pays all outstanding assessments, the comprehensive enforcement hearing officer may review the work order, and modify the same to reflect the objective of the sentence.

h. As used in this section:

    (1) "Comprehensive enforcement program" means the program established pursuant to the "Comprehensive Enforcement Program Fund Act," P.L.1995, c.9 (C.2B:19-1 et seq.).

    (2) The terms "labor assistance program" and "enforced community service" have the same meaning as those terms are defined in section 5 of the "Comprehensive Enforcement Program Fund Act," P.L.1995, c.9 (C.2B:19-5).

    (3) "Public entity" means the State, any county, municipality, district, public authority, public agency and any other political subdivision or public body in the State.

## 2C:46-3.  Revocation of fine

A defendant who has been sentenced to pay a fine may at any time petition the court which sentenced him for a revocation of the fine or of any unpaid portion thereof. If it appears to the satisfaction of the court that the circumstances which warranted the imposition of the fine have changed, or that it would otherwise be unjust to require payment, the court may revoke the fine or the unpaid portion thereof in whole or in part.

## 2C:46-4.  Fines, assessments, penalties, restitution; collection; disposition

a. All fines, assessments imposed pursuant to section 2 of P.L.1979, c.396 (C.2C:43-3.1), all penalties imposed pursuant to section 1 of P.L.1999, c.295 (C.2C:43-3.5), all penalties imposed pursuant to section 11 of P.L.2001, c.81 (C.2C:43-3.6), and restitution shall be collected as follows:

    (1) All fines, assessments imposed pursuant to section 2 of P.L.1979, c.396 (C.2C:43-3.1), all penalties imposed pursuant to section 1 of P.L.1999, c.295 (C.2C:43-3.5), all penalties imposed pursuant to section 11 of P.L.2001, c.81 (C.2C:43-3.6), and restitution imposed by the Superior Court or otherwise imposed at the county level, shall be collected by the county probation division except when such fine, assessment or restitution is imposed in conjunction with a custodial sentence to a State correctional facility or in conjunction with a term of incarceration imposed pursuant to section 25 of P.L.1982, c.77 (C.2A:4A-44) in which event such fine, assessment or restitution shall be collected by the Department of Corrections or the Juvenile Justice Commission established pursuant to section 2 of P.L.1995, c.284 (C.52:17B-170). An adult prisoner of a State correctional institution or a juvenile serving a term of incarceration imposed pursuant to section 25 of P.L.1982, c.77 (C.2A:4A-44) who has not paid an assessment imposed pursuant to section 2 of P.L.1979, c.396 (C.2C:43-3.1), a penalty imposed pursuant to section 1 of P.L.1999, c.295 (C.2C:43-3.5) or restitution shall have the assessment, fine or restitution deducted from any income the inmate receives as a result of labor performed at the institution or on any type of work release program or, pursuant to regulations promulgated by the Commissioner of the Department of Corrections or the Juvenile Justice Commission, from any personal account established in the institution for the benefit of the inmate.

    (2) All fines, assessments imposed pursuant to section 2 of P.L.1979, c.396 (C.2C:43-3.1), any penalty imposed pursuant to section 1 of P.L.1999, c.295 (C.2C:43-3.5) and restitution imposed by a municipal court shall be collected by the municipal court administrator except if such fine, assessments imposed pursuant to section 2 of P.L.1979, c.396 (C.2C:43-3.1), or restitution is ordered as a condition of probation in which event it shall be collected by the county probation division.

b. Except as provided in subsection c. with respect to fines imposed on appeals following convictions in municipal courts and except as provided in subsection i. with respect to restitution imposed under the provisions of P.L.1997, c.253 (C.2C:43-3.4 et al.), all fines imposed by the Superior Court or otherwise imposed at the county level, shall be paid over by the officer entitled to collect same to:

   (1) The county treasurer with respect to fines imposed on defendants who are sentenced to and serve a custodial term, including a term as a condition of probation, in the county jail, workhouse or penitentiary except where such county sentence is served concurrently with a sentence to a State institution; or

   (2) The State Treasurer with respect to all other fines.

c. All fines imposed by municipal courts, except a central municipal court established pursuant to N.J.S.2B:12-1 on defendants convicted of crimes, disorderly persons offenses and petty disorderly persons offenses, and all fines imposed following conviction on appeal therefrom, and all forfeitures of bail shall be paid over by the officer entitled to collect same to the treasury of the municipality wherein the municipal court is located.

   In the case of an intermunicipal court, fines shall be paid into the municipal treasury of the municipality in which the offense was committed, and costs, fees, and forfeitures of bail shall be apportioned among the several municipalities to which the court's jurisdiction extends according to the ratios of the municipalities' contributions to the total expense of maintaining the court.

   In the case of a central municipal court, established by a county pursuant to N.J.S.2B:12-1, all costs, fines, fees and forfeitures of bail shall be paid into the county treasury of the county where the central municipal court is located.

d. All assessments imposed pursuant to section 2 of P.L.1979, c.396 (C.2C:43-3.1) shall be forwarded and deposited as provided in that section.

e. All mandatory Drug Enforcement and Demand Reduction penalties imposed pursuant to N.J.S.2C:35-15 shall be forwarded and deposited as provided for in that section.

f. All forensic laboratory fees assessed pursuant to N.J.S.2C:35-20 shall be forwarded and deposited as provided for in that section.

g. All restitution ordered to be paid to the Victims of Crime Compensation Board pursuant to N.J.S.2C:44-2 shall be forwarded to the board for deposit in the Victims of Crime Compensation Board Account.

h. All assessments imposed pursuant to section 11 of P.L.1993, c.220 (C.2C:43-3.2) shall be forwarded and deposited as provided in that section.

i. All restitution imposed on defendants under the provisions of P.L.1997, c.253 (C.2C:43-3.4 et al.) for costs incurred by a law enforcement entity in extraditing the defendant from another jurisdiction shall be paid over by the officer entitled to collect same to the law enforcement entities which participated in the extradition of the defendant.

j. All penalties imposed pursuant to section 1 of P.L.1999, c.295 (C.2C:43-3.5) shall be forwarded and deposited as provided in that section.

k. All penalties imposed pursuant to section 11 of P.L.2001, c.81 (C.2C:43-3.6) shall be forwarded and deposited as provided in that section.

**2C:46-4.1.**    **Application of moneys collected; priority**

Moneys that are collected in satisfaction of any assessment imposed pursuant to section 2 of P.L.1979, c.396 (C.2C:43-3.1), or in satisfaction of restitution or fines imposed in accordance with the provisions of Title 2C of the New Jersey Statutes or with the provisions of section 24 of P.L.1982, c.77 (C.2A:4A-43), shall be applied in the following order:

a. first, in satisfaction of all assessments imposed pursuant to section 2 of P.L.1979, c.396 (C.2C:43-3.1);

b. second, except as provided in subsection f. of this section, in satisfaction of any restitution ordered;

c. third, in satisfaction of all assessments imposed pursuant to section 11 of P.L.1993, c.220 (C.2C:43-3.2);

d. fourth, in satisfaction of any forensic laboratory fee assessed pursuant to N.J.S.2C:35-20;

e. fifth, in satisfaction of any mandatory Drug Enforcement and Demand Reduction penalty assessed pursuant to N.J.S.2C:35-15;

f. sixth, in satisfaction of any anti-drug profiteering penalty imposed pursuant to section 2 of P.L.1997, c.187 (N.J.S.2C:35A-1 et seq.);

g. seventh, in satisfaction of any anti-money laundering profiteering penalty imposed pursuant to section 9 of P.L.1999, c.25;

h. eighth, in satisfaction of restitution for any extradition costs imposed pursuant to section 4 of P.L.1997, c.253 (C.2C:43-3.4);

i. ninth, in satisfaction of any penalty imposed pursuant to section 1 of P.L.1999, c.295 (C.2C:43-3.5);

j. tenth, in satisfaction of any penalty imposed pursuant to section 11 of P.L.2001, c.81 (C.2C:43-3.6); and

k. eleventh, in satisfaction of any fine.

**2C:46-5.**     **Inapplicability of chapter to certain fines and restitutions**

Except as expressly provided, this chapter shall not affect fines and restitutions imposed under Title 39 of the Revised Statutes or in proceedings in the Superior Court, Chancery Division, Family Part, which shall remain as heretofore.

# 47

# ADULT DIAGNOSTIC AND TREATMENT CENTER

**2C:47-1.**  **Referral to adult diagnostic and treatment center; commitment; examination**

Whenever a person is convicted of the offense of aggravated sexual assault, sexual assault, aggravated criminal sexual contact, kidnapping pursuant to paragraph (2) of subsection c. of N.J.S.2C:13-1, endangering the welfare of a child by engaging in sexual conduct which would impair or debauch the morals of the child pursuant to subsection a. of N.J.S.2C:24-4, endangering the welfare of a child pursuant to paragraph (4) of subsection b. of N.J.S.2C:24-4, or an attempt to commit any such crime, the judge shall order the Department of Corrections to complete a psychological examination of the offender, except the judge shall not require a psychological examination if the offender is to be sentenced to a term of life imprisonment without eligibility for parole. The examination shall include a determination of whether the offender's conduct was characterized by a pattern of repetitive, compulsive behavior and, if it was, a further determination of the offender's amenability to sex offender treatment and willingness to participate in such treatment. The court's order shall contain a determination of the offender's legal settlement in accordance with subdivision D of article 3 of chapter 4 of Title 30 of the Revised Statutes.

**2C:47-2.**  **Report on examination**

The Department of Corrections shall conduct the psychological examination required pursuant to N.J.S.2C:47-1 within 30 days after it receives the Presentence Report. Upon completion of the psychological examination, the Department of Corrections shall send to the court a written report of the results of the examination, including a determination of whether the offender's conduct was characterized by a pattern of repetitive, compulsive behavior and, if it was, a further determination of the offender's amenability to sex offender treatment and willingness to participate in such treatment.

**2C:47-3.**  **Disposition**

    a. If the report of the examination reveals that the offender's conduct was characterized by a pattern of repetitive, compulsive behavior and further reveals that the offender is amenable to sex offender treatment and is willing to participate in such treatment, the court shall determine whether the offender's conduct was so characterized and whether the offender is amenable to sex offender treatment and is willing to participate in such treatment and shall record its findings on the judgment of conviction.

    b. If the court finds that the offender's conduct was characterized by a pattern of repetitive, compulsive behavior and that the offender is amenable to sex offender treatment and is willing to participate in such treatment, the court shall, upon the recommendation of the Department of Corrections, sentence the offender to a term of incarceration to be served in the custody of the commissioner at the Adult Diagnostic and Treatment Center for sex offender treatment as provided in subsection h. of this section, or place the offender on probation with the requirement, as a condition of probation, that he receive outpatient psychological or psychiatric treatment as prescribed.

c. A sentence of incarceration or probation imposed pursuant to subsection b. or f. of this section shall be set in accordance with chapters 43, 44 and 45 of this Title.

d. The court shall impose sentence in accordance with chapters 43, 44 and 45 of this Title and not as provided in subsection b. of this section if it shall appear from the report of the examination made of the offender pursuant to section N.J.S.2C:47-1 that the offender's conduct was not characterized by a pattern of repetitive, compulsive behavior or that the offender is not amenable to sex offender treatment. Notwithstanding the provisions of R.S.30:4-140 or R.S.30:4-92 or any other law, a sentence imposed pursuant to this subsection on an offender who is not amenable to sex offender treatment shall not be reduced by commutation time for good behavior or credits for diligent application to work and other institutional assignments.

e. (Deleted by amendment, P.L.1998, c.72).

f. If the court finds that the offender's conduct was characterized by a pattern of repetitive, compulsive behavior and that the offender is amenable to sex offender treatment, but that the offender is not willing to participate in such treatment, the court shall sentence the offender to a term of incarceration to be served in a facility designated by the commissioner pursuant to section 2 of P.L.1969, c.22 (C.30:4-91.2). The offender shall become primarily eligible for parole in accordance with the provisions of N.J.S.2C:47-5; provided, however, no offender shall become primarily eligible for parole prior to the expiration of any judicial or statutory mandatory minimum term. An offender who meets the criteria of this subsection may, on a biennial basis, request to be transferred to the Adult Diagnostic and Treatment Center. Within 90 days after receiving a request for a transfer, the Department of Corrections shall conduct a psychological examination. If, upon the completion of a psychological examination, the Department of Corrections determines that the offender is amenable to sex offender treatment and is willing to participate in such treatment, the commissioner may order the offender to be transferred to the Adult Diagnostic and Treatment Center.

g. Notwithstanding the provisions of R.S.30:4-140 or R.S.30:4-92 or any other law, a sentence imposed pursuant to subsection f. of this section shall not be reduced by commutation time for good behavior or credits for diligent application to work and other institutional assignments for any year or fractional part of a year that the offender is confined in a facility other than the Adult Diagnostic and Treatment Center; provided, however, if the offender is at any time transferred to the Adult Diagnostic and Treatment Center pursuant to subsection f. of this section, the sentence imposed on the offender shall be reduced by commutation time for good behavior and credits for diligent application to work and other institutional assignments for any year or fractional part of a year that the offender is incarcerated at the Adult Diagnostic and Treatment Center following the date of such transfer.

h. An offender sentenced to a term of incarceration pursuant to subsection b. of this section shall be confined as follows:

   (1) If the court imposes a sentence of seven years or less, the Department of Corrections shall confine the offender to the Adult Diagnostic and Treatment Center as soon as practicable after the date of sentence.

   (2) If the court imposes a sentence of more than seven years, the Department of Corrections shall confine the offender in a facility designated by the commissioner

pursuant to section 2 of P.L.1969, c.22 (C.30:4-91.2). At least 30 days prior to the date which precedes the expiration date of the offender's sentence by five years, including any reductions for commutation time for good behavior and credits for diligent application to work and other institutional assignments, the Department of Corrections shall complete a psychological examination of the offender to determine the offender's amenability to sex offender treatment and willingness to participate in such treatment; provided, however, no such examination shall be required if less than two years has elapsed since the Department of Corrections completed a psychological examination pursuant to N.J.S.2C:47-1. If the report of the examination reveals that the offender is amenable to sex offender treatment and is willing to participate in such treatment, the offender shall be transferred to the Adult Diagnostic and Treatment Center as soon as practicable. If the report of the examination reveals that the offender is not amenable to sex offender treatment, the offender shall not be transferred to the Adult Diagnostic and Treatment Center. If the report of the examination reveals that the offender is amenable to sex offender treatment but is not willing to participate in such treatment, the offender shall not be transferred to the Adult Diagnostic and Treatment Center. An offender may, on a biennial basis, request to be transferred to the Adult Diagnostic and Treatment Center. Within 90 days after receiving a request for a transfer, the Department of Corrections shall conduct a psychological examination. If, upon the completion of a psychological examination, the Department of Corrections determines that the offender is amenable to sex offender treatment and is willing to participate in such treatment, the commissioner shall order the offender to be transferred to the Adult Diagnostic and Treatment Center as soon as practicable.

(3) If a sentence is imposed pursuant to section 2 of P.L.1997, c.117 (C.2C:43-7.2) or if any other judicial or statutory mandatory minimum term of more than seven years is imposed, the offender shall be confined in a facility designated by the commissioner pursuant to section 2 of P.L.1969, c.22 (C.30:4-91.2). At least 30 days prior to the date which precedes the expiration date of the mandatory minimum term by five years, the Department of Corrections shall complete a psychological examination of the offender to determine the offender's amenability to sex offender treatment and willingness to participate in such treatment; provided, however, no such examination shall be required if less than two years has elapsed since the Department of Corrections completed a psychological examination pursuant to N.J.S.2C:47-1. If the report of the examination reveals that the offender is amenable to sex offender treatment and is willing to participate in such treatment, the offender shall be transferred to the Adult Diagnostic and Treatment Center as soon as practicable. If the report of the examination reveals that the offender is not amenable to sex offender treatment, the offender shall not be transferred to the Adult Diagnostic and Treatment Center. If the report of the examination reveals that the offender is amenable to sex offender treatment, but is not willing to participate in such treatment, the offender shall not be transferred to the Adult Diagnostic and Treatment Center. An offender may, on a biennial basis, request to be transferred to the Adult Diagnostic and Treatment Center. Within 90 days after receiving a request for a transfer, the Department of Corrections shall conduct a psychological examination. If upon completion of a psychological examination the Department of Corrections determines that the offender is amenable to sex offender treatment and is willing to participate in such treatment, the commissioner shall order the offender to be transferred to the Adult Diagnostic and Treatment Center as soon as practicable.

i. Notwithstanding the provisions of R.S. 30:4-140 or R.S. 30:4-92 or any other law, a sentence imposed pursuant to subsection b. of this section shall not be reduced by commutation time for good behavior or credits for diligent application to work and other institutional assignments for any year or fractional part of a year from the date the Department of Corrections determines, as a result of a psychological evaluation conducted pursuant to paragraph (2) or (3) of subsection h. of this section, that the offender is not amenable to sex offender treatment or not willing to participate in such treatment; provided, however, if the offender is subsequently determined by the Department of Corrections to be amenable to sex offender treatment and willing to participate in such treatment and is transferred to the Adult Diagnostic and Treatment Center, the sentence imposed on the offender shall be reduced by commutation time for good behavior and credits for diligent application to work and other institutional assignments for any year or fractional part of a year that the offender is incarcerated at the Adult Diagnostic and Treatment Center following the date of such transfer.

j. An offender who is sentenced to a term of life imprisonment without eligibility for parole shall not be confined in the Adult Diagnostic and Treatment Center but shall be confined in a facility designated by the commissioner pursuant to section 2 of P.L. 1969, c.22 (C.30:4-91.2).

k. The commissioner shall be required to provide for the treatment of a sex offender sentenced pursuant to N.J.S.2C:47-1 et seq. only when the offender is incarcerated in the Adult Diagnostic and Treatment Center. This requirement shall not apply when the offender is incarcerated in another facility.

## 2C:47-4. Repealed

## 2C:47-4.1. Transfer out of Adult Diagnostic and Treatment Center

a. The commissioner shall order the transfer out of the Adult Diagnostic and Treatment Center of any offender serving a life sentence without eligibility for parole and any offender not participating in or cooperating with the sex offender treatment provided in the Adult Diagnostic and Treatment Center and any offender who is determined by the Department of Corrections to be no longer amenable to sex offender treatment.

b. Any offender transferred out of the Adult Diagnostic and Treatment Center for failure to participate in or cooperate with the sex offender treatment provided there or because of a determination by the Department of Corrections that the offender is no longer amenable to sex offender treatment may, on a biennial basis, request to be transferred back to the Adult Diagnostic and Treatment Center. Within 90 days after receiving a request for a transfer, the Department of Corrections shall conduct a psychological examination. If, upon completion of a psychological examination, the Department of Corrections determines that the offender is amenable to sex offender treatment and is willing to participate in and cooperate with such treatment, the commissioner shall order the offender to be transferred back to the Adult Diagnostic and Treatment Center.

c. Notwithstanding the provisions of R.S.30:4-140 or R.S.30:4-92 or any other law, a sentence imposed on an offender transferred pursuant to subsection a. of this section shall not be reduced by commutation time for good behavior or credits for diligent application to work and other institutional assignments for any year or fractional part of a year following the date of the transfer; provided, however, if the offender is at any time thereafter transferred back to the Adult Diagnostic and Treatment Center pursuant to subsection b. of this section, the sentence imposed on such offender shall be reduced by commutation time for good behavior and credits for diligent application to work and other institutional assignments for any year or fractional part of a year that such offender is incarcerated at the Adult Diagnostic and Treatment Center following the date of such transfer.

**2C:47-4.2.**      **Confinement of female offenders**

An offender sentenced in accordance with the provisions of this chapter who is female shall be confined in a facility designated by the commissioner pursuant to section 2 of P.L.1969, c.22 (C.30:4-91.2), but otherwise shall be subject to the same statutes and rules and regulations as an offender sentenced in accordance with the provisions of this chapter who is male. All statutory references to the Adult Diagnostic and Treatment Center shall be deemed, when applied to a female sentenced in accordance with the provisions of this chapter, to refer to the sex offender treatment program at the facility designated by the commissioner.

**2C:47-5.**      **Parole**

a. Any offender committed to confinement under the terms of this chapter shall become eligible for parole consideration upon referral to the State Parole Board of the offender's case by a special classification review board appointed by the commissioner. The referral shall be based on the determination by the special classification review board that the offender has achieved a satisfactory level of progress in sex offender treatment. The offender shall be released on parole unless the State Parole Board determines that the information supplied in the report filed pursuant to section 10 of P.L.1979, c.441 (C. 30:4-123.54) or developed or produced at a hearing held pursuant to section 11 of P.L.1979, c.441 (C.30:4-123.55) indicates by a preponderance of the evidence that the offender has failed to cooperate in his or her own rehabilitation or that there is a reasonable expectation that the offender will violate conditions of parole imposed pursuant to section 15 of P.L.1979, c.441 (C.30:4-123.59) if released on parole at that time.

b. (Deleted by amendment, P.L.1998, c.73.)

c. Any offender paroled pursuant to this section shall be subject to the provisions of Title 30 of the Revised Statutes governing parole and the regulations promulgated pursuant thereto.

d. When an offender confined under the terms of this chapter has not been paroled in accordance with subsection a. of this section and is scheduled for release, not less than 90 days prior to the date of the offender's scheduled release the Chief Executive Officer shall:

(1) Notify the Attorney General and the prosecutor of the county from which the offender was committed of the scheduled release;

(2) Provide the Attorney General and the county prosecutor with the officer's opinion as to whether the offender may be "in need of involuntary commitment" within the meaning of section 2 of P.L. 1987, c. 116 (C. 30:4-27.2) and as to whether the person may be a "sexually violent predator" within the meaning of section 3 of P.L.1998, c.71 (C.30:4-27.26); and

(3) Without regard to classification as confidential pursuant to regulations of the State Parole Board or the Department of Corrections, provide the Attorney General and county prosecutor with all reports, records and assessments relevant to determining whether the offender is "in need of involuntary commitment" and whether the person is a "sexually violent predator." All information received shall be deemed confidential and shall be disclosed only as provided in section 4 of P.L.1994, c.134 (C.30:4-82.4).

e. Upon receipt of the notice, advice and information required by subsection d. of this section, the Attorney General or county prosecutor shall proceed as provided in section 4 of P.L.1994,c.134 (C.30:4-82.4) or section 5 of P.L.1998, c.71 (C.30:4-27.28), as appropriate.

f. (Deleted by amendment, P.L.1998, c.71.)

**2C:47-5.1.          Revocation of parole**

a.  Whenever the parole of an offender committed to confinement under the terms of this chapter is revoked by the State Parole Board, the Department of Corrections shall, within 90 days of the date of revocation of parole, complete a psychological examination of the offender to determine whether the violation of the conditions of parole reflects emotional or behavioral problems as a sex offender that cause the offender to be incapable of making any acceptable social adjustment in the community and, if so, to determine further the offender's amenability to sex offender treatment and, if amenable, the offender's willingness to participate in such treatment. Not more than 30 days after the date of the examination, the Department of Corrections shall provide a written report of the results to the State Parole Board.

b.  The offender shall be confined in the Adult Diagnostic and Treatment Center if the report of the examination conducted pursuant to subsection a. of this section reveals that the offender's violation of the conditions of parole reflects emotional or behavioral problems as a sex offender that cause the offender to be incapable of making any acceptable social adjustment in the community and further reveals that the offender is amenable to sex offender treatment and is willing to participate in such treatment. The offender shall be eligible for parole pursuant to the provisions of subsection a. of N.J.S.2C:47-5.

c.  The offender shall be confined in a facility designated by the commissioner pursuant to section 2 of P.L.1969, c.22 (C.30:4-91.2) if the report of the examination conducted pursuant to subsection a. of this section reveals that the offender's violation of the conditions of parole reflects emotional or behavioral problems as a sex offender that cause the offender to be incapable of making any acceptable social adjustment in the community and further reveals that the offender is amenable to sex offender treatment, but is not willing to participate in such treatment. The offender shall be eligible for parole pursuant to the provisions of subsection a. of N.J.S.2C:47-5.

d.  (1)  The offender shall be confined in a facility designated by the commissioner pursuant to section 2 of P.L.1969, c.22 (C.30:4-91.2) if the report of the examination conducted pursuant to subsection a. of this section reveals that the offender's violation of the conditions of parole:

    (a)  does not reflect emotional or behavioral problems as a sex offender; or

    (b)  reflects emotional or behavioral problems as a sex offender that cause the offender to be incapable of making any acceptable social adjustment in the community and further reveals that the offender is not amenable to sex offender treatment.

(2)  An offender confined pursuant to the provisions of paragraph (1) of this subsection shall be eligible for parole pursuant to the provisions of Title 30 of the Revised Statutes. However, a parole eligibility date established by the State Parole Board pursuant to section 20 of P.L.1979, c.441 (C.30:4-123.64) or a future parole eligibility date established by the State Parole Board pursuant to section 12 of P.L.1979, c.441 (C.30:4-123.56) shall not be reduced by commutation time for good behavior pursuant to R.S. 30:4-140 or credits for diligent application to work and other institutional assignments pursuant to R.S.30:4-92.

e.  Notwithstanding the provisions of R.S.30:4-92, the balance of the sentence of an offender confined pursuant to subsection c. or subparagraph (b) of paragraph (1) of subsection d. of this section shall not be reduced by credits for diligent application to work and other institutional assignments; provided, however, if the offender is at any time transferred to the Adult Diagnostic and Treatment Center pursuant to subsection f. of this section the balance of the sentence shall be reduced by credits for diligent application to work and other institutional assignments earned by the offender during confinement in the Adult Diagnostic and Treatment Center.

f.  If an offender is confined pursuant to subsection c. or subparagraph (b) of paragraph (1) of subsection d. of this section, the offender may, on a biennial basis, request to be transferred to the Adult Diagnostic and Treatment Center. Within 90 days after receiving a request for a transfer, the Department of Corrections shall conduct a psychological examination. If, upon the completion of a psychological examination, the Department of Corrections determines that the offender is amenable to sex offender treatment and is willing to participate in such treatment, the commissioner shall order the offender to be transferred to the Adult Diagnostic and Treatment Center as soon as practicable. When an offender previously determined not to be amenable to sex offender treatment is transferred to the Adult Diagnostic and Treatment Center, the offender shall be eligible for parole pursuant to the provisions of subsection a. of N.J.S.2C:47-5.

## 2C:47-6.        Repealed

## 2C:47-7.        Cost of maintenance

The Commissioner shall determine and fix the per capita cost of examining and maintaining any offender upon order of the court pursuant to N.J.S.2C:47-1 and shall furnish a copy of the order to the county treasurer of the county in which the offender has a legal settlement as determined in that order, and upon certification of the amount due, the governing body of the county shall make provisions for payment of one-half of the cost thereof to the Adult Diagnostic and Treatment Center, the remaining one-half to be borne by the State. If the order contains a determination that the offender has no legal settlement in any county, the entire cost shall be borne by the State.

## 2C:47-8.        Adult Diagnostic and Treatment Center; "good time"; conditions

Notwithstanding the provisions of section 7 of P.L.1979, c.441 (C.30:4-123.51), R.S.30:4-140, R.S.30:4-92 or any other law, a term of imprisonment imposed on a person confined to the Adult Diagnostic and Treatment Center pursuant to the provisions of chapter 47 of this Title shall not be reduced by progressive time credits or credits for diligent application to work and other institutional assignments for any year or fractional part of a year if the person failed to fully cooperate with all treatment offered to him during that time period. This section shall not prohibit the reduction of a person's term of imprisonment by such credits if the person is entitled to the credits pursuant to the provisions of subsection g. of N.J.S.2C:47-3.

## 2C:47-9.        Establishment of program to record, analyze recidivism of convicted sex offenders

a.  The Commissioner of Corrections shall establish a program to record and analyze the recidivism of all inmates who are released from the Adult Diagnostic and Treatment Center, whether on parole or upon the completion of their maximum sentences. The purpose of this program shall be to assist in measuring the effectiveness of the center in providing specialized treatment to repetitive and compulsive sex offenders pursuant to N.J.S.2C:47-3.

b.  The program shall record the arrests for all offenses committed by releasees for a period of five years following their release and any convictions resulting from these arrests. These data shall be analyzed to determine whether the rates and nature of rearrests and convictions differ according to the criminal histories and personal characteristics of releasees, the treatment they received at the Adult Diagnostic and Treatment Center, length of sentence, conditions of parole, and such other factors as may be relevant to the purposes of this act.

   c.  The program shall also perform a comparative analysis of the recidivism rates and patterns of releasees from the Adult Diagnostic and Treatment Center with those of persons released from this State's general prison population and with sex offenders released in other jurisdictions with specialized programs for the treatment of sex offenders.

   d.  The department shall prepare and disseminate to the Governor and the Legislature reports documenting the program's findings, along with any recommendations it may have for legislation to improve the effectiveness of treatment offered by the Adult Diagnostic and Treatment Center.

**2C:47-10.**    **"Sexually oriented material" defined; receipt by inmates at Adult Diagnostic and Treatment Center, prohibited**

   a.  As used in this act, "sexually oriented material" means any description, narrative account, display, or depiction of sexual activity or associated anatomical area contained in, or consisting of, a picture or other representation, publication, sound recording, live performance, or film.

   b.  An inmate sentenced to a period of confinement in the Adult Diagnostic Treatment Center shall not receive, possess, distribute or exhibit within the center sexually oriented material, as defined in subsection a. of this section. Upon the discovery of any such material within the center, the commissioner shall provide for its removal and destruction, subject to a departmental appeal procedure for the withholding or removal of such material from the inmate's possession.

   c.  The commissioner shall request an inmate sentenced to confinement in the center to acknowledge in writing the requirements of this act prior to the enforcement of its provisions. Any inmate who violates the provisions of subsection b. of this section shall be subject to on-the-spot sanctions pursuant to rules and regulations adopted by the commissioner.

   d.  A person who sells or offers for sale the material prohibited in subsection b. either for purposes of possession or viewing or who receives, possesses, distributes or exhibits any text, photograph, film, video or any other reproduction or reconstruction which depicts a person under 18 years of age engaging in a prohibited sexual act or in the simulation of such an act as defined in section 2 of P.L.1992, c.7 (C.2A:30B-2), within the center shall be considered to have committed an inmate prohibited act and be subject to sanctions pursuant to rules and regulations adopted by the commissioner.

# 48

# CRIMINAL DISPOSITION COMMISSION

**2C:48-1.**     **Composition**

There is hereby created a Criminal Disposition Commission, consisting of 12 members consisting of two members of the Senate, no more than one of whom shall be of the same political party, appointed by the President of the Senate; two members of the General Assembly, no more than one of whom shall be of the same political party, appointed by the Speaker of the General Assembly; the Chief Justice of the Supreme Court or his designee, the Attorney General or his designee, the Public Defender or his designee, the Chairman of the State Parole Board or his designee, the Commissioner of the Department of Corrections or his designee, the President of the New Jersey Prosecutors Association or his designee and two public members to be appointed by the Governor. The legislative members shall serve for terms coextensive with their respective terms as a member of the House of the Legislature from which they are appointed and the two public members shall serve for a term of three years except that one of the initial appointments shall be for a term of one year. Members shall be eligible for reappointment to the commission, and vacancies in the commission shall be filled in the same manner as the original appointment, but for the unexpired term only. The members of the commission shall serve without compensation, but shall only be reimbursed for necessary expenses actually incurred in the performance of their duties under this chapter. The commission shall choose a chairman from among its members.

**2C:48-2.**     **Duties**

It shall be the duty of the commission to study and review all aspects of the criminal justice system relating to the disposition of criminal offenders, including but not limited to terms of imprisonments, fines and other monetary punishments, parole, probation and supervisory treatment.

**2C:48-3.**     **Powers**

The commission shall be entitled to call to its assistance and avail itself of the services of such employees of the State and the political subdivisions thereof as it may require and as may be available to it for said purpose, and to employ such professional, stenographic, and clerical assistants and incur such traveling and other miscellaneous expenses as it may deem necessary in order to perform its duties, and as may be within the limits of funds appropriated or otherwise made available to it for said purposes.

**2C:48-4.**      **Reports**

The commission shall file annually with the Governor and the legislature a report containing its findings and recommendations concerning the disposition of criminal offenders.

# 49

# CAPITAL PUNISHMENT

**2C:49-1.**  **Definitions**

As used in this act:

   a. "Commissioner" means the Commissioner of the Department of Corrections.

   b. "Department" means the Department of Corrections.

   c. "Inmate" means a person who is incarcerated in the department who is sentenced to death pursuant to the provisions of N.J.S. 2C:11-3.

**2C:49-2.**  **Murder; sentence to death; administration of punishment**

When a person is sentenced to death pursuant to the provisions of N.J.S. 2C:11-3, that punishment shall be imposed by continuous, intravenous, administration until the person is dead of a lethal quantity of an ultrashort-acting barbiturate in combination with a chemical paralytic agent in a quantity sufficient to cause death. Prior to the injection of the lethal substance, the person shall be sedated by a licensed physician, registered nurse, or other qualified personnel, by either an oral tablet or capsule or an intramuscular injection of a narcotic or barbiturate such as morphine, cocaine or demerol.

**2C:49-3.**  **Determination of substances and procedure; dispensation of drugs without prescription; execution technicians**

   a. The commissioner shall determine the substances and procedure to be used in an execution. Any imposition of the punishment of death by administration of the required lethal substances in the manner required by section 2 of this act shall not be construed to be the practice of medicine and any pharmacist or pharmaceutical supplier is authorized to dispense drugs to the commissioner or his designee, without prescription, for carrying out the provisions of section 2, notwithstanding any other provision of law to the contrary.

   b. The commissioner shall designate persons who are qualified to administer injections and who are familiar with medical procedures, other than licensed physicians, as execution technicians to assist in the carrying out of executions, but the procedures and equipment utilized in imposing the lethal substances shall be designed to insure that the identity of the person actually inflicting the lethal substance is unknown even to the person himself.

**2C:49-4.**  **Facility**

The department shall provide and maintain a suitable and efficient facility enclosed from public view, within the confines of a designated State prison for the imposition of the punishment of death. That facility shall contain the apparatus and equipment necessary for the carrying out of executions in accordance with the provisions of this act.

**2C:49-5.          Warrant of execution; date**

a. When a person is sentenced to the punishment of death, the judge who presided at the sentencing proceeding or if that judge is unavailable for any reason, then the assignment judge of the vicinage and, if not available, then any Superior Court judge of the vicinage, shall make out, sign and deliver to the sheriff of the county, a warrant directed to the commissioner, stating the conviction and sentence, appointing a date on which the sentence shall be executed, and commanding the commissioner to execute the sentence on that date.

b. If the execution of the sentence on the date appointed shall be delayed while the conviction or sentence is being appealed, the judge authorized to act pursuant to subsection a. of this section, at the conclusion of the appellate process, if the conviction or sentence is not set aside, shall make out, sign and deliver another warrant as provided in subsection a. of this section. If the execution of the sentence on the date appointed is delayed by any other cause, the judge shall, as soon as such cause ceases to exist, make out, sign and deliver another warrant as provided in subsection a. of this section.

c. The date appointed in the warrant shall be not less than 30 days and not more than 60 days after the issuance of the warrant. The commissioner may fix the time of execution on that date.

**2C:49-6.          Delivery of warrant and person sentenced to department; confinement;
physical access; court order; exceptions**

a. Within 10 days after issuance of a warrant as provided in section 5 of this act, the sheriff shall deliver the warrant, and also the person sentenced, if he is not already in the custody of the department, to the department. From the time of the delivery of the warrant and until the imposition of the punishment of death upon him, unless discharged from the sentence, the person shall be kept isolated from the general prison population in a designated State prison.

b. During the confinement and isolation no person shall be allowed physical access to him without a court order which shall not be unreasonably withheld, except corrections officers and officials, his counsel, and the members of his immediate family, and then only in accordance with the department's rules for security. Upon the request of the inmate, a clergyman or a member of the press shall be allowed access to the inmate without a court order but only in accordance with the department's rules for security.

**2C:49-7.          Persons present at execution**

a. The commissioner, the persons designated by the commissioner to act as execution technicians, and one licensed physician shall be present at the execution. The commissioner shall also select and invite the presence of, by at least three days' prior notice, six adult citizens. The names of the execution technicians shall not be disclosed, and the names of the six adult citizens who witnessed the execution shall not be disclosed until after the execution.

b. The commissioner shall, at the request of the person sentenced to death, authorize and permit no more than two clergymen, who are not related to the inmate, to be present at the execution. The commissioner may, at the request of the person sentenced to death, authorize and permit no more than two adult members of the person's immediate family to be present at the execution.

c. The commissioner shall permit four representatives of the news media to be present at the execution, for the purpose of giving their respective newspapers and associations accounts of the execution. The four representatives shall be composed of one representative of the major wire services, one representative of television news services, one representative of newspapers, and one representative of radio news services. Immediately following the execution, the four representatives of the news media may hold a press conference for the purpose of giving other news representatives an account of the execution.

d. The commissioner shall not authorize or permit any person to be present, except those authorized by this section.

e. The commissioner shall authorize and permit no more than four adult members of the victim's immediate family to be present at the execution. The names of the members of the victim's immediate family who witnessed the execution shall not be disclosed.

f. For purposes of this section, "immediate family" means a spouse, parent, stepparent, legal guardian, grandparent, child, or sibling.

g. Nothing in this section shall be construed to give a right to any person to delay or prevent the execution of a sentence of death on the date appointed in the warrant pursuant to N.J.S.2C:49-5.

**2C:49-8.**      **Examination and report; certificate; filing; delegation of duties by commissioner**

a. Immediately after the execution an examination of the body of the inmate shall be made by the licensed physicians present at the execution, and their report in writing stating the nature of the examination and occurrence of death, so made by them, shall be annexed to the certificate hereinafter mentioned and filed therewith.

b. The commissioner shall prepare and sign a certificate setting forth the time and place of the execution and stating that the execution was conducted in conformity to the sentence of the court and the provisions of this act. He shall cause the certificate to be filed, within 10 days after the execution, with the Superior Court in the county in which the person executed was convicted.

c. The commissioner may appoint a deputy within the department to execute the warrant of execution and to perform all the other duties imposed upon the commissioner by this act.

**2C:49-9.**      **Disposition of body**

a. Prior to the execution, the inmate shall be given the opportunity to decide in writing to whom his body shall be delivered after the execution. The commissioner or his deputy designated pursuant to subsection c. of section 8 of this act shall sign and authorize the inmate's request if the request is not contrary to public policy or law. If the inmate does not indicate to whom his body shall be delivered or if his request is contrary to public policy or law, then the body of an inmate who has been legally executed shall be embalmed immediately and so directed by the commissioner, unless prior to execution, the inmate, relative, or bona fide friend indicates that the body is to be cremated or buried within 48 hours after death. If the body is not demanded or requested by a relative or bona fide friend within 72 hours after execution then it shall be delivered to a duly authorized and incorporated pathological and anatomical association in the State, if requested by an authorized association. If the body is requested by a relative or bona fide friend, the State shall pay a fee, not to exceed $25.00 to the mortician for his services in embalming the body for which the mortician shall issue to the State a written receipt. If the body is requested by a duly authorized and incorporated pathological and anatomical association, the association shall pay a fee, not to exceed $25.00 to the mortician for his services in embalming the body for which the mortician shall issue to the association a written receipt. When the receipt is delivered to the commissioner, the body of the deceased shall be delivered to the party named in the receipt or his authorized agent.

b. If the body is not delivered to a relative, bona fide friend, or a duly authorized and incorporated pathological and anatomical association, the commissioner shall cause the body to be decently buried, and the fee for embalming shall be paid by the State, and no religious or other services shall be held over the body after the execution, except within the facility selected for the execution by the department, and no one shall be present at the service except the officers of the prison, the person conducting the services and relatives by blood or marriage of the person executed.

c. The commissioner shall contact the Social Security Administration, Veterans' Administration, Public Welfare, and appropriate insurance companies for any possible death benefits to offset the State incurred burial expenses. The inmate's account may also be used for burial expenses.

**2C:49-10.    Pregnant person; inquisition; suspension of execution of warrant**

a. If there is reasonable ground to believe that a female inmate, sentenced to the punishment of death, is pregnant, the superintendent of the State institution having custody of the inmate shall impanel a jury of three licensed physicians to inquire into her pregnancy. A physician acting as a juror upon this inquisition need not be qualified to serve as a juror in a court of record.

b. The inquisition of the jury shall be signed by the jurors and the superintendent of the institution. If it is found by the jury that the inmate is pregnant, the superintendent shall suspend the execution of the warrant directing her execution until he receives a warrant from the commissioner directing that the convict be executed.

c. The superintendent shall immediately transmit the inquisition to the commissioner, who, as soon as he is satisfied that the inmate is no longer pregnant, shall issue his warrant, appointing a time and place for her execution, pursuant to her sentence.

**2C:49-11.    Rules and regulations**

The department may adopt any rules or regulations necessary to implement the provisions of this act.

**2C:49-12.    Joint committee of legislature to monitor and evaluate implementation of act; report**

The Judiciary, Law, Public Safety and Defense Committee of the General Assembly and the Judiciary Committee of the Senate, or their respective successors, are constituted a joint committee for the purposes of monitoring and evaluating the effectiveness of the implementation of this act. The Commissioner of the Department of Corrections shall, two years from the effective date of this act, report to the joint committee, an evaluation of the effectiveness of this act and the joint committee shall, upon receiving the report, issue as it may deem necessary and proper, recommendations for administrative or legislative changes affecting the implementation of this act.

**Chapter 50—Reserved**

# 51

# LOSS AND RESTORATION OF RIGHTS INCIDENT TO CONVICTION OF AN OFFENSE

**2C:51-1.**  **Basis of disqualification or disability**

    a. No person shall suffer any legal disqualification or disability because of his conviction of an offense or his sentence on such conviction, unless the disqualification or disability involves the deprivation of a right or privilege which is:

        (1) Necessarily incident to execution of the sentence of the court;

        (2) Provided by the Constitution or the code;

        (3) Provided by a statute other than the code, when the conviction is of an offense defined by such statute; or

        (4) Provided by the judgment, order or regulation of a court, agency or official exercising a jurisdiction conferred by law, or by the statute defining such jurisdiction, when the commission of the offense or the conviction or the sentence is reasonably related to the competency of the individual to exercise the right or privilege of which he is deprived.

    b. Proof of a conviction as relevant evidence upon the trial or determination of any issue, or for the purpose of impeaching the convicted person as a witness is not a disqualification or disability within the meaning of this chapter.

**2C:51-2.**  **Forfeiture of public office**

    a. A person holding any public office, position, or employment, elective or appointive, under the government of this State or any agency or political subdivision thereof, who is convicted of an offense shall forfeit such office or position if:

        (1) He is convicted under the laws of this State of an offense involving dishonesty or of a crime of the third degree or above or under the laws of another state or of the United States of an offense or a crime which, if committed in this State, would be such an offense or crime;

        (2) He is convicted of an offense involving or touching such office, position or employment; or

        (3) The Constitution so provides.

b.  A court of this State shall enter an order of forfeiture pursuant to subsection a.:

   (1) Immediately upon a finding of guilt by the trier of fact or a plea of guilty entered in any court of this State unless the court, for good cause shown, orders a stay of such forfeiture pending a hearing on the merits at the time of sentencing; or

   (2) Upon application of the county prosecutor or the Attorney General, when the forfeiture is based upon a conviction of an offense under the laws of another state or of the United States. An order of forfeiture pursuant to this paragraph shall be deemed to have taken effect on the date the person was found guilty by the trier of fact or pled guilty to the offense.

c.  No court shall grant a stay of an order of forfeiture pending appeal of a conviction or forfeiture order unless the court is clearly convinced that there is a substantial likelihood of success on the merits. If the conviction be reversed or the order of forfeiture be overturned, he shall be restored, if feasible, to his office, position or employment with all the rights, emoluments and salary thereof from the date of forfeiture.

   Any official action taken by the convicted person on or after the date as of which a forfeiture of the person's office shall take effect shall, during a period of 60 days following the date on which an order of forfeiture shall have been issued hereunder, be voidable by the person's successor in office or, if the office of the person was that of member of the governing body of a county, municipality or independent authority, by that governing body.

d.  In addition to the punishment prescribed for the offense, and the forfeiture set forth in subsection a. of N.J.S.2C:51-2, any person convicted of an offense involving or touching on his public office, position or employment shall be forever disqualified from holding any office or position of honor, trust or profit under this State or any of its administrative or political subdivisions.

e.  Any forfeiture or disqualification under subsection a., b. or d. which is based upon a conviction of a disorderly persons or petty disorderly persons offense may be waived by the court upon application of the county prosecutor or the Attorney General and for good cause shown.

f.  Except as may otherwise be ordered by the Attorney General as the public need may require, any person convicted of an offense under section 2C:27-2, 2C:27-4, 2C:27-6, 2C:27-7, 2C:29-4, 2C:30-2, or 2C:30-3 of this Title shall be ineligible, either directly or indirectly, to submit a bid, enter into any contract, or to conduct any business with any board, agency, authority, department, commission, public corporation, or other body of this State, of this or one or more other states, or of one or more political subdivisions of this State for a period of, but not more than, 10 years from the date of conviction for a crime of the second degree, or five years from the date of conviction for a crime of the third degree. It is the purpose of this subsection to bar any individual convicted of any of the above enumerated offenses and any business, including any corporation, partnership, association or proprietorship in which such individual is a principal, or with respect to which such individual owns, directly or indirectly, or controls 5% or more of the stock or other equity interest of such business, from conducting business with public entities.

   The State Treasurer shall keep and maintain a list of all corporations barred from conducting such business pursuant to this section.

g.  In any case in which the issue of forfeiture is not raised in a court of this State at the time of a finding of guilt, entry of guilty plea or sentencing, a forfeiture of public office, position or employment required by this section may be ordered by a court of this State upon application of the county prosecutor or the Attorney General or upon application of the public officer or public entity having authority to remove the person convicted from his public office, position or employment. The fact that a court has declined to order forfeiture shall not preclude the public officer or public entity having authority to remove the person convicted from seeking to remove or suspend the person from his office, position or employment on the ground that the conduct giving rise to the conviction demonstrates that the person is unfit to hold the office, position or employment.

## 2C:51-2.1.    Applicability of act

a. Any person who forfeited or was disqualified from holding any public office, position, or employment, elective or appointive, under the government of this State or any agency or political subdivision thereof, by a court of competent jurisdiction, prior to the effective date of this act shall continue to be disqualified or continue to forfeit such office, position or employment.

b. Any person holding any public office, position, or employment, elective or appointive, under the government of this State or any agency or political subdivision thereof, on the effective date of this act, shall be subject to disqualification or forfeiture of that public office, position, or employment only pursuant to N.J.S.2C:51-2 and not pursuant to a statute other than the criminal code.

## 2C:51-3.    Voting and jury service

A person who is convicted of a crime shall be disqualified

a. From voting in any primary, municipal, special or general election as determined by the provisions of R.S. 19:4-1; and

b. From serving as a juror as determined by the provisions of N.J.S. 2A:69-1.

## 2C:51-4.    Repealed

## 2C:51-5.    Forfeiture, suspension of license; exceptions

a. (1) A practitioner convicted of health care claims fraud pursuant to subsection a. of section 3 of P.L.1997, c.353 (C.2C:21-4.3) or a substantially similar crime under the laws of another state or the United States shall forfeit his license and be forever barred from the practice of the profession unless the court finds that such license forfeiture would be a serious injustice which overrides the need to deter such conduct by others and in such case the court shall determine an appropriate period of license suspension which shall be for a period of not less than one year. If the court does not permanently forfeit such license pursuant to this paragraph, the sentence shall not become final for 10 days in order to permit the appeal of such sentence by the prosecution.

(2) Upon a first conviction of health care claims fraud pursuant to subsection b. of section 3 of P.L.1997, c.353 (C.2C:21-4.3) or a substantially similar crime under the laws of another state or the United States, a practitioner shall have his license suspended and be barred from the practice of the profession for a period of at least one year.

(3) Upon a second conviction of health care claims fraud pursuant to subsection b. of section 3 of P.L.1997, c.353 (C.2C:21-4.3) or a substantially similar crime under the laws of another state or the United States, a practitioner shall forfeit his license and be forever barred from the practice of the profession.

b. A court of this State shall enter an order of license forfeiture or suspension pursuant to subsection a. of this section:

    (1) Immediately upon a finding of guilt by the trier of fact or a plea of guilty entered in any court of this State; or

    (2) Upon application of the county prosecutor or the Attorney General, when the license forfeiture or suspension is based upon a conviction of an offense under the laws of another state or of the United States. An order of license forfeiture or suspension pursuant to this paragraph shall be effective as of the date the person is found guilty by the trier of fact or pleads guilty to the offense.

        This application may also be made in the alternative by the Attorney General to the appropriate licensing agency.

        The court shall provide notice of the forfeiture or suspension to the appropriate licensing agency within 10 days of the date an order of forfeiture or suspension is entered.

c. No court shall grant a stay of an order of license forfeiture or suspension pending appeal of a conviction or forfeiture or suspension order unless the court is clearly convinced that there is a substantial likelihood of success on the merits. If the conviction is reversed or the order of license forfeiture or suspension is overturned, the court shall provide notice of reinstatement to the appropriate licensing agency within 10 days of the date of the order of reinstatement. The license shall be restored, in accordance with applicable procedures, unless the appropriate licensing agency determines to suspend or revoke the license.

d. In any case in which the issue of license forfeiture or suspension is not raised in a court of this State at the time of a finding of guilt, entry of a guilty plea or sentencing, a license forfeiture or suspension required by this section may be ordered by a court or by the appropriate licensing agency of this State upon application of the county prosecutor or the Attorney General or upon application of the appropriate licensing agency having authority to revoke or suspend the professional's license. The fact that a court has declined to order license forfeiture or suspension shall not preclude the appropriate licensing agency having authority to revoke or suspend the professional's license from seeking to do so on the ground that the conduct giving rise to the conviction demonstrates that the person is unfit to hold the license or is otherwise liable for an offense as specified in section 8 of P.L.1978, c.73 (C.45:1-21).

e. If the Supreme Court of the State of New Jersey issues Rules of Court pursuant to this act, the Supreme Court may revoke the license to practice law of any attorney who has been convicted, under the laws of this State, of health care claims fraud pursuant to section 3 of P.L.1997, c.353 (C.2C:21-4.3), or an offense which, if committed in this State, would constitute health care claims fraud.

f. Nothing in this section shall be construed to prevent or limit the appropriate licensing agency or any other party from taking any other action permitted by law against the practitioner.

# 52

# EXPUNGEMENT OF RECORDS

**2C:52-1.**     **Definition of expungement**

    a. Except as otherwise provided in this chapter, expungement shall mean the extraction and isolation of all records on file within any court, detention or correctional facility, law enforcement or criminal justice agency concerning a person's detection, apprehension, arrest, detention, trial or disposition of an offense within the criminal justice system.

    b. Expunged records shall include complaints, warrants, arrests, commitments, processing records, fingerprints, photographs, index cards, "rap sheets" and judicial docket records.

**2C:52-2.**     **Indictable offenses**

    a. In all cases, except as herein provided, wherein a person has been convicted of a crime under the laws of this State and who has not been convicted of any prior or subsequent crime, whether within this State or any other jurisdiction, and has not been adjudged a disorderly person or petty disorderly person on more than two occasions may, after the expiration of a period of 10 years from the date of his conviction, payment of fine, satisfactory completion of probation or parole, or release from incarceration, whichever is later, present a duly verified petition as provided in section 2C:52-7 to the Superior Court in the county in which the conviction was entered praying that such conviction and all records and information pertaining thereto be expunged.

        Although subsequent convictions for no more than two disorderly or petty disorderly offenses shall not be an absolute bar to relief, the nature of those conviction or convictions and the circumstances surrounding them shall be considered by the court and may be a basis for denial of relief if they or either of them constitute a continuation of the type of unlawful activity embodied in the criminal conviction for which expungement is sought.

    b. Records of conviction pursuant to statutes repealed by this Code for the crimes of murder, manslaughter, treason, anarchy, kidnapping, rape, forcible sodomy, arson, perjury, false swearing, robbery, embracery, or a conspiracy or any attempt to commit any of the foregoing, or aiding, assisting or concealing persons accused of the foregoing crimes, shall not be expunged.

        Records of conviction for the following crimes specified in the New Jersey Code of Criminal Justice shall not be subject to expungement: Section 2C:11-1 et seq. (Criminal Homicide), except death by auto as specified in section 2C:11-5; section 2C:13-1 (Kidnapping); section 2C:13-6 (Luring or Enticing); section 2C:14-2 (Aggravated Sexual Assault); section 2C:14-3a (Aggravated Criminal Sexual Contact); if the victim is a minor, section 2C:14-3b (Criminal Sexual Contact); if the victim is a minor and the offender is not the parent of the victim, section 2C:13-2 (Criminal Restraint) or section 2C:13-3

(False Imprisonment); section 2C:15-1 (Robbery); section 2C:17-1 (Arson and Related Offenses); section 2C:24-4a. (Endangering the welfare of a child by engaging in sexual conduct which would impair or debauch the morals of the child); section 2C:24-4b(4) (Endangering the welfare of a child); section 2C:28-1 (Perjury); section 2C:28-2 (False Swearing) and conspiracies or attempts to commit such crimes.

Records of conviction for any crime committed by a person holding any public office, position or employment, elective or appointive, under the government of this State or any agency or political subdivision thereof and any conspiracy or attempt to commit such a crime shall not be subject to expungement if the crime involved or touched such office, position or employment.

c. In the case of conviction for the sale or distribution of a controlled dangerous substance or possession thereof with intent to sell, expungement shall be denied except where the crimes relate to:

    (1) Marijuana, where the total quantity sold, distributed or possessed with intent to sell was 25 grams or less, or

    (2) Hashish, where the total quantity sold, distributed or possessed with intent to sell was five grams or less.

d. In the case of a State licensed physician or podiatrist convicted of an offense involving drugs or alcohol or pursuant to section 14 or 15 of P.L.1989, c.300 (C.2C:21-20 or 2C:21-4.1), the court shall notify the State Board of Medical Examiners upon receipt of a petition for expungement of the conviction and records and information pertaining thereto.

## 2C:52-3.        Disorderly persons offenses and petty disorderly persons offenses

Any person convicted of a disorderly persons offense or petty disorderly persons offense under the laws of this State who has not been convicted of any prior or subsequent crime, whether within this State or any other jurisdiction, or of another three disorderly persons or petty disorderly persons offenses, may, after the expiration of a period of 5 years from the date of his conviction, payment of fine, satisfactory completion of probation or release from incarceration, whichever is later, present a duly verified petition as provided in section 2C:52-7 hereof to the Superior Court in the county in which the conviction was entered praying that such conviction and all records and information pertaining thereto be expunged.

## 2C:52-4.        Ordinances

In all cases wherein a person has been found guilty of violating a municipal ordinance of any governmental entity of this State and who has not been convicted of any prior or subsequent crime, whether within this State or any other jurisdiction, and who has not been adjudged a disorderly person or petty disorderly person on more than two occasions, may, after the expiration of a period of 2 years from the date of his conviction, payment of fine, satisfactory completion of probation or release from incarceration, whichever is later, present a duly verified petition as provided in section 2C:52-7 herein to the Superior Court in the county in which the violation occurred praying that such conviction and all records and information pertaining thereto be expunged.

## 2C:52-4.1.        Juvenile delinquent; expungement of adjudications and charges

a. Any person adjudged a juvenile delinquent may have such adjudication expunged as follows:

    (1) Pursuant to N.J.S. 2C:52-2, if the act committed by the juvenile would have constituted a crime if committed by an adult;

    (2) Pursuant to N.J.S.2C:52-3, if the act committed by the juvenile would have constituted a disorderly or petty disorderly persons offense if committed by an adult; or

    (3) Pursuant to N.J.S. 2C:52-4, if the act committed by the juvenile would have constituted an ordinance violation if committed by an adult.

        For purposes of expungement, any act which resulted in a juvenile being adjudged a delinquent shall be classified as if that act had been committed by an adult.

  b. Additionally, any person who has been adjudged a juvenile delinquent may have his entire record of delinquency adjudications expunged if:

    (1) Five years have elapsed since the final discharge of the person from legal custody or supervision or 5 years have elapsed after the entry of any other court order not involving custody or supervision;

    (2) He has not been convicted of a crime, or a disorderly or petty disorderly persons offense, or adjudged a delinquent, or in need of supervision, during the 5 years prior to the filing the petition, and no proceeding or complaint is pending seeking such a conviction or adjudication;

    (3) He was never adjudged a juvenile delinquent on the basis of an act which if committed by an adult would constitute a crime not subject to expungement under N.J.S. 2C:52-2;

    (4) He has never had an adult conviction expunged; and

    (5) He has never had adult criminal charges dismissed following completion of a supervisory treatment or other diversion program.

  c. Any person who has been charged with an act of delinquency and against whom proceedings were dismissed may have the filing of those charges expunged pursuant to the provisions of N.J.S. 2C:52-6.

**2C:52-5.**     **Expungement of records of young drug offenders**

Notwithstanding the provisions of sections 2C:52-2 and 2C:52-3, after a period of not less than one year following conviction, termination of probation or parole or discharge from custody, whichever is later, any person convicted of an offense under chapters 35 or 36 of this title for the possession or use of a controlled dangerous substance, convicted of violating P.L. 1955, c. 277, s. 3 (C. 2A:170-77.5), or convicted of violating P.L. 1962, c. 113, s. 1 (C. 2A:170-77.8), and who at the time of the offense was 21 years of age or younger, may apply to the Superior Court in the county wherein the matter was disposed of for the expungement of such person's conviction and all records pertaining thereto. The relief of expungement under this section shall be granted only if said person has not, prior to the time of hearing, violated any of the conditions of his probation or parole, albeit subsequent to discharge from probation or parole, has not been convicted of any previous or subsequent criminal act or any subsequent or previous violation of chapters 35 or 36 of this title or of P.L. 1955, c. 277, s. 3 (C. 2A:170-77.5) or of P.L. 1962, c. 113, s. 1 (C. 2A:170-77.8), or who has not had a prior or subsequent criminal matter dismissed because of acceptance into a supervisory treatment or other diversion program.

    This section shall not apply to any person who has been convicted of the sale or distribution of a controlled dangerous substance or possession with the intent to sell any controlled dangerous substance except:

    1. Marihuana, where the total sold, distributed or possessed with intent to sell was 25 grams or less, or

    2. Hashish, where the total amount sold, distributed or possessed with intent to sell was 5 grams or less.

**2C:52-6.**    **Arrests not resulting in conviction**

a. In all cases, except as herein provided, wherein a person has been arrested or held to answer for a crime, disorderly persons offense, petty disorderly persons offense or municipal ordinance violation under the laws of this State or of any governmental entity thereof and against whom proceedings were dismissed, or who was acquitted, or who was discharged without a conviction or finding of guilt, may at any time following the disposition of proceedings, present a duly verified petition as provided in section 2C:52-7 to the Superior Court in the county in which the disposition occurred praying that records of such arrest and all records and information pertaining thereto be expunged.

b. Any person who has had charges dismissed against him pursuant to P.L.1970, c. 226, s. 27 (C. 24:21-27) or pursuant to a program of supervisory treatment, shall be barred from the relief provided in this section until 6 months after the entry of the order of dismissal.

c. Any person who has been arrested or held to answer for a crime shall be barred from the relief provided in this section where the dismissal, discharge, or acquittal resulted from a determination that the person was insane or lacked the mental capacity to commit the crime charged.

**2C:52-7.**    **Petition for expungement**

Every petition for expungement filed pursuant to this chapter shall be verified and include:

a. Petitioner's date of birth.

b. Petitioner's date of arrest.

c. The statute or statutes and offense or offenses for which petitioner was arrested and of which petitioner was convicted.

d. The original indictment, summons or complaint number.

e. Petitioner's date of conviction, or date of disposition of the matter if no conviction resulted.

f. The court's disposition of the matter and the punishment imposed, if any.

**2C:52-8.**    **Statements to accompany petition**

There shall be attached to a petition for expungement:

a. A statement with the affidavit or verification that there are no disorderly persons, petty disorderly persons or criminal charges pending against the petitioner at the time of filing of the petition for expungement.

b. In those instances where the petitioner is seeking the expungement of a criminal conviction, a statement with affidavit or verification that he has never been granted expungement, sealing or similar relief regarding a criminal conviction by any court in this State or other state or by any Federal court. "Sealing" refers to the relief previously granted pursuant to P.L.1973, c. 191 (C. 2A:85-15 et seq.).

c. In those instances where a person has received a dismissal of a criminal charge because of acceptance into a supervisory treatment or any other diversion program, a statement with affidavit or verification setting forth the nature of the original charge, the court of disposition and date of disposition.

**2C:52-9.**    **Order fixing time for hearing**

Upon the filing of a petition for relief pursuant to this chapter, the court shall, by order, fix a time not less than 35 nor more than 60 days thereafter for hearing of the matter.

**2C:52-10.**        **Service of petition and documents**

A copy of each petition, together with a copy of all supporting documents, shall be served pursuant to the rules of court upon the Superintendent of State Police; the Attorney General; the county prosecutor of the county wherein the court is located; the chief of police or other executive head of the police department of the municipality wherein the offense was committed; the chief law enforcement officer of any other law enforcement agency of this State which participated in the arrest of the individual; the superintendent or warden of any institution in which the petitioner was confined; and, if a disposition was made by a municipal court, upon the magistrate of that court. Service shall be made within 5 days from the date of the order setting the date for the hearing upon the matter.

**2C:52-11.**        **Order expungement where no objection prior to hearing**

If, prior to the hearing, there is no objection from those law enforcement agencies notified or from those offices or agencies which are required to be served under 2C:52-10and no reason, as provided in section 2C:52-14, appears to the contrary, the court may, without a hearing, grant an order directing the clerk of the court and all relevant criminal justice and law enforcement agencies to expunge records of said disposition including evidence of arrest, detention, conviction and proceedings related thereto.

**2C:52-12.**        **Denial of relief although no objection entered**

In the event that none of the persons or agencies required to be noticed under 2C:52-10 has entered any objection to the relief being sought, the court may nevertheless deny the relief sought if it concludes that petitioner is not entitled to relief for the reasons provided in section 2C:52-14.

**2C:52-13.**        **When hearing on petition for expungement shall not be held**

No petition for relief made pursuant to this section shall be heard by any court if the petitioner, at the time of filing or date of hearing, has a charge or charges pending against him which allege the commission of a crime, disorderly persons offense or petty disorderly persons offense. Such petition shall not be heard until such times as all pending criminal and or disorderly persons charges are adjudicated to finality.

**2C:52-14.**        **Grounds for denial of relief**

A petition for expungement filed pursuant to this chapter shall be denied when:

   a. Any statutory prerequisite, including any provision of this chapter, is not fulfilled or there is any other statutory basis for denying relief.
   b. The need for the availability of the records outweighs the desirability of having a person freed from any disabilities as otherwise provided in this chapter. An application may be denied under this subsection only following objection of a party given notice pursuant to 2C:52-10 and the burden of asserting such grounds shall be on the objector.
   c. In connection with a petition under section 2C:52-6, the acquittal, discharge or dismissal of charges resulted from a plea bargaining agreement involving the conviction of other charges. This bar, however, shall not apply once the conviction is itself expunged.
   d. The arrest or conviction sought to be expunged is, at the time of hearing, the subject matter of civil litigation between the petitioner or his legal representative and the State, any governmental entity thereof or any State agency and the representatives or employees of any such body.

e. A person has had a previous criminal conviction expunged regardless of the lapse of time between the prior expungement, or sealing under prior law, and the present petition. This provision shall not apply:

    (1) When the person is seeking the expungement of a municipal ordinance violation or,

    (2) When the person is seeking the expungement of records pursuant to section 2C:52-6.

f. The person seeking the relief of expungement of a conviction for a disorderly persons, petty disorderly persons, or criminal offense has prior to or subsequent to said conviction been granted the dismissal of criminal charges following completion of a supervisory treatment or other diversion program.

## 2C:52-15. Records to be removed; control

If an order of expungement of records of arrest or conviction under this chapter is granted by the court, all the records specified in said order shall be removed from the files of the agencies which have been noticed of the pendency of petitioner's motion and which are, by the provisions of this chapter, entitled to notice, and shall be placed in the control of a person who has been designated by the head of each such agency which, at the time of the hearing, possesses said records. That designated person shall, except as otherwise provided in this chapter, insure that such records or the information contained therein are not released for any reason and are not utilized or referred to for any purpose. In response to requests for information or records of the person who was arrested or convicted, all noticed officers, departments and agencies shall reply, with respect to the arrest, conviction or related proceedings which are the subject of the order, that there is no record information.

## 2C:52-16. Expunged record including names of persons other than petitioner

Any record or file which is maintained by a judicial or law enforcement agency, or agency in the criminal justice system, which is the subject of an order of expungement which includes the name or names of persons other than that of the petitioner need not be isolated from the general files of the agency retaining same if the other persons named in said record or file have not been granted an order of expungement of said record, provided that a copy of the record shall be given to the person designated in 2C:52-15 and the original shall remain in the agency's general files with the petitioner's name and other personal identifiers obliterated and deleted.

## 2C:52-17. Use of expunged records by agencies on pending petition for expungement

Expunged records may be used by the agencies that possess same to ascertain whether a person has had prior conviction expunged, or sealed under prior law, when the agency possessing the record is noticed of a pending petition for the expungement of a conviction. Any such agency may supply information to the court wherein the motion is pending and to the other parties who are entitled to notice pursuant to 2C:52-10.

## 2C:52-18. Supplying information to violent crimes compensation board

Information contained in expunged records may be supplied to the Violent Crimes Compensation Board, in conjunction with any claim which has been filed with said board.

## 2C:52-19. Order of superior court permitting inspection of records or release of information; limitations

Inspection of the files and records, or release of the information contained therein, which are the subject of an order of expungement, or sealing under prior law, may be permitted by the Superior Court upon motion for good cause shown and compelling need based on specific facts. The motion or any order granted pursuant thereto shall specify the person or persons to whom the records and information are to be shown and the purpose for which they are to be utilized. Leave to inspect shall be granted by the court only in those instances where the subject matter of the records of arrest or conviction is the object of litigation or judicial proceedings. Such records may not be inspected or utilized in any subsequent civil or criminal proceeding for the purposes of impeachment or otherwise but may be used for purposes of sentencing on a subsequent offense after guilt has been established.

**2C:52-20.**   **Use of expunged records in conjunction with supervisory treatment or diversion programs**

Expunged records may be used by any judge in determining whether to grant or deny the person's application for acceptance into a supervisory treatment or diversion program for subsequent charges. Any expunged records which are possessed by any law enforcement agency may be supplied to the Attorney General, any county prosecutor or judge of this State when same are requested and are to be used for the purpose of determining whether or not to accept a person into a supervisory treatment or diversion program for subsequent charges.

**2C:52-21.**   **Use of expunged records in conjunction with setting bail, presentence report or sentencing**

Expunged records, or sealed records under prior law, of prior arrests or convictions shall be provided to any judge, county prosecutor, probation department or the Attorney General when same are requested for use in conjunction with a bail hearing or for the preparation of a presentence report or for purpose of sentencing.

**2C:52-22.**   **Use of expunged records by parole board**

Expunged records, or sealed records under prior law, of prior disorderly persons, petty disorderly persons and criminal convictions shall be provided to the Parole Board when same are requested for the purpose of evaluating the granting of parole to the person who is the subject of said records. Such sealed or expunged records may be used by the Parole Board in the same manner and given the same weight in its considerations as if the records had not been expunged or sealed.

**2C:52-23.**   **Use of expunged records by department of corrections**

Expunged records, and records sealed under prior law, shall be provided to the Department of Corrections for its use solely in the classification, evaluation and assignment to correctional and penal institutions of persons placed in its custody.

**2C:52-24.**   **County prosecutor's obligation to ascertain propriety of petition**

Notwithstanding the notice requirements provided herein, it shall be the obligation of the county prosecutor of the county wherein any petition for expungement is filed to verify the accuracy of the allegations contained in the petition for expungement and to bring to the court's attention any facts which may be a bar to, or which may make inappropriate the granting of, such relief. If no disabling, adverse or relevant information is ascertained other than that as included in the petitioner's affidavit, such facts shall be communicated by the prosecutor to the hearing judge.

**2C:52-25.**   **Retroactive application**

This chapter shall apply to arrests and convictions which occurred prior to, and which occur subsequent to, the effective date of this act.

**2C:52-26.** **Vacating of orders of sealing; time; basis**

If, within 5 years of the entry of an expungement order, any party to whom notice is required to be given pursuant to section 2C:52-10 notifies the court which issued the order that at the time of the petition or hearing there were criminal, disorderly persons or petty disorderly persons charges pending against the person to whom the court granted such order, which charges were not revealed to the court at the time of hearing of the original motion or that there was some other statutory disqualification, said court shall vacate the expungement order in question and reconsider the original motion in conjunction with the previously undisclosed information.

**2C:52-27.** **Effect of expungement**

Unless otherwise provided by law, if an order of expungement is granted, the arrest, conviction and any proceedings related thereto shall be deemed not to have occurred, and the petitioner may answer any questions relating to their occurrence accordingly, except as follows:

a. The fact of an expungement, sealing or similar relief shall be disclosed as provided in section 2C:52-8b.

b. The fact of an expungement of prior charges which were dismissed because of the person's acceptance into and successful completion of a supervisory treatment or other diversion program shall be disclosed by said person to any judge who is determining the propriety of accepting said person into a supervisory treatment or other diversion program for subsequent criminal charges; and

c. Information divulged on expunged records shall be revealed by a petitioner seeking employment within the judicial branch or with a law enforcement or corrections agency and such information shall continue to provide a disability as otherwise provided by law.

**2C:52-27.1.** **Petition to rescind order of debarment for health care claims fraud**

a. If an order of expungement of records of conviction under the provisions of chapter 52 of Title 2C of the New Jersey Statutes is granted by the court to a person convicted of health care claims fraud in which the court had ordered the offender's professional license be forfeited and the person be forever barred from the practice of the profession pursuant to paragraph (1) of subsection a. of section 4 of P.L.1997, c.353 (C.2C:51-5), the person may petition the court for an order to rescind the court's order of debarment if the person can demonstrate that the person is sufficiently rehabilitated.

b. If an order to rescind the court's order of debarment is granted, the person granted the order may apply to be licensed to practice the profession from which the offender was barred.

**2C:52-28.** **Motor vehicle offenses**

Nothing contained in this chapter shall apply to arrests or conviction for motor vehicle offenses contained in Title 39.

**2C:52-29.** **Fee**

Any person who files an application pursuant to this chapter shall pay to the State Treasurer a fee of $30.00 to defer administrative costs in processing an application hereunder.

**2C:52-30.** **Disclosure of expungement order**

Except as otherwise provided in this chapter, any person who reveals to another the existence of an arrest, conviction or related legal proceeding with knowledge that the records and information pertaining thereto have been expunged or sealed is a disorderly person. Notwithstanding the provisions of section 2C:43-3, the maximum fine which can be imposed for violation of this section is $200.00.

## 2C:52-31.      Limitation

Nothing provided in this chapter shall be interpreted to permit the expungement of records contained in the Controlled Dangerous Substances Registry created pursuant to P.L.1970, c. 227 (C. 26:2G-17 et seq.), or the registry created by the Administrative Office of the Courts pursuant to section 2C:43-21.

## 2C:52-32.      Construction

This chapter shall be construed with the primary objective of providing relief to the one-time offender who has led a life of rectitude and disassociated himself with unlawful activity, but not to create a system whereby periodic violators of the law or those who associate themselves with criminal activity have a regular means of expunging their police and criminal records.

### Chapters 53 to 57—Reserved

# 58

# LICENSING AND OTHER PROVISIONS RELATING TO FIREARMS

**2C:58-1.**       **Registration of manufacturers and wholesale dealers of firearms**

a. **Registration.** Every manufacturer and wholesale dealer of firearms shall register with the superintendent as provided in this section. No person shall engage in the business of, or act as a manufacturer or wholesale dealer of firearms, or manufacture or sell at wholesale any firearm, until he has so registered.

Applications for registration shall be made on such forms as shall be prescribed by the superintendent, and the applicant shall furnish such information and other particulars as may be prescribed by law or by any rules or regulations promulgated by the superintendent. Each application for registration or renewal shall be accompanied by a fee of $150.00.

The superintendent shall prescribe standards and qualifications for the registration of manufacturers and wholesalers of firearms, for the protection of the public safety, health and welfare. He shall refuse to register any applicant for registration unless he is satisfied that the applicant can be permitted to engage in business as a manufacturer or wholesale dealer of firearms without any danger to the public safety, health or welfare.

The superintendent shall issue a certificate of registration to every person registered under this section, and such certificate shall be valid for a period of 3 years from the date of issuance.

b. **Wholesale dealer's agent.** Every registered wholesale dealer of firearms shall cause each of his agents or employees actively engaged in the purchase or sale of firearms to be licensed with the superintendent as a wholesale dealer's agent. Applications for agents' licenses shall be submitted on such forms as shall be prescribed by the superintendent, and shall be signed by the registered wholesale dealer and by the agent. Each application shall be accompanied by a fee of $5.00, and each license shall be valid for so long as the agent or employee remains in the employ of the wholesale dealer and the wholesale dealer remains validly registered under this section. The superintendent shall prescribe standards and qualifications for licensed wholesale dealers' agents, for the protection of the public safety, health and welfare.

c. **Revocation of certificate of registration or license.** The superintendent may, after reasonable notice to all affected parties and a hearing if requested, revoke any certificate of registration or agent's license if he finds that the registered or licensed person is no longer engaged in the business of manufacturing or wholesaling firearms in this State or that he can no longer be permitted to carry on such business without endangering the public safety, health or welfare. A certificate or license may be canceled at any time at the request of the registered or licensed person.

d. **Appeals.** Any person aggrieved by the refusal of the superintendent to register him as a manufacturer or wholesale dealer or a wholesale dealer's agent, or by revocation of his certificate or license, may appeal to the Appellate Division of the Superior Court.

e. **Records of sales.** Every manufacturer and wholesale dealer shall keep a detailed record of each firearm sold by him. The record shall include the date of sale, the name and address of the purchaser, a description of each firearm and the serial number thereof. The records shall be available for inspection at all reasonable times by any law enforcement officer.

## 2C:58-2.      Retailing of firearms; licensing of dealers and their employees

a. **Licensing of retail dealers and their employees.** No retail dealer of firearms nor any employee of a retail dealer shall sell or expose for sale, or possess with the intent of selling, any firearm unless licensed to do so as hereinafter provided. The superintendent shall prescribe standards and qualifications for retail dealers of firearms and their employees for the protection of the public safety, health and welfare.

Applications shall be made in the form prescribed by the superintendent, accompanied by a fee of $50.00 payable to the superintendent, and shall be made to a judge of the Superior Court in the county where the applicant maintains his place of business. The judge shall grant a license to an applicant if he finds that the applicant meets the standards and qualifications established by the superintendent and that the applicant can be permitted to engage in business as a retail dealer of firearms or employee thereof without any danger to the public safety, health and welfare. Each license shall be valid for a period of three years from the date of issuance, and shall authorize the holder to sell firearms at retail in a specified municipality.

In addition, every retail dealer shall pay a fee of $5.00 for each employee actively engaged in the sale or purchase of firearms. The superintendent shall issue a license for each employee for whom said fee has been paid, which license shall be valid for so long as the employee remains in the employ of said retail dealer.

No license shall be granted to any retail dealer under the age of 21 years or to any employee of a retail dealer under the age of 18 or to any person who could not qualify to obtain a permit to purchase a handgun or a firearms purchaser identification card, or to any corporation, partnership or other business organization in which the actual or equitable controlling interest is held or possessed by such an ineligible person.

All licenses shall be granted subject to the following conditions, for breach of any of which the license shall be subject to revocation on the application of any law enforcement officer and after notice and hearing by the issuing court:

(1) The business shall be carried on only in the building or buildings designated in the license, provided that repairs may be made by the dealer or his employees outside of such premises.

(2) The license or a copy certified by the issuing authority shall be displayed at all times in a conspicuous place on the business premises where it can be easily read.

(3) No firearm or imitation thereof shall be placed in any window or in any other part of the premises where it can be readily seen from the outside.

(4) No rifle or shotgun, except antique rifles or shotguns, shall be delivered to any person unless such person possesses and exhibits a valid firearms purchaser identification card and furnishes the seller, on the form prescribed by the superintendent, a certification signed by him setting forth his name, permanent

address, firearms purchaser identification card number and such other information as the superintendent may by rule or regulation require. The certification shall be retained by the dealer and shall be made available for inspection by any law enforcement officer at any reasonable time.

(5) No handgun shall be delivered to any person unless:

(a) Such person possesses and exhibits a valid permit to purchase a firearm and at least seven days have elapsed since the date of application for the permit;

(b) The person is personally known to the seller or presents evidence of his identity;

(c) The handgun is unloaded and securely wrapped;

(d) Except as otherwise provided in subparagraph (e) of this paragraph, the handgun is accompanied by a trigger lock or a locked case, gun box, container or other secure facility; provided, however, this provision shall not apply to antique handguns. The exemption afforded under this subparagraph for antique handguns shall be narrowly construed, limited solely to the requirements set forth herein and shall not be deemed to afford or authorize any other exemption from the regulatory provisions governing firearms set forth in chapter 39 and chapter 58 of Title 2C of the New Jersey Statutes; and

(e) On and after the first day of the sixth month following the date on which the list of personalized handguns is prepared and delivered pursuant to section 3 of P.L.2002, c.130 (C.2C:58-2.4), the handgun is identified as a personalized handgun and included on that list or is an antique handgun. The provisions of subparagraph (d) of this section shall not apply to the delivery of a personalized handgun.

(6) The dealer shall keep a true record of every handgun sold, given or otherwise delivered or disposed of, in accordance with the provisions of subsections b. through e. of this section and the record shall note whether a trigger lock, locked case, gun box, container or other secure facility was delivered along with the handgun.

b. **Records.** Every person engaged in the retail business of selling, leasing or otherwise transferring a handgun, as a retail dealer or otherwise, shall keep a register in which shall be entered the time of the sale, lease or other transfer, the date thereof, the name, age, date of birth, complexion, occupation, residence and a physical description including distinguishing physical characteristics, if any, of the purchaser, lessee or transferee, the name and permanent home address of the person making the sale, lease or transfer, the place of the transaction, and the make, model, manufacturer's number, caliber and other marks of identification on such handgun and such other information as the superintendent shall deem necessary for the proper enforcement of this chapter. The register shall be retained by the dealer and shall be made available at all reasonable hours for inspection by any law enforcement officer.

c. **Forms of register.** The superintendent shall prepare the form of the register as described in subsection b. of this section and furnish the same in triplicate to each person licensed to be engaged in the business of selling, leasing or otherwise transferring firearms.

d. **Signatures in register.** The purchaser, lessee or transferee of any handgun shall sign, and the dealer shall require him to sign his name to the register, in triplicate, and the person making the sale, lease or transfer shall affix his name, in triplicate, as a witness to the signature. The signatures shall constitute a representation of the accuracy of the information contained in the register.

e. **Copies of register entries; delivery to chief of police or county clerk.** Within five days of the date of the sale, assignment or transfer, the dealer shall deliver or mail by certified mail, return receipt requested, legible copies of the register forms to the office of the chief of police of the municipality in which the purchaser resides, or to the office of the captain of the precinct of the municipality in which the purchaser resides, and to the superintendent. If hand delivered a receipt shall be given to the dealer therefor.

Where a sale, assignment or transfer is made to a purchaser who resides in a municipality having no chief of police, the dealer shall, within five days of the transaction, mail a duplicate copy of the register sheet to the clerk of the county within which the purchaser resides.

### 2C:58-2.1.          Guidelines for delivery of handguns

The Superintendent of State Police, in consultation with the Attorney General, shall promulgate guidelines to effectuate the purposes of P.L.1999, c.233.

### 2C:58-2.2.          Findings, declarations relative to sale of handguns

a.  The Legislature finds:

New Jersey's commitment to firearms safety is unrivaled anywhere in the nation;

New Jersey was the first state to require retail dealers to include, as part of every handgun sale, either a State Police approved trigger lock or a locked case, gun box, container or other secure facility;

To encourage all firearms owners to practice safe storage, the State has waived all sales taxes on trigger locks, firearms lock-boxes and vaults and, under the "KeepSafe" program, offers an instant $5 rebate to all retail firearms purchasers who buy a compatible trigger locking device along with their firearm;

New Jersey was the first state to require all firearms dealers to prominently display State-provided firearms information and safety warnings;

New Jersey was one of the first states to make parents and guardians statutorily responsible for unwittingly or carelessly permitting minors under their control to gain access to loaded firearms;

New Jersey statutorily prohibits anyone under the age of 18 years from purchasing or otherwise acquiring a firearm and permits such minors to possess or carry a firearm only in a very limited number of strictly defined situations and under the direct supervision of a qualified parent, guardian or instructor;

To enforce this strict regulatory scheme, New Jersey imposes harsh penalties, including a mandatory minimum prison term of three years, on anyone who knowingly sells, transfers or gives a firearm to a person under the age of 18 years; and

New Jersey was the first state to allocate, as part of its annual Appropriations Act, moneys dedicated exclusively for the development of personal handgun technology, and the amount so allocated, $1,000,000, was one-fifth the total amount the federal government allocated toward the development of this important firearms safety technology in the same fiscal year.

b.  The Legislature, therefore, declares:

It is within the public interest, and vital to the safety of our families and children, for New Jersey to take the bold and innovative step of fostering the development of personalized handguns by firearms manufacturers. To accomplish this objective, the Legislature determines that it should enact legislation designed to further enhance firearms safety by requiring that, within a specified period of time after the date on which these new personalized handguns are deemed to be available for retail sales purposes, no other type of handgun shall be sold or offered for sale by any registered or licensed firearms dealer in this State.

**2C:58-2.3.**     **Reports as to availability of personalized handguns**

    a. On the first day of the sixth month following the effective date of P.L.2002, c.130 (C.2C:58-2.2 et al.), the Attorney General shall report to the Governor and the Legislature as to the availability of personalized handguns for retail sales purposes. If the Attorney General determines that personalized handguns are not available for retail sales purposes, the Attorney General, every six months thereafter, shall report to the Governor and the Legislature as to the availability of personalized handguns for retail sales purposes until such time as the Attorney General shall deem that personalized handguns are available for retail sales purposes and so report to the Governor and the Legislature. In making this determination, the Attorney General may consult with any other neutral and detached public or private entity that may have useful information and expertise to assist in determining whether, through performance and other relevant indicators, a handgun meets the statutory definition of a personalized handgun set forth in N.J.S.2C:39-1.

    b. For the purposes of this section, personalized handguns shall be deemed to be available for retail sales purposes if at least one manufacturer has delivered at least one production model of a personalized handgun to a registered or licensed wholesale or retail dealer in New Jersey or any other state. As used in this subsection, the term "production model" shall mean a handgun which is the product of a regular manufacturing process that produces multiple copies of the same handgun model, and shall not include a prototype or other unique specimen that is offered for sale.

**2C:58-2.4.**     **List of personalized handguns**

    a. On the first day of the 24th month following the date on which the Attorney General reports that personalized handguns are available for retail sales purposes pursuant to section 2 of P.L.2002, c.130 (C.2C:58-2.3), the Attorney General shall direct the Superintendent of State Police to promulgate a list of personalized handguns that may be sold in the State. This list shall identify those handguns by manufacturer, model and caliber.

    b. The list required under subsection a. of this section shall be prepared within six months of the Attorney General's directive to the superintendent and a copy thereof made available to registered and licensed firearms dealers in this State. Whenever a handgun is determined to meet the statutory definition of a personalized handgun as set forth in N.J.S.2C;39-1, the Attorney General shall report that determination in writing to the Governor and the Legislature within 60 days. The superintendent shall promptly amend and supplement the list to include handguns which meet the statutory definition of a personalized handgun as set forth in N.J.S.2C:39-1 or to remove previously listed handguns, if appropriate. Registered and licensed retail firearms dealers in this State shall be notified forthwith of any such changes in the list. The notice shall be given in a manner prescribed by rule and regulation. The Attorney General shall promulgate rules and regulations establishing a process for handgun manufacturers to demonstrate that their handguns meet the statutory definition of a personalized handgun set forth in N.J.S.2C:39-1 and request that their handgun be added to this list. These rules and regulations may require that the handgun manufacturer: (1) deliver a handgun or handguns to the Attorney General or his designee for testing; (2) pay a reasonable application fee; and (3) pay any reasonable costs incurred in, or associated with, the testing and independent scientific analysis of the handgun, including any analysis of the technology the manufacturer has incorporated within the handgun's design to limit its operational use, that is conducted to determine whether the handgun meets the statutory definition of a personalized handgun set forth in N.J.S.2C:39-1.

**2C:58-2.5.**        **Sale of personalized handguns, inapplicability**

a.  On and after the first day of the sixth month following the preparation and delivery of the list of personalized handguns which may be sold in the State pursuant to section 3 of P.L.2002, c.130 (C.2C:58-2.4), no person registered or licensed by the superintendent as a manufacturer, wholesale dealer of firearms, retail dealer of firearms or agent or employee of a wholesale or retail dealer of firearms pursuant to the provisions of N.J.S.2C:58-1 or N.J.S.2C:58-2 shall transport into this State, sell, expose for sale, possess with the intent of selling, assign or otherwise transfer any handgun unless it is a personalized handgun or an antique handgun.

b.  The provisions of this section shall not apply to handguns to be sold, transferred, assigned and delivered for official use to: (1) State and local law enforcement officers of this State; (2) federal law enforcement officers and any other federal officers and employees required to carry firearms in the performance of their official duties and (3) members of the Armed Forces of the United States or of the National Guard.

c.  The provisions of this section also shall not apply to handguns to be sold, transferred, assigned and delivered solely for use in competitive shooting matches sanctioned by the Civilian Marksmanship Program, the International Olympic Committee or USA Shooting. The Attorney General may promulgate rules and regulations governing the scope and application of the exemption afforded under this section. The Attorney General, by rule and regulation, may require, at a minimum, that a person acquiring a handgun pursuant to this section submit valid proof of participation in these sanctioned shooting matches.

d.  No later than 30 days after the preparation and delivery of the list of personalized handguns which may be sold in the State pursuant to section 3 of P.L.2002, c.130 (C.2C:58-2.4), there shall be established a seven-member commission in the Department of Law and Public Safety that shall meet at least once a year to determine whether personalized handguns qualify for use by State and local law enforcement officers. The Governor shall appoint the following six members of the commission: a county sheriff; a county law enforcement officer; a county prosecutor; one local law enforcement officer who shall be an active member of the New Jersey Fraternal Order of Police; one local law enforcement officer who shall be an active member of the New Jersey State Policemen's Benevolent Association; and an experienced firearms instructor qualified to teach a firearms training course approved by the Police Training Commission. The seventh member of the commission shall be the Superintendent of State Police.

   The commission shall issue a report to the Attorney General upon its determination that personalized handguns qualify for use by State and local law enforcement officers. In making this determination, the commission shall consider any advantages and disadvantages to using these weapons in the performance of the official duties of law enforcement officers and shall give due regard to the safety of law enforcement officers and others. The commission shall expire thereafter. The Attorney General shall be authorized to promulgate rules and regulations that apply the provisions of this section to handguns to be sold, transferred, assigned and delivered for official use to State and local law enforcement officers upon a determination by the commission that personalized handguns qualify for use by State and local law enforcement officers.

e.  A person who knowingly violates the provisions of this section is guilty of a crime of the fourth degree.

**2C:58-2.6.**        **Rules, regulations**

The Attorney General, in accordance with the provisions of the "Administrative Procedure Act," P.L.1968, c.410 (C.52:14B-1 et seq.), shall promulgate rules and regulations to effectuate the purposes of this act.

**2C:58-3.**      **Purchase of firearms**

a. **Permit to purchase a handgun.** No person shall sell, give, transfer, assign or otherwise dispose of, nor receive, purchase, or otherwise acquire a handgun unless the purchaser, assignee, donee, receiver or holder is licensed as a dealer under this chapter or has first secured a permit to purchase a handgun as provided by this section.

b. **Firearms purchaser identification card.** No person shall sell, give, transfer, assign or otherwise dispose of nor receive, purchase or otherwise acquire an antique cannon or a rifle or shotgun, other than an antique rifle or shotgun, unless the purchaser, assignee, donee, receiver or holder is licensed as a dealer under this chapter or possesses a valid firearms purchaser identification card, and first exhibits said card to the seller, donor, transferor or assignor, and unless the purchaser, assignee, donee, receiver or holder signs a written certification, on a form prescribed by the superintendent, which shall indicate that he presently complies with the requirements of subsection c. of this section and shall contain his name, address and firearms purchaser identification card number or dealer's registration number. The said certification shall be retained by the seller, as provided in section 2C:58-2a., or, in the case of a person who is not a dealer, it may be filed with the chief of police of the municipality in which he resides or with the superintendent.

c. **Who may obtain.** No person of good character and good repute in the community in which he lives, and who is not subject to any of the disabilities set forth in this section or other sections of this chapter, shall be denied a permit to purchase a handgun or a firearms purchaser identification card, except as hereinafter set forth. No handgun purchase permit or firearms purchaser identification card shall be issued:

    (1) To any person who has been convicted of a crime, whether or not armed with or possessing a weapon at the time of such offense;

    (2) To any drug dependent person as defined in section 2 of P.L.1970, c.226 (C.24:21-2), to any person who is confined for a mental disorder to a hospital, mental institution or sanitarium, or to any person who is presently an habitual drunkard;

    (3) To any person who suffers from a physical defect or disease which would make it unsafe for him to handle firearms, to any person who has ever been confined for a mental disorder, or to any alcoholic unless any of the foregoing persons produces a certificate of a medical doctor or psychiatrist licensed in New Jersey, or other satisfactory proof, that he is no longer suffering from that particular disability in such a manner that would interfere with or handicap him in the handling of firearms; to any person who knowingly falsifies any information on the application form for a handgun purchase permit or firearms purchaser identification card;

    (4) To any person under the age of 18 years for a firearms purchaser identification card and to any person under the age of 21 years for a permit to purchase a handgun;

    (5) To any person where the issuance would not be in the interest of the public health, safety or welfare;

    (6) To any person who is subject to a court order issued pursuant to section 13 of P.L.1991, c.261 (C.2C:25-29) prohibiting the person from possessing any firearm; or

    (7) To any person who as a juvenile was adjudicated delinquent for an offense which, if committed by an adult, would constitute a crime and the offense involved the unlawful use or possession of a weapon, explosive or destructive device or is enumerated in subsection d. of section 2 of P.L.1997, c.117 (C:2C:43-7.2)

d. **Issuance.** The chief of police of an organized full-time police department of the municipality where the applicant resides or the superintendent, in all other cases, shall upon application, issue to any person qualified under the provisions of subsection c. of this section a permit to purchase a handgun or a firearms purchaser identification card.

Any person aggrieved by the denial of a permit or identification card may request a hearing in the Superior Court of the county in which he resides if he is a resident of New Jersey or in the Superior Court of the county in which his application was filed if he is a nonresident. The request for a hearing shall be made in writing within 30 days of the denial of the application for a permit or identification card. The applicant shall serve a copy of his request for a hearing upon the chief of police of the municipality in which he resides, if he is a resident of New Jersey, and upon the superintendent in all cases. The hearing shall be held and a record made thereof within 30 days of the receipt of the application for such hearing by the judge of the Superior Court. No formal pleading and no filing fee shall be required as a preliminary to such hearing. Appeals from the results of such hearing shall be in accordance with law.

e. **Applications.** Applications for permits to purchase a handgun and for firearms purchaser identification cards shall be in the form prescribed by the superintendent and shall set forth the name, residence, place of business, age, date of birth, occupation, sex and physical description, including distinguishing physical characteristics, if any, of the applicant, and shall state whether the applicant is a citizen, whether he is an alcoholic, habitual drunkard, drug dependent person as defined in section 2 of P.L.1970, c.226 (C.24:21-2), whether he has ever been confined or committed to a mental institution or hospital for treatment or observation of a mental or psychiatric condition on a temporary, interim or permanent basis, giving the name and location of the institution or hospital and the dates of such confinement or commitment, whether he has been attended, treated or observed by any doctor or psychiatrist or at any hospital or mental institution on an inpatient or outpatient basis for any mental or psychiatric condition, giving the name and location of the doctor, psychiatrist, hospital or institution and the dates of such occurrence, whether he presently or ever has been a member of any organization which advocates or approves the commission of acts of force and violence to overthrow the Government of the United States or of this State, or which seeks to deny others their rights under the Constitution of either the United States or the State of New Jersey, whether he has ever been convicted of a crime or disorderly persons offense, whether the person is subject to a court order issued pursuant to section 13 of P.L.1991, c.261 (C.2C:25-29) prohibiting the person from possessing any firearm, and such other information as the superintendent shall deem necessary for the proper enforcement of this chapter. For the purpose of complying with this subsection, the applicant shall waive any statutory or other right of confidentiality relating to institutional confinement. The application shall be signed by the applicant and shall contain as references the names and addresses of two reputable citizens personally acquainted with him.

Application blanks shall be obtainable from the superintendent, from any other officer authorized to grant such permit or identification card, and from licensed retail dealers.

The chief police officer or the superintendent shall obtain the fingerprints of the applicant and shall have them compared with any and all records of fingerprints in the municipality and county in which the applicant resides and also the records of the State Bureau of Identification and the Federal Bureau of Investigation, provided that an applicant for a handgun purchase permit who possesses a valid firearms purchaser identification card, or who has previously obtained a handgun purchase permit from the same licensing authority for which he was previously fingerprinted, and who provides other reasonably satisfactory proof of his identity, need not be fingerprinted again; however, the chief police officer or the superintendent shall proceed to investigate the application to determine whether or not the applicant has become subject to any of the disabilities set forth in this chapter.

f. **Granting of permit or identification card; fee; term; renewal; revocation.** The application for the permit to purchase a handgun together with a fee of $2.00, or the application for the firearms purchaser identification card together with a fee of $5.00, shall be delivered or forwarded to the licensing authority who shall investigate the same and, unless good cause for the denial thereof appears, shall grant the permit or the identification card, or both, if application has been made therefor, within 30 days from the date of receipt of the application for residents of this State and within 45 days for nonresident applicants. A permit to purchase a handgun shall be valid for a period of 90 days from the date of issuance and may be renewed by the issuing authority for good cause for an additional 90 days. A firearms purchaser identification card shall be valid until such time as the holder becomes subject to any of the disabilities set forth in subsection c. of this section, whereupon the card shall be void and shall be returned within five days by the holder to the superintendent, who shall then advise the licensing authority. Failure of the holder to return the firearms purchaser identification card to the superintendent within the said five days shall be an offense under section 2C:39-10a. Any firearms purchaser identification card may be revoked by the Superior Court of the county wherein the card was issued, after hearing upon notice, upon a finding that the holder thereof no longer qualifies for the issuance of such permit. The county prosecutor of any county, the chief police officer of any municipality or any citizen may apply to such court at any time for the revocation of such card.

There shall be no conditions or requirements added to the form or content of the application, or required by the licensing authority for the issuance of a permit or identification card, other than those that are specifically set forth in this chapter.

g. **Disposition of fees.** All fees for permits shall be paid to the State Treasury if the permit is issued by the superintendent, to the municipality if issued by the chief of police, and to the county treasurer if issued by the judge of the Superior Court.

h. **Form of permit; quadruplicate; disposition of copies.** The permit shall be in the form prescribed by the superintendent and shall be issued to the applicant in quadruplicate. Prior to the time he receives the handgun from the seller, the applicant shall deliver to the seller the permit in quadruplicate and the seller shall complete all of the information required on the form. Within five days of the date of the sale, the seller shall forward the original copy to the superintendent and the second copy to the chief of police of the municipality in which the purchaser resides, except that in a municipality having no chief of police, such copy shall be forwarded to the superintendent. The third copy shall then be returned to the purchaser with the pistol or revolver and the fourth copy shall be kept by the seller as a permanent record.

i. **Restriction on number of firearms person may purchase.** Only one handgun shall be purchased or delivered on each permit, but a person shall not be restricted as to the number of rifles or shotguns he may purchase, provided he possesses a valid firearms purchaser identification card and provided further that he signs the certification required in subsection b. of this section for each transaction.

j. **Firearms passing to heirs or legatees.** Notwithstanding any other provision of this section concerning the transfer, receipt or acquisition of a firearm, a permit to purchase or a firearms purchaser identification card shall not be required for the passing of a firearm upon the death of an owner thereof to his heir or legatee, whether the same be by testamentary bequest or by the laws of intestacy. The person who shall so receive, or acquire said firearm shall, however, be subject to all other provisions of this chapter. If the heir or legatee of such firearm does not qualify to possess or carry it, he may retain ownership of the firearm for the purpose of sale for a period not exceeding 180 days, or for such further limited period as may be approved by the chief law enforcement officer of the municipality in which the heir or legatee resides or the superintendent, provided that such firearm is in the custody of the chief law enforcement officer of the municipality or the superintendent during such period.

k. **Sawed-off shotguns.** Nothing in this section shall be construed to authorize the purchase or possession of any sawed-off shotgun.

l. Nothing in this section and in N.J.S.2C:58-2 shall apply to the sale or purchase of a visual distress signalling device approved by the United States Coast Guard, solely for possession on a private or commercial aircraft or any boat; provided, however, that no person under the age of 18 years shall purchase nor shall any person sell to a person under the age of 18 years such a visual distress signalling device.

**2C:58-3.1.**    **Temporary transfer of firearms**

a. Notwithstanding the provisions of N.J.S.2C:39-9, N.J.S.2C:58-2, N.J.S.2C:58-3 or any other statute to the contrary concerning the transfer or disposition of firearms, the legal owner, or a dealer licensed under N.J.S.2C:58-2, may temporarily transfer a handgun, rifle or shotgun to another person who is 18 years of age or older, whether or not the person receiving the firearm holds a firearms purchaser identification card or a permit to carry a handgun. The person to whom a handgun, rifle or shotgun is temporarily transferred by the legal owner of the firearm or a licensed dealer may receive, possess, carry and use that handgun, rifle or shotgun, if the transfer is made upon a firing range operated by a licensed dealer, by a law enforcement agency, a legally recognized military organization or a rifle or pistol club which has filed a copy of its charter with the superintendent and annually submits to the superintendent a list of its members and if the firearm is received, possessed, carried and used for the sole purpose of target practice, trap or skeet shooting, or competition upon that firing range or instruction and training at any location.

A transfer under this subsection shall be for not more than eight consecutive hours in any 24-hour period and may be made for a set fee or an hourly charge.

The firearm shall be handled and used by the person to whom it is temporarily transferred only in the actual presence or under the direct supervision of the legal owner of the firearm, the dealer who transferred the firearm or any other person competent to supervise the handling and use of firearms and authorized to act for that purpose by the legal owner or licensed dealer. The legal owner of the firearm or the licensed dealer shall be on the premises or the property of the firing range during the entire time that the firearm is in the possession of the person to whom it is temporarily transferred.

The term "legal owner" as used in this subsection means a natural person and does not include an organization, commercial enterprise, or a licensed manufacturer, wholesaler or dealer of firearms.

b. Notwithstanding the provisions of N.J.S.2C:39-9, N.J.S.2C:58-2, N.J.S.2C:58-3 or any other statute to the contrary concerning the transfer and disposition of firearms, a legal owner of a shotgun or a rifle may temporarily transfer that firearm to another person who is 18 years of age or older, whether or not the person receiving the firearm holds a firearms purchaser identification card. The person to whom a shotgun or rifle is temporarily transferred by the legal owner may receive, possess, carry and use that shotgun or rifle in the woods or fields or upon the waters of this State for the purposes of hunting if the transfer is made in the woods or fields or upon the waters of this State, the shotgun or rifle is legal and appropriate for hunting and the person to whom the firearm is temporarily transferred possesses a valid license to hunt with a firearm, and a valid rifle permit if the firearm is a rifle, obtained in accordance with the provisions of chapter 3 of Title 23 of the Revised Statutes.

The transfer of a firearm under this subsection shall be for not more than eight consecutive hours in any 24-hour period and no fee shall be charged for the transfer.

The legal owner of the firearm which is temporarily transferred shall remain in the actual presence or in the vicinity of the person to whom it was transferred during the entire time that the firearm is in that person's possession.

The term "legal owner" as used in this subsection means a natural person and does not include an organization, commercial enterprise, or a licensed manufacturer, wholesaler or dealer of firearms.

c. No firearm shall be temporarily transferred or received under the provisions of subsections a. or b. of this section for the purposes described in section 1 of P.L.1983, c.229 (C.2C:39-14).

d. An owner or dealer shall not transfer a firearm to any person pursuant to the provisions of this section if the owner or dealer knows the person does not meet the qualifications set forth in subsection c. of N.J.S.2C:58-3 for obtaining or holding a firearms purchaser identification card or a handgun purchase permit. A person shall not receive, possess, carry or use a firearm pursuant to the provisions of this section if the person knows he does not meet the qualifications set forth in subsection c. of N.J.S.2C:58-3 for obtaining or holding a firearms purchaser identification card or a handgun purchase permit.

## 2C:58-3.2. Temporary transfer of firearm for training purposes

a. Notwithstanding the provisions of N.J.S.2C:39-9, N.J.S.2C:58-2, N.J.S.2C:58-3 or any other statute to the contrary, a person who is certified as an instructor in the use, handling and maintenance of firearms by the Police Training Commission, the Division of Fish, Game and Wildlife and the State Park Service in the Department of Environmental Protection, the Director of Civilian Marksmanship of the United States Department of the Army or by a recognized rifle or pistol association that certifies instructors may transfer a firearm temporarily in accordance with the terms of this section to a person participating in a training course for the use, handling and maintenance of firearms by the Police Training Commission, the Division of Fish, Game and Wildlife, the Director of Civilian Marksmanship or by a recognized rifle or pistol association that certifies instructors. The person to whom a firearm is transferred by a certified instructor in accordance with the terms of this section may receive, possess, carry and use the firearm temporarily during the sessions of the course for the purpose of training and participating in the course.

b. A transfer of a firearm under this section may be made only if:

   (1) the transfer is made upon a firearms range or, if the firearm is unloaded, in an area designated and appropriate for the training;

   (2) the transfer is made during the sessions of the firearms course for the sole purpose of participating in the course;

   (3) the transfer is made for not more than eight consecutive hours in any 24-hour period; and

   (4) the transferred firearm is used and handled only in the actual presence and under the direct supervision of the instructor.

c. The transfer permitted by this section may be made whether or not the person participating in the course holds a firearms license, firearms purchaser identification card or a handgun purchase permit. However, an instructor shall not knowingly transfer a firearm under the terms of this section to a person who does not meet the qualifications set forth in subsection c. of N.J.S.2C:58-3 for obtaining or holding a firearms purchaser identification card or a handgun purchase permit, and a person who knows that he does not meet such qualifications shall not receive the transferred firearm under the terms of this section.

d. No firearm shall be transferred or received under the provisions of this section for purposes described in section 1 of P.L.1983, c.229 (C.2C:39-14).

**2C:58-4.        Permits to carry handguns**

a. **Scope and duration of authority.** Any person who holds a valid permit to carry a handgun issued pursuant to this section shall be authorized to carry a handgun in all parts of this State, except as prohibited by section 2C:39-5e. One permit shall be sufficient for all handguns owned by the holder thereof, but the permit shall apply only to a handgun carried by the actual and legal holder of the permit.

All permits to carry handguns shall expire 2 years from the date of issuance or, in the case of an employee of an armored car company, upon termination of his employment by the company occurring prior thereto whichever is earlier in time, and they may thereafter be renewed every 2 years in the same manner and subject to the same conditions as in the case of original applications.

b. **Application forms.** All applications for permits to carry handguns, and all applications for renewal of such permits, shall be made on the forms prescribed by the superintendent. Each application shall set forth the full name, date of birth, sex, residence, occupation, place of business or employment, and physical description of the applicant, and such other information as the superintendent may prescribe for the determination of the applicant's eligibility for a permit and for the proper enforcement of this chapter. The application shall be signed by the applicant under oath, and shall be indorsed by three reputable persons who have known the applicant for at least 3 years preceding the date of application, and who shall certify thereon that the applicant is a person of good moral character and behavior.

c. **Investigation and approval.** Each application shall in the first instance be submitted to the chief police officer of the municipality in which the applicant resides, or to the superintendent, (1) if the applicant is an employee of an armored car company, or (2) if there is no chief police officer in the municipality where the applicant resides, or (3) if the applicant does not reside in this State. The chief police officer, or the superintendent, as the case may be, shall cause the fingerprints of the applicant to be taken and compared with any and all records maintained by the municipality, the county in which it is located, the State Bureau of Identification and the Federal Bureau of Identification. He shall also determine and record a complete description of each handgun the applicant intends to carry.

No application shall be approved by the chief police officer or the superintendent unless the applicant demonstrates that he is not subject to any of the disabilities set forth in 2C:58-3c., that he is thoroughly familiar with the safe handling and use of handguns, and that he has a justifiable need to carry a handgun. If the application is not approved by the chief police officer or the superintendent within 60 days of filing, it shall be deemed to have been approved, unless the applicant agrees to an extension of time in writing.

d. **Issuance by Superior Court; fee.** If the application has been approved by the chief police officer or the superintendent, as the case may be, the applicant shall forthwith present it to the Superior Court of the county in which the applicant resides, or to the Superior Court in any county where he intends to carry a handgun, in the case of a nonresident or employee of an armored car company. The court shall issue the permit to the applicant if, but only if, it is satisfied that the applicant is a person of good character who is not subject to any of the disabilities set forth in section 2C:58-3c., that he is thoroughly familiar with the safe handling and use of handguns, and that he has a justifiable need to carry a handgun. The court may at its discretion issue a limited-type permit which would restrict the applicant as to the types of handguns he may carry and where and for what purposes such handguns may be carried. At the time of issuance, the applicant shall pay to the county clerk of the county where the permit was issued a permit fee of $20.00.

e. **Appeals from denial of applications.** Any person aggrieved by the denial by the chief police officer or the superintendent of approval for a permit to carry a handgun may request a hearing in the Superior Court of the county in which he resides or in any county in which he intends to carry a handgun, in the case of a nonresident, by filing a written request for such a hearing within 30 days of the denial. Copies of the request shall be served upon the superintendent, the county prosecutor and the chief police officer of the municipality where the applicant resides, if he is a resident of this State. The hearing shall be held within 30 days of the filing of the request, and no formal pleading or filing fee shall be required. Appeals from the determination at such a hearing shall be in accordance with law and the rules governing the courts of this State.

If the superintendent or chief police officer approves an application and the Superior Court denies the application and refuses to issue a permit, the applicant may appeal such denial in accordance with law and the rules governing the courts of this State.

f. **Revocation of permits.** Any permit issued under this section shall be void at such time as the holder thereof becomes subject to any of the disabilities set forth in section 2C:58-3c., and the holder of such a void permit shall immediately surrender the permit to the superintendent who shall give notice to the licensing authority.

Any permit may be revoked by the Superior Court, after hearing upon notice to the holder, if the court finds that the holder is no longer qualified for the issuance of such a permit. The county prosecutor of any county, the chief police officer of any municipality, the superintendent or any citizen may apply to the court at any time for the revocation of any permit issued pursuant to this section.

**2C:58-4.1.**        **Employee of armored car company; application; letter from chief executive officer**

In addition to the requirements of N.J.S. 2C:58-4 any application to carry a handgun by an employee of an armored car company shall be accompanied by a letter from the chief executive officer of the armored car company verifying employment of the applicant; endorsing approval of the application; and agreeing to notify the superintendent forthwith upon the termination of the employee of any person to whom a permit is issued and to obtain from the employee the permit which shall thereupon be surrendered to the superintendent.

**2C:58-5.**        **Licenses to possess and carry machine guns and assault firearms**

a. Any person who desires to purchase, possess and carry a machine gun or assault firearm in this State may apply for a license to do so by filing in the Superior Court in the county in which he resides, or conducts his business if a nonresident, a written application setting forth in detail his reasons for desiring such a license. The Superior Court shall refer the application to the county prosecutor for investigation and recommendation. A copy of the prosecutor's report, together with a copy of the notice of the hearing on the application, shall be served upon the superintendent and the chief police officer of every municipality in which the applicant intends to carry the machine gun or assault firearm, unless, for good cause shown, the court orders notice to be given wholly or in part by publication.

b. No license shall be issued to any person who would not qualify for a permit to carry a handgun under section 2C:58-4, and no license shall be issued unless the court finds that the public safety and welfare so require. Any person aggrieved by the decision of the court in granting or denying an application, including the applicant, the prosecutor, or any law enforcement officer entitled to notice under subsection a. who appeared in opposition to the application, may appeal said decision in accordance with law and the rules governing the courts of this State.

c. Upon the issuance of any license under this section, true copies of such license shall be filed with the superintendent and the chief police officer of the municipality where the licensee resides or has his place of business.

d. In issuing any license under this section, the court shall attach thereto such conditions and limitations as it deems to be in the public interest. Unless otherwise provided by court order at the time of issuance, each license shall expire one year from the date of issuance, and may be renewed in the same manner and under the same conditions as apply to original applications.

e. Any license may be revoked by the Superior Court, after a hearing upon notice to the holder thereof, if the court finds that the holder is no longer qualified for the issuance of such a license or that revocation is necessary for the public safety and welfare. Any citizen may apply to the court for revocation of a license issued under this section.

f. A filing fee of $75.00 shall be required for each application filed pursuant to the provisions of this section. Of this filing fee, $25.00 shall be forwarded to the State Treasury for deposit in the account used by the Violent Crimes Compensation Board in satisfying claims and for related administrative costs pursuant to the provisions of the "Criminal Injuries Compensation Act of 1971," P.L.1971, c.317 (C.52:4B-1 et seq.).

g. Any license granted pursuant to the provisions of this section shall expire two years from the date of issuance and may be renewed in the same manner and under the same conditions as apply to original applications. If the holder of a license dies, the holder's heirs or estate shall have 90 days to dispose of that firearm as provided in section 12 of P.L.1990, c.32 (C.2C:58-13).

h. If an assault firearm licensed pursuant to the provisions of this section is used in the commission of a crime, the holder of the license for that assault firearm shall be civilly liable for any damages resulting from that crime. The liability imposed by this subsection shall not apply if the assault firearm used in the commission of the crime was stolen and the license holder reported the theft of the firearm to law enforcement authorities within 24 hours of the license holder's knowledge of the theft.

i. Nothing in P.L.1990, c.32 (C.2C:58-12 et al.) shall be construed to abridge any exemptions provided under N.J.S.2C:39-6.

## 2C:58-6.     Repealed

## 2C:58-6.1.     Possession of firearms by minors; exceptions

a. No person under the age of 18 years shall purchase, barter or otherwise acquire a firearm and no person under the age of 21 years shall purchase, barter or otherwise acquire a handgun, unless the person is authorized to possess the handgun in connection with the performance of official duties under the provisions of N.J.S.2C:39-6.

b. No person under the age of 18 years shall possess, carry, fire or use a firearm except as provided under paragraphs (1), (2), (3) and (4) of this subsection; and, unless authorized in connection with the performance of official duties under the provisions of N.J.S.2C:39-6, no person under the age of 21 years shall possess, carry, fire or use a handgunexcept under the following circumstances:

(1) In the actual presence or under the direct supervision of his father, mother or guardian, or some other person who holds a permit to carry a handgun or a firearms purchaser identification card, as the case may be; or

(2) For the purpose of military drill under the auspices of a legally recognized military organization and under competent supervision; or

(3) For the purpose of competition or target practice in and upon a firing range approved by the governing body of the municipality in which the range is located or the

National Rifle Association and which is under competent supervision at the time of such supervision or target practice or instruction and training at any location; or

(4) For the purpose of hunting during the regularly designated hunting season, provided that he possesses a valid hunting license and has successfully completed a hunter's safety course taught by a qualified instructor or conservation officer and possesses a certificate indicating the successful completion of such a course.

c. A person who violates this section shall be guilty of a crime of the fourth degree. For purposes of this section the fact that the act would not constitute a crime if committed by an adult shall not be deemed to prohibit or require waiver of family court jurisdiction pursuant to N.J.S.2C:4-11 or to preclude a finding of delinquency under the "New Jersey Code of Juvenile Justice," P.L.1982, c.77 (C.2A:4A-20 et seq.), P.L.1982, c.79 (C.2A:4A-60 et seq.), P.L.1982, c.80 (C.2A:4A-76 et seq.) and P.L.1982, c.81 (C.2A:4A-70 et seq.).

**2C:58-7.** **Persons possessing explosives or destructive devices to notify police**

a. Any person who becomes the possessor of any explosive, destructive device, or ammunition therefor, which is or may be loaded or otherwise dangerous, except such as is possessed for any lawful commercial or other purpose in connection with which the use of explosives is authorized or as is authorized in subsection d. of N.J.S. 2C:39-6, shall within 15 days notify the police authorities of the municipality in which he resides or the State Police that the same is in his possession and shall present the same to them for inspection.

b. When any such ammunition, explosive or destructive device is presented for inspection it shall be inspected to ascertain whether or not it is loaded or of a dangerous character, and if it is found to be loaded or of dangerous character, it shall be destroyed or be unloaded or so processed as to remove its dangerous character before being returned to the possessor.

c. Any police officer having reasonable cause to believe that any person is possessed of any such ammunition, explosive, or destructive device shall investigate, under a proper search warrant when necessary, and shall seize the same for the purpose of inspection, unloading, processing or destruction, as provided in this section, and the same shall not be returned to the possessor thereof until it has been unloaded or so processed.

**2C:58-8.** **Certain wounds and injuries to be reported**

a. Every case of a wound, burn or any other injury arising from or caused by a firearm, destructive device, explosive or weapon shall be reported at once to the police authorities of the municipality where the person reporting is located or to the State Police by the physician consulted, attending or treating the case or the manager, superintendent or other person in charge, whenever such case is presented for treatment or treated in a hospital, sanitarium or other institution. This subsection shall not, however, apply to wounds, burns or injuries received by a member of the armed forces of the United States or the State of New Jersey while engaged in the actual performance of duty.

b. Every case which contains the criteria defined in this subsection shall be reported at once to the police authorities of the municipality where the person reporting is located, or to the Division of State Police, by the physician consulted, attending, or treating the injury, or by the manager, superintendent, or other person in charge, whenever such case is presented for treatment or treated in a hospital, sanitarium or any other institution, facility, or office where medical care is provided. This subsection shall not apply to injuries received by a member of the armed forces of the United States or the State of New Jersey while engaged in the actual performance of duty.

The defined criteria shall consist of a flame burn injury accompanied by one or more of the following factors:

(1) A fire accelerant was used in the incident causing the injury and the presence of an accelerant creates a reasonable suspicion that the patient committed arson in violation of N.J.S.2C:17-1.

(2) Treatment for the injury was sought after an unreasonable delay of time.

(3) Changes or discrepancies in the account of the patient or accompanying person concerning the cause of the injury which creates a reasonable suspicion that the patient committed arson in violation of N.J.S.2C:17-1.

(4) Voluntary statement by the patient or accompanying person that the patient was injured during the commission of arson in violation of N.J.S.2C:17-1.

(5) Voluntary statement by the patient or accompanying person that the patient was injured during a suicide attempt or the commission of criminal homicide in violation of N.J.S.2C:11-1.

(6) Voluntary statement by the patient or accompanying person that the patient has exhibited fire setting behavior prior to the injury or has received counseling for such behavior.

(7) Any other factor determined by the bureau of fire safety in the Department of Community Affairs from information in the burn patient arson registry established under section 4 of P.L.1991, c.433 (C.52:27D-25d3) to typify a patient whose injuries were caused during the commission of arson in violation of N.J.S.2C:17-1.

**2C:58-9.**     **Certain convictions to be reported**

Every conviction under any provision of chapter 39 of this code of a person who is not a citizen of the United States, shall be certified to the proper officer of the United States Government by the county prosecutor of the county in which such conviction was had, or by the Attorney General or his representative.

**2C:58-10.**     **Incendiary or tracer ammunition**

No incendiary or tracer type ammunition shall be discharged anywhere in this State except for law enforcement purposes by law enforcement officers in the course of their official duties or by members of legally recognized military organizations during the actual course of their official duties in or upon military establishments or ranges constructed or maintained for such purposes. Nonincendiary shotgun tracer ammunition may, however, be used on a trap or skeet field for target purposes. Nothing in this section shall prohibit the carrying or possession for distress signal purposes of a visual distress signalling device approved by the United States Coast Guard aboard a private or commercial aircraft or any boat.

**2C:58-11.**     **Repealed**

**2C:58-12.**     **Registration of assault firearms**

a. Within 90 days of the effective date of P.L.1990, c.32 (C.2C:58-12 et al.), the Attorney General shall promulgate a list by trade name of any assault firearm which the Attorney General determines is an assault firearm which is used for legitimate target-shooting purposes. This list shall include, but need not be limited to, the Colt AR-15 and any other assault firearm used in competitive shooting matches sanctioned by the Director of Civilian Marksmanship of the United States Department of the Army.

b. The owner of an assault firearm purchased on or before May 1, 1990 which is on the list of assault firearms determined by the Attorney General to be legitimate for target-shooting purposes shall have one year from the effective date of P.L.1990, c.32 (C.2C:58-12 et al.) to register that firearm. In order to register an assault firearm, the owner shall:

(1) Complete an assault firearm registration statement, in the form to be prescribed by the Superintendent of the State Police;

(2) Pay a registration fee of $50.00 per each assault firearm;

(3) Produce for inspection a valid firearms purchaser identification card, a valid permit to carry handguns, or a copy of the permit to purchase a handgun which was used to purchase the assault firearm which is being registered; and

(4) Submit valid proof that the person is a member of a rifle or pistol club in existence prior to the effective date of P.L.1990, c.32 (C.2C:58-12 et al.).

Membership in a rifle or pistol club shall not be considered valid unless the person joined the club no later than 210 days after the effective date of P.L.1990, c.32 (C.2C:58-12 et al.) and unless the rifle or pistol club files its charter with the Superintendent no later than 180 days following the effective date of P.L.1990, c.32 (C.2C:58-12 et al.). The rifle or pistol club charter shall contain the name and address of the club's headquarters and the name of the club's officers.

The information to be provided in the registration statement shall include, but shall not be limited to: the name and address of the registrant; the number or numbers on the registrant's firearms purchaser identification card, permit to carry handguns, or permit to purchase a handgun; the name, address, and telephone number of the rifle or pistol club in which the registrant is a member; and the make, model, and serial number of the assault firearm being registered. Each registration statement shall be signed by the registrant, and the signature shall constitute a representation of the accuracy of the information contained in the registration statement.

c. For an applicant who resides in a municipality with an organized full-time police department, the registration shall take place at the main office of the police department. For all other applicants, the registration shall take place at any State Police station.

d. Within 60 days of the effective date of P.L.1990, c.32 (C.2C-58-12 et al.), the Superintendent shall prepare the form of registration statement as described in subsection b. of this section and shall provide a suitable supply of statements to each organized full-time municipal police department and each State Police station.

e. One copy of the completed assault firearms registration statement shall be returned to the registrant, a second copy shall be sent to the Superintendent, and, if the registration takes place at a municipal police department, a third copy shall be retained by that municipal police department.

f. If the owner of an assault firearm which has been registered pursuant to this section dies, the owner's heirs or estate shall have 90 days to dispose of that firearm in accordance with section 12 of P.L.1990, c.32 (C.2C:58-13).

g. If an assault firearm registered pursuant to the provisions of this section is used in the commission of a crime, the registrant of that assault firearm shall be civilly liable for any damages resulting from that crime. The liability imposed by this subsection shall not apply if the assault firearm used in the commission of the crime was stolen and the registrant reported the theft of the firearm to law enforcement authorities within 24 hours of the registrant's knowledge of the theft.

h. Of the registration fee required pursuant to subsection b. of this section, $20.00 shall be forwarded to the State Treasury for deposit in the account used by the Violent Crimes Compensation Board in satisfying claims and for related administrative costs pursuant to the provisions of the "Criminal Injuries Compensation Act of 1971," P.L.1971, c.317 (C.52:4B-1 et seq.).

**2C:58-13.** **Transfer of assault firearm to another; rendering inoperable; voluntarily surrendering**

    a. Any person who legally owns an assault firearm on the effective date of this act and who is unable to register or chooses not to register the firearm pursuant to section 11 of P.L.1990, c.32 (C.2C:58-12) may retain possession of that firearm for a period not to exceed one year from the effective date of this act. During this time period, the owner of the assault firearm shall either:

        (1) Transfer the assault firearm to any person or firm lawfully entitled to own or possess such firearm;

        (2) Render the assault firearm inoperable; or

        (3) Voluntarily surrender the assault firearm pursuant to the provisions of N.J.S.2C:39-12.

    b. If the owner of an assault firearm elects to render the firearm inoperable, the owner shall file a certification on a form prescribed by the Superintendent of the State Police indicating the date on which the firearm was rendered inoperable. This certification shall be filed with either the chief law enforcement officer of the municipality in which the owner resides or, in the case of an owner who resides outside this State but stores or possesses an assault firearm in this State, with the Superintendent of the State Police.

    c. As used in this section, "inoperable" means that the firearm is altered in such a manner that it cannot be immediately fired and that the owner or possessor of the firearm does not possess or have control over the parts necessary to make the firearm operable.

**2C:58-14.** **Annual report on assault firearms**

Within 180 days of the enactment of P.L.1990, c.32 (C.2C:58-12 et al.), and annually thereafter, the Attorney General shall present a report to the Legislature which includes the types and quantities of firearms surrendered or rendered inoperable pursuant to section 12 of this act and the number and types of criminal offenses involving assault firearms and any recommendations, including additions or deletions to the inventory of assault firearms delineated in N.J.S.2C:39-1, which the Attorney General believes should be considered by the Legislature.

**2C:58-15.** **Minor's access to a loaded firearm; penalty, conditions**

    a. A person who knows or reasonably should know that a minor is likely to gain access to a loaded firearm at a premises under the person's control commits a disorderly persons offense if a minor gains access to the firearm, unless the person:

        (1) Stores the firearm in a securely locked box or container;

        (2) Stores the firearm in a location which a reasonable person would believe to be secure; or

        (3) Secures the firearm with a trigger lock.

    b. This section shall not apply:

        (1) To activities authorized by section 14 of P.L.1979, c.179, (C.2C:58-6.1), concerning the lawful use of a firearm by a minor; or

        (2) Under circumstances where a minor obtained a firearm as a result of an unlawful entry by any person.

    c. As used in this act, "minor" means a person under the age of 16.

**2C:58-16.**     **Retailer's written warnings; wholesaler's warning; violation, penalty**

a. Upon the retail sale or transfer of any firearm, the retail dealer or his employee shall deliver to the purchaser or transferee the following written warning, printed in block letters not less than one-fourth of an inch in height: "IT IS A CRIMINAL OFFENSE, PUNISHABLE BY A FINE AND IMPRISONMENT, FOR AN ADULT TO LEAVE A LOADED FIREARM WITHIN EASY ACCESS OF A MINOR."

b. Every wholesale and retail dealer of firearms shall conspicuously post at each purchase counter the following warning, printed in block letters not less than one inch in height: "IT IS A CRIMINAL OFFENSE TO LEAVE A LOADED FIREARM WITHIN EASY ACCESS OF A MINOR."

c. Violation of this section by any retail or wholesale dealer of firearms is a petty disorderly persons offense.

**2C:58-17.**     **"KeepSafe" program established**

a. There is established a "KeepSafe" program to encourage and stimulate the safe storage of firearms in the State of New Jersey by providing instant rebates to firearms purchasers who purchase trigger locking devices.

Under the program, a person who purchases a firearm from a retail dealer licensed under the provisions of N.J.S.2C:58-2 shall be eligible for a $5 instant rebate when a compatible trigger locking device is purchased along with that firearm. The licensed retail dealer shall deduct the rebate from the price of the compatible locking device in order to reduce by $5 the cost of the device for the purchaser.

b. The Superintendent of State Police, in conjunction with the Attorney General, shall adopt guidelines in accordance with the Administrative Procedure Act, P.L.1968, c.410 (C.52:14B-1 et seq.), to effectuate the purposes of this act.

In addition, the superintendent shall prepare and deliver to each licensed retail firearms dealer in the State the forms necessary to record and report participation in the program. The forms, which shall set forth the name, address, telephone number, State tax number and State license number of the retail firearms dealer, the name of the firearms purchaser and his firearms purchaser identification card number or permit to purchase a handgun number, the make and model number of the compatible trigger locking device purchased and the date of the sale, shall be in duplicate. One copy shall be retained by the retail dealer for his records. The other shall be submitted to the Attorney General for reimbursement. The reimbursement copies shall be submitted monthly at a time prescribed by the superintendent. The submitting retail dealer shall be entitled to a reimbursement of $5 for each trigger locking device sold as part of the KeepSafe program. To help defray any administrative costs, each participating retail dealer shall receive, in addition to the reimbursement, $0.50 for each valid reimbursement copy submitted.

The superintendent also shall provide each licensed retail firearms dealer with a sign to be prominently displayed at a conspicuous place on the dealer's business premises where firearms are offered for sale. The sign shall state substantially the following:

(1)   "KEEP NEW JERSEY FIREARMS SAFE.

(2)   TO ENCOURAGE NEW JERSEY GUN OWNERS TO

(3)   STORE THEIR FIREARMS SAFELY, THE STATE IS

(4)   OFFERING A $5 INSTANT REBATE WHEN YOU

(5)   PURCHASE A COMPATIBLE TRIGGER LOCK ALONG

(6)   WITH YOUR FIREARM.

(7)  REMEMBER—THE USE OF A TRIGGER LOCK IS

(8)  ONLY ONE ASPECT OF RESPONSIBLE FIREARM

(9)  STORAGE. FIREARMS SHOULD BE STORED,

(10)  UNLOADED AND LOCKED IN A LOCATION THAT IS

(11)  BOTH SEPARATE FROM THEIR AMMUNITION

(12)  AND INACCESSIBLE TO CHILDREN.

(13)  NEW JERSEY's FAMILIES AND CHILDREN ARE

(14)  PRECIOUS—KEEP THEM SAFE!!"

**2C:58-18.**          **Report on "KeepSafe" program**

On the first day of the thirteenth month following the effective date of this act, the superintendent shall submit a report on the effectiveness of the KeepSafe program to the Governor and Legislature. In addition to those matters the superintendent deems appropriate and necessary, the report shall include the superintendent's assessment of whether the program should be expanded to include sales of trigger locking devices which are not part of firearm purchases.

**Chapters 59 to 61—Reserved**

# 62

# WILLFUL NONSUPPORT

**2C:62-1.**     **Support orders for willful nonsupport**

    a. **Order for support pendente lite.** At any time after a sworn complaint is made charging an offense under section 2C:24-5 and before trial, the court may enter such temporary order as may seem just, providing for the support of the spouse or children, or both, pendente lite, and may punish a violation of such order as for contempt.

    b. **Order for future support; release on recognizance conditioned on obeying order; periodic service of sentence.** Before trial, with the consent of the defendant, or after conviction, instead of imposing the penalty provided for violation of section 2C:24-5, or in addition thereto, the court, having regard to the circumstances and the financial ability or earning capacity of the defendant, may make an order, which shall be subject to change by the court from time to time as circumstances may require, directing the defendant to pay a sum certain periodically to the spouse, or to the guardian or custodian of the minor child or children, or to an organization or individual approved by the court as trustee. The court may release the defendant from custody on probation, upon his or her entering into a recognizance, with or without surety, in such sum as the court may order and approve. The condition of the recognizance shall be such that if the defendant shall personally appear in court whenever ordered to do so, and shall comply with the terms of the order, or of any modification thereof, the recognizance shall be void, otherwise it will remain in full force and effect. The court may, in addition to or in place of any order under this section, order and direct that any sentence of imprisonment be served periodically, instead of consecutively, during periods of time between Friday at 6 p.m. and Monday at 8 a.m. or at other times or on other days, whenever the court determines the existence of proper circumstances and that the ends of justice will be served thereby. Any person so imprisoned shall be given credit for each day or fraction of a day to the nearest hour actually served.

    c. **Violation of order.** If the court be satisfied by information and due proof under oath that the defendant has violated the terms of the order, it may forthwith proceed with the trial of the defendant under the original charge, or sentence the defendant under the original conviction or plea of guilty, or enforce the suspended sentence or punish for contempt, as the case may be. In case of forfeiture of a recognizance, and the enforcement thereof by execution, the sum recovered may, in the discretion of the court, be paid in whole or part to the spouse, or to the guardian, custodian or trustee of such minor child or children.

    d. **Proof of marriage; husband and wife as witness.** No other or greater evidence shall be required to prove the marriage of such husband and wife, or that the defendant is the father or mother of such child or children, than is required in a civil action. In no prosecution under this chapter shall any existing statute or rule of law prohibiting the disclosure of confidential communications between husband and wife apply, and both husband

and wife shall be competent and compellable witnesses to testify against each other as to any and all relevant matters, including the fact of the marriage and the parentage of the child or children.

e. **Place of residence confers jurisdiction of offense.** The place of residence at the time of the desertion of the spouse, child or children, under the provisions of this chapter, shall confer jurisdiction of the offense set forth therein, upon the county, county district, or juvenile and domestic relations court having territorial jurisdiction of the place of such residence, until the deserted party shall establish a legal residence in some other county or State.

**Chapter 63—Reserved**

# 64

# FORFEITURE

**2C:64-1.**     **Property subject to forfeiture**

    a.  Any interest in the following shall be subject to forfeiture and no property right shall exist in them:

        (1)  Controlled dangerous substances, firearms which are unlawfully possessed, carried, acquired or used, illegally possessed gambling devices, untaxed cigarettes and untaxed special fuel. These shall be designated prima facie contraband.

        (2)  All property which has been, or is intended to be, utilized in furtherance of an unlawful activity, including, but not limited to, conveyances intended to facilitate the perpetration of illegal acts, or buildings or premises maintained for the purpose of committing offenses against the State.

        (3)  Property which has become or is intended to become an integral part of illegal activity, including, but not limited to, money which is earmarked for use as financing for an illegal gambling enterprise.

        (4)  Proceeds of illegal activities, including, but not limited to, property or money obtained as a result of the sale of prima facie contraband as defined by subsection a. (1), proceeds of illegal gambling, prostitution, bribery and extortion.

    b.  Any article subject to forfeiture under this chapter may be seized by the State or any law enforcement officer as evidence pending a criminal prosecution pursuant to section 2C:64-4 or, when no criminal proceeding is instituted, upon process issued by any court of competent jurisdiction over the property, except that seizure without such process may be made when not inconsistent with the Constitution of this State or the United States, and when

        (1)  The article is prima facie contraband; or,

        (2)  The property subject to seizure poses an immediate threat to the public health, safety or welfare.

    c.  For the purposes of this section:

        "Untaxed special fuel" means diesel fuel, No. 2 fuel oil and kerosene on which the motor fuel tax imposed pursuant to R.S.54:39-1 et seq. is not paid that is delivered, possessed, sold or transferred in this State in a manner not authorized pursuant to R.S.54:39-1 et seq. or P.L.1938, c.163 (C.56:6-1 et seq.).

**2C:64-2.**     **Forfeiture procedures; prima facie contraband**

Except as provided in N.J.S. 2C:35-21, prima facie contraband shall be retained by the State until entry of judgment or dismissal of the criminal proceeding, if any, arising out of the seizure. Thereafter, prima facie contraband shall be forfeited to the entity funding the prosecuting agency involved, subject to the rights of owners and others holding interests pursuant to section 2C:64-5.

**2C:64-3.        Forfeiture procedures**

a.  Whenever any property other than prima facie contraband is subject to forfeiture under this chapter, such forfeiture may be enforced by a civil action, instituted within 90 days of the seizure and commenced by the State and against the property sought to be forfeited.

b.  The complaint shall be verified on oath or affirmation. It shall describe with reasonable particularity the property that is the subject matter of the action and shall contain allegations setting forth the reason or reasons the article sought to be or which has been seized is contraband.

c.  Notice of the action shall be given to any person known to have a property interest in the article. In addition, the notice requirements of the Rules of Court for an in rem action shall be followed.

d.  The claimant of the property that is the subject of an action under this chapter shall file and serve his claim in the form of an answer in accordance with the Rules of Court. The answer shall be verified on oath or affirmation, and shall state the interest in the property by virtue of which the claimant demands its restitution and the right to defend the action. If the claim is made in behalf of the person entitled to possession by an agent, bailee or attorney, it shall state that he is duly authorized to make the claim.

e.  If no answer is filed and served within the applicable time, the property seized shall be disposed of pursuant to N.J.S.2C:64-6.

f.  If an answer is filed, the Superior or county district court shall set the matter down for a summary hearing as soon as practicable. Upon application of the State or claimant, if he be a defendant in a criminal proceeding arising out of the seizure, the Superior or county district court may stay proceedings in the forfeiture action until the criminal proceedings have been concluded by an entry of final judgment.

g.  Any person with a property interest in the seized property, other than a defendant who is being prosecuted in connection with the seizure of property may secure its release pending the forfeiture action unless the article is dangerous to the public health, safety and welfare or the State can demonstrate that the property will probably be lost or destroyed if released or employed in subsequent criminal activity. Any person with such a property interest other than a defendant who is being prosecuted, prior to the release of said property shall post a bond with the court in the amount of the market value of the seized item.

h.  The prosecuting agency with approval of the entity funding such agency, or any other entity, with the approval of the prosecuting agency, where the other entity's law enforcement agency participated in the surveillance, investigation or arrest which is the subject of the forfeiture action, may apply to the Superior Court for an order permitting use of seized property, pending the disposition of the forfeiture action provided, however, that such property shall be used solely for law enforcement purposes. Approval shall be liberally granted but shall be conditioned upon the filing of a bond in an amount equal to the market value of the item seized or a written guarantee of payment for property which may be subject to return, replacement or compensation as to reasonable value in the event that the forfeiture is refused or only partial extinguishment of property rights is ordered by the court.

i.  If the property is of such nature that substantial difficulty may result in preserving its value during the pendency of the forfeiture action, the Superior or county district court may appoint a trustee to protect the interests of all parties involved in the action.

j. Evidence of a conviction of a criminal offense in which seized property was either used or provided an integral part of the State's proofs in the prosecution shall be considered in the forfeiture proceeding as creating a rebuttable presumption that the property was utilized in furtherance of an unlawful activity.

## 2C:64-4. Seized property; evidentiary use

a. Nothing in this chapter shall impair the right of the State to retain evidence pending a criminal prosecution.

b. The fact that a prosecution involving seized property terminates without a conviction does not preclude forfeiture proceedings against the property pursuant to this chapter.

## 2C:64-5. Seized property; rights of owners and others holding interests

a. No forfeiture under this chapter shall affect the rights of any lessor in the ordinary course of business or any person holding a perfected security interest in property subject to seizure unless it shall appear that such person had knowledge of or consented to any act or omission upon which the right of forfeiture is based. Such rights are only to the extent of interest in the seized property and at the option of the entity funding the prosecuting agency involved may be extinguished by appropriate payment.

b. Property seized under this chapter shall not be subject to forfeiture if the owner of the property establishes by a preponderance of the evidence that the owner was not involved in or aware of the unlawful activity and that the owner had done all that could reasonably be expected to prevent the proscribed use of the property by an agent. A person who uses or possesses property with the consent or knowledge of the owner is deemed to be the agent of the owner for purposes of this chapter.

c. Property seized under this chapter shall not be subject to forfeiture if the property is seized while entrusted to a person by the owner or the agent of the owner when the property has been entrusted to the person for repairs, restoration or other services to be performed on the property, and that person, without the owner's knowledge or consent, uses the property for unlawful purposes.

## 2C:64-6. Disposal of forfeited property

a. Property which has been forfeited shall be destroyed if it can serve no lawful purpose or it presents a danger to the public health, safety or welfare. All other forfeited property or any proceeds resulting from the forfeiture and all money seized pursuant to this chapter shall become the property of the entity funding the prosecuting agency involved and shall be disposed of, distributed, appropriated and used in accordance with the provisions of this chapter.

The prosecutor or the Attorney General, whichever is prosecuting the case, shall divide the forfeited property, any proceeds resulting from the forfeiture or any money seized pursuant to this chapter with any other entity where the other entity's law enforcement agency participated in the surveillance, investigation, arrest or prosecution resulting in the forfeiture, in proportion to the other entity's contribution to the surveillance, investigation, arrest or prosecution resulting in the forfeiture, as determined in the discretion of the prosecutor or the Attorney General, whichever is prosecuting the case. Notwithstanding any other provision of law, such forfeited property and proceeds shall be used solely for law enforcement purposes, and shall be designated for the exclusive use of the law enforcement agency which contributed to the surveillance, investigation, arrest or prosecution resulting in the forfeiture.

The Attorney General is authorized to promulgate rules and regulations to implement and enforce the provisions of this act.

b. For a period of two years from the date of enactment of P.L.1993, c.227 (C.26:4-100.13 et al.), 10% of the proceeds obtained by the Attorney General under the provisions of subsection a. of this section shall be deposited into the Hepatitis Inoculation Fund established pursuant to section 2 of P.L.1993, c.227 (C.26:4-100.13).

c. Beginning two years from the date of enactment of P.L.1993, c.227 (C.26:4-100.13 et al.) and in subsequent years, 5% of the proceeds obtained by the Attorney General under the provisions of subsection a. of this section shall be deposited into the Hepatitis Inoculation Fund established pursuant to section 2 of P.L.1993, c.227 (C.26:4-100.13).

## 2C:64-7.        Vesting of title in forfeited property

Title to property forfeited under this chapter shall vest in the entity funding the prosecuting agency involved at the time the item was utilized illegally, or, in the case of proceeds, when received.

If another entity's law enforcement agency has participated in the surveillance, investigation, arrest or prosecution resulting in the forfeiture, then the prosecutor or the Attorney General, whichever is prosecuting the case, shall vest title to forfeited property, including motor vehicles, by dividing the forfeited property with the other entity in proportion to the other entity's contribution to the surveillance, investigation, arrest or prosecution resulting in the forfeiture, as determined in the discretion of the prosecutor or the Attorney General. If the property, including motor vehicles, cannot be divided as required by this section, then the prosecutor or the Attorney General, whichever is prosecuting the case, shall sell the property, including motor vehicles, and the proceeds of the sale shall be divided with the other entity in proportion to the other entity's contribution to the surveillance, investigation, arrest or prosecution resulting in the forfeiture, as determined in the discretion of the prosecutor or the Attorney General.

## 2C:64-8.        Seized property; statute of limitations on claims

Any person who could not with due diligence have discovered that property which he owns was seized as contraband may file a claim for its return or the value thereof at the time of seizure within 3 years of the seizure if he can demonstrate that he did not consent to, and had no knowledge of its unlawful use. If the property has been sold, the claimant receives a claim against proceeds.

## 2C:64-9.        Forfeited weapons with military value; donation to National Guard Militia Museum

Any weapon with present or historical military value that has been forfeited pursuant to the provisions of chapter 64 of Title 2C of the New Jersey Statutes may be donated to the National Guard Militia Museum of New Jersey at Sea Girt by the law enforcement agency retaining it.

# 65

## DISPOSITION
## OF STOLEN PROPERTY
## AND DOCUMENTARY
## EXHIBITS

**2C:65-1.**  **Procedure to be followed by law enforcement agencies when stolen property is taken into custody**

When any article of property alleged to be stolen comes into the custody of a law enforcement agency, that agency shall enter in a suitable book a description of that article and shall attach a number to each article, and make a corresponding entry thereof. The agency shall also make and retain a complete photographic record of the property. The photographic record, upon proper authentication, may be introduced as evidence in any court in lieu of the property.

**2C:65-2.**  **Release of stolen property prior to final determination of proceeding**

    a. A law enforcement agency, upon satisfactory proof of ownership of property held pursuant to this section, and upon presentation of proper personal identification, may release the property to the person presenting such proof pursuant to the provisions of subsection b. The release shall be without prejudice to the State or to the person from whom custody of the property was taken or to any person who may have a claim against the property. Any such delivery shall be noted in the book required by 2C:65-1. The person to whom the property is delivered shall sign a sworn declaration of ownership which shall be retained by the agency.

    b. Nothing in this section shall prohibit a law enforcement agency from immediately returning property to its rightful owner where the agency is satisfied that there is no colorable dispute as to ownership; provided, however, that where the law enforcement agency has reason to believe that there is a dispute concerning ownership of property, or if the person from whom custody of the property was taken shall claim ownership, or if any other person shall claim ownership, the property shall not be released to any person claiming it until a hearing has been held pursuant to subsection c.

    c. The court having jurisdiction over the case in which the stolen property is involved, upon application by the person from whom possession was taken, or the person claiming ownership, shall review the matter and order the property to be delivered to the person claiming ownership, or to be retained by the law enforcement agency upon a finding that the person claiming ownership of the property is not entitled thereto.

2C:65-3.        **Disposition of stolen property after final determination of proceeding**

    a. After final determination of any action or proceeding, the court, on application of the person claiming ownership, or an agent designated in writing by the person, may order all property, other than documentary exhibits, to be delivered to the person.

    b. After the expiration of 6 months from the final determination of the action, if the person entitled to the property is unknown, or fails to apply, the court in which the case was tried, upon application of the law enforcement agency in possession of the property, shall make an order specifying what property may be released from the custody of the agency without prejudice to the State. Upon receipt of the order, the clerk of the court shall transfer the property for disposal at public sale to the State, county or municipality, whichever was the prosecuting authority. The property shall not be transferred where it consists of money or currency, but it shall be deposited immediately in the general fund of either the State, county or municipality.

2C:65-4.        **Disposition of documentary exhibits**

No exhibit shall be destroyed or otherwise disposed of until 60 days after the clerk of the court has posted a notice conspicuously in three places in the county, referring to the order for the disposition, describing briefly the exhibit, and indicating the date after which the exhibit will be destroyed or otherwise disposed of.

# 66

# DEPOSITED FUNDS

**2C:66-1.**    **Attachment of deposited funds**

    a. As used in this act:

        "Financial institution" means a state or federally chartered bank, savings bank or savings and loan association or any other financial services company or provider, including, but not limited to, broker-dealers, investment companies, money market and mutual funds, credit unions and insurers.

    b. Upon application by the Attorney General, a court may issue an attachment order directing a financial institution to freeze some or all of the funds or assets deposited with or held by the financial institution by or on behalf of an account holder when there exists a reasonable suspicion that the account holder has committed or is about to commit the crime of terrorism in violation of section 2 of P.L.2002, c.26 (C.2C:38-2) or soliciting or providing material support or resources for terrorism in violation of section 5 of P.L.2002, c.26 (C.2C:38-5).

**2C:66-2.**    **Application by Attorney General**

Application. The application of the Attorney General required by this act shall contain:

    a. a statement of the approximate financial loss caused by the account holder in the commission of the crime of terrorism in violation of section 2 of P.L.2002, c 26 (C.2C:38-2) or soliciting or providing material support or resources for terrorism in violation of section 5 of P.L.2002, c.26 (C.2C:38-5);

    b. a statement of facts relied upon by the Attorney General, including the details of the particular offense that is about to be committed or that has been committed; and

    c. identification of the account holder's name and financial institution account number.

**2C:66-3.**    **Issuance of an order**

If the court finds that:

    a. there exists a reasonable suspicion that the account holder has committed or is about to commit the crime of terrorism in violation of section 2 of P.L.2002, c.26 (C.2C:38-2) or the crime of soliciting or providing material support or resources for terrorism in violation of section 5 of P.L.2002, c.26 (C.2C:38-5);

    b. the accounts of the account holder are specifically identified; and

    c. it is necessary to freeze the account holder's funds or assets to ensure eventual restitution to victims of the alleged offense,

        the court may order the financial institution to freeze all or part of the account holder's deposited funds or assets so that the funds or assets may not be withdrawn or disposed of until further order of the court.

As part of the consideration of an application in which there is no corroborative evidence offered, the judge shall inquire in camera as to the identity of any informants or any other additional information concerning the basis upon which the Attorney General has applied for the attachment order which the judge finds relevant in order to determine if there exists a reasonable suspicion pursuant to this act.

**2C:66-4.**     **Duty of financial institutions**

Upon receipt of the order authorized by this act, a financial institution shall not permit any funds or assets that were frozen by the order to be withdrawn or disposed of until further order of the court.

**2C:66-5.**     **Release of funds**

a. The account holder may, upon notice and motion, have a hearing to contest the freezing of funds or assets and to seek the release of all or part of them.

b. The account holder is entitled to an order releasing all or part of the funds or assets by showing:

(1) that the account holder has posted a bond or other adequate surety, guaranteeing that, upon conviction, adequate funds or assets will be available to pay complete restitution to victims of the alleged offense;

(2) that there does not exist a reasonable suspicion that the account holder has committed or is about to commit the alleged offense;

(3) that the amount of funds or assets frozen is more than is necessary to pay complete restitution to all victims of the alleged offense; or

(4) that the funds or assets should be returned in the interests of justice.

c. It is not grounds for the release of funds or assets that the particular accounts frozen do not contain funds or assets that were proceeds from or used in the commission of the crime of terrorism in violation of section 2 of P.L.2002, c.26 (C.2C:38-2) or soliciting or providing material support or resources for terrorism in violation of section 5 of P.L.2002, c.26 (C.2C:38-5).

**2C:66-6.**     **Disposition of funds**

a. The court may order the financial institution to remit all or part of the frozen funds or assets to the court.

b. If the account holder is acquitted or the charges are dismissed with prejudice, the court shall issue an order releasing the freeze on the funds or assets.

c. If the account holder is not acquitted or the charges are not dismissed, the frozen funds or assets shall become the property of the State and shall be used to provide restitution to victims of terrorism, to fund State law enforcement anti-terrorism programs and activities and for other law enforcement purposes.

**2C:66-7.**     **Time limit**

The freeze permitted by this act expires 24 months after the date of the court's initial attachment order unless the time limit is extended by the court in writing upon a showing of good cause by the Attorney General.

**2C:66-8.**     **Notice**

Within ten days after a court issues an attachment order under this act, the Attorney General shall send a copy of the order to the account holder's last known address or to the account holder's attorney, if known.

**2C:66-9.** **Rights and remedies of financial institution**

A financial institution that is directed to block, freeze or encumber an account pursuant to this act shall be entitled during the period that the account is blocked, frozen or encumbered to exercise any right or remedy with respect to the account as provided by law, or in the deposit agreement and rules or regulations of the financial institution applicable to the account. The provision of this act shall not be construed to preclude a financial institution from exercising its right of set-off or to charge back or recoup a deposit to an account.

**2C:66-10.** **No liability for freezing funds**

Notwithstanding any other law to the contrary, a financial institution shall not be liable to any person for blocking, freezing, encumbering or refusing to release any funds or assets held by the financial institution in response to an order issued by a court, or for any other action taken by the financial institution in good faith to comply with the requirements of this act. A financial institution shall not be required to give notice to an account holder or customer that the financial institution has taken any action pursuant to this act and shall not be liable for failure to provide the notice.

**2C:66-11.** **Construction of act**

Nothing contained in this act shall be construed to abrogate or affect the status, force or operation of the forfeiture provisions of the "New Jersey Code of Criminal Justice," N.J.S.2C:64-1 et seq., or any other provision of law.

**Chapters 67 to 97—Reserved**

# 98

# REPEALERS, ALLOCATIONS AND EFFECTIVE DATE

**2C:98-1.**   **Construction**

The provisions of R.S. 1:1-8 and R.S. 1:1-11 to 1:1-21, both inclusive, shall be applicable to the enactment and operation of said Title 2C. The enactment of this law shall not, due to the repeal set forth in section 2C:98-2:

    a.  Be deemed to revive any common law right or remedy abolished by any sections, acts or parts of acts repealed thereby; or

    b.  Affect any right now vested in any person pursuant to the provisions of those sections, acts or parts of acts, nor any remedy where an action or proceeding thereunder has heretofore been instituted and is pending on the effective date of said repeal.

**2C:98-2.**   **Repealer**

All acts and parts of acts inconsistent with this act are hereby superseded and repealed, and without limiting the general effect of this act in superseding and repealing acts so inconsistent herewith, the following sections, acts and parts of acts, together with all amendments and supplements thereto, are specifically repealed:

New Jersey Statutes sections:

2A:85-1 to 2A:85-5 both inclusive;
2A:85-6 to 2A:85-14 both inclusive;
2A:86-1 to 2A:88-1 both inclusive;
2A:89-1 to 2A:90-3 both inclusive;
2A:91-1 to 2A:94-3 both inclusive;
2A:95-1 and 2A:95-2;
2A:96-1 to 2A:96-4 both inclusive;
2A:97-1 to 2A:98-2 both inclusive;
2A:99-1 and 2A:99-2;
2A:100-1 to 2A:102-12 both inclusive;
2A:103-1 to 2A:104-12 both inclusive;
2A:105-1 to 2A:105-4 both inclusive;
2A:106-1 to 2A:108-8 both inclusive;
2A:109-1 to 2A:111-21 both inclusive;
2A:111-22 to 2A:111-24 both inclusive;

2A:112-1 to 2A:115-1 both inclusive;

2A:115-2;

2A:115-3;

2A:115-4 and 2A:115-5;

2A:116-1 to 2A:119-5 both inclusive;

2A:119-6 to 2A:119-8 both inclusive;

2A:119-9;

2A:120-1 to 2A:121-5 both inclusive;

2A:122-1 to 2A:122-9 both inclusive;

2A:123-1 and 2A:123-2;

2A:124-1 to 2A:127-3 both inclusive;

2A:128-1 to 2A:134-1 both inclusive;

2A:135-1 to 2A:145-1 both inclusive;

2A:146-2 to 2A:148-22 both inclusive;

2A:150-1;

2A:151-1 to 2A:151-9 both inclusive;

2A:151-12;

2A:151-14 to 2A:151-28 both inclusive;

2A:151-31 to 2A:151-41 both inclusive;

2A:151-42 to 2A:151-44 both inclusive;

2A:151-45 to 2A:151-57 os, (inclusive);

2A:151-58 to 2A:151-61 both inclusive;

2A:152-5 to 2A:152-9 both inclusive;

2A:152-10 and 2A:152-11;

2A:152-14;

2A:159-1 to 2A:159-3 both inclusive;

2A:163-2;

2A:163-3;

2A:164-2 to 2A:164-13 both inclusive;

2A:164-14 to 2A:164-23 both inclusive;

2A:164-25 to 2A:164-28 both inclusive;

2A:165-1 to 2A:165-12 both inclusive;

2A:166-1 to 2A:166-7 both inclusive;

2A:166-11;

2A:166-14 to 2A:166-16 both inclusive;

2A:167-1 to 2A:167-3 both inclusive;

2A:168-1 to 2A:168-4 both inclusive;

2A:169-1 and 2A:169-2;

2A:169-4 to 2A:169-10 both inclusive;

2A:170-1 to 2A:170-3 both inclusive;

2A:170-4 to 2A:170-7 both inclusive;

2A:170-9 to 2A:170-11 both inclusive;

2A:170-14;

2A:170-16 to 2A:170-19 both inclusive;

2A:170-21 and 2A:170-25;

2A:170-26 to 2A:170-30 both inclusive;

2A:170-31;

2A:170-32 to 2A:170-41 both inclusive;

2A:170-42 to 2A:170-44 both inclusive;

2A:170-46 to 2A:170-49 both inclusive;

2A:170-53;

2A:170-55 to 2A:170-64 both inclusive;

2A:170-65 to 2A:170-67 both inclusive;

2A:170-68 and 2A:170-69;

2A:170-70 to 2A:170-76 both inclusive;

2A:170-86 to 2A:170-90 both inclusive;

2A:170-93 to 2A:170-96 both inclusive;

2A:171-1;

2A:171-2;

2A:171-4 and 2A:171-5;

2A:171-6 to 2A:171-12 both inclusive;

Pamphlet Laws:

Laws of 1971, c. 450 (C. 2A:85-5.1);

Laws of 1973, c. 191 (C. 2A:85-15 to C. 2A:85-23 both inclusive);

Laws of 1964, c. 74 (C. 2A:88A-1);

Laws of 1962, c. 39 (C. 2A:90-4);

Laws of 1971, c. 314 (C. 2A:94-4);

Laws of 1954, c. 219 (C. 2A:95-3);

Laws of 1961, c. 53 (C. 2A:98-3 and C. 2A:98-4);

Laws of 1960, c. 177 (C. 2A:99A-1 to C. 2A:99A-4 both inclusive);

Laws of 1970, c. 131 (C. 2A:99B-1);

Laws of 1959, c. 98 (C. 2A:102-12.1);

Laws of 1964, c. 265 (C. 2A:104-13 and C. 2A:104-14);

Laws of 1968, c. 83 (C. 2A:105-5);

Laws of 1964, c. 179 (C. 2A:111-21.1);

Laws of 1952, c. 332 (C. 2A:111-25 to C. 2A:111-27 both inclusive);

Laws of 1954, c. 58 (C. 2A:111-28 to C. 2A:111-31 both inclusive);

Laws of 1960, c. 62 (C. 2A:111-32 and C. 2A:111-33);

Laws of 1964, c. 294 (C. 2A:111-34 to C. 2A:111-36 both inclusive);

Laws of 1968, c. 253 (C. 2A:111-37 and C. 2A:111-38);

Laws of 1968, c. 260 (C. 2A:111-39);

Laws of 1968, c. 300 (C. 2A:111-40 to C. 2A:111-51 both inclusive);

Laws of 1962, c. 165 (C. 2A:115-1.1);

Laws of 1971, c. 449 (C. 2A:115-1.1a and C. 2A:115-1.1b);

Laws of 1971, c. 446 (C. 2A:115-1.6 to C. 2A:115-1.12 both inclusive);

Laws of 1971, c. 447 (C. 2A:115-2.1 to C. 2A:115-2.4 both inclusive);

Laws of 1971, c. 448 (C. 2A:115-2.5 to C. 2A:115-2.9 both inclusive);

Laws of 1953, c. 392 (C. 2A:115-3.1);

Laws of 1962, c. 166 (C. 2A:115-3.3 and C. 2A:115-3.5 to C. 2A:115-3.10 both inclusive);

Laws of 1971, c. 376 (C. 2A:116-6);

Laws of 1965, c. 52 (C. 2A:119-5.1 to C. 2A:119-5.5 both inclusive);

Laws of 1962, c. 201 (C. 2A:119-8.1);

Laws of 1968, c. 349 (C. 2A:119A-1 to C. 2A:119A-4 both inclusive);

Laws of 1961, c. 39 (C. 2A:121-6);

Laws of 1971, c. 87 (C. 2A:122-9.1 and C. 2A:122-9.2);

Laws of 1960, c. 5 (C. 2A:122-10);

Laws of 1960, c. 69 (C. 2A:122-11);

Laws of 1967, c. 72 (C. 2A:122-12);

Laws of 1964, c. 86 (C. 2A:127-5);

Laws of 1957, c. 49 (C. 2A:148-22.1);

Laws of 1967, c. 182 (C. 2A:149A-1);

Laws of 1968, c. 395 (C. 2A:149A-2 and C. 2A:149A-3);

Laws of 1968, c. 147 (C. 2A:151-10.1);

Laws of 1969, c. 157 (C. 2A:151-41.1 and C. 2A:151-41.2);

Laws of 1966, c. 60 (C. 2A:151-44.1 and C. 2A:151-44.2);

Laws of 1966, c. 60 (C. 2A:151-57.1 and C. 2A:151-57.2);

Laws of 1952, c. 5 (C. 2A:151-62 and C. 2A:151-63);

Laws of 1962, c. 160 (C. 2A:152-9.1 to C. 2A:152-9.5 both inclusive);

Laws of 1952, c. 212 (C. 2A:152-15 and C. 2A:152-16);

Laws of 1952, c. 74 (C. 2A:159-4);

Laws of 1968, c. 279 (C. 2A:169-11);

Laws of 1971, c. 315 (C. 2A:170-3.1 to C. 2A:170-3.3 both inclusive);

Laws of 1955, c. 105 (C. 2A:170-20.8);

Laws of 1953, c. 67 (C. 2A:170-25.2);

Laws of 1954, c. 147 (C. 2A:170-25.3);

Laws of 1955, c. 213 (C. 2A:170-25.4);

Laws of 1955, c. 250 (C. 2A:170-25.5);

Laws of 1959, c. 194 (C. 2A:170-25.7);

Laws of 1964, c. 178 (C. 2A:170-25.8);

Laws of 1966, c. 150 (C. 2A:170-25.14 and C. 2A:170-25.15);

Laws of 1970, c. 133 (C. 2A:170-25.16);

Laws of 1973, c. 258 (C. 2A:170-25.18 to C. 2A:170-25.20 both inclusive);

Laws of 1972, c. 159 (C. 2A:170-30.1);

Laws of 1956, c. 185 (C. 2A:170-31.1);

Laws of 1972, c. 160 (C. 2A:170-41.1);

Laws of 1956, c. 195 (C. 2A:170-50.1 to C. 2A:170-50.3 both inclusive);

Laws of 1965, c. 184, sections 3 to 5 (C. 2A:170-50.4 to C. 2A:170-50.6 both inclusive);

Laws of 1957, c. 203 (C. 2A:170-54.1);

Laws of 1968, c. 324 (C. 2A:170-54.2);

Laws of 1953, c. 68 (C. 2A:170-64.1);

Laws of 1961, c. 139 (C. 2A:170-64.2);

Laws of 1954, c. 16 (C. 2A:170-67.1);

Laws of 1954, c. 137 (C. 2A:170-69.1);

Laws of 1958, c. 170 (C. 2A:170-69.1a and C. 2A:170-69.1b);

Laws of 1955, c. 245, sections 2 and 3 (C. 2A:170-69.2 and C. 2A:170-69.3);

Laws of 1964, c. 53 (C. 2A:170-69.4 to C. 2A:170-69.6 both inclusive);

Laws of 1968, c. 288 (C. 2A:170-69.7 and C. 2A:170-69.8);

Laws of 1962, c. 178 (C. 2A:170-97 to C. 2A:170-101 both inclusive);

Laws of 1968, c. 256 (C. 2A:170-102 and C. 2A:170-103);

Laws of 1958, c. 138 (C. 2A:171-5.1 to C. 2A:171-5.7 both inclusive).

**2C:98-3.**        **Allocations**

Pending enactment of acts to revise, repeal or to compile the same in Title 2C of the New Jersey Statutes, the following sections, acts or parts of acts, together with all amendments and supplements thereto, shall remain in full force and effect for use, administration and enforcement as heretofore:

New Jersey Statutes sections:

2A:127-4;

2A:149-1;

2A:151-10 and 2A:151-11;

2A:152-1;

2A:152-2;

2A:152-3;

2A:152-4;

2A:152-12;

2A:152-13;

2A:153-1 to 2A:153-3 both inclusive;

2A:154-1 to 2A:154-3 both inclusive;

2A:155-1 to 2A:156-4 both inclusive;

2A:157-1 to 2A:158-1 both inclusive;

2A:158-2 to 2A:158-10 both inclusive;

2A:158-13;

2A:158-15;

2A:158-16;

2A:158-18;

2A:158-19 and 2A:158-20;

2A:160-1 to 2A:162-8 both inclusive;

2A:163-1;

2A:164-1;

2A:164-24;

2A:166-8 to 2A:166-10 both inclusive;

2A:166-12 and 2A:166-13;

2A:166-17 to 2A:166-19 both inclusive;

2A:167-4 to 2A:167-12 both inclusive;

2A:168-5 to 2A:168-17 both inclusive;

2A:169-3;

2A:170-20;

2A:170-51;

2A:170-77;

2A:170-78 to 2A:170-85 both inclusive;

2A:170-91 and 2A:170-92;

Pamphlet Laws:

Laws of 1952, c. 121 (C. 2A:96-5);

Laws of 1966, c. 12 (C. 2A:96-5.1);

Laws of 1957, c. 182 (C. 2A:102-13 to C. 2A:102-17 both inclusive);

Laws of 1952, c. 95 (C. 2A:108-9);

Laws of 1953, c. 267 (C. 2A:123-3 to C. 2A:123-15 both inclusive);

Laws of 1971, c. 412 (C. 2A:150A-1 to C. 2A:150A-5 both inclusive);

Laws of 1973, c. 354 (C. 2A:150A-6);

Laws of 1956, c. 134 (C. 2A:152-17 to C. 2A:152-19 both inclusive);

Laws of 1968, c. 427 (C. 2A:154-4);

Laws of 1967, c. 171 (C. 2A:153-4);

Laws of 1968, c. 409 (C. 2A:156A-1 to C. 2A:156A-26);

Laws of 1970, c. 6 (C. 2A:158-1.1 and C. 2A:158-1.2);

Laws of 1970, c. 6 (C. 2A:158-15.1 and C. 2A:158-15.2);

Laws of 1957, c. 128 (C. 2A:158-16.1);

Laws of 1953, c. 307 (C. 2A:158-18.1 and C. 2A:158-18.2);

Laws of 1964, c. 168 (C. 2A:158-21);

Laws of 1967, c. 43 (C. 2A:158A-1 to C. 2A:158A-5 both inclusive);

Laws of 1974, c. 33 (C. 2A:158A-5.1 and C. 2A:158A-5.2);

Laws of 1967, c. 43 (C. 2A:158A-6 to C. 2A:158A-20 both inclusive);

Laws of 1967, c. 43 (C. 2A:158A-22);

Laws of 1968, c. 371 (C. 2A:158A-23 to C. 2A:158A-25 both inclusive);

Laws of 1958, c. 12 (C. 2A:159A-1 to 2A:159A-15 both inclusive);

Laws of 1952, c. 163 (C. 2A:162-9 and C. 2A:162-10);

Laws of 1960, c. 24 (C. 2A:166A-1 to 2A:166A-4 both inclusive);

Laws of 1953, c. 83 (C. 2A:168-18 to C. 2A:168-25 both inclusive);

Laws of 1968, c. 282 (C. 2A:168A-1 to C. 2A:168A-3 both inclusive);

Laws of 1954, c. 181 (C. 2A:170-20.1 to C. 2A:170-20.4 both inclusive);

Laws of 1956, c. 230 (C. 2A:170-20.9 and C. 2A:170-20.10);

Laws of 1975, c. 183 (C. 2A:170-20.11 and C. 2A:170-20.12);

Laws of 1952, c. 106 (C. 2A:170-25.1);

Laws of 1965, c. 41 (C. 2A:170-25.9 to C. 2A:170-25.13 both inclusive);

Laws of 1972, c. 143 (C. 2A:170-25.17);

Laws of 1955, c. 48 (C. 2A:170-77.2);

Laws of 1962, c. 174 (C. 2A:170-77.2a and C. 2A:170-77.2b);

Laws of 1955, c. 277 (C. 2A:170-77.3 to C. 2A:170-77.7 both inclusive);

Laws of 1962, c. 113 (C. 2A:170-77.8 to C. 2A:170-77.11 both inclusive);

Laws of 1964, c. 230 (C. 2A:170-77.12 to C. 2A:170-77.14 both inclusive);

Laws of 1966, c. 314 (C. 2A:170-77.15);

Laws of 1977, c. 215 (C. 2A:170-77.16 to C. 2A:170-77.18 both inclusive);

Laws of 1966, c. 114 (C. 2A:170-90.1 and C. 2A:170-90.2);

Laws of 1975, c. 182 (C. 2A:170-90.3 to C. 2A:170-90.5 both inclusive);

Laws of 1955, c. 254 (C. 2A:171-1.1 and C. 2A:171-1.2);

Laws of 1959, c. 119 (C. 2A:171-5.8 to C. 2A:171-5.18 both inclusive).

**2C:98-4.**        **Effective date**

This act shall take effect the first day of the thirteenth month following enactment.

**Chapters 99 to 103—Reserved**

# 104

# MATERIAL WITNESSES

**2C:104-1.**     **Definitions**

    a. A material witness is a person who has information material to the prosecution or defense of a crime.

    b. A material witness order is a court order fixing conditions necessary to secure the appearance of a person who is unlikely to respond to a subpoena and who has information material to the prosecution or defense of a pending indictment, accusation or complaint for a crime or a criminal investigation before a grand jury.

**2C:104-2.**     **Application for material witness order**

    a. The Attorney General, county prosecutor or defendant in a criminal action may apply to a judge of the Superior Court for an order compelling a person to appear at a material witness hearing, if there is probable cause to believe that: (1) the person has information material to the prosecution or defense of a pending indictment, accusation or complaint for a crime or a criminal investigation before a grand jury and (2) the person is unlikely to respond to a subpoena. The application may be accompanied by an application for an arrest warrant when there is probable cause to believe that the person will not appear at the material witness hearing unless arrested.

    b. The application shall include a copy of any pending indictment, complaint or accusation and an affidavit containing: (1) the name and address of the person alleged to be a material witness, (2) a summary of the facts believed to be known by the alleged material witness and the relevance to the criminal action or investigation, (3) a summary of the facts supporting the belief that the person possesses information material to the pending criminal action or investigation, and (4) a summary of the facts supporting the claim that the alleged material witness is unlikely to respond to a subpoena.

    c. If the application requests an arrest warrant, the affidavit shall set forth why immediate arrest is necessary.

**2C:104-3.**     **Order to appear**

    a. If there is probable cause to believe that a material witness order may issue against the person named in the application, the judge may order the person to appear at a hearing to determine whether the person should be adjudged a material witness.

    b. The order and a copy of the application shall be served personally upon the alleged material witness at least 48 hours before the hearing, unless the judge adjusts the time period for good cause, and shall advise the person of

(1) the time and place of the hearing; and

(2) the right to be represented by an attorney and to have an attorney appointed if the person cannot afford one.

**2C:104-4.**        **Arrest with warrant**

a. If there is clear and convincing evidence that the person named in the application will not be available as a witness unless immediately arrested, the judge may issue an arrest warrant. The arrest warrant shall require that the person be brought before the court immediately after arrest. If the arrest does not take place during regular court hours, the person shall be brought to the emergency-duty Superior Court judge.

b. The judge shall inform the person of:

(1) the reason for arrest;

(2) the time and place of the hearing to determine whether the person is a material witness; and

(3) the right to an attorney and to have an attorney appointed if the person cannot afford one.

c. The judge shall set conditions for release, or if there is clear and convincing evidence that the person will not be available as a witness unless confined, the judge may order the person confined until the material witness hearing which shall take place within 48 hours of the arrest.

**2C:104-5.**        **Arrest without warrant**

a. A law enforcement officer may arrest an alleged material witness without a warrant only if the arrest occurs prior to the filing of an indictment, accusation or complaint for a crime or the initiation of a criminal investigation before a grand jury, and if the officer has probable cause to believe that:

(1) a crime has been committed;

(2) the alleged material witness has information material to the prosecution of that crime;

(3) the alleged material witness will refuse to cooperate with the officer in the investigation of that crime; and

(4) the delay necessary to obtain an arrest warrant or order to appear would result in the unavailability of the alleged material witness.

b. Following the warrantless arrest of an alleged material witness, the law enforcement officer shall bring the person immediately before a judge. If court is not in session, the officer shall immediately bring the person before the emergency-duty Superior Court judge. The judge shall determine whether there is probable cause to believe that the person is a material witness of a crime and, if an indictment, accusation or complaint for that crime has not issued or if a grand jury has not commenced a criminal investigation of that crime, the judge shall determine whether there is probable cause to believe that, within 48 hours of the arrest, an indictment, accusation or complaint will issue or a grand jury investigation will commence. The judge then shall proceed as if an application for a warrant has been made under N.J.S.2C:104-4.

**2C:104-6.**        **Material witness hearing**

a. At the material witness hearing, the following rights shall be afforded to the person.

(1) the right to be represented by an attorney and to have an attorney appointed if the person cannot afford one;

(2) the right to be heard and to present witnesses and evidence;

(3) the right to have all of the evidence considered by the court in support of the application; and

(4) the right to confront and cross-examine witnesses.

b. If the judge finds that there is probable cause to believe that the person is unlikely to respond to a subpoena and has information material to the prosecution or defense of a pending indictment, accusation or complaint for a crime, or a criminal investigation before a grand jury, the judge shall determine that the person is a material witness and may set the conditions of release of the material witness.

c. If the judge finds by clear and convincing evidence that confinement is the only method that will secure the appearance of the material witness, the judge may order the confinement of the material witness.

d. The judge shall set forth the facts and reasons in support of the material witness order on the record.

## 2C:104-7.    Conditions of release; confinement

a. A confined person shall not be held in jail or prison, but shall be lodged in comfortable quarters and served ordinary food.

b. The conditions of release for a material witness or for a person held on an application for a material witness order shall be the least restrictive to effectuate the appearance of the material witness. A judge may:

(1) place the witness in the custody of a designated person or organization agreeing to supervise the person;

(2) restrict the travel of the person;

(3) require the person to report;

(4) set bail; or

(5) impose other reasonable restrictions on the material witness.

c. A person confined shall be paid $40.00 per day, and when the interests of justice require, the judge may order additional payment not exceeding the actual financial loss resulting from the confinement. The party obtaining the material witness order bears the cost of confinement and payment unless the party is indigent.

## 2C:104-8.    Deposition

A material witness may apply to the Superior Court for an order directing that a deposition be taken to preserve the witness's testimony. After the deposition is taken, the judge shall vacate the terms of confinement contained in the material witness order and impose the least restrictive conditions to secure the appearance of the material witness.

## 2C:104-9.    Orders appealable

A material witness order shall constitute a final order for purposes of appeal, but, on motion of the material witness, may be reconsidered at any time by the court which entered the order.

# INDEX